W9-ABZ-268

Sex Bias in the Schools

The

Edited by

RUTHERFORD • MADISON • TEANECK
FAIRLEIGH DICKINSON UNIVERSITY PRESS
LONDON: ASSOCIATED UNIVERSITY PRESSES

SEX BIAS IN THE SCHOOLS

Research Evidence

Janice Pottker and Andrew Fishel

Associated University Presses, Inc.
Cranbury, New Jersey 08512

Associated University Presses
Magdalen House
136–148 Tooley Street
London SE1 2TT, England

Library of Congress Cataloging in Publication Data

Main entry under title:

Sex bias in the schools.

Includes bibliographical references and index.
1. Sex differences in education—Addresses, essays, lectures.
2. Education of women—United States—Addresses, essays, lectures.
I. Pottker, Janice. II. Fishel, Andrew.
LC212.2.S48 1977 376 74-200
ISBN 0-8386-1464-7

PRINTED IN THE UNITED STATES OF AMERICA

Contents

Preface

This reader is intended for those people who are concerned about sexism in the schools, whether or not they are working within the educational system. Obviously, teachers, members of professional staffs, and administrators of public schools should be directly concerned with the issues presented in this book, as school board members, parents, and concerned laymen should also be. Both undergraduate and graduate education majors should find the topics included here relevant. Teachers and students of women studies will also find this book informative about one critically important area of sexism in American society.

The readings in this anthology have been selected to reveal how it is possible to document specific practices of sexism in the schools. Although considerable media attention has been given to feminist charges that schools are sex biased, much of the public remain unconvinced that these accusations are based on fact. Others, while in agreement with the general charge of sex discrimination, do not know exactly how or where it exists, and, more importantly, do not know how to go about proving its existence with empirical evidence. Without substantiating charges, few changes can be made.

These selections utilize a wide variety of research methods to identify, quantify, and verify the existence of discrimination against girls and women in schools. The readings that are included will inform those individuals not previously cognizant of the existence of sexist practices and policies in the schools; the selections will also provide guidance to those individuals seeking information about the direction and nature of changes needed to achieve equality for girls and women in American education.

Acknowledgments

We would like to thank all those of our colleagues and friends who provided us with thoughts, insights, and motivation for this book: David E. Wilder, Donna E. Shalala, Robert A. Dentler, Mary F. Williams, Frances K. Heussenstamm, E. Edmund Reutter, Jr., Vincent Tinto, George Z. F. Bereday, Rozanne Marel, Rodney Riffel and F. Dale Einhorn. To our editor, George E. Magee, goes tremendous gratitude for his skillful and painstaking service of editing this reader. And last, we thank the authors for permission to reprint their stimulating papers.

Introduction

The articles in this reader establish the subtle and invidious distinctions made by American educators between the role enactments of being male or being female, as well as educators' blatant discrimination against girls and women in the schools. In fact, the techniques used by educators are usually not even perceived by the recipients—girls and women—nor are they perceived by parents or even the educators themselves. This is what makes translating sexism in the schools so difficult for the general public; only when case after case is documented is the point driven home.

It would be far easier to convince the public of school sexism if girls did not attain high scholastic achievement. For example, the poor academic records of certain racial and ethnic minorities demonstrate that schools do not meet their needs. But since girls do much better in school than boys, it is difficult for many to see how girls could be the object of discriminatory school policies.

Another problem is that sexism in the schools supports some of society's most cherished traditions: that males and females are different in almost every aspect. This is why even documentation of school sex bias often brings only a shrug from many people. The belief that the sexes are different enables many individuals to reconcile sex-biased treatment of boys and girls. By such reasoning, girls are not being discriminated against, but rather being treated in an appropriate, natural, and correct fashion for future biological and social roles.

National attention was paid to the teacher who separated blue-eyed and brown-eyed children, and gave one group privileges that were denied the other. This was lauded as a tremendously exciting way to teach children the effects of race discrimination. But what would happen if a teacher told the girls in the class that few of them could ever aspire to be doctors, few would receive high educational degrees, few would have the independence and freedom that their brothers would have, most would have complete responsibility for household chores as adults, and they would consistently receive sixty percent of a man's salary for doing the same job? The resentment that the girls would feel upon hearing this would be understandable.

And if the teacher then separated the girls from the boys, denying the girls certain privileges, this would demonstrate sex discrimination as truly as the former teacher taught race discrimination. But what would be the reaction of administrators who might even have supported the earlier scheme that showed race discrimination? It is doubtful that it would approve the sex-discrimination exercise, because discrimination due to sex is considered natural and is supported by the schools.

COOLING OUT THE FEMALE

Our concern in this introduction is not so much to convince the reader of school sex bias, but rather to illustrate the complexity and the extent of sex bias. Invidious forms of discrimination against females permeate the entire operation of the American school system. Schools systematically, ingeniously, and sometimes unconsciously act along the socially accepted norm of relegating girls and women to subordinate positions.

Erving Goffman, in "On Cooling the Mark Out,"[1] presents an analysis of the individual's adaption to failure. He looks at the individual's concept of himself or herself and shows how this self-concept is determined by relativistic constructs. That is, how self-concepts and actions are explained by the behavior of the people surrounding us.

The confidence game is used by Goffman as an example. A person called the *mark,* who is the victim of the con game, is almost always a loser. When the mark loses, he must quietly accept his losses and not complain or take action against the operators of the con game. In order for this to happen, he has to be made to accept his losses and, indeed, blame them on himself rather than on some outside force, such as the con game or man. If the mark did not internalize his unhappiness and if he blamed his unhappiness on some other person, he might then complain and seek retribution from those who made him a loser. Obviously for those in the con game, this reaction must be avoided.

The process that the mark goes through in order that he not complain is called the *cool out* or *cooling the mark out;* the system consists of measures taken by the operators of the con game to insure that the mark blames himself and not the operators of the game for his losses.

Burton Clark has shown that the analogy of the con game can be applied to the educational system.[2] It is also possible to apply Goffman's and Clark's theories on cooling the mark out to describe how schoolgirls are cooled out by the schools. The methods of control of women used by educators (and, of course, many of these are *women*) are similar to the methods of control of the mark used by the operators of the confidence game. The irony of the situation is that this reflects a final condition that is socially approved, for discrimination against women is part of the American way of life. This is the danger of sexism in the schools and why its effect is lethal.

Let us look at who does what in this process of cool out in the school system. In Goffman's confidence game, certain facts are sometimes purposely misrepresented to the mark. In the school system, vocational and academic training stresses to boys that they must choose a career or pick a vocation and so on, but this is not emphasized to girls. The assumption is that if girls do work, their work will be temporary and unimportant, and will terminate upon marriage. Schools also show what they consider men's work and women's work to be when they track *all* of the girls into home economics classes, and *all* of the boys into shop classes. Labor statistics show that today's schoolgirl will work at least twenty-five years, and that she will also find the monetary rewards of this work of great importance to her. Therefore, the misrepresentation of essentials she receives from her school will most likely harm her in later life.

Facts are distorted for girls, facts that are vital to them in planning their futures. Yet these facts of life for girls are disregarded for a more socially approved myth: that girls will grow up, work a year or two, then marry and totally retire from the business world for the rest of their lives. This can easily be seen from the textbooks girls read in which working women are grossly underrepresented.

Not all of the school personnel who come into contact with girls are actually aware of what they are doing. Probably few of them realize either their own motivation for their actions or the implications these actions have for women and society. For example, most schools allot quite a large budget providing an extracurricular athletic program for their male students' after-school activities. Few schools have after-school programs that involve as many girls as boys, therefore not nearly as much money is being spent for activities that include girls as for activities that include boys. This unequal expenditure is detrimental both to the girl students and to their teachers. For example, those teachers who are in charge of girls' activities or coed activities are paid less than those in charge of boys' activities.

Coolers also exist, in both the confidence game and the educational system, who are aware of what they are doing. Most of these people are acting in good faith, either sincerely believing that girls will not have a long work span or substituting their emotions for logic. Perhaps they believe women to be happier as housewives, and therefore they orient females toward the home, despite the low odds that the girls will actually follow this nonwork pattern.

Stereotyping does not leave the scene even when it is recognized that girls will work. Girls learn about jobs that are traditionally female, whether they learn from textbooks that show women working as teachers or nurses, or whether they learn from their own school's example that teachers are female and principals and superintendents are male. A narrow vision for girls is shown them in limited job counseling, whether formal or informal. But often good faith is intended here. There are surely some teachers and publishers, for example, who honestly believe that women are happier as secretaries rather than as business executives or as teachers rather than as principals.

Another tactic used by educators to cool girls is called *alternative achievement.* Alternative achievement would have girls give up one type of achievement, usually job success, for another. It is obvious that the other type is the achievement of marriage and motherhood. Girls are taught that it is good and fulfilling to be only housewives and mothers, and they are advised to find their success in marriage.

And for women, this alternative achievement is couched in either-or terms. How often are girls greeted with a "choice": the choice to be either a wife or mother or to have a career. The concepts of "wife" and "mother," and of "career woman," are totally different. Girls are only shown several statuses that are possible for them to hold within their status-set, whereas boys are told that they have a wide range from which to choose. Boys realize that they can be both school superintendent and husband and father, while girls receive the message that career and motherhood are not compatible statuses. And yet who would suggest that men be satisfied with being only a good husband and father?

But often women resign temporarily from their jobs not upon marriage, but rather upon motherhood. For many women this is not necessarily an option; once pregnant, they must cope with the loss of their jobs and they must also realize how few child-care arrangements exist in this country. The school system has traditionally turned against its own women teachers by forcing them out of teaching if they became pregnant. Then women were denied higher administrative jobs in the school system, the rationale being that they would have to leave if pregnant. However, women are consoled with the certainty that the raising of a child by one person is "the most important job there is," although it is apparently not important enough for men to bother themselves with. This belief—that they are doing something unique and crucial—represses women's anger at society for shutting them out of their occupation.

What is peculiar about alternative achievement is that usually working women are also wives and mothers. In fact, the teachers and counselors who do not advise girls into making a serious commitment to one or another future vocation are often working mothers themselves. Here again we can see how girls receive a message dysfunctional to their development and future life-style.

For those girls who escape this primary cooling-out feature of alternative achievement and insist upon a career, there is a second cooling-out feature. If the girl maintains an interest in achieving and attaining a job outside the home, her options are limited. She is told what jobs she should hold. The jobs that she is told that she should want are primarily service jobs: teaching (below the college level), nursing, and social work. She is told that it is womanly and fulfilling to help rectify society's wrongs rather than, as it is implied, cause more wrongs to be committed by working at whatever she wishes to work at. To be selfish, worldly, nonnurturing, and female is quickly shown to be evil by the schools. Schools teach girls to be acquiescent and docile.

Schools also want their women teachers to be passive conformists. Women are encouraged to stay within the teaching ranks and are discouraged from seeking principalships. When they do seek administrative jobs, they are rarely given them: in fact, it takes the average woman eight years longer to become a principal than it does the average man.

The school's second tactic, gradual disengagement, is related to alternative achievement. Throughout their schooling, girls are gradually disengaged from what the schools do not want them to be. Girls must mirror the image perceived of them by educators, and they are admonished if they do not fit this image.

At certain times this gradual disengagement does not work and a period of crisis takes place. This usually occurs when the girl and the school are at a point of disagreement. For the school's purpose, it is preferable not to be open in disengaging the girl's aims, whatever they might be. The school neither wants to show its hand nor, indeed, admit that it holds one. There are myths about schools as well as about women, and one school myth is that schools exist for the students' benefit. It is difficult for the school to subscribe to this belief and yet openly block a student's wishes.

Another myth regarding the school is that schools treat all people equally. Indeed, this creed of equality is one that the schools are supposed to teach their students. Yet we know that women seeking school promotions are discriminated against in favor of men. Usually some justification for this is given, such as that men teachers dislike working for a woman principal. Never is the school administration at fault; it won't take the blame, but rather attributes its actions to someone else's bias.

Open crisis is to be avoided because gradual disengagement is better; the schools cool the female much more effectively if cooling is done slowly and subtly. It is more effective if the school can imply throughout its socialization of the girl that she would be much happier in a job that requires less training and education and fewer responsibilities than to tell her only that happiness lies in being a lab technician rather than a chemist. Malcolm X's final break with white society came when he told his school counselor that he wanted to be a lawyer when older. The counselor replied by suggesting that he become a carpenter instead. The similarity between Malcolm X's experience and the experience of many women is striking.

A third tactic the school uses is through its agents of consolation. These agents, to be fully successful, should themselves believe in the value of the alternative course for girls. They should not question the assumption that the cooling out of a girl's ambitions is natural and necessary for the fulfillment and inner happiness of the student. These agents are represented most often today by school counselors, who are gaining more and more importance in the schools. Indeed, this consoling function is crucial to the role of the counselor.

The fourth and most important device utilized by the schools is the sense of guilt they cause nonconforming females to feel. Guilt leads to a sense of insecurity, and once the mark is insecure, once her belief in herself is shaken, it becomes even easier to cool her out. Guilt is employed by the school when the girl or woman show signs of not having been properly cooled out already. How many women have been made to feel as if they would not be good mothers upon stating that they would rather continue teaching than stop work when pregnant? Instead of concentrating on the question of what constitutes a proper policy regulation, the school hints to the teacher that she is an abnormal and unnatural woman.

Always the rebellious female is made to feel that there is something wrong with her rather than with the school. However, girls and women should never be allowed to question the cooling process: the cooler should never let the mark reach this stage of disillusionment and awareness. The female, if she does reach this point, is told that she is "different"; indeed, she will then perceive herself as different. The tragedy is that, having not been shown how to utilize this difference as an asset, she will turn it inward, against herself.

THE FEMINIZED MALE: AND FEMALE?

A current theory in educational circles is that the schools *feminize* boys. New critics of education charge that most males are made docile and compliant by the school system, and that those boys who manage to remain independent of the teacher's attempted molding meet with school failure. To be independent (and masculine) does not lead to school success, as does being acquiesent (and feminine).

It is well documented that successful children in schools are those who tend to be acquiesent and that girls are more docile than boys and therefore more successful (this, however, does not totally explain the reasons for girls' greater achievement). However, a few thoughts need to be added to this explanation.

If boys become feminized in schools and if this feminization means conformity, passivity, docility, and obedience, then educators should be just as concerned about the feminization of girls as they are about the feminization of boys. If certain "feminine" characteristics have negative overtones, then why should they no longer be transmitted by schools to boys but still allowed to be transmitted to girls? If certain modes of behavior impede growth, they should not be fostered in boys or girls.

No child should be encouraged into passivity. Independence and self-reliance must be encouraged in all schoolchildren, whether male or female. Breaking the spirit of boys is a crime, to be sure, but it is no less an offense to break the spirit of girls, although not many educators seem concerned about the girls.

Sexism enters when those school critics who rightly favor the teaching of independence rather than dependence in schoolchildren stress the teaching of independence only to males. In fact, the problem of docility is stated just in terms of males; it is deemed proper for girls to continue their role of docility. This one-sided view shows a concern that is tinged with *machismo*: how terrible it is that boys are stifled! Our reply is that it is deplorable for *children* to be stifled, whether male *or* female. The schools' purpose should be to enable *all* children to realize their full potential, not just the boys' potential.

The irony is that children are told that school achievement will bring future life success, which is not true for girls. Having developed the characteristics that are necessary for successful careers in school, once out of school girls are limited by society's bias from attaining positions for which they are qualified. But most girls never realize to what extent they are restricted and discriminated against because the school has done such an effective job in cooling them out. The schools, acting as agents for the existing social order, contribute to the maintenance of a society where sex rather than ability determines the limits of a person's accomplishments. The perpetration of this system in American schools is clearly not only unjust to girls and women, but it also perpetuates a great loss of American talent.

NOTES

1. Erving Goffman, "On Cooling the Mark Out: Some Aspects of Adaption to Failure," *Psychiatry: Journal for the Study of Interpersonal Processes* 15 (November 1952).
2. Burton R. Clark, "The 'Cooling-Out' Function in Higher Education," *The American Journal of Sociology* 65 (May 1960).

Sex Bias in the Schools

Preschool and Elementary Education

The articles in this section focus on sex-role behavior of girls and boys from the nursery school through elementary school. Most sex-role socialization outside of the family takes place in the schools, and unfortunately the sex-stereotypes taught by many parents to their children are being reinforced by the schools. As Carol Joffe's article, "Sex Role Socialization and the Nursery School: As the Twig is Bent," points out, even in schools that are careful not to reinforce stereotyped sex-role behavior, a considerable amount still appears. Interestingly, she found that teachers would categorize children's sex-typed behavior for the purpose of discipline and control ("Act like a lady"). This is one way in which teachers may unconsciously teach "appropriate" sex-role behavior.

Ruth E. Hartley and Armin Klein examine the "Sex-Role Concepts Among Elementary-School-Age Girls" who were from socioeconomically average homes and attended progressive schools. These children had definite beliefs as to how women and men should act, and these ideas were conservative and traditional. Although there was some evidence that the girls perceived women as favoring certain activities, the girls themselves rejected these activities for themselves. This might eventually lead girls to a conflict situation as they become older, similar to the one perceived by college girls in Matina Horner's studies of fear of success.

"Sex Differences in the Self-Concepts of Elementary-School Children," by Cheryl Reed, Donald W. Felker, Richard S. Kay, and Douglas J. Stanwyck, notes that boys and girls from middle-class and lower-class backgrounds marked self-concept items differentially. The lower-class boys reported a significantly higher self-concept than did lower-class girls, while no significant differences between boys and girls were found in total self-concept scores within the middle-class sample. Teachers enrolled in graduate classes indicated that they believe girls to have higher self-concepts than boys. The authors call for alternatives to total scores when measuring self-concepts that differ by sex.

Richard L. Krebs, in "Girls—More Moral than Boys or Just Sneakier," describes a common classroom situation—cheating—where teachers' unconscious sex-typed opinions of boys and girls determine their attitudes toward them. Girls cheat just as much as boys, but teachers perceive boys as cheating more often than girls. Krebs raises questions as to how sex-typed beliefs are transmitted to children.

In all of these articles sex-typed behavior is shown to be harmful, and very often it is the schools that are perpetuating this damage. Joffe points out that schools reinforce sex-typed behavior, especially in terms of discipline. Reed shows that lower-class girls display significantly less self-confidence than lower-class boys, while teachers believe that girls have higher self-concepts. Again, teachers have been shown to hold differential views of boys and girls: Krebs notes that teachers perceive girls as cheating less often than boys, although there is often no factual basis for this belief.

Reed's finding of lower-class girls' low self-esteem dispels a popular belief among educators that it is mostly lower-class boys who suffer from low self-concepts due to the "feminizing" effects of schools and, sometimes, matriarchal family structure. Recent reading studies have also shown that there are significant groups of girls, along with the boys, in the school systems who have severe reading problems. Educators must be cognizant of girls' needs as well as boys' when trying to improve school programs.

Teachers' and administrators' beliefs of what is sex-appropriate are impairing children's self-esteem and self-actualization, particularly the self-actualization of girls. The elementary schools are setting the stage for children's adult behavior, and if girls grow up to be less ambitious and less successful than boys, it is the elementary school that we can turn to as the precursor of girls' failure. It is unclear what specific effect teachers' attitudes have on students regarding sex-appropriate behavior. It is obvious, however, that the teacher is an important role model for children and transmits values to them. While federal guidelines can eradicate formal sex bias, attitudinal changes of teachers must also take place simultaneously.

It is for this reason that teachers and administrators must immediately analyze their attitudes and conduct toward sex-role stereotyping. As Joffe has shown, even those schools directed toward eliminating sex-typed behavior still exhibit a considerable amount; therefore all schools must rigorously examine themselves and conduct activities to eradicate these behaviors. These pursuits might include: consciousness-raising sessions on the part of teachers and administrators, encompassing reverse sex-role-playing; workshops on sexism incorporating what the federal guidelines against sex discrimination are; reviewing the number of boys and girls included in school functions, such as street-crossing guards and audio-visual aides; role-playing activities and discussions about being a boy or a girl within the classroom; and an increased sensitivity to the needs of those children who are not middle-class.

Sex-role Socialization and the Nursery School: As the Twig Is Bent*

CAROLE JOFFE

A problem within the field of socialization that has recently been raised with new urgency is that of sex roles. This renewed attention is coming about in large part as a result of issues currently being raised in the women's movement; a central theme of the analysis emanating from this movement is that American society demands the socialization of both men and women into fixed sex roles, at great cost to the individual needs of members of both sexes.[1] This socialization is said to be omnipresent, literally starting at birth with the proverbial blue or pink blanket that is given to the newborn infant. But although the women's movement has caused a new focus of attention on this phenomenon of early socialization into sex roles, certain social scientists have long given attention to the same topic. Kagan, for example, has noted the significance of the differential treatment accorded male and female infants and the effects this has for the child's subsequent sexual identity.[2] But although it is generally agreed—both by those who adopt a critical stance and those who seemingly are interested only in description—that sex-role socialization is everywhere, certain institutions are, of course, more crucial in the cultural transmission of these expectations than others. Two of the most centrally

* Carole Joffe, "Sex Role Socialization and the Nursery School: As the Twig is Bent," © copyright 1971, National Council on Family Relations, from *Journal of Marriage and the Family* 33 (August 1971): 467–75. Reprinted with permission of National Council on Family Relations and the author. The author wishes to express gratitude to Sheldon Messinger and Norman Donzin.

involved agencies in the sex-role socialization of the young (and hence two that are currently undergoing severe criticism) are the family and the schools. This study will discuss experiences of children with respect to socialization in one of these institutions—the nursery school. For many children, it must be remembered, their attendance at nursery school marks their first institutional contact outside of the home and, thus, this kind of school can justifiably be seen as performing critical socialization functions. The analysis will attempt to demonstrate both what the school seemed to be demanding from the children in terms of sex-appropriate behavior and how the children themselves conceived of their sex-role obligations. It is hoped that a close look at the quality of sex-role socialization received by persons in their first institutional setting will not only enlighten us further as to the meaning of sex roles in American society, but also, for those of us committed to some form of change in the institutions serving our children, such a study might suggest some policy implications.

Before proceeding to my own findings, I will briefly comment on work done to date on nursery schools and socialization into sex roles. Although no major work appears to have been done specifically on nursery schools as *facilitators* of sex roles,[3] there has recently been some attention paid to other educational institutions as they relate to sex roles. Several writers have noted the significance of the fact that at the elementary school level most teachers are women and the effects this has on children of both sexes in terms of classroom behavior.[4] Because elementary schools are geared, in Silberman's term, toward "docility," this reinforces cultural messages about appropriate behavior little girls are already receiving elsewhere; in the case of little boys, this sets up a conflict in view of their masculine-oriented socialization, with the result being that some claim the only boys who do well academically at the elementary level are those who become "feminized."[5] But other than noting these two quite important facts—that most primary school teachers are female and that the school situation puts forth an ideal of docility among students—there do not yet seem to be accounts of the *specific* ways in which schools foster socialization into sex roles. Certainly there remains a gap in studies of the nursery school in this respect. Through my research, I will attempt to pinpoint various structural and ideological features of the pre-school and discuss their relationship to this kind of socialization.

A final digression before I begin will be to make clear my own bias about the issues under discussion, "sex roles." The treatment of sex roles in this study will be substantially different from that which it receives in much of the socialization literature. A common feature of the huge number of studies of preschool children and sex roles is that, for the most part, what constitutes appropriate "sex roles" is not made problematic.[6] The researchers had a preconceived idea of what the content was of proper masculine and feminine roles and tested the children to see how well they conformed to these already existing measures.[7] Thus, for the majority of the researchers in this field, there is a seeming acceptance of prevailing ideas about maleness and femaleness: children who don't comply with these concepts become listed as deviants. I will be taking the position that the idea of sex roles, particularly for children of preschool age,[8] is a very problematic matter and should be approached with great skepticism. The reader should understand that what will be discussed is how the school fosters contemporary *notions* of sex roles and what use of these notions the children make; I will not be speaking to the issue of what the "real" differences between the sexes are and therefore what would constitute legitimate sex-role socialization. An additional bias that will occur is that in spite of the lack of discussion about what sex-role socialization *should* be, I nevertheless will take a position against what I feel are the most blatantly damaging forms of sex-role socialization that are the norm now, e.g., channeling members of each sex into restrictive roles that limit the life options and behavioral choices of each. Accordingly, in this study the "good" school will be one in which these attempts at imposing such damaging sex roles are minimized while the "bad" school is one that encourages them.

A CASE STUDY OF ONE SCHOOL

In this section is reported two separate periods of participant observation at a nursery school. Although at the time of the observations I was also concerned with other factors, I will deal here exclusively with the findings on sex-role socialization and how the children themselves conceived sex roles. I will first briefly describe the research situation.

The first series of observations were made over a period of two months in the spring of 1970 at a parent-nursery school in the San Francisco Bay area. (A parent-nursery is one in which, in addition to two full-time teachers, each of the participating parents takes a weekly shift at the school.) The school I observed was affiliated with a Bay area school district, although some of the parents paid tuition. There were regular teacher-parent meetings and parents were encouraged to help formulate school policy.

The children observed in the first series consisted of 22 students, 9 male and 13 female, ranging in age from 3½ to 4½. The school was racially mixed, consisting of about an equal number of children of white professionals and graduate students, and black children from lower-income families. The second set of observations, accomplished in January-February 1971, were of the afternoon session of the same parent-nursery and thus a certain proportion of children who had been seen in 1970 were seen again almost a year later. Twelve of the children observed during the afternoon session had initially been seen earlier and nine had not been seen before. In this second group, there were fourteen females and nine males, with the percentage of black children being somewhat higher than it had been in the previous group. The age of the children in this group covered a span from four and one half to five.

Each of the classes had two full-time female teachers (one black and one white in each case) and each day from three to five mothers would also work. (The school claimed to be eager to have fathers of the children participate as well, but except on a very sporadic basis, e.g., emergencies, fathers did not participate during the periods of my observation.) As an observer, I essentially took the role of a participating mother (*albeit* without a child), e.g., watching children in the yard, reading stories, etc. Additionally I attended parent-teacher meetings and had opportunities for extended conversations with both teachers and parents.

I will start my discussion by offering in broadest terms an analysis of the school's overall "attitude" toward sex roles and the type of behavior that seemed to be expected from the children in this respect. In each of the sessions I observed, there was an extremely positive (in terms of the value bias mentioned earlier) orientation toward sex roles: there was no active move to impose any notion of correct sex-typed behavior and, most impressive, there was a very relaxed response towards those children who violated normal expectations about members of their sex group. Clearly then, the school I happened to study represents a negative case in terms of any attempt to show dramatically how damaging socialization takes place in nursery schools. I do believe, however, that such a school is useful to us in spite of its atypical quality. First, in examining such a "good" school, it is possible to draw out policy implications for other less-liberated institutions; second, even in a school committed to avoiding imposition of these notions of sex stereotypes, inadvertent sex-role socialization does take place.

Starting a discussion of sexism in the schools in reverse, therefore, I will list the features of this particular school that are indicative of its policy of not stressing sex roles. Most generally, there was no structural indication of two separate categories of persons: bathrooms, for example, were not segregated and often children of both sexes would use them at the same time; all activities in the school program were officially open to both sexes and the participation of all children in some of the more traditionally sex-typed activities (e.g., cooking, washing dishes) was consistently encouraged. Most striking, as I already indicated, was the tolerance shown those children whose behavior showed varying degrees of sex-identity "confusion," e.g., those children who with regularity would dress as members of the opposite sex and assume the "wrong" sexual identity in games of "house." The school's most notable example of what elsewhere might be termed as "deviation" was K., a Polynesian male who frequently dressed in women's clothes, occasionally wore his hair in "feminine" fashion, and, in games with the other children, often assumed female identities, e.g., "sister." There is a certain variation among the children as to how K's behavior was received. In terms of his teachers, however, I was struck by the firm commitment on their part to noninterference. Both felt it would be unnecessarily upsetting, both to K. and to the other children, to in any way make an issue out of this behavior. Rather, in discussion with the observer, one of the teachers stressed she viewed such behavior as very creative and emotionally beneficial—"it's good for him to have all kinds of experiences." Both of the teachers referred to K.'s foreign background as a factor which, although not entirely understood by them, might conceivably explain some of his actions, particularly his mode of dancing. In summary, then, the vocabulary of motive that seemed to be in operation among the teachers with regard to sex-identity "switching" was that it was common to many children; it was in many aspects a "creative" exercise; it would only be to all the children's detriment to have such action questioned by adults.

What I have described above is the school's official position towards socialization into sex roles; I believe that this represents a type of institution, on an imaginary continuum of "bad" to "good" schools, that is, in ideological terms, impressively free from sexism. However, special attention must be paid to the variety of ways in which inadvertently sex-typing nonetheless does take place in this school. The first point to make is that while it is easy to gain a sense of the teacher's policies, one cannot as readily presume to summarize all the parents' attitudes. As mentioned, this school is one in which parents work a weekly shift, and thus, each child was exposed regularly to approximately eighteen-twenty different women. To understand all the subtle influences playing on the children, ideally one would have to determine systematically each of these women's own attitudes about sex roles. While observations suggest that most of the mothers shared the teachers' assumptions in this regard,[9] there nevertheless occurred a series of small events in the interactions between children and mothers (and teachers to a certain degree as well) that in a cumulative sense could well serve to convey to the children messages about sex-role expectations. One of these seemingly trivial events, which occurred fairly often, was the acknowledgment of the girls' clothing:

> M. walks in wearing a dress she has not worn before. One of the mothers says to her, "M., what a pretty little lady you are today."

One might argue of course that admiring a child is not the same thing as sex-typing her. Nor will I suggest that admiring a child is "wrong" and should not be done. I have to point out, however, that in some cases this unavoidably has consequences for the child's self-conception in terms of gender identity. Not surprisingly, the pattern I noted of compliment giving was that girls were more frequently admired than boys, and moreover, girls received more compliments on days they wore dresses rather than pants. It is outside the context of this study to consider how ultimately damaging it is for little girls to be responded to in this way. I use this example simply as an illustration of one of the variety of subtle ways in which girls (and boys) get cues as to differing social images of femininity and masculinity. An event that I observed far less frequently and that conceivably served the same function of transmitting cues as to appropriate sex-linked behavior was the occasional positive reinforcement a boy would get when he ably defended himself against a physical attack, as in the following:

> L. and N. have been arguing over the use of a spade. N. pushes L. and L. responds by delivering a solid punch to N.'s chest. A mother who has witnessed the scene says to the observer (within hearing of L.), "Did you see the punch L. gave N.? He really can take care of himself like a man."

Because there is such strong prohibition against fighting in the school, in fact incidents like the above do not occur very often, i.e., the fights occur, but most mothers would not give this kind of approval; but whether in this context or in others, e.g., physical-strength contests in games, there no doubt occurs a differential amount of reinforcement accorded to boys' physical exploits than to girls, with the obvious implications for self-concept of each sex.

A far more clear-cut example of damaging sex-roles socialization offered to the children can be found in the quality of the media in use at the nursery school. There is clearly a lag—perhaps somewhat unavoidable—between the school's own attitudes toward sex-typing and the quality of materials in use at the school. The story books read to the children, the songs taught them at music time, the traditional children's games they play[10]—all contain, to a great extent, vestiges of dominant social attitudes toward sex roles. For example, a mother leading the children in singing, sings a form of the typical children's song in which each character performs a different task:

> And the daddy went spank-spank, and the mommy went "shh-shhh."
> (The song concerned a child who had made noise on a bus.)

The lag, as I stated, is at least in part unavoidable. There simply do not yet exist adequate nursery-school materials, especially story books, that are free from sex-typing.[11] An accommodation made by some who work in the nursery school is simply to alter the stories as they read them to the children.[12] But until the same serious effort is made to prepare materials that are free from sexism that recently appears to have at least been started in the preparation of nonracist material, the quality of children's objects in the school (here I am including both literature and toys) will remain a major source of traditional sex role.

Another factor in the school that I see as inadvertently contributing to an unfortunate notion of sex specialization is the fact that all the adults working there are female. Again, this is something that the school itself does not prefer, but rather it is a reflection both of the structure of the individual families participating in the school program and the job arrangements that presumably most of the children's fathers have. We can speculate about several possible consequences the all-female population of the school might have on the children's conceptions of sex roles. I would suspect that for these children the main consequence of this situation is the realization that in our society child care is exclusively a female function. For these children, their school life is essentially a continuation of their family life, in that they predominantly spend time with their mothers (and other females) and rarely see adult males. In a situation such as this, one can readily understand the source of the pattern noted by many —that children make clear distinctions between expectations from father and mother.[13] For those working toward a future in which there is meaningful sharing of child-care responsibilities between parents, the lack of men at institutions such as these makes the attainment of such a goal more difficult. We can see how the unfortunate cycle of American family life as it now exists is maintained in these and similar situations: fathers, due both to their own lifelong socialization that has stressed extensive interest in nurturant functions as "unmasculine" and to their actual job situations, don't participate in this type of school; mothers, even with cooperative schools such as these, don't have careers and spend far more time with the child than the father does. The father takes on a somewhat formal role, seen largely as the final authority in disciplinary matters—thus it ultimately becomes somewhat a bizarre deal to all concerned (father, mother, child) to have men take an active role in child care.[14]

AWARENESS OF SEX ROLES AMONG CHILDREN

In this section will be discussed how the children seemed to respond to the school's efforts to minimize sex-role imperatives and to the inadvertent socialization that nonetheless took place. The reader should bear in mind that how children perceived sex roles is, of course, not simply a function of what transpired in the school; their own families as well as numerous other influences in their lives (e.g., television)[15] also contributed to this awareness.

On the basis of my observations, I conclude that while all the children in the school had correct knowledge about their gender identity,[16] there did not exist among these children any patterned recognition of appropriate sex roles; the children as a group did not perceive certain activities or modes of behavior as being the exclusive property of one sex. Although there were no systematic efforts to articulate the rights of males and females, on a more sporadic basis the simple fact of sex difference itself would occasionally be invoked as an attempt at behavior control. Under the appropriate conditions, e.g., an encounter between persons of both sexes, one of the parties would sometimes point to the fact of sex difference as an attempt to justify his actions. The following is an example of this use of sex categories as an "ideology of control."

> C. and two other girls are playing on top of a large structure in the yard. A. (male) comes over and C. screams, "girls only!" to which A. screams back, "No, boys only!"

I think the above example is especially useful because it emphasizes the reciprocal (and thus in a sense, meaningless) character of these exchanges. "Girls only" is immediately countered with "boys only" and thus one can reasonably conclude that to neither of the contestants is there any serious belief in an essential "male" or "female" aspect of the structure under dispute. Rather, sex differences are called forth as a seeming last-ditch effort to impose one's will when the other means of behavior control typically in use have not been effective.

Further evidence that this use of sex categories is quite unrelated to the child's actual perception of sex-appropriate behavior can be found in the behavior of K., the boy who was mentioned earlier as often assuming the identity of a female. K., who elsewhere tampered with quite fundamental assumptions about proper "male" conduct, nonetheless used sex categories in the same way as mentioned in the previous case.

> S. (female) is playing the guitar. K. comes over and asks her to let him play it. When she refuses, K. says, "that's for boys, not girls."

In general then the pattern is that the children will make reference to sex categories when there is a reason to do so (which usually means when a piece of property is under dispute). It should also be pointed out that this ideology was consistently quite unsuccessful; I never in fact saw a child yield to his or her opponent, simply because sex categories were cited, although other ideologies, e.g., the value of sharing, in similar situations, sometimes do work. In summary, we might look at the use of sex as an ideology of control in childhood as a revealing caricature of the adult world and its usage of sex categories. Like these children, adults also invoke sex as a means of behavior control; the crucial differences are that, among adults, the two categories are utilized in a patterned way (some would call it male supremacy) and both male and female adults—unlike these children—actually behave in accordance with this ideology.

The only other regular mention of sexual categories that I observed on the part of the children came in the reactions of some to the sex identity "switching" of K. and several others (in addition to K., I noted about five others—one male and four females—who also periodically assumed roles of the opposite sex).[17] For example, upon seeing K. dressed in feminine apparel, a typical comment would be, "Hey, that's for *girls*." However, neither K.'s nor any of the other children's violations of behavioral expectations in this matter ever became a major issue in the school for the remainder of the children (in large part, I believe, because of the low-keyed reaction of the adults in the school). Thus, for example, although in games of "house" the clear majority of the children chose identities consistent with their sex, there was minimal or no questioning of the fact that some of their playmates acted in the opposite way. It might be concluded, therefore, that on a daily basis, a conscious awareness of different sexual categories was not a dominant theme in the life of this nursery school—although comparative studies suggest that the situation can be very different in other pre-schools.[18]

MALE AND FEMALE SUBCULTURES

Although the children themselves did not articulate sex categories as a major factor in their school lives, I, as an observer, did nonetheless see very intriguing patterns of "sex differences" in terms of friendship networks and play preferences. A small percentage of the school population (4-5 girls and 3-4 boys) assumed on a fairly consistent basis elements of what might be called *traditional sex roles*. The boys in question established a form of "masculine subculture," playing mainly with each other out of doors, and while the girls I refer to did not establish so exclusive a social grouping, they did spend a great deal of time in an all-female society, and for the purposes of discussion, we can analyze their activities in terms of a female subculture. In this section will further be described each of these so-called subcultures, exploring the possible relationships to male and female groupings found later in the life cycle, and finally asking what these subcultures reveal about the school itself as a facilitator of sex roles.

The group I have designated as the "male subculture" consisted of a friendship circle of three boys, L., P., and G., all black, with the occasional participation of W., also black (the four made up the entire black male population of the school; thus, as will be discussed later, race is obviously a central factor here also). It is on the following grounds that I have chosen to see this group in this particular light: they, of all the other individuals or informal groups in the school, spend the greatest amount of time outdoors, mainly playing at very active games, e.g., racing tricycles; they are the most "aggressive" persons in the school, judged simply on the number of physical fights they have with one another and with outsiders; their speech, finally, contains frequent use of phrases of "toughness" that one does not as often hear from the other children, e.g., "don't mess with me," "I'm gonna take care of you," etc.

This group neither exclusively plays with each other nor only plays at active outdoor games. It is interesting to note though that in their interactions both with other children and with other activities, they typically bring their "masculine" mode of behaving to the new situation. In other words, when they play with other children, they immediately attempt to assert dominance; when at cooking sessions, they will demand to be first, take the other children's materials as they are needed, etc. Finally, perhaps most interesting—although least susceptible to generalization—is the quality of the friendship I noted between one member of this group, L., and a black female, V. I noted that on those occasions that L. breaks away from his friends and plays separately with V., and they both refer to themselves as the "L. Brothers." In other words, this seems to suggest that V. is accepted as long as she literally becomes one of the boys. In general, then, I am arguing that both in terms of the large amount of time this group chooses to spend solely with each other and in view of their prevailing interpersonal style, it is useful for us to consider them as a masculine subculture within this school. (It should be stressed that this decision is partially reached by comparing them with the other males in the school, who show a far greater range of behavior.)

The group I consider as the female subculture participated to a far greater extent in a variety of activities and associated with persons of both sexes outside of their immediate circle than did the males mentioned above. I am treating them in this light because of the very definite group identity that existed among them, and more particularly, because of the daily recurring rituals that took place within the group. These rituals included, for each member, the scheduling of individual actions in relation to the group and also the constant location of oneself in the group's very powerful social hierarchy. Although they often made forays to persons and events outside of the group, members seemed to return periodically to a "quorum" (e.g., at least two out of the five), both to report on themselves and to reaffirm their group ties. In the following example, we can see a case of the most simple function performed by this group, e.g., members' use of one another to orient themselves to school life:

> M. arrives at school and immediately goes up to J. and H. (both also part of this circle) and says, "Hi, J., I'm playing with you today, right?" J. answers, "No, I'm playing with H. now."

It should thus be noted that although the group is looked to as a primary source of companionship, it is also the constant source of rejections, because persons trying to maintain places in the social hierarchy of the group drop low-status friends for higher ones. In the next example, there is a more dramatic case of a group member rejecting her companion of the moment (who actually is only a marginal member of the group), but then attempting some accommodation:

> H. and A. (marginal member) are playing together in the yard. J. and a group of others call out to H. to join them at the swing. Although A. hasn't been invited, she goes along also and hangs around on the fringes of the group. H. looks at A. sheepishly and then says to the observer standing nearby, "Carole, would you play with A. for awhile?"

The reader might very well question at this point my labeling as "female" this tendency toward exclusion and social ranking. As I have reported elsewhere, in fact, nearly all the children engaged in it on occasion;[19] the point is that it appeared to be only within this group that this behavior was so regularly tied to the same persons and hence had meaning in a *social group*.

Our next task is to see the resemblances that exist between the male and female subcultures I have described and those that occur elsewhere in the life cycle. In fact there does seem to be a quite uncanny resemblance between the behavior noted in the nursery school and that observed by Henry in his study of adolescent culture in a high school. Speaking of the differing nature of male and female friendship groups, Henry said:

> Boys flock; girls seldom get together in groups above four. . . . Boys are dependent on masculine solidarity . . . the emphasis is on masculine unity; in girls' cliques the purpose is to shut out other girls.[20]

In the behavior of these nursery-school children we appear, then, to have a case of what might be seen as anticipatory socialization; the male and female subcultures noted in the nursery can almost be considered embryonic forms of those that occur in adolescence. What do these recurring patterns tell us about the "nature" of males and females, and more specifically, about the role of the varying institutions providing behavior settings for the children and the adolescents? The first point to be stressed is that for Henry, the differences in male and female culture he saw were directly traceable to the different social circumstances of each of the groups. The tendency of the boys to "flock" was attributable to the fact that the most significant activity in their lives was team sports; the girls' competitive behavior was basically due to a variety of circumstances that all converged to make the chief task of their lives an overwhelming necessity to be "popular," i.e., compete for boyfriends and other affirmations of their "femininity." Obviously, in such a developed form, these same circumstances do not have meaning at the nursery-school level: the boys do not play team sports and the girls are not involved with courtship. To understand why, therefore, such similar patterns were observed at the nursery, we have to first consider the possible salience of some factors not directly related to sex itself, but mainly we have to take fresh account of the strength of the sex-role socialization that has already imposed itself by the age of five.

In explaining the particular cases of male and female subcultures that were observed in this school, we have also to consider the relevance of race as a contributing factor in the former and conceivably "idiosyncrasy" in the case of the latter. As mentioned, all participants in the male subculture were black, and counting the fourth occasional member, this group included the entire black male population of the school. While the question of the situation of black children in a nursery school such as this one deserves far more extended consideration, initial observations suggest that it is very likely that the group in question, in its impetus to establish a separate identity, was at the very least attempting to assert a mixture of both maleness *and* blackness. As for the idiosyncratic nature of the female subculture, it should be remembered that in a nursery school of a fairly small and stable population, one child can establish a tone that is picked up by others and becomes a part of school ritual. In the case of the exclusionary behavior that I mentioned as being a central aspect of the female society, I noted in the first set of observations that it appeared to be J., a member of this group, who initially introduced the particular vocabulary of exclusionary categories to the entire school. Thus, in its particular forms in this school, it might be reasonably said that this behavior was partially due to one or two children.

To the extent that the behavior I noted goes beyond the limits imposed by race and idiosyncrasy (and certainly in the case of the girls, I am convinced it does), and can be validly related to sex, I think that what we have is eloquent testimony not to the "differences" between the sexes, but to the degree to which these chidren have somehow picked up notions of how their society both expects and encourages separate cultures of male and female. Going beyond this initial fact of separateness, the differing characters of each of the societies suggests evidence of the very early age at which at least some children perceive the existence of differing assumptions of correct male and female behavior. Somehow, the little boys I observed "knew" that a comfortable sense of self,[21] in relation to masculine identity, was achieved by at least partial isolation from female things and by disproportionate aggressive behavior. Similarly the notion had somehow been conveyed to the little girls in question that one defines oneself by one's friends and, if necessary, betrays one's friends. Seen in a certain way, the lack of female solidarity—which has both been put forward as a central theme of the analysis of many in women's liberation and which also has started to yield as a result of the exposure of many women to the movement—can be seen to have taken root among some females at an astonishingly early age.

To end the discussion with an attempt to link these arguments to the nursery school—specifically to determine the extent to which the school itself is accountable for this situation—on the surface, the findings are puzzling. I have shown a "good" school—one that in no way appeared to consciously foster notions of sex stereotypes—and yet some of the children acted in traditional ways. This leads to two quite obvious conclusions: The first is that the nursery school does not exist in a vacuum; teachers, parents, and children all bring to the school experiences from outside settings, e.g., the family, which often have drastically different conceptions about sex roles. The second conclusion is simply that this study has actually learned very little about the *mechanisms* by which sex-role expectations are transmitted. We have seen very clear-cut policies adopted in this school to minimize children's awareness of sexual differentiation, but we have seen their limitations. In terms of research strategy, it would seem that to understand completely how sex-role socialization takes place, especially in such a good setting, participant observation is only the first of several necessary lines of action. A final comment pertinent to further research is to reiterate that the present study represents a task only half completed. It is imperative next to study a "bad" traditional school and examine its structural and ideological aspects as well as its students' responses. It is only by such a comparative approach that we will be able to gain a fuller sense of the role actually played by the school itself in the transmission of sexual stereotypes.

REFERENCES

Clausen, John. 1968. *Socialization and society.* Boston: Little, Brown.

Denzin, Norman K. 1970. Children and their caretakers. Paper prepared for Social Science Research Council, Self-Concept Work Group of the "Learning and the Educational Process Subcommittee on Compensatory Education."

Greenwald, Susan. 1970. A study of sex identity, self-imposed sex segregation and the peer group in pre-school children. Unpublished paper.

Hamburg, David, and Lunde, Donald T. 1966. Sex hormones in the development of sex differences in human behavior. In *The development of sex differences,* ed. Eleanor Maccoby. Stanford: Stanford University Press.

Hartley, Ruth. 1959. Sex-role concepts among elementary-school-age girls. *Marriage and family living* 21:59–64.

Henry, Jules. 1963. *Culture against man.* New York: Vintage.

Joffe, Carole. 1970. Taking young children seriously. Paper presented to the 1970 American Sociological Association meeting.

Kagan, Jerome. 1964. The acquisition and significance of sex-typing. In *Review of child development research.* ed. M. Hoffman. New York: Russell Sage.

Millet, Kate. 1970. *Sexual politics.* New York: Doubleday.

Oetzel, Roberta. 1966. Annotated bibliography of research on sex differences. In *Development of sex differences,* ed. Eleanor Maccoby. Stanford: Stanford University Press.

Seward, George, and Williamson, Robert E. 1970. *Sex roles in changing society.* New York: Random House.

Sexton, Patricia. 1969. *The femininized male.* New York: Vintage.

Silberman, Charles. 1970. *Crisis in the classroom.* New York: Random House.

NOTES

1. For example, Millet's statement: "Because of our social circumstances, male and female are really two cultures and their life experiences are utterly different. . . . Implicit in all the gender identity development which takes place through childhood is the sum total of the parents', the peers', and the culture's notions of what is appropriate to each gender by way of temperament, character, interests, status, worth, gesture, and expression. Every moment of the child's life is a clue as to how he or she must think and behave to attain or satisfy the demands which

gender places upon one." Kate Millet, *Sexual Politics* (New York: Doubleday, 1970), p. 31.

2. Jerome Kagan, "The Acquisition and Significance of Sex-typing," in *Review of Child Development Research,* ed. M. Hoffman (New York: Russell Sage, 1964).
3. Although there has, of course, been a huge amount of work done on nursery school-age children in the area of "sex differences."
4. John Clausen, *Socialization and Society* (Boston: Little Brown, 1968); Patricia Sexton, *The Feminized Male* (New York: Vintage, 1969); and Charles Silberman, *Crisis in the Classroom* (New York: Random House, 1970).
5. Sexton, *Feminized Male.*
6. Roberta Oetzel, "Annotated Bibliography on Research on Sex Differences," in *Development of Sex Differences,* ed. Eleanor Maccoby (Stanford: Stanford University Press, 1966).
7. A pleasant exception to this genre is the work of Ruth Hartley, who tested *conceptions* of sex roles among children, and found, among other things, that children of working mothers sex-typed fewer items than those of nonworking mothers. Ruth Hartley, "Sex-role Concepts Among Elementary-school-Age Girls." *Marriage and Family Living* 21 (1959): 59–64.
8. Even for those who take the fact of physiological differences between the sexes as a legitimate basis for the establishment of fixed sex roles, it is generally agreed that the physiological differences that exist between children of preschool age are of minimal significance. See David Hamburg and Donald T. Lunde, "Sex Hormones in the Development of Sex Differences in Human Behavior," in *The Development of Sex Differences,* ed. Eleanor Maccoby (Stanford: Stanford University Press, 1966).
9. One teacher told me of having at one point had some difficulty persuading some parents to accept the idea of nonsegregated bathrooms.
10. To gain a sense of the extent to which sex-typing occurs in traditional children's games, see Iona Opie and Peter Opie, *The Lore and Language of Children* (Oxford: Clarendon Press, 1959).
11. One might argue though that the situation is better in nursery schools than in elementary schools because so much of nursery-school literature is concerned with animals and fantastic adventures, etc. It is in the elementary-school textbooks that the worst offenses take place, with the very stereotyped notions of sex roles presented in the family scenes. A movement is currently starting in California to take legislative action against these textbooks.
12. Norman K. Denzin, "Children and Their Caretakers." Paper prepared for Social Science Research Council, Self-concept Work Group of the "Learning and the Educational Process Subcommittee on Compensatory Education."
13. One of Henry's most revealing findings was that although children made these sharp differentiations between role of mother and father, they in fact were very unhappy about them! "But many expressions of traditional masculinity and femininity are now felt by children to be intolerable." Jules Henry, *Culture Against Man* (New York: Vintage, 1963), p. 137.
14. Henry, *Culture Against Man.*
15. With regard to television, it must be mentioned that the favorite program of nearly all the children in the schools I studied, "Sesame Street"—although in other respects excellent—does very little, if anything, to challenge traditional conceptions of sex roles.
16. It is generally believed that children gain a sense of gender at approximately

eighteen months. See Hamburg and Lunde, "Sex Hormones."

17. An additional tribute to the strength of sex-role socialization in our society can be seen in the fact that in a nonthreatening environment such as this, only 5–6 children regularly experimented with assuming opposite sexual roles.
18. Susan Greenwald, "A Study of Sex Identity, Self-imposed Sex Segregation and the Peer Group in Preschool Children," (unpublished paper, 1970).
19. Carole Joffe, "Taking Young Children Seriously," (paper delivered at the 1970 American Sociological Association meeting).
20. Henry, *Culture Against Man.*
21. I use this word *comfortable,* of course, in a very tentative way. I am trying to convey the idea that acting in such ways as they did clearly fulfilled some notion they had of "what made sense."

Sex-role Concepts Among Elementary-school Age Girls*

RUTH E. HARTLEY and ARMIN KLEIN

The data on which this paper is based were reported as part of a symposium on the psychological implications of changing sex roles at the 1957 annual convention of the American Psychological Association. The section of the investigation described here was conducted under Grant M959 (C-1) from the U.S. Public Health Service.

The materials forming the basis for this article are part of the data being collected in an intensive study, which is presently in process, of the development of children's concepts of women's social roles. Although the study is primarily focused on girls, some data were also collected from boys, to be used as an aid in evaluating the information obtained from girls. With these data it will be possible to make some limited comparisons between girls' and boys' concepts.

The study as a whole was largely inspired by growing evidence of widespread difficulties encountered by women in defining and adjusting to their social roles. Since difficulties of adjustment in adulthood usually have roots in the developmental process, it was necessary to try to find out, by using systematic methods of investigation, what happens to girls in the course of growing up to promote the pronounced and unresolved ambivalence evidenced so widely by adult women.

About a third of the projected total of 150 subjects have thus far been seen, and of these, the majority come from middle- or upper-mid-

* Ruth E. Hartley and Armin Klein, "Sex-Role Concepts among Elementary-School-Age Girls," © copyright 1971, National Council on Family Relations, from *Journal of Marriage and Family Living* 21 (February 1959): 59–64. Reprinted with permission of National Council on Family Relations and the authors.

dle-class homes. Hence, any observations will have to be stated very tentatively and without undue generalization. It is necessary to emphasize this point particularly because these findings are at variance with findings reported by several other workers; let it suffice to say that these findings refer to a small specific sample, described in more detail below.

As one of the means of attaining the basic objectives, it was important to have a clear picture of what the world of men and women looked like to the subjects and how their perceptions of that world fitted into their own concepts of themselves, their needs, abilities, and desires. To do this, an informal inventory was made of the principal roles in which adults are expected to function in our society; this was then broken down further into activities, places, and objects symbolizing, signifying, or otherwise central to, these roles. These items were then presented to the subjects for sorting into categories that could be designated as characteristically male, characteristically female, or not sex-linked (that is, belonging to both or to neither). Responses to this technique provided tentative answers to such questions as these: To what extent do children at different age levels perceive the world of behavior as being divided into sex-appropriate categories? To what extent are their perceptions consonant with the intentions and expectations of the adult world that is socializing them? Adaptations of this approach were designed to yield answers to more affectively oriented questions like the following: Are sex-connected behaviors perceived as carrying integral rewards or privations? What awareness do the children have of the feelings adults have toward the roles they implement? What is the nature of the impact of certain adult-implemented social roles on the children themselves? And, finally, what connections can we identify between the quality of the children's perceptions of social roles and their projections of self-roles for the future?

Preliminary analysis has been carried out on part of the data collected from twenty-seven eight- and eleven-year-old girls and eleven eight- and eleven-year-old boys. These subjects were obtained mainly from private "progressive" schools in New York City. All live in homes where they have an opportunity to see the implementation of male and female roles, and they come from upper-middle-class backgrounds. This article will center on the girls, with some comparisons in lesser detail involving the smaller number of boys.

It is to be noted first that, contrary to many recent assertions on this topic, the subjects have very explicit and comprehensive ideas about the sex-typing of behaviors in this culture. On a 133-item inventory of a wide range of behaviors in this culture that could be sex-typed, the average percentage of items reported by the girls as belonging specifically to the province of men or of women was 70. A group of twenty-five adult men and women, elementary schoolteachers from the northeastern part of the country, whose mean age was thirty-two, estimated 67 percent of these behaviors to be sex-typed when they responded to the same inventory.

The content, furthermore, of the girls' sex-typing was essentially the same as the adult group's estimation. Behaviors related to child care, care of the interior of the house, and of clothes and food, were assigned to women. Behaviors related to the manipulation of the physical environment, machines, transportation, the structure of a house, many kinds of recreation, and most kinds of occupations were assigned to men. Recreational behaviors dominate the list of behaviors that were not sex-typed, along with a few out-of-the-home occupations that have been traditionally open to women, such as cooking and waiting on table, selling in retail stores, caring for the sick, and doing office work. Where the girls did disagree with the estimated cultural norm of the adults, the disagreements were matters of weighting rather than a jump from one major category to another. For example, one group might categorize a given behavior as belonging definitely in the area of women's functioning, and the other group might be unable to reach a consensus as to that item's category. A further contradiction to the assertions that children no longer know how to differentiate between what is expected of men and what is expected of women appeared in the direction of these disagreements: compared with the adult sample, these young female subjects tended to sex-type *more* rather than fewer behaviors.

To determine the relationship between their self-concepts and their perceptions of sex-connected roles, the girls were given an independent inventory of equivalent items, with directions to "show what you would like to do when you grow up." Almost without exception, they rejected for themselves the behaviors that, in response to the technique described above, they assigned to men. As exceptions, they said that they would like to play with their male children (a responsibility that they assigned to fathers) and they were ambivalent about a few recreational behaviors involving vigor and daring, and about the directing of household repairs, items they also assigned to men. On the other hand, they looked forward to performing the behaviors they assigned to women, with a few exceptions. Among household activities, the girls rejected the washing of floors, of dishes, and of clothes, and among vocational occupations, that of telephone operator and of beauty technician.[1]

Thus, contrary to the expectations that might stem from the many assertions that have been made about the envy with which girls regard masculine roles, these female subjects did not want to do the things that they perceived as appropriate for men, and they liked, for the most part, the prospect of doing the things that they thought were for women. To give some specific illustrations, these subjects liked the prospect of the different aspects of child care and the home behaviors related to food care and home planning. As a group they were ambivalent about, but tended towards liking, vacuuming, ironing, and making clothes. They were ambivalent about a few occupations—nursing, teaching children, and medicine—with a trend toward disliking office work, clerking, laboratory work, college teaching, and entertaining. All other occupational roles in the inventory were completely rejected. It is interesting to note, at this point, that of twenty-six of the girls who were asked, twenty-four said they planned to marry and have children and twenty said they planned to work after marriage. Only one subject said she planned not to marry and have children, and only two subjects said specifically that they planned not to work.

The small group of boys showed trends similar to those of the girls. Their average percentage of sex-typed items was 72 as compared with the adults' estimate of 67 percent and the girls' average of 70 percent. The content of their categorizations appeared not to differ from that of the girls or from the adult-estimated cultural norm. When they did differ from the estimated norm, they did so mainly by "desegregating" items that the adults assigned to women. In other words, when the boys "desegregated" behaviors at all, these were behaviors that the adult group perceived as being feminine by cultural definition. These behaviors were dominated by child-care items. The same picture presented itself when the item differences between the boys and the girls were examined. The boys tended to assign to both sexes child-care items that were assigned to women by the girls. If these data are prophetic, they indicate a re-entry of men into the home rather than a further exodus of women, but we must remember they were obtained from a very small and specialized sample.

The relationship between the age of the subjects and their concepts and that existing between their mothers' work status and the latter were also explored. No statistically significant differences appeared between the girls who were eight years old and those who were eleven, but some trend in the direction of more sex-typing by the eight year olds was apparent.[2] (Data are being collected from a five-year-old sample that will eventually extend our exploration of the effect of age.)

The degree of sex-typing of role behaviors shown by the girls whose mothers worked did not differ significantly from the adult-estimated norm, but the difference that did appear was in a direction that might have been expected. The average percentage of sex-typing in their responses was 63, as compared to the adults' estimate of 67 percent.

The group of girls whose mothers did not work also did not differ significantly (by statistical test) from the adult group in the degree of sex-typing they evinced, although in general they sex-typed an average of 83 percent of the activities as compared to the average of 67 percent by the adult group. In the items on which they did differ, however, these girls showed a striking trend toward sex-typing behaviors estimated as "desegregated" by the adult sample. These items did not group themselves into any generalized categories; they seemed merely to be reflecting a greater degree of rigidity concerning sex-role concepts on the part of these subjects.

Similar results were obtained when the responses of this group were compared with those of the girls with working mothers. The girls whose mothers were not in the labor force tended to sex-type more items than did the girls with working mothers: 83 percent versus 63 percent. This trend toward more sex-typing, however, did not emphasize any particular role-behaviors.

To approach another aspect of the subjects' identification with their perception of the role-behaviors appropriate to their own sex, we asked the girls to indicate which activities they thought women enjoyed. These conjectured preferences were then compared with their own expressed attitudes toward the same activities. The results of this comparison seem to suggest a degree of individual selection operating within a general framework of agreement with the world of adult women. The girls perceived women as liking all the activities they thought they themselves would like. They did not think, however, that women dislike everything that *they* anticipated disliking. They definitely rejected for themselves some of the things they perceived women as liking to do. Some of these rejections are probably related to their high socioeconomic identifications, such as those involved in the occupations of sales clerk, dressmaker, telephone operator, and beauty parlor technician. Others may relate to a maturational requirement of self-confidence not yet attained: teaching college classes, performing before audiences, and speaking at meetings. Still others might be indicative of a subgroup bias: for example, this sample thought that most women liked to go to church but that they themselves would not.

Although the preliminary analysis of grouped data described above suggested that the process of role differentiation is associated with certain factors in the individual's experience, it obscured striking individual differences. It was believed that a careful analysis of individual protocols would add to understanding the dynamic processes involved in this aspect of socialization. Accordingly, two cases were selected that might illustrate variations in sex-role concepts and throw light on the individual processes and determinants at work in their development. Both subjects were eleven years old, but one was described by her teachers as being extremely "boyish" and the other as "quite feminine."

In contrast to the grouped data discussed above, the responses of the "boyish" girl indicated a liking for only 9 percent of the role behaviors she perceived as typically feminine. This figure takes on added meaning when it is compared with a preference for 50 percent of female-segregated roles displayed by the "feminine" girl of the same age. On the other hand, when the responses to role-behaviors perceived as appropriately masculine by each child were examined, the "boyish" subject liked 23 percent of these items while her more "feminine" peer owned to a liking for only 5 percent.

The greatest contrast between these two girls appeared in the relationship between their own preferences for activities and the attitudes toward these activities that they assigned to adult women. The "feminine" girl was almost completely in agreement with her perceptions of the attitudes of adult women. She indicated dislike for only one activity that she assumed adult women liked, and uncertainty about six. Our "boyish" subject, on the other hand, disliked nineteen activities that she assumed adult women liked, and showed uncertainty about the same number. In her total listing of "things ladies like to do," she also included nine items that she had designated as typically masculine activities. Only two such items appeared in a similar listing by the "feminine" subject.

The general impression created by these data is that one child is comfortably adjusted to the world of sex-roles as she sees it, while the other clearly lacks anchorage. The latter sees herself as disliking a substantial area of activity she perceives as part of the feminine role, and she sees women frustrated over being deprived of activities they would like. The lack of anchorage, however, is not acknowledged openly by this subject in any of her spontaneous verbal materials. The closest she comes to such acknowledgement is by innuendo. Discussing how girls feel about their sex-identity, she says she likes being a girl; then, in response to the question, "Why?", she refuses to pursue the topic with "Don't ask me why—I have no choice." Clearly, analysis of grouped data will tell only a small part of the story in this study.

Another aspect of the study that has yielded some interesting data is that relating to the way eight- and eleven-year-old subjects perceive and react to the implementation of roles that involve separation, an experience that should be important in the determination of their own role concepts. In this part of the study the subjects were shown pictures representing, respectively, a woman leaving a small child, a man leaving a small child, a man leaving a woman, and two children at home. The subjects were told in each case that the departing person was going to work, and were then queried concerning the feeling of each individual in each picture about the event taking place.

In this sample, including both boys and girls, there was no consensus on how the people who were leaving for work felt, but all those who were being left were described as feeling badly. While 100 percent of the subjects thought the child felt badly about the mother's leaving, 81 percent also thought the child felt similarly about its father's leaving, and 55 percent thought that the wife felt badly about her husband's leaving for work. No systematic variation was found in feelings associated with subjects' sex, age, or whether the subject's mother worked or not.

Some trends were perceptible in the children's interpretations of the attitudes of those who were described as going to work. The girls with working mothers reported the mother in the picture as feeling more favorable about going to work than did the girls with nonworking mothers. The boys saw the father as feeling significantly more positive about leaving his wife for work than did the girls, although they did not differ from the girls in interpretation when the picture showed a child being left behind.

These pictures may be tapping an interactional process involving both projection and identification. It may be that when the role-behavior of an adult releases intense negative feelings in a child, the latter's perception of that behavior and its attitudinal components is inaccurate and identification with the role may be impeded. Further work will be needed to check this hypothesis.

In general, it seems to us that the subjects are maintaining quite traditional concepts of sex-connected roles, often in conflict with their own self-definitions. Their responses to questions concerning what "most men" and "most women" do are often quite different from what happens in their own primary social groups. It is almost as if they discount their immediate personal experiences in favor of some impersonal criterion impinging on them from an unspecified external source. They may, of course, be encouraged in this by the attitudes, if not the behavior, of their adult intimates.

Some of the data derived from parent interviews supports this possibility. The working mothers of the subjects, in this small upper-middle-class sample, tend to report that they tell their children that they are working out of the home because of financial need. They express guilt about their working and appear to hold quite traditional concepts of appropriate "feminine" behavior that they feel they are violating. An example is provided by a well-to-do working mother who obviously loves her work but told her daughter that she works because of financial necessity. When asked why she doesn't let her daughter know she enjoys her work, she answered, "Well, then what excuse would I have for working?"

It seems that many sex-role difficulties in the current social scene may be due more to the lack of change in sex-role concepts in the face of a changing reality than to changes in concepts.

A hopeful note arises out of the perceptiveness of a few of the subjects. When asked why some mothers go to work, they, in general, tended to talk about financial need. Occasionally, however, a response like the following was timidly offered: "Some of them work for the money, some of them work because they like to, and some of them work to get away from the children." If more mothers could accept the validity of the second reason, perhaps there would be less need for children to believe the third.

SUMMARY

In summary, the experience with the first small sample of subjects in this exploratory study of the development of concepts of women's roles suggests that, contrary to assumptions that are currently receiving a good deal of acceptance, children of this generation have quite explicit ideas concerning the respective assignment of specific behaviors to men and to women. Furthermore, these concepts may well be quite traditional and conservative and agree quite closely with adult expectations. These observations are based on data collected through extended interviews with twenty-seven girls and eleven boys, eight- and eleven-years old, attending "progressive" schools and coming from above-average socioeconomic family backgrounds. Within this sample, the influence of age or sex on role-concepts seems to be less decisive than the work status of the mother. Subjects with working mothers and those with mothers who are not in the labor force differ from each other in their concepts of sex-appropriate behavior more than either group differs from an adult sample.

The female subjects in the study seem to accept for themselves the role-behaviors they perceive as characteristic of adults of their own sex.

They reject the activities they see as belonging to men and respond positively to those they perceive as primarily for women. They also anticipate implementing much the same attitudes they attribute to adult women.

In addition, these subjects think that the separations from parents caused by the out-of-the-home working role produces negative responses in children and that there is almost as much bad feeling about fathers leaving for work as about mothers—this despite the subjects' conservative concepts that it is men who generally go to work and that women usually do not.

NOTES

1. The rejection of these two occupations may be a function of the relatively high socio-economic level of the subjects.
2. This may be due to differences in the composition of the respective samples—60 per cent of the eleven-year-old subjects had working-mothers while only 50 per cent of the eight-year-olds did.

Sex Differences in the Self-Concepts of Elementary-school Children*

CHERYL L. REED, DONALD W. FELKER,
RICHARD S. KAY, and DOUGLAS J. STANWYCK

Many research workers have confirmed the popular belief that the male is regarded more highly than the female by both men and women.[1] Women evaluate women less favorably than they do men and also women evaluate themselves less favorably than men evaluate themselves.[2] It has also been found that a larger proportion of women would prefer to be men than vice versa.[3] McKee and Sherriffs suggested that the differences in esteem with which the two sexes are regarded will be reflected in the self-concepts of men and women.[4]

Since children as young as five or six are aware of sex differences in power and prestige,[5] one might hypothesize that elementary-school girls would have a poorer self-concept than elementary-school boys. However, total self-concept scores for boys and girls have frequently been found to be equal.[6] Even though total self-concept scores are the same, the scores are not equally predictive for the sexes. For example, Lekarczyk and Hill found no differences in self-esteem scores of boys and girls in the fifth and sixth grades.[7] However, self-esteem was significantly negatively correlated to test anxiety for boys but not for girls and high self-esteem was

* Cheryl L. Reed, Donald W. Felker, Richard S. Kay, and Douglas J. Stanwyck, "Sex Differences in the Self-Concepts of Elementary-School Children." Reprinted with permission of the authors. A slightly different version of this article was presented at the 1973 Annual Meeting of the American Educational Research Association.

positively related to verbal learning for boys but not for girls. Sears found that femininity in both boys and girls was related to poor self-concept, although there were no sex differences in self-concept.[8] These findings may indicate that boys and girls report their self-concepts differently, perhaps in relation to sex appropriateness of the items as identified by peers or significant others.

Sex differences in self-concept may also be confounded by differences in socioeconomic groups. Soares and Soares in a study of fourth- through eighth-grade students, found that advantaged girls tended to be higher than advantaged boys and disadvantaged boys tended to be higher than advantaged girls in self-perceptions.[9] Zirkel reviewed several studies that indicated that differences between reported self-concepts of black subjects and white subjects disappeared when socioeconomic class was taken into account.[10] Thus, past research indicates differences in self-concept may exist between various socioeconomic groups. However, these differences have not been related to differences in sex appropriateness of the items.

Coopersmith found that although boys and girls had the same self-concept scores, teachers rated girls significantly higher than boys on a self-concept scale.[11] A study of nursery-school children indicated that teachers more often reinforced feminine-type behaviors than masculine behaviors, although they did reinforce boys but not girls when children performed masculine behaviors.[12] These differential expectations of teachers may also influence the student's conception of the sex appropriateness of various self-concept items. The present study investigated how lower- and middle-class boys and girls differ in self-concept and related these differences to stereotypic ideals set by teachers. The specific purposes were:

1. To identify how lower-class, inner-city boys and girls differ in reported self-concept.
2. To identify how middle-class, rural and urban boys and girls differ in reported self-concept.
3. To compare the sex differences in reported self-concept found in differing socioeconomic classroom environments.
4. To identify how teachers believe elementary-school boys and girls differ in self-concept.
5. To compare the teachers' stereotypic beliefs of boys' and girls' self-concepts to differences in boys' and girls' reported self-concepts.

METHODS

The Piers-Harris self-concept scale was administered in group sessions to subjects in three samples.[13] Sample one consisted primarily of lower-class students, grades three through six from eight inner-city, predominantly black elementary schools. Sample two consisted primarily of middle-class students, grades three through six from four middle-class predominantly white elementary schools. These included three rural, small-town schools and one urban school. The self-concept scale was administered to both samples by a university tester reading each item to intact classroom groups. Sample sizes for the first two samples by grade and sex are presented in Table 1. Sample three consisted of elementary and secondary teachers (sixty-six females and thirty-six males) enrolled in graduate-level education courses. These teachers were asked to mark each item as a "typical" or "average" elementary-school boy (or girl) would mark it. These instructions were designed to elicit "stereotypic" responses from the teachers about boys' and girls' self-concepts. Fifty-eight teachers were asked to respond as a "typical boy" and forty-four were asked to respond as a "typical girl."

Table 1

Sample Sizes by Sex and Grade

Grade	Lower Class		Middle Class	
	Boys	Girls	Boys	Girls
3	152	112	193	170
4	132	125	192	159
5	112	108	101	101
6	87	102	108	110

In order to identify how the sexes differ in self-concept within samples one and two (purposes 1 and 2), a chi-square test was applied to individual item results. Boys' and girls' item responses within each grade and within each sample were compared in this manner. Differentiating items will be referred to as "male positive" or "female positive" depending on which group (boys or girls) more frequently marked the item in the manner indicative of positive self-concept. Differences in total self-concept scores were tested in each sample using a two-way analysis of variance with sex and grade (four levels) as factors. Bartlett's test of homogeneity of variance was applied to the eight age and sex groups in each sample. Homogeneity of variance was found to hold in each sample.

A variety of techniques were used to compare the sex differences in reported self-concept found in differing socioeconomic classroom environments (purpose 3). Identified sex differences were compared across groups using various methods of item classification. Items were classified by grade and sample according to which sex most frequently answered in the positive direction. Each of the factors developed by Piers and Harris was discussed in relation to whether it contained primarily male-positive or female-positive items.[14] The six factors included in the test were "Behavior" (eighteen items), "Intellectual and School Status" (eighteen items), "Physical Appearance and Attributes" (twelve items), "Anxiety" (thirteen items), "Popularity" (twelve items), and "Happiness and Satisfaction" (nine items). Also, Newman Keuls tests were used at each grade level to identify significant differences in total self-concept scores of boys and girls in the two samples within each grade.[15]

Differences in teachers' total ratings of a "typical" boy's or girl's self-concept (purpose 4) were identified using a one-way analysis of variance. A chi-square analysis was used to identify sex-discriminating items based on teacher ratings of "typical" boys and girls. Finally, teachers' stereotypic beliefs of "typical" students' self-concepts were compared to sex differences in self-concept identified in each sample of students (purpose 5). This was done by comparing the male-positive and female-positive items found in the student samples to the male-positive and female-positive items identified from teacher ratings.

RESULTS

The first purpose of this study was to identify how lower-class, inner-city boys and girls differ in reported self-concept. The chi-square tests by items within grades resulted in sixty-eight significant differences[16] (.05 level or beyond) in boys' and girls' item responses (only sixteen would be expected by chance). Item results indicate more male-positive items than female-positive items (see Table 2).

Table 2

Distribution of Item Differences by Grade Within Samples

		GRADE				
		3	4	5	6	Items Overall
Lower[17] Class Sample	Male Positive	12	9	12	22	28
	Female Positive	1	4	4	2	9
Middle Class Sample	Male Positive	10	11	12	12	19
	Female Positive	28	11	8	11	33

The number of male-positive and female-positive items found in each factor is given in Table 3.

Table 3

Distribution of Sex Differences on Items by Factor

	Lower-Class Sample[18]		Middle-Class Sample	
Factor	Male Positive	Female Positive	Male Positive	Female Positive
I. Behavior	1	8	1	16
II. School	7	0	4	6
III. Appearance	8	0	3	4
IV. Anxiety	7	0	8	0
V. Popularity	2	0	3	2
VI. Happiness	2	0	1	1
None of the factors	5	2	3	6

The existing female-positive items were almost exclusively items belonging to the "Behavior" factor identified by Piers and Harris.[19] The female-positive behavior items included items such as "I am well behaved in school.", "I behave badly at home.", and "I get into a lot of fights." Each of the remaining five factors contained more male-positive than female-positive items. In general, lower-class girls report a more negative view of themselves than do lower-class boys, except in terms of behavior. The boys more than girls take a positive view of themselves in terms of "Physical Appearance and Attributes" (e.g., "I am strong." and "I am a leader in games and sports."); "Intellectual and School Status" (e.g., "I get nervous when the teacher calls on me." and "I can give a good report in front of the class."); "Anxiety" (e.g., "I give up easily." and "I am often afraid."); and to a lesser extent in terms of "Popularity" items (e.g., "I am popular with boys." and "I have many friends.") and "Happiness and Satisfaction" items (e.g., "I am unhappy." and "I am unlucky."). In the lower-class sample, girls had significantly lower total self-concept scores than boys. There were no significant grade or grade by sex differences. The means and standard deviations by grade are presented in Table 4.

Table 4

Means and Standard Deviations of Total Self-Concept Scores

		Lower-Class Sample		Middle-Class Sample		
Grade		Males (M1)	Females (F1)	Males (M2)	Females (F2)	(Differences in Means)
3	Mean	56.16	53.98	53.91	56.61	N.S.
	S.D.	(12.40)	(12.14)	(12.74)	(13.54)	
4	Mean	52.91	51.98	55.37	56.28	F 2 > F 1
	S.D.	(11.51)	(12.21)	(14.37)	(14.13)	
5	Mean	54.36	51.47	57.24	55.83	M 2 > F 1
	S.D.	(12.89)	(13.74)	(13.68)	(15.04)	
6	Mean	55.55	49.84	55.16	55.99	F 2 > F 1, M 2 > F 1 M 1 > F 1
	S.D.	(14.01)	(14.16)	(12.10)	(13.36)	

The second purpose of this study was to identify how middle-class rural and urban boys and girls differ in reported self-concept. The chi-square tests by item within grade resulted in 109 significant differences (.05 level or beyond). The distribution of items exhibiting sex differences by grade are presented in Table 2. In third grade there were more female-positive than male-positive items. However, in grades four through six the number of male- and female-positive items were almost the same. The distribution of items exhibiting sex differences by factor is given in Table 3. Girls more frequently answered the "Behavior" items in a positive direction while boys responded to "Anxiety" related items more positively. No significant differences were found in the total self-concept scores by sex, by grade, or by sex and grade interaction in this sample. Means and standard deviations by sex and grade are presented in Table 4.

The third purpose of this study was to compare the differences in reported self-concepts of lower- and middle-class students. A notable difference between the two samples was the lower self-concept reported by lower-class girls. This is evidenced by lower total self-concept scores and fewer female-positive items. In the lower-class sample boys had a significantly higher self-concept than girls, while in the middle-class sample no significant differences were found. The results of the Newman Keuls tests that compared means of boys and girls in both samples within grades are presented in Table 4. In every grade except third, lower-class girls had significantly lower self-concepts than at least one group from the middle-class sample. Lower-class boys tended to take an especially positive view of themselves (in relation to lower-class girls) in terms of "Physical Appearance and Attributes" and "Intellectual and School Status" (see Table 3). Middle-class boys and girls appeared to have approximately the same number of positive views of themselves in these two areas. The two samples were similar in that girls responded to those items relating to "Behavior" while boys responded to items relating to "Anxiety" in the manner suggesting a positive self-concept. In other words, girls reported themselves to be more anxious and better behaved than boys in both samples. Piers also reported finding similar sex differences.[20] Six items were found to be female positive in the middle-class sample and male positive in the lower-class sample. These items were "I am an important member of my family.", "I have nice hair.", "I have a pleasant face.", "I have many friends.", I have a good figure.", and "I am always dropping or breaking things." There were no items that were female positive in the lower-class sample but male positive in the middle-class sample.

The fourth purpose of this study was to identify teachers' perceptions of differences in self-concept between elementary-school boys and girls. The present study found no significant differences in total teacher-rated "typical boy" (mean = 55.5) and "typical girl" (mean = 57.4) self-concept scores. Still, fifteen items were found to differentiate "typical" boys and girls. Ten of these fifteen items identified were female positive, i.e., indicating that teachers would expect girls to answer more frequently than boys in the direction of positive self-concept.

The fifth purpose of this study was to compare teachers' stereotypic beliefs of sex differences in self-concept to the previously identified differences in boys' and girls' reported self-concepts (purpose 5). The items identified by teachers as differentiating were all identified as differentiating boys and girls in the middle-class sample but not in the lower-class sample (see Table 5). This is partially due to the lower self-concept scores of lower-class girls. Teachers were best at identifying male-positive and female-positive items related to the "Achievement and School Status" factor (60% success on the items differentiating middle-class boys and girls). They also identified all the (middle-class) male-positive items on the "Physical Appearance and Attributes" factor.

Table 5

Factor Structure of Teacher-Identified Differentiating Items[21]

Factors	Lower-Class		Middle-Class	
	Males	Females	Males	Females
I: Behavior	0	2	0	3
II: School	1	0	2	4
III: Appearance	3	0	3	1
IV: Anxiety	1	0	1	0
V: Popularity	1	0	1	1
VI: Happiness	0	0	0	0

DISCUSSION AND IMPLICATIONS

Sex-appropriate behavior is an aspect of socially desirable behavior that will differentiate the appropriateness of specific acts for boys and girls. Since self-concept and social desirability measures are correlated one might expect reported self-concept scores to have a different meaning for boys and girls to the extent that differentially sex-appropriate items exist on the scale.[22] The results of this study indicate that many items on the self-concept measure are marked differentially by boys and girls in both lower and middle classes. However, it is impossible to conclude from this study whether the differences result from "differential sex-appropriate items" or "differential self-perceptions" that are sex related. In either case, this indicates the existence of a sex-by-item interaction, resulting in total-score comparisons for the two sexes being inappropriate.[23] Several alternatives to total scores are being investigated by the authors at the present time. The use of factor scores rather than total scores may partially account for sex differences. The use of item responses as the basic data for analyses in repeated measures designs would identify when sex-item interaction existed.[24]

Further research is needed to identify why boys and girls respond differently to some items. It is likely that self-evaluation in areas of the most importance to an individual are the most important determiners of the individual's self-concept. It may be that girls value good behavior more than boys. If this is true, negative self-evaluations by a girl on behavior items would imply a much lower self-concept than the same self-evaluations by a boy who values behavior less. Bardwick gives a good example of how these differences in values may influence boys' and girls' responses to the school environment.[25] Girls appear to have an advantage in elementary school because they tend to behave and do what the teacher tells them. Because good behavior is so important to a girl's self-concept, girls tend to be conformists. Bardwick suggests, that since conformity or good behavior are not important to boy's self-concept, boys are freer to develop creativity than girls.[26]

Teachers can help students to develop their self-concepts. Felker, Stanwyck, and Kay have enumerated five principles for teachers to use to cultivate a positive self-concept in children.[27] These are:

(1) Adults: praise yourselves
(2) Help children evaluate realistically
(3) Teach children to set reasonable goals
(4) Teach children to praise themselves
(5) Teach children to praise others.

Teachers may be able to overcome some of the negative effects of values determined by sex appropriateness using these principles. For example, teachers could praise themselves and teach children to praise themselves and others for accomplishments regardless of their sex appropriateness.

REFERENCES

Bardwick, J. M. 1971. *Psychology of women.* New York: Harper & Row.

Clarkson, F. E.; Vogel, S. R.; Broverman, I. K.; Broverman, D. M.; and Rosenkrantz, P. S. 1969. Family size and sex-role stereotypes. *Science* 167: 390–92.

Coopersmith, S. 1967. *The antecedents of self-esteem.* San Francisco: Freeman.

Fagot, B. I., and Patterson, G. R. 1969. An *in vivo* analysis of reinforcing contingencies for sex-role behaviors in the preschool child. *Developmental psychology* 1: 563–68.

Farls. R. 1966. Unpublished data received from Freedom Area School District, Freedom, Pennsylvania. In 1969 *Manual for the Piers-Harris children's self-concept scale.* Nashville: Counselor Recordings and Tests.

Felker, D. W.; Stanwyck, D. J.; and Kay, R. S. 1973. The effects of a teacher program in self-concept enhancement on pupils' self-concept, anxiety, and intellectual achievement responsibility. *Journal of educational research* 66: 443–45.

Guardo, C. J. 1969. Sociometric status and self-concept in sixth graders. *Journal of educational research* 62: 320–22.

Horowitz, R. 1943. A pictorial method for study of self-identification in pre-school children. *Journal of genetic psychology* 62: 135–48.

Jarrett, R. F., and Sherriffs, A. C. 1953. Propaganda, debate, and impartial presentation as determiners of attitude change. *Journal of abnormal and social psychology* 48: 33–41.

Kohlberg, L. 1966. A cognitive-developmental analysis of children's sex-role concepts and attitudes. In *The development of sex differences* ed. E. E. Maccoby. Stanford: Stanford University Press, pp. 82–173.

Lekarczyk, D. L., and Hill, K. L. 1969. Self-esteem, test anxiety, stress, and verbal learning. *Developmental psychology* 1: 147–54.

Lynn, D. B. 1959. A note on sex differences in the development of masculine and feminine identification. *Psychological review* 66: 126–35.

Mandeville, G. K. 1972. A new look at treatment differences. *American educational research journal* 9: 311–21.

McKee, J. P., and Sherriffs, A. C. 1957. The differential evaluation of males and females. *Journal of personality* 26: 356–71.

———. 1959. Men's and women's beliefs, ideals & self-concepts. *American journal of sociology* 64: 356–63.

Millen, L. 1966. The relationship between self-concept, social desirability, and anxiety in children. Unpublished M.Sc. thesis, Pennsylvania State University. In 1969 *Manual for the Piers-Harris children's self-concept scale.* Nashville: Counselor Recordings and Tests.

Piers, E. V. 1965. Children's self-ratings and rating by others. Unpublished paper. In 1969 *Manual for the Piers-Harris children's self-concept scale.* Nashville: Counselor Recordings and Tests.

———. 1969. *Manual for the Piers-Harris children's self-concept scale.* Nashville: Counselor Recordings and Tests.

——— and Harris, D. B. 1964. Age and other correlates of self-concept in children. *Journal of educational psychology* 55: 91–95.

Rosenkrantz, P.; Vogel, S.; Bee, H.; Broverman, I., and Broverman, D. M. 1968. Sex-role stereotypes and self-concepts in college students. *Journal of consulting and clinical psychology* 32: 287–95.

Sears, R. R. 1970. Relation of early socialization experiences to self-concepts and gender role in middle childhood. *Child development* 41: 267–89.

Soars, A. T., and Soars, L. M. 1969. Self-perceptions of culturally disadvantaged children. *American educational research journal* 6: 31–45.

Stanwyck, D. J., and Felker, D. W. 1971. Intellectual achievement responsibility and anxiety as a function of self-concept of third- to sixth-grade boys and girls. A paper presented at the Annual Meeting of the American Educational Research Association, New York.

Steinmann, A.; Levi, J.; and Fox, D. J. 1964. Self-concept of college women compared with their concept of the ideal woman and men's ideal woman. *Journal of counseling psychology* 11: 370–74.

Winer, B. J. 1972. *Statistical principles in experimental design.* New York: McGraw-Hill.

Zirkel, P. A. 1971. Self-concept and the "disadvantage" of ethnic group membership and mixture. *Review of educational research* 41: 271–75.

NOTES

1. R. F. Jarrett and A. C. Sherriffs, "Propaganda, Debate, and Impartial Pre-

sentation as Determiners of Attitude Change," *Journal of Abnormal and Social Psychology* 48 (1953) : 33–41; J. P. McKee and A. C. Sherriffs, "The Differential Evaluations of Males and Females," *Joural of Personality* 26 (1957) : 356–71; and P. Rosenkrantz et al., "Sex-role Stereotypes and Self-concepts in College Students," *Journal of Consulting and Clinical Psychology* 32 (1968) : 287–95.

2. F. E. Clarkson et al., "Family Size and Sex-role Stereotypes," *Science* 167 (1969) : 39–92; J. P. McKee and A. C. Sherriffs, "Men's and Women's Beliefs, Ideals, and Self-concepts," *American Journal of Sociology* 64 (1959) : 356–63; Rosenkrantz et al., "Sex-role Stereotypes"; and A. Steinmann, J. Levi, and D. J. Fox, "Self-concept of College Women Compared with Their Concept of the Ideal Woman and Man's Ideal Woman," *Journal of Counseling Psychology* 11 (1964) : 370–74.
3. D. B. Lynn, "A Note on Sex Differences in the Development of Masculine and Feminine Identification," *Psychological Review* 66 (1959) : 126–35.
4. McKee and Sherriffs, "Men's and Women's Beliefs."
5. R. Horowitz, "A Pictorial Method for Study of Self-identification in Pre-school Children," *Journal of Genetic Psychology* 62 (1943) : 135–48; and L. Kohlberg, "A Cognitive-developmental Analysis of Children's Sex-role Concepts and Attitudes," in *The Development of Sex Differences,* ed., E. E. Maccoby (Stanford: Stanford University Press, 1966) pp. 82–173.
6. S. Coopersmith, *The Antecedents of Self-esteem* (San Francisco: Freeman, 1967) ; R. Farls, unpublished data received from Freedom Area School District, Freedom, Pennsylvania, in *Manual for the Piers-Harris Children's Self-concept Scale* (Nashville: Counselor Recordings and Tests, 1969) ; D. L. Lekarczyk and K. L. Hill, "Self-esteem, Test Anxiety, Stress, and Verbal Learning," *Developmental Psychology* 1 (1969) : 147–54; L. Millen, "The Relationship Between Self-concept, Social Desirability, and Anxiety in Children" (M.Sc. thesis, Pennsylvania State University, 1966) , cited in *Manual for the Piers-Harris Children's Self-concept Scale* (Nashville: Counselor Recordings and Tests, 1969) ; E. V. Piers, "Children's Self-ratings and Ratings by Others," unpublished paper cited in *Manual for the Piers-Harris Children's Self-concept Scale* (Nashville: Counselor Recordings and Tests, 1969) ; E. V. Piers and D. B. Harris, "Age and Other Correlates of Self-concept in Children," *Journal of Educational Psychology* 55 (1964) : 91–95; and R. R. Sears, "Relation of Early Socialization Experiences to Self-concepts and Gender Role in Middle Childhood," *Child Development* 41 (1970) : 267–89.
7. D. L. Lekarczyk and K. L. Hill, "Self-esteem."
8. Sears, "Relation of Early Socialization."
9. A. T. Soars and L. M. Soars, "Self-perceptions of Culturally Disadvantaged Children," *American Educational Research Journal* 6 (1969) : 31–45.
10. P. A. Zirkel, "Self-concept and the 'Disadvantage' of Ethnic Group Membership and Mixture," *Review of Educational Research* 41 (1971) : 271–75.
11. Coopersmith, *Antecedents.*
12. B. I. Fagot and G. R. Patterson, "An *In Vivo* Analysis of Reinforcing Contingencies for Sex-role Behaviors in the Preschool Child," *Developmental Psychology* 1 (1969) : 563–68.
13. Piers and Harris, "Age and Other Correlates."
14. Ibid.
15. B. J. Winer, *Statistical Principles in Experimental Design* (New York: McGraw-Hill, 1972) .

16. The specific results of the chi-square tests by item have not been presented here due to the large number of differences found. A complete table of the findings may be obtained by writing the first author.
17. One item was omitted in the tabulation of items in the lower-class sample because it was marked male positive in one grade and female positive in another.
18. Ibid.
19. Piers and Harris, "Age and Other Correlates."
20. Piers, "'Children's Self-ratings."
21. Only items identified as differentiating by both teacher and student samples are included.
22. Miller, "Relationship Between Self-concept."
23. G. K. Mandeville, "A New Look at Treatment Differences," *American Educational Research Journal* 9 (1972) : 311–21.
24. Ibid.
25. J. M. Bardwick, *Psychology of Women* (New York: Harper and Row, 1971).
26. Ibid.
27. D. W. Felker, D. J. Stanwyck, and R. S. Kay, "The Effects of a Teacher Program in Self-concept Enhancement of Pupils' Self-concept, Anxiety, and Intellectual Achievement Responsibility," *Journal of Educational Research* 66 (1973) : 443–45.

Girls—More Moral Than Boys or Just Sneakier?*

RICHARD L. KREBS

"Sugar and spice and everything nice . . . ," the cultural stereotype of girls being good and boys being bad is part of our folklore. In talking with teachers and reading the education literature one gets the impression that teachers are strongly influenced by this stereotype.[1] The following research was undertaken both to check on the existence of the impression that teachers do see girls as more moral than boys and also to assess the accuracy of the teachers' perceptions.

A random sample of sixth-grade children was selected from ten classes in a middle-class and a working-class school to fit a balanced factorial design with two factors, sex and social class. The boys and girls groups were controlled for IQ. The IQ scores were obtained from the school records and were based on standardized group intelligence tests. While the design called for 132 Subjects, only 127 Subjects were obtained. (Five working-class boys were lost during the study).

To assess the influence of the cultural stereotype on the teachers' perceptions of boys and girls, teachers were asked to rate the Subjects on three scales of morality previously used by Kohlberg: trustworthiness, obedience, and respect for others' rights.[2]

To assess the accuracy of the teachers' perceptions, two behavioral measures of morality were employed: Kohlberg's moral judgment inventory and three cheating tests. Kohlberg's moral judgment inventory uses a series of ten hypothetical moral dilemmas to identify a child's level of moral judgment. This level of moral judgment has, in turn, been found to be related to other indices of morality, such as nondelinquency.

The three cheating tests consisted of an individual test and two group

* Reprinted with permission of the author.

tests. In the individual cheating test the Subjects played a ray-gun and a model-house game, while the experimenter sat at a table some distance from the game working on some papers. The ray-gun game was similar to the one developed by Grinder and consisted of a revolving target that the subject tried to shoot with a ray gun.[3] In the model-house game the subject was supposed to arrange furniture in a series of rooms.

If the subject obtained a score of twenty-five points in the games, he received a prize; a sharp shooter's medal for the ray-gun game and an ID bracelet for the model-house game. Each subject recorded his own score. The games had been programmed so that it was necessary to cheat in order to win the prize.

The two group tests were adaptations of Hartshorne and May's Improbable Achievement Tests. The first of the two tests consisted of rows of small circles in which the subject was supposed to write the numbers one through ten with his eyes closed. While the children took the test, the experimenter stood with his back to the class and looked at the clock on the wall to time the test. On the second group test the subject was given a sheet of paper with drawings of blocks piled on top of one another. The subject was supposed to decide how many blocks were touching a block with an x on it and write that number next to the x. At the end of the test, a confidant called the experimenter out of the room for three minutes. In both the individual and group-testing situations the experimenter appeared indifferent to the child's behavior and made no clear demands beyond a brief explanation of the rules of the games.

RESULTS

Table 1 shows that on the teacher ratings of morality, girls were rated as more moral than boys on all three scales for both middle-class and working-class children.

Turning to the behavioral indices of morality we find that on Kohlberg's moral judgment inventory, Table 2, girls were not more moral than boys. In fact, in the middle-class group, boys were more moral than girls.

Table 3 shows that there were no significant differences between middle-class boys and girls on the three cheating tests. Table 3 indicates that in the working-class group, girls *were* more moral than boys on one of the three cheating tests.

The results suggest that teachers do view girls as more moral than boys, but the teachers' viewpoint is not supported by behavioral evidence. The latter results are in general agreement with previous research on differential moral behavior in boys and girls. Most previous researchers have found no difference in cheating behavior in boys and girls although some did find a few cases in which boys were more honest than girls and girls gave more service to other people than boys did.[4]

If girls are not more moral than boys, why do teachers persist in thinking that they are?

One possible explanation is that girls are more conforming than boys. Terman and Tyler's review indicates that girls have lower delinquency rates than boys and they get into less trouble at home and at school than boys do.[5] Apparently, girls conform to external adult standards better than boys do. However, when these standards are not clearly indicated by an authority, as is the case in both the moral judgment inventory and the cheating tests, girls do not act any more morally than boys.

In addition to needing more clearly defined standards, it is also possible that girls respond more to the apparent interest of the authority than boys do. Hartshorne and May found that girls cheated more than boys when the tests were of the take-home variety.[6] Mutterer found that girls cheated more on tests when the rewards were made publicly than they did when the rewards were made in private, while boys cheated at the same rate regardless of the way the reward was presented.[7] Girls perform less well, when they are responding to an authority who appears disinterested and is not making clear demands.

Apparently, girls do look better than boys do when the teacher is present and making demands, but teachers have mistakenly assumed that girls are generally more moral than boys; that they are more moral not only when the teacher is present, but also when she is absent. Not only when she is concerned about her students' behavior, but also when she is disinterested.

If this were the end of the proposed causal chain then the research would not have been of much importance. I would have had a neat little study that showed that teachers have been falsely influenced by a cultural stereotype and by the overt behavior of their students. Teachers have assumed girls are more moral, when in fact they are only more conforming. However, the research of Ausubel has suggested that there may be another step in the causal chain.[8] Fourth- and fifth-grade girls see themselves as more accepted and intrinsically worthwhile than boys do. Katz and Zigler also found similar results in fifth-grade children regarding a discrepancy between real self and self as seen by others.[9] There are two ways to interpret the fact that boys have lower self-esteem than girls do. Perhaps the message has been getting through to the children that the stereotype of boys is less moral than girls and is being perpetuated by the teachers at the cost of lowered self-esteem in boys. Another interpretation is suggested by the work of Zigler who found that feelings about the self are related to increased maturity. He found that there was a decrease in the relationship between the real self and the ideal self with increased age. As children get older, they realize that they aren't what they want to be. This increased discrepancy is apparently related both to an increased ideal self (i.e., higher standards) and increased cognitive differentiation.

If Zigler's analysis is correct, then perhaps the causal chain should not go from teacher to student but rather from student to teacher. It is possible that the boys' lowered self-esteem reflects his greater maturity in this developmental variable and the teacher is responding to the boys' lowered self-esteem rather than creating it.

The question of causation cannot really be answered by this study. However, the study does raise interesting questions about the nature of the relationship between transmitted cultural stereotypes, moral behavior, and self-perceptions in children.

Table 1

Teacher Ratings of Morality—Middle-Class Subjects

Scale	N	X	S2	t	P
Trustworthiness—	BOYS -33	11.26	10.22		
	GIRLS-33	22.39	10.32	10.91	<.001
Obedience	BOYS -33	12.63	11.88		
	GIRLS-33	23.83	10.48	13.49	<.001
Respect for	BOYS -33	8.77	8.21		
Others' Rights	GIRLS-33	15.50	10.13	6.94	<.001

Teacher Ratings of Morality—Working-Class Subjects

Scale	N	X	S2	t	P
Trustworthiness—	BOYS -28	20.88	18.73		
	GIRLS-33	41.52	25.00	13.58	<.001
Obedience	BOYS -28	18.53	12.57		
	GIRLS-33	23.27	9.95	5.27	<.001
Respect for	BOYS -28	16.32	12.24		
Others' Rights	GIRLS-33	20.18	11.24	4.20	<.001

Table 2

Behavioral Indices of Morality—Kohlberg's Moral Judgment Inventory

Scale	N	X	S2	t	P
Middle Class	BOYS -33	278	11.36		
	GIRLS-33	263	9.91	4.54	<.001
Working Class	BOYS -28	243	7.21		
	GIRLS-33	256	6.14	.40	N.S.

Table 3

Behavioral Indices of Morality—Cheating Tests—Middle Class

Scale	N	X	S2	t	P
Individual Test	BOYS -33	4.88	10.62		
	GIRLS-33	5.17	13.56	.26	N.S.
Group Test—Circles	BOYS -33	5.94	4.81		N.S.
	GIRLS-33	7.94	5.83	1.10	
Group Test—Blocks	BOYS -33	10.55	3.48		
	GIRLS-33	10.49	4.15	.08	N.S.

Behavioral Indices of Morality—Cheating Tests—Working Class

Scale	N	X	S2	t	P
Individual Test	BOYS -28	5.47	10.65		
	GIRLS-33	2.31	8.14	5.45	<.001
Group Test—Circles	BOYS -28	6.47	6.30		
	GIRLS-33	5.97	2.83	.94	N.S.
Group Test—Blocks	BOYS -28	10.80	3.99		
	GIRLS-33	11.17	3.94	.76	N.S.

REFERENCES

Ausubel, D. 1954. Perceived parents' attitudes as determinants of children's ego structures. *Child development* 25: 173–83.

Burton, R. V.; Maccoby, Eleanor E.; and Allinsmith W. 1961. Antecedents of resistance to temptation in four-year-old children. *Child development* 32: 689–710.

Grinder, R. E. 1961. New techniques for research in children's temptation behavior. *Child development* 32: 679–88.

———. 1962. Parental childrearing practices, conscience, and resistance to temptation of sixth-grade children. *Child development* 33: 803–20.

Hartshorne, H., and May, M. 1928–30. *Studies in the nature of character*. New York: MacMillan.

Johnson, L. 1943. Pupil cheating. *Education digest* 9: 32–33.

Katz, P., and Zigler, E. 1967. Self-image disparity: a developmental approach. *Journal of personality and social psychology* 5, no. 2: 186–95.

Kohlberg, L. 1958. The development of modes of moral thinking and choice in the years ten to sixteen. Unpublished doctoral dissertation, University of Chicago.

Krebs, R. 1967. Some relationships between moral judgment, attention, and resistance to temptation. Unpublished doctoral dissertation, University of Chicago.

Meyer, W., and Thompson, G. 1956. The differences in the distribution of teacher approval and disapproval among sixth-grade children. *Journal of educational psychology* 47: 385–96.

Mutterer, M. 1965. Factors affecting the specificity of preadolescents' behavior in a variety of temptation situations. Unpublished master's thesis, University of Wisconsin.

Nelson, E.; Grinder, R.; and Howard, J. 1967. Resistance to temptation and moral judgment; behavioral correlates of Kohlberg's measure of moral development. Paper presented at the Society for Research in Child Development, New York, March 1967.

Terman, L., and Tyler, L. 1946. Psychological sex difference. In *Manual of child psychology,* ed. L. Carmichael. New York: John Wiley.

NOTES

1. L. Terman and L. Tyler, "Psychological Sex Difference," in *Manual of Child Psychology,* ed. L. Carmichael (New York: John Wiley, 1946); W. Meyer and G. Thompson, "The Differences in the Distribution of Teacher Approval and Disapproval Among Sixth-grade Children," *Journal of Educational Psychology* 47 (1956): 385–96.
2. L. Kohlberg, "The Development of Modes of Moral Thinking and Choice in the Years Ten to Sixteen" (Ph.D. diss., University of Chicago, 1958).
3. R. E. Grinder, "New Techniques for Research in Children's Temptation Behavior, *Child Development* 32 (1961): 679–88.
4. M. Mutterer, "Factors Affecting the Specificity of Preadolescents' Behavior in a Variety of Temptation Situations" (M.A. thesis, University of Wisconsin, 1965); E. Nelson, R. Grinder, and J. Howard, "Resistance to Temptation and Moral Judgment: Behavioral Correlates of Kohlberg's Measure of Moral Development" (Paper delivered at the Society for Research in Child Development, New York, March 1967); and R. V. Burton, Eleanor Maccoby, and W. Allensmith, "Antecedents of Resistance to Temptation in Four-year-old Children," *Child Development* 32 (1961): 689–710; L. Johnson, "Pupil Cheating," *Education Digest* 9 (1943): 32; and H. Hartshorne and M. May, *Studies in the Nature of Character* (New York: MacMillan, 1928–30).
5. Terman and Tyler, "Psychological."
6. Hartshorne and May, *Studies.*
7. Mutterer, "Factors."
8. D. Ausubel, "Perceived Parents' Attitudes as Determinants of Children's Ego Structures," *Child Development* 25 (1954): 173–83.
9. P. Katz and E. Zigler, "Self-image Disparity: A Developmental Approach," *Journal of Personality and Social Psychology* 5 (1967): 185–95.

Secondary Education

The articles in this section are devoted to students' sex-typed attitudes regarding each other, and how these attitudes are enforced or reinforced by junior and senior high schools.

James Coleman asks what attributes of girls are most desirable in the high-school culture. Unfortunately, the answer is "attractiveness." Both boys and girls emphasize superficial qualities such as appearance in regard to popularity with boys and success in school. This means that attractiveness is placed in a category of school success. How is the school combating the effects of an adolescent social system that emphasizes girls as "desirable objects" for boys? ("Desirable objects" would probably translate as "sex object" in today's terminology.)

Coleman shows that the training of girls as objects for boys will lead to life maladjustments, unless, as he shockingly concludes, the girls become models or call girls. Coleman concludes that coeducation, since it produces these unhealthy and artificial values for girls, possibly promotes serious adjustment problems for girls later in life.

In Mary Jean Gander's "Sex-Typing in the High School," high-school girls were significantly more liberal in their sex-typing attitudes than were high-school boys. Senior girls were the most liberal, while sophomore boys were the most conservative. Gander noted that, in general, there was a sufficient amount of liberal feeling among the students to warrant less rigid sex-typing policies in high schools. Gander's questionnaire will be of interest to those who need instruments to measure sex bias.

Andrew Fishel and Janice Pottker's "Sex Bias in Secondary Schools: The Impact of Title IX" discusses the effect of new federal regulations in high schools. Those school areas that will be most influenced are: admission to vocational schools, admission to classes, and participation in physical education and extracurricular programs.

Girls traditionally have been offered fewer vocational courses than boys, and these have led girls to lower-paying jobs. Girls will not be barred from industrial-arts courses, nor will boys be barred from home-economics classes.

But the major impact of Title IX will be on physical-education programs. Since under Title IX activities cannot be restricted to one sex, physical-education classes will become coeducational. It will be illegal to restrict participation in noncontact sports to one sex: teams will either become coeducational, or each sex will have its own team. Since girls' sports have had little support in comparison to boys' sports, Title IX regulations will dramatically change the sports picture for girls.

A. J. H. Gaite studied "Teachers Perceptions of Ideal Male and Female Students: Male Chauvinism in the Schools" and found that teachers' descriptions of what activities excellent male and female students would be engaged in at ages twenty-one and thirty-one are widely disparate. Males were portrayed as pursuing higher education, job success, and political or community activities. Family life was ancillary to males' pursuits, while females were described as having marriage and children as their only interest. Although boys were given a wide range of jobs, girls' jobs were limited to that of nurse, elementary schoolteacher, secretary, and shop assistant.

Teachers' perceptions of female students' adult lives are discouraging, especially when one realizes that these girls were described as being ideal students. If talented, friendly, and bright, girls are all destined to be housewives in their teachers' minds, the attitudes of educators would then seem to be instrumental in causing society to lose the talents of bright women.

The articles in this section have documented a great deal of institutional support for sex bias within the schools. Coleman points to girls serving as cheerleaders, an activity totally ancillary to boys' participation in sports. Gander notes that high-school students probably are more willing to accept policies that are not sex typed than are their school policy-makers. Fishel and Pottker show how schools have barred girls from many vocational programs, and offered them inferior programs instead. Girls' sports activities have also been shockingly undersponsored by the schools. Gaite has shown that no matter how talented a student, if the student is female she will be perceived by her teachers, without exception, as being a future housewife.

Schools heavily contribute to the support of sex bias in society. School structure forces students into modes of behavior that are sex typed because students conform to what they believe to be socially acceptable behavior as represented by school practices. Instead of encouraging students to develop their individual personalities and interests, secondary schools narrow students' options.

With the passage of Title IX, federal law will for the first time mandate schools to be free of formal, sex-biased practices. Unfortunately, these readings show how entrenched and ingrained are sex-stereotyped attitudes of teachers and administrators. Without a concurrent attitudinal change on the educators' part, the impetus of revised policies due to Title IX will be weakened.

The Adolescent Culture*

JAMES COLEMAN

THE GENERAL INTERESTS AND ACTIVITIES OF TEENAGERS

Because adolescents live so much in a world of their own, adults remain uninformed about the way teenagers spend their time, the things that are important to them, and the things that friends have in common. Several questions were asked in the study that give a picture of these patterns of activities and interests. Every boy and girl was asked: "What is your favorite way of spending your leisure time?"

The boys' responses (see Table 1) indicate that boys like to spend a great deal of their time in fairly active outdoor pursuits, such as sports, boating, and just going around with the fellows. They also spend time on hobbies—the most frequent of which is working on their car—and on such passive pursuits as movies, television, records, and the like. Being with girls does not, as adults sometimes think, constitute a large part of their leisure activities—although it comes to occupy more time as they go from the freshman year to the senior year.

Girls' leisure-time activities show a sharp contrast in some categories. Girls' favorite leisure activities less often include the active outdoor pursuits of boys. More frequent are activities like "just being with their friends," watching television and movies, attending games, reading, and listening to records. Their more active pursuits include one that never exists for boys—dancing among themselves. Perhaps this is an activity that substitutes for the sports on which boys spend their time; in part, it is certainly preparation for dancing with boys. In any case, it suggests the oft-heard quip that boys are interested in sports and girls are interested in boys.

The general pattern of these leisure pursuits, showing considerably more

---

* Reprinted with permission of Macmillan Publishing Co., Inc. from *The Adolescent Society* by James Coleman. Copyright © 1961 by The Free Press.

Table 1

Leisure activities of boys and girls in the nine public high schools

	Boys	*Girls*
1. Organized outdoor sports—including football, basketball, tennis, etc.	22.0%	6.9%
2. Unorganized outdoor activities—including hunting, fishing, swimming, boating, horseback riding	14.7	11.3
3. "Being with the group," riding around, going up town, etc.	17.2	32.5
4. Attending movies and spectator events—athletic games, etc.	8.5	10.4
5. Dating or being out with opposite sex	13.6	11.6
6. Going dancing (girls only)		12.0
7. Hobby—working on cars, bicycles, radio, musical instruments, etc.	22.5	20.1
8. Indoor group activities—bowling, playing cards, roller skating, etc.	8.0	8.1
9. Watching television	19.4	23.6
10. Listening to records or radio	11.2	31.7
11. Reading	13.7	35.5
12. Other, e.g., talking on telephone	7.1	9.3
13. No answer	8.1	3.7
Number of cases	(4,020)	(4,134)

activity among the boys, is indicative of a situation that seems to be quite general in the adolescent community: boys have far more to *do* than girls. Whether it is athletics, or cars, or hunting, or model-building, our society seems to provide a much fuller set of activities to engage the interests of boys. Thus, when girls are together, they are more often just "with the group" than are boys. A frequent afternoon activity is simply "going up town" to window shop and walk around.[1]

There is a point of particular interest in these responses, in relation to the school. Only one of the categories, organized sports, has any direct relation to school. Some of the hobbies and other activities may, of course, have their genesis in school, but except for such hobbies and organized sports, school-related activities are missing. No one responds that doing homework is his favorite way of spending his leisure time. This is at least in part because homework is assigned work, and cannot be leisure. Yet athletics, which involves work during practice, manages to run over into leisure time, breaking the barrier that separates work from leisure. Perhaps it is not too much to expect that other in-school activities directly tied to learning could—if the right way were found—similarly spill over into leisure and be a favored way of spending free time.

Another glimpse of teen-age interests, and the way these interests differ for boys and girls, may be obtained from answers to the following question: "What do you and the fellows (girls) you go around with here at school have most in common—what are the things you do together?"

Table 2

Activities and interests that friends have in common, for boys and girls in the nine public schools

(Listed in the table are all the categories of activities or interests mentioned by at least 10 percent of the boys or girls.)

	Boys	*Girls*
1. Organized outdoor sports—including football, basketball, tennis, etc.	34.5%	8.2%
2. Unorganized outdoor activities—including hunting, fishing, swimming, boating, horseback riding	11.7	6.6
3. In-school activities, interests, clubs	8.9	19.2
4. Attending spectator events		
a) School-related games and events	5.4	22.1
b) Out-of-school—movies, etc.	17.8	33.0
5. Eating together at lunch or taking classes together	9.1	13.7
6. Dating together or going to dances together	19.7	39.6
7. Having parties together (girls only)		10.6
8. "Hanging around together," "going uptown"	13.4	26.8
Number of cases	(4,020)	(4,134)

The activities and interests that friends share, as seen in Table 2, show similar patterns to the leisure interests expressed in Table 1. Missing, of course, are the activities carried on alone, such as watching television and reading. Again, there is the striking difference in outdoor activities; girls seldom engage in them, while they are the focus of common interests for a large proportion of the boys. This time, however, activities carried on in school show up in several ways: friends attend games and other events together; they engage in school clubs and activities together; and some of them merely eat together at lunch or see each other in the halls. All of these school-related activities are more nearly a basis of friendship among girls than they are among boys; for boys, the one activity within the school that overwhelms all others as a common interest of friends is athletics. This can be seen also by examining the activities of boys who name each other as friends. The one factor most related to boys' friendship was being out for football. The measure of similarity on this attribute was near 0.5 in every school (using an index where chance association is zero, and the maximum possible is 1.0), higher than any other interest or activity among either boys or girls—except being in the same grade.

Table 2 does show a greater amount of activity within school among friends than does Table 1. The fact that this is most true among girls (except for the one activity of athletics for boys) indicates a rather general characteristic: in all these schools, the clubs and activities were more the province of the girls than of the boys. For example, in almost every school of the more than fifty whose yearbooks were examined during this study, a girl was editor of the yearbook and a girl was editor of the school newspaper.

Some activities, of course, are either solely for boys (such as the Hi-Y clubs) or are largely populated by boys (such as a chemistry club or photography club). However, in general, it seems that there is a kind of tacit division of labor in most schools: activities and clubs are for the girls, athletics are for the boys.

BOY-GIRL RELATIONS AND THEIR IMPACT ON THE CULTURE

Let us suppose that the girls in a school valued good grades more than did the boys. One might expect that the presence of these girls would be an influence on the boys toward a higher evaluation of studies. Yet the data say *not;* they say that a boy's popularity with girls is based less on doing well in school, more on such attributes as a car, than is his popularity with other boys. Similarly for girls—scholastic success is much less valuable for their popularity with boys than for their popularity with other girls.

We have always known that the standards men and women use to judge each other include a large component of physical attractiveness, and a smaller component of the more austere criteria they use in judging members of their own sex. Yet we seem to ignore that this is true in high schools just as it is in business offices, and that its cumulative effect may be to deemphasize education in schools far more than we realize.[2] In the normal activities of a high school, the relations between boys and girls tend to increase the importance of physical attractiveness, cars, and clothes, and to decrease the importance of achievement in school activities. Whether this *must* be true is another question; it might be that schools themselves could so shape these relations to have a *positive* effect, rather than a negative one, on the school's goals.

The general research question is this: what kinds of interactions among boys and girls lead them to evaluate the opposite sex less on grounds of physical attraction, more on grounds that are not so superficial? It seems likely, for example, that in some private schools where adolescents engage in common work activities, bases develop for evaluating the opposite sex that are quite different from those generated by the usual activities surrounding a public high school. The question of practical policy, once such a research question has been answered, is even more difficult: what can a school do to foster the kinds of interactions that lead boys and girls to judge the opposite sex on grounds that implement the school's goals?

It is commonly assumed, both by educators and by laymen, that it is "better" for boys and girls to be in school together during adolescence—if not better for their academic performance, then at least better for their social development and adjustment. But this may not be so; it may depend wholly upon the kinds of activities within which their association takes place. Coeducation in some high schools may be inimical to *both* academic achievement and social adjustment. The dichotomy often forced between "life adjustment" and "academic emphasis" is a false one, for it forgets that most of the teenager's energy is not directed toward either of these goals. Instead, the relevant dichotomy is cars and the cruel jungle of rating and dating versus school activities, whether of the academic or life-adjustment variety.

But perhaps, at least for girls, this is where the emphasis *should* be: on making themselves into desirable objects for boys. Perhaps physical beauty, nice clothes, and an enticing manner are the attributes that should be most important among adolescent girls. No one can say whether girls should be trained to be wives, citizens, mothers, or career women. Yet in none of these areas of adult life are physical beauty, an enticing manner, and nice clothes so important for performing successfully as they are in high school. Even receptionists and secretaries, for whom personal attractiveness is a valuable attribute, must carry out their jobs well, or they will not be able to keep them. Comparable performance is far less important in the status system of the high school, with its close tie to the rating and dating system. There, a girl can survive much longer on personal attractiveness, an enticing manner, and nice clothes.

The adult women in which such attributes *are* most important are of a different order from wives, citizens, mothers, career women, secretaries: they are chorus girls, models, movie and television actresses, and call girls. In all these activities, women serve as *objects of attention* for men and, even more, objects to *attract* men's attention. These are quite different from the attributes of a good wife, which involve less superficial qualities. If the adult society wants high schools to inculcate the attributes that make girls objects to attract men's attention, then these values of good looks and nice clothes, discussed above, are just right. If not, then the values are quite inappropriate.

A second answer to what's wrong with these values is this: nothing, so long as they do not completely pervade the atmosphere, so long as there are *other* ways a girl can become popular and successful in the eyes of her peers. And there are other ways, as indicated by emphasis on "a nice personality." Yet the overall responses to these questions suggest that in adolescent cultures these superficial, external attributes of clothes and good looks do pervade the atmosphere to the extent that girls come to feel that this is the only basis or the *most important* basis on which to excel.

Effects on Girls of the Emphasis on Attractiveness

Further consequences of this emphasis on being attractive to boys are indicated by responses to a set of sentence-completion questions. Comparing the boys' responses and the girls' gives some indication of the degree to which the high-school culture impresses these matters upon girls. The questions are listed in Table 3, together with the proportions responding in terms of popularity with the opposite sex or relations with the opposite sex.

To each one of these sentence-completion questions, girls gave far more responses involving popularity and relations with others than did boys. These responses suggest that the emphasis on popularity with boys has powerful consequences for these girls' attitudes toward life and themselves. A further indication that success with boys is tied to rather superficial external qualities is shown by the great proportion of girls who say that they worry most about some personal characteristic—most often an external attribute such as weight or figure or hair or skin, but also including such attributes as "shyness."

One might suggest, however, that the girls' concern with popularity and with the physical attributes that help make them popular would be just as strong in the absence of the adolescent culture. A simple comparison of these four sentence-completion questions suggests that this is not so. The question in which girls *most* often give responses involving relations with the opposite sex is the one referring directly to the school life: "The best thing that could happen to me this year at school would be. . . ." When the question refers to life in general ("The most important thing in life is . . ."), then the boy-girl differential is sharply reduced. This suggests that it is within the adolescent social system itself that relations with boys and physical attractiveness are so important to girls.

Table 3
Boys' and girls' sentence-completion responses related to popularity—totals for nine schools

(These questions were asked in a supplementary questionnaire, filled out in the nine schools by the 6,289 students who completed the basic fall questionnaire early.)

	Boys	*Girls*
s.11. More than anything else, I'd like to		
Responses involving popularity with opposite sex	5.4%	10.8%
Responses involving popularity, unspecified	5.3	11.4
Total codable responses	(2,343)	(2,776)
s.12. The best thing that could happen to me this year at school would be		
Responses involving relations with opposite sex	4.5	20.7
Responses involving relations with others, unspecified	3.2	9.0
Total codable responses	(2,222)	(2,702)
s.13. The most important thing in life is		
Responses involving popularity with opposite sex	6.3	7.4
Responses involving popularity, unspecified	4.6	7.9
Total codable responses	(2,151)	(2,737)
s.14. I worry most about . . .		
Responses involving popularity with opposite sex	9.2	13.9
Responses involving personal attributes related to popularity (weight, hair, figure, etc.)	2.7	8.6
Total codable responses	(2,201)	(2,803)

The emphasis on popularity with the opposite sex has other effects on the girls, of which we have only the barest knowledge. One of the effects is on her feelings about herself. We may suppose that if a girl found herself in a situation where she was not successful in "the things that count," she would be less happy with herself, and would want to change, to be someone different. On the other hand, the more successful she was in the things that counted, the more she would be satisfied with herself as she was.

We have no measure of the objective beauty of girls, and we are not able to separate out those who are particularly unattractive in dress or beauty, to see the impact that these values have upon their conceptions of themselves. However, we can pick out those girls who are, in the eyes of their classmates, the best-dressed girls. This will allow an indirect test of the effect of the emphasis on clothes. On the questionnaire, we asked every girl: "Of all the girls in your grade, who is the best dressed?" The girls named most often by their classmates are at one end of the continuum. Thus, if this is an important attribute to have, these girls should feel considerably better about themselves than do their classmates. Table 4 below shows that they do, and that those named most often felt best about themselves.

Table 4
If I could trade, I would be someone different from myself

	Percent who agree	*Number*
All girls	21.2	(3,782)
Girls named 2–6 times as best dressed	17.0	(282)
Girls named 7 or more times as best dressed	11.2	(98)

The effect of being thought of as "best dressed" by her classmates is quite striking, reducing by nearly half the likelihood of her wanting to be someone different. Or, to put it differently, the effect of *not* being thought of as "best dressed" by her classmates nearly doubles a girl's likelihood of wanting to be someone different.

To see the strength of this effect, relative to the effect of competing values, it is possible to compare these responses with those of girls who were highly regarded by their classmates, but in other ways. The following questions were asked along with the "best-dressed" question: "Of all the girls in your grade, who . . . is the best student? . . . do boys go for most?"

The girls who were named most often by their classmates on these two questions and the previous one can be thought of as "successful" in each of these areas—dress, studies, and relations with boys. Insofar as these things "count," they should make the girls feel happier about themselves—and conversely, make the girls who are not successful less happy about themselves.

Figure 1 indicates the relative effectiveness of these three values, the degree to which they "count" in making a girl happy or unhappy about herself. For each of the three values, the girl who is named as "best" seven times or more is least likely to want to be someone different. It is apparent that all three values have some effect. However, success with boys apparently has the most effect; being thought of as best dressed—which seems to be important largely because it contributes to being successful with boys

—is somewhat less effective; and being thought of as best student is apparently least effective of the three. The results of the companion questions for boys are shown along with those for the girls, to indicate that this result is not simply due to the personality of those popular with the opposite sex. For boys, athletics is apparently most effective, more so than popularity with girls.

Altogether, then, it appears that the role of girls as objects of attention for boys is emphasized by the adolescent values in these schools. Its consequences are multifarious, and we have only touched upon them, but one point is clear: just "putting together" boys and girls in the same school is not necessarily the "normal, healthy" thing to do. It does not necessarily promote adjustment to life; it may promote, as is indicated by these data, adjustment to the life of a model or chorus girl or movie actress or call girl. It may, in other words, promote *mal*adjustment to the kind of life that these girls will lead after school.

Common sense is not enough in these matters. It is not enough to put boys and girls in a school and expect that they will be a "healthy influence" on one another. Serious research is necessary in order to discover the kinds of activities and the kinds of situations that will allow them to be such, rather than emphasizing the superficial values of a hedonistic culture.

Figure 1

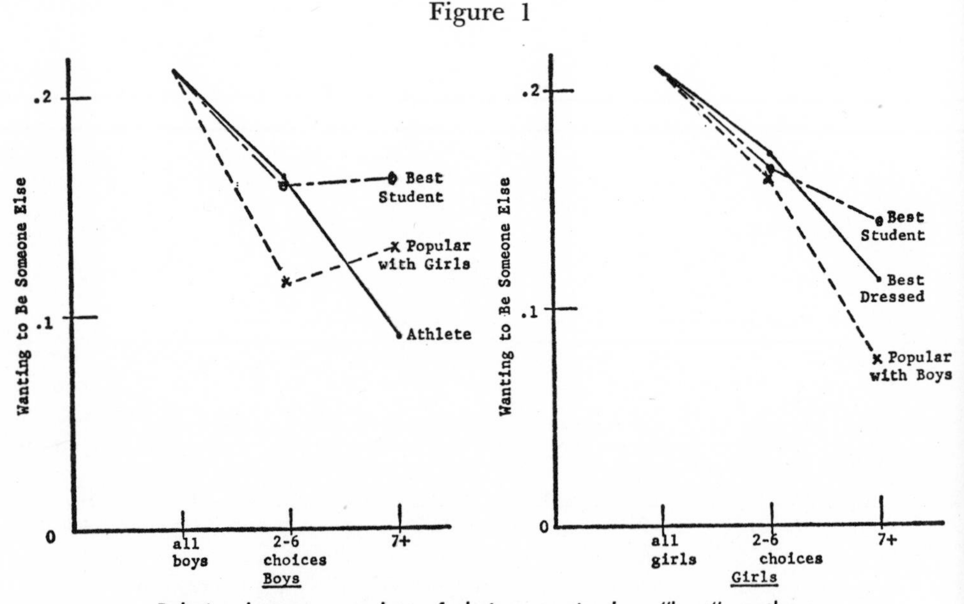

Relation between number of choices received as "best" on three criteria and proportion wanting to be someone else.

NOTES

1. A teen-age girl comments: This greater activity among boys is the reason that "being accepted" or being in the "right clique" means more to the girls, who have less to occupy their leisure time. Boys engaged in many activities have many different kinds of friends. They have different interests in common with different friends. Although they are friends they may have only one interest in common with a certain other boy and therefore could not be in a successful clique with all their friends. Because girls have fewer interests, they form small cliques according to these interests.
2. One cannot infer from the above considerations that single-sex high schools would produce more attention to academic matters. One other matter is the tendency of some adolescents in a single-sex school to have few interests in school. The opposite sex in a school pulls interests toward the school, and then partly diverts it to nonscholastic matters.

Sex-typing in the High School*

MARY JEAN GANDER

THE RESEARCH

The majority of investigations of sex typing in education have been in the area of sexist literature, the discrimination against young boys in elementary school, and vocational counseling for girls. Few studies have investigated sex typing in high school or what the students themselves think about it.

The following study was made in an attempt to identify:

A) some of the sex typing now going on in high school
B) how aware of this sex typing high-school students are
C) their reaction to it,
   1. when it is pointed out to them and
   2. when they see it for themselves
D) and if there are any sex differences or age differences in students' reactions to sex typing in the school.

To accomplish this, two types of questionnaires were used. Throughout the study four specific areas were examined in particular for sex typing. These were physical education, home economics, industrial arts, and guidance counseling. The subjects were 148 sophomore and senior high-school students in a small, Midwestern town of about 6,000 white, middle-class people. The two types of questionnaires will be discussed separately because of their different orientations and analyses.

---

* Mary Jean Gander, "Sex-typing in the High School," reprinted with permission of the author. This article is a greatly expanded version of a paper entitled, "Student Attitudes Toward Sex-typing Practices in High School," presented by Mary Jean Gander and A. J. H. Gaite at the 1973 Annual Meeting of the American Educational Research Association.

Questionnaire No. 1

This questionnaire was designed to find out what sex-typing practices students recognize in their high school and to assess students' opinions of this sex typing. In addition, two questions were included concerning the women's liberation movement.

Method

The subjects were forty-eight male and female sophomore and senior high-school students. Each subject was given questionnaire no. 1, which consisted of six items. Item 1 dealt with student reported sex typing in five areas: home economics, industrial arts, physical education, guidance counseling, and sex typing in general. Item 2 asked for the subject's opinion of sex typing. Items 3 and 4 asked what advantages girls had over boys, and boys had over girls in their school, as well as their opinion of these advantages. The final two questions concerned their opinion of the women's liberation movement and whether or not it has had any impact on their lives.

Results and Discussion

Due to the subjective nature of the questionnaire, the results were analysed in terms of percentage of students making certain responses and all responses were considered relevant.

In home economics it was the general consensus that girls were expected to have already developed many of the skills needed and to know more than the boys. They were allowed to choose from a much wider variety of projects and had preference in getting into most home-economics courses (except "Boys' Chef," a course set up and named to attract boys because of its masculine orientation and upgrading of "cooking"). It was suggested that home economics was expected to be taken more seriously by girls because they would someday be homemakers, whereas boys just took it for fun and to learn skills that might be useful. One girl thought boys were expected to "goof off" and be clumsy (i.e., not take it seriously) to "maintain their masculinity." About 20% of the students thought girls had more privileges than boys in this class. Of the sophomore boys, 50% complained of being treated as "dummies" and only allowed to do easy projects. They felt boys were not given credit for their abilities. Two each sophomore girls and boys said that boys were mocked or made fun of sometimes for electing home economics.

In industrial-arts education the observations were just the reverse. Girls were expected to be "stupid" and not to be able to learn many of the necessary skills. About 75% of the girls complained of being treated as if they could not do anything; for example, they were not allowed to use the machines and could only make simple projects. They were not expected to take industrial arts seriously or to "out do" the boys in any projects. Four students (a girl and a boy in each class) said girls who elected to take industrial arts were either pampered or harrassed by the boys. Boys were treated as if they knew more and had more sophisticated projects, had use of all the machines, and had preference in getting into the classes.

Over 80% of the students thought that girls had much easier exercises and sports in physical education than the boys. Four students described boys' sports as rougher. Eight students felt boys were expected to be better in physical education and more physically fit, whereas girls were expected to be weaker and have less ability and coordination. Over 20% of the girls complained that the boys had more freedom, variety, equipment, and fun in physical education than they did; three sophomore girls even complained of having to do everything the easy way. It was the opinion of one senior boy that by the time girls graduate from high school, they are out of shape. One senior girl suggested that coeducational physical education might be a good idea.

The students were more vague about the ways in which boys and girls were treated differently by the guidance counselor. A sophomore boy suggested that boys needed more help and it was more important for them to find a job so they were given more attention. Over half of the girls (55%) complained they were not able to talk to the male counselor about certain things and that he would not understand their problems. They definitely wanted a female counselor in addition to the male counselor.

In a general question about sex typing in any other classes or in interaction with teachers and administrators, many of the students (32%) felt girls were treated more leniently, that boys were disciplined more harshly and could get away with less. Of the boys, 42% complained of teachers "babying" the girls. One girl complained that the school officials were men; she felt there was no good reason for this. A sophomore girl felt that boys in athletics were treated with more respect. One senior girl described herself as a "doer" and said the teachers and administrators were amazed at her self-confidence and forcefulness because she was a girl. Another senior girl stated rather vaguely that "boys seem somehow superior" and "somehow get seniority in most classes."

When questioned as to what, if any, advantages girls have over boys or boys have over girls in high school, about 63% of the students (including 80% of the sophomore boys) thought girls were treated more leniently and trusted more. Some students felt this was as it should be, others felt it was unfair and should be changed. Nearly half of the students felt boys had an advantage over girls in that they could go out for sports. Many students thought this was very discriminatory, a few sophomore boys and many girls (both seniors and sophomores) felt girls should have organized sports, too. One sophomore girl wanted to be able to go out for sports without being labeled a "sweatie." Another sophomore girl expressed the opinion that girls had no choice about being "babied," that "this is what society puts on you so you have no choice." A senior girl said she was not afraid to admit that boys were superior because the Bible says they are.

When asked if boys should be treated differently from girls in high school, the students expressed mixed opinions. About half the students (66.6% of the sophomore boys, 60% of the sophomore girls, 50%

of the senior girls, and 42% of the senior boys) felt they should be treated the same. In their opinions, boys and girls were both in school to learn and so they should have the same rights, penalties, and opportunities. One senior girl expressed the opinion that humans are "created equal." Those who felt girls should be treated differently from boys often added, "different but equal." Many of these students felt there were so many important differences between the sexes, they could not and should not be treated the same.

In the item dealing with women's liberation, nearly 75% of the students preferred answer (B), men and women are equal but different. This shows liberalism but is not a very realistic answer because of the built-in conflict. Men and women cannot be regarded as equals if the old stereotypes about their differences are retained, yet by not choosing (C), they show they are not in complete agreement with these stereotypes. These students do not see the woman as being suppressed. Perhaps these students realize some of the inequalities that exist now and want them corrected without changing the sex roles to any great extent. The women's liberation movement has received much bad publicity and it shows up in these students; none of them care to be connected in any way to the movement. About two-thirds of the students felt the movement had not had any effect on their lives.

Summary

This questionnaire revealed that the high-school students studied were aware of many of the obvious and some of the subtle ways girls are treated differently from boys in their high school. The differences mentioned most often included preferential treatment of girls by teachers, particularly in matters of discipline, and the greater opportunity to participate in athletics for boys. About half of the students seemed to agree with sex-typing practices in general, although some of them expressed disagreement with specific types. The remaining students felt girls and boys should be treated equally and have the same rules, penalties, and opportunities. The sex typing recognized by these students in the five areas examined and their reactions to it tend to support earlier discussions about sex typing in high school.

Questionnaire No. 2

This questionnaire was given in an attempt to assess students' opinions of sex-typing practices in the school when they were pointed out. It was predicted that senior women would be the most liberal in regard to opinions about sex typing because one would expect them to be the most enlightened, with the sophomore boys the most conservative due to a combination of their heightened anxiety about their masculinity and their naiveté. Girls would be more liberal, on the average, than boys in regard to sex typing because deviation on the part of females is more acceptable than by males and men are more anxious about their masculinity, which may tend to make them exaggerate behaviors, values, attitudes, and interests accepted as masculine. One might expect seniors to be more enlightened, thus more liberal than sophomores. In this context a liberal individual would be one who accepts a wider range of behaviors for each sex, that is, more overlap of the masculine and feminine domains. A conservative individual would be one who accepts traditional sex-role stereotypes.

Method

The subjects were 100 male and female sophomore and senior high-school students. Four groups were taken into consideration: sophomore males, sophomore females, senior males, and senior females (n=25). Each student was given questionnaire no. 2, which consisted of 46 items. Of the 46 items, 23 were statements about sex-typing practices typically found in high schools in one of 6 areas; home economics, industrial arts, physical education, guidance counseling, elementary education, and general sex typing. In order to obtain unbiased results, the remaining 23 items were parallel statements to the first 23 items, only leaning in the opposite direction. After reading each item a subject was confronted with a four-point Likert Scale. Either the subject strongly agreed, agreed, disagreed, or strongly disagreed with the statement (no neutral choice was provided).

Results

Initially a "liberation" score was calculated for each subject, the lower the score the more liberal the subject was in his opinions about sex typing; the higher the score, the more conservative were his opinions. The mean liberation score and standard deviation for each of the four categories of subjects are found on Table 1. To determine if there were any significant sex, age, or interaction effects, a two-way analysis of variance with fixed effects was performed on the data. The results of this analysis are summarized in Table 2. It is clear from Table 2 that there are highly significant sex differences. Age differences were not found to be significant. However, they were in the predicted direction. Interaction effects were not significant.

A second analysis was done on strength of feeling behind the subject's opinion. The number of "strongly agree" and "strongly disagree" opinions were tabulated for each subject and a one-tailed T-test was performed on the data. This analysis is summarized in Table 3. The female subjects showed significantly stronger feelings about sex typing in their school than did the males.

Discussion

It would seem that the girls are more liberal in regard to sex typing than the boys, with the senior girls being the most liberal and the sophomore boys the most conservative. The seniors were somewhat more lib- as a group than the sophomores. Taking all students into account, there are very few who are quite conservative, but several who are very liberal.

Table 1
Means and Standard Deviations

	Males	Females
Seniors	M = 99.90	M = 88.40
	s = 11.85	s = 12.08
Sophomores	M = 103.20	M = 89.90
	s = 11.59	s = 12.27

Table 2
Two-way ANOVA with Fixed Effects

Source	SS	df	MS	F
Rows (Sex)	3844.00	1	3844.00	26.18*
Columns (Age)	146.41	1	146.41	.997
Interaction	20.25	1	20.25	.138
Error	14091.88	96	146.79	
Totals	18102.54	99		

*Significant at .01

Table 3

Girls	Boys
$M_1 = 15.28$	$M_2 = 9.92$
$S^2_1 = 85.82$	$S^2_2 = 76.27$

Est. Ódiff = 1.82

$$t = \frac{(M_1 - M_2) - E(M_1 - M_2)}{\text{est. Ódiff}} = \frac{(15.28 - 9.92) - 0}{1.82} = 2.95^*$$

df = 98

*Significant at .01

This suggests that students might welcome a loosening of sex-role stereotyping in the school. In general, the girls felt more strongly about their opinions than did the boys, perhaps because they appear to be the oppressed group due to the male role being preferred. Thus, they would want certain sex-role stereotypes changed more readily. It would appear from the data, however, that the girls would like to "have their cake and eat it, too." That is, they seem to want more advantages they see boys as having, but do not always want the added responsibilities or work. For example, many girls want the same amount of equipment in physical education as the boys, but some do not want to do as strenuous exercises as the boys. Though many girls seem quite liberal about sex typing on some items, they show successful indoctrination by society on other items. For example, the majority of girls feel more women should be employed in positions of authority in the school, but many still feel that it is more important to send a son to college than a daughter, and there were mixed feelings about having a male home-economics teacher or the need for more women teaching physics. They felt boys have a need for home economics but it should not be a requirement for them even if it is for the girls.

Nearly all students felt pregnant girls should not be discriminated against in school. Also, nearly all students felt sex-education classes, home-economics classes, and industrial-arts classes should be coeducational. Over half of all students felt coeducational physical education was a good idea.

The boys showed much more conservatism on statements about vocations. Even though many of them felt that college-oriented girls should be given information on traditionally masculine majors (math, engineering, science, etc.), many did not think boys could use information on traditionally feminine fields (nursing, home economics, elementary education) and that the noncollege-oriented girls would have little use for information on plumbing, construction work, management, etc.

The two items dealing with importance of sex-role acquisition brought interesting results. Though some students were very definite about their opinions on these statements, many students showed mixed feelings. Even though they agreed that rigid sex-role stereotyping should be eliminated from elementary school, they also agreed that it was very important that elementary children develop a strong identification with traditionally masculine or feminine roles, and know how to act.

The majority of sophomore boys did not feel they should be required to take home economics even if the girls were. Over half of them thought boys needed math, science, and industrial arts more than girls. However, a definite majority felt that girls should have the same opportunities to use physical education equipment as the boys and that girls should have athletics if they want them. Sophomore boys showed a good deal of liberalism on many items in spite of their conservatism in certain areas. A summary of the data for questionnaire no. 2 is located at the end of this article.

QUESTIONNAIRE NO. 1: SAMPLE

Senior_________ Male_________

Soph._________ Female_________

1. List as many ways as you can think of that girls are treated differently from boys:

   in home economics:

   in industrial arts:

   in physical education:

   in guidance counseling:

   in any other classes or in interacting with teachers and administrators:

2. Do you think the school should treat boys and girls differently?

   _________Yes

   _________No.

   Please explain why or why not.

3. List as many ways as you can think of that the girls have advantages over the boys in school.

   What is your opinion of this?

4. List as many ways as you can think of that the boys have advantages over the girls in school.

   What is your opinion of this?

5. What is your general opinion of the women's liberation movement?

   _________ (A) I think it was necessary. Women have not enjoyed many of the privileges, opportunities, and wages that men in our society have. This must be corrected. To effect any changes, women had to organize.

   _________ (B) I am indifferent to the movement, perhaps there is a need of improvement in equal wages for equal work, but women enjoy plenty of freedom in our society. I don't think they are oppressed. If they want a career they have to work for it just as men have to. I believe in equality but differences between the sexes.

   _________ (C) I disagree with the movement; man is the head of the home and woman is the heart. It is vitally important for girls and boys to develop a strong identification as feminine or masculine. This movement seeks to neutralize the sexes, masculinize women and feminize men, to the detriment of everyone.

6. Do you feel that the women's liberation movement has had some impact on you.
   ________Yes
   ________No.
   Please explain.

QUESTIONNAIRE NO. 2: SAMPLE

Senior________ Male________

Soph.________ Female________

	Percent Males Agree	Percent Females Agree
1. High schools should have more women teachers in math, science, and industrial arts.	42	58
2. High schools should have more male teachers in home-economics and/or family-living courses.	34	54
3. Schools should employ more women in positions of authority, such as principal, superintendent, etc.	56	86
4. Math, science, and industrial arts are usually taught by men because they are mentally and physically better adapted for these areas than women.	52	18
5. Women most often teach home-economics and/or family-living courses, men would look silly teaching such courses.	60	22
6. Positions of authority in the school such as principal or superintendent are usually held by men because they are better equipped mentally and physically for jobs that require decision-making and leadership.	36	18
7. A pregnant girl should not be allowed to attend regular classes, but the boy who got her pregnant should *not* be expelled.	36	12
8. A pregnant girl should be allowed to attend regular classes, as long as she can and as soon after the birth of the child as possible, just as the boy who got her pregnant is able to do.	92	98

	Percent Males Agree	Percent Females Agree
9. A vocational counselor should feel it is more important to send a son to college than a daughter because he may have to support a family someday.	50	22
10. It would be silly for a vocational counselor to give college-oriented boys information on nursing, elementary education, or home economics; there are no opportunities for men in these "feminine" fields.	34	6
11. It would be a waste of time for a vocational counselor to give a college-oriented girl information on computer science, medical school, or engineering; girls are rarely interested in these fields.	12	6
12. A vocational counselor who thinks it is more important to send a boy to college than a girl is prejudiced.	76	68
13. A vocational counselor who gives college-oriented boys information on computer science, engineering, medical school, etc., but never tells them about opportunities for men in fields such as nursing, elementary education, or home economics, etc., is not allowing them complete freedom of choice.	74	88
14. A vocational counselor should give college-oriented girls information on engineering and computer science as well as elementary education and social work.	86	86
15. A counselor or teacher who is not aware of the changing sex roles in our society and adjusting their counseling or teaching accordingly may be detrimental to the full development of their students.	88	90
16. The sex roles in our society are not changing; movements like women's liberation come and go but can not change such basic things as what our society sees as feminine or masculine.	68	44
17. More girls should be encouraged to take industrial arts, math, and science.	74	84

	Percent Males Agree	Percent Females Agree
18. If girls are required to take home-economics and/or family-living courses, boys should also have this requirement.	44	58
19. Boys need courses like industrial arts, math, and science more than girls do.	48	42
20. Boys would have no use for a home-economics or family-living course.	8	2
21. School personnel should see students first as individuals and secondly as male or female.	90	96
22. It is only natural and right that school personnel immediately categorize students as male and female, and treat them accordingly.	28	24
23. Though boys usually have a "gang" shower, girls need more privacy and should have separate shower stalls.	16	58
24. It is ridiculous for a school to have separate shower stalls for the girls but a common shower room for the boys.	74	42
25. A school should separate the boys from the girls during sex-education classes or movies to avoid embarrassment.	12	14
26. In sex-education classes, lectures, or movies, students should be informed primarily about their own sex with little emphasis on the other sex.	8	12
27. Boys and girls should *not* be separated for sex-education and/or family-life education classes or movies, and therefore, they should be presented with information on both sexes.	90	90
28. In physical education, schools should not expect as much physical exertion, stamina, and coordination from the girls as from the boys.	54	40
29. Girls should have separate physical-education classes from the boys, they are not able to compete with the boys.	54	44

	Percent Males Agree	Percent Females Agree
30. In physical education, schools should expect as much physical stamina, coordination, and exertion (not strength) from the girls as from the boys: too many girls are in poor physical condition when they graduate from high school.	74	70
31. Physical education should be coeducational. If girls and boys take physical education together, they can develop teamwork, cooperation, and similar interests in sports and recreational activities, thus promoting more understanding between the sexes.	80	70
32. Girls should have the same opportunities to use physical education equipment as the boys.	90	98
33. Girls should be allowed to compete in interscholastic athletics, thus having the same opportunity for prestige and recognition in their school and home town as the boys have. By the same token, boys should be allowed to try out for cheerleading and not made fun of for doing so.	68	98
34. Boys need more physical education equipment than the girls.	38	24
35. Schools should not be expected to have interscholastic, competitive sports for the girls on the same scale that they have for the boys. It would be "unfeminine" for girls to engage in such strenuous, physical competition.	26	12
36. Schools should separate classes for boys and girls in industrial arts and home economics (that is, if boys are allowed to take home economics and the girls are allowed to take industrial arts).	20	22
37. Industrial-arts and home-economics classes should be coeducational.	92	92

	Percent Males Agree	Percent Females Agree
38. A vocational conuselor should give vocationally oriented girls information about opportunities for women in plumbing, construction work, management, etc., as well as in clerical work, practical nursing, etc., so they have a more complete idea of the possibilities open to them and, thus, more freedom of choice.	80	94
39. A vocational counselor should give vocationally oriented boys information on opportunities for men in clerical work, practical nursing, etc., as well as in areas such as plumbing, construction work, management, etc.	86	96
40. Giving vocationally oriented girls information on plumbing, management, or construction work is a waste of time; girls do not want to know about these fields, just as it would be silly to give vocationally oriented boys information on nursing or clerical work.	24	8
41. Elementary schools need more male teachers.	64	82
42. Elementary schoolteaching is a woman's job; men would not be as adapted to this sort of work.	16	4
43. Little girls and boys should not be segregated on the playground; elementary teachers should make more effort to orient them toward coeducational sports, games, and activities.	80	92
44. Little boys do not like the same sports and games as little girls do and should not be expected to play with the little girls on the playground.	58	38
45. Children's literature that reflects traditional, rigid, and exaggerated feminine and masculine roles should be eliminated from the elementary schools.	28	40

	Percent Males Agree	Percent Females Agree
46. It is important that elementary boys and girls be shown what is traditionally feminine and masculine so that they will develop a strong identification with their own sex and know how to act.	70	70

Sample Sizes: Males N=50
Females N=50

Sex Bias in Secondary Schools: The Impact of Title IX

ANDREW FISHEL and JANICE POTTKER

Very few Americans were aware of the enactment of the Education Amendments of 1972 in June 1972. Yet Title IX of these Amendments will eventually produce revolutionary changes in American education. The language of Title IX is deceptively simple: "No person shall, on the basis of sex, be excluded from participation in, be denied the benefits of, or be subjected to discrimination under any education program or activity receiving federal financial assistance. . . ."

The importance of Title IX lies in the fact that it is the first comprehensive antisex discrimination law that covers students. Although most of the attention given to the law since its passage has focused on its impact on colleges, Title IX will have the greatest impact on the elementary and secondary levels of education, since all school districts in the country receiving federal funds will be required to abide by Title IX regulations if they want to continue receiving these funds.

The Office of Civil Rights in the Department of Health, Education, and Welfare was given the responsibilty of devising the specific regulations to implement the general wording of Title IX in July 1972. The issues involved in writing these regulations were so complex that it was not until June 1974 that the proposed regulations were released for public comment, and it is expected to be at least until January 1975 before the contents of the regulations are finalized. As a result, Title IX had minimal impact during the 1972–73 and 1973–74 school years. Although the implementing regulations are expected to be issued during the 1974–75 school year, the actual force of the regulations will probably not be widely felt until the 1975–76 school year.

This legislation does not prohibit different entrance requirements for boys and girls to schools for the academically or artistically talented, nor does it prohibit single-sex schools, except for vocational schools if comparable schools are available for both sexes. However all other aspects of public-school policy will in one way or another be affected by Title IX.

Although the implementing regulations of Title IX have not been finalized, from the proposed regulations released in June 1974, it is possible to determine the type of school policies that will require changes. Specifically, Title IX will prohibit discrimination on the basis of sex in admission to public vocational schools. Similarly, it will prohibit discrimination on the basis of sex in school programs and activities. This last requirement, in effect, mandates that once a student is admitted to a school, all facets of student programs and activities must be free of sex bias. This includes sex bias in course offerings, appraisal and counseling materials, and extracurricular and athletic programs.

Because of the scope of the policies covered, the number of existing school policies that will be in violation of Title IX is very large. For example, requiring girls to take one course and boys another will no longer be legal, nor will having different admissions requirements for boys and girls wanting to take the same course. Even if courses are technically open to both sexes on an equal basis, a violation of Title IX would occur if members of either sex are discouraged by formal or informal counseling on the part of teachers or guidance counselors from enrolling in a course. In addition, the use of sex-biased counseling materials will be prohibited, as will the offering of athletic and extracurricular activities for only one sex although separate athletic teams are allowed.

While both formal and informal policies that are sex-biased are prohibited under Title IX, it is obvious that it will be nearly impossible to monitor counseling practices and teacher behavior in all school districts to determine if discrimination is occurring. Because of this, the major impact of Title IX will be to bring about changes in formal, school-district policies rather than in informal practices.

As the Citizen's Advisory Council on the Status of Women has pointed out, girls are afforded inferior educational opportunities at all levels of the public education system.[1] However, the treatment of schoolgirls and boys is more differentiated at the secondary level than at the elementary level, so that it is at this level that Title IX can be expected to mandate the greatest number of policy changes. The areas of secondary education involving students that will be most strongly affected by Title IX fall into three categories: 1) policies regarding admissions to vocational schools; 2) policies regarding admissions to classes; and 3) policies regarding physical education and extracurricular activities. Only by viewing the existing institutional policies and practices in these areas will it be possible to appreciate the scope of the changes Title IX will require in American secondary education.

ADMISSION TO VOCATIONAL SCHOOLS

Although it is commonly accepted that separate-but-equal facilities for black and white students are inherently inequal, it has not yet been accepted that separate facilities for boys and girls are inherently unequal. There are many public schools today that still admit students of only one sex. When single-sex schools exist, the girls' schools usually do not even meet the standard of being separate but equal: they are separate and unequal.

Most single-sex schools are special types of high schools, used either for vocational training or for the education of the academically or artistically talented. Under Title IX, only sex bias in admissions to vocational schools is prohibited. This means that it will still be possible for school districts to restrict the number of girls admitted to schools for the academically or artistically talented as long as a comparable school is available for girls.

The extent of the impact of the Title IX prohibition against discrimination in admission to vocational schools is unclear due to the lack of nationwide data on the number of single-sex vocational schools.[2] However, from state and local surveys it is clear that in many localities vocational training is available to more boys than girls, and that vocational schools offer male students a much wider range of vocational courses than are offered to girls. For example, a study of Massachusetts schools found that the total places for boys in vocational training schools was three times greater than the number of places for girls.[3] In the newly built modern regional vocational schools, the imbalance was found to be even greater, with four times as many male students as female students attending these contemporary schools. As a result, most of the girls attending vocational school were placed in old buildings that were not nearly as well-equipped as the schools attended by male students.

Similar discrimination in admission to vocational schools was found in the New York City Public Schools. In the nation's largest school system, there are eighteen sex-segregated vocational high schools: thirteen are available to boys and only five are available to girls.[4]

Not only are girls denied admittance to certain vocational schools, but also the schools girls are permitted to attend usually offer a narrower range of vocational programs than is offered in the boys' vocational schools. It is common practice to offer girls programs that only prepare them for traditionally female occupations. Even in vocational schools that are attended by both girls and boys, the sexes are in separate programs. The preliminary and unofficial results of a national survey made by the Office of Civil Rights found that over half of all classes in coeducational vocational schools were comprised entirely of students of the same sex.

The total enrollment in secondary school vocational educational programs for 1972–73 is shown in Table 1. As can be seen from this table, fifty-seven percent of the six million students enrolled in vocational programs are girls. Due to the sex-stereotyping and restrictions on course enrollments, girls comprise the overwhelming majority of students in four programs (health, homemaking, occupational home economics, and office/business). In contrast, boys constitute the overwhelming majority in three programs (agriculture, technical education, and trades/industry). Only in the distributive education program is there an even balance of male-female enrollees.

Table 1
Sex of Secondary-level Vocational Education Enrollees, 1972–73[5]

Program	Total Students Enrolled	Percent of Enrollees Who Are Male	Percent of Enrollees Who Are Female
Agriculture	647,081	93.7	6.3
Distributive Education	341,644	48.1	51.9
Health	75,002	19.3	80.7
Home Economics/Homemaking	1,529,370	9.8	90.2
Home Economics/Occupational	261,530	14.5	85.5
Office/Business	1,623,793	16.8	83.2
Technical Education	242,224	88.1	11.9
Trades/Industry	1,300,742	85.6	14.4
TOTAL	6,021,387	42.7	57.3

Table 2 shows the percent of boys and girls enrolled in the eight vocational programs. As this table shows, seventy-nine percent of all girls in vocational education programs are in either a homemaking or an office/business program.[6] Since the homemaking program is not intended to prepare the enrollees for jobs outside the home, it is difficult to even consider this as vocational training. The girls who complete the office/business programs usually graduate to low-paying and dead-end clerical and secretarial jobs. As a result, two and three-quarter million girls enrolled in homemaking and office/business programs are not being prepared to compete in the job market for higher-paying jobs.

The discrimination against girls in admission to vocational schools, in the programs offered them in sex-segregated vocational schools, and in the sex-typing of programs in coeducational vocational schools certainly contributes to the large gap that exists between the male and female vocational graduates' income. The boys who have received training for jobs in trade and industry will earn far higher wages than the girls who have been trained for clerical and service positions. For example, a study of one city's vocational schools found that the average expected wage for the occupations being taught to girls was forty-seven percent lower than the average salary for the trades in which boys were receiving training.[7]

While Title IX will end discrimination against girls in admission to

Table 2
Percent of Male/Female Secondary-level Vocational Education Enrollees in Each Program

Program	Percent of All Male Vocational Enrollees	Percent of All Female Vocational Enrollees
Agriculture	24	1
Distributive Education	6	5
Health	1	2
Home Economics/ Homemaking	6	40
Home Economics/ Occupational	1	7
Office/Business	11	39
Technical Education	8	1
Trades/Industry	43	5
TOTAL	100	100

vocational schools and vocational courses, it cannot end the informal school and peer pressures on students to conform to stereotyped vocational roles. Therefore, the extent to which Title IX will actually result in the broadening of vocational choices by boys and girls is unclear. However, the freedom of boys and girls to choose the roles they wish will be broadened by these regulations.

COURSE REQUIREMENTS AND ADMISSION TO CLASSES

Title IX regulations state that there can be no preference shown to either sex in admission to classes. Therefore, classes will no longer be restricted to one sex. The most common example of this is when girls were enrolled in home economics while boys enrolled in industrial arts. How many girls will continue to voluntarily take home-economics courses is not clear, but the likelihood of massive changes in these course enrollments appears quite high. At present, five million students are enrolled in home economics classes while five million are enrolled in industrial-arts classes.[8] Since industrial arts is one of the few teaching areas where there is still a teacher shortage rather than a surplus, any change in the enrollment ratio between industrial arts and home economics would result in an even more drastic shortage of qualified industrial-arts teachers. At the same time, it would also result in an overabundance of home-economics teachers. It is ironic that the opening of industrial-arts classes to girl students will hurt the women who teach home economics as the decline in home-economics enrollments will undoubtedly cost many of these women their jobs.

Not only will it be prohibited to require girls to take home economics unless boys are also required to do so, but it will be illegal to give preference to either sex in admission to classes. It is sometimes allowed for certain classes to be open to both sexes, while boys receive preference if there is a limitation on the number of students who can enroll. This occurs most often when girls want to take a class in industrial arts, but also occurs in academic classes such as physics, where laboratory space is limited, and in advanced math courses, where qualified teachers are in short supply. This practice means that boys are more likely to receive the type of scientific and mathematical training in high school that is needed to major in these areas in college. Considering that seventy-three percent of all students enrolled in high-school physics and sixty-six percent of all students enrolled in high-school trigonometry are boys,[9] it is not surprising how few girls are math or science majors in college or that few women enter math or science oriented occupations after graduating from college.

While Title IX cannot change the attitudes that have identified industrial arts, math, and science as masculine interests, it will ban all formal regulations that prohibit or restrict enrollment of girls in these courses. However, if the experience in Massachusetts is any indication, Title IX will require strict enforcement in order to actually open all classes offered by schools to girls. Despite a state law forbidding sex discrimination in schools, a study of Massachusetts schools found that one-quarter of the schools in the state did not admit both sexes to all classes.[10]

PHYSICAL EDUCATION, SPORTS AND EXTRACURRICULAR ACTIVITIES

Title IX will have a major impact on the treatment of girls in the areas of physical education, competitive sports, and extracurricular activities. Under Title IX it will no longer be possible to restrict participation in extracurricular activities, such as band or other special interest clubs, to one sex. All honor societies must also be open to both sexes.

The impact of Title IX on competitive team sports is more complicated. However, it definitely will make it illegal to restrict participation in noncontact sports to one sex without offering the other sex a chance to participate in the sport. This can be done through a coed team or through separate teams for each sex. If a school operates teams for boys and girls, it will not be allowed to provide the boys' team with certain services, such as paid coaches, uniforms, equipment, and transportation to games, if it does not provide these same services to the girls' team.

Because girls' sports teams are undersupported by most school districts, a far greater number of boys are able to participate on competitive teams than are girls. A national survey made by the National Federation of

State High School Associations of participation on high-school teams found that more than five times as many boys as girls are on all interscholastic high-school teams.[11] Table 3 shows the number of schools and the number of participants on boys' and girls' teams by sport.

Table 3
High School Interscholastic Sport Teams, 1973

	BOYS		GIRLS	
	Number of Schools	Number of Participants	Number of Schools	Number of Participants
Archery	70	420	339	4,019
Badminton	1,070	10,293	1,271	14,469
Baseball	12,860	371,783	16	480
Basketball	19,468	667,928	8,718	203,207
Bowling	736	8,237	769	10,330
Cross Country	9,383	180,674	433	4,921
Curling	874	6,214	570	3,337
Decathlon	234	770	0	0
Fencing	65	419	35	267
Field Hockey	37	1,003	1,572	45,252
Football—11 Man	14,314	969,635	0	0
— 8 Man	561	13,171	1	20
— 6 Man	112	2,304	0	0
— 9 Man	211	5,582	0	0
—12 Man	545	33,599	2	45
— Flag	8	245	0	0
Golf	9,250	129,115	1,228	10,106
Gymnastics	1,636	32,918	2,154	35,224
Ice Hockey	672	24,250	29	144
Lacrosse	231	6,055	94	3,123
Riflery	304	4,458	53	589
Rugby	93	6,766	0	0
Skiing	535	10,749	261	4,509
Soccer	2,582	77,141	245	5,174
Softball	328	5,947	4,251	81,379
Swimming	3,553	90,076	2,079	41,820
Tennis	6,828	103,035	4,219	53,940
Track and Field (indoor)	1,521	42,544	407	8,191
Track and Field (outdoor)	16,774	640,344	7,292	178,209
Volleyball	2,100	36,803	6,158	108,298
Water Polo	302	9,119	0	0
Wrestling	8,403	279,024	1	5
TOTAL	115,660	3,770,621	42,196	817,058

SOURCE: National Federation of State High School Associations, *1973 Sports Participation Survey* (Elgin, Illinois: NFSHSA, 1973).

As Table 3 shows there are 115,660 boys' high-school teams in the country but only 42,196 girls' teams. This means that of the 157,856 teams, twenty-seven percent are girls teams. Of the 4,587,679 participants on all high-school teams, eighteen percent are girls. While a total of 1,024,572 boys compete on football teams alone, there are only 817,058 participants in all girls teams. This means that there are more boys on football teams in the fall than there are girls on all teams throughout the school year. High schools give unequal treatment to girls' tennis and golf, although professional women athletes are now competing

Table 4
Percentage of All High Schools Offering Sport

Sport	Percentage of All High Schools With A Boys' Team	Percentage of All High Schools With A Girls' Team
Archery	/	2
Badminton	5	6
Baseball	58	0
Basketball	88	40
Bowling	3	3
Cross Country	43	0
Curling	4	/
Decathlon	1	0
Fencing	/	/
Field Hockey	/	7
Football	72	/
Golf	42	6
Gymnastics	7	10
Ice Hockey	3	/
Lacrosse	1	/
Riflery	1	/
Rugby	/	0
Skiing	2	1
Soccer	12	1
Softball	1	19
Swimming	16	9
Tennis	31	19
Track and Field (Indoor)	7	2
Track and Field (Outdoor)	76	33
Volleyball	10	28
Water Polo	1	0
Wrestling	38	/

NOTE: Less than one percent denoted by /
SOURCE: Calculated from National Federation of State High School Associations, *1973 Sports Participation Survey* (Elgin, Illinois: NFSHSA, 1973).

heavily in these sports. For example, of all tennis teams, sixty-two percent are for boys and only thirty-eight percent are for girls, while eighty-eight percent of all golf teams are for boys and twelve percent are for girls. The imbalance between boys' and girls' teams can be shown by comparing the percent of all high schools in the country that offer each sport.

As Table 4 shows, basketball is the most frequently offered sport for girls, being offered by forty percent of the high schools in the country. The only sports offered by more than a third of high schools for girls to compete on at the interscholastic level are basketball and outdoor track and field. In contrast, seven sports for boys to compete on at the interscholastic level are offered by more than a third of the high schools. While seventy-six percent of the high schools have a boys' outdoor-track-and-field team, only thirty-three percent have a girls' team in this sport. Other areas where the discrepancy between boys' and girls' teams is great are golf and baseball. While forty-two percent of the high schools have a boys' golf team, only six percent have a team for girls. Similarly, there are boys' baseball teams in fifty-eight percent of the high schools in the country, but only nineteen percent of the high schools have a girls' softball team.

When the sports offered by high schools are classified by those operating in the fall, winter, and spring, as shown in Table 5, it becomes clear how many boys and girls are participating on competitive teams.

Table 5
Participation in Sports By Season

Season	Number of Boys on Teams	% of All-Boy Students	Number of Girls on Teams	% of All-Girl Students	Total Students on Teams	% of All Students
Fall	1,290,100	18	55,432	1	1,345,532	10
Winter	1,212,739	17	415,921	6	1,628,660	12
Spring	1,267,762	18	345,725	5	1,613,487	11

NOTE: There are 14,100,000 students in regular public schools in fall, 1973 according to *Digest of Educational Statistics* (Washington, D.C.: U.S. Government Printing Office, 1974). There are an equal number of boys and girls in public high schools according to the 1970 Census as cited in Charles E. Johnson, Jr. and Jerry T. Jennings, "Sex Differentials in School Enrollment and Educational Attainment," *Education* (September/October 1971).

SOURCE: Calculated from National Federation of State High School Associations, *1973 Sports Participation Survey* (Elgin, Illinois: NFSHSA, 1973).

As Table 5 shows, around seventeen or eighteen percent of high-school boys are on athletic teams throughout the school year, while the participation rate for girls varies from a low of one percent in the fall to a high of six percent in the winter. Thus, during the fall, eighteen times as many boys as girls participate in interscholastic sports, while around three times as many boys as girls compete in sports during the winter and spring. More importantly, this table shows that only between ten and twelve percent of all high-school students are on teams during any one season. As such, the expenditure of large sums of money for competitive sports results in these funds being used for the benefit of only a small minority of the country's high-school students.

Although Title IX will not require equal spending on sports for boys' and girls' teams, the present spending levels will become more balanced. It is possible to get an indication of the present ratio of spending for girls' and boys' sports from several local surveys, as shown in Table 6.

Table 6
Spending Ratio on Boys and Girls Interscholastic Teams in Selected School Districts

School District	Spending Ratio Boys:Girls
Ann Arbor, Michigan[12]	10:1
Fairfax, Virginia[13]	9:1
Kalamazoo, Michigan[14]	8:1
Minneapolis, Minnesota[15]	20:1
New Brunswick, New Jersey[16]	11:1
State College, Pennsylvania[17]	10:1
Syracuse, New York[18]	450:1
Waco, Texas[19]	100:1

In addition to these local studies, a Massachusetts state analysis also found ratios with local expenditures for boys' sports sometimes being one hundred times greater than the expenditures for girls' sports.[20] In addition, until recently no money at all was spent for girls' interscholastic sports in the states of Utah and Nevada.[21] The extent of the inequities can be illustrated by the example of Minneapolis, where the cost of equipping one high-school football team was greater than the total expenditure for girls' sports at all eleven of the city's eleven high schools.[22] Despite statistics and examples such as these, nearly one-quarter of the local superintendents of schools in a nationwide survey did not believe that girls athletic programs were being shortchanged on funding, facilities, or coaches.[23]

The reason many educators do not believe that girls are being shortchanged is not one of factual misinformation, but rather of attitude. Educators are not unaware that girls' sports receive less money than boys' sports, but rather they often do not believe that boys and girls should receive equal sports expenditures. For example, the Director of Physical Education for the State of Georgia has said: "I don't think the phys.[ical] ed.[ucation] program on any level should be directed toward making an athlete of a girl."[24] The man who is director of girls' athletics in Iowa has commented: "I know the men who head the high-school athletic associations in all fifty states and I don't think there are more than three or four of them who genuinely want to see a girls' program comparable to that of boys'."[25]

Even when there is an impetus from the state level to change, there is usually resistance to change at the local level. For example, a year after the New Jersey Athletic Association issued a policy allowing girls to play on teams with boys, one-third of the local school districts in the state were still refusing to allow girls to compete on the same teams with boys.[26] Because of this resistance to change at the state and local levels, it has taken court orders in New Jersey, Michigan, Indiana, Connecticut, Minnesota, and Nebraska to mandate schools to allow girls to participate on teams with boys when there is no team in the sport provided for girls.[27] This resistance exists in spite of the fact that the majority of parents belive girls should be permitted to participate in noncontact sports on the same team with boys.[28]

Unfortunately, the prospects for voluntary change are low because of tight budgets. Many local school systems have been cutting back on their athletic programs in recent years as a means of holding down school costs. It is therefore unrealistic to expect the new funds that will have to be raised to support better athletic programs for girls to come from an increase in the total school budget. As a result, the only way to finance new programs for girls in many school districts will be to take away funds from the programs now operated exclusively for the benefit of boys. It must be emphasized that when cutting the athletic budget for boys is necessary this will not actually affect very many students. As noted earlier, only around eighteen percent of all male students are on athletic teams during any season. The changes required by Title IX will not affect the great majority of boys and girls who do not participate on interscholastic teams. Hopefully, Title IX will encourage school districts to reconsider the emphasis they place on competitive sports and instead emphasize the recreational value of sports. This change in emphasis would be in the best interest of the overwhelming majority of high-school students, both male and female.

Even if exact compliance with Title IX regulations on interscholastic sports by local school districts occurs, changes in student attitudes will be needed before the majority of girls will take advantage of the opportunity to participate in team sports. But the transition from girls' present roles as passive supporters while spectators or cheerleaders to active participants, may not be as difficult as is commonly believed. A study in Kalamazoo found that eighty-seven percent of girls thought that team sports are as appropriate for girls as boys, and eighty-one percent believed girls should be given equal treatment in the use of physical-education facilities. In contrast, only thirty-two percent of boys believed team sports were as appropriate for boys as girls and only fifty percent believed that girls should have equal use of physical-education facilities.[29] This lack of social approval on the part of boys for girls' competition in sports will present more impediments to girls' sport participation than will girls' own attitudes. Girls will not take full advantage of their opportunity to compete in sports until it becomes as socially acceptable and desirable for girls to be interested and talented in sports as it is for boys.

ENFORCEMENT OF TITLE IX

The gap between present school policies and what Title IX will require regarding course requirements, admission to vocational schools, enrollment in classes, and extracurricular and physical-education activities is large. Unfortunately, the Office of Civil Rights, in charge of enforcing Title IX in 18,000 local school districts, is not scheduled to get any major increases in staff or budget in order to carry out its enforcement duties. Out of necessity, most of the compliance with Title IX by local school districts will have to be voluntary. Only in cases regarding the largest school districts or the most flagrant violations of Title IX will the Offiice of Civil Rights be able to institute formal review procedures that are required before federal funds can be cut off due to noncompliance. This means that it will take a concerted effort on the part of educators, parents, and students to ensure compliance of their school district to Title IX. The lack of public attention given to this Act will certainly make public pressure for compliance slow in forming. However, as the requirements of Title IX become more widely known, the demands for change will increase and can be expected to eventually mandate major changes in the operation of American schools.

NOTES

1. Citizen's Advisory Council on the Status of Women, *Need for Studies of Sex Discrimination in Public Schools* (Washington, D.C.: U.S. Department of Labor, 1972).
2. The Office of Civil Rights, U.S. Department of Health, Education, and Welfare, did begin collecting this type of information in 1974 for the first time.
3. Governor's Commission on the Status of Women, Commonwealth of Massachusetts, *Report of Task Force on Education,* 1973. The complete report of this study is contained in this volume.
4. U.S. Office of Education, *Report of the Commissioner's Task Force on the*

Impact of Office of Education Programs on Women, November 1972.
5. Nicholas A. Osso, *Characteristics of Students and Staff in Vocational Education 1972* (Washington, D.C.: U.S. Government Printing Office, 1974).
6. Ibid.
7. "Women's Liberation Expected to Reach Locker Room Soon," *Phi Delta Kappan* 55 (May 1974): 643.
8. National Center for Education Statistics, *Patterns of Course Offerings and Enrollments in Public Secondary Schools, 1970–71* (Washington, D.C.: U.S. Government Printing Office, 1972).
9. U.S. Office of Education, *Digest of Educational Statistics, 1973* (Washington, D.C.: U.S. Government Printing Office, 1974).
10. Governor's Commission, *Report.*
11. The National Federation of State High School Associations, *1973 Sports Participation Survey* (Elgin, Illinois: NFSHSA, 1973).
12. Marcia Federbush, *Let Them Aspire: A Plea and Proposal for Equality of Opportunity for Males and Females in the Ann Arbor Public Schools* (Pittsburgh: KNOW Inc., 1973).
13. Robert E. L. Balien, "Fairfax Unit Finds School Sexual Bias," *Washington Post,* 13 April 1974.
14. Committee to Study Sex Discrimination in the Kalamazoo Public Schools, *Report of the Physical Education/Athletic Task Force* (Kalamazoo, Mich.: Kalamazoo Public Schools, 1973).
15. Emma Willard Task Force on Education, *Sexism in Education* (Minneapolis, Minn.: Emma Willard Task Force on Education, 1973).
16. Bil Gilbert and Nancy Williamson, "Sport Is Unfair to Women," *Sports Illustrated,* (28 May 1973): 88, 90–98.
17. National Education Association, *Education for Survival* (Washington, D.C.: NEA, 1973).
18. Ibid.
19. Kathleen M. Engle, "The Greening of Girls' Sports," *Nation's Schools,* (September 1973): 27.
20. Governor's Commission, *Report.*
21. Gilbert and Williamson, "Unfair."
22. Emma Willard Task Force, *Sexism.*
23. Engle, "Greening."
24. Gilbert and Williamson, "Unfair."
25. Bil Gilbert and Nancy Williamson, "Women In Sport: Programmed to be Losers," *Sports Illustrated,* (11 June 1973): 60–62, 65–66. 68, 73.
26. Phyllis Zatlin Boring, "Girl Sports: Not Equal," *New Directions for Women in New Jersey* 2 (Spring 1973): 3.
27. Brenda Feigen Fasteau, "Giving Women a Sporting Chance," *Ms,* (July 1973), p. 56–58, 103.
28. George H. Gallup, "Fourth Annual Gallup Poll of Public Attitudes Toward Education," *Phi Delta Kappan* 54 (September 1974).
29. Committee to Study Sex Discrimination in the Kalamazoo Public Schools, *Report.*

Teachers' Perceptions of Ideal Male and Female Students: Male Chauvinism in the Schools*

A. J. H. GAITE

It is well established that females do not achieve, in the conventional sense of the word, as much as do males in our society. In our schools there are clearly established male and female patterns of performance, wherein female students with high ability tend not to do well in math and scientific subjects. In later life the phenomenon of gifted and talented females who apparently have no interest in achieving in a particular field is well recognized. The recent development of women's groups interested in examining the position of females in our society and bringing about changes in it has once again focused attention on these kinds of differences between males and females, and raises the question of how and why they occur. This study is an attempt to assess the likely effect that high-school teachers have in influencing students' attitudes toward achievement and life style.

---

* A. J. H. Gaite, "Teachers' Perceptions of Ideal Male and Female Students: Male Chauvinism in the Schools," text of paper delivered at the 1972 Annual Meeting of the American Educational Research Association.

METHOD

A written description of an ideal senior student was prepared. The description was such that it described a student who had most of the qualities typically considered as desirable in our society. Thus, the student was both excellent in scholastic achievement and athletics, friendly and extroverted, liked by fellow students and by teachers, a student leader in both formal and informal activities. These characteristics were then incorporated in several descriptions of students; half of the profiles describing male students and half female students. The descriptions were essentially identical except for the names of the students that were either clearly male or clearly female. These idealized student profiles were presented to fifty high-school teachers who were invited to write a short account of what they perceived as a possible later career and life-style for the students. In addition to this relatively free response, the teachers responded to a specific questionnaire asking for details of the students' lives when they (the students) were twenty-one years old and thirty-one years old. The sample of teachers was drawn from two high schools located in small towns in southeast Wisconsin.

RESULTS

The results clearly illustrate the different perception that teachers have of male and female students. Without exception, teachers described male students at age twenty-one years as engaging in some kind of further education and at thirty-one years as actively and usually successfully pursuing some job or career. In contrast, teachers rarely described female students as going on for further education, and all teachers *without exception* described female students at thirty-one years as being married, with children, and looking after a home. A comparison of the kinds of jobs or careers that male and female students were following at twenty-one years indicated a very restricted range of activities for female students, a range that did not go beyond: nurse, elementary teacher, secretary, and shop assistant. In contrast, teachers perceived male students as following a very wide range of activities and jobs. No teacher ever described a female either at twenty-one years or at thirty-one years as engaging in any kind of political or community activity, while males were often so described. Overall, the picture of male students that teachers presented was one of purposeful behavior directed toward achieving money, power, and status. Females were described only in terms of marriage and a home and were perceived as essentially subordinate to and an appendage of their husbands. For example, females were never described as owning property or playing anything other than a minor role in where a family lived. The results showed no significant differences between the responses of male and female teachers, except that female teachers more often described female students as working as a teacher or a nurse prior to marriage and children than did male teachers.

CONCLUSION

It might be argued that the responses of teachers in this study are a true and realistic forecast of what awaits male and female students. Thus, the restricted activities and achievement that has characterized teachers' descriptions of female students could be seen as an accurate perception on the part of the teachers of how most females' lives develop. On the other hand, it seems likely that there is some cause here as well as effect. This study clearly shows that teachers do not have the same expectations for female students that they have for male students, and it seems reasonable to suggest that this in itself is a contributory cause of the low achievement and restricted opportunities that face females in our society. Discussion of these results with teachers in the study and with other teachers shows that few teachers are consciously aware of the different ways in which they perceive students' opportunities. It would seem, then, that a necessary first step in widening the opportunities for achievement for female students is to educate teachers to perceive the possibility that a woman may pursue a career and have a life-style similar to that which is currently perceived as a preserve for men only.

Textbooks

Textbooks present an occupational and social picture of the outside world to children. Distorted or negative representations of the people who inhabit this world affect children's self-esteem. This has long been apparent regarding the portrayal of minority groups in textbooks. Today, texts are being examined for sex stereotyping as well as for race and ethnic stereotypes.

Janice Pottker, in "Psychological and Occupational Sex Stereotypes in Elementary-School Readers" analyzed third-grade readers for personality and occupational stereotypes of females. Females' personalities were representative of the "most feminine" woman imagined. The work world of women was grossly distorted, especially in terms of class, and it was concluded that this constant and pervasive distortion would negatively affect girls' future vocational training.

The majority of women in texts were homemakers, although the majority of American women have not been homemakers since before World War II. The greatest number of working women in textbooks were elementary schoolteachers. Girls are being told that they can be only homemakers or elementary schoolteachers when they grow up. In twenty texts, only sixteen different jobs for women existed (fewer than one different occupation per textbook), but men were portrayed in over 100 different jobs. Men also worked and were married with children: not one married woman in textbooks worked. Since the schoolgirls studying these books will marry, have children, and work (in occupations other than elementary schoolteacher), these textbooks are not helping them form any accurate idea as to what their future will be. In fact, the textbooks are promoting adjustment problems for girls.

One might think that math texts would be free of sexism: one and one adds to two. However, it is through pictures and story questions that sex-role stereotypes are included. As Winifred Jay shows in "Sex Stereotyping in Elementary-school Mathematics Textbooks" significantly more famous men than famous women are shown in elementary math books. Similarly, the men in math textbooks are shown in a far greater number of different occupations than are the women. It is thus obvious that even in mathematics texts used at the elementary level, sex bias and sex stereotypes are present.

Janice Law Trecker in "Women in U.S. History Textbooks" analyzed American history texts and found that women are ignored in U.S. history. When they are mentioned, they are treated perfunctorally. Women who played leading roles in certain phases of American life, such as the labor movement, are not acknowledged. Women are treated as being supplementary to American history, rather than being integral to it.

Why should we be so critical of the female image in textbooks? One reason is that texts can lower girls' self-esteem. When girls see that women are not important in history, they realize that they are not important. Men's daring acts are shown, but women apparently took no part in them.

Textbooks also present a poor picture of schoolgirls. Girls are rarely shown doing the interesting things that the boys are doing. While the boys repair generators, study rock samples, and take part in a dozen other activities, the girls only observe through a microscope. In fact, in some texts girls are portrayed as admiring boys for performing feats that are seemingly impossible for girls. Girls exposed to this image of themselves will scarcely grow up to be active, inquiring, challenging adults.

This type of representation of girls is also harmful to boys. If girls are always passive, then boys must always be active. If girls are dumb, then boys must be smart. Men must perform all the world's work, since women do none of it. This type of burden is too heavy for men to carry, and boys realize it. The adulation of males can only make boys feel uneasy, at best, and at worst, makes boys feel unequal and inferior to the image that they are told they must live up to.

Girls are also being prepared for a vocational world that does not exist. Millions of American women are not homemakers or elementary schoolteachers. Married women do work, and so do women with children. Girls consistently show a poorer vocational knowledge than boys, and textbooks are a cause of this.

Textbooks don't just exhibit a sex-stereotyped portrayal of women, they show a portrayal that is grossly inaccurate. Texts do not even represent the reality of working women. When parents today are concerned that their daughters be shown pictures of women doctors as well as nurses, it is ironic that texts don't even show the nurses. School policy-makers should insist on textbooks that do not distort women and their activities. It is desirable that texts present a favorable image of women and it is essential that they at least present an accurate picture.

Psychological and Occupational Sex Stereotypes in Elementary-school Readers[1]

JANICE POTTKER

This study determined how girls and women were presented in elementary-school reading textbooks.[2] There were four principle areas studied: 1) what type of personal characteristics girls and women were presented as having in elementary-school reading textbooks, 2) what occupations were women presented as having, with reference to type and class, in elementary-reading textbooks, 3) to what extent were the personal characteristics of girls and women shown in the elementary-reading textbooks an accurate reflection of the characteristics attributed to the most feminine woman imagined, and 4) to what extent was the occupational status of women as shown by elementary-school reading textbooks an accurate reflection of the occupational status of women in the United States. The methodology of this study was in two parts. First, the personality characteristics of the textbook females were identified and categorized according to Jenkin and Vroegh's list of the most feminine woman imagined.[3] Secondly, the occupations of textbook women were listed and compared with the occupations of American women in the labor force.

ANALYSIS OF THE PERSONALTY DATA

In each of the twenty textbooks studied, each story was read and each major female character was classified as possessing one major personality characteristic for that story. Jenkin and Vroegh's adjective list was used for the purpose of identifying and categorizing each major female's personality characteristic. (The adjective "feminine" was not ranked for textbook characters.)

Table 1
Personality List—Rank and Total Number

(The characteristics that received "0" textbook total number were not necessarily characteristics absent from the female character, but rather not her primary characteristic. The only characteristic that received a "0" and was totally absent from any textbook character was "sexually responsive.")

Jenkin and Vroegh Rank	Jenkin and Vroegh Adjective	Textbook Total Number	Textbook Rank
1	affectionate	37	2
2.5	charming	33	3.5
2.5	feminine	—	—
4.5	appreciative	44	1
4.5	attractive	22	5
6	courteous	17	7
8	graceful	7	15.5
8	gracious	14	10
8	sexually attractive	0	—
10	sociable	7	15.5
11.5	considerate	33	3.5
11.5	gentle	10	12.5
13.5	understanding	18	6
13.5	warm	3	18
16.5	good figure	0	—
16.5	poised	2	21
16.5	sexually responsive	0	—
16.5	thoughtful	13	11
21	cooperative	15	9
21	emotionally stable	0	—
21	good-natured	10	12.5
21	intelligent	16	8
21	sense of humor	6	17
24	well-groomed	0	—
26	healthy	0	—
26	motherly	0	—
26	personable	0	—
28.5	dependable	0	—
28.5	vivacious	2	21
32	active	2	21
32	artistic	1	24
32	calm	9	14
32	sentimental	2	21
32	tactful	2	21

The total number of occurrences of each textbook personality characteristic was numerically tabulated and is shown in Table 1, as is the rank order of these personality characteristics.

These textbook characteristics were evaluated to see if they were representative of Jenkin and Vroegh's list, which described the most feminine woman imagined. As is shown in Table 1, the rank order of Jenkin and Vroegh's characteristics and of the textbook characteristics is very similar.

Table 1 shows that the textbook-females do represent Jenkin and Vroegh's description of the most feminine woman imagined. The textbook-woman is best characterized by being called appreciative, affectionate, charming, and considerate. She is also attractive and understanding, but she is not usually artistic or calm. What is significant is that Jenkin and Vroegh's list of characteristics is not descriptive of the typical woman or the average woman or even an unfeminine woman, but rather the most feminine woman imagined. Since the textbook-females are significantly represented on this list, it is assumed, therefore, that they are representative of the most feminine woman imagined. The textbook-writers have shown extreme examples of femininity. Any character representative of an extreme, any character that is accurately described as the "most . . . imagined" of any category, is bound to appear stereotyped and unreal. Examples from the twenty textbooks analyzed will further show how women are characterized as being extremely feminine.

Examples of Textbook Females' Personality

Girls in textbooks stories are often younger sisters who display a "ninny syndrome."[4] "The typical family constellation includes a younger sister."[5] Little sisters were found in thirty-four percent of the stories Blom, et al., analyzed, but little brothers were only found in six percent of these same stories.[6] Brothers were constantly helping their sisters out of tough situations in the stories. These sisters act as a foil for the boys' greater knowledge and experience.

Since boys are "portrayed as smarter, with greater initiative and achievement,"[7] it is not surprising that girls and women go to males to help them with their problems. "Males are being portrayed as the bearers of knowledge and wisdom."[8]

The storywriters are careful to sex-type play.[9] One text-story told of a group of boys who found a box to play in, and later abandoned it to a group of girls. When the boys played in the box it was a truck, and when the girls played in the box, it was a dollhouse.[10] Zimet pointed out that textbook-stories between 1921 and 1966 have portrayed "a very limited and restricted prototype of sex behavior."[11]

Some of the examples of the little-sister syndrome in the twenty texts studied include a crying girl who has lost her cup in the water and asks

Pablo to retrieve it (which he does by merely putting his hand in the water and picking it up),[12] a boy named Bill who frightens his little sister Sandra with his monster imitations,[13] girls who are frightened in the haunted house because they are without the company of their brothers,[14] and a girl named Judy who asks Nick to protect her from "The Boys Around the Corner":

> "I'd be afraid to do that," Judy said. "They're too big to punch. I'd even be afraid to talk back to them the way you did. I bet they won't keep picking on you. They know you're brave."
>
> "Oh, I'm not so brave," said Nick.
>
> But he felt braver, just because of Judy. "If you want," he said, "I'll walk to school with you in the morning."[15]

Is bolstering male egos an appropriate task for eight-year-old girls?

Females are helped out of their many dilemmas by males, and sometimes these males are far younger than the females they are saving. In one story, a mother is distraught over her leaking pipes and, unable to figure out what to do by herself, calls in her eight-year-old son to solve her problem.[16]

With a mixture of chivalry, paternalism, and condescension, a policeman and a young boy come to the rescue of the owner of a pet shop:

> "The fact is—I need somebody to help," sobbed Miss Peasley.
>
> "I'd suggest that you allow Tandy and me to solve this puzzle," said the policeman. He winked at Tandy, and Tandy winked back.[17]

One story tells of how Mother had to have the doorman help her open a suitcase,[18] and another story ends with the girls watching the boys rescue the goats that the girls had lost.[19]

In "Timmy Pretend,"[20] a mouse appeared while Timmy was dreaming of baseball, while Father was reading, while Mother was sewing, and while sister Katherine was baking cakes.

> "It *is* a real mouse," cried Mother, dropping her sewing. "Do something, somebody." She ran to the other side of the house. She was no help.
>
> "Don't let it come near me. Keep it away," screamed Katherine. She ran quickly to the other side of the room. She was no help at all.[21]

Father and Timmy chased the mouse out of the house.

Not content to portray the women as nurturant and maternal, the textwriters also have to attribute these characeristics to girls. Belinda emphasizes that she would rather take care of babies then play with the boys: "I like to take care of babies."[22]

In 1898, Charlotte Perkins Gilman wrote:

> Boys are encouraged from the beginning to show the feelings supposed to be proper to their sex. When our infant son bangs about, roars, and smashes things, we say proudly that he is "a regular boy." When our infant daughter coquettes with visitors, or wails in maternal agony because her mother has broken her doll, we say proudly that "she is a perfect little girl already!" What business has a little girl with the instincts of maternity? No more than the little boy should have with the instincts of paternity.[23]

None of the little boys in any of the stories are encouraged to take a paternal interest in children.

Just as the mother is shown to be weak, passive, and vacillating,[24] the father is portrayed as a firm figure in the stories. "Father was kind, but he was also master of his house."[25] Kristen says to his wife, "I am master of the farm, and I decide what is to be done."[26] Mother told Bob that *Father* would have to decide whether or not Bob could go sailing.[27] Another story is entitled "What the Old Man Does Is Always Right."[28] When Becky invited the Indian women inside her house, "they made no move but looked to their men, and three braves followed her instead,"[29] showing that even Indian women are subservient to their husbands.

An air of male superiority permeates some of the stories. Otto tells us, "girls and little boys have snowsuits. But not big boys like me"[30] Charles announces, "I'm not going to any girl party."[31] A Negro boy named Lincoln tells his sisters Sissy and Sassy (the degree of ethnic sophistication in texts is not high) that it was more important for *him* to travel than for them to travel.[32]

In summary, the female textbook-character mirrors the characteristics of the most feminine woman imagined by being overwhelming, affectionate, appreciative, charming, and attractive. Her place in the family is secondary in importance to that of her husband, her brother, or even her male children, and she is dependent upon their aid. She is a cardboard figure to her readers and a sugarspun bore. Ray Bradbury's description of Martian robots fits her: "sexed, but sexless, and borrowing from humans everything but humanity."[33] She is the female eunuch[34].

ANALYSIS OF THE OCCUPATIONAL DATA

Almost fifty-seven percent of the women in textbooks were housewives,[35] as seen in Table 2. The majority of text-women were shown as housewives, although it has been over twenty years since the majority of

Table 2
Occupations of Textbook Women

Occupation	Total Number	Percentage	Salaried Percentage
Housewife	59	56.76	—
Elementary Schoolteacher	19	18.27	42.22
Nurse	5	4.80	11.11
Small-store Owner	4	3.84	8.89
Secretary	2	1.92	4.44
Housekeeper	2	1.92	4.44
Service Worker	2	1.92	4.44
Trapeze Artist	2	1.92	4.44
Operative	1	.96	2.22
Baker	1	.96	2.22
Landlady	1	.96	2.22
Librarian	1	.96	2.22
Clerical Worker	1	.96	2.22
Elephant Trainer	1	.96	2.22
Waitress	1	.96	2.22
Recreation Director	1	.96	2.22

American women have been housewives.[36] Only thirty-nine percent of American women are homemakers, while forty-four percent of the women are in the labor force, with seventeen percent of women who are students, ill, or unemployed.[37] Textbooks show fifty-seven percent of women as housewives, which is almost twenty percent more than are in the country.

Since most women in textbooks are in their early thirties and since many have small children, it was thought that possibly women with these characteristics in the labor market were the women who were housewives. This would help explain why there were so many more housewives shown in the texts than exist in the labor market.

But forty-nine percent of all mothers in the population work, and over one-third of these women have children under six years of age. The median age for a working woman is thirty-nine years. The women in the population who are not working are women in their fifties and sixties.[38] Therefore, the age of the textbook-women is not related to their occupational status.

Looking at Table 2, elementary schoolteachers hold 42.22% of the salaried occupations in the texts, but in the real labor force, women who are teachers comprise only 6.1% of the labor force (and this includes both elementary and secondary schoolteachers).[39]

Slightly over eleven percent of textbook-women are small-store owners, while fewer than .9% of American women are small-store owners.[40]

Almost four-and-a-half percent of textbook-women are secretaries, stenographers, or typists, as compared to over twelve percent of employed women.[41] The percentage of housekeepers in the texts (4.4%) is exactly the percentage of housekeepers in the labor market.[42] Although 9.9% of women in the labor force are service workers, only 4.4% of text-women are service workers.[43]

There are 4.4% of employed textbook-women who are trapeze artists, and although the percentage of women workers who are trapeze artists is not known, it is ludicrous that textbooks present as many women trapeze artists as secretaries.

All other textbook occupations had 2.2% of women in them, so that there were only 2.2% of text-women who were operatives as compared with fifteen percent in the labor force, 2.2% of text-women who were clerical workers as compared with 21.6% in the labor force, and 2.2% of text-women who were waitresses as compared to 5.7% in the labor force.[44] It can be seen here that the type of blue-collar jobs that lower-middle-class and lower-class women hold are grossly underrepresented in textbooks.

There was a similar percentage of women librarians in the texts and in the labor market. In the texts, as many women were shown to be elephant trainers as waitresses or operatives.

Table 3 shows a comparison of the occupations of textbook-women to women in the labor force. A great deal more textbook-women were

Table 3
Comparison of Occupations of Text-women to Women in Labor Force

Overrepresentation Greatly More	More	Same	Fewer	Underrepresentation Greatly Fewer
Housewife	Nurse	Librarian	Secretary	Clerical Worker
Elementary School-teacher	Small-store Owner	Housekeeper	Service Worker	Waitress
Trapeze Artist	Recreation Director			
Elephant Trainer	Baker			
	Landlady			

shown as homemakers and elementary schoolteachers than exist in the labor market. Although the percentage of textbook trapeze artists and elephant trainers was far smaller than the percentage of textbook housewives and elementary schoolteachers, there were far more trapeze artists and elephant trainers shown in the texts than there are in real life. Also overrepresented in the textbooks were nurses, small-store owners, recreation directors, bakers, and landladies. Librarians and housekeepers were shown in equal percentages in textbooks and in the labor force, while secretaries and service workers were underrepresented in the texts. There were far fewer clerical workers and waitresses shown in the textbooks than are in the labor force.

These results show that there is an overemphasis in textbooks on women who are housewives and professional workers, and an underemphasis on clerical and operative workers. Ninety-seven percent of all stenographers and typists are women, and almost seventy percent of all waitresses, clerks, and other clerical workers are women.

What is most interesting is that these texts are not just sex biased, they are sex biased *and* class biased at the same time. The stereotyped female occupations shown are predominately middle class. A lower-class schoolgirl reading these texts is shown a work force and life-style in which she will probably not be able to play a part.

And textbooks are the major source of instruction in the schools. Approximately seventy-five percent of classroom time is spent working with texts, and ninety-five percent of homework time is spent with textbooks. Also, some children read only textbooks; the only reading material that lower-class children might be exposed to is textbooks. It is therefore extremely important that textbooks be free, as far as possible, from biased and inaccurate portrayals of any group of people. However, it seems that children from working-class homes are served least well by the texts.

Textbooks are also so oriented to the middle class that upper-class life is distorted, too. One reader showed a queen, complete with crown and ermine cape, cooking dinner for her family!

Not only are text-women's jobs sex stereotyped, but these jobs are few in number. In the twenty third-grade readers included in this study, women were shown to have only seventeen occupations (including that of housewife). That is fewer than one different women's job per textbook. An informal list was made of men's occupations in these twenty texts, and this list included more than *ninety* occupations.

These textbook-men's occupations included such diverse jobs as doctor, veterinarian, cameraman, reporter, college teacher, astronaut, construction worker, scientist, farmer, business executive, engineer, pilot, telephone lineman, policeman, truck driver, and radio announcer. Again, these are mostly upper-middle-class jobs. If a person had to choose a job for himself or herself, and if he or she could have a choice of either the textbooks' list of jobs of women or the textbooks' list of jobs of men, which list would it be more likely that he or she would choose? Perhaps the portrayal of women's jobs is a cause of girls' poorer vocational knowledge.

Women's Occupations in Textbooks

Textbook-women are excluded from many different jobs, whereas men assume a wide variety of roles and activities. It has been stated that women are shown in sixteen salaried jobs whereas men are shown in over ninety jobs. Most of these jobs are interspersed throughout the stories and are not central to them. However, there are some stories dealing exclusively with occupations, and these stories never include women.

In "The Latest News," almost a dozen different types of newspaper occupations are shown and all of the jobs are held by men. Not one woman works for that newspaper,[45] although one-third of all reporters are women.

Scientists and doctors are always men. "Our Fishy Future" shows caveman fishermen, male scientists, pilots, and Asian sea farmers.[46] Only men are concerned with space projects, as shown in "Pioneers in Space,"[47] and "Laika, Sam, Miss Sam, and Ham."[48] One text tells its readers, "men who work in science are called scientists," and pictures only male scientists.[49] Charley says, "Dad's a doctor. People need him. Mother's a nurse, and nurses are always needed."[50] However, Mother only works when Dad needs her at the hospital. Apparently nurses are not needed too much, at least if they are also mothers.

Again, readers are told that scientists are men:

> The scientists are also finding ways to live more safely and more comfortably in that cold part of the world. In the future they will be able to take their families there. The penguins may have to make room for women and children, as well as for scientists![51]

"The First Bread" shows a caveman experimenting with grain, and a cavewoman baking his product. All the current agricultural workers shown are also men, although the story ends with, "ask your mother to bake it for you."[52]

Women who work apparently cannot be identified by their occupation. In "Cow Concert," two people are discribed as "a baker and his wife" even though they are both pictured working in the bakery.[53]

Although women are excluded from certain types of jobs, they are assigned other jobs. "Come to the Library" pictures a male librarian, but the text of the story always uses the pronoun "she" when referring to librarians.[54] Women are identified as housewives for no apparent reason. In Mr. Y and Mr. X's store, "the first customer to come the next morning was a housewife."[55] " 'But they're always two for a quarter,' said the housewife,"[56] and "village housewives with their market baskets" shopped often.[57]

Even if women are not housewives, they are shown to be concerned with domestic details. The teacher who holds a conference with her pupil's mother asks for a recipe.[58] The girls in another story are praised for being domestic: "She could wash the dishes and help keep the house clean. But best of all, she liked to cook,"[59] and:

> Agnes wasn't a bad girl. She was really very good most of the time. She did her lessons well in school. She had learned to cook, to bake bread, to make jam and jelly, and to sew a little. She helped her mother wash clothes and clean house, and she never complained about doing that work.[60]

These girls' jobs are certainly not also boys' jobs. Billy explains that he had to take care of his baby brother, Teddy: "Well, Mom had to go to town, so she asked me to take care of Teddy 'til she gets back. Besides, she's going to give me a dollar."[61]

"Chuka's Hawk" tells the reader of the low status of "women's jobs."

> When they were done, Chuka helped his mother clear away the dishes and wash them. "Little boys do women's work," said Big Brother.[62]

The teacher's edition to this text, which includes both questions and answers, hardly speaks of the need for equality between men and women:

> Discussion and Reading
> Role
> What did mother do?
> (cooked dinner,
> cleared things away,
> and washed up)
> Did Big Brother help?
> (no)
> Attitude and Inference
> What is his attitude
> about women's work?
> (looks down on it) [63]

Kami, in "The Great Wave," expressed the same concept for women's jobs:

> It wasn't fair, he thought. His father and his older brother would spend their day on the ocean, doing the work of men. They were fishermen. But he, Kami, had to stay home and do the chores of a woman. He was almost as much of a man as his brothers. Why couldn't he do a man's work?
>
> Kami looked at his little sister. "Women's work," he thought.[64]

Kami then saves his sister from drowning, and his mother tells him:

> "You are indeed a man! Tonight I shall speak to your father. You will spend every day in the fishing boat. No more chores around here."
> "A man's work," he thought. He had done a man's work this morning, Kami knew.
> Kami grinned at his mother. "Oh," he said, "I guess fishing is all right. But a man has to do his job, and my job's right here."[65]

Kami has now turned the morning activities, watching the baby, from a woman's work to a man's work, by virtue of the importance of watching the baby. If the work is important, Kami infers, then it is a man's work.

The teacher's guide apparently agrees with this philosophy of *machismo*:

> How did his experience influence his attitude toward women's chores? (What he had called women's chores was really a man's work).[66]

The message is clear: important work is not women's work, but man's work.

Amory points out that women in texts are "almost exclusively portrayed as mothers and teachers,"[67] but he does not point out that textbook-women are rarely mothers and teachers at the same time. In the twenty textbooks analyzed, sixteen women teachers were unmarried (assuming that the title "Miss" is an indication of marital status) and one was married. These teachers are almost the only women who were addressed by name: therefore, the image of working women in the textbooks is that they are unmarried.

The only working *mother* given any attention in the text was the country bunny. She delighted in being the world's Easter bunny, until she had little bunnies: "Now, children, since I have such a lovely big family, I'll have to stop thinking about being an Easter bunny who hops all over the world with beautiful eggs for little boys and girls. I'll have to stay at home and take care of my babies."[68]

The message for children is clear: good mothers, even bunny mothers, stay home with their children.

Famous Women in Textbooks

Many of the texts had stories devoted to famous people, but most of these famous people were men. *Better than Gold, Ideas and Images,* and *Friends Far and Near* did not include any women in their famous people category. Pocahontas was the only woman in *Basic Goals in Reading,* and it was difficult to tell if she was supposed to be the token woman or the token Indian. Nancy Hanks, who achieved her fame through motherhood, was the only woman in *More Roads to Follow,* while Betsy Ross was in *Round the Corner.* Joan of Arc was represented in *A Trip Around the World.* And with the same sophistication that included George Washington Carver as the only Negro in the unit "Famous People" in *A Magic World,* the only woman included was Florence Nightingale.

Pocahontas achieved fame by loving a man (or so the legend goes), Nancy Hanks by bearing a child, Betsy Ross by virtue of her sewing (which is historically inaccurate), and Florence Nightingale by being the Lady with the Lamp. If text-writers admire teachers, why not include Prudence Crandell? And perhaps Elizabeth Blackwell just as well represents women in the medical profession as does Florence Nightingale. Interestingly, the picture of Florence Nightingale shown was that of a kind, motherly woman taking care of wounded soldiers, when in reality Nightingale was an administrator, not a "motherly" nurse. As one nursing student said, "It's all such a sham: Florence Nightingale died of syphilis—we *all* know *that!*"[69]

CONCLUSION

Women's personalities and occupations are grossly distorted in textbooks. Women's and girls' personalities in the texts are representative of the "most feminine" woman imagined. They are displayed in the texts as being appreciative and affectionate at the expense of being active or artistic. Women's occupations are also distorted in terms of sex stereotypes: women are shown as elementary schoolteachers, and not as college teachers, and they are shown as nurses rather than doctors. Within the realm of sex stereotyping also comes class stereotyping: women in texts are middle-class and therefore hold middle-class jobs. Few text-women are shown as clerks or waitresses.

Further research should be conducted on the harm sex and class steretypes inflict upon schoolchildren. Bettleheim has spoken of texts as anxiety-producing agents for children that contribute to a negative self-image.[70] Children compare themselves to the characters they read about in texts, and realize that they are not like them. For example, some cannot imagine themselves as the sort of passive homemakers shown in texts, and many children also realize that they will not be able to go to college and become teachers.

Textbooks today portray to children a distorted, inaccurate picture of women in the work world. Most textbook publishers have not yet realized that they have a duty to present views of social life that are not warped beyond recognition to many children.

Parents are concerned that their daughters be shown women dentists and not just hygienists, but the texts do not even show the hygienists. Although it is fine and commendable to show girls and boys through the texts that women can be lawyers, it is also important not to eliminate the job many women hold as legal secretary. It is ironic that texts would not be half so bad as they are if they just mirrored the occupations that women hold in today's society. This possible portrayal of the status quo, while not representing the very best that can be done, would at least be better than the warped work-world of women shown today in texts.

There is also the danger of presenting female role-models in textbooks that are inaccessible for many girls, especially girls of working-class homes. Texts comprised solely of women doctors and astronauts would be class biased. The girl whose mother is a dime-store clerk needs strong female figures with whom to identify, but she will probably identify little with Matina Horner, whose status is next to unattainable for her. A more representative, and less class-biased, array of women's jobs and personality characteristics is strongly called for.

NOTES

1. This paper was adapted from the author's M.A. thesis, "Female Sex-role Stereotypes in Elementary-school Readers," University of Maryland, 1971, and from "Sex and Class Occupational Stereotypes in Elementary Readers" presented at the 1973 Annual Meeting of the American Sociological Association, New York. The author would like to thank the following for their helpful suggestions: Daniel P. Huden, University of Maryland; Barbette Blackington, International Institute of Women Studies; Rita Seiden Miller, Rhode Island College; and the Feminist Research Group, New York City.
2. The study dealt with a simple random sample of those elementary-school reading textbooks approved for use in the 1969–70 school year by the Montgomery County Public Schools, Maryland, for the third grade. Twenty texts, or approximately 2,000 stories, were analyzed. Only the occupations of women, and not girls, were classified in the study, and only the occupations that are found in the *Dictionary of Occupational Titles* were classified.
3. Noel Jenkin and Karen Vroegh, "Contemporary Concepts of Masculinity and Femininity," *Psychological Reports* 25 (1969) : 679–97.
4. Joan Beck, "The Feminist Movement Hits Children's Books," *Chicago Tribune,* 21 January 1971, sec. 2, p. 1.
5. Cleveland Amory, "Trade Winds," *Saturday Review,* 20 March 1971, p. 16.
6. Gaston E. Blom, Sarah Zimet, and Richard R. White, "Ethnic Interaction and Urbanization of a First-grade Reading Textbook: A Research Study," *Psychology in the Schools* 4 (1967) : 176–81.
7. Amory, "Trade Winds," p. 16.
8. Gaston E. Blom, Richard R. Waite, and Sarah Zimet, "Content of First-grade Reading Books," *The Reading Teacher* 21 (1968) : 217–323.
9. Irvin Child, Elmer H. Potter, and Estelle M. Levine, "Children's Textbooks and Personality Development: An Exploration in the Social Psychology of Education," *Psychological Monographs* 60 (1946) : 1–53.
10. Virginia Kidd, ' "Now You See," Said Mark," ' *New York Review of Books* 15 (2 September 1970) : 35–36.
11. Sarah F. Zimet, "Little Boy Lost," *Teachers College Record* 72 (1970) : 31–40.

12. David H. Russell, Theodore Clymer and Gretchen Wulfing, *Friends Far and Near* (Boston: Ginn and Co., 1966), pp. 208–9.
13. Bank Street College of Education, *City Sidewalks* (New York: Macmillan, 1966), p. 32.
14. Bank Street College of Education, *Around the Corner* (New York: Macmillan, 1966), p. 32.
15. Bank Street College, *City Sidewalks*, p. 32.
16. Ibid., pp. 211–21.
17. Paul McKee, et al., *Climbing Higher* (Boston: Houghton Mifflin, 1966), p. 142.
18. Helen M. Robinson, et al., *More Roads to Follow* (Chicago: Scott, Foresman, and Co., 1965), p. 57.
19. Ibid., p. 42.
20. Marjorie Seddon Johnson, et al., *High and Wide* (New York: American Book Co., 1968), pp. 156–63.
21. Ibid., pp. 160–61.
22. Josephine L. Wright, Albert J. Harris, and Mae Knight Clark, *Better Than Gold* (New York: Macmillan, 1965), p. 220.
23. Charlotte Perkins Gilman, *Women and Economics* (New York: Harper and Row, 1966, originally published by Small and Maynard, 1898), p. 56.
24. Beck, "Feminist Movement," p. 1.
25. William D. Sheldon and Mary C. Austin, *Story Caravan* (Boston: Allyn and Bacon, 1959), p. 9.
26. Bank Street College, *City Sidewalks*, p. 168.
27. Russell, *Friends*, p. 13.
28. Ibid., pp. 255–64.
29. Glenn McCracken and Charles C. Walcutt, *Basic Reading* (Phila.: Lippincott 1964), p. 183.
30. Helen M. Robinson, et al., *Roads to Follow* (Chicago: Scott, Foresman, and Co., 1965), p. 71.
31. Robinson, *More Roads*, p. 44.
32. Helen M. Robinson, et al., *Speeding Away* (Chicago: Scott, Foresman, and Co., 1968), p. 120.
33. Ray Bradbury, *The Martian Chronicles* (New York: Bantam Books, 1970), p. 111.
34. Germain Greer, *The Female Eunuch* (New York: McGraw-Hill, 1971).
35. This is a conservative estimate of the number of housewives in the texts, since a woman was not coded as a housewife unless it was obvious that she was at home or engaged in leisure activities during the weekday. Women who were at home with their children after school were not coded as housewives because they presumably could have work hours allowing them to be free in the afternoon.
36. Robert W. Smuts, *Women and Work in America* (New York: Columbia University Press, 1959), p. 1.
37. U.S. Department of Labor, Women's Bureau (Washington, D.C.: U.S. Government Printing Office, 1971).
38. U.S. Department of Labor, Women's Bureau, *Who Are The Working Mothers?* (Washington, D.C.: U.S. Government Printing Office, 1970), p. 2.
39. U.S. Department of Labor, Women's Bureau, *1969 Handbook of Women Workers* (Washington, D.C.: U.S. Government Printing Office, 1969), p. 90.
40. Ibid.

41. Valerie Kincade Oppenheimer, "The Sex Labeling of Jobs," *Industrial Relations* 7 (1968) : 220.
42. U.S. Department of Labor, *1969 Handbook*, p. 90.
43. Ibid.
44. Oppenheimer, "Sex Labeling," p. 220.
45. Bank Street College, *Around the Corner*, pp. 139–44.
46. Wright, *Better Than Gold*, pp. 139–44.
47. Robinson, *Speeding Away*, pp. 102–105.
48. Bank Street College, *City Sidewalks*, pp. 14–16.
49. William Kottmeyer and Kay Ware, *Basic Goals in Reading 3–1*, (Phila.: Lippincott Co., 1964), pp. 44–48.
50. Robinson, *More Roads*, p. 40.
51. Wright, *Better Than Gold*, p. 280.
52. Bank Street College, *City Sidewalks*, pp. 222–27.
53. McKee, *Climbing Higher*, pp. 7–27.
54. Bank Street College, *City Sidewalks*, pp. 114–17.
55. McCracken and Walcutt, *Basic Reading*, p. 81.
56. Ibid., p. 82.
57. Ibid., p. 105.
58. Bank Street College, *City Sidewalks*, p. 60.
59. Sheldon, *Story Caravan*, p. 25.
60. McKee, *Climbing Higher*, p. 96.
61. Johnson, *High and Wide*, p. 241.
62. Ibid., p. 90.
63. Marjorie Seddon Johnson, Roy A. Kress, and P. J. Hutchins, *High and Wide: Teacher's Annotated Edition* (New York: American Book Co., 1968), p. 62.
64. Marjorie Seddon Johnson, Roy A. Kress, and P. J. Hutchins, *Ideas and Images: Teachers Annotated Edition* (New York: American Book Co., 1968), p. 62.
65. Ibid., p. 69.
66. Ibid.
67. Amory, "Trade Winds," p. 16.
68. Sheldon, *Story Caravan*, p. 108.
69. Cynthia Kruger, "Do Bad Girls Become Good Nurses?," *Transaction* 5 (1968) : 32.
70. Bruno Bettleheim, "The Decision to Fail," *School Review* 69 (1961) : 377–412.

Sex Stereotyping in Elementary-school Mathematics Textbooks*

WINIFRED TOM JAY

THE PROBLEM

Given the renewed societal concern regarding equal educational opportunity for all, it is logical to scrutinize commercially prepared instructional materials used by children to determine whether heretofore commonly accepted formats may not, in fact, perpetuate sex stereotyping. The basic assumption underlying this proposition is that the removal of sex bias, if it exists in printed materials, will move educators and schools in society closer toward the pedagogical goal of fully individualized instruction, and as a consequence toward the societal goal of equal opportunity and realization of potential.

Several related assumptions underlie this investigation. First, the textbooks used by children in elementary mathematics are not neutral in their contribution to the development of interests, self-image, cultural role, and even career choices. Second, foundations for life-long interest in mathematics are likely formed in the early years. Finally, the existence of sex

* Winifred Tom Jay, "Sex Stereotyping in Elementary-school Mathematics Textbooks," reprinted with permission of the author. Originally appeared as part of a Ph.D. dissertation at the University of Oregon, 1973.

stereotyping in elementary-school mathematics texts would contribute to girls' historical lack of interest in mathematics, role assumption, repression of ability, aspirations, and so forth.

Specifically, the purpose of this study was to analyze for sex stereotyping selected mathematics textbooks now being used in Grades 2, 4, and 6. To fulfill the stated purpose of this investigation, answers to the following questions were sought:

Does sex stereotyping exist in mathematics word problems and illustrations?

Do boys and girls make the same judgments about sex stereotyping?

Do fathers and mothers make the same judgments about sex stereotyping?

Do children make the same judgments about sex stereotyping as adults?

What is the most common response (boy, girl, either) to each of the mathematics problems as determined by children? by adults?

Are there significantly more famous men than famous women in math textbooks?

Are there significantly more occupations for men than for women in math textbooks?

Do the textbooks feature men and women in unusual, nonstereotyped roles?

BASIC RESEARCH PROCEDURE

Elementary-school mathematics texts from four publishers were examined. The principal format for gathering data was provided by an adaptation of Berelson's content-analysis technique. The approach calls for the establishment of categories (units to count and variables) for efficacy in examining the manifest content of printed material. The following categories were established for this study:

1. Word problems and illustrations featuring items of interest to a boy, a girl, or either
2. Word problems and illustrations featuring famous people: males and females
3. Word problems and illustrations featuring occupations for males and females

4. Word problems and illustrations featuring unusual ways the textbooks handled traditional roles for males and females.

A two dimensional approach, *i.e.,* adaptation of Berleson, was actually applied to gather data for this study. To control for investigator bias, the data-gathering process for *Category 1* utilized a school survey involving students and parents. The more conventional approach was used to gather data for *Categories 2, 3,* and *4.* Two adult coders were asked to analyze six textbooks each, in the search for famous people, occupations, and unusual roles.

METHODS AND PROCEDURES FOR DATA COLLECTION

Elementary-school mathematics textbooks for Grades 2, 4, and 6 were selected for analysis in this investigation. The materials of four commercial publishers that appear on Hawaii's *Approved Instructional Material List* were chosen. This resulted in an examination of a total of twelve pupil editions.

The textbooks analyzed are as follows:

Publisher	*Title*
Addison-Wesley Publishing Co., Copyright 1971	*Elementary School Mathematics,* Grades 2, 4, and 6
Holt, Rinehart & Winston, Inc., Copyright 1970	*Exploring Elementary Mathematics,* Grades 2, 4, and 6
Houghton Mifflin Co. Copyright 1970	*Modern School Mathematics* Grades 2, 4, and 6
Silver Burdett Co. Copyright 1970	*Modern Mathematics Through Discovery,* Grades 2, 4, & 6

CATEGORIES

Generating categories is a first step in content analysis. They serve as common denominators to be applied to the material being analyzed. They also serve as units of measurement so that if the study is to be repeated, other analysts can apply the dimensions to the same content for verification. Four categories delineated for this study are:

Category 1—Word problems and illustrations featuring items of interest to a boy, a girl, or either

Category 2—Word problems and illustrations featuring famous people: males and females

Category 3—Word problems and illustrations featuring occupations for males and females

Category 4—Word problems and illustrations featuring unusual ways the text handles traditional roles for males and females.

OBJECTIVITY

A second requirement in content analysis is maintaining objectivity. In order to keep investigator bias to a minimum the research was executed by using adults and students as coders. Two approaches were used for coding, or analysis of the textbook material. For *Category 1,* parents and students were asked to classify material according to gender. The content of *Category 1* was derived through the random selection of five pages from each of twelve texts. Results were reported in terms of agreement and disagreement between boys and girls; between fathers and mothers; between students and parents. For *Categories 2, 3,* and *4,* two adult coders unrelated to the school in any way were asked to analyze six textbooks each, for famous males and females, occupations for males and females, and unusual ways the texts handled traditional roles for males and females. Results in the second approach were reported in terms of relative frequencies.

It is pertinent to indicate here that at the beginning of the study, the investigator had planned to ask the two adult coders to analyze for all four categories. In attempting to develop coding rules for identifying items as boy, girl, or either, it became evident that the rules, though necessary for consistency in analysis, would carry the biases of the investigator. Hence, the survey was designed to sample the thinking of students and parents, thereby freeing the investigator from projecting preconceived notions on the coding task.

The coding rules which were finally developed for the two adult coders were in reality directions for the task of analyzing for *Categories 2, 3,* and *4.* These categories required little or no judgment on sex stereotyping. That is, the coders were merely asked to report what exists, without having to rate items as to sex appeal.

THE SURVEY

The subjects for the school survey (*Category 1*) consisted of parents and students from an elementary school in Honolulu, Hawaii. One class from each of Grades 2, 4, and 6 or a total of 81 children participated. At a time convenient for the classes involved, the investigator presented the survey directions and an illustrative practice sheet. Subsequently, each class spent approximately thirty minutes to complete the survey under the direction of the investigator.

Parents of the school were reached through the Parent-Teacher Association. A total of 30 adults (10 per Grades 2, 4, and 6) spent approximately 20 minutes one evening to complete the survey, which is the identical one used on the students. It was not possible to match the children and parents in terms of grade level. Half of the group consisted of fathers, and the other half were mothers.

The participants were not informed of the purpose of the study beyond the fact that they might be contributing to the improvement of education. The task was to classify each word problem and/or illustration according to one of three possibilities (see Figure 1):

_________Boy _________Girl _________Either

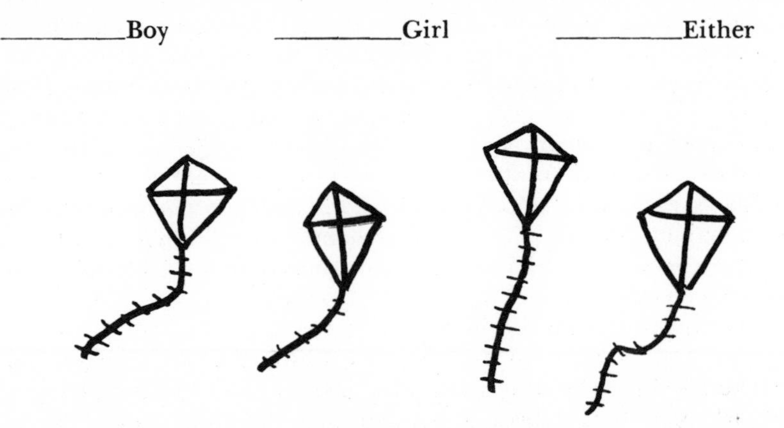

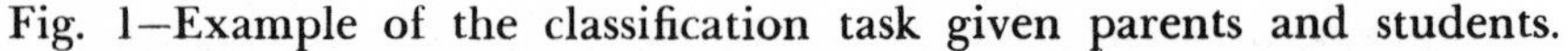

Fig. 1—Example of the classification task given parents and students.

The survey format was developed by using items appearing on selected pages of pupil's texts. A sample of five pages was chosen from each of the textbooks through the use of a random numbers table.

In the random selection of pages, the writer excluded from the sample, pages that had the following characteristics:

1. Pages with numerals only
2. Pages with clock faces
3. Pages with coins and currency appearing as illustrations. (These items were included in *Category 2* because of the "famous people" featured)
4. Pages with geometric shapes (cylinders, squares, circles, etc.)
5. Pages with measurement tools (rulers, measuring cups, etc.)

It was necessary to omit pages with the above features in order to secure an adequate variety of items that fit the category being analyzed, namely, "items of interest to a boy, a girl, or either." The material was considered to be neutral. Further, with the decision to select only five pages from each text, it was not appropriate that any of those selected pages be neutral.

QUANTIFICATION

A third requirement of content analysis is that there be a system of quantification. In content analysis, *relative frequencies* is the usual form of reporting units of measure. As the survey in the study consisted of a random sampling of five pages from each of twelve books, the end result varied from the usual type of content-analysis reporting. Instead of relative frequencies, the findings for *Category 1* are reported in terms of agreement and disagreement on sex stereotyping of items. For *Categories 2, 3,* and *4,* data are reported in the conventional form used in content analysis.

After the survey results for *Category 1* were grouped and tabulated, a percent agreement formula was applied to both the student and parent responses. For *Category 1,* median and modal responses were also noted.

A probability test was applied to determine the likelihood of chance affecting the findings in all categories. The Table of Probabilities was used when N was under 25. The chi-square one-sample test was used when N was greater than 25.

ANALYSIS OF DATA

Content analysis was the technique employed in this investigation. Four categories were established to guide coders in the examination of the selected textbooks. To maintain objectivity, parents and students were asked to assist in the analysis of *Category 1.* The content of *Category 1* was derived through the random selection of five pages from each of twelve texts. Responses of parents and students are reported in Part One. Part Two focuses on the findings of the two adult coders who analyzed *Category 2,* famous males and females; *Category 3,* occupations for males and females; and *Category 4,* unusual ways the texts handled traditional roles for males and females.

PART ONE

Category 1

The material classified by parents and students is reported in terms of modal responses and percent of agreement. A summary of the modal responses resulting from the classification of items by gender is presented in Table 1.

Table 1
Summary Data: Category 1
Word Problems and Illustrations

Classification of Content		Student Responses				Parent Responses			
		GRADE							
		Two N≡56	Four N=54	Six N=50	Totals N=160	Two N≡56	Four N=54	Six N=50	Totals N=160
Masculine	N	14	12	6	32*	9	13	6	28*
	%	23%	22%	12%	20%	18%	24%	12%	17%
Feminine	N	7	5	2	14*	9	2	1	12*
	%	13%	9%	4%	9%	16%	4%	2%	8%
Neutral	N	35	37[a]	42[a]	114	38[b]	39[c]	43[d]	120
	%	64%	69%	84%	71%	66%	72%	86%	75%
TOTALS	N	56	54	50	160	56	54	50	160
	%				100%				100%

a Includes one item split equally between "boy" and "either."
b Includes three items split equally between "boy" and "either."
c Includes one item "girl-either" and two items "boy-either."
d Includes two items "girl-either"; seven items "boy-either."
* $P < .02$

Modal Responses

In this investigation a modal response represents the highest number of votes that students as a group, or parents as a group assigned to individual items that appeared in *Category 1.* In cases where the vote was split equally between "boy-either" or "girl-either," the count was included in the neutral classification and a notation was made.

Scrutiny of Table 1 reveals that the respondents found approximately two-thirds of the material in Grade 2 to be neutral. It further indicates that the respondents felt approximately four-fifths of the material in Grade 4, and approximately nine-tenths of the material in Grade 6 to be neutral.

Beyond the neutral material, however, the next greatest proportion of material was classified as masculine. The respondents found nearly one-fourth of the material in Grade 2 and Grade 4 to be masculine. Approximately one-eighth of the material in Grade 6 was labeled masculine.

The least amount of material was classified as feminine. In the Grade 2 material less than 10 out of 56 items were identified as feminine. In the Grade 4 material, students and parents designated only 2 of 54 items as feminine. In the Grade 6 material, students found 2 and parents found 1 out of 50 items to be feminine. However, they did not agree on the identical items.

Using the chi-square one-sample test (Table 2) on the masculine and feminine totals, probability of items appearing in the proportions indicated in Table 1 was $p < .02$. That is, the obtained totals for male and female items are significant, and cannot be attributed to sampling error.

Table 2 Chi-square With Yates Correction

$$X^2 = \frac{(|O - E| - .5)^2}{E}$$

Where O = Observed number of cases
E = Expected number of cases
.5 = Yate's correction

Table 3 represents a summary of the collective modal responses of students and adults.

Table 3
Collective Modal Responses of Students and Parents

Response	Number			Total	Percent
	Grade 2	Grade 4	Grade 6		
Masculine	8	11	4	23	14%
Feminine	7	2	0	9	6%
Neutral	35a	37b	41c	113d	71%
Disagreement	6	4	5	15	9%
TOTAL	56	54	50	160	100%

a Includes 3 bimodal responses*
b Includes 4 bimodal responses*
c Includes 9 bimodal responses*
d Includes 16 bimodal responses*

* The reader should be aware that the inclusion of bimodal responses in the neutral classification has the effect of inflating that classification and deflating the masculine and feminine classifications.

When the coding for *Category 1* was completed, students and parents made identical classifications for 145 out of 160 items presented. In short they agreed 91% of the time.

On only 15 items or 9% was there disagreement regarding the classification. The specific items on which there was disagreement appear in Table 4.

Table 4
Items of Disagreement

	Description of Problem	Responses* Students	Parents
GRADE 2	Bowling pins	3	1
	Cars in the parking lot	1	3
	Doctors	3	1
	Indian headbands	3	1
	Beads on string	1	2
	Fingernail file	1	2
GRADE 4	Jane walks to Sally's house	2	1
	"If you washed 8 cups and 7 saucers . . ."	2	1
	A 5,000-pound delivery truck carries oil	1	3
	John, Ralph, and Ted helped their father pick apples	3	1
GRADE 6	Mrs. Saunders bought a coat	2	1
	Susan bought cupcakes and ice cream for a party	1	2
	Jim earns money for Mother's gift	1	3
	Earth, Sun, Mars, and space ship	3	1
	Jack and Neil run on the racetrack	1	3

*CODE: 1 = neutral
2 = feminine
3 = masculine

Examination of the 15 items in Table 4 does not generate a consistent or obvious rationale that might explain why students or parents have disagreed on the classification of these items.

Table 5 lists the specific items students and parents classified as feminine. Nine items or 6% of the 160 were so identified. There was a decreasing number starting with seven items in Grade 2 and ending with none in Grade 6. Stereotyping was evident in that jewelry, doll dresses, and jacks were singled out. So were flowers, barrettes, rope jumping, and Mrs. Brown baking pies.

Table 5
Items Classified as Feminine by Students and Parents

GRADE	*DESCRIPTION OF PROBLEM*
2	A girl pulling a wagon
	A ring (jewelry)
	Ann's doll dresses
	Jacks
	Barrettes
	Flowers
	Helen and girls jumjing rope
GRADE	*DESCRIPTION OF PROBLEM*
4	Mrs. Brown baked pies
	Girls made paper baskets
GRADE	*DESCRIPTION OF PROBLEM*
6	None

The twenty-three items or 14% of the total that were classified as masculine by students and parents seem to have been determined by factors such as the use of masculine names (Bill, Tom, Jim, Mr. Jordan, etc.) ; the reference to traditionally acceptable masculine activities (such as fishing, mowing the lawn, and carpentry) ; and the use of boys' toys (such as marbles, autos, and model airplanes). Table 6 presents a summary of those items.

Table 6
Items Classified as Masculine by Students and Parents

GRADE	*DESCRIPTION OF PROBLEM*
2	Helicopters
	Jeeps
	Boy pulling a wagon
	Pilots
	Toy auto
	Baseball, catcher's mitt, football and helmet
	Bill and Tom fishing
	Hats for cowboys, firemen, baseball players
4	Carpenter cuts a piece of board
	7 astronauts
	Satellite in orbit
	Jim mows the lawn
	Gerald has marbles
	David and his dad go fishing
	Mr. Kennison measures his path
	Bob and Ben have marbles
	The gas station sells tires
	Jim mows the lawn
	John belongs to a club of boys
6	Al and model airplane
	John and Harold have model cars
	Mr. Jordan's wire fence
	Bill wants to build a fence

Percent of Agreement

STUDENT RESPONSES

In determining the percent of agreement, responses from only ten children per grade were used. From an alphabetical list, boys and girls segregated, every third name was selected to yield five boys' and five girls' names. The responses of these randomly selected children were used in the calculations.

At each grade level, the response to each item by each of the ten students was recorded and the persent of agreement among students was determined by the formula:

$$\text{Percent of Agreement} = \frac{(\#\text{ items both completed}) - (\#\text{ items disagreed})}{\#\text{ items both completed}}$$

To illustrate: A total of 56 items were presented to the second graders. Responses of B1 (Boy 1) were compared with B2 (Boy 2). They disagreed on 14 items.

$$\text{Percent of Agreement} = \frac{56 - 14}{56} \quad \text{or } 75\%$$

The procedure was repeated for all pairs of subjects, reulting in a total of forty-five pairs per class.

Table 7 reveals the median percent of agreement in Grade 2 among

Table 7
Percent of Agreement Among Students and Parents

	Grade	Boys % Agreement	Girls % Agreement	Total Grade % Agreement
STUDENTS	2	.73 — .91	.73 — .89	.68 — .91
	Median	.81	.83	.84
	4	.44 — .70	.41 — .69	.41 — .78
	Median	.61	.57	.57
	6	.56 — .82	.44 — .86	.40 — .86
	Median	.62	.59	.62

	Grade	Men % Agreement	Women % Agreement	Total Grade % Agreement
PARENTS	2	.59 — .82	.70 — .93	.59 — .93
	Median Percent	.68	.80	.74
	4	.43 — .74	.56 — .78	.41 — .80
	Median Percent	.61	.63	.63
	6	.30 — .76	.46 — .86	.30 — .90
	Median Percent	.58	.66	.60

10 pairs of boys was .81; among 10 pairs of girls it was .83; and for the total grade (45 pairs of boys and girls) the median percent of agreement was .84. For Grade 4, the median percent of agreement among 10 pairs of boys was .61; among 10 pairs of girls it was .57; and for the total grade (45 pairs of boys and girls) the median percent of agreement was .57. Within Grade 6, the median percent of agreement among 10 pairs of boys, 10 pairs of girls and for the total grade were .62, .59, and .62 respectively.

The highest percent of agreement occurred among second grade boys and girls (.84). The next highest was among sixth graders (.62). The lowest percent of agreement was among fourth graders (.57).

PARENT RESPONSES

Percent of agreement among parents was determined by using the same formula applied to student responses. Table 7 reveals for Grade 2, the median percent of agreement among 10 pairs of men was .68; among 10 pairs of women it was .80; and for the total grade (45 pairs of men and women), the median percent of agreement was .74. For Grade 4, the median percent of agreement among 10 pairs of men was .61; among 10 pairs of women it was .63; and for the total grade (45 pairs of men and women) the median percent of agreement was .63. With Grade 6, the median percent of agreement among 10 pairs of men, 10 pairs of women, and for the total grade were .58, .66, and .60 respectively.

The median percent of agreement for both men and women was highest in Grade 2 (.74). The median percent of agreement in Grades 4 and 6 was about equal, .63 and .60 respectively.

PART TWO

For *Categories 2, 3,* and *4* two adult coders were asked to analyze six textbooks each. The traditional approach to content analysis was used in that the units of measure were in terms of relative frequencies.

Upon completion of the task that involved examining a total of 4,104 pages, the two coders submitted their data to the investigator, who checked the results. Each coder examined approximately 2,050 pages of text material. A summary of the findings appears in Table 8.

Table 8
Summary Data *Categories 2, 3,* and *4*

Classification of Content	Relative Frequencies GRADES Two	Four	Six	Totals
Category 2				
Famous Males	**6	*34	*22	46
Famous Females	0	0	3	3
Category 3				
Male Occupations	*30	*55	*31	86
Female Occupations	5	13	5	18
Category 4				
Unusual Role – Males	1	1	0	2
Unusual Role – Females	0	1	1	2

NOTE: Totals for each *category* represent single entry for all grades combined; excluded were any duplications appearing in Grades 2, 4, or 6.

* P — .01
** P = .02

Category 2

From 4,104 text pages the coders identified 49 famous people, 46 of whom were males. The three famous females found in two Grade 6 textbooks were Queen Elizabeth I, Florence Nightingale, and Nellie Bly. A fourth famous female, Alice-in-Wonderland, was referred to but not included in the count. Personalities famous in fiction, though not many in number, were excluded from the study.

Among the famous men whose names were featured in the twelve textbooks analyzed, presidents of the United States appeared most frequently. One explanation is that their pictures are on coins, currency, and postal stamps—appropriate objects for lessons dealing with money.

Next in frequency of appearance on the list of famous men was a group of inventors. Their birthdates and the year of the respective invention evidently offer opportunities for arithmetical computations.

The balance of the list of famous men consisted of explorers, scientists, mathematicians, ancient rulers, and men who contributed to history through sports or a special event.

In the analysis, the coders found cities, states, buildings, and mountains named after famous people. Since the study did not include a category for famous land sites, namesakes for such places as Jamestown, Virginia, John Hancock Building, Rockefeller Center, Mt. Everest, Mt. McKinley Verrazano-narrows Bridge, and Marianas Trench were omitted from the tabulation.

The binomial test for small populations demonstrates for all grades the following probabilities:

Number of Famous People

Grade	*Male*	*Female*	*Probability*
2	6	0	$p < .02$
4	34	0	$p < .01$
6	22	3	$p < .01$

In terms of the data obtained, there are significantly more famous males than famous females in the twelve texts analyzed.

Category 3

Within the 4,104 text pages, the two coders identified a total of eighty-six occupations for adult males and eighteen occupations for adult females.

The chi-square one-sample test was applied to determine whether there was a significant difference between the number of male and female occupations found in the textbooks. Findings after application of the formula were:

Occupation:

Number of Instances

Grade	*Male*	*Female*	X^2
2	30	5	$p < .01$
4	55	13	$p < .01$
6	31	5	$p < .01$

At each grade level, the probability of obtaining a difference between the number of male and female occupations by chance alone as extreme as that obtained is $p<.01$.

Category 4

In analyzing the twelve textbooks for unusual, nonstereotyped roles, the coders found a total of four cases. Two were for males, and two for females.

Male teachers were referred to in the texts for Grades 2, 4 and 6. Having male teachers in the elementary grades was considered an unusual role. However, these teachers taught mathematics science, and physical education, traditionally male-oriented subjects. In one instance, a male teacher took the second-grade children on a field trip.

The second case of males in unusual roles referred to fathers marketing. The unusualness had its limitations in that the fathers shopped for meat and steaks. No mention was made of fathers shopping for other supermarket items.

Males cooking may be considered a third case, but was not tallied for two reasons. Fathers who cooked did so at cookouts or camps, not in kitchens. Secondly, when Mr. Green baked bread and cupcakes baking was rated as neutral by both students and parents. Hence Mr. Green was not credited with an unusual role.

The first unusual role identified for females referred to girls painting a meeting room. Seven girls were pictured painting the wall and floor. Painting houses, like carpentry, is generally considered a male task.

The second incidence of an unusual female role was that of a girl swimming from one end of the pool to another in 7.8 seconds. Generally speaking, boys were engaged in sports and girls were spectators in the texts.

It was not possible to apply probability tests due to the small numbers representing unusual roles.

CONCLUSIONS

Category 1

Do boys and girls make the same judgments about sex stereotyping? Results show the highest median percent of agreement (.84) occurred among boys and girls in Grade 2. In Grades 4 and 6, the students agreed among themselves slightly better than 50% of the time. The median percent of agreement was .57 and .62 respectively.

The above data indicate boys and girls in Grade 2 make the same judgments about sex stereotyping a high percentage of the time. There is also evidence that students in Grade 2 were especially discerning when it came to classifying certain items. Toys in general may be neutral, but to the students some toys are definitely earmarked for boys and some for girls. For example, beach balls and balloons were classified as neutral but footballs and baseballs were classified as masculine. Jacks and dolls are for girls. Hats and shoes are utilitarian objects for everyone, but hats for cowboys, firemen, and baseball players are masculine. Cowboy boots featured with ladies' shoes were classified as neutral.

In Grades 4 and 6, the students do not appear to agree as readily on sex stereotyping as did the second graders. A possible explanation for the lower percentage of agreement in Grades 4 and 6 is that material for the two upper grades contained much more reading content and fewer illustrations. Where pictures appeared, scenes were sometimes complicated and unlike the one-concept illustrations featured in Grade-2 material. Thus, it appears material for the two upper grades required a higher level of reading and interpretative skill, which contributed to the lower percent of agreement in Grades 4 and 6.

Do fathers and mothers make the same judgments about sex stereotyping? Results indicate there is a high correlation in the judgments made by fathers and mothers who helped classify the selected material. Parents classifying Grade-2 material demonstrated the highest median percent of agreement (.74). Parents who classified Grade 4 and Grade 6 material showed a lower percent of agreement. The percentages of agreement were .63 and .60 respectively. Results indicate fathers and mothers responding to Grade-2 material made the same judgments about sex stereotyping nearly three-fourth of the time. Again, it may be hypothesized that the higher percent of agreement found in Grade 2 may be the result of material being easier to classify at that grade level. Material for the two upper grades was much more difficult to classify. For example, there were picture clues and word clues to sort out.

Respondents were probably influenced by names and pictures used. Often the sex of the child appearing in a picture seemed the determining factor in the classification. A good example was in the Grade-2 material. *A boy* pulling a wagon and a *girl* pulling a wagon were classified masculine and feminine respectively, by both student and parent groups. The wagon by itself may have been classified neutral.

Do children make the same judgments about sex stereotyping as adults? Based on the 91% agreement of parents and students in the classification of 160 items according to gender, the conclusion is that both groups in this study appear to make the same judgments. The respondents disagreed on the classification of only 15 items or 9% of the 160 items presented. Examination of the 15 items did not generate a consistent or obvious rationale that might explain why students or parents disagreed on the classification of these items. Items such as bowling pins "Mrs. Saunders bought a coat," and "Jane walks to Sally's house" are representative of the items where disagreement was found.

What is the most common response to each of the choice situations as determined by children? by adults? Of the three choices, masculine, feminine, and neutral, both student and parent groups agreed that 113 items or 71% were neutral or nonstereotyped. A possible explanation for the high percentage of neutral items classified is that in the community sampled a good number of the children came from homes where both parents were salaried. Other studies on sex stereotyping show that in homes where both parents work, attitudes of children toward traditional roles tend to be more liberal. Married couples who work also feel less bound by cultural expectations and find it easier to share home responsibilities. By the same token, the women have more freedom outside of the home, and are more independent than nonworking mothers. Fathers are more inclined to help with marketing, cooking and even doing the laundry on their days off in these settings. Thus, it is not surprising that the respondents in the study would classify as neutral such items as "bathythermograph and underwater temperature," "the weight of objects on Earth and Mars." These two examples are representative of science and mathematics, two subjects that are traditionally considered "masculine" interests.

A final example of parental enlightenment may be found in the Grade-4 material. "If you washed 8 cups and 7 saucers . . ." was classified as feminine by students and as neutral by parents. Seemingly, parents are more liberal as to sex roles and responsibilities, whereas boys and girls in Grade 4 are faced with the reality of life, and it is girls who wash dishes at home.

In general neutral items could be grouped into larger classifications such as *food,* which includes fruits, hot dogs, candy; *toys,* which include balloons, whistles blocks; *school activities,* which include references to spelling, geography, physical education; *birds and animals*; and *utilitarian objects,* which include toothbrushes, spoons, money.

Following the neutral classification, the next highest classification was masculine items. There were 23 settings or 14% of the 160 items in which the identified choice was masculine. This was more than twice as many classified as feminine items. Respondents agreed that 9 items or 6% of the total were feminine.

Category 2

Are there significantly more famous men than famous women in the selected elementary-mathematics textbooks? Out of 4,104 textual pages from twelve elementary-school mathematics texts, coders found forty-nine famous people, forty-six of whom were male. The three famous females referred to in the two Grade-6 textbooks were Queen Elizabeth I, Florence Nightingale, and Nellie Bly. Based on these findings the conclusion must be there are significantly more famous men than famous women featured in the textbooks chosen for analysis in this study. Furthermore, tests of probability on the ratio of famous men to famous women showed for Grade 2, $p<.02$; for Grades 4 and 6, $<p.01$.

Category 3

Are there significantly more male occupations than female occupations? The coders found 86 occupations for males and 18 for females in the 12 textbooks analyzed. For men the jobs literally ranged from A to Z, from acrobat to zoo keeper. In between were the astronaut, doctor, inventor, lawyer, mathematician, president, scientist, weatherman, and men who perform services in the community. None of the above male occupations appeared on the female list of occupations. For women, jobs not duplicated on the male list included: a buyer, cafeteria manager, cook, dressmaker, doughnut maker, journalist, librarian nurse, queen, and ticket seller.

The test for probability indicated at each grade level the number of occupations found for both sexes was $p<.01$. That is, more than chance was in effect, and sex stereotyping does exist in the twelve mathematics texts analyzed.

Category 4

Do textbooks feature men and women in unusual, nonstereotyped roles? Within the twelve textbooks or 4,104 pages analyzed, the coders found only four cases, two males and two females featured in what could be termed *unusual* roles. In the first case, male teachers were found in elementary schools. However, they were featured teaching mathematics, science, and physical education, traditionally male-oriented subjects.

The second case identified as an unusual male role was fathers marketing. Even at that role, fathers only shopped for meats and steaks. Traditionally father is considered the breadwinner. He is too busy earning a living to go marketing at the end of the work day. Mother is home all day so she is the one who follows the advertisements and shops for the family.

The two unusual roles identified for females featured girls painting a room and a girl swimming across a pool. These cases appeared to be nonstereotyped roles, because girls are usually featured as spectators or helpers.

Considering the conclusions of previous questions and by examining the coders' data, the following generalizations appear appropriate.

Sex stereotyping exists in the mathematics textbooks as evidenced by the fact boys play with autos, boats, and rockets. Boys play in the sand pile, take part in baseball and football games, and run in track meets. Boys earn money after school by delivering newspapers, cleaning yards, mowing lawns, shoveling snow, washing cars, moving furniture, shining shoes. Conversely, girls play with dolls and jacks. They jump rope, practice on the piano, write poetry, do cut-and-paste work, and help mother.

In terms of adults, fathers go fishing, camping, and hunting. Fathers earn money, buy varnish, lumber, fencing, steaks, and hamburgers.

Mothers make fudge, sandwiches, bread, and cookies. Mothers go marketing, sew on buttons, collect trading stamps. Mothers buy wax paper, butter, and sugar. Together, girls and mothers bake, cut, and serve pies. Boys and fathers eat the pies.

In conclusion, for *Category 1,* though parents and students classified 71% of the randomly selected material (60 pages or 160 items) as neutral, the balance of the material analyzed by parents and students favors males over females.

Beyond the nature and character of the settings used in mathematics examples, illustrations, story problems, in analyzing *Categories 2, 3,* and *4,* coders found abundant examples of sex stereotyping in people and occupations and no truly unusual roles for males and females.

Women in U.S. History High-school Textbooks*

JANICE LAW TRECKER

Early in our history, enterprising groups of English gentlemen attempted to found all-male colonies. The attempts were failures, but the idea of a society without women appears to have held extraordinary appeal for the descendants of those early colonists. Throughout our history, groups of intrepid males have struck off into the wilderness to live in bachelor colonies free from civilization and domesticity.

The closing of the frontier and the presence, even from the earliest days, of equally intrepid females ended these dreams of masculine tranquility. Yet, the hopeful colonists may have had their revenge. If women have had their share in every stage of our history, exactly what they did and who they were remains obscure. Ask most high-school students who Jane Addams, Ida Tarbell, or Susan B. Anthony were, and you may get an answer. Ask about Margaret Sanger, Abigail Duniway, or Margaret Brent, and you will probably get puzzled looks. Sojourner Truth, Frances Wright, Anna Howard Shaw, Emma Willard, Mary Bickerdyke, Maria Mitchell, Prudence Crandall, and scores of others sound like answers from some historian's version of "trivia."

Interest in the fate of obscure Americans may seem an esoteric pursuit, but this is not the case. History, despite its enviable reputation for presenting the important facts about our past, is influenced by considerations other than the simple love of truth. It is an instrument of the greatest social utility, and the story of our past is a potent means of transmitting

* Reprinted with permission of the National Council for the Social Studies and Janice Law Trecker from *Social Education* 35 (March 1971): 249–61+.

cultural images and stereotypes. One can scarcely doubt the impact of history upon the young in the face of recent minority groups' agitation for more of "their history."

Minority groups are perhaps not the only ones with a complaint against the historians and the schools, nor are they the only ones to show the effects of stereotypes. Consider the most recent reports of the President's Commission on the Status of Women. According to the 1968 report of the Commission, *American Women,* in the fall of 1968 only forty percent of entering college freshmen were women. The lag in female participation in higher education is even more noticeable at the graduate level. Statistics from the Commission's 1968 report indicated that women earned only one in three of the B.A. degrees and M.A. degrees granted and only one in ten of the doctorates. It is seldom noted that this represents a percentage decline from the 1930s when women received two in five B.A. degrees and M.A. degrees, and one in seven Ph.D. degrees. The loss of potential talent this represents is clear from the Commission's information that among the top ten percent of our high-school seniors, there are twice as many girls as boys with no college plans.

Able girls are not entering science and mathematics in any great number, and, according to the *Conant Report,* they fail to take courses and programs commensurate with their abilities. There seems to be a clear need for an examination of the factors that permit the loss of considerable amounts of female talent.

The Education Committee of the President's Commission on the Status of Women was concerned about this loss, noting that:

> Low aspirations of girls are the result of complex and subtle forces. They are expressed in many ways—even high achievement—but accompanied by docility, passivity, or apathy. The high motivation found in the early school years often fades into a loss of commitment and interest, other than in the prospect of early marriage.

The Committee found that some of the reasons for this loss of motivation are the stereotypes of women in our culture and in the lingering ideas of female inferiority.

Educators should be aware that the school is one of the means by which the stereotypes of women and their capacities are transmitted. As one of the main cultural forces in the society, the school shares a responsibility for the diminished aspirations of its female students. Looking at the position of women in our society, one would have to be very sanguine to say that the education of American girls needs no improvement. Something is wrong when women are concentrated in a relatively few, lower-paid positions; when there are few women represented in the upper levels of government and industry; and when the symptoms of discontent and frustration are all too clearly manifesting themselves among militant young women.

Something is indeed wrong, and educators should begin a rigorous investigation of their programs and practices in order to discover if they are reinforcing the cultural pressures that discourage talented girls.

ANALYSIS OF HIGH-SCHOOL TEXTBOOKS

A reasonable place to start, considering the admitted obscurity of most women in American history, is the United States history text. Are the stereotypes that limit girls' aspirations present in high-school history texts?

The answer is *yes*. Despite some promising attempts to supplement the scant amount of information devoted to women in American history texts, most works are marred by sins of omission and commission. Texts omit many women of importance, while simultaneously minimizing the legal, social, and cultural disabilities that they faced. The authors tend to depict women in a passive role and to stress that their lives are determined by economic and political trends. Women are rarely shown fighting for anything; their rights have been "given" to them.

Women are omitted both from topics discussed and by the topics chosen for discussion. For example, while only a few women could possibly be included in discussions of diplomacy or military tactics, the omission of dance, film, and theater in discussions of intellectual and cultural life assures the omission of many of America's most creative individuals.

Women's true position in society is shown in more subtle ways as well. While every text examined included some mention of the "high position" enjoyed by American women, this is little more than a disclaimer. Wherever possible, authors select male leaders and quote from male spokesmen. Even in discussions of reform movements, abolition, labor—areas in which there were articulate and able women leaders—only men are ever quoted. Even such topics as the life of frontier women are told through the reminiscences of men. When they are included, profiles and capsule biographies of women are often introduced in separate sections, apart from the body of the text. While this may simply be a consequence of attempts to update the text without resetting the book, it tends to reinforce the idea that women of note are, after all, optional and supplementary. Interestingly enough, the increase in the amount of space devoted to black history has not made room for the black woman. In these texts black history follows the white pattern, and minimizes or omits the achievements of the black woman. Like the white woman, she is either omitted outright, or is minimized by the topics selected.

These assertions are based upon the examination of over a dozen of the most popular United States history textbooks. Most were first copyrighted in the sixties, although several hold copyrights as far back as the early fifties, and one text is copyrighted back to 1937. Included are the following:

Textbooks

Baldwin, Leland D., and Warring, Mary. 1965. *History of our republic.* Princeton: D. Van Nostrand Co., Inc.

Bragdon, Henry W., and McCutchen, Samuel P. 1965. *History of a free people.* New York: The Macmillan Company.

Brown, Richard C.; Lang, William C.; and Wheeler, Mary A. 1966. *The American achievement.* Morristown, New Jersey: Silver Burdett Company.

Canfield, Leon H., and Wilder, Howard B. 1964. *The making of modern America.* Boston: Houghton Mifflin Company.

Frost, James A.; Brown, Ralph Adams; Ellis, David M.; and Fink, William B. 1968. *A history of the United States.* Chicago: Follett Educational Corporation.

Graff, Henry E., and Krout, John A. 1959. *The adventure of the American people.* Chicago: Rand McNally.

Hofstadter, Richard; Miller, William; and Aaron, Daniel. 1957. *The United States—the history of a republic.* Englewood Cliffs, New Jersey: Prentice-Hall, Inc.

Kownslar, Allan O., and Frizzle, Donald B. 1964. *Discovering American history.* 2 Vols. New York: Holt, Rinehart and Winston.

Noyes, H. M., and Harlow, Ralph Volney. 1964. *Story of America.* New York: Holt, Rinehart & Winston.

Todd, Lewis Paul, and Curti, Merle. 1966. *Rise of the American nation.* 1 Vol. and 2 Vol. editions. New York: Harcourt, Brace & World. 2 Vol. edition includes selected readings.

Williams, T. Harry, and Wolf, Hazel C. 1966. *Our American nation.* Columbus, Ohio: Charles E. Merrill Books, Inc.

Collections of documents

Hofstadter, Richard. 1958. *Great issues in American history.* 2 Vols. New York: Vintage.

Meyers, Marvin; Kern, Alexander; and Carvelti, John G. 1961. *Sources of the American republic.* 2 Vols. Chicago: Scott, Foresman, & Company.

All entries indexed under "Women" were examined and various other sections and topics where information about women might reasonably be expected were examined. Particular attention was paid to women in colonial and revolutionary times, education, the women's rights movement and suffrage, reform movements, abolition, the Civil War, labor, frontier life, the World Wars, family patterns, the present position of women, and all sections on intellectual and cultural trends. The resulting picture is a depressing one.

On the basis of information in these commonly used high-school texts, one might summarize the history and contributions of the American woman as follows: Women arrived in 1619 (a curious choice if meant to be their first acquaintance with the new world). They held the Seneca Falls Convention on Women's Rights in 1848. During the rest of the nineteenth century, they participated in reform movements, chiefly temperance, and were exploited in factories. In 1923 they were given the vote. They joined the armed forces for the first time during the Second World War and thereafter have enjoyed the good life in America. Add the names of the women who are invariably mentioned: Harriet Beecher Stowe, Jane Addams, Dorothea Dix, and Frances Perkins, with perhaps Susan B. Anthony, Elizabeth Cady Stanton, and, almost as frequently, Carrie Nation, and you have the basic "text." There are variations, of course, and most texts have adequate sections of information on one topic, perhaps two, but close examination of the information presented reveals a curious pattern of inclusions and neglects, a pattern that presents the stereotyped picture of the American woman—passive, incapable of sustained organization or work, satisfied with her role in society, and well supplied with material blessings.

1. Revolutionary and early federal periods

There is little information available in most texts concerning the colonial woman, or on her daughters and granddaughters in the revolutionary and early federal periods. The amount of information ranges from one textbook's two paragraphs on women's legal and social position to another textbook's total absence of anything even remotely pertaining to women during the early years of American history. Most texts fall in between. Some attention is commonly paid to the legal disabilities inherited from English law, although one textbook limits itself to "tobacco brides" and a note about William Penn's wife. Usually, little is said about the consequences of the social, political, and legal disabilities of the colonial woman, although the sharp limitations of the nineteenth century and the exploitation of the working-class women in the early industrial age were a direct result of woman's lack of political influence and her gradual exclusion from "professional" and skilled jobs. The texts are especially insensitive to the problem of religious and clerical prejudices against women. The long opposition of most American religious groups to women's rights is almost never suggested.

The perfunctory notice taken of women's education in the early period is discussed below. It should be noted, however, that few texts take any note of sectional differences in women's education or in other aspects of the position of women.

Although a number of texts mention the high regard in which the colonial woman was held, few are named and only one gives much information about the amount of work done outside the home by colonial women. Women mentioned are Pocahontas and Anne Hutchinson. Sections on Pocahontas tend to favor discussion of such questions as, "Did Pocahontas really save John Smith?", rather than on any information about her life or the lives of other Indian women. Anne Hutchinson is almost always subordinated to Roger Williams. In one book, for example, she is described as another exile from Massachusetts. In more generous texts, she may receive as much as a short paragraph.

In general, the treatment of the early periods in American history stresses the fact that the America of the colonies, and early republic, was a "man's world." The authors wax eloquent over the "new breed of men." Any doubt that this might be merely linguistic convention is soon removed. The colonial farmer is credited with producing his own food, flax, and wool, in addition to preparing lumber for his buildings and leather goods for himself and his family. What the colonial farmer's wife (or the female colonial farmer) was doing all this time is not revealed, although plenty of information exists. Such passages also convey the unmistakable impression that all the early planters, farmers, and proprietors were male.

Education is important in consideration of the position of women because, as Julia Cherry Spruill points out in *Women's Life and Work in the Southern Colonies,* lack of opportunities for education finally ended women's employment in a variety of areas as technology and science made true "professions" of such occupations as medicine. In the early days, women, despite stringent legal restrictions, participated in almost all activities save government, the ministry of most religions, and law (although the number who sued and brought court cases is notable).

Usually, if any notice at all is taken of the education of girls and women, it is limited to a bland note that "girls were not admitted to college" or "most Americans thought it unnecessary or even dangerous to educate women." These statements are presented without explanation. A mention of the existence of the dame schools completes the information on women and education.

After the colonial-revolutionary period, it is rare for more than one paragraph to be devoted to the entire development of education for women. Often, none of the early educators are mentioned by name. The facts that women literally fought their way into colleges and universities, that their admission followed agitation by determined would-be students, and that they were treated as subservient to male students even at such pioneering institutions as Oberlin, are always absent. The simple statement that they were admitted suffices.

2. Sections on rights and reforms

The most information about women appears in two sections, those on women's rights and suffrage and general sections on reform. Yet a full page on suffrage and women's rights is a rarity and most texts give the whole movement approximately three paragraphs. The better texts include something on the legal disabilities that persisted into the nineteenth century. These sections are sometimes good, but always brief. Most of them end their consideration of the legal position of women with the granting of suffrage, and there is no discussion of the implications of the recent Civil Rights legislation that removed some of the inequities in employment, nor is there more than a hint that inequities remained even after the Nineteenth Amendment was passed.

Leaders most commonly noted are Susan B. Anthony, Elizabeth Cady Stanton, and Lucretia Mott. Aside from passage of the Nineteenth Amendment, the only event noted is the Seneca Falls Convention of 1848. Even less space is devoted to the later suffrage movement. Anna Howard Shaw is seldom mentioned and even Carrie Chapman Catt is not assured of a place. The western ladies like Abigail Duniway are usually absent as are the more radical and militant suffragettes, the members of the Woman's Party. Alice Paul, leader of the militants, is apparently anathema.

This is perhaps not too surprising, for the tendency in most texts is to soncentrate on the handicaps women faced and to minimize their efforts in their own behalf. One textbook, which dutifully lists Seneca Falls, Stanton, Mott, Wright, Anthony, Stone, and Bloomer, tells very little about what they did, noting "the demand for the right to vote made little headway, but the states gradually began to grant them more legal rights." The text mentions that by 1900 most discriminatory legislation was off the books and describes the post-Civil War work of the movement in these terms: "the women's rights movement continued under the leadership of the same group as before the war and met with considerable success." Later two lines on suffrage and a picture of a group of suffragettes complete the story. Lest this be considered the most glaring example of neglect, another textbook devotes two lines, one in each volume, to suffrage, mentioning in volume one that women were denied the right to vote and returning to the topic in volume two with one line on the Nineteenth Amendment in the middle of a synopsis of the twenties. This book actually includes more information on the lengths of women's skirts than on all the agitation for civil and political rights for women.

Other texts show a similar lack of enthusiasm for the hundred years of work that went into the Nineteenth Amendment. One places woman suffrage fifth in a section on the effects of the progressive movement. Catt, Anthony, and Stanton are mentioned in a line or two, while whole columns of text are devoted to Henry Demarest Lloyd and Henry George.

At times there appears to be a very curious sense of priorities at work even in textbooks that give commendable amounts of information. One book uses up a whole column on the Gibson Girl, describing her as:

> Completely feminine, and it was clear that she could not, or would not, defeat her male companion at golf or tennis. In the event of a motoring emergency, she would quickly call upon his superior knowledge . . . .

The passage goes on to point out that this "transitional figure" was politically uninformed and devoted to her traditional role. One would almost prefer to learn a little more about the lives of those other "transitional figures," the feminists, yet there is almost no mention of their lives, their work, or their writings.

Only one text quotes any of the women's rights workers. It includes a short paragraph from the declaration of the Seneca Falls Convention. The absence in other texts of quotes and of documentary material is all the more striking, since a number of the leaders were known as fine orators and propagandists. Books of source materials, and inquiry method texts, are no exception; none of those examined considers woman suffrage worthy of a single document. One book is exceptional in including one selection, by Margaret Fuller, on the topic of women's rights.

The reformers and abolitionists are slightly more fortunate than the feminists. Three women are almost certain of appearing in history texts: Harriet Beecher Stowe, Jane Addams, and Dorothea Dix. Addams and Stowe are among the few women quoted in other source books or regular texts and, along with the muckraking journalist Ida Tarbell, they are the only women whose writings are regularly excerpted. Addams and Dix are usually given at least one complete paragraph, perhaps more. These are sometimes admirably informative, such as in certain sections on Dix. Other reformers, including the women abolitionists, both white and black, are less fortunate. The pioneering Grimké sisters may rate a line or two, but just as often their only recognition comes because Angelina eventually became Mrs. Theodore Weld. None of the female abolitionists, despite their contemporary reputations as speakers, is ever quoted. Interest in black history has not made room for more than the briefest mention of Harriet Tubman, whose Civil War services are deleted. Sojourner Truth and the other black lecturers, educators, and abolitionists are completely absent. The texts make little comment about the nineteenth century's intense disapproval of women who spoke in public, or of the churches' opposition (excepting always the Quakers, from whose faith many of the early abolitionists came).

Women journalists are given even less notice than the early lecturers. The women who ran or contributed to newspapers, periodicals, or specialized journals and papers for abolition, women's rights, or general reform are rarely included.

The reform sections of these high-school texts frequently show the same kind of capriciousness that in sections on the twenties assigns more space to the flapper than to the suffragette. In discussions on reform movements, they give more prominence to Carrie Nation than to other more serious, not to say more stable, reformers. The treatment of temperance is further marred by a failure to put women's espousal of temperance in perspective. Little stress is placed on the consequences for the family of an alcoholic in the days when divorce was rare, when custody of children went to their father, and when working women were despised. Nor is there much mention of the seriousness of the problem of alcoholism, particularly in the post-Civil War period.

3. Neglected areas

The most glaring omission, considering its impact on women and on society, is the absence of a single word on the development of birth control and the story of the fight for its acceptance by Margaret Sanger and a group of courageous physicians. The authors' almost Victorian delicacy in the face of the matter probably stems from the fact that birth control is still controversial. Yet fear of controversy does not seem a satisfactory excuse. The population explosion, poverty, illegitimacy—all are major problems today. Birth control is inextricably tied up with them as well as with disease, abortion, child abuse, and family problems of every kind. Considering the revolution in the lives of women that safe methods of contraception have caused, and the social, cultural, and political implications of that revolution, it appears that one important fact of the reform movement is being neglected.

A second, largely neglected area is the whole question of woman's work and her part in the early labor movement. Although the American woman and her children were the mainstays of many of the early industries, for a variety of social and political reasons she received low wages and status and was virtually cut off from any hopes of advancement. The educational limitations that gradually forced her out of a number of occupations that she had held in preindustrial days combined with prejudice to keep her in the lowest paid work. Whether single, married, or widowed, whether she worked for "pin money" or to support six children, she received about half as much as a man doing the same or comparable work.

Obviously under these conditions, women had exceptional difficulties in organizing. Among them were the dual burden of household responsibilities and work, their lack of funds, and in some cases their lack of control over their own earnings, and the opposition of male workers and of most of the unions.

Despite these special circumstances, very little attention is paid to the plight of the woman worker or of her admittedly unstable labor organizations. Information on the early labor leaders is especially scanty; one textbook is unique with its biographical information on Rose Schneiderman. On the whole, the labor story is limited to the introduction of women workers into the textile mills in the 1840s. As a caption in one book so concisely puts it, "Women and children, more manageable, replaced men at the machines." Others note the extremely low pay of women and children, one text calling women "among the most exploited workers in America." Anything like a complete discussion of the factors that led to these conditions, or even a clear picture of what it meant to be "among the most exploited," is not found in the texts.

Several things about women and labor are included. Lowell mills receive a short, usually complimentary, description. The fact that the Knights of Labor admitted women is presented. There then follows a hiatus until minimum wage and maximum hour standards for women workers are discussed. The modern implications of this "protective legislation" is an area seldom explored.

Despite the fact that abundant source material exists, the sections on labor follow the familiar pattern: little space is devoted to women workers, few women are mentioned by name, and fewer still are quoted. Most texts content themselves with no more than three entries of a few lines each.

The absence of information on the lives of women on the frontier farms and settlements is less surprising. In the treatments of pioneer settlements from the colonial era on, most texts declare the frontier "a man's world." This is emphasized by the importance the authors place on descriptions and histories of such masculine tools as the Pennsylvania rifle and the ax, the six-shooter, and the prairie-breaker plow. One textbook is perhaps the most enthralled with these instruments, devoting five pages to the story of the six-shooter. Scarcely five lines are spent on the life of the frontier woman in this text, and most other works are also reticent about the pioneer woman.

Only "man's work" on the frontier is really considered worthy of description. This is particularly puzzling, since there was little distinction in employment, and marriage was a partnership with lots of hard work done by each of the parents. On pioneer farms, typical "woman's work" included, in addition to all the housework, the care of poultry; the dairy—including milking, feeding, tending to the cows, and making butter and cheese; the care of any other barnyard animals; the "kitchen" or vegetable garden; and such chores as sewing, mending, making candles and soap, feeding the hired hands, and working in the fields if necessary.

Considering these chores, it is hard to see why discussions of pioneer farming content themselves with descriptions of the farmer's struggles to plow, plant, and harvest. The treatments of the frontier period also omit mention of the women who homesteaded and claimed property without the help of a male partner. According to Robert W. Smuts in *Women and Work in America,* there were thousands of such women. Information about the women on the frontier tends either to short descriptions of the miseries of life on the great plains frequently quoted from Hamlin Garland or to unspecific encomiums on the virtues of the pioneer women. One text states: "[the women] turned the wilderness into homesteads, planted flowers, and put curtains in the windows. It was usually the mothers and schoolteachers who transmitted to the next generation the heritage of the past."

The relationship between women's exertions on the frontier and their enlarged civil and political liberties in the Western states and territories is often noticed. Their agitation for these increased privileges is generally unmentioned.

With little said about women's life in general, it is not surprising that few are mentioned by name. Sacajawea, the Indian guide and interpreter of the Lewis and Clark expedition, shares with Dix, Stowe, and Addams, one of the few solid positions in United States history texts. Occasionally the early missionaries to Oregon territory, like Nerissa Whitman and Eliza Spaulding, are included, and one book even adds a "profile" of Nerissa Whitman. Most, however, only mention the male missionaries, or include the fact that they arrived with their wives.

4. Civil War period

Like the frontier experience, the Civil War forced women from all social strata into new tasks and occupations. In *Bonnet Brigades,* a volume in the *Impact of the Civil War Series,* Mary Elizabeth Massey quotes Clara Barton's remark that the war advanced the position of women by some fifty years. Great numbers of women dislocated by the war were forced into paid employment. The war saw the entry of women into government service, into nursing, and into the multitude of organizations designed to raise money and supplies for the armies, to make clothing, blankets, and bandages. The result of this activity was not only to force individual women outside of their accustomed roles, but to provide the experience in organization that was to prove valuable for later suffrage and reform movements. The war helped a number of women escape from the ideas of gentility that were robbing women in the East of much of their traditional social freedom, and brought women of all classes into the "man's world." In addition to the few women who served as soldiers, women appeared in the camps as nurses, cooks, laundresses, adventurers; they served in the field as spies, scouts, saboteurs, and guides; they worked in the capitals as the "government girls"—the first female clerks, bookkeepers, and secretaries. Women opened hospitals, set up canteens, and developed the first primitive forms of what we know as USO clubs and services. After the war, they served as pension claims agents, worked to rehabilitate soldiers, taught in the freedman's schools, entered refugee work, or tried to find missing soldiers and soldiers' graves.

Of all these activities, women's entry into nursing is the only one regularly noticed in the texts. The impact of the war upon women, and upon the family structure, is barely mentioned, although a few texts include a paragraph or two on the hardships that women faced during the conflict. The only women mentioned by name are Clara Barton and

Dorothea Dix, who held the position of superintendent of women nurses. Other women, like Mary Bickerdyke, who was known both for her efforts during the war and for her work for needy veterans afterwards, are omitted. No other women, black or white, are named, nor is there any information on the variety of jobs they held. The special problems of black women in the postwar period rarely get more than a line, and the efforts by black women to set up schools and self-help agencies are omitted.

5. The Two World Wars

While women in the Civil War era receive little attention, even less is given to them during the two World Wars. In both cases, their wartime service is glowingly praised, but few details are presented. At least half of the texts examined make no note at all of women's wartime activities during the First World War; in a number of others, the story of women's entry into what were formerly labeled "men's jobs" is dealt with in a captioned picture.

As for social changes between the wars, a number of texts devote several paragraphs to the "liberation of women" and to their changing status. In one textbook there are four paragraphs devoted to these liberated ladies—the only two mentioned being Irene Castle and Alice Roosevelt. Like other texts, this one devotes a considerable amount of space to fashions and flappers and to the social alarm that they occasioned.

There is little about the later stages of the rights movement, although two textbooks note the relationship between women's wartime service and the increasing willingness of the nation to grant rights and privileges to women. One limits itself to three sentences, noting women's work "in factories and fields" and their efforts behind the lines overseas. "Women's reward for war service was the Nineteenth Amendment which granted them the franchise on the eve of the 1920 election." Readers might wish for greater elaboration.

The period from the Depression to the present day receives the same laconic treatment in the texts. The one woman sure of notice in this period is Frances Perkins, Roosevelt's Secretary of Labor. She receives at least a line in most texts and some devote special sections to her. Frances Perkins appears to be the "showcase" woman, for no other American woman is regularly mentioned—this includes Eleanor Roosevelt, who is omitted from a surprising number of texts and who is mentioned only as Roosevelt's wife in quite a few more.

The World War II era marked the beginning of the Women's Military Corps. This fact is invariably mentioned, usually with a captioned picture as an accompaniment. As in World War I, women entered factories, munitions plants, and "men's jobs" in great numbers. This development rarely gets more than a paragraph and the differences between the experience in World

War I and the longer exposure to new jobs in World War II are seldom elucidated. The impact of the war on women and specific information about the variety of jobs they held is sketchy or nonexistent.

Information on women in the postwar era and in the present day is hardly more abundant. The history texts definitely give the impression that the passage of the Nineteenth Amendment solved all the problems created by the traditional social, legal, and political position of women. Contemporary information on discrimination is conspicuously absent. The texts are silent on current legal challenges to such practices as discriminatory hiring and promotion and companies' failures to comply with equal-pay legislation. They do not take account of agitation to change laws and customs that weigh more heavily on women than on men. There is nothing about recent changes in jury selection, hitherto biased against women jurors, or reform of discriminatory practices in criminal sentences; there is no information on the complex problems of equitable divorce and guardianship, nor on the tangled problem of separate domicile for married women.

A number of texts do, however, provide good information on changes in the structure of the family, or provide helpful information on general social and political changes. The impression, insofar as these sections deal directly with American women, is a rosy picture of the affluence and opportunities enjoyed by women. Many books note the increasing numbers of women employed in the learned professions, but never the percentage decline in their numbers. While women undoubtedly enjoy more rights, opportunities, and freedoms than in many previous eras, the texts give an excessively complacent picture of a complex and rapidly changing set of social conditions.

6. Intellectual and cultural achievements

A final glimpse of the position of the American woman may be gained from sections dealing with intellectual and cultural trends and achievements. Since most texts extol the role of women in preserving culture and in supporting the arts, one might expect women to be well represented in discussions of the arts in America. A number of factors, however, operate against the inclusion of creative women. The first, and one that deprives many creative men of notice as well, is the extreme superficiality of most of these discussions. Intellectual and cultural life in America is limited to the mention of a few novelists and poets, with an occasional musician or playwright. Only a few individuals in each category are ever mentioned, and the preference for male examples and spokesmen, noticeable in all other topics, is evident here as well. In individual texts, this leads to such glaring omissions as Emily Dickinson and Margaret Fuller. To be fair, the text guilty of ignoring Miss Dickinson appears to feel that John Greenleaf Whittier was one of our greatest poets, yet ignorance of American poetry is hardly an acceptable excuse.

Dickinson and Fuller, however, are among the small, fortunate circle including Harriet Beecher Stowe, Willa Cather, and Margaret Mitchell who are usually named. The principles governing their selection and decreeing the omission of other writers like Edith Wharton, Ellen Glasgow, Eudora Welty, and Pearl Buck are never explained. Apparently their presence or absence is determined by the same caprice that decrees Edna St. Vincent Millay the only modern female poet.

Only a handful of texts discuss painters and sculptors, but of those that do make some effort to include the visual arts, only one reproduces a painting by Mary Cassatt. Georgia O'Keeffe is also represented in this text. Other texts, even when including Cassatt's fellow expatriates, Sargent and Whistler, omit her—an exclusion inexplicable on grounds of quality, popularity, or representation in American collections. Contemporary art is totally ignored and everything after the Ashcan School is left in limbo. This omits many painters of quality and influence, including the many women who have entered the arts in the twentieth century.

More serious than the sketchy treatment given to the arts covered by the texts is the omission of arts in which women were dominant or in which they played a major part. Dance is never given as much as a line. This leaves out the American ballerinas, and, even more important, it neglects the development of modern dance—a development due to the talents of a handful of American women like Isadora Duncan, Martha Graham, and Ruth St. Denis.

There is a similar neglect of both stage and screen acting. If film or drama are to be mentioned at all, directors and writers will be noted. It hardly seems necessary to point out that acting is an area in which women have excelled.

Music sees a similar division with similar results. Composers and instrumentalists, chiefly men, are mentioned. Singers, men and women, are omitted. This particularly affects black women. Only one textbook mentions Marian Anderson and Leontyne Price. White classical singers are ignored as are the black women jazz singers.

If intellectual and cultural developments are limited to areas in which men were the dominant creative figures, it is obvious that American women will not receive credit for their contributions. It also seems clear that such superficial accounts of the arts are of questionable value.

SUMMING UP

Although it is tempting to imagine some historical autocrat sternly decreeing who's in and who's out—giving space to Harriet Beecher Stowe but not to Marianne Moore; to Dorothea Dix but not Mary Bickerdyke; to Pocahontas but not Margaret Brent; to Susan B. Anthony but not Abigail Duniway—the omission of many significant women is probably not a sign of intentional bias. The treatment of women simply reflects the attitudes and prejudices of society. Male activities in our society are considered the more important; therefore male activities are given primacy in the texts. There is a definite image of women in our society, and women in history who conform to this image are more apt to be included. History reflects societal attitudes in all topics, hence the omission of potentially controversial persons like Margaret Sanger or that militant pioneer in civil disobedience, Alice Paul. Sensitivity to social pressure probably accounts for the very gentle notes about religious disapproval of women's full participation in community life and for omission of contemporary controversies, especially on sexual matters, which would offend religious sensibilities.

Another factor that affects the picture of women presented in these texts is the linguistic habit of using the male pronouns to refer both to men and to men and women. While this may seem a trivial matter, it frequently leads to misunderstanding. Discussing the early colonists, for example, solely in terms of "he" and "his" leads to the implication that all early proprietors, settlers, planters, and farmers were men. Given the cultural orientation of our society, students will assume activities were only carried on by men unless there is specific mention of women.

To these observations, authors of high-school texts might reasonably respond that their space is limited, that they seek out only the most significant material and the most influential events and individuals; that if dance is omitted, it is because more people read novels, and if such topics as the role of female missionaries or colonial politicians are neglected, it is for lack of space. One is less inclined to accept this view when one notices some of the odd things that authors do manage to include. One feels like asking, "How important was Shays's Rebellion?". Should the Ku Klux Klan receive reams of documentary material and woman suffrage none? Do we want to read five pages on the six-shooter? Is two columns too much to give to Empress Carlotta of Mexico, who lived most of her life in insanity and obscurity? Is the aerialist who walked a tightrope across Niagara Falls a figure of even minor importance in American history? Is Henry Demarest Lloyd more important than Carrie Chapman Catt? Are the lengths of skirts significant enough to dwarf other information about women?

There are other questions as well: How accurate is the history text's view of women and what images of women does it present? The texts examined do very little more than reinforce the familiar stereotypes.

It should be clear, however, that changes in the construction of high-school-level history texts must go beyond the insertion of the names of prominent women and even beyond the "profiles" and "special sections" employed by the more liberal texts. Commendable and informative as these may be, they are only the beginning. Real change in the way history is presented will only come after those responsible for writing it, and for interpreting the finished product to students, develop an awareness of the bias against women in our culture, a bias so smooth, seamless, and pervasive, that it is hard to even begin to take hold of it and bring it into clear view. Until this awareness is developed, until the unquestioned dominance of male activities and the importance of male spokesmen and examples are realized, texts will continue to treat men's activities and goals as history, women's as "supplementary material."

One sees this quite clearly in the existence of sections dealing with women's rights, women's problems, and women's position, as if women's rights, problems, and position were not simply one half of the rights, problems, and position of humanity as a whole, and as if changes in women's position and work and attitudes were not complemented by changes in the position, work, and attitudes of men. A sense of the way the lives and duties and achievements of people of both sexes are intermeshed is needed in expositions of life in all periods of American history.

To do this it is clear that material hitherto omitted or minimized must be given more consideration. For example, information about mortality rates, family size, and economic conditions must be included, along with more information on the impact of technological change, on the mass media, and on moral and religious ideas. More information about how ordinary people lived and what they actually did must be included as well as information drawn from the ideas and theories of the educated classes.

This is not to deny that certain developments have had far more effect on women than on men, or that women's experience might be different from men's: for example, the early struggles to form unions. Nor is it to deny that more information on women leaders is needed and more space for their particular problems and achievements. More information on all aspects of women's life, work, and position—legal, social, religious, and political—is needed, but more information alone, no matter how necessary, will not really change histories. What is needed, besides more information, is a new attitude: one that breaks away from the bias of traditional views of women and their "place" and attempts to treat both women and men as partners in their society; one that does not automatically value activities by the sex performing them; and one that does not relate history from the viewpoint of only half of the human family.

Role Formation: Occupational, Social, and Political

The articles in this section elucidate and define boys' and girls' attitudes toward appropriate work roles, political roles, and social roles for males and females. Nancy K. Schlossberg and Jane Goodman, in "A Woman's Place: Children's Sex Stereotyping of Occupations," study curriculum material to see the degree to which it is sex typed and the causation of children's sex stereotyping of occupations. They found toys whose apparent purpose was to reinforce sex typing. Kindergarten and sixth-grade students indicated that while they realized that women worked, they believed that men and women held different occupations. Interestingly, men were perceived as able to do "women's work" more often than women were perceived as able to do "men's work." Many children also stated that women could perform certain jobs if they had special training, whereas no special training was cited as a prerequisite for men. The authors stress that it is easier to expand a woman's options through elementary-school training rather than waiting until she is middle-aged: school administrators should be cautious of the type of play and curricular materials that are given to children.

Claire Lynn Fleet Siegel, in "Sex Differences in the Occupational Choices of Second Graders," found that boys listed almost twice as many preferred jobs as did girls. Girls' choices also showed a smaller range than boys' choices: sixty-nine percent of the girls wanted to be either teachers or nurses. It is relevant to note how closely these occupational choices reflect the occupations boys and girls are shown in the texts, as seen in Pottker's study. Siegel's article makes it obvious that girls' vocational outlook is narrow.

Lynne B. Iglitzin's "Sex-Typing and Politicization in Children's Attitudes" finds that there is little difference between boys' and girls' responses in terms of reversing traditionally sex-typed jobs, but that significantly more girls answered that both men and women should hold a particular job. (It is curious to note that girls were far less willing to see men as fifth-grade teachers than were boys.) Children's views of which parent performs certain household chores was also sex typed.

Girls and boys both gave traditional answers to questions regarding different personality traits of the sexes, but more girls than boys attributed certain traits to both boys and girls. In terms of children's future jobs, the range of jobs boys selected for themselves was smaller than the range of jobs girls selected for themselves. However, the job choices of girls and boys were basically sex typed. Significantly, boys gave details pertaining to work when asked to describe a typical day in their adult life, while girls answered in terms of domestic chores.

The second part of Iglitzin's study regards politicization of children. Iglitzin found significant differences among boys and girls in response to questions pertaining to jobs in politics and government, although children's holding of stereotyped social attitudes was not correlated with a low level of political awareness. In the last section, Iglitzin provides valuable commentary on sexist language used in political socialization questionnaires, and the concentration on the macrolevel of politics and on formal power by political scientists when surveying children.

Selma Greenberg analyzes "Attitudes Toward Increased Social, Economic, and Political Participation by Women as Reported by Elementary and Secondary Students." Girls' answers were more liberal than were boys' answers, and the girls were definitely more favorable to the women's rights movement than were boys. Upper-grade students' answers were more egalitarian than were lower-grade students' answers. Children for the lower class did not exhibit more traditional ideas than children from the upper class, to the surprise of the author. However, this corresponds to Entwisle's and Greenberger's study discussed below: the bright, middle-class boys were the most traditional in their attitudes.

Doris R. Entwisle and Ellen Greenberger show how "Adolescents' View of Women's Work-role" is stereotyped. They found that boys always responded more conservatively to women's occupational role than did girls, and that high IQ boys who were middle class responded the most conservatively. It is interesting that blacks were more liberal than whites regarding working women, and that it was the middle-class white boys and girls who differed the most in their answers.

This would help to show why the women's liberation movement tends to be a white and middle-class movement: perhaps black males are less traditional in their thinking, causing black women to feel less sex-role stress, while white middle-class women experience the greatest amount of strain between their own work views and the views of the men they know. The fact that middle-class, high IQ boys were the most rigid in their views might help to explain the cause of professional men's tension with professional women.

The schools must help boys become more aware of females' changing social and economic status. Programs for both boys and girls that deal with nonbiased career options will help strengthen girls' identity and hopefully broaden boys' outlook on women's role in society. The hostility and tension that may result from childhood misconceptions about which roles members of the opposite sex should play can be avoided with the school's help. These stereotyped views of work that children exhibit show what has to be overcome by the schools in order to enable girls to expand their horizons, and to enable boys to view women's new occupational roles positively, rather than with hostility.

What these articles have shown is not just the sex-typed opinions of schoolage boys and girls, nor how the schools' curriculum reinforces this. Earlier it was mentioned that girls' self-image and self-esteem would suffer due to certain discriminatory school practices. It was noted that they would also be "maladjusted" for their future work-roles.

This section has strengthened previous findings and added to them. Not only will girls have a poor self-esteem and be unprepared for work, but if they deviate from this passive role, they can expect hostility from their male counterpart. The harm done to girls by this role rigidity, and the tension it will cause between women and men in adult life, is scarcely something that should be perpetuated by the schools, which claims as one of their goals "healthy" relationships between boys and girls.

A Woman's Place: Children's Sex Stereotyping of Occupations*

NANCY K. SCHLOSSBERG and JANE GOODMAN

From birth, males and females are viewed differently, often in a way suggestiong inferiority for women.[1] The handling in infancy, the number and kinds of toys in toddlerhood, the encouragement of dependence or independence during preschool years all reinforce the conclusion one little five-year-old made to her mother, "Boys have more chances than girls." Toys for very young children seem to be designed to reinforce these role limitations and stereotypes. Girls get miniature mothering or household-work items or nurse's kits; boys get cars and trucks and doctor kits.

Several studies of five-year-olds demonstrate the degree to which contemporary society differentially socializes boys and girls. One reported in Maccoby shows that when five-year-olds were exposed to a series of paired pictures depicting sex-appropriate activities, both sexes knew what little boys and little girls were expected to do.[2] Mothers cook and clean; fathers work.

This stereotyping at age five is continued in adolescence. In studying the occupational fantasy-life of adolescents, Douvan and Adelson found that "the bulk of girls' choices (ninety-five percent) fall into the following

---

four categories: personal aide, social aide, white collar traditional, and glamor fashion."[3]

Adolescents who enter college maintain the notion of differential achievement for boys and girls. A recent experiment with two groups of college students illustrates this. The experimenter asked one group to complete a story based on the clue, "After first term finals, John finds himself at the top of his medical school class." The other group had the same assignment, but "Anne" was substituted for "John." The group story about John was very positive. In dealing with Anne the students were less enthusiastic. Typical comments were: "Anne is an acne-faced bookworm . . . her fellow classmates are so disgusted with her behavior that they jump on her in a body and beat her. . . . Anne doesn't want to be No. 1 in her class . . . she drops downs to ninth in the class and then marries the boy who graduates No. 1."[4]

This early socialization of women partially explains why women are employed, for the most part, in jobs that are extensions of the work they do at home. "Over half the women workers are employed in only 21 of the 250 distinct occupations listed in the Bureau of Census. One-fourth of all employed women were in five occupations—secretary-stenographer, household worker, bookkeeper, elementary schoolteacher, and waitress."[5] It is obvious that the job openings do not, in themselves, make it easy for women, or for those who counsel them, to abandon traditional occupations for untried areas of endeavor. As the present study demonstrates, girls, as well as boys, believe that a woman's opportunities in the world of work are more limited than a man's.

PROCEDURE

This study was designed to discover the degree to which elementary schoolchildren hold stereotypes about occupations based on sex. The differences between kindergartners and sixth graders, between boys and girls, and between two elementary schools—one predominantly middle- and upper-middle class, the other a model-cities project school—were studied. All children in the kindergarten and the sixth grade of the two schools were asked to respond to twelve drawings, representing work settings of six occupations traditionally considered feminine and six occupations traditionally considered masculine. The occupations were classified as "feminine" or "masculine" according to the major sex represented in the occupation. Of the feminine occupations, the ones chosen for this study were those employing over a fourth of all employed women—secretary-bookkeeper, household worker, elementary schoolteacher, waitress, and nurse. The masculine jobs are prominent among those identified as fields in which there will be a need for more personnel in the 1970s—a need that cannot be filled by men alone.[6] The masculine fields included in this study were doctor, dentist, architect-draftsman, television-radio repairman, mechanic, and laboratory scientist.

To discover the degree to which children stereotype occupations, the children were helped to identify the picture by the interviewer, who said, for example: "This is where a person works who fixes televisions and radios. Could a man work here? Could a woman work here?" The order of these questions, as well as the order of the pictures, was random. The working "could" rather than "does" or "should" was used to enable the children to free themselves from their perceptions of present occupational segregation and from their feelings about sex-appropriate occupations. In addition, each child was asked, "What do you want to be when you grow up?"

RESULTS

A child's response was considered to be stereotyped when the child said, "No, a man could not work here," about one of the feminine occupations, or, "No, a woman could not work here," about one of the masculine occupations. The data were analyzed in terms of number of stereotyped responses. The results from the model-cities kindergarten are not included, for the children did not seem to relate to the study in a meaningful way, possibly because the interviewer was white or possibly because the interviewer was middle class.

The data indicate: (a) no appreciable increase in stereotyping from kindergarten to sixth grade; (b) the sixth graders at the model-cities school held more stereotypes than those at the middle-income school; (c) the children were more ready to exclude women from men's jobs than to exclude men from women's jobs; (d) with few exceptions, the children chose jobs for themselves that fall within the usual stereotypes, e.g., most children felt either men or women could be doctors or nurses, but the boys all chose to be doctors and the girls, nurses; (e) there was some disparity between the amount of stereotyping of one occupation and another.

Kindergarten and sixth grade stereotyping.

There was no significant difference between the role stereotypes held by the middle-class sixth graders and those held by the middle-class kindergartners. Although it might be expected that the sixth graders, with their greater experience of the world, would be more aware of the real sexual division of labor, it was apparent that they also were more responsive to the difference between the interviewer's "could" and their perception of reality as it "is." They frequently expressed this in comments such as, "Sure, a woman *could* fix cars, but she wouldn't like it much," or, "She *could,* if she got some overalls."

Model-cities and middle-income sixth graders.

The middle-income sixth graders were consistently less stereotyped than the model-cities sixth graders. The middle-income elementary school is in a community where many of the mothers work at professional jobs, and this perhaps enables the children to view women as having more capabilities than do the model-cities project schoolchildren, whose community includes women working almost exclusively at low-level, women's jobs.

Feminine and masculine occupations.

The boys and girls interviewed excluded women from men's jobs more than they excluded men from women's jobs. There were seventy-eight responses indicating that only a woman could do one of the women's jobs. There were 156—or twice as many responses—indicating that only a man could do one or another of the men's jobs. To state it another way, women were considered unable to do men's work twice as often as men were considered unable to do women's work.

A tentative explanation for this phenomenon is that the children believe that while a "man can do anything," a woman's powers are more limited. Evidence for this is found in many of the children's informal comments. Even when the children's responses did not exclude a woman from a man's occupation (and therefore do not show up as stereotyped responses in the data), they often added qualifying comments. For example, when shown the picture depicting an architect-draftsman and asked if a man could do that, all the children said yes. When asked if a woman could do that, many of those who said yes added, "if she had special training," of, "if she went to a special school," or some similar statement. Somehow, a man was assumed to have all the expertise necessary. Not a single child specified special training or any other qualifications for a man for either the masculine or feminine occupations. In several cases where a child said a woman *could* work in an occupation, it was clear that he felt she *should not.* For example, one boy, when asked if a woman could be an auto mechanic, said, "Sure, she could, if she were one of these 'woman's lib' types."

Stereotyping of children's own career plans.

Eighty-three percent of the girls and ninety-seven percent of the boys who chose any occupation chose an occupation traditionally reserved for their sex. Although approximately seventy-five percent of the children felt men could be nurses, no boy chose this occupation. (Ten of the girls said they wished to be nurses when they grew up.) Although approximately eighty-nine percent of the children felt women could be doctors, none of the girls chose this occupation. (Seven of the boys wanted to be doctors when they grew up.)

Relative stereotyping of different occupations.

A striking aspect of the data is the disparity between the amount of stereotyping of one occupation and another. One hundred percent of the model-cities project sixth graders, boys and girls, said a woman could not fix televisions and radios or cars. Only ten percent said she could not be a doctor. Seventy-six percent said a man could not be a housekeeper; only five percent excluded him from the teaching profession.

In the middle-class sixth grade, forty-eight percent of the children felt a woman could not be an auto mechanic, only five percent that she could not be a doctor. Thirty-eight percent said a man could not be a housekeeper; none said he should be excluded from waiting on tables, or teaching.

Similar disparities were demonstrated in the middle-class kindergarten. Fifty-nine percent of the children excluded women from fixing cars, only eleven percent from fixing teeth. Nineteen percent said a man could not be a housekeeper; none excluded him from secretarial work.

CONCLUSION

According to the children we interviewed, a woman's place was clearly *not* fixing autos or television sets or designing buildings. The children, however, said she could work as a waitress, nurse, or librarian. Clearly the issue was not that they felt a woman's place was in the home, but rather that it was in certain specified occupations. By contrast, they did not feel that men had to be similarly limited. A man could fix automobiles or teach children or even be a nurse. A woman was not granted this freedom. And often when women were not actually excluded, they were thought to need special training that men did not need. Although the children were asked, "*Could* a woman do that?" and, "*Could* a man do that?", they evidently responded in terms of *do* men or women do these things.

The sex typing of occupations "reflects—and perpetuates—the differential status of male and female."[7] Thus, children's early notions of differential achievement for men and women need to be changed. It is much easier for elementary-school personnel to keep options open than it is to convince a forty-year-old woman that it is appropriate for her to achieve. This study looked at one small dimension of a complex problem, but the dimension studied can be rectified. If children are to develop the flexibility required to deal with tomorrow's world, they must learn to make the transition between *do, could,* and *will*—and educators can influence this learning.

REFERENCES

Dornbush, S. M. 1968. Afterward to *The development of sex differences* ed. E. E. Maccoby. Stanford: Stanford University Press.

Dowan, E., and Adelson, J. 1966. *The adolescent experience.* New York: Wiley.

Horner, M. S. 1969. Woman's will to fail. *Psychology today* 3 (November 1969) : 33–38, 62.

Hedges, J. N. 1970. Woman at work, woman workers, and manpower demands in the 1970s. *Monthly labor review* 93, no. 6: 19–34.

Maccoby, E. E., ed. 1968. *The development of sex differences.* Stanford: Stanford University Press.

Moore, L. 1971. Allocation of rewards and minority member recipients. Mimeographed. Detroit: Wayne State University.

Polk, B. 1970. Socialization of little girls. Speech given at Wayne State University Teach-in on Women, Detroit, October 1970.

NOTES

1. B. Polk, "Socialization of Little Girls," from a speech given at Wayne State University Teach-in on Women, Detroit, October 1970.
2. S. M. Dornbush, Afterword to *The Development of Sex Differences* (Stanford: Stanford University Press, 1968) .
3. E. Dowan and J. Adelson, *The Adolescent Experience* (New York: Wiley, 1966) .
4. M. S. Horner, "Woman's Will to Fail," *Psychology Today* 3 (November 1969) : 36–38, 62.
5. J. N. Hedges, "Women at Work, Woman Workers, and Manpower Demands in the 1970s," *Monthly Labor Review* 93, no. 6 (1970) : 19–34.
6. Ibid.
7. L. Moore, "Allocation of Rewards and Minority Member Recipients," mimeographed (Detroit: Wayne State University, 1971) .

Sex Differences in the Occupational Choices of Second Graders*

CLAIRE LYNN FLEET SIEGEL

Existing career development theories generally do not differentiate between men and women. Yet research comparing the sexes indicates that from middle-elementary school grades through college, women and men modally develop different types of occupational career-interest patterns.[1] To a large extent interests in occupations appear to be conditioned by adherence to the traditional definitions of sex-role patterns[2] with women selecting both a smaller range and different types of occupations than men.[3] In order to extend the normative data available, the present research investigated sex differences in the occupational choices of children in primary-school grades, a younger age group than had been studied previously.

METHOD

An open-ended questionnaire was administered to sixty-one second graders in a middle-class suburb of Boston, Massachusetts. The children were asked if they had thought about what occupation they would like to enter when they "grew up," what kind of work their father did, what kind of work they would most like to do when they "grew up," and what kind of work they least wanted to do when they "grew up."

Table 1
Occupations Students Most Preferred

Boys (N=32)		Girls (N=29)	
Policeman	7	Teacher	12
Construction	3	Nurse	8
Storekeeper	2	Ballerina	2
Scientist	2	Brownie	1
Baseball player	2	Biologist	1
Don't know	2	Babysitter	1
Doctor	1	Stewardess	1
Chemist	1	Skin diver	1
Electrical engineer	1	Marcher	1
Space man	1	Princess	1
Teacher	1		
Manager airport	1		
Foreman	1		
Fireman	1		
Pilot	1		
Marine	1		
Drive train	1		
Milkman	1		
Farmer	1		
Build log cabins	1		

RESULTS

Ninety-seven percent of students questioned said that they had thought about what occupation they would like to enter when they "grew up." All of the girls said they had thought about their occupational choice, while two of the thirty-two boys said they had not thought about their occupational choice.

Students were asked if they knew what kind of work their father did. Paternal occupations were ascertained through school records. Eighty-eight percent of the boys, and seventy-six percent of the girls accurately knew their father's occupation.

Table 1 refers to students' occupational choices. Boys chose almost twice the number of occupations than girls chose. The spread over the occupations was greater for boys than it was for girls; i.e., of twenty-nine girls, twenty selected either "teacher" or "nurse." In contrast, of thirty-two boys, except for seven who chose "policeman," not more than three boys were in any single category. There was no overlap between those occupations selected by boys and those selected by girls. The sole exception was a boy who selected "teacher." He had been previously referred to guidance with the complaint that he was "too feminine."

Table 2
Occupations Students Least Preferred

Boys (N=32)		Girls (N=29)	
Teacher	3	Nurse	4
Garbageman	3	Teacher	3
Janitor	3	Storekeeper	2
Policeman	3	Slave	2
Baker	2	Doctor	2
Don't know	2	Robber	2
Banker	1	Maid	2
Lawyer	1	Cab driver	1
Astronaut	1	Pickpocket	1
Engineer	1	Kiss	1
Principal	1	Fight	1
Painter	1	Go to war	1
Singer	1	Train lion	1
Telephone man	1	"Ordinary housewife"	1
Army	1	Singer	1
Barber	1	Stewardess	1
Fireman	1	Write	1
Reader	1	Movie star	1
Slave	1	Don't know	1
Robber	1		
Burglar	1		
Pay taxes	1		

Table 2 presents those occupations the students least wanted. Boys chose twenty-one occupations while girls chose eighteen. Again there was little overlap in occupations chosen by boys and girls ("teacher" and "robber" being the only two mentioned by both groups).

DISCUSSION

The results of this study indicated that distinct sex differences in occupational choices appear to be operative by second grade. The patterns revealed in the study; i.e., girls chose a smaller range and different types of occupations than boys, are similar to those reported by other investigators on older age groups.[4]

The occupations selected most often, *i.e.*, "policemen," "teacher," and "nurse" were those found by Meyer to be traditionally "masculine" and "feminine" occupations.[5] Hartley has demonstrated that children were able to assign one group of activities to men, another to women, and some equally to both sexes.[6] It is as if by the second grade, children have absorbed the societal expectations of "sex-appropriate" work, are aware of their own sexual identity at some level, and have selected the traditional cultural stereotype.

That fewer girls than boys accurately knew their father's occupations is of note. However, fully seventy-six percent of the girls knew their father's occupation yet chose, on the whole, traditionally "feminine" occupations. From this, one might infer the following set of hypotheses: (a) In general, more information about paternal occupations is communicated to sons than daughters; (b) of the information that is communicated, different messages (expectations) are attached to the content depending on the child's sex; (c) those message expectations that are communicated most often reflect traditional cultural expectations; (d) parental expectations are reinforced by the child's observations from other adults, TV, books, schools, and other societal institutions; (e) the end result being that knowledge about particular occupations does not legitimize those occupations as being true potential choices (this process is true for both sexes); and (f) the information that then is communicated to the child about occupations may be selectively heard in light of the above process. "Sex-appropriate" occupations are a simpler solution than are dystonic occupations.

The preceding hypotheses need further investigation. If they are correct, there would be many implications for vocational counseling at the primary-grade level.

REFERENCES

Bailyn, L. 1959. Mass media and children: a study of exposure habits and cognitive effects. *Psychological monographs* 73, no. 471.

Clark, E. T. 1967. Influence of sex and social class on occupational preference and perception. *Personnel and guidance journal* 45: 440–41.

Empey, L. T. 1958. Role expectations of young women regarding marriage and a career. *Marriage and family living* 20: 152–55.

Hartley, R. E. 1961. Current patterns in sex roles: children's perspectives. *National association of women deans and counselors journal* 25: 3–13.

Lehman, H. C., and Witty, P. A. 1930. Some factors which influence the child's choice of occupations. *Elementary school journal* 31: 285–91.

Meyer, Marilyn M. 1969. Patterns of perceptions and attitudes toward traditionally masculine and feminine occupations through childhood and adolecsence. Ed.D. dissertation Michigan State University.

Nelson, R. C. 1963. Knowledge and interests concerning sixteen occupations among elementary and secondary students. *Educational and psychological measurement* 23: 741–54.

O'Hara, R. P. 1962. The roots of careers. *Elementary school journal* 62: 277–80.

Powell, M., and Bloom, V. 1962. Development of and reasons for vocational choices of adolescents through the high-school years. *Journal of educational research* 56: 126–33.

Shuval, J. T. 1963. Occupational interests and sex-role congruence. *Human relations* 16: 171–82.

NOTES

1. L. Bailyn, "Mass Media and Children—A Study of Exposure Habits and Cognitive Effects," *Psychological Monographs* 73 (1959) ; E. T. Clark, "Influence of Sex and Social Class on Occupational Preference and Perception," *Personal and Guidance Journal* 45 (1967) : 440–41; L. T. Empey, "Role Expectations of Young Women Regarding Marriage and A Career," *Marriage and Family Living* 20 (1958) : 152–55; Marilyn M. Meyer, "Patterns of Perceptions and Attitudes Toward Traditionally Masculine and Feminine Occupations Through Childhood and Adolescence" (Ed.D. diss., Michigan State University, 1969) ; R. C. Nelson, "Knowledge and Interests Concerning Sixteen Occupations Among Elementary and Secondary Students," *Educational and Psychological Measurement* 23 (1963) : 741–54; and R. P. O'Hara, "The Roots of Careers," *Elementary School Journal* 62 (1962) : 277–80.
2. H. C. Lehman and P. A. Witty, "Some Factors which Influence the Child's Choice of Occupations," *Elementary School Journal* 31 (1930) : 285–91; Nelson, "Knowledge and Interest,"; and J. T. Shuval "Occupational Interests and Sex-role Congruence," *Human Relations* 16 (1963) : 171–82.
3. Clark, "Influence of Sex," Nelson, "Knowledge and Interest," and M. Powell and V. Bloom, "Development of and Reasons for Vocational Choices of Adolescents Through the High School Years," *Journal of Educational Research* 56 (1962) : 126–33.
4. Clark, "Influence of Sex"; Powell and Bloom, "Development"; and O'Hara, "Roots."
5. Meyer, "Patterns."
6. R. E. Hartley, "Current Patterns in Sex Roles: Children's Perspectives," *National Association of Women Deans and Counselors Journal* 25 (1961) : 3–13.

Sex-typing and Politicization in Children's Attitudes*

LYNNE IGLITZIN

This is a report of a two-phase study that was conducted on schoolchildren in three suburbs of the city of Seattle. Two hundred ninety children (141 boys, 149 girls) in the fifth grade (ages 10-11) were tested by questionnaire in spring 1971; 147 fifth graders (67 girls, 80 boys) were tested in spring 1972. Fifth grade was selected because the children were considered old enough to be articulate about themselves and social roles, yet not to have experienced the hormonal and physiological changes and sex differentiation of puberty. The 1971 and 1972 studies differed in emphasis and will be discussed separately. In 1971, the study (in collaboration with sociologist Judith Fiedler) concentrated on the degree to which traditional feminine values and sex-typing dominated the thinking of girls. The 1972 study was designed to compare these feminine values with the level of politicization in girls.

THE 1971 STUDY: SEX-TYPING AND FEMININITY

One of the clearest areas in which to explore the holding of traditional values is that of the sexual division of labor. Cross-cultural anthropological research, dating back as early as 1937, indicates that the notion of "wom-

 Prepared for delivery at the 1972 Annual Meeting of the American Political Science Association, Washington, D. C. The author wishes to extend her appreciation to her colleagues, Judith Lamare and Philip Meranto, for their comments and criticisms on an earlier draft of this study.

en's work" and "men's work" is virtually universal.[1] But there is also wide variation from culture to culture as to what constitutes such work—in some societies, for example, it is the men who cook, sew, raise the children, tend the hearth. Thus, each culture needs to socialize its members concerning "proper" work for the sexes. This was corroborated in our study: these children overwhelmingly expressed a strongly stereotyped view of social roles consonant with dominant norms and expectations.

The study involved the construction of a series of questions designed to show sex-stereotyping based on views of career and employment patterns for oneself and others; social roles in home and family; the child's view of his/her own future life as an adult. Sex stereotyping (as measured by the response "men" or "women" rather than the open access "either" or "both") was found in each of these measures for both boys and girls. However, significantly higher proportions of girls gave nonstereotyped responses in all the categories. The girls in this sample were much more open than the boys to the idea of divorcing a wide variety of social roles from rigid sex categories.

Career and employment patterns

Children were provided with a list of jobs, ranging from professional to manual labor, and asked to indicate whether "men," women," or "both men and women" should perform them. Sex-typing was extremely strong: the majority of children saw men as doctors, bosses, taxi drivers, mayors, factory workers, lawyers, college professors, and clerks; and women as cooks, teachers, artists, nurses, and house cleaners. (See Table 1.) Stereotyping was common for both boys and girls—in fact, in some cases, girls were even *less* inclined than boys to see women in traditionally masculine jobs. For example, 3.6% of the boys said women should be mayors, but only 2% of the girls said this; 5.7% of the boys said women should be college professors, compared to only 1.3% of the girls.

Although, as Table 1 indicates, girls are as little inclined as boys to reverse sex roles in traditionally sex-tied jobs, they are much more willing to see jobs open to either sex. A significantly higher proportion of girls gave the nonstereotyped, open access answer "both men and women" on every one of the job categories.

Home and family

The concern of this part of the study was with the strength of traditional values and sex-stereotyping within home and family tasks, from rearing and guiding the children to cleaning floors and taking out the garbage. The results showed that fifth graders have thoroughly inculcated a sex-typed view of home and household: women wash dishes, cook, dust, scrub floors, and get up with a sick child. (See Table 2.) Men pay bills, fix things, and weed the yard. Their list is much smaller than the woman's—even taking out the garbage, usually thought of as a male chore, is bestowed by our children on women! Girls' views are as traditional as the boys, though there is a slightly greater tendency for girls to see both parents performing these tasks.

Other questions asked children to say which tasks boys and girls ought to perform in conjunction with their parents, and in these answers the picture of distinctly male (men and boys) and female (women and girls) functions is even stronger. The role of the father is a limited one, revolving mainly around the abstract task of paying bills (although important, somewhat removed from the routine of daily life). Boys are seen as emulating fathers, helping simply to weed the yard and to fix things. Girls see themselves, on the other hand, as involved in the multitude of daily household chores as their mothers.

Personality traits

As with the boys, the girls in our study view one another with a high degree of sex-typing of personality traits and approved roles. They see girls as kinder, better behaved, more serious, while they see boys as fighting more, figuring better, and exerting the best leadership. Most traits are seen as distinctly masculine or feminine by the majority of all the children. The most striking example is the aggression-gentleness continuum: close to 90% of all the children see boys as fighting more and about 80% see girls as kinder (*see* Table 3). Although the girls in the sample are traditional in their sex-typed view of personality traits, more of them also see both sexes exhibiting these traits. On almost every characteristic significantly more girls checked the "both boys and girls" category, part of a pattern that emerged throughout the study.

Sex-typing in girls' view of their own future

The pattern of traditional sex-typing that emerged in girls' views of social roles and personality traits was carried over into their own career aspirations and description of their lives as adults. (See Table 4.) While the boys wanted to be engineers, scientists, sportsmen, and pilots, the girls chose teacher, artist, stewardess, and nurse. Many girls choose specifically glamor-type jobs, such as model or stewardess, while others focused on food-oriented jobs such as cooking or waitressing. Fourteen percent of the girls chose veterinarian compared to none of the boys, while only 2% of the girls opted for doctor or dentist. One wonders whether girls see their ambition in the healing professions appropriate to animals but not to people, or whether it is simply that their medical interest is diverted into nursing (chosen by 15% of the girls).

The overwhelming preponderance of girls compared to boys who choose teaching as a career raises an interesting question of role-modeling. It is true that, things being as they are, the children in the sample may never have seen a male nurse or a female dentist. The opportunity to assimilate nontraditional sexes in these roles is minimal, and the children may not even be able to imagine their portrayal. Yet why did only girls choose a career as teachers? This particular group of children had been exposed to both male and female teachers. Four of the twelve teachers of the children in the sample were men, while male teachers presided over other classes in the same buildings. In spite of the fact that male and female role-models were available, the failure of boys to select "teacher" seems to confirm the strength of sex-typing for both sexes.

Overall, the girls had varied job and career aspirations, albeit heavily weighted toward traditional female occupations. They seemed in little doubt that they would have careers. Only six percent said they would be simply a mother or homemaker. At age eleven, these girls expressed firm career choices (much firmer than the boys) in which home-housewife-family plays only a minor role. Yet when we correlated the career-choice question with an open-ended essay at the end, "Imagine you are grown up. Describe how you would spend a typical day," a different picture emerged. The girls showed a marked discrepancy between their stated career goals and their description of an actual day in their lives when grown, compared to the boys in the sample. Five dimensions were used to analyze the essays: emphasis on marriage and family; specific details of family life; job or career details; private vs public interest; recreation vs work emphasis.

Emphasis on marriage and family is much higher among girls than among the boys in our sample. Despite the small number (6%) who said they would be housewives and mothers in question 1, well over 25% of the girls make marriage and family the predominant focus of their projected day, while an even larger group, 37.2%, emphasize details of family life in their descriptions. (*See* Table 5.) In contrast, boys overwhelmingly ignored domestic life—well over 83% gave no details at all of family activities and fewer than one-fourth even mentioned marriage or family.

Typical of comments of many of the girls were extensive and detailed accounts of their homemaker routine. Even girls who had chosen a variety of careers in the earlier question ("what do you want to be when you grow up?") saw themselves doing traditional "women's work" around the house. In fact, for many, the description of the household chores seemed far more salient than the job. Here is a girl who had said she wanted to be "an artist, maybe a beautician" describing her typical day:

> "I would start the morning after getting out of bed by eating breakfast. Then I would clean house. If I was done before lunch I would probably visit a friend. Then eat lunch. After lunch I would go shopping. Then I would come home and rest for a while. When my husband came home (if I was married), he would probably tell me how

> his day went and I would tell him how mine went. If he was in a real good mood he would take me out to dinner. When we were done with dinner, we would go to a movie. Then we would go home and go to bed."

Or another, whose career choice was "actress": "I would do what I would be doing for about four hours. Then I would go home and, if I were married, I'd go clean house and prepare our evening dinner and maybe go shopping before that!" Perhaps most succinct is the following:

> "If I were a grown-up, I would be working as a teacher and I would have to have a lot of patience. I would have to clean the house, make dinner, make breakfast, and make the beds."

Boys tend much more (25% as against 35%) to focus exclusively on details of job and career. Quite typical is this boy who wants to be a lawyer, and who never discusses marriage, family, or home.

> "I would talk to my clients on what their problems were. If I thought his thoughts were right I would explain the right procedures to take depending on his problem, and I would fight for his thoughts."

Within the three largest categories of career choice, girls show a significantly lower emphasis on details of job activities, and the general level of their responses on this question are far less job and career oriented than are the boys. Also noticeable was the tendency of girls to see their career choice largely or solely in terms of its utility to their homes and families. The response of the girl who, when asked to describe her typical day, answered, "I would be a nurse and keep my family nice and healthy," was not atypical.

The public versus private category was intended to distinguish between comments that indicated a concern with life outside the home as against those centered on the family. While roughly equivalent numbers of boys and girls mentioned *only* private items in their descriptions, substantially fewer girls saw themselves engaged in activities that could be categorized as public. The most striking privatized responses came from those girls who said they wanted to be "housewives" and whose essays consisted of a listing, by number, of the daily chores. One such essay begins as follows:

> 1. Get up
> 2. Get dressed
> 3. Straighten up house
> 4. Get husband's lunch ready
> 5. Get husband up
> 6. Help husband up
> 7. Help him off to work
> 8. Get big girl up
> 9. Get her off to work . . .

And so on, through number forty-one, with a similarly detailed routine that involved babies, naps, meals, dirty clothes, even feeding the pets!

Outstanding among the comments of these girls were elements that could be described as typical of persons leading what has been called the "contingent life",[2] that of seeing one's actions as being derived from and dependent on others. Thus, statements such as, "I would try to please my husband," or "if my children wanted to . . . ," are common.

Summary

This first study indicated that the degree of traditional sex stereotyping of the major social roles in society is very strong by the fifth-grade level. A clear demarcation of roles exists both at home and in the outside world, and even personality traits are thought of in male and female terms. Girls see themselves largely in traditional female jobs, such as nurses and teachers, and, regardless of occupation choice, expect to spend most of their "typical day" when grown-up on home, children, and husband. The high-status, powerful roles in both home (correcting and teaching children) and community (doctor, lawyer, mayor) are monopolized by men.

Of particular interest was the fact that so many of the girls in our study so clearly opt for career choices that they appear to be unwilling or unable to translate into consequences in their own lives. It is true that girls have experienced women in the role of housewives in their own homes. Boys, however, have been equally exposed to men in the roles of husbands, participating to a greater or lesser degree in household work and management. They do not reflect this domestic side of life. Furthermore, the children in our sample are the products of homes in which forty percent of the mothers are presently working outside the home, and it can be assumed that a larger number have done so at some time in their lives. Yet unlike their fathers, their mothers are not seen in terms of their occupational identities. Responses to other items on the questionnaire clearly indicate that this association of women with housework and traditional female occupations is maintained.

What is the explanation for the dichotomy between career choice and visualization of future life that our data showed applied unequally to the boys and girls in our sample? Some research exists that corroborates our finding of a discrepancy between girls' desires for the future and their realistic appraisals of attaining it.[3] It appears that girls are restricted in expressing a free choice of future roles by social stereotypes. If this is true, it may be that the first question, "what would you like to be when you grow up. . . ," by suggesting that such decisions are possible, permitted the girls freedom to state their wildest wishes. The latter question, however, brings them down to earth by asking them to imagine a typical day. The realities of societal pressure take over, they see themselves doing things women always do, and thus fall back into the traditional activities they sense are sanctioned by society.

In our view, the most significant finding of all was that consistently the girls were less stereotyped in their views than the boys, more willing to view personality traits and social roles as neutral, and not the exclusive prerogative of one sex or the other. More girls saw traditionally male roles as ones that should be played by both men and women and this pattern held true for the classroom, the locus of moral authority in the home, or the burden of household chores. This is a puzzling finding that we were at a loss to explain, particularly in view of the literature that attests to women as traditional bearers and upholders of conservative values. One variable that did seem to be relevant in determining which children had less traditional sex-stereotyped attitudes about the role of men and women in society, turned out to be whether or not their mothers worked. As other studies have shown,[4] our data indicate that children with working mothers had more liberalized views on roles of men and women in society. Girls, in particular, seemed to reflect this relationship.

1972 STUDY: SEX, STEREOTYPING, AND POLITICIZATION

A year later a follow-up study was accomplished in the same schools and with the same age children. The emphasis here was to determine what effect, if any, the strongly stereotyped views that children hold, have on their political attitudes and beliefs. More particularly, the interest was with girls, who had always emerged as less politically interested and aware than boys in previous socialization studies. Is there a relationship between strong adherence to traditional feminine values and weak political interest among girls?

Like the 1971 study, the new questionnaire dealt with children's own view of their future roles in job and family, the degree of openness/stereotyping in their view of social roles for men and women, and, new in this study, a series of questions designed to explore their political information and awareness. Several hypotheses were tested that had been developed out of the earlier study. These were:

1) that there would be marked, sex differences in children's responses to the political, as well as the economic and social questions;
2) that the holding of stereotyped views of the world has a negative effect on the level of political awareness and information, i.e., those children who hold the most egalitarian views (social roles least tied to sex) would score higher on political awareness and information;
3) that the girls most highly trained in "femininity" (most strongly adhering to traditional norms regarding the woman's role) would have the lower politicization scores.

As will be seen, only the first hypothesis received conclusive support.

Findings on the other two were ambiguous and subject to various interpretations.

Sex differences and political responses

A number of questions attempted to deal with the degree of stereotyping in children's views of both public and private roles. I was curious to see if the sexual division of labor that we had seen extended into family and social roles also held true for the civil and political arena. The democratic norm of equal opportunity implies that anyone can be president, a goal theoretically thus open to both sexes. Which was more salient for the girls, the rhetoric of equal access or the reality of male dominance in virtually all positions of political power? For boys, the log cabin-to-presidency myth or an impenetrable "power elite"? Furthermore, to what degree do eleven-year-olds perceive a barrier between the nebulous figures in Washington, D. C., who "run things" and themselves? Do they find the prospect of becoming powerful political leaders someday attractive? What degree of realism do they have about their actual chances of attaining such a post?

To get answers to some of these queries, a number of questions were asked dealing with national and local politics. First was the extent of the child's personal identification. They were asked to assume that they were grown and could choose any political job, such as president, governor, judge, head of the school board, and mayor. The most striking result was that well over half of all the children picked none of the posts. (*See* Table 6.) Strong sex differences were apparent: although about the same small proportion of boys and girls picked president, a sizeable number of boys wanted to be the mayor, yet not a single girl chose this. For girls, the most popular choice was head of the school board and, in second place, judge.

Immediately following this question was another in which the children were asked to assess which of the positions they thought they had a *realistic* chance of attaining. Here the notion being explored was that girls, more than boys, would sense the impossiblity of achieving these high prestige roles in our society. This pattern did not occur—the percentages were almost identical to the previous question. Several interpretations are possible. Probably many of the children did not understand the concept of "realistic" and simply copied the answer they had given in the previous question. Or else, their political concepts are still so naive that they truly think they can become anything they want. Perhaps a third speculation is in order. Maybe their initial choices are already calibrated to what is possible: they sense the impossiblity of the "you, too, can be President someday" myth and refuse to play that game.

Other sex differences emerged that were in line with previous socialization studies. When asked, "who runs the country?", girls in the present study were twice as likely as the boys to respond that the president does, while boys were much more likely to choose the Congress. (*See* Table 7.) When asked to decide for what reason they might vote for a candidate for public office, girls were more likely to choose candidates who were peace oriented and honest and sincere. (*See* Table 8.) Twice as many boys as girls chose the candidate whose ideas would contribute to the country's economic wealth.

Finally, a composite index was drawn up to include the determinants of political information and awareness. The information score consisted of correct answers to the various political identification questions; the awareness score was composed of any response other than "don't know" to the various questions dealing with voting and elections. On each of these scores, the girls did more poorly than the boys. (*See* Table 9.)

In areas beside the political, sex-stereotyping was as strong in the attitudes of these children as it had been in their counterparts a year ago (and this in spite of a year of active women's liberation activities in the media and press). When grown, girls saw themselves marrying and having children, boys thought in terms of jobs. (*See* Table 10.) Over half of the children thought there were jobs in society only men should do and only women should do. When asked if they thought a woman ought to work away from the house, girls were even more emphatic than boys in approving a woman's working only if her children are grown-up or if she has no children. A very low 10.6% of the girls and 14.7% of the boys said a woman should work "anytime she wants to."

Stereotyping and politicization

Once the existence of sex differences had been established, the attempt was made to see if a common variable, stereotyping, could be isolated as a determinant of low politicization. The measurement of stereotyping was the degree to which the children saw social roles (protection of city, housework, medical care, etc.) in the traditional terms of sexual dichotomy. For all the children, the stereotyping index was matched against the separate political information and awareness indices and, in addition, for girls, the femininity index (measured by their adherence to traditional female careers and values) was matched against the political scores. Results were inconclusive. Stereotyping clearly exists, but the data did not show any strong relationship with level of political information and awareness except in a few cases at the extremes. For example, those children with the least stereotyped views did score the highest on political information. Two-thirds of the children in the least stereotyped group ranked at the high end of the information scale, compared to one-half of the most stereotyped who were also high on information. No correlations appeared significant for the whole middle grouping between stereotyping and awareness other than what could have been expected in a random distribution.

The main concern was to see the effect of stereotyping and feminizing influences upon the girls. Here girls did seem more strongly affected than did the boys. There were some indications that girls who had the least narrowly feminine aspirations scored higher on political information and awareness, but the relationship was weak. Similarly, the occupation of the mother (housewife or working at a job) clearly affected the girls' aspirations and degree of stereotyping, but was less apparent in influencing their politicization scores. In contrast to the earlier study, such a small percent of the mothers were job-holders (of the 67 girls tested, 77.3% had mothers who were housewives) that it would be misleading to draw any conclusions based on the daughters of the six working-mothers.

In conclusion, the findings of this study were viewed with mixed feelings. On the one hand, the expected strong sex differences on political, social, and economic roles in society had emerged. Moreover, the existence of very strong sex-typing in children's views of jobs and functions in the world, as well as their own personal role within it, had been again confirmed. But the hoped-for correlations between stereotyping and feminization in the girls as an explanation for their low politicization scores had proved inconclusive.

EPILOGUE: THE STUDY THAT NEVER WAS, OR, WHO IS GOING TO RESOCIALIZE THE SOCIALIZERS?

Reflecting at length about the implications of these findings compared with previous political socialization studies, some anomalies may be perceived. The specific hypotheses with respect to the correlation between feminine aspirations, sex-typing, and low political interest and awareness in girls had not received any conclusive support. Nonetheless, the data confirmed the existence of all of these variables even though their interrelatedness had not been proved. The study was orthodox in its findings on sex differences and performance: girls scored lower in information and awareness (Greenstein), personalized authority (Hess and Torney; Easton and Dennis), saw their identity linked with marriage rather than job (Andrain), and were less wealth oriented than boys (Andrain).

In an earlier paper, the idea had been suggested that women have really received a "noneducation" when it comes to the civic awareness considered the hallmark of the good citizen.[5] As long as all the socializing agents of society, such as parents, teachers, and the media, subtly continue to inculcate the idea that politics is the exclusive province of men, boys will continue to strive toward active political roles. Girls, encouraged to turn inward to home and family, will continue to indicate little interest and identification with (male) political concerns. This theory provided the basis for the study just discussed. Unless the standard explanations for women's apolitical behavior (biologically unsuited; psychologically predisposed to domesticity; emotionally unable to cope with the rough-and-ready political world, etc.) were correct, women ought to differ in their political orientation according to the effectiveness of their feminization.

Yet such a relationship had not emerged in any significant degree. Two alternative explanations can be advanced for this failure. On the one hand, since virtually all the girls were feminized, choosing traditional female occupations and strongly believing that there are certain jobs only men should do and only women should do, no valid comparisons were possible. Very few of the girls identified themselves in terms other than marriage and family: there will be no women lawyers or lady engineers and only two women doctors among all the girls, according to their present aspirations. Thus, efforts to prove the hypothesis had not succeeded, first of all, because the training in femininity had proved more effective than had been realized: the sample failed to turn up more than a tiny handful of girls not caught in its net, so there was nothing substantial enough for comparisons.

Yet another explanation seemed in order. Perhaps all of these questionnaires reflected an unconscious ideology of sexism, which would result in disadvantaging the girls. Such an ideology would be reflected in two dimensions: the sexist language in which questionnaires were written, and the sexist subject matter with which they concerned themselves.

Before undertaking the 1972 study, it had been attempted to control for sexist language. In the first place, a content analysis was made of questionnaires used in three of the best-known political studies in recent years, choosing only those studies that explicitly devoted some space to sex roles and sex differences in politicization and all of which had findings that indicated lower politicization for girls.[6] Considered evidences of sexist language were such things as the exclusive use of the masculine pronoun, references to fathers only, males and females shown in only traditional roles, and an unconscious assumption that *men* do the important things in society. The results indicate that sexist language was widespread. (*See* end of article.)

Convinced that language is symbolic of underlying ideological views and thus important, a conscious attempt was made to use a sex-neutral questionnaire in the second study.[7] "He/she" was used instead of the ubiquitous "he," women were included as examples of political leaders, and the possibility was suggested that men and women could play unconventional social roles. In the 1971 study, the questionnaire used was typical of the ones cited at the end of this article in asking only for father's job. But the 1972 questionnaire assumed that either father or mother could be home doing housework or out at a full-time job, and asked appropriate questions for each. Furthermore, the question that aroused the most interest among the children as evinced in discussions afterwards, was the one that listed different jobs people do and asked "in every case, put a check by the best person who should do the job." Jobs were listed by function: housework, protecting the city, caring for sick people, running the country, raising the children, and coaching sports. In each case it was possible to choose a man, a woman, or either. Most interest and controversy was created by the use of the term "househusband" to denote a man who spends his day doing housework (presumably married, with a wife to support the family).

In spite of these efforts, the girls still made a poor showing on the political information and awareness scales. All political socialization tests had found girls relatively less knowledgeable and interested in politics than boys, and now my study had shown this, also. Maybe there really *was* something innate about the female of the species that constitutionally indisposed her for politics? Finding this answer unacceptable, further reflection was in order about the subject matter of all the questionnaires, the ones for this study as well as the predecessors.

Perhaps, as Fred Greenstein had put it, even when they are still very young, these girls had clearly come to the realization that "politics is a man's business";[8] but furthermore, perhaps all these questionnaires were serving to confirm that realization. Perhaps the typical questions that test for political information and awareness are male designed and male oriented: who runs the country, political party labels, names of mayors and governors—male oriented, because these posts have historically always been occupied by men. How many girls, set the task of memorizing the names of the Presidents of the United States, will visualize themselves in that role? If this is one's perspective, it could seem quite rational that many young girls and women would be disinterested and care little about politics. When politics is conceptualized in terms of power, aggression, and conflict, it is not surprising that women, trained in submissiveness, dependence, and passivity, should find little in it to interest them.

Table 1

Appropriate Sex Roles in Occupations

"For each job, check if you think a *man* should do this job, or if a *woman* should, or if *both* men and women should."

Job		*Men* (%)	*Women* (%)	*Both* (%)
Doctor	Boys	38.6	.7	60.0 *
	Girls	26.5	0.0	73.5
Cook	Boys	2.9	36.4	60.7
	Girls	2.6	35.1	62.3
Fifth-grade Teacher	Boys	20.7	17.1	62.1 **
	Girls	3.3	19.2	76.2
Boss	Boys	79.3	.7	19.3 **
	Girls	64.9	2.0	33.1 **
Taxi Driver	Boys	56.9	5.1	38.0 **
	Girls	62.0	0.0	38.0
Artist	Boys	11.6	13.8	74.6
	Girls	4.1	9.4	86.5 *
Mayor	Boys	86.4	3.6	10.0 **
	Girls	78.1	2.0	19.2
Factory Worker	Boys	63.6	5.7	30.0
	Girls	59.3	4.0	36.7
Nurse	Boys	2.9	91.3	5.7
	Girls	4.0	84.1	11.3
Lawyer	Boys	77.1	1.4	20.7 **
	Girls	57.6	.7	41.7
Office Worker	Boys	26.1	13.8	60.1 **
	Girls	10.7	14.7	74.7
College Professor	Boys	45.0	5.7	47.9 *
	Girls	49.6	1.3	56.3
House Cleaner	Boys	2.1	85.7	11.4 **
	Girls	2.6	76.8	20.5
Clerk in a Store	Boys	15.7	9.3	72.1
	Girls	17.2	7.3	74.8

* Differences significant below .05
** Differences significant below .01

N=290

Table 2

Appropriate Sex Roles in Household Tasks

"Here is a list of jobs that people do *at home*. Who do you think is the best one to do each of the jobs?"

Task		Appropriate sex (%)* *Male*	*Female*	*Both*
Washing dishes	Boys	1.5	82.1	16.1
	Girls	.7	81.9	17.3
Taking out the garbage	Boys	5.2	81.3	13.4
	Girls	2.0	87.0	10.9
Grocery shopping	Boys	79.5	11.6	8.8
	Girls	90.8	3.5	5.4
Paying bills	Boys	55.0	15.2	29.6
	Girls	59.6	10.2	33.1
Cooking	Boys	2.3	81.3	15.8
	Girls	2.8	86.2	11.1
Fixing things around the house	Boys	63.4	26.2	10.5
	Girls	55.3	31.5	13.3
Dusting	Boys	2.3	92.5	5.3
	Girls	2.1	94.4	3.5
Scrubbing floors	Boys	6.0	91.2	3.6
	Girls	4.2	86.7	9.1
Getting up at night with a sick child	Boys	3.7	70.0	26.3
	Girls	6.0	64.0	29.8
Weeding the yard	Boys	52.7	16.4	31.0
	Girls	41.4	10.1	48.5

* Male includes Men and Boys
Female includes Women and Girls

N=290

Table 3

Personality Traits Assigned to Boys and Girls

"Tell who you think best fits these descriptions, boys, or girls."

Trait		*Boys (%)*	*Girls (%)*	*Both (%)*
Kinder	Boys	20.7	75.3	3.6 *
	Girls	3.4	85.2	11.4
Fights most	Boys	88.6	7.9	3.6
	Girls	89.9	4.0	6.0
Behaves best	Boys	22.1	71.4	6.4 *
	Girls	4.0	84.6	10.7
Figures out things best	Boys	70.7	20.0	7.9 *
	Girls	26.2	57.7	15.4
Gets their own way	Boys	32.1	59.3	6.4 *
	Girls	44.3	41.6	11.4
Most serious	Boys	52.1	42.1	5.7 *
	Girls	23.6	66.2	10.1
Works hardest	Boys	72.1	18.6	8.6 *
	Girls	38.3	45.6	15.4
Best in science	Boys	75.7	12.9	11.4 *
	Girls	59.7	21.5	18.1
Best in math	Boys	57.1	30.7	11.4 *
	Girls	18.8	62.4	17.4
Best in social science	Boys	48.6	40.0	10.7 *
	Girls	34.2	44.3	18.8
Best in leadership	Boys	65.3	25.7	8.9 *
	Girls	41.4	42.3	14.4

* Differences significant below .01

N=290

Table 4

Career Aspirations Named by Boys and Girls

"What do you want to do when you grow up and finish your education?"

Career	*Girls* (%) (n=149)	*Boys* (%) (n=141)
Teacher	20.0	.71
Nurse, social worker	15.33	
Stewardess	14.67	
Veterinarian, raise animals	14.00	
Artist, writer	7.33	2.13
Marriage, family, housewife	6.00	1.42
Actor, singer, model	4.00	
Get (or have) a job	3.33	7.10
Skilled or semiskilled craft	5.33	16.33
Engineer, scientist	2.67	5.68
Secretary	2.67	
Doctor, lawyer, dentist	2.0	11.36
Police, military	1.34	3.55
Sport	1.33	24.85
Pilot	0.0	10.65
Business or store	0.0	4.26
Undecided, no answer, etc.	.67	9.23
Irrelevant answer	.67	2.84

Table 5

Children's View of their own Futures

"Imagine you are grown. Describe how you would spend a typical day."

	Boys (%)	*Girls (%)*
Marriage and Family		
No mention or only incidental mention	74.8	46.2
Predominant or only subject	10.2	26.2
Details of Family Life		
Housework, spouse, child	13.8	37.2
Household finances	3.1	0.0
No details given	83.1	62.8
Job or Career Details		
No mention or only incidental mention	29.1	35.7
Predominant or only subject	52.0	35.0
Private vs Public Emphasis		
Private only	14.4	16.1
Public only	28.8	18.9
Mixed	56.8	65.0
Recreation vs Work Emphasis		
Recreation only	11.2	8.5
Work only	36.0	36.2
Mixed	52.8	55.3

N=290

Table 6

Sex Differences in Children's Desire for Jobs in Politics and Government

"Here are some jobs that relate to politics and government. Assume you could be anything, which of these jobs would you *like* to have?"*

	Girls (%)	*Boys (%)*
President of country	9.0	11.5
Governor	3.0	7.7
Mayor	0.0	15.4
Judge	10.4	6.4
Head of school board	22.4	2.6
None	55.2	56.4
	100.0	100.0

N=145

* Differences significant below .01

Table 7

Sex Differences in Children's View of National Power

"Who do you think does the most to run our country?"*

	Girls (%)	*Boys* (%)
President	65.4	36.1
Supreme Court	1.9	8.3
Congress	21.2	48.6
Don't know	11.5	5.6
	100.0	100.0
		N=124

* Differences significant below .01

Table 8

Sex Differences in Orientation to Political Candidates

"If you were old enough to vote, why would you vote for a particular person?"

	Girls (%)	*Boys* (%)
Member of political party I like	1.5	1.3
Person will make country wealthier	10.4	23.7
He/she is honest and sincere	37.3	30.3
Person promises to work for peace	41.8	32.9
Other	1.7	1.3
Don't know	6.0	10.5
		N=143

Table 9

Sex Differences in Children's Political Information and Awareness

*Political Information**	*Girls (%)*	*Boys (%)*
Low (score 2 or below)	77.7	66.3
High (score 3 or above)	22.4	33.8
		n = 147
*Political Awareness***		
Low (score 2 or below)	35.8	22.5
High (score 4)	34.3	45.0
		N = 147

* Composite index, 0–5, based on number of *correct* answers to questions on identifying national and local political figures, being able to name some things governor and mayor do.

** Composite index, 0–4, based on any response other than "don't know" to such questions as reasons for voting, who runs the country, choice of presidential candidates, identification with a political party.

Table 10

Sex Differences in Children's View of the Future

"Imagine you are grown. Check which one you are *most* sure you will do."*

	Girls (%)	*Boys (%)*
Get a job	29.9	64.1
Get married and have children	56.7	15.3
Be rich	4.5	9.0
Have fun	7.5	7.7
All	1.5	2.6
		N = 145

* Differences significant below .01

NOTES

1. Jessie Bernard, *Women and the Public Interest* (Chicago: Aldine/Atherton Press, 1970), pp. 105–109.
2. Cynthia Epstein, *Women's Place* (Berkeley, Calif.: University of California Press, 1970).
3. M. S. Horner, "Femininity and Successful Achievement: A Basic Inconsistency," in *Roles Women Play: Readings Towards Women's Liberation*, Garskof, ed. (Belmont, Calif.: Brooks/Cole, 1971).
4. Women whose mothers were employed had higher estimation of their own competence as shown in R. S. Vogel, et al., "Sex-role Stereotypes: A Current Appraisal," *Journal of Social Issues* (Summer 1972); see also, E. T. Peterson, "The Impact of Maternal Employment on the Mother-daughter Relationship and on the Daughter's Role-orientation" (Ph.D. dissertation, University of Michigan, 1950).
5. Lynne Iglitzin, "Political Education and Sexual Liberation," *Politics and Society* (Winter 1972).
6. Focusing only on these three questionnaires should not imply that these are the only ones using sexist language nor that they are even the worst offenders. They are chosen simply as examples of what is undoubtedly a widespread phenomenon. A more extended and more precise content analysis would turn up more and worse examples—but what is the point of continuing to document what we already know?
7. At least one other researcher has made a similar attempt to modify our sexist language. Jack Masson, in a recent study of political socialization of Seattle children, emphasizes mother and father, rather than just father; where the respondent is female, he suggests the possibility of policewomen as well as policemen. One might only suggest that women as policewomen or authority figures is a possibility that ought to be placed before boys, too, if we are going to counteract sex-typing in children's views. Jack Masson, "Political Socialization Study of Seattle Children" (Ph.D. dissertation, University of Washington, 1971).
8. Fred I. Greenstein, *Children and Politics* (New Haven, Conn.: Yale University Press, 1965), p. 119.

SEXISM IN SOME POLITICAL SOCIALIZATION QUESTIONNAIRES

Questionnaires used in three surveys were studied: Robert D. Hess and Judith V. Torney, *The Development of Political Attitudes in Children* (Garden City, N.Y.: Anchor Books, 1967); Fred I. Greenstein, *Children and Politics* (New Haven, Conn.: Yale University Press, 1965); and Charles F. Andrain, *Children and Civic Awareness* (Columbus, Ohio: Charles E. Merrill Publishing Co., 1971). They are each indentified in parentheses.

I. Adult models are presented only in traditionally sex-typed social and political roles

(Hess and Torney) "Here are some people. Which ones work for the government?" (Pictures shown—*male* milkman, policeman, soldier, judge, postman.)

"Does the teacher work for the government?" (Female picture.)

"Who helps you and your family the most?" (Pictures of policeman, soldier, father, president—males; teacher—female.)

(Andrain) "What person represents your hope for America's future?" (Choices: astronaut, peace-corps worker, army general, president of a large company.)

II. Politics is a man's business

(Andrain) "Which of the following does NOT work for the government?" (Postman, policeman, telephone repairman, soldier—all males.)

"Which of the following is a NATIONAL political leader?" (Male choices only.)

"Of the following four men, which one is a Republican?" (Males only.)

"Who has the most control over military action in Vietnam?" (Male choices only.)

"What do you think is the most important purpose of political parties?" (One response: "To let people choose the best man to run the government.")

III. The belief is fostered and maintained that only the father in the family deals with politics and authority questions

(Hess and Torney) "If you think a policeman is wrong in what he tells you to do, what would you do?" (Among the responses that deal with compliance with the request is : "Do what he tells you, but tell your *father* about it.")

"Think of *Your Father* as he really is . . . (i.e., helper, decision-maker, knows things, promises, has power, etc.).

"Think of *Your Father* as he really is . . . (makes mistakes, is a leader, punishes, works hard, protects, etc.).

THERE ARE NO EQUIVALENT QUESTIONS FOR THE MOTHER!

"Put an X beside the sentence which comes closest to telling what your *father's* job is." (No category for mother.)

IV. Women are addressed only indirectly; women get vicarious satisfaction through their husband's status

(Hess and Torney) "If the President came to your school, to give a prize to two *boys* who were the best citizens and the teacher offered him these boys, which two boys would he pick?" (Choices among boys helping others, getting good grades, working hard, etc., etc.) (Emphasis added.)

NO EQUIVALENT QUESTION FOR GIRLS!

(Greenstein) "Check all the jobs you would like when you are older." (Girls can also check jobs they would want their husbands to have.)

Attitudes Toward Increased Social, Economic, and Political Participation by Women as Reported by Elementary and Secondary Students*

SELMA GREENBERG

BACKGROUND

The women's rights movement has as its aim full and equal participation of women in all spheres: economic, political, and social. Opponents of this movement base their opposition on many different factors including: biological, social, and traditional ones. However, one of the arguments most persistently presented by the movement's opponents is simply that both women and men prefer to retain the present societal arrangements that focus women's interest on home, children, and family, while focusing men's interest on the larger economic, political, and social spheres. Thus, one aim of this study was to surface students' attitudes toward woman's increased

* Reprinted with the permission of the author. This article is a slightly revised version of a paper presented at the 1972 Annual Meeting of the American Educational Research Association in Chicago. Among the many helpful persons who assisted in the collection, coding, and analyzing of the data the following played a major role: Ann Braile, Marcia Brieger, Joseph Notturno, Cynthia and Heide Stutz, and Sally Storrs.

participation in fields typically thought of as male. The attitudes were assessed by means of a questionnaire. The questionnaire was developed by Ms. Sally Storrs, a graduate student, while working in a course with the author. Ms. Storrs tested her own sixth-grade class with the questionnaire and found systematic and significant differences in responses between boys and girls. At that time it was believed that these differences were chance ones and would not exist in a larger, more random group. With Ms. Storrs's permission, the questionnaire was given to an additional 100 students. The same systematic differences were found as had been reported by Ms. Storrs. Intrigued, it was decided to proceed with a large-scale study of male/female attitudes using this questionnaire as the investigative instrument.

PROBLEM

Are there systematic and significant group differences in responses to the questions posed by this questionnaire? Are these differences a function of grade or age, socioeconomic status, and/or sex?

SAMPLE

Because the students participating in the study were required to read the questionnaire, grade four was chosen as the earliest grade with which to begin. It was believed that an efficient way to continue would be to secure a sample from every other grade; thus, students in fourth grade, sixth grade, eighth grade and tenth grade composed the sample. By choosing various school districts on Long Island, New York, representative of differing social-class membership, the variable of social class was examined. Initially 100 students in each of four social classes were sampled in each of four grades. Thus, a total of 1,600 students were sampled, approximately 800 females and 800 males. After the data was collected, it was decided that there was insufficient justification for maintaining the four social-class distinction and, thus, the original four classes were combined into two —an upper- and a lower-social-class group.

RESULTS

An interval score was calculated on each subject by converting the answers on items 1–19 into an egalitarian score. Answers to question 20 were excluded from the egalitarian score. For although the patterns of male/ female responses is quite dissimilar, the meaning of the responses were difficult to evaluate in terms of their egalitarian dimension. Thus, answering *yes* to items 1–12, and 16–19 and *no* to items 13-15 were all scored as

Positive on the egalitarian score. A three-way analysis of variance was then performed on the data. No differences exist between members of the two social classes. Some significant differences were revealed in analyzing the answers by grade. Males in grades 6, 8, and 10 had higher egalitarian scores than males in grade 4. Females in grades 8 and 10 had higher egalitarian scores than females in grades 4 and 6 (these differences were significant at the .01 level). However, in all age and social-class groups, females had consistently and significantly more egalitarian scores (significant at the .01 level) than males.

In analyzing the questionnaire item by item, the following percentages of female/male answers were calculated.

Item 1

Do you think that it's fair for a woman to have the same chance as a man (equal opportunity) to apply for and work at any job she wants if she is qualified?
Female Response Yes *92%* No *8%* Male Response Yes *80%* No *20%*

Item 2

Do you feel that a female doctor or dentist would be as good as a male?
Female Response Yes *81%* No *19%* Male Response Yes *70%* No *30%*

Item 3

Should radio and TV stations hire more female announcers and newscasters?
Female Response Yes *66%* No *34%* Male Response Yes *52%* No *48%*

Item 4

Should we have more female jockeys at the race track?
Female Response Yes *46%* No *54%* Male Response Yes *30%* No *70%*

Item 5

Are lady scientists as smart as male scientists?
Female Response Yes *86%* No *14%* Male Response Yes *66%* No *34%*

Item 6

Would a trained female garage mechanic be as good as a man if your car needed fixing?

Female Response Yes *50%* No *50%* Male Response Yes *33%* No *67%*

Item 7

Should we have female astronauts?
Female Response Yes *58%* No *42%* Male Response Yes *35%* No *65%*

Item 8

Should more women be encouraged to become lawyers, judges, and senators?
Female Response Yes *82%* No *18%* Male Response Yes *41%* No *59%*

Item 9

Do you think that we will ever have a woman president?
Female Response Yes *60%* No *40%* Male Response Yes *39%* No *61%*

Item 10

Are women as intelligent as men?
Female Response Yes *94%* NO *6%* Male Response Yes *71%* No *29%*

Item 11

Do you think that most female teachers are as good as most male teachers?
Female Response Yes *91%* No *9%* Male Response Yes *78%* No *22%*

Item 12

Do you feel that a female would be as good a school principal as a male?
Female Response Yes *73%* No *27%* Male Response Yes *53%* No *47%*

Item 13

Do women become upset more easily than men?
Female Response Yes *83%* No *17%* Male Response Yes *85%* No *15%*

Item 14

Would you mind working for a woman boss?
Female Response Yes *25%* No *75%* Male Response Yes *47%* No *53%*

Item 15

Is it right that men should be expected to open doors and take off their hats for women if women have equal jobs?
Female Response Yes *68%* No *32%* Male Response Yes *48%* No *52%*

Item 16

Do you think that men should be allowed to hold jobs that women usually do, such as airline stewards as well as male secretaries?
Female Response Yes *48%* No *52%* Male Response Yes *39%* No *61%*

Item 17

Do you think that women in all countries of the world should have equal rights to men?
Female Response Yes *81%* No *19%* Male Response Yes *63%* No *37%*

Item 18

Should women in all countries be allowed to vote for their leaders if men do?
Female Response Yes *81%* No *19%* Male Response Yes *70%* No *30%*

Item 19

Do you feel that women are as talented as men in art, music, the theater (acting)?
Female Response Yes *95%* No *5%* Male Response Yes *80%* No *20%*

Item 20

Is it better to be a man or woman in the United States today?

Female Response		Male Response	
Man	*19%*	Man	*48%*
Woman	*22%*	Woman	*12%*
Both are Equal	*59%*	Both are Equal	*40%*

DISCUSSION

Although concerned with the difficulty of some of the wording of several questions, i.e., "Would you mind working for a woman boss?", and the unconscious antiwomen bias in other questions, i.e., "Are women as intelligent as men?", it was decided to proceed with the Storrs questionnaire because it was both reliable and capable of revealing attitudinal differences. Since the completion of this study, another study undertaken by a student from a neighboring college yielded results congruent with both Ms. Storrs's pilot study and this one, thus giving further evidence of the questionnaire's usefulness.

The significant change toward more egalitarian answers after grade four by males and after grade six by females may be due to greater sophistication and understanding of social issues or a better ability to understand the language and thrust of the questions themselves.

The absence of social-class differences in responses even after the four classes were reduced to two is a surprising one. It argues against the notion of a more liberal posture toward social change among more privileged males (at least on this issue) and also against the notion that the women's rights movement reflects only the perceived interests of more privileged females.

The difference between responses of male and female students on questions that dealt with knowledge of objective fact or the ability to analyze objective reality was interesting. Thus, "Are women as intelligent as men?", and, "Will there ever be a woman president?", are not questions that tap personal preference or belief in quite the same way as, "Should we have female astronauts?" Yet the former questions were responded to in the same pattern as the latter, i.e., females said yes more often than males.

CONCLUSION

This study demonstrated that systematic and significant differences exist between responses of groups and that these differences of responses are primarily a function of the sex of the respondent and somewhat a function of the grade level. Thus, females are more likely to give an egalitarian response than males and upper-grade students (after grade four in the case of males, after grade six in the case of females) are more likely to give egalitarian responses than lower-grade students.

Generally then, female students see women more positively and more optimistically than do males. Additionally they are more favorable to the concept of social change that will grant women greater participation in the social, economic, and political spheres.

AFTERWARD

After the completion of the main study, the questionnaire was distributed to four sixth-grade classes. This time the effects upon children's responses of having a mother who is gainfully employed was examined. When the data was looked at in this way the following was discovered. In ranking groups from most to least egalitarian, the girls of employed mothers were most egalitarian, girls of nonworking mothers ranked second in egalitarianism, boys of working mothers ranked third, and boys of nonworking mothers ranked fourth or last. Additionally, it was found that whether or not a mother was employed was much more likely to affect the responses of boys than the responses of girls.

In considering the ramifications of all the above information, certain questions come to mind. If, in this study, female respondents saw women more positively and optimistically than male respondents, perhaps we can speculate that these differences may be true for adults as well. We might then ask, do male teachers, male principals, and the male decision-making hierarchy convey differential expectations to female teachers and female students?

Further, if the children of employed mothers do, as this study suggests, see women in a more positive and egalitarian fashion than do the children of mothers engaged in housework, how authentic is the often voiced societal approval of the stay-at-home mother?

Last, might it not be that the drive toward a more positive view of woman has been fueled by the image of the competent, well-educated professional women all young children intimately know, the female elementary schoolteacher.

Adolescents' Views of Women's Work-role*

DORIS R. ENTWISLE and ELLEN GREENBERGER

Role theorists have shown much concern with role-models and with the processes by which roles are internalized, whether by imitation, by identification, or both. There has been much less concern with the *substance* of roles—what specific behaviors, attitudes, or value systems are acquired, or with the effect of the "audience" upon role acquisition. In the learning of a feminine role, for example, role theorists would emphasize the proximity of suitable female figures (the mother, other female relatives, the teacher) in the child's life-space and the psychological dynamics involved in the child's imitation of, or identification with, such figures. Another crucial factor, however, in shaping girls' attitudes about woman's role is probably the "audience," their school classmates including the set of young boys they view as potential mates. There has been some emphasis lately on the learning of "what not to do" in the latter stages of sex-role development. Girls, according to this view, tend to learn *not* to engage in sexually aggressive behavior rather than learning what specific female behaviors they should display. For this kind of negatively based learning, the presence and actions of a suitable male audience are equivalent to a set of negative role-models who can invoke powerful sanctions in a way that is probably quite different from that of positive role-models (mothers, teacher, etc.).

The main focus of this study is upon the acquisition of a few specific attitudes or beliefs: whether women should work, what kinds of jobs women should hold, and whether women are intellectually curious. In particular, we are interested in what opinions young adolescent girls and boys hold in these specific areas on woman's role, how their opinions vary as a function of social class or residential locus, and in what ways there is congruence or incongruence between the opinions of girls and boys of the same age on these topics.[1]

METHOD

Procedure

As part of a large survey of Maryland ninth-grade students in the spring of 1968, three questions on woman's role were included. These questions, part of a large battery of tests, appeared together in the form below:

Check one and only one answer to the statements below. Also tell how strongly you feel about the answer you check.

1. What do you think women should be like?

_______Women should do many things including being leaders in politics, the professions, and business (the same work as men).

_______Women should center their lives in the home and family and their jobs should be in such fields as teaching, nursing, and secretarial service (different work from men).

Check how strongly you feel about your answer.

(very weak) ____ ____ ____ ____ (strong)
1 2 3 4

2. How do you think women see the world?

_______Women are interested in things but not usually to the point of following them up seriously. Working on problems isn't what they get satisfaction from.

_______Women are curious about many things, try to learn more about these things, and get a lot of satisfaction from working on these problems.

Check how strongly you feel about your answer.

(very weak) ____ ____ ____ ____ (strong)
1 2 3 4

3. What do you think women should do?

_______It is not a good idea for women to work. They should devote themselves to their home and family.

_______It is a good idea for women to work. They don't have to devote themselves only to their homes and family.

Check how strongly you feel about your answer.

(very weak) ____ ____ ____ ____ (strong)
1 2 3 4

Each question can be scored from one (least favorable or least liberal) to nine (most favorable or most liberal). For example, if a respondent chooses the first alternative in Question 1, the liberal alternative, he automatically receives five po:nts plus the number he checks on the intensity scale. If he chooses the second alternative in Question 1, he automatically receives five less the number of checks on the intensity scale.

Table 1

Characteristics of the Samples of Respondents

Group Name		Number of Boys	Number of Girls	Average Years Of Schooling Completed By Adults*	Average Income*
Inner-City	Black	58	69	8.2	$4,608
Inner-City	White	16	16	7.0	3,528
Blue-Collar	Black	48	52	10.3	6,629
Blue-Collar	White	49	60	8.7	5,953
Rural	White	49	58	9.2	5,829
Middle-Class	White	50	50	12.6	9,828

*Data are approximate, obtained by averaging census-tract figures (1960) for neighborhoods schools serve.

Subjects

Altogether, 270 boys and 305 girls answered the women's-role questions. Respondents were selected by locating schools whose students typify certian social class or racial strata of the U.S. population. For example, the blue-collar white school was located in a typically blue-collar white neighborhood in the suburbs of Baltimore near the Cheasapeake Bay where much heavy shipbuilding and steel manufacturing industry is located. Homes in this area are "row houses," sometimes owned by the occupants, which in 1960 sold in the range from $8000 to $12,000 new. Educational and economic data characterizing families of respondents (TABLE 1) is taken from 1960 census-tract statistics for the neighborhoods served by the six schools. To facilitate discussion, the groups of students have been given the labels shown at the left in TABLE 1.

Within schools, subjects were selected to fulfill certain aptitude or achievement criteria according to test scores procured earlier by the school system. These "IQ" strata are labeled and defined in TABLE 2. The strata present for a school indicate the IQ composition of the school. In schools where no "low IQ" stratum is listed, there were not enough students fulfilling the "low IQ" requirement to form a stratum. Similarly, in schools where no "high IQ" stratum is listed, there were not enough students of that type to form a stratum.

RESULTS

TABLE 2 gives the average score for each question for each subgroup. Several variance analyses were carried out to clarify trends seen there, and the main findings of these analyses will be discussed in turn. They are too lengthy to present in their entirety, but involve repeated measures-analyses (three questions) of the fixed-effect factors of sex, school (residential locus, social class, race), and IQ level. Four main designs are possible: 1) six schools for average IQ groups; 2) three white schools with average IQ and high IQ strata; 3) four schools with race (black, white)

Table 2

Mean Scores by Subgroups For Women's Role Questions*

Type School	Race	IQ Level	Boys N	Boys Ques 1	Boys Ques 2	Boys Ques 3	Girls N	Girls Ques 1	Girls Ques 2	Girls Ques 3	Total Boys	Total Girls
Inner-City	Black	Lo IQ	30	1.47	6.53	4.43	30	2.33	6.83	6.00	12.43	15.16
		Med IQ	28	2.43	6.00	4.25	39	3.74	7.03	5.97	12.68	16.74
	White	Med IQ	16	1.69	5.94	3.94	16	2.94	6.94	6.37	11.57	16.25
Blue-Collar	Black	Lo IQ	22	1.86	6.00	3.82	22	2.41	7.14	6.73	11.68	16.28
		Med IQ	26	2.54	5.62	4.58	30	2.50	7.03	5.40	12.74	14.93
	White	Med IQ	30	2.10	5.37	2.50	30	2.30	7.40	2.80	9.97	12.50
		Hi IQ	19	3.05	5.32	2.84	30	4.83	7.60	6.17	11.21	18.60
Rural	White	Med IQ	29	1.45	5.24	2.17	28	2.14	6.36	4.29	8.86	12.79
		Hi IQ	20	2.40	5.20	4.90	30	3.97	7.77	6.10	12.50	17.84
Middle-Class	White	Med IQ	20	2.45	5.85	3.70	20	4.05	6.45	4.15	12.00	14.65
		Hi IQ	30	2.23	4.90	3.73	30	4.17	6.63	6.90	10.36	17.70

* "Average IQ" students have IQs (mostly CTMM) in the range 95 to 114 *or* SCAT scores between 39th and 60th percentile on national norms. "Low IQ" students have IQs in the range 70–85. "High IQ" students have IQs in the range 128-up *or* SCAT scores above the 92nd percentile on national norms.

and social class (inner-city, blue collar) in a 2x2 design for average IQ students; and 4) two black schools where social class (inner-city, blue collar) and IQ level (medium and low) form a 2x2 design. Findings of least-squares analyses (unequal cell sizes) were in all cases confirmed when randomly selected subsets of subjects were formed to yield cells with proportional numbers.

INTERACTIONS BETWEEN QUESTION, RESIDENTIAL LOCUS, IQ, AND SEX FOR WHITE NINTH-GRADERS OF MEDIUM OR HIGH IQ (DATA FROM TABLE 2)

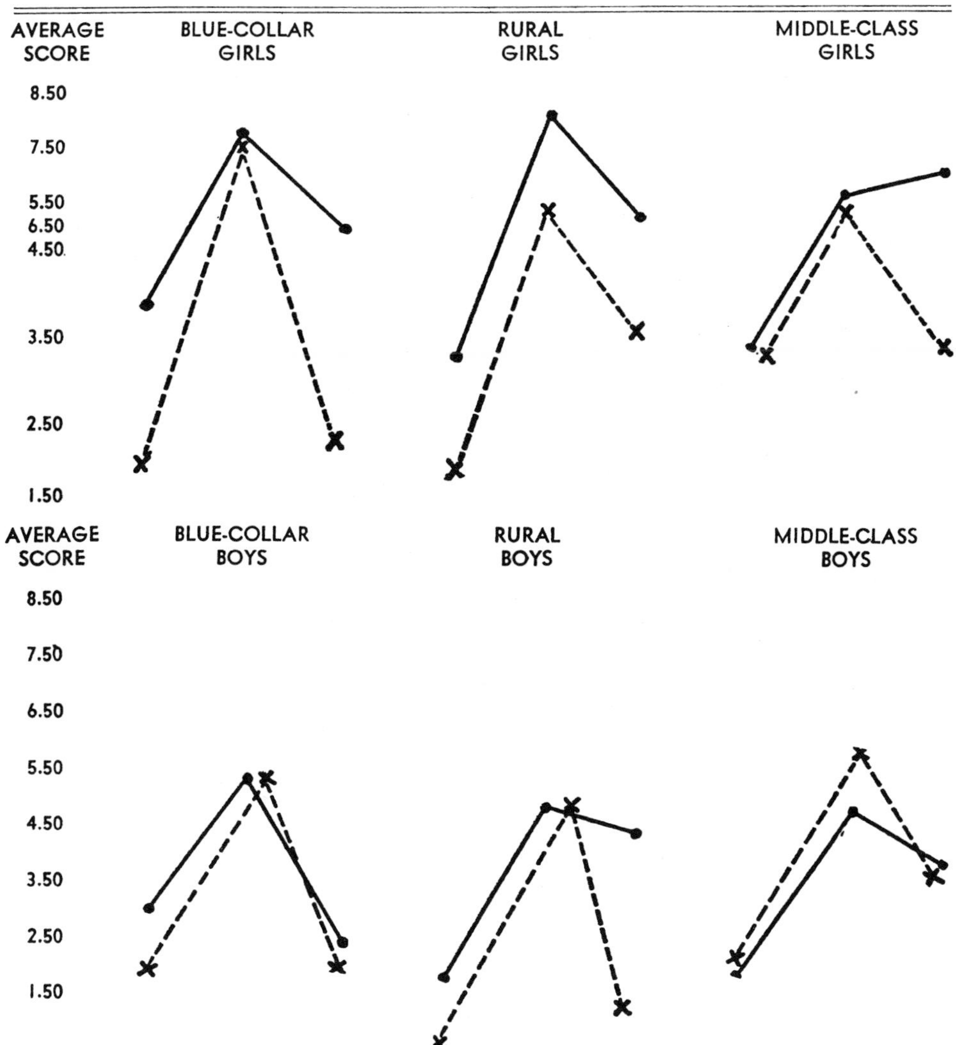

Figure 1—Relation between number of choices as "best" on three criteria and proportion wanting to be someone else. (Broken lines indicate Medium IQ; solid lines High IQ. Diagram reflects responses to all three questions relating women's work roles; see *Procedures.)*

Sex

There are consistent, large sex differences. Of thirty-three comparisons possible between sexes for matched subgroups of boys and girls in TABLE 2, in only one instance are boys more "liberal" than girls. In all four variance analyses examining factorial designs that can be formed from subsets of the data, sex is uniformly significant beyond the .01 level.

With two exceptions, the variance analyses yield no significant interaction effects involving sex. The first exception appears in an analysis of data for white students of average or high IQ, from schools of blue-collar, rural, and middle-class neighborhoods. The interaction is complex and can be seen in detail in FIGURE 1. Generally, higher IQ students of both sexes are more liberal than medium IQ students (an exception is middle-class white boys), but the IQ differential is more pronounced for girls. Perhaps the most important component of this interaction is the difference between high IQ middle-class boys and girls on Question 3 (whether women should work). This particular difference is large (almost five scale points) and highly significant ($p<.001$).

The second exception, involving social class, will be discussed in the next section.

Social Class or Residential Locus

For average IQ students over six schools, school and the question-*x*-school interaction are significant. "School" includes race (black-white), social class (middle-class, blue-collar, inner-city), and rural-urban differences. The totals for inner-city and blue-collar youngsters of average IQ in TABLE 2, display the question-*x*-school interaction—inner-city totals range from 11.57 to 16.74, while blue-collar totals are considerably lower, ranging from 9.97 to 14.93. Blue-collar respondents are more conservative. Again it is Question 3 (whether women should work) that produces differences—blue-collar girls are more conservative ($p<.05$) on this issue than inner-city girls, about two scale points. On the first question (what kinds of jobs women should hold), inner-city boys are more conservative than blue-collar boys, whereas for girls this effect reverses, the blue-collar girls being more conservative.

Rather surprisingly, as the school effect is analyzed further in a comparison of white-rural, blue-collar, and middle-class groups, school differences are minimal, except for the four-way interaction involving school, IQ, sex, and question discussed under "sex" above. The differences between rural and other groups are well within chance expectation. It is also worth noting that blue-collar black males and middle-class white males, matched on IQ, look very similar.

Race

Only one comparison allows race to be included as a factor along with social class while IQ is held constant. This comparison of inner-city and blue-collar blacks and whites shows social class to be significant beyond the five percent level, as already mentioned, but the race factor does not attain significance. None of the interactions with race is significant. No effect of race per se seems to be present in the answers to the questions of this survey.

IQ

As mentioned earlier, certain IQ levels could not be obtained in some schools. For black students sampled only at medium and low levels of IQ, IQ is not a significant source of variance. Stratifying on medium and high levels of IQ reveals large differences associated with IQ for white students. IQ interacts with question, sex, and school, as discussed earlier. It also interacts with question, with sex, and is highly significant ($p<.01$) as a main effect. Although generally a liberalizing factor, IQ is associated with greater differences for girls than for boys. High-IQ white girls generally are positively disposed toward women working, whereas medium-IQ white girls are not, and all white boys, whether of medium or high IQ, feel women should not work. All white girls are below five on the topic of women holding men's jobs, but boys are even more negatively disposed on this issue.

Although there are no significant correlations between white boys' answers to the three questions on women's work role and boys' grades, there are a number of significant correlations between white girls' grade and their answers to these questions. In particular, when girls' grades in four major subjects (mathematics, English, social studies, and science) are correlated with answers to each of the three questions, eight of twelve possible correlations (four correlations in three schools) are positive and significant beyond the .01 level. No correlations with grades appear for black girls.

DISCUSSION

There is a marked difference in opinion between boys and girls about women's role, with boys consistently holding more conservative opinions. Some general trends emerge if subgroup differences are temporarily ignored. Both sexes are decidedly on the negative side for Question 1 (women holding men's jobs), with boys about one scale point lower than girls. Both sexes are on the positive side for Question 2 (how women see the world) with boys slightly positive and girls about 1.5 points higher. On the third question (whether women should work) most of the girls are mildly positive, boys are consistently negative, and almost two points separate them.

As a group, black boys appear more liberal in their attitudes toward women than whites, but this stems from a social-class-related willingness for women to work that is shared by inner-city whites. Social class, not race, was associated with willingness for women to work and probably reflects the need in high poverty areas for women to work in order to achieve subsistence.

Surprisingly, the relatively most liberal views on women holding men's jobs are expressed by high-IQ blue-collar white students of both sexes, but the boys' score (3.05) indicates opposition nonetheless. Middle-class white boys are even more conservative on this issue, and about two points lower than middle-class girls. For those girls most able to be upwardly mobile occupationally (high-IQ white), then, there is potential negative peer-group pressure by mates, because boys are much more traditional in views they express about women's working and what jobs women should hold. As this question was expressed, the jobs are "leaders in politics, the professions, and business," the presumed vocational targets of the high-IQ white middle-class males. That blue-collar boys of high IQ express a slightly more liberal view than middle-class boys toward women holding "men's" jobs (3.05 *vs* 2.23) has already been noted, but perhaps this is because the jobs listed are somewhat unrealistic in terms of the vocational aspirations of blue-collar students. Thus, to imagine a woman holding such a job may not be personally threatening, nor even be conceived by blue-collar boys in terms of their own girl classmates holding such jobs.

The differences in sex-role orientation by social class so frequently cited, blue collar being more conservative than middle class, are seen in the present data more for girls than for boys. Girls from the various residential groups are very different—blue-collar girls have views close to the views of their male classmates. The middle-class girls, on the other hand, hold the most favorable views toward women working of any group of girls, and this view is markedly discrepant (3.67 points) from that of their male classmates.

The favorable attitudes of blacks towards women holding jobs may be a direct consequence of their being socialized in families with female heads, or in families where two wage earners are required to achieve subsistence. Work expectations for blacks are not coupled with a desire to see women in positions of leadership, even though blacks generally are a little more favorable toward this idea than whites.

Adolescent girls' sex-role behaviors probably conflict with goals of high-school achievement in two major respects: a) role behaviors for girls do not emphasize, and in some cases devalue, school achievement (the "blue stocking" image) ; b) to compete for grades a girl must express aggressive tendencies—a masculine image—and express these tendencies *against* her male classmates. Since a very effective way for boys to reduce competition and thereby to increase their own likelihood of obtaining good grades is to invoke sanctions against girls who achieve, and since these sanctions at adolescence can be phrased in terms of other, more central, female achievement values (physical attractiveness, dating, and so on), the academically achieving girl is working against strong odds. There is evidence in the data reported here of potential pressure against middle-class girls' academic achievement in the strong conservative views of their male classmates.

The development of young people in terms of occupational roles is one of the least studied aspects of the entire socialization process. Borow suggests that this is because occupational phenomena have been examined mostly when they are explicit and within the formal setting of work itself—the overt choice of an occupation or overt performance on a job by adults.[2] Social patterns now formally exclude youth from early labor force participation. Younger persons are not studied, then, because it is impossible to study them in the institutional context of work. The lack of research, however, does not mean that occupational developments are not occurring or that they are unimportant.

The present data suggest that the occupational aspirations of females may be subject to considerable shaping by peer-group pressure. One wonders what the longitudinal course of these pressures may be. At what age are they first apparent? At later ages are the differences of opinion between the sexes smaller or larger? Some evidence suggests that differences continue to increase as age increases.[3]

Some of the issues raised here are important for education. In many respects, the educational system through college pretends to prepare males and females for the same occupational roles, but these roles are not scripted in the society at large. Davis,[4] after a review of what little is written on this topic, suggests that women's role in America is "properly" that of domesticity and child rearing, with the implication that careers for women are both difficult and ill-advised. Many persons have noted that women seldom achieve eminence, even in traditionally feminine fields. This failure has its most appealing explanation in terms of role congruence, for modern American society seems to be intolerant of the intellectually aspiring or intellectually achieving woman, and devalues the role of women generally. Role incompatibility as an explanation for women's lack of eminence is suggested by such findings as Milton's.[5] He notes that a sex difference in problem-solving, often viewed as the sphere of men exclusively, is abolished when problems are expressed in terms that are role-compatible. Specifically, girls' performance is better on problems that involve objects or activities traditionally considered to fall in the female domain than on problems that require exactly the same reasoning processes but mention more "male" objects.

Many have noted that the educational system is not functionally attuned to the needs of society in terms of preparing women for work roles (see, e.g., Komarovsky).[6] The issues are far too numerous and complex even to raise in a small study of this kind, but the data suggest that present socialization practices are leading to large differences in males' and females' conceptions of female work roles. Furthermore the sex discrepancies in work expectations are greatest in the very groups that may produce females with high occupational aspirations and the ability to implement these aspirations.

REFERENCES

Borow, H. 1968. Development of occupational motives and roles. In *Review of child development research,* vol. 2, eds. L. Hoffman and M. Hoffman. New York: Russell Sage Foundation.

Davis, A. 1969. Women as a minority group in higher education. *American sociology* 4: 95.

Komarovsky, M. 1946. Cultural contradictions and sex roles. *American journal of sociology* 52: 184.

Milton, G. 1957. The effects of sex-role identification upon problem-solving skill. *Journal of abnormal social psychiatry* 55: 208.

Stein, A., and Smithells, J. 1969. Age and sex differences in children's sex-role standards about achievement. *Developmental psychology* 1: 252.

NOTES

1. This research was supported by funds from the United States Office of Education, Department of Health, Education, and Welfare to the Center for Social Organization of Schools, The Johns Hopkins University. Grant no. OEG–2–7–061610–0207, Project no. 61610–03–04.
2. H. Borow, "Development of occupational motives and roles," in *Review of Child Development Research,* vol. 2, ed. L. Hoffman and M. Hoffman (New York: Russell Sage, 1068).
3. A. Stein and J. Smithells, "Age and Sex Differences in Children's Sex-role Standards about Achievement," *Developmental Psychology* 1: 252.
4. A. Davis, "Women as a Minority Group in Higher Academics," *American Sociology* 4: 95.
5. G. Milton, "The Effects of Sex-role Identification upon Problem-solving Skill," *Journal of Abnormal Social Psychiatry* 55: 208.
6. M. Komarovsky, "Cultural Contradictions and Sex Roles," *American Journal of Sociology* 52: 184.

Counseling

In his *Autobiography,* Malcolm X defines the very moment when he turned against white American society. It was when he told his high-school counselor that he was thinking of becoming a lawyer. His counselor replied:

> "Malcolm, one of life's first needs is for us to be realistic. A lawyer —that's no realistic goal for a nigger. You need to think about something you *can* be. Why don't you plan on carpentry?"
>
> The more I thought afterwards about what he said, the more uneasy it made me. It just kept treading around in my mind.
>
> It was a surprising thing that I never thought of it that way before, but I realized that whatever I wasn't, I *was* smarter than nearly all those white kids. But apparently I was still not intelligent enough, in their eyes, to become what I wanted to be.
>
> It was then that I began to change—inside.[1]

Inept counseling can have many consequences: Malcolm X is an extreme case. But in a one-to-one situation, where the pervading note is one of intimacy and care for the individual, a vocational rebuff can insult and damage a student's spirit. John F. Pietrofesa and Nancy K. Schlossberg, in "Counselor Bias and the Female Occupational Role," stated that although counselors purport to treat girls' and boys' vocational aims equally, in practice they do not.

Counselors, both male and female, are biased against women entering "masculine" jobs. The less "masculine" the job is, the less biased are the counselors against women occupying this job. Different reasons were given to the girls stating why they shouldn't enter "masculine" jobs: family reasons, working conditions, educational preparation, and so on. Interestingly, some counselors were biased in favor of women working in certain areas, and almost all of these counselors were women.

Ann Steinmann, in "Female Role Perception as a Factor in Counseling," points out the scarcity of counseling regarding women's working roles. Girls are unable to plan their future working lives as best they could because their ideas on marriage and work seem to be drawn almost entirely from their parents. Counselors must fill the gaps between students' ideas of self, their parents' attitudes toward work, and the structure of society.

William C. Bingham and Elaine W. House's study, "Counselors View Women and Work: Accuracy of Information," shows that secondary-school counselors harbor misinformation about women's work-roles. Only forty-eight percent of the items were marked correctly by the respondents. Women counselors were better informed as to women's work-roles than were male counselors, significantly so on twenty-eight percent of the items. The authors suggest that counselors' incorrect answers may be based on negative attitudes rather than on misinformation.

Bingham and House's later study, "Counselors' Attitudes Toward Women and Work," found that male, secondary-school counselors had more negative attitudes than did female counselors. Sex differences were present on twenty-two percent of the items, with the most widely divergent opinions shown on the subjects of whether there is a "place in modern American society for upwardly mobile women" and whether "the most important function of women is being 'mother'." Male counselors gave many negative answers even when, in general, they replied positively. The authors conclude that this type of counselor ambiguity may leave the girls they counsel confused as to their position.

Carol Kehr Tittle, Karen McCarthy, and Jane Faggen Steckler's "Women and Educational Testing," finds that the language usage (nouns and pronouns) of the most frequently used achievement tests included, in general, far more male than female references. When analyzed for sex-role stereotyping of activities, achievement tests closely parallel other school curriculum in showing women's and girls' narrow interests and limited activities.

The authors note that at least two million students take either the CEEB or the ACTP tests each year, and that these tests (and the counselor's guide that accompany them) are sex-biased in favor of males. Tittle, McCarthy, and Steckler suggest specific methods that the test publishers can utilize in order to present a more equitable view of girls and women.

Title IX will mandate changes in achievement tests and vocational tests. Tittle's article has pointed out how easily achievement tests can be amended for a more equitable presentation of males and females. Vocational tests will also have to be amended: boys and girls should receive the same tests. For example, the Strong vocational test should be changed to add the careers of school superintendent and psychiatrist to girls' options and to add the careers of elementary schoolteacher and actor to the boys' options.

There is also a manifest need for better undergraduate and graduate training in counseling. Courses that discuss developmental sex differences should be mandatory, and the changing image of women, both psychological and occupational, should be stressed. Training would have to be extensive in order to combat the subtle and unconscious attitudes present regarding sex-appropriate behavior.

Counselors are shown in these selections to be vocationally inept sources of negative attitudes and misinformation for schoolgirls. Counselors' own bias toward the proper role of women in society seems to be a major criteria for how they advise students. Male counselors, especially, may have a more deleterious effect on the girls whom they counsel.

Counselors must be retrained with an increased sensitivity to the scope of women's options. Since counselors are precisely the schoolpeople who should be without prejudice regarding students' vocational choices, it is ironic that they display bias. In fact, counselors should be in the forefront of fighting school sexism. Counselors in particular should be the professionals helping to make aware and to change classroom teachers' own sex-typed attitudes.

NOTES

1. Malcolm X., *The Autobiography of Malcolm X* (New York: Grove Press, Inc., 1966), p. 36–37.

Counselor Bias and the Female Occupational Role*

JOHN J. PIETROFESA and
NANCY K. SCHLOSSBERG

INTRODUCTION

Even though a large percentage of women work, and a large percentage of workers are women, the startling fact is the decline in their position in recent years. For example:

> There are nearly twenty-eight million female workers in 1966 representing over one-third of the country's work force, and yet "women are concentrated to a considerable extent in low-skilled, low-paid jobs" and "their representation among professional workers has actually declined from 40 percent in 1950 to 37 percent in 1966.[1]

Furthermore, women receive proportionately fewer Master's degrees and Doctorates today than in the 1920s, and women hold proportionately fewer technical and professional positions today than in 1940[2] and in 1967.[3] Complicating the picture is the fact that each sex occupies different levels on the status hierarchy and the sexes are unevenly distributed as to field of endeavor. It has been substantiated that

---

* John J. Pietrofesa and Nancy K. Schlossberg, "Counselor Bias and the Female Occupational Role." Reprinted with permission of John J. Pietrofesa and Nancy K. Schlossberg. This article was originally presented at the 1970 Annual Meeting of the American Educational Research Association.

> American education is blighted by a sex-split in its curriculum. At present the whole field of knowledge is divided along tacit but well-understood sex lines. Those subjects given the highest status in American life are "masculine"; those given the lowest are "feminine" . . . thus math, the sciences . . . business administration . . . are men's subjects . . . and the humanities are relegated . . . "suitable to women."[4]

> Furthermore, women receive lower salaries than their male counterparts. In 1965 women employed full-time had a median wage of $3,800 in contrast to nearly $6,400 for men.[5]

> Discrimination in the world of work can be easily seen when one examines the number of women in certain high-status fields. For example, only 208 are women listed among the 6,597 members of the American Institute of Physics. One-half of the women are employed as physics teachers. Of the 600,000 people classified as in engineering and related technical fields, only 6,000 are women. About seven percent of chemists, three percent of all dentists, and four percent of the doctors are women[6].

This unbalanced occupational distribution of the sexes is easy to understand when one considers legislation like the Vocational Education Act that reflects and reinforces the cultural bias against women by providing training for girls, but in the traditional areas of dental assistant, licensed practical nurse, and hairdresser.

As counselor educators, our concern deals with the degree to which counselors aid and abet this situation.

PROBLEM

Since many high-school and college women discuss their choice of major and occupation with counselors, the question arises—what do counselors feel the role of women should be? In discussing this question with counselors-in-training, they voice a partial egalitarian view—women should do whatever they want to do. Since actions speak louder than words, it was decided to study actual interviews of counselors-in-training with a female client who was deciding between a "feminine" and "masculine" occupational role. The assumption was that through careful analysis of verbatim interviews, the degree of counselor bias would be revealed. Thus, this study was conceived as an investigation of the counselor's bias in the total process of role-stereotyping of women. If counselors do display bias, the ramifications of such a fact would have to be taken into account in counselor-education programs.

METHOD

Introduction

In order to test the hypothesis that counselors are biased against women entering a "masculine" occupation, the investigators arranged interviews between counselor trainees in the counseling practicum at Wayne State University [Detroit] and a coached female counselee. During the counseling session, the counselee informed the counselor that she was a transfer student to Wayne State University, that she was entering her junior year of college and could not decide whether to enter the field of engineering, a "masculine" occupation, or enter the field of education, a "feminine" occupation.

Each interview was tape recorded. At the end of the interview the counselor was informed that the counselee had been coached and that the sessions and tapes were to be used for a research study. Counselors were informed not to mention their interviews to other counselors. After all counselors had conducted interviews, a brief discussion was held among the counselor group concerning their feelings about the counseling sessions. No other information was given to the counselors.

The Subjects

The subjects (counselors) in the study were students in the practicum, fall and winter quarters, 1968–1969. The counselor group, then, consisted of twenty-nine people, i.e., sixteen males and thirteen females.

The Procedure

The tapes were reviewed and tabulated as to their bias by a male graduate student in guidance and counseling, a male counselor-educator with a solid background in counseling practicum, and a female college professor, former school psychologist with a research specialty. Frequencies and percentages were calculated and chi square was then used in a variety of configurations. The final stage of the project involved a content analysis of all biased statements.

The raters designated a counselor's statement as biased or prejudicial against the female counselee when she expressed interest in the "masculine" field and the counselor rejected this interest in favor of the "feminine" vocation. Statements of rejection then included disapproval of the female counselee's desire to enter the "masculine" field—comments that implied disadvantages in entering that field, etc. A counselor's statement was considered biased for the female counselee when she expressed interest in the masculine occupation and the counselor supported or reinforced this expressed interest. Statement of positive bias toward females included direct approval to statements that subtlely implied advantages in entering the masculine field.

RESULTS AND DISCUSSION

The results of this study indicated that counselor bias exists against women entering a masculine occupation. (*See* Tables 1 and 2.)

The data suggest that counselors do hold bias against women entering a so-called masculine occupation. Female counselors, interestingly enough, displayed as much bias as did their male counterparts. The results tend to suggest that male and female counselors both display more statements "biased against females" than "biased for females." The three ratings combined showed a significant difference at the .01 level of confidence. Percentage results strongly reinforce the conclusion that counselors are biased. against women entering masculine fields. Of the total bias statements, 81.3% are against women, whereas only 18.7% are biased for women. The tables, containing percentages, further demonstrate quite vividly the disparity between bias for and bias against females.

A content analysis of the seventy-nine biased statements made by the counselors in this study reveals that most negatively biased statements emphasized the masculinity of the field. (*See* Table 3.) Working conditions and promotional opportunity were a far second and third.

Out of a total of seventy-nine items classified by content analysis as biased statements, only five were positive and most of those were made by women. Thus, the pressures against women working in a field stereotyped as masculine were prevalent among this group.

In order to tabulate the statements, ten categories were devised so that negative bias (NB) and positive bias (PB) statements could be classified as to content. The following examples of bias statements will give the flavor of the kinds of pressures counselors imposed.

Salary—Amount of monetary return

(NB) "Money isn't everything."
(PB) "You could make much more money as an engineer."

Status—Perception of self in vocation

(NB) "The status of a woman is higher in the field of teaching."
(PB) "There is more prestige in becoming an engineer."

Marriage and Family—Family Attachment

(NB) "Would your husband resent you being an engineer?"

(NB) "You would only be gone from home during school hours if you taught school."
(PB) "Being an engineer would not interfere with you becoming married."

Parents—Parental Support

(NB) "How do your parents feel about you entering engineering instead of education?"
(PB) "I am glad your parents want you to become an engineer."

Educational Time—Amount of time necessary for preparation to enter the vocational field.

(NB) "Engineering would take five years and elementary education would be four years. . . . These are things you might want to consider."
(PB) "It may take longer to become an engineer but it is well worth it."

Educational Preparation—Classes one must take to enter the field and the kinds of classes already taken.

(NB) "The course work in engineering would be very difficult."
(PB) "Your classwork up to now shows that you would do well as an engineer."

Promotional Opportunities—Advancement in position

(NB) "There might be a holding of you back because you are a woman."
(PB) "Your chances of promotion would be good in engineering."

Hiring—Opportunity to enter field

(NB) "They are not supposed to discriminate against women, but they still get around it."
(PB) "The opportunities for a woman in engineering are good."

Working Conditions—Where, with whom, what kind of work, and/or under what conditions work is done.

(NB) "Engineering . . . it is very, you know, technical, and very, I could use the term 'unpeopled'."
(PB) "You could work at a relaxed pace as an engineer."

Masculine Occupation—Identification of occupation as masculine

(NB) "You normally think of this as a man's field."
(PB) "There is no such thing as a man's world anymore."

IMPLICATIONS

Hopefully, counselors would not reflect in their interaction with their female counselees the prejudices and biases of the larger society. Counselors should be made aware of sex biases entering into the process. Westervelt wrote:

> Male counselors and student counselors who express the conviction that women's primary and socially essential roles are domestic and maternal and take place in the home may be reflecting a covert need to keep them there. Girls and women in the lower socioeconomic brackets who particularly need counseling help to recognize and plan for paid employment—will get little assistance from such counselors. Nor, of course, will these counselors help intellectually and educationally privileged girls to use their gifts and training to best advantage. . . .
>
> No formal, university sponsored, graduate-level, degree-awarding program in counselor education requires even a one-semester course in social and psychological sex differences that affect development or provides any focus on sex differences in a practicum or internship in counseling. . . .
>
> The trends toward the integration into counselor education, at basic levels, of more subject matter from social psychology, anthropology, sociology, and economics would also provide more exposure to materials on psychosocial sex differences and changing sex roles. Again, however, the effect of such exposure will depend on the student's initial sympathetic interest, since the material will be only a small part of a much larger whole.[7]

Westervelt makes reference to the role, and moreso, the importance of the practicum in the training of counselors:

> Counselors, guidance workers, and student-personnel workers who are planning to work chiefly with girls and women should have as many opportunities as possible to counsel with females—and, ideally, with females of all ages, in order that, no matter what the age level with which they eventually work, they get an opportunity to observe at first-hand the patterns of continuity and discontinuity in feminine development. Counseling experience should not, however, be limited to working with females; opportunity to counsel with boys and men is most important, both because it will provide insights into psychosocial sex differences and because it will provide a chance to explore useful variations in approaches to counseling the two sexes. All counselors-in-training should be helpful to identify, understand, and work with sex differences in their counseling practicum or internship. . . . There is a need for practice or field-work programs in educational/vocational counseling that will focus on this kind of counseling with adults (men as well as women, of course).[8]

The implications of the study are quite clear—counselors, both male and female, hold biases against female counselees entering an occupation characteristically associated with males. Counselor-education programs must take this into account and attempt to bring into the open such biased feelings, so that counselors are able to control them, or better yet, remove them from their counseling and human encounters.

SUMMARY

This study attempted to determine if counselors, both male and female, are biased against women entering what is considered a "masculine" occupation. Counseling sessions were arranged between counselor trainees and a coached female counselee. Counseling tapes were analyzed by a (1) graduate student in counselor education. (2) male counselor-educator with extensive supervisory background in the practicum and (3) female professor with a research background.

The following conclusions may be drawn:

1. Counselors display more bias against female counselees than for females entering a so-called masculine occupation.
2. Female counselors display as much bias against females as their male counselor counterparts.
3. Content analysis of bias statements indicate that major stress is placed upon the "masculinity" of the occupation.

Women should have an equal opportunity to compete in the world of work with their male counterparts. Yet discriminatory practices still exist. Further, subtle pressures and influences against entering so-called masculine occupations by parents, as well as teachers and counselors, may do more harm than discriminatory practices by employers. Self-fulfillment for women is not an insubstantial and irrational dream; it can be achieved.

Table 1

Classification of Biased Comments For and Against Women Entering the "Masculine" Occupation of Engineering

(All Raters Combined)

Group	Bias For Women	Bias Against Women	Total Bias Statements
Males	6	62	68
Females	22	60	82
	28	122	150

$X^2 = 7.94$ (Significant at the .01 level of confidence.)

Table 2

Percentage of Total Biased Statements For and Against Women Entering the Occupation of Engineering

(All Raters Combined)

Percentages

Group	Bias For Women	Bias Against Women
Males	4.0	41.3
Females	14.7	40.0
Total	18.7	81.3

Table 3

Content Analysis of Negative and Positive Bias Statements*

	Female Negative	Male Negative	Female Positive	Male Positive	Total
Salary	1	0	1	0	2
Status	1	0	0	0	1
Marriage and Family	1	2	0	0	3
Parents	0	2	0	0	2
Educational Time	2	2	0	0	4
Educational Preparation	0	2	0	0	2
Promotional Opportunity	1	4	0	0	5
Hiring	0	3	0	0	3
Working Conditions	6	3	0	0	9
Masculine Occupation	16	28	3	1	48
Total	28	46	4	1	79

* Not all statements were classifiable and several were appropriate to more than one division.

SELECTED REFERENCES

Berelson, B. R. 1954. Content analysis. In *Handbook of social psychology*, vol. 1, ed. G. Lindzey, Reading, Mass.: Addison-Wesley.

Cassara, B. 1962. *American women: the changing image*. Boston: Beacon Press.

Manpower Report of the President. 1967. Washington, D. C.: Department of Labor.

Millett, K. 1968. *Token learning: a study of women's higher education in America*. New York: National Organization for Women.

Stone, D. J. 1966. *The general inquirer: a computer approach to content analysis.* Cambridge, Mass.: Massachusetts Institute of Technology Press.

Westervelt, E. 1963. The recruitment and training of educational/vocational counselors of girls and women. Background paper for Subcommittee on Counseling, President's Commission of the Status of Women.

NOTES

1. Manpower Report of the President (Washington, D. C.: Department of Labor, 1967), p. 133.
2. K. Millett, *Token Learning: A Study of Women's Higher Education in America* (New York: National Organization for Women, 1968), p. 8.
3. Manpower Report, p. 133.
4. Millett, p. 14.
5. Manpower Report, p. 133.
6. B. Cassara, *American Women: The Changing Image* (Boston: The Beacon Press, 1962), p. 77.
7. E. Westervelt, "The Recruitment and Training of Educational/Vocational Counselors of Girls and Women," background paper for the Subcommittee on Counseling, President's Commission of the Status of Women, pp. 21–22.
8. Westervelt, pp. 26–28.

Female-role Perception as a Factor in Counseling*

Anne Steinmann

According to the *Wall Street Journal* of 16 September 1969, guidance counselors pay "little or no attention" to job-oriented high-school students. Counseling has been employed almost solely for academic purposes, while youngsters who do not plan to go to college are ignored. This problem is particularly acute with regard to the counseling of young women.

Although women now enjoy an unprecedented number of opportunities for careers, it appears that these opportunities produce severe conflicts for many of them. There is considerable evidence to suggest that women feel they must choose, at an early age, between a career and a family, between self-realization and home-orientation.[1] The idea has been advanced that the reason women experience conflict and confusion in deciding what to do as adults is that as a result of the many social and psychological changes that have taken place in a very short time, there exists no explicit definition of the female role.[2]

In counseling young women, especially in high school and junior high school, special attention must be paid to the issue of conflict between young women's perceptions of their roles as homemakers and career women. Steinmann administered an inventory of female values to a sample of college women and found that the young women desired a balance between intra- and extra-familial activities.[3] They felt they were able to do both, but they thought an "ideal" woman would be more home-oriented than self-assertive. They felt, even more strongly, that an ideal woman, as men see her, would stay at home and raise children.

These findings have been confirmed in studies both in the United States[4] and abroad.[5] Irrespective of age, marital status, race, education, or socioeconomic status, women seem to be ambivalent with respect to home and career. It is incumbent upon counselors to identify this problem at an early age and to help young women make appropriate choices in resolving it. Unlike the counselor of a generation ago, whose basic role was to advise students about curriculum, counselors must now be able to grasp the nature of the intrapsychic conflicts of students. This task is particularly urgent in counseling young women, and since role conflicts are so prevalent, the need for early counseling in school is especially urgent. Without such help, women are likely to experience frustration in whatever role they ultimately choose.[6]

It is important to look closely at the responses given by women on inventories of female values. What factors are responsible for women choosing a career? Why do women believe that an ideal woman is home-oriented? What influence do men's attitudes have on women's behavior? These, and other questions pertaining to female-role perception, must be answered if counselors are to deal successfully with problems presented by young women. Although it was previously held that only married women in particular circumstances suffered from ambivalence about their roles,[7] Steinmann demonstrated that the problem is almost universal.[8]

In an attempt to uncover the bases for the responses given by women on inventories of female values, an investigation was undertaken with a group of college women. It was felt that their ability to articulate feelings would provide insight into the pattern of responses discussed above.

METHOD AND SUBJECTS

The instrument used in this investigation was the *Inventory of Feminine Values.* It consists of thirty-four statements, each of which expresses a particular value related to women's activities and satisfactions. Agreement or disagreement is indicated on a five-point scale, ranging from "completely agree" to "completely disagree," through a midpoint of "I have no opinion." Items are sometimes worded positively, sometimes negatively, to avoid the influence of response sets.[9]

Of the 34 statements, 17 provide the respondent the opportunity to delineate a family-oriented woman, while the other 17 delineate a self-achieving woman. The score on the inventory represents the difference in strength of agreement with the 17 family-oriented and 17 self-achieving items.

Three forms of the inventory were used, the first requiring subjects to respond in terms of how they themselves felt. On a second administration, subjects were asked to respond as they thought their ideal woman would respond. Finally, they were asked to respond as they thought men would want women to respond.

Some of the items reflect women's feelings about being assertive; for instance: "I argue against people who try to assert their authority over me." Another example of this kind of item: "I would rather not marry than sacrifice some of my essential beliefs and needs in order to adjust to another person." Another set of statements samples women's feelings about being skillful at whatever they try; for example, "A woman who works cannot possibly be as good a mother as the one who stays at home, even though the child may go to school." Also, "I believe that a capable woman has the duty to be active in a field of endeavor outside the home." Some of the statements assess the degree of rivalry between husband's and wife's achievements: "Unless single, women should not crave personal success, but be satisfied with their husband's achievements." Again, "It is unfair that women are obliged to compromise their personal goals and ideas for the sake of a good marital relationship, more than men are."

The subjects in this study were 51 young women enrolled in sociology courses at a liberal arts college in a suburb of New York City. All subjects were between 17 and 22 years of age, and unmarried. They had all received guidance at the high-school or junior-high-school level. All could be considered middle class, according to the occupations of their fathers. Both fathers and mothers of the young women were interviewed intensively regarding their feelings on women working, as well as their own experiences in this respect. Most of the parents were high-school graduates, between 45 and 54 years of age. All the men were employed, while 41 of the mothers were housewives. Of the ten women who were working, three had professional occupations, two worked in industry, and five had white-collar positions. The responses given by parents were compared with those of their daughters in order to study the relationship between parents' attitudes and those of their children.

FINDINGS

In the present sample of college women, although all were prepared for high-level employment, most did not feel that working was important in their lives. Of the 51 subjects, 35 indicated that they might work after marriage, but 20 of these 35 stated that they would work only if their husbands needed financial assistance in order to support the family. Of the 15 young women who listed self-expression as one of the reasons for working, only 8 considered it the primary reason. Twice this number were certain that they would not work after marriage. The modal attitude is illustrated in the following interview:

Q. Would you want to work before you had children?
A. Yes, I would, just to get settled. If you are financially set, you can start raising your family right away. If not, I think you should set up a home and the right kind of place to raise children.
Q. Would you work after you had children?
A. Not for a long time. Not until they had started school. I would never leave them at an early age.
Q. Would you consider working even if you didn't need the money?
A. No, if I didn't need the money I wouldn't.

Most of the young women surveyed were willing to sacrifice a career for a family. They did not indicate that having a family satisfied their need for self-expression. Instead, they seemed to view the responsibility of raising children as a *fait accompli*. Most of the subjects placed the interests of their families above their own.

In trying to discover the reasons for this set of attitudes, a survey of mothers was taken, which indicated that most of them believed that working after marriage was a tremendous burden. The two reasons cited most often by mothers were the difficulties of raising children and the husband's objections to having a working wife. Both reasons were stated with approximately equal frequency, by about two-thirds of the mothers. An illustration of the typical attitude expressed by the mothers is the following excerpt from an interview:

Q. Did you ever think of working outside the home?
A. I have often thought of it.
Q. Did you ever work?
A. Yes, a long time ago, for economic reasons.
Q. Why did you stop?
A. Too many responsibilities at home.
Q. Did it affect your family?
A. In order to work, I had to leave my child with my parents, which was a burden to family and child.

In some cases, the women were deterred from working largely by their husbands' attitudes, for example:

Q. What do you think of working wives?
A. I think a woman's place is in the home. If she has to help out earning a living, then it is okay.
Q. Have you ever thought of working outside the home?
A. Well, I didn't when the children were little, but even now my husband doesn't believe in it.

Only three mothers in the entire sample did not object to women working after children had arrived. All three expressed the belief that it was essential for a woman to keep up her vocational activities because they made her a more stimulating person. However, the emphasis was on being a good wife or mother, not being self-assertive. These women also had the support of their husbands with regard to working.

Although there appeared to be considerable regret among the mothers about their own unfulfilled potential, over two-thirds felt that their daughters should not work after having children. One mother, when asked if she would live her life differently if given a second chance, expressed ambivalence between the desire to express herself and her feeling of devotion to family:

Q. On the basis of your experience as a mother, would you pattern life differently if you had a chance?
A. In a sense, yes. But if you mean would I have married and raised a family, yes, I would. But I would have turned my talent in many directions. Unfortunately, I frittered it away. But my husband thinks I have talent for making a home, so it worked out.

Among fathers, the most common attitude was that women should not work after marriage, until the children are grown. Ten of the fathers believed women should not work at all. Only three fathers felt it was not harmful to the children for a woman to work. It is interesting to note that the wives of these men are the three women who believed work is essential because it makes a woman more stimulating. The more prevalent attitude among the fathers was expressed by the following man:

Q. How do you feel about mothers working?
A. So long as there are no children, it's good to get out and do something or she just works for her husband and home. But married women with children, that's different. No one can give growing children more care than the mother. After the children grow up, if she still has the interest, she can go back.

Of the 16 young women who said they definitely would not work after marriage, 9 had fathers who felt that women should not work at all after marriage. There appears to be a definite relationship between the attitudes of fathers and those of their daughters with regard to women working. The relationship is not quite as clear in the case of mothers. Most of the mothers actually had worked at some time or other during marriage, but it was a result of financial need, and they experienced working as a hardship. At the same time, they seemed to feel that they had not achieved as much in their lives as they would have liked to.

The notions held by young women regarding work and family seem to reflect both the views and the actions of their parents. Characteristically, the young women adopt the view that they are capable of working and raising a family at the same time. This probably reflects, to a large extent, their mothers' unfulfilled aspirations in terms of working. However, most young women do not feel working is important in their lives, which most likely reflects their mothers' experiences with work and the difficulties involved in doing so. When the young women assert that an ideal woman would be home-oriented, they seem to be expressing the views of their fathers. In most of the families in this study, fathers felt that children would suffer if mothers worked. In some cases, however, the men seemed threatened by having a working wife. A few of the men expressed their apprehension about women being taken advantage of in the business world. Several others indicated a fear that their wives would achieve more than they did.

Among the eight young women who listed self-expression as a primary reason for working, five had fathers who were apparently threatened by the prospect of their wives working. Possibly, the young women sensed the feelings of inadequacy underlying their fathers' assertions about women not working. It would be interesting to know what kinds of choices these young women make for husbands. If they are simply reacting to the views held by their fathers, they may choose men who frown on women working. If, however, they actually feel a desire to work, they may choose husbands who encourage this feeling.

IMPLICATIONS FOR COUNSELORS

Most young women in educational settings are unaware of the problems they will face with respect to work and family. They may be intellectually acquainted with the issue, but have no idea of the sources of their views, or how to plan their actions in order to minimize frustration. Here, the role of counselors is extremely important. The choices made by young women at a comparatively early age largely determine the course of their lives. This is especially true for young women who bear children, perhaps illegitimately, when they are young, and who must spend ten years receiving welfare aid, in the home, often without a husband. The problem also exists for college women, who may develop interests and aspirations that an early marriage, producing children, thwarts. It is imperative that counselors help young women be fully aware of the difficulties they will face in raising a family and pursuing a career.

Evidence from the present study suggests strongly that counselors must consider the potential life-style of young women clients against the background of the views and life-styles of their parents. Parents' attitudes represent both a direction and a limitation for young women. Every young woman must be helped to make an early start at assessing her own needs and measuring these needs in relation to the environment. Some girls may harbor illusions about careers, the result of shortsightedness with regard to bearing children. Others may want children too soon, before being able to exercise mature judgment on the matter. The counselor must probe the roots of these problems and must help clients plan realistically for their solution.

If, for one reason or another, a woman is forced to suppress her need for self-expression, she will experience a loss of self-esteem; she will become less effectual in all spheres of her life. For a woman to obtain gratification in her life, she must continually develop deep reservoirs of intellectual and spiritual strength. Counselors must encourage this development, but in order to do so, they must be aware of their own attitudes and feelings about women's roles. A study by Steinmann, Fox, and Farkas revealed that men as well as women suffer from discrepancies between what they are and what they would like to be, or what they think they should be.[10] Unless men resolve their problems, including their feelings about what women should do, they will be unable, as counselors, husbands, or fathers, to help women decide what to do with their lives.

The problem of counseling young women is complicated by the circumstances in which they live. Many are victimized by prejudices regarding birth control, by racial prejudice, and by prejudice against women as workers. The issue of the *Wall Street Journal* cited at the outset mentions an instance of a large Dallas company that lost its first female management trainee to marriage. A high executive of that company said: "Don't even talk to me about bringing more women into our training program." In addition to helping young women plan at an early age for the problems they will face working and raising a family, all individuals concerned with this problem must continually stress the need for universal, free day care. Ultimately, only this will give women the opportunity to choose freely between home and career.

REFERENCES

Brammer, L. M., and Shostrom, E. L. 1960. *Therapeutic psychology: fundamentals of counseling and psychotherapy*. Englewood Cliffs, N. J.: Prentice-Hall.

Couch, A., and Keniston, K. 1960. Yeasayers and naysayers: agreeing response set as a personality variable. *Journal of abnormal and social psychology:* 60.

Commission on the Education of Women, American Council on Education. 1954. *Plan for a study of american women as individuals*. Washington D. C.: the Commission.

Kluckhohn, F. 1954. Dominant and variant value orientation. *Personality in nature, society, and culture*. Edited by C. K. Kluckhohn and H. A. Murray. New York: Alfred A. Knopf.

Kluckhohn, F. 1955. *How fare american women?* Washington, D. C.: Commission on the Education of Women. American Council on Education, 10 April 1955.

Parsons, T. 1954. Age and sex in the social structure of the United States. *Personality in nature, society, and culture*. New York: Alfred A. Knopf.

Steinmann, A. 1963. A study of the concept of the feminine role of 51 middle-class American women. *Genetic psychology monographs* 67: 275–352.

Steinmann, A. 1966. Guidance personnel and the college woman. *Personnel journal* 45: 294–99.

Steinmann, A. 1968. The counselor: a guide for the misbegotten. Paper presented at "Counseling Girls in Vocational and Life Opportunities: A Conference." Los Angeles: University of California Extension. Downtown Center. March 1968.

Steinmann, A., and Fox, D. J. 1966. Male-female perceptions of the female role in England, France, Greece, Japan, Turkey, and the United States: a cross-cultural study. *International mental health research newsletter* 8: 7–8, 13–16.

Steinmann, A.; Fox, D. J.; and Farkas, R. 1968. Male and female perceptions of male sex-roles. *Proceedings of the 76th annual convention of the American psychological association*, 1968, pp. 421–22.

Steinmann, A.; Fox, D. J.; and Levi, J. 1965. Specific areas of agreement and conflict in women's self-perceptions and their perceptions of men's ideal woman in the United States, Peru, and Argentina. *International mental health research newsletter* 7: 1–4.

Steinmann, A.; Levi, J.; and Fox, D. J. 1964. Self-concept of college women compared with their concept of ideal woman and men's ideal woman. *Journal of counseling psychology* 11: 330–74.

NOTES

1. Commission on the Education of Women, American Council on Education, *Plan for a Study of American Women as Individuals* (Washington, D. C.: the Commission, 1954) ; F. Kluckhorn, "Dominant and Variant Value Orientation," in *Personality in Nature, Society, and Culture*, ed. C. K. Kluckhorn and H. A. Murray (New York: Alfred A. Knopf, 1954); and F. Kluckhorn, *How Fare American Women?* (Washington, D. C.: Commission on the Education of Women, American Council on Education, 10 April 1955) .
2. T. Parsons, "Age and Sex in the Social Structure of the United States," in *Personality in Nature, Society, and Culture*, ed. C. K. Kluckhorn and H. A. Murray (New York: Alfred A. Knopf, 1954) .
3. A. Steinmann, "A Study of the Concept of the Feminine Role of 51 Middle-class American Women," *Genetic Psychology Monographs* 67 (1963) : 275–352.
4. A. Steinmann, J. Levi, and D. J. Fox, "Self-concept of College Women Compared with Their Concept of Ideal Woman and Men's Ideal Woman," *Journal of Counseling Psychology* 11 (1964) : 370–74.
5. A. Steinmann and D. J. Fox, "Male-female Perceptions of the Female Role in England, France, Greece, Japan, Turkey, and the United States: a Cross-cultural Study," *International Mental Health Research Newsletter* 8 (1966): 7–8, 13–16; and A. Steinmann, D. J. Fox, and J. Levi, "Specific Areas of Agreement and Conflict in Women's Self-perception and Their Perceptions of Men's

Ideal Women in the United States, Peru, and Argentina," *International Mental Health Research Newsletter* 7 (1965) : 1–4.

6. A. Steinmann, "The Counselor: A Guide for the Misbegotten," paper presented at "Counseling Girls in Vocational Life Opportunities: A Conference," Los Angeles, University of California Extension, Downtown Center, March 1968.
7. L. M. Brammer and E. L. Shostrom, *Therapeutic Psychology: Fundamentals of Counseling and Psychotherapy* (Englewood Cliffs, N.J.: Prentice-Hall, 1960).
8. Steinmann, "Middle-class Women."
9. A. Couch and K. Keniston, "Yeasayers and Naysayers: Agreeing Response Set as a Personality Variable," *Journal of Abnormal and Social Psychiatry,* 1960, p. 60.
10. A. Steinmann, D. J. Fox, and R. Farkas, "Male and Female Perceptions of Male Sex-roles," *Proceedings of the 76th Annual Convention of the American Psychological Association,* 1968, pp. 421–22.

Counselors View Women and Work: Accuracy of Information*

WILLIAM C. BINGHAM and ELAINE W. HOUSE

In recent years, the status of women in the United States has received unaccustomed attention. Even though some advances have been made in elevating their status, it is clear that women have not attained true equality with men with respect to occupational status. "Progress . . . has been impeded . . . because of a prevalence of misinformation . . . and widely held negative attitudes."[1] In the present social context, it is important to know how counselors compare with other groups: How knowledgeable are they about women and work? Are they informed about recent reports concerning working women? Are their attitudes supportive of women who are trying to overcome obstacles? This report is the first in a series of efforts to address such questions and to examine the extent to which misinformation and negative attitudes prevail among counselors and counselor-educators.

In the spring of 1970, before much of the present protest about women's status had crystallized into social action, the authors were involved in two ventures that represented efforts to inform counselors about the changing status of women and, perhaps, to influence the direction that changes in counselors' related attitudes might take. Both authors were in-

* Reprinted with the permission of the American Personnel and Guidance Association and William C. Bingham and Elaine W. House from *Vocational Guidance Quarterly* 21 (June 1973): 262–68, © copyright 1973 by the National Vocational Guidance Association.

volved directly in planning for the 27th Rutgers Guidance Conference, held October 1970 and addressed to vocational problems of women. They were also involved in the activities of the NVGA (National Vocational Guidance Association) Commission on the Occupational Status of Women, which had been charged by the NVGA Board of Directors to investigate the attitudes of counselors and counselor-educators respecting the occupational status of women. Since it is likely that attitudes can be influenced by information, it was decided to study factual knowledge as well.

PROCEDURE

Since no suitable instrument was known to exist, the authors constructed one especially for this study. Two graduate classes in counselor education were invited to contribute to an item pool by writing statements or questions about either facts or attitudes related to the employment of women. Those statements were rewritten and submitted to a panel of advanced students in both vocational-technical education and counseling psychology and to counselor-educators for two purposes: to check the clarity of expression and to rate each item as either factual or attitudinal. From the pool of approximately 100 items, 25 judged factual and 25 judged attitudinal were selected for variety of content and arranged in random order. Accuracy of the factual items was verified by consulting publications of the Bureau of Labor Statistics and the Women's Bureau, as well as news media.

The questionnaire was mailed to a ten percent sample of the secondary-school counselors listed in a New Jersey State Department of Education Directory.[2] The list was entered randomly, and then every tenth name was selected. Of the 205 counselors contacted, 135 (66 percent) responded, and 93 percent of those responses (126: 67 male and 59 female) were usable.

While no specific hypotheses were formulated, it was expected that, in general, counselors would be accurately informed in terms of factual data, but that there might be some indication of negative attitudes, particularly among males. Since the first expectation was not realized, this report is limited to responses to the 25 factual items; analysis of the attitudinal items is in process and will be reported at a later date. The 25 items analyzed are listed in Figure 1, numbered as they appeared in the complete instrument, except that the correct response is indicated below.

RESULTS

On 12 of the 25 items examined, counselors manifested accurate information. They tended to know that most women will work at some time in their lives (Item #23) and will often face restrictions imposed by employers (#29), that women can be accommodated in many occupations where they are not usually employed (#18), and that they will find opportunities to move into supervisory positions primarily in occupations already dominated by women (#44). They were also accurately informed that, as homemakers, women are not counted in the labor force (#15), and they find some jobs closed to them because working hours are not compatible with homemaking responsibilities (#30). In addition, they knew that women who complete college usually marry (#17) and do not need clerical skills to find employment (#21). They knew, as well, that women perform as adequately as men in most occupations (#38), but receive lower wages (#1), are less likely to be covered by Social Security benefits (#19), and find more jobs closed to them (#22) than men do.

Of the 13 items reflecting inaccurate counselor information, 6 are shown in Table 1. Four revealed approximately equal division among the respondents as to the proportion of women who work (#25), the extent to which women are discriminated against (#41), whether employers change job titles to lower women's wages (#45), and whether women share equal professional status with men at colleges and universities (#46). On the other two items, respondents manifested high agreement but endorsed the incorrect answer. Apparently they were misinformed as to the increasing discrepancy between men's and women's income (#28) and the probability that women will advance to leadership positions in the foreseeable future (#43).

Figure 1

THE EFFECT OF SEX AND ABILITY ON AN APPLICANT'S OPPORTUNITY FOR AN INTERVIEW

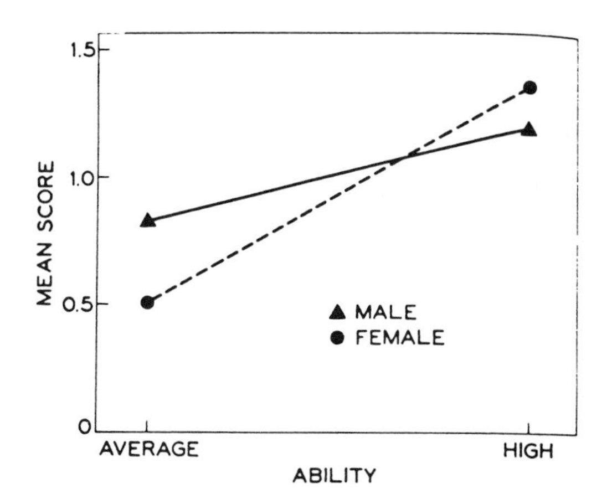

Factual Items from the Questionnaire on the Occupational Status of Women

Item No.	Statement	Answer
1.	More than half of the women working in the U.S. today earn less than $5,000 per year.	True
4.	Women need more alternatives for employment than are currently available to them.	True
11.	Most women are capable of performing well as both worker and homemaker.	True
13.	In general, women are less able than men.	False
14.	Employment practices clearly discriminate against women.	True
15.	In the U.S. Census, women who are homemakers are considered as not in the labor force.	True
17.	Approximately 40% of American women who hold collgee degrees never marry.	False
18.	There is no reasonable way to facilitate the employment of women in jobs such as welder, night watchman, truck driver, etc.	False
19.	Women are more likely than men to work in jobs not adequately covered by Social Security benefits.	True
21.	Female college graduates need clerical skills as well as a diploma to get employment.	False
22.	There are more jobs in the U.S. that are totally closed to men than there are that are totally closed to women.	False
23.	According to present estimates, 90% of the women in the U.S. can be expected to work some time in their lives.	True
25.	Approximately ⅔ of the married women in the U.S. today are working for income.	True
26.	In the U.S. today, there are few jobs that cannot be performed equally well by men and women.	True
28.	The discrepancy between salaries received by men and women for doing the same work is increasing.	True
29.	In spite of legislation that makes it illegal to do so, many companies continue to restrict employment opportunities for women.	True
30.	Because typical working hours are not compatible with women's other responsibilities, many job opportunities are "automatically" closed.	True
33.	On the average women spend about 25 years in the labor force	True
38.	In most occupational situations, women perform as adequately as men.	True
41.	Some statistics indicate that women suffer more from discrimination than blacks do.	True
43.	In the foreseeable future, women will fill only very limited leadership roles in work settings.	True
44.	Women tend to advance into supervisory positions almost exclusively in those occupations in which there is already a predominance of women.	True
45.	Employers change job titles so they can pay women lower wages or salaries.	True
46.	One area in which women have gained equality is college teaching; they are just as likely to be full professors as are men.	False
49.	Many companies make fringe benefits available to male and female workers.	True

The other seven items reflecting inaccuracy (in Table 2) offer a basis for some dramatic observations. On each of those items, the difference between the responses of male and female counselors was significant beyond the .05 level. Even more striking is the fact that in every case more female than male counselors endorsed the correct answer. Male counselors appear to be less accurately informed than females as to the occupational alternatives needed by women (#4), the ability of women to be both worker and homemaker (#11), the general ability of women (#13), whether women are clearly discriminated against (#14), the number of jobs that cannot be performed equally well by women and men (#26), the length of time women spend in the labor force (#33), and that many companies make fringe benefits available to women (#49).

Table 1

Counselors' Equivocal and Incorrect Responses to Questionnaire Items

Item No.	*N*	Answer	Sex	Agree	Disagree	x^{2*}
25	121	T	M	28	37	
			F	30	26	.75
41	118	T	M	29	32	
			F	26	31	.07
45	122	T	M	31	33	
			F	33	25	.87
46	125	F	M	30	36	
			F	30	29	.36
28	122	T	M	10	54	
			F	10	48	.06
43	126	T	M	12	55	
			F	13	46	.36

* All x^2 values are nonsignificant.

DISCUSSION

As the questionnaire used to collect data for this study was not tested regarding reliability and validity, results should be interpreted with caution. Since accuracy of the factual items was verified through dependable information sources, the content validity appears satisfactory. Factual accuracy aside, the distinct and consistent differences between counselors of opposite sex need to be explained, along with other findings.

On the two items that elicited nearly unanimous endorsement of the incorrect response, there may have been misinterpretation by respondents. Events reported by the news media of instances where the discrepancy between male and female income has been reduced may attract attention without reflecting the national averages reported by Lansing and intended as the relevant base for responding to Item #28.[3] Respondents may not have used the same definition of "foreseeable" (Item #43) as that used by the Bureau of Labor Statistics. Besides, being in error on four percent of the content does not appear to be condemnable or unreasonable. Furthermore, since the two items in question address matters not closely associated with entry level occupations, counselor actions taken on the basis of misinformation of this kind may not be especially damaging. The fact that these incorrect responses were almost unanimous, however, may weaken the above considerations.

One might be tempted to attribute the equivocal responses elicited by Items #25, #41, #45, and #46 to ambiguous word usage in the item content. Careful reading of the items, however, reveals that they are lucid and straightforward enough so that their intention can hardly be misleading. Only one of them, that women suffer more from discrimination than do blacks,[4] requires careful reading to be sure of interpretation. Since both women and blacks have been subjected to a great deal of discrimination, it may be unfair to demand that the required distinction be made.

Table 2

Differences Between Male and Female Counselors' Responses to Questionnaire Items

Item No.	*N*	Answer	Sex	Agree	Disagree	x^2
4	122	T	M	34	31	
			F	41	16	4.94*
11	125	T	M	37	30	
			F	47	11	9.40**
13	126	F	M	13	54	
			F	1	58	9.96**
14	124	T	M	39	28	
			F	43	14	4.08*
26	125	T	M	35	32	
			F	42	16	5.21*
33	122	T	M	18	46	
			F	35	23	12.86**
49[a]	125	T	M	43	23	
			F	59	0	25.95**

* Significant at the .05 level.
** Significant at the .01 level.
[a] Yates's Correction used.

The facts needed to make the differentiation may also be remote enough that they are not common knowledge. It can be argued with much conviction, on the other hand, that counselors ought to be possessors of uncommon knowledge about labor-market conditions.

The other items with equivocal responses leave no room for misinterpretation. That two-thirds of married women work, that employers change job titles, and that discrimination against women is common in college and university teaching are widely known and widely published facts. Failure to be aware of them probably has to be regarded as the result of some selective perception process, a process operating strongly in approximately half of the counselors, both male and female, who responded to this questionnaire. It seems reasonable to conclude, or at least to hypothesize, that the apparent misinformation in this case is a function of negative attitudes, of response tendencies tuned to deny the obvious information.

Some of the items that evoked sex differences are of particular interest in considering attitudes about women working. It is entirely conceivable that the idea that women are as able as men, can do most jobs as well as men, are capable of performing in dual roles, and are in need of more occupational opportunities may very well be threatening to some men, especially when attitudes like those described in the previous paragraph are in operation.

Item #14 is impossible to interpret with certainty because responses to it are inconsistent with responses to other items. In the cases of employers' restriction of opportunities for women (#29) and jobs totally closed to women (#22), male counselors' willingness to acknowledge discrimination against women was not significantly different from that of female counselors. On the other hand, there was a significant difference between males and females as to whether women are clearly discriminated against, with about 75 percent of the females agreeing that they are and about 25 percent not agreeing, while males were approximately equally divided. Thus, differences between the sexes about the existence of discrimination seem to emerge less clearly in terms of relatively specific illustrations of it than in the general case. Perhaps the general situation permits underlying sex differences to surface more readily than a specific one does.

Men's responses to Items #33 and #49 are also difficult to interpret. The length of time women spend in the labor force and the fact that many companies offer benefits to women seem to be free from emotional content, so the attitudinal explanation does not make as much sense as it did in some other items. It would appear, in these cases, that male and female counselors were differentially informed, and that with respect to Item #33, the male counselors were just categorically misinformed.

Whether counselors—and males much more than females—are simply misinformed about women and work or they harbor negative attitudes, the implications for counselor education are clear. Some kind of change is in order. To the extent that the problem is purely informational, solutions are not difficult to find. The necessary information can be provided. The ready availability of relevant information about women, however, suggests that the problem is attitudinal. In that case, solutions are likely to be more elusive. Present data does not permit determination of the sources of negative attitudes. Different change strategies are indicated if counselors have these attitudes before they begin professional preparation, acquire them from their counselor-educators, or learn them on the job.

REFERENCES

Bingham, W. C., ed. 1970. *Proceedings of the 27th rutgers guidance conference.* New Brunswick, N.J.: Rutgers University Press.

Francis, D. R. 1970. U.S. women's pay indicates bias. *Christian science monitor,* 13 April 1970.

Lansing, D. 1970. Job surveys support unfair-to-women charge. *Christian science monitor,* 1 April 1970.

New Jersey State Department of Education. 1969. *Directory of guidance personnel in approved New Jersey secondary schools, 1969–70.* Trenton, N.J.: Division of Curriculum and Instruction.

NOTES

1. W. C. Bingham, ed., *Proceedings of the 27th Rutgers Guidance Conference* (New Brunswick, N. J.: Rutgers University Press, 1970), p. 1.
2. Division of Curriculum and Instruction, New Jersey State Department of Education, *Directory of Guidance Personnel in Approved New Jersey Secondary Schools, 1969–70* (Trenton, N. J.: 1969).
3. D. Lansing, "Job Surveys Support Unfair-to-women Charge," *Christian Science Monitor,* 1 April 1970.
4. D. R. Francis, "U.S. Women's Pay Indicates Bias," *Christian Science Monitor,* 13 April 1970, p. 12.

Counselors' Attitudes Toward Women and Work*

WILLIAM C. BINGHAM and ELAINE W. HOUSE

This report is the second in a series of efforts to examine the extent to which misinformation and negative attitudes about women and work prevail among counselors and counselor educators. In the first report,[1] counselor responses to twenty-five factual questions about women and some of the working conditions and employment opportunities they face were analyzed, revealing that some counselors are misinformed and that there are notable sex differences in information. Attitudes of the same counselors are the focus of the present analysis.

Although no specific hypotheses were formulated, it was anticipated that some negative attitudes would be found, especially among male counselors. In the analysis of factual responses, it was concluded that some misinformation (particularly in males) probably resulted from selective processes influenced by attitudes. This observation supported the expectation that negative attitudes would be found in male counselors.

PROCEDURES

The 50-item questionnaire used to collect data was constructed especially for this study. It was mailed to a ten percent sample of the secondary-school counselors listed in a New Jersey State Department of Education

---

* Reprinted with the permission of the American Personnel and Guidance Association and William C. Bingham and Elaine W. House from *Vocational Guidance Quarterly* 22 (September 1973): 16–23, © copyright 1973 by the National Vocational Guidance Association.

Directory.[2] The list was entered randomly, and then every tenth name was selected. Of the 205 counselors contacted, 135 (66 percent) responded, and 93 percent of the responses (126: 67 male and 59 female) were usable. Subjects were instructed to agree or disagree with each item.

Responses to 25 items on factual information were analyzed in the earlier report.[3] The remaining 25 items, regarded by judges as attitudinal, are the subject of this report. They are shown in Table 1, numbered as they appeared in the complete instrument, except that a key, determined by the authors, has been added to correspond to each item. Items keyed with a plus (+) sign are those in which an "Agree" response reflects a positive attitude; in those keyed with a minus (–) sign, an "Agree" response reflects a negative attitude.

RESULTS

To facilitate analysis, responses to the 25 attitudinal items have been grouped into three categories: those on which there was essential agreement among subjects, those on which no clear trends could be discerned, and those on which there were significant sex differences. Agreement was arbitrarily defined as endorsement by 80 or more subjects, i.e., approximately two-thirds of the respondents.

Essential agreement among subjects was observed on eight attitudinal items (see Table 2). Approximately equal numbers of male and female counselors agreed that women perform better than men on some jobs typically considered "for men only" (Item #20). They also agreed that it is not difficult for counselors to work effectively with girls when so many occupations are closed to them (#24), and that it is not more difficult to do vocational counseling with girls than with boys (#5). About the same number disagreed that women use job demands primarily as a "smokescreen" (#3), are too emotional to fill high government posts (#6), and that sex-role identification problems can be attributed to women's competing in business (#31). Both males and females endorsed the notions that women must be superior to men in ambition as well as intelligence to succeed in some fields (#36) and that men find it difficult to marry women who are more educated than themselves (#40).

Those items on which responses were rather evenly distributed are shown in Table 3. Respondent opinion about some labor market conditions was divided as to whether complete equality for women can realistically be expected (#9), whether jobs should be closed to women because of physical requirements (#10), and whether school principals pay more attention to male rather than female teachers' requests and suggestions (#42). There was also divided opinion concerning women's preferences and feelings with respect to a real desire for equality (#39), guilt about absence from family (#35), and wanting to "have their cake and eat it, too" (#12).

Table 1

Attitudinal Items from the Questionnaire on the Occupational Status of Women

Item No.	Statement	Key
2.	No man really prefers to have a female boss.	—
3.	Women's demands for equality are really a "smokescreen"; they already enjoy many advantages in the labor force such as earlier retirement, maternity leave, more liberal sick-leave privileges, shorter working hours, special lounge facilities, etc.	—
5.	Vocational counseling is much more difficult with high-school girls than it is with boys.	+
6.	Women are too emotional to fill high positions in government.	—
7.	The time and money spent on training women for high-level jobs is largely wasted.	—
8.	When a man with a family to support and a single woman perform the same work, the man should be paid more.	—
9.	Complete equality for women is unrealistic.	—
10.	Many jobs should be closed to women because of the physical requirements.	—
12.	Women today want to have their cake and eat it, too.	—
16.	Women in business are good administrators and supervisors.	+
20.	Many women can perform better than men in some jobs that are presently considered "for men only."	+
24.	It is difficult for counselors to work effectively with girls when so many occupations are closed to them.	+
27.	There is no place in modern American society for upwardly mobile women except in very specialized fields.	—
31.	One of the major reasons so many young people today have sex-role identification problems is that too many women try to compete in business on equal terms with men.	—
32.	The most important function of women is being "mother"; all other roles are secondary.	—
34.	As a rule, men make better counselors than women.	—
35.	Working women feel guilty about being away from their homes and children.	—
36.	In order to succeed in a field traditionally considered a man's domain, women must surpass men in both ambition and intelligence.	—
37.	Something must be "wrong" with a woman who wishes to perform a traditionally male job.	—
39.	Down deep, most women don't want equality.	—
40.	Men find it difficult to marry women who have more education than they do.	—
42.	School principals pay more attention to requests or suggestions that come from male teachers than to those that come from female teachers.	—
47.	It is acceptable for women to work to supplement family income; it is unrealistic for them to expect meaningful implementation of vocational self-concepts.	—
48.	Since most women marry and depend on their husbands, it is appropriate that boys be better educated than girls.	—
50.	Women excel in fields requiring awareness of and sensitivity to the needs of others.	—

Table 2

Attitudinal Items Endorsed by Counselors

Item No.	*N*	Key	Sex	Agree	Disagree	x^{2*}
3	126	–	M	24	43	
			F	13	46	2.85
5	125	+	M	24	42	
			F	19	40	24
6	126	–	M	14	53	
			F	8	51	1.38
20	124	+	M	48	18	
			F	43	15	.03
24	124	+	M	13	53	
			F	6	52	2.08
31	125	–	M	22	45	
			F	12	46	2.32
36	125	–	M	49	20	
			F	47	9	3.59
40	126	–	M	56	11	
			F	48	11	.11

* All x^2 values are nonsignificant.

Sex differences emerged on the 11 items in Table 4 (p. 20). On two of them, opinions were widely divided as to whether there is a place in American society for upwardly mobile women (#27) and whether the primary function of a woman is being a mother (#32). Men, more often than women, disagreed that there is no place for upward mobile women outside of specialized fields, but they more often agreed that all other female roles are secondary to motherhood.

On two other items, subjects agreed that no man really prefers to have a female boss (#2) and that women excel in fields requiring awareness of and sensitivity to the needs of others (#50). It should be noted that the statistically significant difference between the sexes on these items is accounted for by the difference in the "Disagree" column.

On seven of the items reported in Table 4, the majority endorsed the response keyed as the positive attitude. Thus, the observed sex differences reflected in the reported chi-square values emerged because of the differences in numbers of males and females who endorsed the "incorrect" response. On each of these items, males more frequently than females expressed the undesirable attitude. More males than females expressed negative attitudes about economic issues by agreeing that training women for high-level jobs is wasteful (#7), married men should receive more pay than

Table 3

Items Reflecting Divided Opinion among Counselors

Item No.	*N*	Key	Sex	Agree	Disagree	x^2*
9	125	—	M	30	36	
			F	33	26	.05
10	123	—	M	41	24	
			F	31	27	1.17
12	123	—	M	26	39	
			F	21	37	.19
35	122	—	M	35	29	
			F	27	31	.81
39	124	—	M	43	23	
			F	32	26	1.29
42	123	—	M	23	42	
			F	22	36	.09

* All x^2 values nonsignificant.

single women doing the same work (#8), and boys should be better educated than girls (#48). Similar positions respecting the competency of women were reflected in their disagreement that women make good business administrators (#16) and just as good counselors as men (#34). Males also more frequently than females said that it is unrealistic for women to expect meaningful implementation of vocational self-concepts (#47) and that something must be "wrong" with a woman who wants to do a traditionally male job (#37).

DISCUSSION

Because the reliability and validity of the instrument used to collect data for this study have not been established, results need to be interpreted with caution. In spite of that, however, the high level of agreement among counselors on some items is impressive. In addition, the consistent differences between the sexes need especially careful consideration.

On 11 items (#s 3, 6, 7, 8, 16, 20, 31, 34, 37, 47, and 48), positive attitudes were endorsed by at least 80 of the respondents. Even though the opinions were not unanimous, these counselors generally expressed positive opinions about the content tapped by these particular items. That is the strongest and most important trend in the data, but it is equivocal. Sex

Table 4

Items Reflecting Sex Differences among Counselors

Item No.	N	Key	Sex	Agree	Disagree	x^2
2	126	—	M	46	21	
			F	50	9	4.48*
7	126	—	M	14	53	
			F	2	57	8.67**
8	125	—	M	18	49	
			F	3	55	10.47**
16	124	+	M	47	20	
			F	50	7	5.58*
27	125	—	M	21	45	
			F	31	28	5.51*
32	124	—	M	43	24	
			F	26	31	4.30*
34	126	—	M	19	48	
			F	4	55	9.79**
37	126	—	M	9	58	
			F	2	57	3.97*
47	124	—	M	19	46	
			F	6	53	6.98**
48	126	—	M	22	45	
			F	6	53	9.33**
50	125	—	M	43	23	
			F	49	10	5.19*

* Significant at the .05 level.
** Significant at the .01 level.

differences on seven of these items (#s 7, 8, 16, 34, 37, 47, and 48) occurred because, in every case, more males than females endorsed the negative attitude. The same trend is clear in three of the other four items (#s 3, 6, and 31) and is just barely present in the remaining one (#20). The uniformity of this trend is compelling, particularly so with regard to those seven items where the difference was significant. On those, the negative response to each item was endorsed by fewer than 10 women, with endorsement rates ranging from 3.4 to 12.3 percent. Only one negative response was endorsed by fewer than 10 men, with endorsement rates ranging from 13.4 to 33.3 percent. Thus, on these seven items, the lowest male endorsement rate (13.4 on #37) of the negative attitude was higher than the highest female endorsement rate (12.3 on #16). Even in the context of generally positive attitudes, there is evidence that substantial numbers of men have negative response sets.

On six items (#s 2, 5, 24, 36, 40, and 50), counselors endorsed the keyed negative attitude. It is possible, of course, that with attitudinal items their responses are more "accurate" than those keyed by the authors. It is conceivable, for example, that in the case of Items #2 and #50, subjects responded as if the items represented fact rather than opinion. Certainly everyone can cite examples of men who do not prefer a female boss and of women who excel in jobs requiring sensitivity. That kind of personal experience can hardly be regarded as representative of the labor force, and the tendency to generalize from it has to be regarded much more as a matter of attitude than information.

The same tendency to generalize from personal experience may operate with respect to Items #36 and #40. Examples of women who have felt the need to demonstrate excessive superiority in order to succeed and men with better educated wives who have had marital difficulties are not hard to find. To respond to a test item, however, as if that kind of illustration represents the norm seems to be more a matter of attitude than effective use of information. Perhaps the attitudinal thrust of the items would be particularly clear if the extremes were considered. If the items read: "women must *always* surpass men" or "men *always* find it difficult," then the very transparency would permit few endorsements. The omission of "always" probably has little effect on the meaning to which subjects respond.

It may be argued, of course, that more than personal experience can be invoked to illustrate that opportunities are restricted to women in many occupations. That is indeed true enough. A weakness in the argument, though, is the absence of evidence that it is, in fact, superior intelligence and ambition that have made the difference in those cases where women have managed to succeed in spite of obstacles. Clinical experience suggests very strongly that superiority in any number of other personal attributes may also be associated with success.

Responses to Items #5 and #24 may be particularly illustrative of greater "accuracy" of responses as compared to the authors' key. It may be that counselors regard vocational counseling with girls as no more difficult than with boys. It would be reasonable to take the position that the two tasks are equally difficult. The authors' key may simply be in error. The idea, however, that restricted opportunity does not make it more difficult to work effectively with girls is not easy to accept. Even the fact that 84.7 percent of the subjects answered the same way is not convincing. If the task is not more difficult for another reason—because counselors are not concerned about the implementation of self in occupational terms—then there should have been general agreement with Item #47; 99 subjects disagreed. Perhaps the explanation lies in the word "effectively." If counselors regard themselves as engaging in effective vocational counseling when young women accept obstacles to meaningful employment, then the responses to this item would be understandable. If that were the case, however, it seems reasonable to expect more general evidence of negative attitudes in the sample. Perhaps it is just a poor item.

It is remarkable that there was so much divided opinion on the items reported in Table 3. Both the labor-market conditions and the women's preferences covered in those items were described, for the most part, in very general terms. Perhaps the ambiguity permitted respondents to "read in" their own response sets. Such a tendency may be desirable in measuring attitudes, but what the subjects actually did respond to is unclear. What is clear is that opinion was divided and that women made the undesirable response about as often as men did. Of course, it may be that the generality of the item content itself is what permitted the negative attitudes to surface.

Another pair of items (#27 and #32) produced divided opinions and sex differences, as well. The fact that men disagreed that there is no place in American society for upward-mobile women except in very specialized fields seems to be inconsistent with their endorsement of motherhood as the most important function of women. Perhaps it is possible to regard motherhood as a "most important function" without perceiving it as restrictive of opportunities for occupational fulfillment, but this seems unlikely. It makes more sense to expect counselors (who presumably favor meaningful implementation of occupational self-concepts for all people) to support the idea that each woman should be free to decide for herself how important motherhood is to be in her own life. Counselors who believe in that type of autonomy ought to find it difficult to agree with Item #32.

Five of the items listed in Table 4 yielded sex differences at the .01 level of significance. In each of these items, there was some particularly value-laden term: "appropriate," "unrealistic," "better," "family to support," "wasted." Is it possible that such terms are more likely to evoke negative responses from men than from women?

IMPLICATIONS

The data analyzed here poses some important questions that warrant further investigation. The central meaning of the findings, however, has to be sought in terms of implications for counseling practice. In that regard, some general observations are possible.

By and large, the counselors in the study expressed more positive than negative attitudes toward women and work. In some respects, their attitudes were less clearly defined than was expected. Such lack of definition may leave some clients, especially girls, with feelings of uncertainty about where they stand with their counselors. On the basis of the data analyzed here, it can be concluded that girls who do feel uncertain about their counselors might anticipate greater support on some important dimensions of vocational behavior from female rather than from male counselors. That kind of support is not tantamount to more productive counseling, but it is a good start.

Questions about effective counseling inevitably raise parallel questions about counselor preparation. Data now being collected on the attitudes of counselor educators may suggest whether the attitudes of counselors are influenced by their teachers. In any event, the education that counselors receive should certainly help them to make their professional services equally effective for all prospective clients without regard to their sex.

REFERENCES

Bingham, W. C., and House, E. W. 1973. Counselors view women and work: Accuracy of information. *Vocational guidance quarterly* 21: 262–268.

New Jersey State Department of Education. 1969. *Directory of guidance personnel in approved New Jersey secondary schools, 1969–70* Trenton, N. J.: Division of Curriculum and Instruction.

NOTES

1. W. C. Bingham and E. W. House, "Counselors View Women and Work: Accuracy of Information," *Vocational Guidance Quarterly* 21: 262–68.
2. Division of Curriculum and Instruction, New Jersey State Department of Education, *Directory of Guidance Personnel in Approved New Jersey Secondary Schools, 1969–70* (Trenton, N. J.: 1969).
3. Bingham and House.

Women and Educational Testing*

CAROL KEHR TITTLE, KAREN McCARTHY, and JANE FAGGEN STECKLER

BACKGROUND

Several types of educational materials have been examined for discrimination against women. Studies have examined children's books,[1] sex roles in early reading textbooks,[2] described ways to evaluate sexism in readers and textbooks,[3] and surveyed the research in instructional materials and literature.[4]

In general, these studies show a considerable amount of sex-role stereotyping and, in the larger sense, a prejudiced or biased presentation of girls and women. For example, males were main characters in three times as many stories as females in readers and first and second-grade textbooks. Women were observed in occupations outside the home in about one-fourth as many stories as were males. While males were engaged in many types of work, females were only in eleven occupations, all of which were traditional female jobs, such as teacher, nurse, etc. Few stories show fathers as "homemakers-shoppers" and girls are more frequently seen as less active, giving up easily, and lacking competence in many tasks, where the reverse portrait is drawn of boys.[5]

* Carol Kehr Tittle, Karen McCarthy, and Jane Faggen Steckler, "Women and Educational Testing," From *Women and Educational Testing: A Selective Review of the Research Literature and Testing Practices* (Princeton, N. J.: Educational Testing Service, in collaboration with the Association for Measurement and Evaluation in Guidance, 1974). Reprinted with the permission of Carol Kehr Tittle.

The role of male and female in children's books was examined by Key.[6] It seems clear that the prejudices and myths held in society can be found throughout children's literature. The male is also placed in a stereotyped role, often not permitted a full range of emotions or allowed to make mistakes. The full range of career choices is restricted for males and females.

While children's books, textbooks, and readers have been examined for sex-role stereotyping and content bias, educational achievement tests have not been. In view of these earlier analyses, it seemed reasonable to see if educational achievement tests, too, contribute to the stereotyping of male and female roles—that is, were males and females considered to typify or conform to unvarying patterns, and were boys and girls reinforced in their development of fixed and unvarying ideas about men and women?

Sex-role stereotyping, then, is one area to be examined in educational achievement tests. The second area is language usage. An estimate of content bias may be obtained by determining if males are referred to more often than females. Reading comprehension, social studies, science, and other tests may well cite male novelists much more frequently than female, describe male scientists' activities more frequently, and so build, or rather reinforce, the view of the world as male oriented.

There is some evidence that bias may largely arise through content selection. Counts of word frequencies have been made for school instructional materials. The preparation of the new *American Heritage Dictionary* involved a computer analysis of 10,000 500-word samples from 1,000 of the most frequently used publications in representative schools across the country.[7] The analysis of these school materials showed evidence of male orientation. The word "boy" or "boys" appears 4,700 times versus 2,200 for "girl" or "girls." Of the 20 given names most frequently used, 13 were male and 7 female.

These are specific instances of male orientation in school materials. Several writers have discussed the general male orientation of the English language, and what appears to be sex-typed use of language. Strainchamps[8] and Key[9] have discussed the stereotyped characterization of English as masculine. Key has outlined some of the preliminary work in language with regard to male and female usage and several studies have examined classroom transcripts of four female and four male social-studies teachers.[10] These latter studies begin to suggest the type of linguistic analysis that may be required to understand more fully the relationship between attributes of the language, language usage, and continuation of prejudice against women.

Until the linguistic analysis methods are applied to educational materials, a rough estimate of the weighting of content toward males or toward females is obtained by computing ratios of frequency of usage of male nouns and pronouns to female nouns and pronouns.[11] One factor that apparently contributes to prejudice is that the English language has no singular pronouns equivalent to the plurals *they, their,* and *them.* Common usage tends to attribute "maleness" to references to most professional occupations. For example, the counselor . . . "he," the writer (author) . . . "he," etc. It might be argued that what appears to be bias is only the result of common language usage.

To summarize, bias could arise in selecting item content; bias could be mainly a function of usage—such as generic pronouns—and not subject to change by the test publisher; or bias could result from a combination of selection and usage. The present study attempts to determine whether bias arises in selecting content or is more a function of usage. In order to examine the source of bias, the language usage counts in this study were done both including and excluding generic nouns and their pronoun references (*i.e.,* references to such nouns as mankind, chairman, fisherman, alderman).

Language usage is the ratio of counts of frequencies of male nouns and pronouns to female nouns and pronouns. Generic nouns and pronouns are included in a total count (*all* nouns and pronouns) and excluded in a second count (*regular* nouns and pronouns).

The comparison of *all* versus *regular* ratios of male to female nouns and pronouns tests the hypothesis that bias is in selection of test content rather than usage. If bias is largely a function of content selection, it is readily subject to change.[12]

Sex-role stereotyping is examined in light of the discussion at the beginning of this section. Do females appear in other than traditional jobs as teachers, nurses, etc.? Are girls shown as active and independent? The hypothesis, here, is that educational achievement tests will contain the same type of sex-role stereotypes of women that are present in other educational materials.

PROCEDURES

The procedures followed in developing and using the instructions for male-female noun and pronoun counts of language usage and examples of stereotyping were developed in the following manner. Two doctoral students in educational psychology, with a specialization in measurement, did a pilot analysis of a test from each of the major test publishing companies. This preliminary analysis was used to develop the recording instructions. These recording instructions were then used by two college graduates to analyze a series of achievement tests.

A. Language Usage

A form was prepared on which both nouns and pronouns and content stereotypes were recorded. Each subtest in a test battery was examined; the recorder listed each noun and pronoun occurring that specifically referred to a male or female; these were tallied later as regular nouns and pronouns. Each generic pronoun was identified by a (g) and tallied as *generic.*

Included in the count of regular nouns were words occurring in usage such as: The writer rewrote his story four times. In this context, *writer* would be recorded as *writer* (m), and tallied as a male noun, regular. While the noun itself is not sex-referenced, it is sex-designated by the pronoun following it.

An example of generic usage is: Western man wrote his history as if it were the history of the entire human race. Here the noun and pronoun would be followed by a (g) in recording, and tallied as generic nouns and pronouns (man [g], his [g]). It could be argued that examples such as *Western man wrote his history* . . . are not intentional examples of sex bias on the part of the test developer. That is, the inclusion of these nouns and pronouns as sex-referenced would arbitrarily distort the estimate of bias since this is a built-in bias in usage of English. Therefore, the count of these generic nouns and pronouns was established separately. This permitted a total ratio of *all* nouns and pronouns (regular plus generic) and a *regular* ratio (excluding the counts of generic nouns and pronouns) to be compared.

Once the lists of nouns and pronouns identified as regular and generic had been made, a summary was prepared for each subtest in the achievement test battery and for the total battery. Complete data for each battery contains the following: name of subtest, total number of items in the test (and number of sample items), the *frequencies* and *ratios* for *all* male nouns and pronouns to *all* female nouns and pronouns, and the frequencies and ratios of the *regular* male nouns and pronouns to *regular* female nouns and pronouns. The data for *regular* nouns and pronouns *exclude* nouns and pronouns where used generically (*i.e.,* with no reference to a specific person).

B. Sex-role stereotypes

In addition to indicating language usage as described above, recorders were asked to identify stereotypic content, and list instances on the same form used to record nouns and pronouns.

General guidelines were given to recorders to suggest the types of sex-role stereotypes that might occur in the test content. *Stereotyped activities* for women were to be identified: Mary helped her mother set the table.

Women mentioned in a *stereotyped profession* were also listed: The teacher . . . Mrs. Jones; the secretary . . . Miss Ward. Items or descriptions that assign women to a *secondary or helpless status* were included as stereotypic content: Bob was elected class president and Susan was elected secretary.

Two other categories listed as identifying stereotypic content were those that *limit female occupational pursuits* and references to activities that were *items distinctly male or female oriented.* An example of content limiting women's occupational goals is: The delegates discussed the qualifications a man must have to be suitable for the Presidency. Male-female oriented activities were illustrated by the statement: Repairing a carburetor is not as complicated as you might assume.

The results of the data gathered by these procedures are summarized below. The quantitative data on language usage are presented first. The more qualitative listing of sex-role stereotyping of content is then given through a series of examples. No attempt has been made here to quantify the number and/or type of stereotyping listed on the recording forms. Elimination of stereotypes is dependent on specific review of new tests under development. Overall bias in content weighting of tests may, however, be usefully studied through quantitative methods, such as the language-usage counts in this study. More technically accurate and sophisticated methods of linguistic analysis for content bias are being developed. These may well provide test developers with methods useful for determining whether test content is sex biased.

RESULTS FOR LANGUAGE USAGE

Table 1 shows the ratio of male noun and pronoun referents to female noun and pronoun referents for the educational achievement test batteries analyzed. These total battery data are obtained by summing the male/female references for all the tests in the battery and computing the ratios for these total counts. Ratio figures greater than 1.00 indicate proportionally more male noun and pronoun referents than female.

Before describing the data, one major finding can be pointed out. There are few differences between the conclusions that would be drawn by using the ratios based on *all* nouns and pronouns and those based on *regular* nouns and pronouns only. That is, the content bias in favor of males does *not* appear to be primarily a function of language usage, but rather of content selection. Deleting the generic pronouns used (according to customary usage at this time) reduces a few of the ratios, but the reductions seem of little practical significance. The *Sequential Tests of Educational Progress,* Forms 1A, has a ratio of 14.00 with *all* nouns and pronouns and a ratio of 12.19 with the *regular* nouns and pronouns only. Similarly, the *Comparative Guidance and Placement Program,* Form

Table 1

Ratios of Male Noun and Pronoun Referents to Female Noun and Pronoun Referents—Educational Achievement Test Batteries

Test	Total No. of Test Items	Nouns and Pronouns			
Test	Items	All		Regular	
		nM/nF	=Ratio	nM/nF	=Ratio
California Achievement Tests					
Level 3 Form A (Gr. 4–6)	343	190/47	4.04	190/47	4.04
Level 4 Form A (Gr. 6–9)	337	84/46	1.83	84/46	1.83
Level 5 Form A (Gr. 9–12)	349	93/36	2.58	93/36	2.58
Comparative Guidance and Placement Program					
Form TPG (Gr. 13–14)	391	127/9	14.11	106/9	11.77
Form UPGX3 & UPGX4 (Gr. 13–14)	275	121/34	3.56	111/33	3.36
Iowa Tests of Basic Skills					
Form 6 (Gr. 3–8)	1232	1221/368	3.31	1211/368	3.29
The Iowa Tests of Educational Development					
Form Y5 (Gr. 9–12)	330	262/195	1.34	219/195	1.12
Metropolitan Achievement Tests					
Primary I Form F (Gr. 1.5–2.4)	174	51/59	.86	48/54	.89
Primary II Form F (Gr. 2.5–3.4)	257	137/86	1.59	137/86	1.59
Elementary Form F (Gr. 3.5–4.9)	300	124/42	2.95	121/42	2.88
Intermediate Form F (Gr. 5.0–6.9)	534	181/44	4.11	178/44	4.05
Advanced Form F (Gr. 7.0–9.5)	524	198/51	3.88	195/51	3.82
Sequential Tests of Educational Progress					
Series II Form 4A (Gr. 3–5)	420	366/103	3.55	322/98	3.29
Series II Form 3A (Gr. 6–9)	420	443/150	2.95	408/149	2.74
Series II Form 2A (Gr. 9–12)	470	468/134	3.49	360/120	3.00
Series II Form 1A (Gr. 13–14)	320	448/32	14.00	390/32	12.19
SRA Achievement Series					
Level 1–2 Form D (Gr. 1–2)	320	179/88	2.03	179/88	2.03
Level 2–4 Form D (Gr. 2–4)	276	333/241	1.38	330/234	1.41
Multilevel Form D (Gr. 4–9)	1070	1513/231	6.55	1462/229	6.38
Stanford Early School Achievement Test					
Level I (Gr. K–1)	126	217/93	2.33	217/93	2.33
Level II (Gr. 1)	259	192/168	1.14	190/168	1.13
Stanford Achievement Test					
Primary I Form W (Gr. 1.5–2)	251	134/53	2.52	123/51	2.41
Primary I Form X (Gr. 1.5–2)	251	119/78	1.53	115/78	1.47
Primary II Form W (Gr. 2–3)	409	209/89	2.34	192/87	2.20
Primary II Form X (Gr. 2–3)	409	143/87	1.64	143/87	1.64
Intermediate I Form W (Gr. 4–5)	540	221/83	2.66	198/71	2.78
Intermediate II Form W (Gr. 5–6)	544	171/58	2.95	166/58	2.96
Advanced Form W (Gr. 7–9)	532	181/46	3.93	157/46	3.11
High School Basic Battery					
Form X (Gr. 9–12)	478	245/40	6.13	242/39	6.21

TPG, has a ratio of 14.11 for *all* nouns and pronouns and 11.77 for *regular* nouns and pronouns. Comparing the size of the ratios in the *all* column with those in the *regular* leads to the conclusion that the content of educational achievement tests is selectively biased, and as such amenable to change through awareness of the bias on the part of test developers and publishers.

Each test battery shows a higher frequency of male nouns and pronouns than female nouns and pronouns, with the exception of the *Metropolitan Achievement Tests,* Primary I, Form F. The range of the ratios is from a low of .86 for the *Metropolitan Achievement Tests,* Primary I, to a high of 14.11 for one form of the *Comparative Guidance and Placement Program* test (grades 13-14) and 14.00 for the *Sequential Tests of Educational Progress* (STEP) Series II, Form 1A (grades 13-14). For the low ratio of .86, there were a few more female references than male. For the high ratios of 14.00 and 14.11, there were 14 times as many references to male nouns and pronouns as to female.

The distribution of ratios of *all* nouns and pronouns shows 8 of the 29 batteries analyzed have ratios of male to female below 2 to 1. Twenty-one of the batteries show males being referred to with a ratio of greater than 2 to 1. The subtests within the individual batteries show considerable variability.

There is a tendency for the test batteries developed for the early grade levels, kindergarten through grade three or four, to have lower ratios than the test batteries for the higher grades. This is largely because the tests at the early grades have fewer extended reading passages. Another reason for the low ratio may be the "home orientation" of primary education. Examples and discussion may revolve more around the home and mother.

The total battery figures substantiate the general impression obtained from scanning the test content for stereotyping and bias. Educational achievement tests reflect the general bias in school instructional materials, referring much more frequently to males and their world, rather than balancing the references and drawing on content equally for the two sexes.

Some indication of the consistency of these ratios throughout the batteries is given in Table 2. Table 2 shows the number of subtests in each series of achievement tests that had a ratio below 1.00, that is, where there were more female nouns and pronouns used than male nouns and pronouns. The range of subtests within a battery showing ratios below 1.00 is from 0, for the *Iowa Test of Basic Skills* and the *Stanford High School Battery,* to 5 subtests out of 9 for the *Stanford Early School Achievement Test,* Levels I and II. The small number of subtests with ratios below 1.0 is another indication of the imbalance in references to males and females in these educational achievement tests.

The extent of the imbalance that exists in some of the subtests of the educational achievement tests is indicated in Table 3. Table 3 shows the subtests with the highest male to female ratios. All five subtests include measures with a heavy verbal or reading content. There are three reading tests, a social studies test, and a science test. The most biased content selection, in terms of the ratios computed here, was for the reading comprehension test of the *California Achievement Tests*: a ratio of 84 to 1 was recorded. The same ratio was obtained for the reading section of a form of the *Comparative Guidance and Placement Program.*

It had been suggested that perhaps alternate forms of the same tests might be balanced for sex bias. That is, although one form of a test might refer more to males than to females, an alternate form of the test for the same subject and grade level might refer more to females than

Table 2

Number of Subtests with M/F Ratios of Noun and Pronoun Referents Below 1.00

Test	Number of Subtests with Ratio Below 1.00	Total Number of Subtests*
California Achievement Tests (Levels 3, 4, 5)	4	21
Comparative Guidance and Placement Program (Forms TPG: UPGX3, UPGX4)	0	5
Iowa Tests of Basic Skills	0	5
The Iowa Tests of Educational Development	1	7
Metropolitan Achievement Tests (Primary I, II; Elementary; Intermediate; Advanced)	4	28
Sequential Tests of Educational Progress (Levels 1–4)	1	22
SRA Achievement Series (Levels 1–9)	2	13
Stanford Early School Achievement Test (I, II)	5	9
Stanford Achievement Test		
Primary I, II, Intermediate I, II, Form W	2	30
Primary I, II, Form X	3	13
Advanced, Form W	2	6
High School Basic Battery, Form X	0	7

* Only subtests including any male or female nouns or pronouns are counted here.

to males. In order to provide a check on this, the social studies tests for the *Stanford Achievement Test* were analyzed at the Intermediate Level for Form X and Form W. The comparison of the alternate forms is shown in Table 4. At the Intermediate I level, the ratio of male to female for *all* nouns and pronouns was 3.40 and 5.33. At the Intermediate II level, the ratios were 16.33 and 8.67. Although Form W was half the ratio (8.67) of the alternate Form X (16.33), both ratios are still highly biased from a practical viewpoint.

Table 3

Five Subtests with Highest M/F Ratios

Test	Number of Items	Nouns and Pronouns	
		nM/nF	Ratio
California Achievement Tests			
Reading Comprehension, Level 3, Form A	42	84/1	84.00
Comparative Guidance and Placement Program			
Reading, Section 4, Form TPG	35	84/1	84.00
Sequential Tests of Educational Progress			
Social Studies, Series II, Level 4A	50	41/1	41.00
SRA Achievement Series			
Science, Multilevel, Form D	90	33/1	33.00
Stanford Achievement Test			
Paragraph Meaning, Advanced Battery, Form W	60	69/1	69.00

Table 4

Comparison of Alternate Forms for Social Studies Subtests

	Number of Items	Nouns and Pronouns			
		All		Regular	
		nM/nF	= Ratio	nM/nF	= Ratio
Stanford Achievement Test					
Social Studies					
Intermediate I, Form X	49	17/5	3.40	17/4	4.25
Intermediate I, Form W	49	16/3	5.33	16/3	5.33
Intermediate II, Form X	74	49/3	16.33	49/2	24.45
Intermediate II, Form W	74	26/3	8.67	25/1	25.00

As shown in Table 1, the Primary I and II levels of the Stanford Achievement Test were also analyzed for two forms—W and X. The male/female ratios for these batteries are much lower. Primary I, Form W, 2.52, Form X, 1.53; Primary II, Form W, 2.34, Form X, 1.64. These batteries are apparently more closely balanced in content, from the standpoint of these ratios. However, the alternate forms do not have either identical ratios or one highly male and the other highly female. Generally speaking, however, it is apparent that the ratios in the alternate-forms analysis remain fairly similar. There is no correction of extreme imbalance from one form to another. The similarity of these figures also indicates that analysis of alternate forms of other achievement tests may not provide very different data from those that are presented here.

EXAMPLES OF SEX-ROLE STEREOTYPING

Sex-role stereotypes were recorded for each test analyzed. This section presents examples of the stereotypes found and makes some general inferences about the way women are presented.

Women are portrayed almost exclusively as homemakers or in the pursuit of hobbies (e.g., "Mrs. Jones, the President of the Garden Club . . . ").[13] Young girls carry out "female chores" (e.g., Father helps Betty and Tom build a playhouse; when it's completed, "Betty sets out dishes on the table, while Tom carries in the chairs . . . ").[14]

In numerous activity-centered items, boys are shown playing, climbing, camping, hiking, taking on roles of responsibility and leadership. Girls help with the cooking, buy ribbon and vegetables and when participating in any active pursuit, take the backseat to the stronger, more qualified boys. (E.g., Buddy says to Clara, "Oh, I guess it's all right for us boys to help girls. I've done some good turns for girls myself, because I'm a Scout.")[15]

Some items imply that the majority of professions are closed to women. A reading comprehension passage about the characteristics and qualifications required for the Presidency begins with the statement: "In the United States, voters do not directly choose the man they wish to be President"; and repeatedly says "*he* must be," "he must have. . . ."[16] Most short biographies turn out to be written about men. Practically all teachers are listed as female, while professors, doctors, and presidents of companies are listed as male. If a team of players is mentioned, usually it has all-male members.

Another example of bias is reflected in the reading comprehension items, which tend to be male oriented in subject matter. The *Sequential Tests of Educational Progress* (STEP) uses familiar literature excerpts that are predominantly male authored. One of the few female-authored sections is an excerpt from *People and Places* by Margaret Mead. Yet even this positive example is flawed: One of the comprehension questions following the Mead passage says, "The writer acts as if *he* were. . . ."[17] Other items appear that cannot be categorized as stereotypes, but must be mentioned as reinforcements of the existing downgraded female role in our culture (e.g., "In many countries men rarely ever help their wives with household chores.").[18]

The examination of the test content for sex-role stereotypes indicates that the educational achievement tests do not differ from other instructional materials in education. Most of the tests analyzed contain numerous sex-role stereotypes.

SUMMARY OF TEST ANALYSES

The analysis of the educational achievement tests shows content bias, as indicated by the analysis of language usage, and sex-role stereotyping of women. The male/female ratios of noun and pronoun references vary widely from subtest to subtest for the tests examined. The subtest data and the overall ratios for the test batteries clearly indicate that there are more frequent references to males than to females.

The analysis and criticism of tests described here is aimed at presenting a more equitable or less prejudiced view of women. This can be done by a fairer representation of women in the test content and by showing women in a variety of occupations and activities. These changes can be readily made by test publishers through a review procedure initiated very early in the test-development process. Specifications to item writers can encourage a less stereotyped presentation of women and the use of examples in history, literature, science, and other areas where women have made contributions. After the item-writing specifications, test editors can again review the content before items are tried out. After the tryouts, and when a test is assembled, a check on the balance in presentation for males and females can be instituted.[19] These suggestions do not deal with the more technical problems of deciding whether usage is biased, but suggest minimum standards for lack of bias and sex-role stereotyping in the content of educational achievement tests.

COLLEGE ADMISSIONS TESTS AND MANUALS

The use of tests in the college admissions process was mentioned in the introduction. As a conservative estimate, probably 2,000,000 students take one of the tests of the College Entrance Examination Board (CEEB) or American College Testing Program (ACTP) each year. While the tests themselves were not available for analysis, some publications of the testing programs were.

For the student booklets for both the CEEB and ACTP, most of the copy is directed to "you." However, in the ACTP *Student's Booklet* (1971/72), the main example, which runs through the booklet, is of a student named Joseph Astro, so that much of the discussion is done in terms of "Joe's" report, "his" first college choice, etc. In the *Student Bulletin* (1972/73) for the admissions testing program of the CEEB, again, most of the text is directed to the student as "you." However, references to the candidate are consistently "he." An examination of the CEEB bulletin on the *Achievement Tests* (1972/73) shows the following bias in presentation of sample items to students. These items are intended to be representative of the content of the tests. For example, in the English test, the references are primarily to males (Thoreau, Hamilton, and Jefferson) and few examples with women's names or female pronouns appear. For history and social studies, there are male citations and references almost exclusively. One exception is a picture of a king and queen of ancient Egypt, but there are no examples of women in, or influencing, history. In the modern foreign languages, the item illustrations show males and females in stereotyped roles. In the sciences section, with few exceptions, these items are neutral and do not refer to people. The exceptions include one item referring to "you"; an animal breeder—"he"; a student—"he."

Two manuals from the ACT Program were examined: the *ACT Counselor's Handbook,* 1972/73 and *Using ACT on the Campus,* 1972/73. The *ACT Counselor's Handbook* shows a mixed usage in referring to the student as "he" or "his/her." An item writer is referred to as "he"; the student is also referred to as "he." More usually, the form "his/her" has been used, but the manual is inconsistent in this usage. The sample reports and profiles used to illustrate the materials are of male cases, for the most part (with one exception on page 16), and the discussion of "visuals for group guidance" again uses a male example, Joseph Astro (p. 21).

In the publication, *Using ACT on the Campus,* 1972/73 edition, there is reference to the item writer, "he." The student is also referred to as "he." Again, all the sample profiles and student examples given are male.

Materials for the *Comparative Guidance and Placement Program (CGP)* of the CEEB were examined also. The study of the CGP test item content was reported in the preceding section. The interpretive materials and user materials accompanying this program tend to be consistent in referring to a counselor, a faculty advisor, a student, the CGP coordinator, all as male. Materials examined include the *Interpretive Manual for Counselors, Administrators, and Faculty* (1969/70); a *Counselor's Guide to CGP* (1971/72); and a publication providing sample items, *CGP, A Program for Two-Year Colleges and Vocational-Technical Institutes* (1971/72). In this latter publication, the sample profile is for Thomas Garcia who scores high in mathematics, physical sciences, engineering and low in secretarial, business, social sciences (p. 14–15). A sample reading passage quotes a New York City official without noting whether the official is male or female, yet the question refers to the official as "he" (p. 6).

The student answer form for the *Comparative Guidance and Placement Program* (copyrighted 1971), shows a few interest items that are stereotyped. Item 28 refers to an executive—"him"; item 33 refers to successful *men* discussing their fields; item 68 refers to a nurse—"she"; items 152 and 153 refer to crafts*men*.

These brief analyses of some of the materials accompanying the major college admissions testing programs indicate that these materials should be carefully reviewed for stereotyped content, the balance between references to males and females, and the portrayal of women as a part of American culture. It is possible to prepare manuals and reports that are more balanced in their use of language. *The Report of the Commission on Tests: I. Righting the Balance* is a publication that illustrates this point.[20] Applicants, counselors, and so on, are referred to in the plural, thus avoiding the use of pronouns that specify male or female. In the few instances where these nouns were used in the singular, a *his/her* form has been used.

SUMMARY

This report provides a survey of several aspects of educational testing with a view toward identifying discrimination against women. Two major ways in which discrimination can occur are examined in educational testing: reinforcement of sex-role stereotypes and restriction of individual choice. Discrimination also occurs through selective bias of test content or user materials—reading passages are about men more often than women, and scientists are referred to consistently as male, rather than identified also as female.

It is important to examine tests and their possible discrimination against women for several reasons. Educational tests are a part of the schools' materials, along with textbooks and other instructional materials, and tests are used in guidance as well as in evaluating student progress. A more quantitative indication of the importance of educational tests is the number in use on an annual basis. Holmen and Docter estimate that 200 million achievement test forms and answer sheets are used in the United States annually.[21] In addition to the widespread use of educational tests, there is other evidence of their importance. Students, parents, teachers, and other users of test scores tend to believe that they are fairly accurate and should be used in decision-making.[22]

ANALYSIS OF EDUCATIONAL ACHIEVEMENT TESTS

Studies of children's books, early reading textbooks and other instructional materials used in education show a considerable amount of sex-role stereotyping.[23] Another survey of classroom materials showed evidence of male orientation—counts showed that some male nouns were used about twice as frequently as female nouns.[24] These studies indicate that bias can arise in selecting test content as well as in sex-role stereotyping. In the present study, major educational achievement test batteries were analyzed for evidence of bias against women.

Educational achievement test batteries were analyzed for two sources of bias: selective content bias against women as measured by language usage; and examples of sex-role stereotyping of women. While bias can arise in selecting test content, some bias might be a function of usage not subject to change by the test developer, such as generic nouns and pronouns (mankind, chairman, fisherman, alderman). In order to examine the source of bias, the language usage counts were done both including and excluding generic nouns and their pronoun references.

Ratios of counts of frequencies of male nouns and pronouns to female nouns and pronouns were computed; one ratio includes *all* nouns and pronouns, a second ratio includes only *regular* nouns and pronouns (generics excluded). The results of the analysis of the most widely used educational achievement tests show:

1. There are few differences between conclusions that would be drawn based on ratios using *all* nouns and pronouns and those based on *regular* nouns and pronouns only. Content bias in favor of males does *not* appear to be primarily a function of language usage, but rather of content selection.
2. With one exception, each test battery shows a higher frequency of usage of male nouns and pronouns than of female nouns and pronouns. The range of ratios was from a low of .86 (slightly more female references than male) to a high of 14.11 and 14.00 for two batteries (14 times as much usage of male nouns and pronouns as female).
3. The number of subtests in each achievement test series with ratios below 1.00 (where more female nouns and pronouns were used than male) ranged from none (0 out of 7) to a high of 5 subtests (out of 9). The majority of batteries showed few subtests with ratios at or be-

low 1.00, another indication of the imbalance in references to males and females in the educational achievement tests analyzed.

4. The extent of the imbalance is shown in the five subtests with the highest frequencies of male nouns and pronouns to female—84:1; 84:1; 69:1; 41:1; and 33:1. These figures show that in two subtests, for example, 84 male nouns and pronouns were counted and only one female noun or pronoun.
5. Alternate forms of two test batteries and two social studies subtests were compared. There does not appear to be a correction of imbalance in ratios from one form to an alternate form. The alternate forms of the tests analyzed were not balanced for sex bias in content selection.

Numerous examples of sex-role stereotyping were recorded; women are portrayed almost exclusively as homemakers or in the pursuit of hobbies. Boys are shown playing, climbing, taking on roles of responsibility and leadership. Girls help with the cooking, buy ribbon and vegetables, and take the backseat to the stronger, more qualified boys.

The total battery analyses substantiate the general impression obtained from scanning the test content and recording examples of stereotyping. Educational achievement tests reflect the general bias in school instructional materials, referring much more frequently to males and their world, rather than balancing the references and drawing on content equally appropriate for the two sexes.

Some materials from the college admissions testing programs were examined. Materials from the College Entrance Examination Board (CEEB) programs tend to show the same bias that exists in the educational achievement tests. Sample items show references to males rather than females and student booklets refer to candidates as male (*he*) unless the copy is directly addressed to the student (*you*). Counselors, faculty advisors, and coordinators of testing programs are referred to as male (*he*). Materials from the American College Testing Program (ACTP) show a mixed usage; one handbook refers to the student as *he* in some parts and uses the form *his/her* in other sections of the manual. Sample reports and profiles are almost exclusive in the use of male cases.

An analysis of the items for the tests used in the college admissions testing programs will probably show the same examples of sex-role stereotyping and bias in content selection that were found for educational achievement tests. The college admissions tests were not available for analysis, with the exception of the *Comparative Guidance and Placement Program* (*CGP*) of the CEEB. Subtests of the CGP show content bias as measured by language usage. Test development and review procedures can eliminate the obvious discrimination against women in test content.

The concern in this report has been to examine and report on examples of discrimination against women in educational testing. This has been done through a study of content bias in tests and evidence of sex-role stereotypes in tests. These surface aspects of discrimination against women and other subgroups *can* be changed. Hopefully, the use of sex as a basis on which to categorize and classify individuals to insure "fair" treatment is a temporary phenomenon. Studies of human abilities typically show extensive overlap in score distributions between subgroups. This means that, for example, while boys on the average score higher than girls on tests of mathematics aptitude, there are still many girls who score higher than the average for boys. The extensive overlap indicates that sex as a classification variable will probably not provide a large improvement in prediction work or in devising more effective instructional treatments (although, the use of sex as a classification variable may suggest other, seemingly sex-related variables for study).

Over the long term, understanding of human behavior and the development of individuals to their fullest will not occur when they are categorized on the basis of a variable such as sex. Rather, variables specified in psychological theories and amenable to development and modification will replace the classification of individuals on variables such as sex and race.

REFERENCES

Barron, N. 1971. Sex-typed language: the production of grammatical cases. *Acta sociologica* 14: 24–42.

———; Loflin, M. D.; and Biddle, B. J. 1972. *Sex-role and the production of case frames.* Columbia, Mo.: Univ. of Mo.

———, and Marlin, M. J. 1972. Sex of the speaker and the grammatical case and gender of referenced persons. *Technical report C153.* Columbia, Mo.: Center for Research in Social Behavior, Univ. of Mo.,

Frasher, R., and Walker, A. 1972. Sex in early reading textbooks. *The reading teacher* 25: 741–49.

Grambs, J. D. 1972. Sex-stereotypes in instructional materials, literature, and language: a survey of research. *Women studies abstracts* 1: 1–4, 91–94.

Gunderson, D. V. 1972. Sex roles in reading and literature. Paper presented at the meeting of the American Educational Research Association, Chicago, April 1972.

Jacobs, C., and Eaton, C. 1972. Sexism in the elementary school. *Today's Education* 61: 20–22.

Key, M. R. 1971. The role of male and female in children's books—dispelling all doubt. *Wilson library bulletin* 46: 167–76.

Malcolm, A. H. 1971. Most common verb in schools, study finds, is . . . is. New York: *New York Times,* 4 September 1971, p. 22.

Strainchamps, E. 1971. Our sexist language. *Women in sexist society*, ed. V. Gornick and B. K. Moran. New York: Basic Books.

NOTES

1. M. R. Key, "The Role of Male and Female in Children's Books—Dispelling All Doubt," *Wilson Library Bulletin* 46 (1971) : 167–76.
2. R. Frasher and A. Walker, "Sex in Early Reading Textbooks," *The Reading Teacher* 25 (1972): 741–49.
3. C. Jacobs and C. Eaton, "Sexism in the Elementary School," *Today's Education* 61 (1972) : 20–22.
4. J. D. Grambs, "Sex-stereotypes in Instructional Materials, Literature, and Language: A Study of Research," *Women Studies Abstracts* 1 (1972) : 1–4, 91–94.
5. Frasher and Walker.
6. Key.
7. A. H. Malcolm, "Most Common Verb in Schools, Study Finds, Is . . . Is," *New York Times*, 4 September 1971, p. 22.
8. E. Strainchamps, "Our Sexist Language," in *Women in Sexist Society*, ed. V. Gornick and B. K. Moran (New York: Basic Books, 1971) .
9. Key.
10. N. Barron, "Sex-typed Language: The Production of Grammatical Cases," *Acta Sociologica* 14 (1971) : 24–42; N. Barron and M. J. Marlin, "Sex of the Speaker and the Grammatical Case and Gender of Referenced Persons," *Technical Report C153* (Columbia, Mo.: Center for Research in Social Behavior, University of Missouri Press, 1972); and N. Barron, M. D. Loflin, and B. J. Biddle, *Sex Role and the Production of Case Frames* (Columbia, Mo.: University of Missouri Press, 1972) .
11. The idea that language usage should be examined for tests was suggested by a review presented by D. V. Gunderson, "Sex Roles in Reading and Literature," in his paper presented at the meeting of the American Educational Research Association, Chicago, April 1972.
12. Additionally, there are nouns that are not sex designated, in and of themselves, but are designated by a pronoun following them. Here, the test publisher can provide a balance in designating sex in such context as, the doctor—*she*, the lawyer—*she*, etc.
13. *California Achievement Tests*—Language Usage, Level 5, Form A, 1970, item no. 43, p. 43.
14. *SRA Achievement Series*—Reading 1–2, Form D, 1963, p. 17.
15. *SRA Achievement Series*—Grammatical Usage, Multilevel Edition, Form D, 1963, p. 45.
16. *SRA Achievement Series*—Reading, Multilevel Edition, Form D, 1963, p. 76. See also, *Sequential Tests of Educational Progress*, Series II Reading, Form 1A, 1969, p. 18.
17. *Sequential Tests of Educational Progress*, Series II Reading 4A, 1969, p. 7. Here the item writer has adopted "he" in a context that demands the specific "she."
18. *Sequential Tests of Educational Progress*, Series II English Expression, Form 4A, 1969, item 25, p. 6.

19. C. Jacobs and C. Eaton; these researchers have described a form for evaluating sexism in readers. A similar form could be developed for test content, considering the illustrations, main characters, and characteristics of children and adults.
20. *Report of the Commission on Tests: Righting the Balance* (New York: College Entrance Examination Board, 1970).
21. M. G. Holmen and R. F. Doctor, *Education and Psychological Testing: A Study of the Industry and Its Practices* (New York: Russell Sage Foundation, 1972).
22. O. G. Brim, et al., *American Beliefs and Attitudes About Intelligence* (New York: Russell Sage Foundation, 1969); D. A. Goslin, *Teachers and Testing* (New York: Russell Sage Foundation, 1967).
23. Grambs.
24. Malcolm.

Policymakers

Teacher organizations, both associations and unions, have not been active concerning the professional problems and concerns of women teachers, as disclosed in Andrew Fishel and Janice Pottker's "Women Teachers and Teacher Power." Various claims about women teachers are proven to be fallacious. For example, the charge that the high turnover rate of women teachers keeps teacher organizations from becoming strong is shown to be false because women teachers have the same turnover rate as male teachers. It is suggested that the reason why so many women teachers do not actively support their teacher organization is because the actions of these organizations have favored male members at the expense of female members. Salary aims and maternity-leave policies are two examples of the male bias of teacher organizations.

There is sex discrimination in promotion to school administration as shown in "Performance of Women Principals: A Review of Behavioral and Attitudinal Studies." Over eighty-six percent of principals in the country are men, although fewer than one-third of American teachers are male. As the grade level rises, and as the status of the administrative position rises, fewer and fewer women are found in leadership positions. Many studies have concluded that women not only are as qualified as men to be principals, but that they are often more qualified than men to hold such positions. Specifically, studies have shown women principals to be more capable than male principals in supervising and administering a school and maintaining good relations with students and parents.

Even though women have been shown to be qualified as principals, they are rarely promoted. As a result, the one-third of the teaching force that is male fills almost all administrative positions. Sex, and not ability, is the most important determinant of whether a teacher becomes an administrator.

Suzanne Saunders Taylor, in "The Attitudes of Superintendents and Board of Education Members Toward the Employment and Effectiveness of Women as Public School Administrators," concludes that there are sex differences in attitudes toward women in administration, with women board members reacting more favorably toward women than male members. Opportunities for women in administration are limited, although there are no written policies against their promotion.

In "School Boards and Sex Bias in American Education" the authors call attention to the fact that American school boards are, and always have been, dominated by men. Today only twelve percent of all school-board members are women, and over half of all boards in the country have no women members. This male domination of local boards of education is shown as resulting in policies that discriminate against women teachers and female students. The unequal treatment of women will not end until more women are represented on school boards.

"Sex Discrimination as Public Policy: The Case of Maternity Leave for Teachers" points out that almost all teachers in the country have, in the past, been forced to leave teaching if they became pregnant, and were often prohibited from returning after giving birth. These maternity-leave policies were based on irrational reasoning and myths about pregnancy, and not on scientific or medical knowledge. These policies worked financial hardship upon women and helped to disqualify them from promotions. While being harmful to women teachers, the policies enabled school districts to cut back on the total number of teachers they employed and to pay less money overall in teacher salaries. Despite challenges to maternity-leave policies, local school boards refused to change their policies until required to by the U.S. Supreme Court.

The articles in this section demonstrate beyond any doubt that male domination and prejudice against females exists in all levels and positions of decision-making in education. The field of education has been fortunate in that societal pressures have pushed hundreds of thousands of intelligent and qualified women into the field of teaching. But it is a fantastic waste of human resources and talent not to allow these professional women to achieve a rank commensurate with their ability. Not only does sexism hurt women in education, but it is also damaging to the schools and society by providing people who are not the best qualified to fill positions of leadership and authority.

Women Teachers and Teacher Power*

ANDREW FISHEL and JANICE POTTKER

In 1956 Myron Lieberman wrote, "The predominance of women in teaching is one of the most important and neglected facts about American education." In spite of this realization, in the years that have passed little attention has been paid to the effects of the feminine role in teaching.

Most of what has been written has concerned itself with the effect of women teachers on the students. Almost nothing has been written directly on the effect of women in teaching on teacher organizations, despite the rise of the women's liberation movement and the subsequent manifold increase in writing on the role of women in American society.

Writers who have dealt with teacher organizations and teacher militancy have almost unanimously seen the presence of women teachers as harmful for teacher organizations.

These statements about women teachers express common attitudes:

> [The number of women in teaching] must be regarded as one of the two or three most important obstacles to the professionalization of education.[1]
>
> The large concentration of women in public school-teaching will decrease the power and effectiveness of teacher organizations[2].
>
> The cause [militant unionism] itself provides unusual opportunities [for women] for association with men.[3]

---

* Reprinted with the permission of the Center for Urban Education and the authors; a slightly different version of this article appeared originally in *The Urban Review* 6 (November/December 1972): 40–44.

Same writers show open hostility toward women:

> Teaching may still be dominated by middle-aged matrons and young women who use the schools as a convenient stop-gap between college and marrying, but these groups will no longer set the tone.[4]
>
> Teaching is not one occupation, but two. There are men teachers and women teachers.[5]

There are two main reasons why women teachers are seen as having a negative effect on teacher organizations. First, it is claimed that the high turnover rate among women teachers makes it difficult for teacher organizations to be effective. Secondly, it is claimed that women are less willing to support the goals and actions of the teacher organizations and thus the women undermine the organizations' operations.

There has not been any real understanding of or sympathy for the women teachers' position. It is necessary to look at the participation of women in teacher organizations with a different perspective.

TURNOVER TRUTHS

The claim that the high turnover rate of women teachers detracts from the effective operation of teacher organizations ignores the turnover rate for male teachers. Actually, the turnover rate for men is only slightly lower than the turnover rate for women. This is true for both elementary and secondary schools.[6] Furthermore, when men teachers leave the profession they stay out. But when women teachers leave they frequently come back, which tends to equalize the teacher turnover ratio for men and women.

It is often claimed that those women who leave teaching view it as an occupation to have for a few years and to be left usually for marriage. Actually, there are other reasons that are as central to the purposes of teacher organizations as the reasons for men leaving. But so far all the attention has been focused on the causes for male dissatisfaction with teaching. For example, all of the plans for differential staffing are centered around the need to keep those males who have not yet become administrators from leaving for higher paying jobs.

MATERNITY POLICIES

Some women who left teaching were forced to leave even though they wanted to continue. A recent report indicated that one-third of the women teachers leaving did so because of maternity.[7] Up until 1974, almost all teacher contracts required a teacher to leave during pregnancy and to stay out of teaching for months (or even years) afterward. Few contracts allowed the teacher to decide whether she wanted to continue teaching.

In most cases, a woman teacher taking a leave of absence was not even guaranteed a position when she wanted to return, unlike male teachers who almost always were guaranteed a position upon returning from serving in the military. Since maternity was not considered a medical disability, women teachers usually could not use their paid sick-leave days for childbirth.

The paternalistic and condescending maternity policies made by the men who run the schools were opposed strongly on the national level by both the AFT's Women's Rights Committee and the NEA's Committee on Professional Rights and Responsibilities, and by many state teacher organizations. But declaring support on the national and state level for better maternity-leave policies is far different from demanding implementation of that policy in contract negotiations on the local level. These changes were not demanded in negotiations.

Although there have been over 400 teacher strikes since 1969, none was ever over the issue of maternity leave. However, many teacher organizations struck over male-oriented issues, such as preparation time for secondary-school teachers. Local teacher organizations usually have been male oriented in their actions and have aimed at achieving goals that primarily benefit male teachers.

Restrictive maternity-leave policies were finally overthrown by the U.S. Supreme Court in 1974.[8] The elimination of discriminatory policies was, therefore, eventually accomplished because of the efforts of individual teachers and their lawyers and not because of the efforts of local teacher organizations in collective bargaining.

It can be seen that a certain portion of the turnover rate for women elementary and secondary schoolteachers in the past would have to be considered involuntary due to the nature of maternity-leave regulations. This is of considerable significance since it affects so many teachers.

DISCRIMINATION IN PROMOTION

There is a second reason why so many women leave teaching. They see that their opportunities for advancement are quite limited.

Although two-thirds of all teachers are women, eighty-seven percent of all principals are men. In elementary schools, where eighty-four percent of the teachers are women, eighty percent of the principals are men. In secondary schools the situation is even worse: women account for only three percent of junior-high principals and one percent of senior-high principals.[9] In addition, it has traditionally taken ten years longer for a woman principal to obtain that position than for a male principal.[10]

Besides these obvious areas of discrimination in education, there are more subtle forms of sex discrimination at work. Women teachers are also discriminated against in pay for extra duties: male teachers receive far higher salary supplementals for coaching sports than women teachers receive for supervising nonathletic activities.[11] Lower pay supplementals for women holds true even when the activities require the same amount of time; this is a dramatic example of unequal pay for equal work.

Preferential treatment is also frequently given to male teachers in terms of tenure and sabbaticals. The total experience of women in teaching has shown that sex discrimination is as great in public employment as it is in private employment.

AMBITION THWARTED

Besides the obvious discrimination in refusing to promote women in education, there is another factor that keeps women almost exclusively in the classroom or that makes them decide to leave teaching. Women see that they have little chance to advance and therefore do not think it is worth the effort to obtain the academic credentials needed to do so. This process can be seen in the fact that women receive three-quarters of all bachelor's degrees in education, but under half of master's degrees and under one-fifth of doctorates in education.[12]

One study of teachers found that only two percent of women teachers aspired to an administrative position, while almost half of men wanted to become school administrators.[13] However, women do not enter teaching with this attitude. Beginning women teachers were more eager to achieve an administrative position than were the more experienced women teachers,[14] who have seen how difficult it is for a woman to obtain such a position. This is, of course, part of the reason for the success that school systems have had in discriminating against women.

There is also an insidious type of discrimination against women in the educational system, especially regarding administrative positions. Many administrators use the protégé system: they choose "their man" from the pool of availables to sponsor. This is often done on a very personal basis, and since the overwhelming number of administrators are men, they choose a man to sponsor.

But if academic qualifications are used as an indicator of ability, women teachers would make better principals than would men teachers. Women in teaching have higher scores on the National Teacher Examination than do men Far more female teachers than male teachers have been National Merit Scholarship Finalists and Semi-finalists.[15] In addition, those studies that have compared the attitudes and performance of women and men principals have concluded that women make better principals in many ways than do men.[16] However, the typical woman teacher, no matter how qualified, will usually begin and end her career as a classroom teacher. Discrimination against women at the principalship level is particularly harmful since the principalship is frequently a steppingstone to higher administrative posts.

ROLE CONFLICT

There is still another factor involved in keeping women from pursuing advancements. This is the conflict some women experience between home and work. Single women teachers make more advancements than do married women teachers.[17] Part of this is due to the greater job discriminations married women face, and part of this is due to women's multiple roles that in this society are conflictive. (Men's roles are not conflictive: no one is surprised at a man who is a husband, father, and school superintendent.)

Women eliminate the strain that results from multiple roles by concentrating on one role, which usually means lowering their career aspirations. If women's role in the family continues to require more than does the family role of men, women will continue to feel it necessary to spend much of their energy in this direction. If men were willing to assume an equal responsibility for child care and household chores then women would not be faced with such an unpleasant choice: work or family.

What exists now is a vicious cycle. Women are told by society from an early age that raising a family should be more important to them than a job, and that to be good wives and mothers they should give it their full-time attention. Up until recently almost all women accepted this as true, even though they may have had families and worked. As a result, women who wanted to have a career along with a family felt guilty about not giving enough attention to their family obligations. This feeling of guilt, along with the realization that they would be discriminated against in their career, results in reduced career aspirations for most women. Women then can be denied advancement because they lack ambition or are thought incapable of handling a higher position.

PUSHED INTO TEACHING

There are other reasons besides maternity policies, failure to receive promotions, and role conflict that cause many women to leave teaching. Many women are simply not suited, nor ever were suited, to be teachers. Teaching is basically defined as a woman's occupation in the United States because so many teachers are women. But teaching is also characterized as feminine because the traits it is identified with, expressiveness and nurturing, are associated with women in this culture. However, when sex-related characteristics of occupations in various countries are analyzed it becomes apparent that the characterization of teaching as feminine in nature is merely a means of supporting the occupational status quo. For example, in countries where teachers are mostly men, teaching is considered a masculine occupation.

The definition of teaching as a feminine occupation in the United States has influenced the supply of teachers. Women in college prepare themselves for jobs that are considered appropriate for them by society and where they know there will be a market for their services. As a result, forty-two percent of all bachelor's degrees earned by women are in education and fifty-nine percent of all masters' and thirty percent of all doctorates awarded to women are in education.[18]

It is also startling that of all women who have graduated from college and are working, over sixty percent are in education.[19] It would be extremely naive to assume that two-thirds of all college-educated women in the United States really want to be teachers.

It is partially because so many intelligent women have been pushed into a "feminine" occupation, for which they are not really suited or which they did not really want, that they are so willing to leave teaching when they get married or have a child.

LACK OF SUPPORT

The second reason why it is claimed that somen have a negative effect on teacher organizations is that they are thought to be less willing to support the goals and actions of the organization.

To begin with, most unions have been unresponsive to the needs of their women members. As a result there is a reluctance on the part of women to join unions in all occupations, not only in education. Over thirty percent of the men in the labor force belong to a union as compared to only twelve percent of the women.[20]

In education the AFT (an AFL-CIO affiliate) when confronted with an issue such as the Equal Rights Amendment for women where it had to choose between taking the position endorsed by the AFL-CIO or taking the position endorsed by the overwhelming majority of women teachers, decided to side with the AFL-CIO. At their 1971 convention the AFT voted not to support the ERA, although a poll had shown that fewer than ten percent of the teachers in the country opposed ERA.[21] After ERA was passed by Congress, the AFT eventually came out in favor of ratification by the states, but did not do so until the AFL-CIO had also changed its position and endorsed the amendment. Even after it had officially endorsed ERA, the teacher unions in many states showed little or no enthusiasm for the amendment. For example, when ratification of ERA was being considered by the Connecticut legislature, the Connecticut Education Association lobbied vigorously for its passage while the Connecticut Federation of Teachers did little to try to develop legislative support for the amendment.[22]

However, there are other factors involved with women's reluctance to join teacher unions—such as social class, mobility aspirations, and political ideology. Two-thirds of New York City teachers who came from a lower-class background expressed a strong belief in unionism, as compared to one-third of the teachers who came from a middle-class background.[23] Since more female teachers than male teachers in the United States came from middle-class backgrounds,[24] it can be assumed that part of the reluctance of women to join teacher unions is due to social origin rather than sex-related characteristics.

Enthusiasm for unionism is clearly related to the individual's aspirations and therefore there are many women teachers who will not become activists until their unions fight, successfully, to eliminate discrimination in promotion policy. Vigorous unionism is supported by only forty percent of teachers who don't look forward to promotion: the category to which most women belong because of the discriminatory ceiling placed on their aspirations. Among teachers who seek advancement, seventy percent are in favor of militant union activity.[25]

In addition, society expects aggressive behavior on the part of men and expects women to be more submissive. Women teachers are thus placed in a position where they must either accept societal expectations of feminine behavior and not support aggressive organization tactics, or else reject society's image of what a woman should act like and support the organization. Men teachers have no such conflict and therefore find it much easier to support militant actions.

Women teachers are more conservative politically than are men teachers,[26] and persons who are more conservative are not too likely to subscribe to the goals or actions of militant teacher unions.

However, women teachers are more likely than male teachers to join the National Education Association.[27] But even though women join more than men they usually do not dominate the leadership. Tables 1 and 2 show how women are represented in various elective and staff positions in NEA and state education associations.

Table 1

Women in Leadership Positions in NEA, 1973[28]

Position	*Total*	*No. of Women*	*Percent Women*
Executive Management	3	1	33.3
Top Management	11	0	0
Other Managerial Positions	70	10	14.3
Executive Committee	10	3	30
Board of Directors	100	24	24

Although almost two-thirds of NEA members are women, Table 1 shows that only eleven out of eighty-four, or thirteen percent, of managerial positions in NEA are held by women. Another fact that the table does not show is that only twenty-five percent of the entire professional staff in NEA are women.[29] As Table 2 shows, in 1973 only fifteen per-

Table 2

Women in Leadership Positions in State Education Associations, 1973[30]

Position	*Total*	*No. of Women*	*Percent Women*
President	54	8	14.8
Executive Secretary	50	0	0
Deputy/Associate/Assistant Executive Secretary	97	5	5.1
Professional or Semiprofessional Staff	790	109	13.7

cent of state education association presidents were women, no state had a woman executive secretary, and only fourteen percent of the entire professional and semiprofessional staff were women. Why women in state education associations can be found in so few leadership positions can be understood from a study made of the Oregon Education Association. The study found that men, although numerically in the minority, used their votes in association elections for the express purpose of keeping women from positions of authority in the organization.[31]

Women, thus excluded from the leadership of the organization to which they belong, have very little control over the direction of the organization. Once in power, male leaders of teacher organizations, whether union or association, use their power to further the aims of the male members.

SALARY AIMS

Salary aims are another way in which unions lose women's support. Teaching is one occupation where salary is determined by specific measurable qualifications regardless of sex. Teacher salaries are determined by the number of years in teaching and the number of hours of graduate work completed. Most teacher organizations, while attempting to uplift the salary of all teachers, have concentrated particularly on decreasing the amount of graduate hours needed between salary increases. A standard method used by the NEA to evaluate how successful a local affiliate has been in its negotiations with its school board is the number of increments given for graduate work. It is thought that a local affiliate that has a pay scale where salary increases are given at the B.A., B.A. plus 15 hours, and B.A. plus 30 hours is better than one where salary changes occur only at the B.A., and the B.A. plus 30 levels.

Since forty-three percent of men teachers have a masters' degree as compared to nineteen percent of women teachers,[32] these efforts clearly benefit male teachers far more than they do women teachers. Not only do most women teachers not benefit from these efforts, but their salary is also less than it would have been otherwise since the money that was spent for more categories of graduate work increments could have been spent on general salary increases.

Since the average woman teacher has twelve-years experience and the average man teacher only ten years,[33] women teachers would benefit significantly if teacher organizations made their aim greater yearly increases rather than yearly and graduate-work increases. As it stands now, even though the average woman teacher has more experience than male teachers, the average salary for women teachers is $8,953 as compared to $9,854 for men.[34] Also forty-three percent of male teachers earn over $10,000 as compared to only twenty-nine percent of women teachers.[35]

The attitude of most men in education regarding women teachers' salaries has been condescending, since so many women in teaching are married, "their salary often is considered a second income and the difference of one or two hundred dollars a year is of little significance."[36] In fact, only two-thirds of women teachers are married with husbands present as compared to eighty percent of men teachers who are married.[37] This previous statement also assumes that all of the married women teachers have husbands who work, and none of the married men have wives who work. Actually only eighty-eight percent of husbands of women teachers work. Of the married male teachers, fifty-five percent of their wives work.[38] This means that for over half of all married male teachers there is a second income.

However, the real financial problem faced by married men teachers results from the fact that even if a male teacher's wife works, she is probably being paid a low salary because of the economic discrimination against women. Therefore, male teachers cannot expect their wives to provide much additional family income. In comparison, the majority of married women teachers are married to a man having an income higher than that of a teacher.[39] As a result, the average household income of married female teachers is $18,510 as compared to $15,006 for the married male teacher.[40] If male teachers could expect their wives to receive a respectable income from their work, they would be less likely to leave teaching if they could not be promoted to an administrative position. Teacher organizations would then have an easier time organizing this more stable teaching force. Again, the general societal discrimination against women plays an important role in undermining the effectiveness of teacher organizations.

SOCIETY'S VIEWS

Another way the economy discriminates against women is in the very low salary paid to teachers. The reason usually given for teachers' low salaries is that the salary level for teaching is a compromise between what is required to attract and hold qualified women and what is required to attract and hold qualified men. Since women have been so discriminated against in other fields, it is often stated that teaching is a better paying job for a woman than a man. However, this is not to say that it is a well-paying job for a well-educated woman. Women's pay for teaching is favorable only when it is compared to the other jobs women typically hold, such as being a secretary, saleswomen, or clerk. Teaching is considered a poorly paid job for a man since it is compared to medicine, law, or business. It is strange that it is conceivable for a college-educated woman to be a clerk, but it is never envisioned that a male teacher would be a clerk. However, the educational establishment apparently accepts this dichotomous view.

Women who are faced with the option of being a secretary, or a clerk, or a teacher view the pay they receive in two ways. Women teachers realize that their salary is indeed far better than that of most other women, but not anywhere near the income they might possibly receive were it not for the sex segregation of occupations. It is little wonder that a woman, pushed into a job in which she may feel her talents are being wasted, while at the same time being told by society that if a woman works she should earn less money than her husband, emphasizes the personal rewards that can be found in teaching rather than becoming concerned with the economic rewards.

CHANGE NEEDED

Prejudice and discrimination against women is a fact in education as in all other aspects of American life. It is harmful certainly to the women who are discriminated against, and it is also harmful to the men who go into what society considers a feminine occupation and thus get low pay. It is also destructive to teacher organizations that are weakened by lack of support from women teachers, and last it is dysfunctional to society as a whole that does not obtain the most qualified persons to act as teachers of its young or administrators of its schools.

Lieberman wrote in 1956, "The harsh unpleasant truth is this. Education will not become a leading profession unless either the proportion of men to women is drastically increased or there occurs a cultural revolution concerning the role of women in American society."[41] When this was written, it appeared that the only possible direction would be to reduce the number of women in the teaching force. Now with the low status of American women receiving so much attention, the dramatic changes necessary for a cultural revolution have become a more likely possibility.

The results of such cultural changes would be fewer women in teaching because more of them will be in school administration or law or medicine. It would also mean more men in teaching, for the stigma of going into a feminine occupation will no longer exist and the salaries paid teachers will have risen at the same time.

If teacher organizations really want to improve the position of teachers, it is imperative that they further the societal changes taking place in regard to the position and role of women in American life. Teacher organizations must also give equal attention to the needs of male and female teachers rather than concentrating on goals benefiting its male members. If teacher organizations do not become more responsive to the needs of women teachers, then they will be failing these teachers, and women teachers will continue to be reluctant to join or support teacher organizations.

NOTES

1. Myron Lieberman, *Education as a Profession* (Englewood Cliffs, N.J.: Prentice-Hall, 1956), p. 241,
2. Michael Moskow, *Teachers and Unions* (Philadelphia: University of Pennsylvania Press, 1966), p. 195.
3. T. M. Stinett, *Turmoil in Teaching* (New York: Macmillan, 1968), p. 83.
4. Robert Doherty and Walter Oberer, *Teachers, School Boards, and Collective Bargaining* (Ithaca, N. Y.: New York School of Industrial and Labor Relations, 1967), p. 8.
5. Oswald Hall, "The Social Structure of the Teaching Profession," in *Struggle For Power in Education,* ed. Frank Lutz and Joseph Azzarell (New York: Center for Applied Research in Education, 1966), p. 42.
6. Moskow, *Teachers and Unions,* p. 63.
7. *Status of the American Public Schoolteacher, 1970–71* (Washington, D. C.: National Education Association, 1972), p. 20.
8. For a complete discussion of this topic see the selection, "Sex Discrimination As Public Policy: The Case of Maternity-leave Policies for Teachers" in this volume.
9. *26th Biennial Salary and Staff Survey of Public-school Professional Personnel, 1972–73* (Washington D. C.: National Education Association, 1973).
10. Neal Gross and Anne Trask, *Men and Women as Elementary-school Principals* (Cambridge, Mass.: Graduate School of Education, Harvard University, 1964), pp. 3–39.
11. "Salary Supplemental for Extra Duties," *NEA Research Bulletin,* (May 1970): 43; and Connecticut Education Association, *Extra Pay for Athletic and Non-athletic Activities in Connecticut Teacher Contracts 1971–72* (Hartford, Conn.: CEA, 1972).
12. Patricia Sexton, *The Feminized Male* (New York: Vintage Books, 1969), p. 139.
13. John Colombutos, *Sources of Professionalism: A Study of High-school Teachers* (Washington, D. C.: U.S. Government Printing Office, 1962), p. 68.
14. Ward Mason, *The Beginning Teacher* (Washington, D. C.: U.S. Government Printing Office, 1961), p. 62.
15. Sexton, *The Feminized Male,* p. 142.
16. For a complete discussion of this topic see the selection, "Performance of Women

Principals: A Review of Behavioral and Attitudinal Studies" in this volume.

17. Richard Simpson and Ida Simpson, "Women and Bureaucracy in the Semiprofessions," in *The Semiprofessions and Their Organizations,* ed. Amitai Etzioni (New York: Free Press, 1969), p. 230.
18. Sexton, *The Feminized Male,* p. 139.
19. U.S. Department of Labor, *Handbook of Women Workers* (Washington, D. C.: U.S. Government Printing Office, 1969), p. 175.
20. Abbot Ferris, *Indicators of Trends in the Status of American Women* (New York: Russell Sage Foundation, 1971), p. 176.
21. "Teacher Opinion Poll—Equal Rights for Women," *Today's Education,* 60 (November 1971): 9. See Appendix for the complete results of this poll.
22. Suzanne S. Taylor, "Educational Leadership: A Male Domain?" *Phi Delta Kappan* 55 (October 1973): 126.
23. Stephen Cole, *The Unionization of Teachers* (New York: Praeger Publishers, 1969), p. 84.
24. *Status of the American Public Schoolteacher,* p. 61.
25. Cole, *Unionization of Teachers,* p. 90.
26. *Status of the American Public Schoolteacher,* p. 89.
27. Ibid., p. 165.
28. Based on information contained in *NEA Handbook 1973* (Washington, D. C.: NEA, 1973).
29. Taylor, "Educational Leadership," p. 126.
30. Based on information contained in *NEA Handbook 1973* (Washington, D. C.: NEA, 1973).
31. Harmon Zeigler, *The Political World of the High-school Teacher* (Eugene, Oregon: Center for the Advanced Study of Educational Administration, 1966), p. 80.
32. *Status of the American Public Schoolteacher,* p. 12.
33. Ibid., p. 15.
34. Ibid., p. 72.
35. Ibid.
36. Moskow, *Teachers and Unions,* p. 195.
37. *Status of the American Public Schoolteacher,* p. 63.
38. Ibid., p. 64.
39. Cole, *Unionization of Teachers,* p. 88.
40. *Status of the American Public Schoolteacher,* p. 78.
41. Lieberman, *Education as a Profession,* p. 242.

Performance of Women Principals: A Review of Behavioral and Attitudinal Studies*

ANDREW FISHEL and JANICE POTTKER

Men, although a minority of the nation's teachers, have assumed the leadership of the nation's schools. The male domination of administrative positions is frequently justified on the grounds that men perform better as principals than do women and that teachers prefer working for male principals. Over the last twenty years a large number of studies have analyzed both the behavior of male and female principals and the differing attitudes of teachers toward principals of either sex. A review of this literature dramatically demonstrates the wide disparity between the popularly held beliefs regarding male and female principals, and the empirical evidence regarding their behavior.

UNDERREPRESENTATION OF WOMEN ADMINISTRATORS

Although two-thirds of American teachers are women, only fourteen percent of school principals are female. While only sixteen percent of ele-

* Reprinted with the permission of the National Association of Women Deans, Administrators, and Counselors and the authors; a slightly different version of this article appeared in the *Journal of National Association of Women Deans, Administrators, and Counselors* 38 (Spring 1975). This is a much broader and greatly expanded version of an earlier article by the authors entitled, "Women Lose Out: Is There Sex Discrimination in School Administration?", which appeared in *The Clearing House* 47 (March 1973): 387–91.

mentary schoolteachers are males, men assume eighty percent of the principalships.[1] The percent of women elementary principals has sharply declined since 1928, as seen in Table 1.

Table 1

Percent of Elementary-school Principals Who Were Women[2]

Year	*Percent Women Principals*
1928	55
1948	41
1958	38
1968	22
1971	21
1973	20

In secondary schools, where women comprise half of the teachers, men constitute ninety-seven percent of junior-high principals and ninety-nine percent of senior-high principals. Women constitute only 12.5 percent of all assistant principals. Women comprise thirty-one percent of the assistant principals in elementary schools, eight percent in junior-high schools, and six percent in senior-high schools.[3]

BEHAVIORAL STUDIES

Women clearly do not fare well in appointments to administrative positions. A popular rationalization for appointing men rather than women as principals is that men are supposedly better suited to be principals. Many studies over the past twenty years have compared various aspects of the behavior of men and women principals. The findings from nine of these studies, listed in Table 2, were reviewed in order to determine what, if any, empirical evidence exists to demonstrate that characteristics of successful principals are sex linked.

Table 2

Major Studies of Sex Differences in Principal Behavior

Author(s)	*Date*	*Location of Study*
Wiles and Grobman[4]	1955	Florida
Hines and Grobman[5]	1956	Florida
Hemphill, Griffith, and Frederickson[6]	1962	———
Gross and Trask[7]	1965	United States
Morsink[8]	1968	Michigan
Hoyle[9]	1969	Texas
Sprence[10]	1971	———
Mann[11]	1971	New York
Van Meir[12]	1973	Suburban Chicago

The most significant results from these studies are categorized according to four areas and are presented below: instructional supervision; relations with students; relations with parents; and community and general administration.

Instructional Supervision

1. Women principals are less tolerant of teachers acting on their own initiative and making their own decisions.[13]

2. Women principals emphasize and bring about a greater amount of productive behavior on the part of their teachers.[14]

3. Women principals influence teachers to use more desirable teaching practices.[15]

4. Women principals exhibit greater knowledge of teaching methods and techniques.[16]

5. Women principals are more concerned with the objectives of teaching.[17]

6. Women principals are more able and willing to assist beginning teachers with instructional problems.[18]

7. Women principals place greater emphasis on recognizing differences between individual pupils.[19]

8. Women principals exhibit a greater concern for the social and emotional development of pupils.[20]

9. There is no difference between male and female principals regarding emphasis placed on maintaining academic standards.[21]

10. Women principals are more aware of potential problem students.[22]

11. Women principals place greater emphasis on evaluating the learning process taking place in their schools.[23]

12. The academic achievement of students in schools with women principals is either equal to[24] or higher than[25] the achievement of students in schools with male principals.

Relations With Students

1. There is higher student morale in schools having women principals.[26]

2. Women principals make greater efforts to involve students in school affairs.[27]

Relations With Parents And Community

1. Parents approve more often of the learning activities and outcomes in schools with women principals.[28]

2. Parents approve more often the way in which women principals handle student discipline.[29]

3. Parents look favorably upon schools with women principals more often than they do upon schools with men principals.[30]

4. Parents whose children are in schools having women principals are involved in school affairs as often[31] or more often[32] than parents whose children are in schools with male principals.

5. Women principals are more often guided by community preferences when deciding on school operations.[33]

General Administration

1. Women principals are generally more democratic in the way they operate their schools.[34]

2. There is no difference between men and women principals in the amount of support given to teachers in conflict with a pupil.[35]

3. There is no difference between men and women principals in the emphasis placed on maintaining school discipline.[36]

4. Women principals display greater respect for the dignity of the teachers in their school.[37]

5. Women principals have better and closer communication with teachers in their school.[38]

6. Teacher morale in schools with women principals is either equal to[39] or higher than[40] in schools with male principals.

7. Women principals speak and act more often as representatives of the group.[41]

8. Women principals maintain a more closely knit organization.[42]

9. Women principals are more effective at resolving conflicts with staff members.[43]

10. Women principals are less rigid in their response to school situations.[44]

11. Women principals are better at reconciling conflicting demands.[45]

12. Women principals exhibit greater foresight in the decisions they make and the actions they take.[46]

13. Women principals more frequently review the results of actions they have taken.[47]

14. Women principals exercise stronger leadership.[48]

15. Women principals generally exhibit more effective administrative techniques.[49]

These behavioral studies clearly indicate that in terms of ability to supervise and administer a school and to maintain good relations with students and parents, the few women who have been able to obtain administrative positions have performed as capably, if not more capably, than their male counterparts.

ATTITUDINAL STUDIES

Because behavioral studies have shown that women principals generally perform more capably than male principals, it is worthwhile to look at the results of studies made of the attitudes of teachers, administrators, and school board members toward women principals. The findings of the twenty-two studies listed in Table 3 were reviewed and categorized according to three areas: teacher attitudes toward women principals; attitudes toward the recruitment and hiring of women principals; and attitudes of women principals toward their job.

Table 3
Major Studies of Attitudes Toward Women as School Administrators

Author(s)	*Date*	*Location of Study*
Barter[50]	1957	Wayne County, Michigan
Krause[51]	1964	New Jersey
Burns[52]	1964	California
Henschel[53]	1964	Utah
Jenkins[54]	1966	Montgomery County, Pa.
Rock & Hemphill[55]	1966	United States
Milanovich[56]	1966	New York
Warwick[57]	1967	Wisconsin
Lemon[58]	1968	———
Cobbley[59]	1970	Six Western States
Taylor[60]	1971	Connecticut
Zimmerman[61]	1971	Pennsylvania
Scriven[62]	1973	United States
Crosby[63]	1973	United States
Neidig[64]	1973	Iowa
Holland[65]	1973	New York
Longstreth[66]	1973	Florida
Matheny[67]	1973	Cook County, Illinois
Peterson[68]	1973	Detroit
Timmons[69]	1973	Indiana
LaBarthe[70]	1973	California
NEA[71]	1973	United States

The major results from these studies, which were carried out over a period of sixteen years, are presented below.

Teacher Attitudes Towards Women Principals

1. Male teachers prefer working for male administrators.[72]

2. Male teachers who have worked with a female administrator are more favorable toward women as principals than those male teachers who have not worked with a woman principal.[73]

3. Women teachers are more favorable toward working with women administrators than are male teachers.[74]

4. Teachers believe there is no difference in the leadership abilities of men and women principals.[75]

Attitudes Toward the Recruitment and Hiring of Women Principals

1. Colleges and universities make no special effort to recruit women for training to become principals.[76]
2. Women teachers receive less encouragement from supervisors to prepare for and to become administrators.[77]
3. There is strong bias against appointing women to administrative positions.[78]
4. Women teachers do not aspire to administrative positions to the same extent that men aspire.[79]
5. Women teachers do not academically prepare themselves for administrative positions as often as male teachers prepare themselves.[80]
6. Women teachers must possess superior qualifications and skills in order to be appointed to an administrative position.[81]
7. Most women who become administrators did not initially seek the position but rather were either offered the position or were encouraged by a supervisor to apply for it.[82]

Attitudes of Women Principals Towards Their Job

1. Women who become administrators do so because of the challenge it offers them and a desire to be in a leadership position.[83]
2. Women in administrative positions feel sensitive about holding a position traditionally held by men.[84]
3. Women who become principals express the same amount of satisfaction with their job as do male principals.[85]

It is frequently argued that the reason there are so few women in authority positions in the schools is not due to male bias, but rather that women teachers have not obtained the academic credentials necessary to hold administrative positions. While it is true, as these studies show, that women teachers do not aspire or prepare for administrative jobs to the same extent as male teachers, these attitudinal studies have also shown that women teachers are discouraged from seeking administrative appointments.

As a result of this discouragement, most women in education who seek positions other than that of a classroom teacher undertake graduate studies in fields other than school administration. This is illustrated by the small number of women who receive doctorates in educational administration, as compared to other education areas. In 1972, only eleven percent of doctorates in education administration went to women, as compared to thirty-two percent in educational psychology, twenty-five percent in counseling, and thirty-eight percent in curriculum.[86] Similarly, from 1960 to 1969 only thirteen percent of the doctorates in education administration went to women as compared to twenty-six percent in educational psychology, and twenty-one percent in counseling.[87]

The results from these attitudinal studies indicate that there is prejudice shown by most male teachers, school superintendents, and school board members against women serving as principals. As a result, the criteria currently used to recruit and hire principals is not related to characteristics needed for effective performance as principal. Sex has been the determinant in appointment to principalship, rather than ability. Although the weight of behavioral evidence indicates that, in many areas, the performance of male principals is inferior to that of women principals, male teachers continue to receive the overwhelming number of appointments to administrative positions.

NOTES

1. National Education Association. *26th Biennial Salary and Staff Survey of Public-school Professional Personnel 1972–1973* (Washington, D. C.: NEA, 1973).
2. Dorothy Johnson, "What is the Future of Women in School Administration?" in *Women: A Significant National Resource* (Washington, D. C. National Council of Administrative Women in Education, 1971), p. 35.
3. National Education Association, *26th Biennial Salary and Staff Survey*.
4. Kimball Wiles and Hulda Gross Grobman, "Principals as Leaders," *Nation's Schools* 56 (October 1955): 75–77.
5. Vynce Hines and Holden Grobman, "The Weaker Sex is Losing Out." *School Board Journal* 132 (March 1956): 100, 102.
6. John Hemphill, Daniel Griffiths, and Herman Frederiksen, *Administrative Performance and Personality* (New York: Teachers College Press, 1962).
7. Neal Gross and Anne Trask, *Men and Women as Elementary-school Principals* (Cambridge, Mass.: Harvard University, Graduate School of Education, 1965).
8. Helen Morsink, "Leader Behavior of Men and Women Secondary-school Principals," *Educational Horizons* (Winter 1968–69), pp. 69–74.
9. John Hoyle, "Who Shall Be Principal—A Man or A Woman?", *National Elementary Principal* (January 1969): 23–24.
10. Betty A. Spence, "Sex of Teachers as a Factor in Their Perception of Selected Leadership Characteristics of Male and Female Elementary-school Principals" (Ph.D. diss., Purdue University, 1971) in *Dissertation Abstracts International* 32 (December 1971): 2,985A.
11. Dale Mann, *Administrative-community-school Relationships in New York State*, Report for the New York State Commission on the Quality, Cost, and Financing of Elementary and Secondary Education, 1971.
12. Edward J. Van Meir, "Leadership Behavior of Male and Female Elementary Principals: A Comparison By Sex," *Marquette University Education Review* 4 (Spring 1973): 8–11.
13. Morsink, "Leader Behavior" and Gross and Trask, *Men and Women*.
14. Wiles and Grobman, "Principals"; Hines and Grobman, "The Weaker Sex"; Morsink, "Leader Behavior"; and Spence, "Sex of Teachers."
15. Hines and Grobman, "The Weaker Sex."
16. Hemphill, Griffiths, and Fredericksen, *Administrative Performance*.

17. Ibid.
18. Ibid.
19. Gross and Trask, *Men and Women.*
20. Ibid.
21. Ibid.
22. Hoyle, "Who Shall Be Principal?"
23. Hemphill, Griffiths, and Fredericksen, *Administrative Performance.*
24. Hines and Grobman, "The Weaker Sex."
25. Gross and Trask, *Men and Women.*
26. Hines and Grobman, "The Weaker Sex."
27. Hemphill, Griffiths, and Fredericksen, *Administrative Performance.*
28. Hines and Grobman, "The Weaker Sex."
29. Ibid.
30. Ibid.
31. Gross and Trask, *Men and Women.*
32. Hemphill, Griffiths, and Fredericksen, *Administrative Performance.*
33. Mann, *Administrative-community-school.*
34. Hines and Grobman, "The Weaker Sex"; Hemphill, Griffiths, and Fredericksen, *Administrative Performance;* Morsink. "Leader Behavior"; and Wiles and Grobman, "Principals."
35. Gross and Trask, *Men and Women.*
36. Ibid.
37. Wiles and Grobman, "Principals."
38. Ibid.
39. Gross and Trask, *Men and Women.*
40. Hines and Grobman, "The Weaker Sex."
41. Morsink, "Leader Behavior."
42. Ibid.
43. Ibid.
44. Hines and Grobman, "The Weaker Sex."
45. Van Meir, "Leadership Behavior."
46. Morsink, "Leader Behavior."
47. Hoyle, "Who Shall Be Principal?"
48. Van Meir, "Leadership Behavior."
49. Hines and Grobman, "The Weaker Sex."
50. Alice S. Barter, "The Status of Women in School Administration—Where Will They Go from Here," *Educational Horizons* 37 (Spring 1959): 72–75.
51. John Ludwig Krause, "A Study of Teacher Attitudes Toward Their Women Secondary-school Principals in New Jersey" (Ed.D. diss., Temple University, 1964) in *Dissertation Abstracts* 25 (August 1964): 967–68A.
52. Dorothy M. Burns, "Women In Educational Administration: A Study of Leadership in California Public Schools" (Ed.D. diss., University of Oregon, 1964) in *Dissertation Abstracts* 25 (November 1964): 2,821–22A.
53. Beverly Jean Smith Henschel, "A Comparison of the Personality Variables of Women Administrators and Women Teachers in Education" (Ed.D. diss., University of Utah, 1964) in *Dissertation Abstracts* 25 (May 1965): 6,313A.
54. William Job Jenkins, "A Study of the Attitudes of Elementary Schoolteachers in Selected Schools in Montgomery County, Pennsylvania, Toward the Woman Elementary-school Principal" (Ed.D. diss., Temple University, 1966) in *Dissertation Abstracts* 25 (November 1966): 1,223–24A.

55. Donald Rock and John Hemphill, *Report of the Junior-high School Principalship* (Washington, D. C.: National Association of Secondary School Principals, 1966).
56. Anthony Milanovich, "Gentlemen Before Ladies?", *New York State Education* 54 (December 1966) : 18–19.
57. Eunice Blowers Warwick, "Attitudes Toward Women in Administrative Positions As Related to Curricular Implementation and Change" (Ph.D. diss., University of Wisconsin, 1967) in *Dissertation Abstracts* 28 (October 1967) : 1,256–57A.
58. Donald K. Lemon, "A Study of the Attitude of Selected Groups Toward The Employment of Women for Administrative Positions in Public Schools" (Ed.D. diss., University of Kansas, 1968) in *Dissertation Abstracts* 29 (December 1968) : 1,718–19A.
59. LeOre Cobbley, "A Study of Attitudes and Opportunities for Women in Six Western States to Become Elementary-school Principals" (Ed.D. diss., Brigham Young University, 1970) in *Dissertation Abstracts International* 31 (March 1971) : 4,409A.
60. Suzanne S. Taylor, "The Attitudes of Superintendents and Board of Education Members In Connecticut Toward the Employment and Effectiveness of Women as Public-school Administrators (Ed.D. diss., University of Connecticut, 1971) . A portion of this study is contained in this volume.
61. Jeanne Noll Zimmerman, "The Status of Women in Educational Administrative Positions within the Central Offices of Public Schools" (Ed.D. diss., Temple University, 1971) in *Dissertation Abstracts International* 32 (October 1971): 1,826A.
62. Alvenin Levine Scriven, "A Study of Women Occupying Administrative Positions in the Central Office of Large School Districts" (Ed.D. diss., University of Florida, 1973) in *Dissertation Abstracts International* 33 (June, 1973) : 6,920A.
63. Jeanie West Crosby, "An Exploratory Study of Women Superintendents" (Ed.D. diss., University of Massachusetts, 1973) in *Dissertation Abstracts International* 34 (January 1974): 3,742A.
64. Marilyn Boyd Neidig, "Women Applicants for Administrative Positions: Attitudes Held by Administrators and School Boards" (Ph.D. diss., University of Iowa, 1973) in *Dissertation Abstracts International* 34 (December 1973) : 2,982–83A.
65. Jacqueline Lois Holland, "Relationships Between the Chief School Administrator's Selection of Principal Candidates and the Candidate's Qualifications, Attitudes on Educational Issues, and Sex" (Ed.D. diss., Fordham University, 1973 in *Dissertation Abstracts International* 34 (November 1973) : 2,213–14A.
66. Catherine Archibald Longstreth, "An Analysis of the Perceptions of the Leadership Behavior of Male and Female Secondary-school Principals in Florida" (Ed.D. diss., University of Miami, 1973) in *Dissertation Abstracts International* 34 (November 1973) : 2,224–25A.
67. Priscilla Herron Pugh Matheny, "A Study of the Attitudes of Selected Male and Female Teachers, Administrators, and Board of Education Presidents Toward Women in Educational Administrative Positions" (Ph.D. diss., Northwestern University, 1973) in *Dissertation Abstracts International* 34 (December 1973) : 2,976A.
68. Marcella Tandy Peterson, "Status and Trends in the Promotion of Women to Secondary-school Principalships with Special Reference to Black Women"

(Ed.D. diss., Wayne State University, 1973) in *Dissertation Abstracts International* 33 (June 1973) : 6,915A.

69. Joseph Edward Timmons, "A Study of Attitudes Toward Women School Administrators and the Aspirations of Women Teachers for Administrative Positions in the State of Indiana" (Ed.D. diss., Indiana University, 1973) in *Dissertation Abstracts International* 34 (February 1974) : 4,660A.
70. Eileen Reid LaBarthe, "A Study of the Motivation of Women in Administrative and Supervisory Positions in Selected Unified School Districts in Southern California" (Ed.D. diss., University of California, 1973) in *Dissertation Abstracts International* 34 (January 1974) : 3,695–96A.
71. National Education Association, "Survey Findings," Research *Action Notes—Resource Center on Sex Role in Education* 1 (4 September 1973) : 4.
72. Matheny, "A Study of the Attitudes of Selected Male and Female Teachers"; Neidig, "Women Applicants"; and National Education Association, "Survey Findings."
73. Barter, "The Status of Women"; Warwick, "Attitudes Toward Women"; and National Education Association, "Survey Findings."
74. Matheny, "A Study of the Attitudes of Selected Male and Female Teachers"; Warwick, "Attitudes Toward Women"; Barter, "The Status of Women"; Krause, "A Study of Teacher Attitudes"; Jenkins, "A Study of the Attitudes of Elementary Schoolteachers"; Lemon, "A Study of the Attitudes of Selected Groups"; and Timmons, "A Study of Attitudes Toward Women." An opposite result was found by National Education Association, "Survey Findings."
75. Barter, "The Status of Women"; Cobbley, "A Study of Attitudes and Opportunities for Women"; Longstreth, "An Analysis of the Perceptions of Leadership Behavior"; and Henschel, "A Comparison of Personality Variables." An opposite result was found by Milanovich, "Gentlemen Before Ladies?"
76. Warwick, "Attitudes Toward Women"; Matheny, "A Study of the Attitudes of Selected Male and Female Teachers"; and Peterson, "Status and Trends."
77. Warwick, "Attitudes Toward Women"; Matheny, "A Study of the Attitudes of Selected Male and Female Teachers"; Jenkins, "A Study of the Attitudes of Superintendents and Board of Education Members."
78. Timmons, "A Study of Attitudes Toward Women"; Matheny, "A Study of the Attitudes of Selected Male and Female Teachers"; Barter, "The Status of Women"; LaBarthe, "A Study of the Motivation of Women"; Cobbley, "A Study of Attitudes and Opportunities for Women"; Longstreth, "An Analysis of the Perceptions"; Warwick, "Attitudes Toward Women"; Neidig, "Women Applicants"; and Taylor, "The Attitudes of Superintendents and Board of Education Members." Opposite results were found by Holland, "Relationships Between Chief School Administrators"; and Zimmerman, "The Status of Women in Educational Administrative Positions."
79. Timmons, "A Study of Attitudes Toward Women"; Zimmerman, "The Status of Women in Educational Administrative Positions"; Cobbley, "A Study of Attitudes and Opportunities for Women"; Barter, "The Status of Women"; Warwick, "Attitudes Toward Women"; Burns, "Women in Educational Administration"; and Peterson, "Status and Trends."
80. Timmons, "A Study of Attitudes Toward Women"; Barter, "The Status of Women"; and Burns, "Women in Educational Administration."
81. Matheny, "A Study of the Attitudes of Selected Male and Female Teachers"; Warwick, "Attitudes of Superintendents and Board of Education Members."

82. Cobbley, "A Study of Attitudes and Opportunities for Women"; Zimmerman, "The Status of Women in Educational Administrative Positions"; and Scriven, "A Study of Women."
83. LaBarthe, "A Study of the Motivation of Women."
84. Ibid.
85. Crosby, "An Exploratory Study"; and Rock and Hemphill, *Report.*
86. National Research Council, *Summary Report: 1972 Doctoral Recipients from United States Universities* (Washington, D. C.: National Research Council, 1973).
87. Council for University Women's Progress at the University of Minnesota, *Proportion of Doctorates Earned by Women, by Area and Field, 1960–1969* (Washington, D. C.: Association of American Colleges, 1971). See Appendix for the complete results of this study.

The Attitudes of Superintendents and Board of Education Members Toward the Employment and Effectiveness of Women as Public-school Administrators*

SUZANNE S. TAYLOR

The purpose of the study was to assess attitudes of superintendents and board of education members in Connecticut toward the employment and effectiveness of women in public-school administration. Two research instruments were used in the investigation: an ARI (Attitude Research Instrument) and a BDQ (Background Data Questionnaire). The population was composed of superintendents and school-board members from 107 of Connecticut's 133 school districts. The usable returns analyzed in the study included 84 superintendents and 321 school-board members. The statistical technique used to analyze the data was the one-way analysis of variance.

* Reprinted with the permission of Suzanne S. Taylor. Article was originally from text of author's dissertation, unpublished, University of Connecticut, 1971.

OPPORTUNITIES FOR WOMEN ADMINISTRATORS

An analysis of the responses to the opinion questions on the Background Data Questionnaire was performed and the data was tabulated in order to develop some conclusions about the opportunities for women in administrative positions in Connecticut public schools. Specifically, five questions (P, Q, R, S, and T) under the heading "Your Opinions" on page two of the Background Data Questionnaire were tabulated in order to provide information concerning promotion policies and opportunities for women in administrative positions within the school system.

Sex of the candidate as a determining criterion

Question P asked, "Do you believe sex of the candidate should be a determining criterion in the selection of personnel for any of these administrative positions: superintendent, central-office supervisor or coordinator, secondary principal, assistant secondary principal, elementary principal, assistant elementary principal?" Table 1 presents the number of responses by superintendents and school-board members to the six categories of administrative positions listed under Question P. A comparison of "yes" and "no" responses of superintendents and school-board members is given in the first and second columns of Table 1 and a similar comparison of male and female school-board members is given in columns four and five. The total number of responses in each category is listed in column three.

Considerable agreement existed between superintendents' and school-board members' opinions concerning sex of the candidate as a determining criterion in the selection of personnel for four of the six administrative positions. Considerable disagreement occurred concerning the positions of superintendent and secondary principal. School-board members were more inclined to believe that sex of the candidate should not be a determining criterion, whereas superintendents were inclined to believe that sex of the candidate should be a determining criterion for these two positions.

More than half of the superintendents (52) thought that sex of the candidate should be a determining criterion for the position of superintendent, whereas more than half of the school-board members (185) thought that sex of the candidate should not be a determining criterion for the position of superintendent. This was true even when the school-board members' opinions were analyzed according to the sex of the respondent. Slightly more than half of the male school-board members (112) and approximately threefourths of the female school-board members (73) stated that sex of the candidate should not be a determining criterion for the position of superintendent. Only two school-board members did not respond to this category of the question, less than half a percent, whereas nine superintendents, ten percent, did not answer the question.

More than half of the superintendents (52) also stated that sex of the

Table 1

Sex of the Candidate as a Determining Criterion in the Selection Of Personnel for Administrative Positions

	Superin-tendents	School-board Member	Total	Male Board Member	Female Board Member
Superintendent					
Yes	52	134	186	102	31
No	23	185	208	112	73
No Response	9	2	11	1	1
Central-Office Supervisor					
Yes	9	47	56	35	11
No	68	269	337	177	92
No Response	7	5	12	3	2
Secondary Principal					
Yes	52	105	157	74	30
No	22	213	235	139	74
No Response	10	3	13	2	1
Assistant Secondary Principal					
Yes	12	47	59	35	11
No	64	271	335	178	93
No Response	8	3	11	2	1
Elementary Principal					
Yes	7	31	38	21	9
No	70	286	356	191	95
No Response	7	4	11	3	1
Assistant Elementary Principal					
Yes	5	18	23	12	5
No	72	299	371	200	99
No Response	7	4	11	3	1
N	84	321	405	215	105

candidate should be a determining criterion for the position of secondary principal, whereas more than half of the school-board members (213) stated that sex of the candidate should not be a determining criterion in the selection of a secondary principal. Of these school-board members, 139 were male and 74 were female. Only three school-board members did not respond to this category of the question, less than half a percent, whereas ten superintendents, 12 percent, did not respond.

The choice of central-office supervisor or coordinator should not be decided with sex of the candidate as a determining criterion according to the large majority of both the superintendents (68) and school-board members (177 men and 92 women, a total of 269). Those not responding to this category included seven superintendents and five school-board members.

Considerable agreement also occurred with respect to the opinions of superintendents and school-board members concerning the selection of an assistant secondary principal. A large majority of both superintendents (64) and school board members (178 men and 93 women, a total of 271) stated that sex of the candidate should not be a determining criterion in the selection of an assistant secondary principal. Those not responding to this category of the question included eight superintendents and three school-board members.

Further agreement was evidenced in the opinions of superintendents and school-board members concerning the positions of elementary principal and assistant elementary principal. A very large majority of superintendents (70) and school-board members (191 men and 95 women, a total of 286) stated that sex of the candidate should not be a determining criterion of the position of elementary principal. Only seven superintendents and four school-board members did not respond to this category of the question. A large majority of the superintendents (72) and school-board members (200 men and 99 women, a total of 299) stated that sex of the candidate should not be the determining criterion for the position of assistant elementary principal.

A comparison of male and female school-board members' opinions showed that the percentage of women who felt that sex of the candidate should not be a determining criterion for any of the six positions was slightly higher than the majority of male school-board members who concurred with this opinion.

The largest variation in the opinions of the two sexes concerned the position of superintendent. Slightly more than half of the male school-board members (52 percent, 112) stated that sex of the candidate should not be a determining criterion for this position, whereas 70 percent of the female school-board members (73) concurred with this statement.

Little difference in the percentages of the male and female school-board members' opinions concerning sex of the candidate as a determining criterion for the other five administrative positions was noted. Concerning the position of central-office supervisor, 82 percent of the male school-board members (177) stated that sex of the candidate should not be a determining criterion, while 88 percent of the female school-board members (92) concurred with this statement. The statement that sex of the candidate should not be a determining criterion for the position of secondary principal was made by 65 percent of the male school-board members (139) and 70 percent of the female school-board members (74). The percentages agreeing with this opinion concerning the position of assistant secondary principal were slightly higher. Eighty-two percent of the male school-board members (178) and 89 percent of the female school-board members (93) stated that sex of the candidate should not be a determining criterion for this position.

Even higher percentages of school-board members stated that sex of the candidate should not be a determining criterion for the positions of elementary principal and assistant elementary principal. Concerning the position of elementary principal, 89 percent of the male school-board members (191) and 90 percent of the female school-board members (95) felt that sex of the candidate should not be considered in the selection of an elementary principal. Concerning the position of assistant elementary principal, 93 percent of the male school-board members (200) and 95 percent of the female school-board members (99) felt that sex of the candidate should not be a determining criterion for this position.

Tables 2, 3, 4, and 5 present the tabulation of the data elicited from questions Q, R, S, and T of the Background Data Questionnaire. Respondents were given the opportunity to answer "yes" or "no" to questions concerning policy in making administrative appointments, encouragement of women to prepare and to apply for administrative positions, and final choice between a male and a female candidate. Responses were tabulated according to the factors of sex and type of position. Table 1 presented a tabulation of opinion on "what should be" and Tables 2, 3, 4, and 5 present a tabulation of opinion on "what is" concerning opportunities for women in public-school administration.

Policy excluding women from administrative appointment

Question Q asked, "Is there a policy, written or unwritten, that excludes women from appointment to administrative positions in your school system?" Table 2 presents the number of responses of superintendents and school-board members to the types of policies suggested in Question Q. A comparison of "yes" and "no" responses of superintendents and school-board members is given in the first and second columns of this table, and a similar comparison of responses of male and female school-board members is displayed in columns four and five. The total number of "yes" and "no" responses is presented in the third column of Table 2.

Considerable agreement was evident between superintendents' and school-board members' opinions concerning policy in making administrative appointments. A majority of superintendents (77) and school-board members (296) stated that there was no written policy that excluded women from appointment to administrative positions in their school systems. No school-board member or superintendent stated that there was a written policy excluding women from appointment to administrative positions in their respective school systems, although 7 superintendents and 25 school-board members did not respond to the question. A majority of superintendents and school-board members also stated that there was no unwritten policy that excluded women from appointment to administrative positions in their school systems. One superintendent and 14 school-board members (5 men and 10 women) stated that there was an unwritten policy, while 7 superintendents and 25 school-board members (14 men and 11 women) did not respond to the question.

Table 2

Written or Unwritten Policy that Excludes Women from Appointment to Administrative Positions

	Superintendents	School-board Members	Total	Male Board Members	Female Board Members
Written					
Yes	0	0	0	0	0
No	77	296	373	204	91
No Response	7	25	32	11	14
Unwritten					
Yes	1	14	15	4	10
No	76	282	358	197	84
No Response	7	25	32	14	11
N	84	321	405	215	105

Encouragement of women to apply for administrative positions

Question R asked, "Are women encouraged to apply for administrative positions in your school system?" Table 3 presents the number of responses from superintendents and school-board members to Question R. A comparison of "yes" and "no" responses of superintendents and school-board members is given in the first and second columns of this table and a similar comparison of responses of male and female school-board members is displayed in columns four and five. The total number of "yes" and "no" responses of the superintendents and school-board members is presented in the third column.

Considerable agreement was evident between superintendents' and school-board members' responses to this question. More than half of the superintendents (46) stated that women were encouraged to apply for administrative positions in their school systems and approximately half of the school-board members (143) concurred, although approximately one-third of the superintendents (25) and school-board members (93) did not respond to the question. Of those who stated that women were not encouraged to apply for administrative positions, 13 were superintendents and 85 school-board members.

A comparison of male and female responses revealed some disagreement between the sexes. Approximately half of the male school-board members (106) stated that women were encouraged to apply for administrative positions, but only a third of the female respondents (37) concurred. Of those who stated that women were not encouraged to apply for administrative positions, 51 were men and 34 were women, although 58 men and 34 women did not respond to the question.

The total number of responses of the 405 subjects indicated that almost half of the respondents (189) stated that women were encouraged to apply for administrative positions in their school systems, while a fourth of the respondents (98) said women were not encouraged to apply for these positions and another fourth (118) did not respond.

Table 3

Encouragement of Women to Apply for Administrative Positions

	Superintendents	School-board Members	Total	Male Board Members	Female Board Members
Yes	46	143	189	106	37
No	13	85	98	51	34
No Response	25	93	118	58	34
N	84	321	405	215	105

Encouragement of women to prepare professionally

Question S asked, "Are women encouraged to prepare themselves professionally for administrative positions in your school system?" Table 4 presents the number of responses to this question by superintendents and school-board members. A comparison of "yes" and "no" responses of school-board members and superintendents is given in the first and second columns of this table, and a similar comparison of responses of male and female school-board members is displayed in columns four and five. The total number of "yes" and "no" responses of the two groups is presented in the third column.

Considerable agreement was evident between superintendents' and school-board members' responses to this question. Slightly less than half of the superintendents (36) and school-board members (142) stated that women were encouraged to prepare themselves professionally for administrative positions in their respective school systems, although approximately one-third of the superintendents (28) and one-third of the school-board members (92) did not respond to the question. Of those who stated that women were not encouraged to prepare themselves professionally for administrative positions, 20 were superintendents and 87 were school-board members.

Table 4
Encouragement of Women to Prepare Themselves Professionally For Administrative Positions

	Superintendents	School-board Members	Total	Male Board Members	Female Board Members
Yes	36	142	178	100	42
No	20	87	107	54	33
No Response	28	92	120	61	30
N	84	321	405	215	105

A comparison of male and female responses revealed agreement between the sexes. Approximately half of the male school-board members (10) and half of the female school-board members (42) stated that women were encouraged to prepare themselves professionally for administrative positions, although 61 male school-board members and 30 female school-board members did not respond to the question. Of those who stated that women were not encouraged to prepare themselves professionally for administrative positions, 54 were men and 33 were women.

The total number of responses from the 405 subjects indicated that slightly less than half of the respondents (178) stated that women were encouraged to prepare themselves professionally for administrative positions, while a quarter (107) of the total respondents stated that women were not encouraged to prepare themselves for these positions, and approximately another quarter (120) did not respond to the question.

Final selection between male and female candidate

Question T asked, "In a choice between two candidates of approximately equal qualilcations and experience, who would be selected for an administrative position in your school system?" Table 5 presents the number of responses of superintendents and school-board members to this question. A comparison of responses of superintendents and school-board members is given in the first and second columns of this table, and a similar comparison of responses of male and female school-board members is displayed in columns four and five. The total number of responses of superintendents and school-board members is presented in the third column of Table 5.

It was difficult to determine if considerable agreement existed between superintendents' and school-board members' responses to this question inasmuch as a large majority of superintendents did not answer this question. Of the 63 superintendents who did not respond to this question, 33 explained that the candidate would be judged solely on the basis of his or her qualifications. Only 20 superintendents stated that with approximately equal qualifications and experience, a man would be selected for an administrative position in their school systems in preference to a woman. School-board members were less reluctant to answer this question, because slightly more than a third (115) did not answer. Those who said that, under the conditions mentioned above, a man would be selected for an administrative position in preference to a woman numbered 205 school-board members. Nonetheless, only one superintendent and one school-board member said that a woman would be selected for an administrative position in preference to a man under the previously stated conditions.

A comparison of male and female responses revealed considerable agreement on this question. A majority of male school-board members (137) and female school-board members (67) stated that with approximately equal qualifications and experience, a man would be selected for an administrative

Table 5

Selection of Administrator in a Choice Between Two Candidates Of Approximately Equal Qualifications and Experience

	Superintendents	School-board Members	Total	Male Board Members	Female Board Members
Man	20	205	225	137	67
Woman	1	1	2	1	0
No Response	63	115	178	77	38
N	84	321	405	215	105

position in preference to a woman. The one school-board member who believed that a woman would be chosen for the administrative position was a male. There were 77 male school-board members and 38 female school-board members who did not respond to this question, approximately a third in each case.

The total number of responses of the 405 subjects indicated that more than half of the respondents (225) stated that with approximately equal qualifications and experience, a man would be selected for an administrative position in their school systems in preference to a woman. Two respondents said that, under the conditions mentioned above, a woman would be selected for an administrative position in their school systems in preference to a man. Forty-four percent of the total number of respondents (178) did not answer the question.

CONCLUSIONS

Several conclusions can be drawn from the findings of this study; they relate to attitudes of superintendents and school-board members included in this study toward women as public-school administrators in Connecticut and to opportunities for women to pursue careers in educational administration in Connecticut.

1. The assumption that attitudes toward women in administrative positions represent a male-female issue is true.
2. Female school-board members evidence favorable attitudes toward women in administrative positions, whereas male school-board members and superintendents evidence attitudes somewhere between neutral and favorable toward women in administrative positions.
3. A significant difference exists in attitudes of male school-board members who have worked for a female administrator and those who have not. Attitudes of male school-board members who have worked for female administrators are more favorable than those who have not worked for female administrators.
4. No significant difference exists in attitudes of superintendents and school-board members toward women as public-school administrators because of type of position held, age, length of experience as a superintendent or school-board member, size of school district, or academic level attained by either a superintendent or school-board member.
5. Women are not precluded from appointment to administrative positions on the basis of attitudes of either male superintendents and school-board members or female school-board members included in this study, although the evidence does not support the likelihood of their being hired.
6. No written policy and very few unwritten policies exist that preclude the appointment of women to administrative positions in school systems included in this study.

7. Women are encouraged to apply for and prepare professionally for administrative positions in approximately half the school systems included in this study, but note that the other half do not encourage them.

8. Opportunities for women to pursue administrative careers appear to be limited. In a choice between two candidates of approximately equal qualifications and experience a man would be chosen in preference to a woman. Women are not likely to be appointed as superintendents or secondary-school principals; they are more likely to be appointed as central-office supervisors, assistant secondary principals, elementary principals, or assistant elementary principals.

School Boards and Sex Bias in American Education*

ANDREW FISHEL and JANICE POTTKER

When a midwest state school-board association sought information last year from its members about attendance at their annual convention, they asked, "Will your wife be attending?", rather than, "Will your spouse be attending?" It is assumed that all school-board members are male, which unfortunately is not far from the truth. Women comprise only a very small minority of school-board members in the United States. This often comes as a surprise to many citizens who assume that since women traditionally have been interested in education, women would be well represented on local boards of education.

MALE DOMINATION OF SCHOOL BOARDS

In reality, the percentage of women school-board members has hovered between ten and fifteen percent from 1920 to the present time. In 1927 George Counts found that there was an increase in women on school boards after the passage of the Nineteenth Amendment in 1920.[1] This led Counts to speculate that women would eventually outnumber men on school boards and thus gain control over school policy. This has proven fallacious, as have most of the beliefs about what women would accomplish once they obtained the vote.

Various studies have shown the sex-ratio composition of school boards.

* Reprinted with the permission of the School of Education, Indiana State University, and the authors. A slightly different version of this article appeared originally in *Contemporary Education* 65 (Winter, 1974): 85–89.

Table 1 provides the percentage of women who have served as school-board members in the last half century. This table shows that the number of women serving as board members has been fairly constant. Any changes in the status of American women that have taken place in the last fifty-five years have not resulted in any substantial increase in the proportion of women in educational policymaking positions.

Table 1

Percentage of School-board Members in the United States Who Have Been Women

Year	*Percent Women*
1920	8
1926	14
1932	14
1946	10
1953	14
1958	18
1960	10
1964	22
1965	15
1967	18
1969	13
1970	24
1971	19
1972	12

(See end of article for complete note on sources for each year.)

The percentages in Table 1 do not represent the fact that around forty percent of the school boards in the United States do not have any women members.[2] This can produce a situation like that in Boise, Idaho, where a school board recently held its meeting in the men's room in order to elude the women reporters who were covering the meeting.[3] An additional thirty-five percent of school boards in the United States have only one woman member.[4] This leads to the question: Who are the women who serve on school boards?

WOMEN ON SCHOOL BOARDS

The variables that have been looked at in regard to women's membership on school boards are state, region, type of school district, organization of school system, and method of obtaining the position. There are definite state variations in the representation of women on local school boards. In 1972 the total number of women on local school boards in the states ranged from a high of forty percent in Alaska to a low of two percent in Arkansas.

Table 2

Percentage of Local School-board Members Who Were Women in 1972 By State[5]

Rank	*State*	*Percent*
1	Alaska	40
2	Vermont	31
3	Maine	29
4	New Hampshire	28
5	Connecticut	27
6	Maryland	25
7	Rhode Island	24
8	Massachusetts	21
9	California	20
10	Hawaii	18
11	Arizona	16
12	Ohio	15
12	Texas	15
12	New Jersey	15
15	Nevada	14
15	New York	14
15	Nebraska	14
18	Oregon	13
18	Wyoming	13
20	Florida	12
20	Delaware	12
22	Virginia	11
22	North Carolina	11
22	Michigan	11
25	Washington	10
25	Illinois	10
25	Wisconsin	10
28	West Virginia	9
28	Missouri	9
30	Idaho	8
30	Pennsylvania	8
30	South Dakota	8
30	Iowa	8
30	Minnesota	8
35	Colorado	7
35	Indiana	7
35	North Dakota	7
35	Oklahoma	7
39	Alabama	6
39	Tennessee	6
41	Kentucky	5
41	Montana	5
43	New Mexico	4
43	Utah	4
43	Georgia	4
43	Louisiana	4
43	Kansas	4
48	Mississippi	3
48	South Carolina	3
50	Arkansas	2

Table 2 shows, in rank order, the percentage of women on local school boards in the states. This table shows that women comprise under ten percent of the board members in nearly half the states, and that there is only one state where women constitute over one-third of the total local board membership.

There are also definite regional variations in the proportion of women in school boards, as shown in Table 3. Women are most likely to be on a school board in the Northeast and least likely to be found on a school board in the West. When looking at the type of community that is more likely to have women board members, it is found that large city school boards are the most likely to have women members. For example, in 1967 eighteen percent of school-board members in large cities were women and by 1970 twenty-four percent of large city board members were women.[6] In contrast, small towns and rural communities are the areas least likely to have women board members.[7]

Table 3

Percentage of Local School-board Members Who Were Women in 1972 by Region[8]

Region	*Percent Women*
Northeast	17
Southern	10
Central	10
Western	9
Pacific	16

The decentralization of urban school systems and the establishment of numerous local community school boards seem to result in an even greater representation of women on large city school boards. Under decentralization in New York City and Detroit, a large number of women have sought and gained election to the community-based boards. As a result, the percentage of women board members in these cities has increased over the number represented on the previously centralized boards.

There exists another characteristic in regard to the proportion of women on school boards, and this characteristic is political in nature: Are the board members elected or appointed? Women are more likely to be on school boards whose members are elected rather than on those boards where women are appointed.[9] Women are less likely to be appointed to school boards than men: only fourteen percent of women on boards are appointed as compared to eighteen percent of male board members.[10] When a woman is appointed, it usually is as a replacement for a boardwoman whose term of office has ended, rather than to replace a male board member.[11] The failure to appoint women is most likely due to the problem of sponsorship, or to use a more colorful word, *cronyism*. Mayors are usually the officials who appoint school-board members, and women are at a great disadvantage here because mayors frequently appoint "one of the boys." As a result, it is easier for a woman to be elected to a school-board position by her community than it is for her to be appointed to this position. The characteristics of women school-board members are summarized in Table 4.

Table 4

Who Is The Woman School-board Member?

She is more likely to be on these school boards	*She is more likely to be on these school boards*
Northeastern	Western
Large City	Small Town and Rural
Decentralized	Centralized
Elected	Appointed

A trait of women board members is that they are usually homemakers. Housewives account for three-quarters of all women school-board members,[12] whereas well under half of all women in the United States are housewives. This overrepresentation of housewives on school-boards is probably due to housewives' greater leisure time that allows them to be more active in community affairs. Working women have a tremendous burden juggling job and family demands, without becoming involved in community affairs as well. Working men, on the other hand, are not as involved in domestic routines as their wives, even if their wives work. Men who serve on a school board can come home from work and find their dinner prepared and the children attended to, so that they can attend board meetings. Usually no one prepares dinner or takes care of the children for the working woman, and therefore her freedom for community involvement is greatly decreased.

TREATMENT OF WOMEN BOARD MEMBERS

Does it matter whether school-board members are male or female? Very little is known about the different values and behavior of men and women board members, or whether men or women perform more effectively as board members. However, the board member's sex has not been found to be related to the individual's motivation for seeking a board position.[13] There also is not any evidence that women board members are any less effective than men board members.[14]

Although there is no reason to believe that women are not as capable as men to be school-board members, many male board members act condescendingly toward women on the board. A study done in 1951 found that a third of male board members thought that women were too emotional to be competent board members.[15] According to a 1972 study, the attitudes of male school-board members toward women board members has changed very little in the last two decades.[16] As a result, those few women who manage to overcome society's sex bias to become school-board members find that the sex bias continues even after they are on the board.

Women school-board members throughout the nation are angered by the patronizing and condescending treatment they often receive from male board members.[17] Women board members complain that they are not taken seriously by the men on the board, that their opinions are frequently ignored, and that it is not uncommon for the male board members to act as if women members were not even present at a meeting.[18] Women board members also are discriminated against in that they are rarely chosen to head a committee set up by the board, and are frequently not even considered when the board deliberates on which member should be chosen to be president or chairperson.[19]

BOARD POLICIES DISCRIMINATE AGAINST WOMEN TEACHERS

It is not surprising that many school policies discriminate against women teachers when it is considered how few women school-board members there are, and how male school-board members treat the women members. Male dominance of school boards is probably an important cause of discriminatory policies regarding women teachers. An excellent example of this is shown by the small number of women teachers who are appointed principals by school boards despite that women teachers have been shown to make superior administrators to male teachers, and despite that women principals have been shown to receive greater approval from the community than male principals.[20] This preference for male administrators on the part of school boards has resulted in eighty-seven percent of all principals being male, although only one-third of teachers are men. In addition, fewer than one percent of local school superintendents are women.[21]

Male domination of school boards has also led to maternity-leave policies that discriminate against women teachers. Up until 1974, almost every school district in the county required pregnant teachers to take a leave of absence months before giving birth and did not allow them to work for months and sometimes years afterward. In most cases, the teacher was not even guaranteed her position back when she wanted to return to work. Despite numerous lawsuits brought by women teachers against their school boards and despite pressure from teacher organizations demanding change in maternity-leave policies, most school boards resisted making changes in their maternity-leave policies until required to do so by a U.S. Supreme Court ruling.[22]

BOARD POLICIES DISCRIMINATE AGAINST FEMALE STUDENTS

Schoolgirls are affected by the predominance of men on school boards, just as are women teachers. Many school systems have established separate course requirements for boys and girls. The most common occurrence is for girls to be required to take home economics and for boys to be required to take industrial arts. This is a case of institutionalized sexism, which discriminates against the girl wishing to enroll in shop, and the boy wishing to enroll in home economics.

Another way girls are discriminated against is that schools spend hundreds of millions of dollars directly for the benefit of male students only. Extracurricular activities in the school are clearly geared toward boys and their sports programs, which exclude girls. There are usually some programs oriented toward girls, such as drama or even sports, but nowhere near the time or money is expended on girls' activities as is expended on boys'. As a result, about three times as many boys participate in extracurricular activities as girls.[23] This shortchanging of girls' activities by school boards exists in spite of the fact that the overwhelming majority of parents favor equal financial support for girls and boys athletic activities.[24]

The very poor representation of women on American school boards has a definite and negative effect on a number of local school district policies. The sex imbalance in the composition of school boards makes it nearly impossible for women board members, who are aware of sex-biased policies and practices, to change this situation. Therefore the presence of sexist policies that discriminate against women teachers and schoolgirls is not likely to end until there are more women on boards of education to represent the interest of their sex. Fortunately, the movement for women's rights has resulted in an increased number of women participating in politics as well as in all phases of American life. As a result of this, the proportion of women school-board members will most likely be increasing in the future. Policies that are less sex biased will stem from these school boards, and a more equitable educational system will be the result.

NOTES

1. George Counts, *The Social Composition of Boards of Education* (Chicago: University of Chicago Press, 1927).
2. National School Boards Association, *Women on School Boards* (Evanston, Illinois: NSBA, 1974).
3. "School Board Hearing Held in a Men's Room," *New York Times*, 6 May 1973, p. 65.
4. National School Boards Association, *Women*.
5. National School Boards Association, *Women*.

6. National School Boards Association, *Survey of Public Education in the Nation's Big City School Districts* (Evanston, Illinois: NSBA, 1972).
7. Alpheus White, *Local School Boards: Organization and Practices* (Washington, D. C.: U.S. Government Printing Office, 1962).
8. National School Boards Association, *Women.*
9. White, *Local School Boards;* and National School Boards Association, *Women.*
10. National School Boards Association, *Women.*
11. Carolyn Mullins, "The Plight of the Boardwoman," *The American School Board Journal* 159 (February 1972).
12. National School Boards Association, *Women;* and Educational Research Service, "Local Boards of Education: Status and Structure." *ERS Circular,* no. 5 (1972).
13. Neal Gross, *Who Runs Our Schools?* (New York: Wiley, 1958); Donald McCarthy, "School Board Membership: Why Do Citizens Serve?", *Administrators Notebook* (September 1959); and National School Boards Association, *Women.*
14. Maurice Stapley, *School-board Studies* (Chicago: University of Chicago Press, 1957); and National School Boards Association, *Women.*
15. Maurice Stapley, *Attitudes and Opinions of School-board Members in Indiana Cities and Towns* (Bloomington, Indiana: Indiana University Press, 1957).
16. Mullins, "The Plight of the Boardwoman."
17. Ibid.
18. Ibid.
19. Ibid.
20. For a complete discussion of this topic, see the selection, "Performance of Women Principals: A Review of Behavioral and Attitudinal Studies" in this volume.
21. National Education Association, Research Division, *26th Biennial Salary and Staff Survey of Public-School Professional Personnel,* 1972–73 (Washington, D. C.: NEA, 1973).
22. For a complete discussion of this topic, see the selection, "Sex Discrimination as Public Policy: The Case of Maternity-leave Policies" in this volume.
23. For a complete discussion of this topic, see the selection, "Sex Bias in Secondary Schools: The Impact of Title IX" in this volume.
24. George H. Gallup, "Sixth Annual Gallup Poll of Public Attitudes Toward Education," Phi Delta Kappan 54 (September 1974). See Appendix A for the results from this poll relating to participation in sports by girls.

Sources for Table 1

1920, 1926

George Counts, *The Social Composition of Boards of Education* (Chicago: University of Chicago Press, 1927).

1932

Claude E. Arnett, *Social Beliefs and Attitudes of American School Board Members* (Ph.D. dissertation, University of Mississippi, 1932) cited in National School Boards Association, *Women on School Boards* (Evanston, Illinois: NSBA, 1974.

1946

National Education Association, *Status and Practices of Boards of Education* (Washington, D. C.: NEA, 1946).

1953

R. H. Brown, "Composition of School Boards, "*American School Board Journal* (August, 1954).

1958

Frank R. Albert, "Selected Characteristics of School-board Members and Their Attitudes Toward Certain Criticism of Public School Education," (Ph.D. diss., University of Mississippi, 1959) cited in Keith Goldhammer, *The School Board* (New York: Center for Applied Research in Education, 1966).

1960

Alpheus White, *Local School Boards: Organization and Practices* (Washington, D. C.: U. S. Government Printing Office, 1962).

1964

National School Boards Association, *Survey of Public Education in the Member Cities of the Council of Big City Boards of Education* (Evanston, Illinois: NSBA, 1964).

1965

Richard L. Strayer, *An Analysis of the Factors Resulting in the Social Composition of the Public Boards of Education in Selected School Districts* (Ph.D. diss., Temple University, 1966) cited in National School Boards Association. *Women on School Boards* (Evanston, Illinois: NSBA, 1974).

1967

National School Boards Association, *Survey of Public Education in the Nation's Big City School Districts* (Evanston, Illinois: NSBA, 1972).

1969

National School Boards Association, *The Fifty State School Boards* (Evanston, Illinois: NSBA, 1969).

1970

National School Boards Association, *Survey of Public Education in the Nation's Big City School Districts* (Evanston, Illinois: NSBA, 1972).

1971

Educational Research Service, "Local Boards of Education: Status and Structure," *ERS Circular,* no. 5 (1972).

1972

National School Boards Association, *Women on School Boards* (Evanston, Illinois: NSBA, 1974).

Sex Discrimination as Public Policy: The Case of Maternity-leave Policies for Teachers*

JANICE POTTKER and ANDREW FISHEL

When the U.S. Supreme Court struck down the maternity-leave policies for teachers in the Cleveland, Ohio, and Chesterfield County, Virginia, school districts in January 1974, it was, in effect, mandating that school districts change their maternity-leave regulations.[1] The questions raised as a result of this decision are why and how could almost every public school district in the country have provisions in their maternity-leave regulations that the Supreme Court described as being arbitrary, irrational, unreasonable, and a clear violation of the due process clause of the U.S. Constitution. The answer to these questions appears to be that sex discrimination is so deeply ingrained in American society that even the laws and regulations made by governing bodies sometimes reflect sex-biased attitudes.

In some cases policymakers, who are almost always male, are not actually conscious that the decisions they make are discriminatory. But this was not the case regarding the issue of maternity-leave policies. Women teachers throughout the country had been struggling for years to get local school boards to change maternity-leave regulations. In spite of claims from women teachers that they were being discriminated against, most school boards in the country steadfastly refused to voluntarily change their policies. Therefore, a regulation that was clearly biased against wom-

* Reprinted with the permission of Kappa Delta Pi and the authors, © copyright 1974, Kappa Delta Pi, from *The Educational Forum* 39, no. 1 (November 1974): 7–15.

en teachers existed as public policy, and would have continued to exist had it not been for the Supreme Court decision.

CONTENT OF MATERNITY-LEAVE REGULATIONS

What were the maternity-leave regulations that women teachers throughout the country had protested against and that school boards were so unwilling to change? Maternity-leave policies exist in virtually all school districts. In some instances, the policy is informal and unwritten, but in most cases the policy is a written regulation, drawn up unilaterally by the school board or by the board in negotiation with the local teacher organization. Prior to 1974, only a small number of policies allowed the teacher to decide for herself when to leave teaching before the birth of her child and how soon to return. The majority of school districts set time limits for her. In contrast, sixty percent of the major corporations in the country allowed their women workers to set their own time limits for maternity leave.[2]

Although time limits varied, most pregnant teachers were required by their school board to leave teaching five or six months prior to giving birth, and to stay out of teaching at least three months after the birth of their child.[3] Many policies went so far as to require a woman to leave teaching immediately upon detection of pregnancy, and to stay out of teaching two years after the birth of her child! Even more extreme was the requirement of one New York school district that a woman report her pregnancy to the school board within ten days of conception.

These time requirements set down in maternity-leave regulations would not have been so offensive to women teachers if they had any basis in medical fact, but they did not. The weight of medical evidence is that pregnant women are far more likely to be incapacitated in the early stages of pregnancy than in later months. In none of the maternity-leave cases that were brought to court was there presented any medical testimony why a teacher whose pregnancy was progressing normally should not have been allowed to continue working up until the expected date of delivery. Maternity-leave policies that were in effect in January 1974 were not based on medical knowledge, but rather on myths and misinformation about pregnancy. It is not just a coincidence that these policies were written mainly by men.

MALE CONTROL OF EDUCATION

Although two-thirds of American teachers are women, women are not in policymaking positions. At the local school-district level where maternity-policy decisions are made, only one-tenth of one percent of local superintendents of schools are women.[4] Women comprise only twelve percent of the school-board members in the United States, and over half of the school boards in the country have no women members.[5] Local teacher organizations also tend to be male dominated and male oriented.[6]

A paternalistic and a condescending attitude on the part of policy-makers probably accounted for the inclusion of restrictions in maternity-leave policies. For example, most maternity policies required a woman teacher to present a physician's statement of her ability to return to work after childbirth. In almost no other instance of medical absence was a teacher required to prove to the school district that he or she was fit to return to work. Other maternity-leave provisions required a woman to present the school system with evidence that her child was satisfactorily cared for before she was allowed to return to work. Another provision sometimes found in maternity-leave regulations was the requirement that a woman, in order to return to teaching after pregnancy, bring in a note from her husband giving his permission for his wife to return to work.

Another way in which women teachers were treated unfairly and unequally by maternity-leave policies was that, almost without exception, women were not allowed to use the paid sick-leave they had accumulated for the time they were absent due to childbirth. *All* other types of medical absences were allowed under paid sick-leave policy. A woman teacher could conceivably take paid sick-leave to have an abortion, in fact, but not to have a baby.

POLICIES HARMFUL TO WOMEN TEACHERS

Maternity-leave regulations imposed a great financial hardship on pregnant teachers. Women were required not only to leave teaching for a considerable period of time before and after childbirth, whether they wanted to or not, but they also had to do this at their own expense. Even more harmful to women was the fact that they were often not guaranteed their old position back when they wanted to return to work. Even worse, in many school districts nontenured teachers had to resign from their jobs when required to leave due to pregnancy, and when they wanted to return to work they had to reapply for the job and were treated as a new applicant. This is in direct contrast to policies regarding men who have military leave; these men usually are assured of getting their jobs back, even after an absence of three years.

Maternity leave, besides working a financial hardship on women teachers, also negatively affected a woman's chances for promotion to an administrative position or a supervisory position. Young women often have not been promoted on the assumption that they would become pregnant and have to leave work. As they became older, women teachers were frequently denied promotions because they had fewer consecutive years of work experience than men due to mandatory maternity-leave requirements. In addition, the interruption in teaching caused by mandatory maternity leave undoubtedly encouraged many women teachers to consider teaching as a temporary job, rather than as a career. After years away from the classroom, women teachers would understandably have less self-confidence and lower aspirations. Making the situation even worse for these teachers was the knowledge that if they became pregnant again, they would once more be forced from their jobs.

SYMBOLIC IMPORTANCE OF THE MATERNITY-LEAVE ISSUE

The requirment of a mandatory maternity leave was an expression of male policymakers' support of the societal norm that women should work only before they had children or after their children were grown. The underlying assumption of maternity policies is that a woman's major role in life should be that of a housewife and mother. This view obviously conflicts with the basic themes of the women's rights movement. As such, it is not surprising that the conflict over maternity-leave policies took on symbolic importance for the school-board members who were defending them and for the women teachers who were challenging them. To the male board members, maternity leaves represented a policy that supported the institution of the family, and any concession to women teachers on this issue would deal a severe blow to the very foundation of the social order. To the women teachers, maternity leaves were a highly visible expression of the restrictive societal roles that had subjugated women for years and that women were attempting to cast off.

POLICIES BENEFICIAL TO SCHOOL DISTRICTS

Maternity policies existed for reasons other than ignorance or paternalism on the part of male policymakers. Such policies remained because they worked to the financial advantage of the school district. School districts often allowed pregnant teachers, who had been forced to resign their regular positions, to do substitute teaching, sometimes on a long-term basis teaching their regular classes. However, since substitute teachers are paid on a per diem basis, which is below the regular teacher's salary, this practice could save the school district money.

In addition, maternity leaves were used by those school districts that were faced with budgetary pressures to cut back on the total number of teachers they employed. By requiring women teachers to leave upon becoming pregnant, these school districts had an easy method of eliminating teaching positions. Even where no teaching positions were being eliminated, school districts sometimes saved money by requiring pregnant teachers to resign. Pregnant teachers could be replaced by a person with little or no teaching experience, thus saving the school district money in salary costs. And maternity-leave regulations were frequently used by newly integrated school districts as a means of eliminating black female teachers who could then legally be replaced by white teachers.

School districts benefited from mandatory maternity-leave policies in another way: fixed time requirements for leave greatly simplified the administrative task of finding a substitute teacher to replace the pregnant teacher. The rights of the woman teacher were sacrificed for the administrative convenience of knowing exactly when a pregnant teacher would be leaving and returning to the classroom.

THE RESPONSE OF TEACHER ORGANIZATIONS

Although this treatment now seems shocking and exploitive of women, for a long time women teachers accepted maternity-leave regulations as an unpleasant fact of life in a society that generally discriminates against women. Women teachers believed that these policies were inevitable, especially in recent years when the policies were supported by their own local teachers' organizations.

It has only been in the last few years, with the advent of the women's rights movement and the resulting changes in the career attitudes of women, that women teachers began to fight unfair maternity-leave regulations as well as other aspects of sex bias in education. The National Education Association and the American Federation of Teachers have recently begun to support women teachers in their efforts to bring about changes in maternity-leave regulations. Both NEA and AFT have passed policy resolutions on the state and national levels calling for the liberalization of maternity-leave policies. In addition, they have provided legal and financial assistance to women teachers challenging discriminatory policies.

In spite of the commitment to change on the state and national levels, most local NEA and AFT affiliates have traditionally shown only nominal concern for the maternity-leave issue. This could be seen when local teacher organizations regularly agreed to maternity-leave provisions in their contract negotiations that were in direct contrast to the policy of their national organization. It was an unusual case when national teacher organizations tried to change a policy through the judicial process because their local affiliates were unwilling to change it through the collective bargaining process.

Seventy percent of school districts in the country that have a contract with a teacher organization at the present time have a maternity-leave provision in their contract.[7] Therefore, maternity leave presents an area where teachers have been effective in inducing their local school board to share decision-making authority, rather than having the board decide district policy unilaterally. A study of maternity-leave policies by the Connecticut Education Association found that almost all negotiated maternity-leave policies in the state violated Connecticut state law, as well as NEA policy.[8] A similar study of negotiated maternity-leave policies in New York State found equally harsh policies being agreed to by NEA and AFT local affiliates.[9] The findings from Connecticut and New York about the restrictiveness of maternity policies in existence in 1972 were similar to the findings of a nationwide study of maternity-leave policies in large school systems made six years earlier.[10]

There was little or no movement on the part of local school districts to change voluntarily their maternity-leave policies between 1966 and 1972. It is apparent that local teacher organizations had not used the collective-bargaining process to require changes to be made. It is interesting to note that, while there have been over four hundred teacher strikes since 1969, none was ever over the issue of maternity leave. However, local teacher organizations did strike over male-oriented issues such as preparation time for secondary schoolteachers and the rate of pay for coaching athletic teams. As a result, women teachers who wanted to change the maternity-leave policy in their school district had no alternative except to file suit with their local Human Rights Commission or to take their school board to court. In fact, court suits on the maternity-leave issue were filed in over twenty states by 1974. It was on two such cases that the Supreme Court ruled in January 1974.

THE SUPREME COURT RULING

The maternity-leave cases heard by the Supreme Court involved a variety of issues, but the most important was the right of school boards to set time restrictions for when a teacher had to leave her job during pregnancy and when she could return after her child was born. The school boards in these two school districts presented numerous arguments to the Court in defense of the time requirements they had established for leave during pregnancy.[11] These arguments included the maintenance of continuity in classroom instruction, the protection of children from teachers who were incapable of performing their duties, administrative convenience, and the protection of the health of the expectant mother and her unborn child.

The Court found all of the arguments of the school boards to be unsupported, and it therefore ruled the regulations on leave policy to be unconstitutional. As the Court noted, the school board regulations were actually counterproductive in that they were more likely to prevent continuity in instruction than to preserve it. Justice Powell, in his concurring opinion, labeled the arguments advanced by the school boards in defense of their leave policy as "after-the-fact rationalizations," which had been developed specifically to meet the legal challenge being made to their policy. Powell said, "The records before us abound with proof that a principal purpose behind the adoption of the regulations was to keep visibly pregnant teachers out of the sight of schoolchildren."

Thus, a public policy that inflicted such great damage on the careers of women teachers was instituted in part because of "outmoded taboos." It is ridiculous today that a policy could be advocated in order to "save pregnant teachers from embarassment at the hands of giggling children," as the superintendent of the Cleveland Public Schools described. Another reason for these policies, advanced by Chesterfield County school-board members, was that it was not healthy for students to see conspicuously pregnant teachers because some students might think that the "teacher swallowed a watermelon."

The Court also ruled that the Cleveland provision requiring a woman to stay out of teaching for three months after childbirth was unconstitutional. The Court described this provision as "wholly arbitrary and irrational," and stated that it unnecessarily penalized women for having children. The Chesterfield County return regulation, in contrast, was upheld by the Court. By reqiring the tueacher to wait to return to teaching until the beginning of the next school year, the Court stated that the goal of continuity in instruction was being achieved.

Among the minor issues resolved by these cases was the right of school boards to: require a teacher to provide substantial advance notice that she is pregnant; require a doctor's certificate of a woman's ability to continue working during pregnancy and to return to work after childbirth; and to require a statement from the teacher that she would devote full attention to her job.

However, the Court's decision left many other legal questions unanswered in regard to maternity-leave policies. For example, it is not clear whether school boards must let each individual teacher decide when to leave teaching during pregnancy or if the board can set a termination date for her during the last few weeks of pregnancy. Similarly, the Court's decision did not even touch on the issue of whether teachers on maternity leave must be paid their normal salary or be provided with other normal benefits, such as health insurance. In addition, the Court did not address the issue of whether maternity leave can be denied altogether to nontenured teachers. Additional lawsuits will undoubtedly be brought by women teachers in the future to clarify these important legal issues.

THE IMPACT OF THE CIVIL RIGHTS ACT ON MATERNITY-LEAVE POLICIES

As the Court noted, the practical impact of its decision in the Cleveland and Chesterfield County cases probably will not be great. Because the teachers involved in these cases were placed on maternity leave prior to the extension of Title VII of the Civil Rights Act of 1964 to cover educational employees, the Court did not consider Title VII regulations when making its decision.

In 1972 Title VII, which prohibits job discrimination on the basis of sex as well as other characteristics, was extended by the Equal Employment Act of 1972 to cover public employees. The Equal Employment Opportunities Commission (EEOC), the federal body that administers Title VII, has issued guidelines that mandate that pregnancy be treated exactly the same as other types of temporary disability. Therefore, under EEOC regulations, maternity leave must be viewed as just another reason for regular paid sick-leave and not as a special and separate category of leave as it usually has been treated.

According to EEOC regulations, women teachers cannot be dismissed from their jobs and cannot be denied the use of sick-leave because of absence due to pregnancy. The EEOC regulations also state that it is entirely up to the pregnant woman and her doctor to decide when she should leave work and when she should return to work after her child is born.

While EEOC regulations do not have to be accepted by the courts, courts have generally supported these regulations. It is inevitable that all future court cases on the maternity-leave issue will be heavily influenced by the EEOC regulations. The regulations being proposed by the Department of Health, Education, and Welfare to implement Title IX of the Education Amendments of 1972 also include a provision on maternity leave. If the language contained in the proposed regulations, released in June 1974, are retained when the regulations are formally adopted, HEW's requirements will be even more strict than those of EEOC.

The HEW regulations will require all school districts to treat pregnancy as a temporary disability for all job-related purposes. This would include commencement, duration and extension of leave, as well as payment of disability income, accrual of seniority, reinstatement, and any fringe benefits offered. Specifically, the HEW regulations will require school districts to allow women teachers to continue teaching as long as they are physically capable of performing their duties, and to return no later than the beginning of the first full academic term after they have given birth. Once the Title IX regulations are adopted, sometime in early 1975, they will then guide all subsequent court decisions on the maternity-leave issue. In the interim, there will continue to be many areas of conflict between women teachers and their school boards over issues relating to maternity leave.

In this regard, it must be emphasized that court decisions on issues relating to maternity leaves merely decide whether school boards have the legal right to institute certain policies. These court decisions do not require school boards to have particular provisions in their regulations, nor do they indicate that it is even wise for school boards to have such policies. For example, the Supreme Court decision that a school board may require a teacher to submit a doctor's certificate as to her ability to return to work after her child is born does not mandate, nor even suggest, that school districts do this.

THE TWO-THIRDS "MINORITY"

School boards are likely to view court decisions upholding provisions in their maternity-leave regulations as providing legal sanction for these policies. As such, school boards are not likely to be inclined to voluntarily change a policy that a court has ruled it has the right to include. As a result, while the judicial process at present offers women teachers their greatest protection, it cannot and should not be relied upon too heavily in the future.

It is of great significance that the basis for the majority opinion in the Supreme Court decision was the due process clause of the U.S. Constitution and not the equal protection clause. The Supreme Court decision in the Cleveland and Chesterfield County cases should indicate to women that the courts are inclined to give school boards wide discretion in setting regulations as long as they are aimed at and achieve legitimate state interests. This comes at the expense of what some observers might call individual rights within the area of sex discrimination. Women teachers will have to rely on the political process, rather than the courts, for adoption of policies they desire.

Despite the fact that two-thirds of all teachers are women, this large group was unable in most school districts to produce a favorable policy on an issue so important to their career as maternity-leave requirements. This example provides dramatic documentation of the powerlessness of women in the educational policymaking process.[12] It is therefore possible to consider women teachers, in spite of their number, as having "minority-group" status in education.

It seems certain from this example of maternity-leave regulations that as long as women are underrepresented in policymaking positions they will not have their interests protected in the policymaking process. Women must expect policies that are unfavorable to their interests to result. The implication for women in education, as in other areas, is clear: women must obtain positions of power if they ever want to be able to determine policy on those issues that directly affect them.

REFERENCES

Barstow, Robbins. 1972. Teacher maternity provisions in Connecticut. In *51% minority: Connecticut conference on the status of women,* pp. 51–53. Washington, D. C.: National Education Association.

Bender, Marilyn. 1973. Many companies revising maternity-leave policies. *New York Times.* 10 December 1973, p. 61.

Bird, Roger. 1974. Title VII and the pregnant employee. *Notre dame lawyer* 49: 568–78.

Cary, Eve. 1973. Pregnancy without penalty. *The civil liberties review* 1: 31–48.

Connecticut Education Association. 1972. *Factors affecting maternity leave in Connecticut teacher contracts.* Hartford: CEA.

Danziger, Joe H. 1972. Mandatory maternity leave of absence policies: an equal protection analysis. *Temple law quarterly* 45: 240–58.

Discriminating against the pregnant teacher. 1971. *Today's education,* pp. 33–35.

Dismissals for pregnancy in government employment. 1973. *Maine law review* 25: 61–87.

Fair employment: is pregnancy alone a sufficient reason for dismissal of a public employee? 1972. *Boston university law review* 52: 196–201.

Fishel, Andrew, and Pottker, Janice. 1974. School boards and sex bias in American education. *Contemporary education* 65: 85–89.

——— 1974. Women in educational governance: a statistical portrait. *Educational researcher* 3: 4–7.

French, Larry. 1973. Can your school district defend a tight maternity policy in court? *American school board journal* 160: 30–31.

Hodges, George R. 1972. Mandatory maternity leaves for teachers—the equal protection clause and Title VII of the civil rights act of 1964. *North Carolina law review* 51: 768–86.

Goodbye mandatory maternity leaves. 1972. *Nation's schools* 90: 10–11, 14.

Greenwald, Carol. 1973. Maternity-leave policy. *New England economic review,* 13–18.

Grubb, Erica B., and McCoy Margarita C. 1972. Love's labors lost: new conceptions of maternity leaves. *Harvard civil rights civil liberties review* 7: 260–97.

Hayden, Trudy. 1973. *Punishing pregnancy: discrimination in education, employment and credit.* New York: American Civil Liberties Union.

Mandatory maternity law for public schoolteachers does not violate equal protection clause. 1974. *University of Richmond law review* 8: 317–24.

Marcus, Phyllis Elayne. 1973. Mandatory maternity-leave policy in the school systems: a survey of cases. *Cleveland state law review* 22: 172–85.

Masters, Carole A. 1972–73. Mandatory maternity leaves and the equal protection clause. *Kentucky law journal* 61: 589–600.

Maternity-leave provisions for classroom teachers in large school systems. 1966. Washington, D. C.: Educational Research Service.

National Education Association, Research Division. 1973. *26th biennial salary and staff survey of public-school professional personnel, 1972–73.* Washington, D. C.: NEA.

Nolte, Chester. 1973. This one's even tougher: pregnant teachers obliterating school board maternity policies. *American school board journal* 160: 28–30.

Portman, Glenn A. 1973. A problem for the school systems: are mandatory maternity-leave rules enforceable? *Southwestern law journal* 27: 542–53.

Pottker, Janice. 1974. *Local education policymaking and the rights of women teachers: the case of maternity-leave regulations in New York state.* Chevy Chase, Maryland: Center for the study of Sex Differences in Education.

Roberts, Charles E. 1972–73. The effect of Title VII and the proposed equal rights amendment on mandatory maternity leaves for teachers. *Journal of family law* 2: 447–58.

Selected maternity-leave provisions contained in comprehensive agreements. 1970. *Negotiation research digest* 4: 24–27.

Shannon, Thomas A. 1974. Your stake mr. (or ms.) administrator in three 1974 supreme court decisions. *Phi delta kappan* 55: 460–61.

Sipser, Margaret Ann. 1973. Maternity leave: judicial and arbitral interpretation 1970–72. *Labor law journal* 24: 173–190.

The effect of new maternity-leave code in negotiation. 1972. *Negotiation research digest* 6: 23–26.

Tilman, Robert C. 1973. Teacher pregnancy: care to look at your contract? *Journal of collective negotiations* 2: 393–403.

NOTES

1. *Cleveland Board of Education vs. LaFleur* (no. 72–777) and *Cohen vs. Chesterfield County School Board* (no. 72–129), U.S. Supreme Court, decided 21 January 1974.
2. Marilyn Bender, "Many Companies Revising Maternity-leave Policies," *New York Times,* 10 December 1973, p. 61.
3. "Selected Maternity-leave Provisions Contained in Comprehensive Agreements," *Negotiation Research Digest* 4 (September 1970) : 24–27.
4. National Education Association, Research Division, *26th Biennial Salary and Staff Survey of Public-School Professional Personnel, 1972–73* (Washington, D. C.: NEA, 1973).
5. Andrew Fishel and Janice Pottker, "School Boards and Sex Bias in American Education," *Contemporary Education* 65 (Winter 1974) : 85–89.
6. Andrew Fishel and Janice Pottker, "Women Teachers and Teacher Power," *The Urban Review* 6 (November/December 1972) : 40–44.
7. "The Effect of New Maternity-leave Code in Negotiation," *Negotiation Research Digest* 6 (September 1972) : 23–26.
8. Connecticut Education Association, *Factors Affecting Maternity Leave in Connecticut Teacher Contracts* (Hartford: CEA, April 1972).
9. Janice Pottker, *Local Educational Policymaking and the Rights of Women Teachers: The Case of Maternity-leave Regulations in New York State* (Chevy Chase, Md.: Center for the Study of Sex Differences in Education, 1974).
10. *Maternity-leave Provisions for Classroom Teachers in Large School Systems* (Washington, D. C.: Educational Research Service, March 1966).
11. The Cleveland policy required the woman teacher to go on leave five months before the birth of her child and the Chesterfield County policy required the teacher to go on leave no later than the fifth month of pregnancy.
12. For a complete discussion of this issue see: Andrew Fishel and Janice Pottker, "Women In Educational Governance," *Educational Researcher* 3 (July/August 1974) : 4–7.

Higher Education

No longer are colleges and universities looked upon as guiltless institutions regarding inequality in American education. Universities are instrumental factors in causing women's low economic status, if only by default.

Margaret M. Clifford and Elaine Walster found that there was overall discrimination against women in "The Effect of Sex on College Admission, Work Evaluation, and Job Interviews." In college admission, male applicants were preferred over females, although not to a significant degree. However, the sex-by-ability interaction was found to be significant: low-ability males were preferred significantly over low-ability females, while high-ability males were not preferred over high-ability females. Similarly, in college employment interviews there was a trend toward discriminating less against the high-ability woman than the low-ability woman. The authors support the contention that a woman must be of exceptional ability in order to succeed.

This study has ramifications for the current feelings in academia of resentment against women: it is assumed, usually by competitive men, that women are being given preferential job treatment over men in colleges and universities. Although most informed educators know this is not true, studies such as Clifford's and Walster's verify that this type of thinking is fallacious.

Another implication of the Clifford and Walster study is that it does prove true a generalization regarding sex discrimination: only the most qualified women can succeed. The woman who can "make it" is very special. Since discrimination did not exist against the most highly qualified women, this generalization would seem to prove accurate. Unfortunately, very few women can compete at this high level.

Gary R. Hanson, Nancy S. Cole, and Richard R. Lamb studied "Sex Bias in Selective College Admissions." Specific selection strategies for admission to college were analyzed, and it was found that each of the four selection strategies would result in the admittance of more freshmen women than men. However, the male/female ratio differed by the type of strategy utilized.

The expected success rates of men would be less than the expected success rates of women, if colleges admitted more men than their particular selection strategy allowed. The authors conclude that the college ethos of maintaining high admission standards is violated due to the interests of admitting a greater proportion of men, and that the result of this would seem to be a quota for undergraduate women's admission to college.

Hazel Markus, in "Continuing Education for Women: Factors Influencing A Return to School and the School Experience," surveyed women counseled by the Center for Continuing Education of Women at the University of Michigan. Although the study is mostly concerned with overall attitudes of returning adult-female students, the role of university faculty is highlighted.

A significant proportion of the faculty did not encourage adult-women students. Almost forty percent of those women who dropped out of school stated that they received no or very little encouragement from their instructors.

When asked to state problems encountered in returning to school, forty-four percent stated that they were due to lack of acceptance by professors, counselors, and advisers (16%), and not feeling a member of the university community (28%). The women reported that their motives for taking classes were questioned by instructors, and that they were discouraged from going to school if they were only part-time students. Older women were more likely to encounter problems with faculty than were younger women.

At the faculty level, Janice Pottker's "Overt and Covert Forms of Discrimination Against Academic Women" shows a myriad of levels of bias toward women in academe. Women are not hired by universities, especially not by Ivy League schools, and if hired, they are not promoted as they should be. They are also not given tenure or job responsibilities equally, nor are they paid the same salaries as their male colleagues of equal rank.

Covert forms of discrimination include nepotism rules, which state that husbands and wives cannot work for the same university. Professional socialization often excludes women, so that they are unable to interact informally with their colleagues and receive these benefits. Women also are not sponsored to the same degree as are men, which negatively affects their employment chances.

In short, women service universities: women enroll as undergraduate and graduate students, enabling universities to hire men to teach them. When they graduate, they are not given an equal chance at employment. If hired, they are not promoted nor are they paid equally. Most American colleges and universities could not exist without women students, but they apparently can exist without women faculty above the level of instructor.

Rodney T. Harnett's "The Female Trustee" examines characteristics of women on governing boards of higher education, and finds that they have fewer advanced degrees than men, are less business oriented, are more liberal, and are more inclined to be Democrats. These characteristics are reflected in women's favorable orientation toward social problems and belief in free faculty expression, and by their less favorable attitudes toward loyalty oaths and administrative control of campus newspapers. It would seem that the addition of women trustees would have a liberalizing effect on governing boards of higher education.

Despite universities' cries supporting admission of the most qualified students, studies by Clifford and Walster, and by Hanson, Cole, and Lamb, have zeroed in on colleges' different admission criteria for men and women. Clifford and Walster also have shown trends in discrimination against women in college employment interviews, while Pottker has shown some of both the obvious and insidious forms of sex bias in academe. Markus points out that within universities the older woman student is sometimes stymied by lack of encouragement and internal regulations. Colleges and universities in the U.S. are now legally required to admit students and offer scholarships and financial aid on the basis of the students' qualifications, regardless of sex. But merely admitting women students on an equal basis with male students does little to bring about changes in the internal regulations of colleges and universities that discriminate against women students after they are enrolled. These internal regulations include residency requirements, refusal to grant transfer credit, lack of day-care facilities, and so on. These rigid rules do not help the university but just serve to impede students' progress, particularly women students' progress. These barriers annoy students and faculty alike, and with the current trend of abandoning other types of requirements for graduation (such as requiring a course in American history) it would seem that these internal regulations could be abandoned also, with no harm to the institution. This is the least that colleges and universities could do to help their students, especially their women students.

Most of these internal policies are and will remain outside the scope of federal laws and regulations. Therefore changes in these internal policies will have to be achieved on an institution by institution basis through the efforts of students and faculty.

Since this is the case, it is particularly important that colleges act to end discrimination against the hiring and promotion of women faculty, and to compensate for past discrimination by making an all-out effort to recruit women faculty and to promote qualified women already employed by the institution. This so called "affirmative action" on the part of colleges has been criticized by white, male professors and administrators as reverse bias, which it is not. The colleges have retained the right to establish whatever minimum requirements and qualifications they want for a particular position: there was no lowering of standards. However under affirmative action, if a man and a woman both applied for a position and both met the requirements established by the institution, then the female was given preference to make up for all the years that colleges refused to hire or promote women, no matter how well qualified they were.

Many white male academicians are hypocritical in their opposition to affirmative action. For all of their academic careers they were willing to benefit from discrimination against women and blacks without raising their voices to protest this type of bias. However, once they no longer benefited by these informal hiring practices, they have become opposed to the use of criteria such as sex or race to decide who gets a job. Many of these same academicians never would have achieved the level of their present position had it not been for the use of sex and ethnicity as criteria for hiring and promotion.

Because of the existence of federal laws and regulations, the legal basis for the elimination of sex discrimination in higher education is provided. The task now becomes one of enforcing these laws on male-dominated institutions that either openly oppose federal laws or at best feel neutral towards them. For example, institutions that are under the threat of losing federal aid if they do not actively recruit women for faculty and administrative positions often only go through the motions of considering women candidates before hiring a man. It is not uncommon for a woman to be invited to travel across the country for an interview for a position, then be kept waiting for hours before the interview, and then summarily dismissed after being interviewed only perfunctorily.

The institution can then show the federal government that it has interviewed a woman, according to affirmative action regulations. It is ironic that these men protest all rules of conduct in affirmative action guidelines and yet by doing their best to circumvent these rules, cause a situation where even more regulations of conduct must be written and enforced.

The enforcement of these laws will require the active participation of women academicians as well as the continued support of federal regulatory agencies such as the Office of Civil Rights and the Equal Employment Opportunity Commission. An informed and active body of women in institutions of higher education combined with sympathetic and powerful male allies remains the most effective means of bringing about an end to sexism in higher education.

The Effect of Sex on College Admission, Work Evaluation, and Job Interviews* [1]

MARGARET M. CLIFFORD and
ELAINE WALSTER

An experiment by Walster, Cleary, and Clifford tested the hypothesis that male candidates would have a better chance of being admitted to college than would comparable female candidates.[2]

The design of the experiment was a simple one. A sample of 240 colleges was randomly selected from *Lovejoy's College Guide*.[3] Applications for admission were prepared for each school. These applications for admission were identical in all respects, except that the sex and ability level of the applicant was randomly varied. Half of the time the applicant claimed to be a male; half of the time a female. One-third of the Subjects were described as high; one-third average; and one-third low in ability.

To generate the materials required for the college applications, we secured the school records of three high-school seniors of different ability levels and with names that were appropriate for either a girl or boy. The sex of the candidate was manipulated by attaching an appropriate photograph to the application and to the copy of the transcript supposedly sent by the high school. The sex code was appropriately indicated whenever it appeared.

* Reprinted with permission of Dembar Educational Research Services and Margaret M. Clifford and Elaine Walster, © copyright 1972, Dembar Educational Research Services, Inc., from *Journal of Experimental Education* 41, no. 2 (Winter 1972): 1–5.

The distinctions between the three ability levels were determined by students' actual records: The *low-ability* candidate ranked 268 in a class of 414 and had a high-school transcript on which this rank and appropriate course grades were recorded. He had an ACT composite score of 10 (09 in English, 18 in mathematics, 07 in social science, and 06 in natural science). His college board results were an SAT verbal score of 404, an SAT mathematics score of 382, and achievement scores of 451 in English, 442 in American history, and 356 in mathematics.

The *average-ability* candidate ranked 135 in a class of 414. He had an ACT composite score of 21 (19 in English, 16 in mathematics, 26 in social science, and 22 in natural science). His college board results were an SAT verbal score of 504, an SAT score of 482 in mathematics, and achievement scores of 531 in English, 522 in American history, and 436 in mathematics.

The *high-ability* candidate ranked 55 in a class of 414. His ACT composite was 25 (23 in English, 22 in mathematics, 29 in social science, and 27 in natural science). His college board results were an SAT verbal score of 604, an SAT mathematics score of 582, and achievement scores of 591 in English, 580 in American history, and 526 in mathematics.

To insure that applications would be as standard as possible, a master form was prepared. This form attempted to provide answers to any question that a college might ask. Included in this application was basic information about the student's background, education, and interests. Also included were essays on his interests and hobbies, and his religious experiences. Letters of reference, appropriate for students of either sex, were prepared. These recommendations were presumably from a minister, teacher, counselor, an employer, and a neighbor. The necessary medical records were prepared by a cooperating physician.

All applications were completed by referring to the master form. Once the documents were prepared, cooperating individuals signed and notarized them when necessary.

Dependent Variable

The colleges' acceptance or rejection of the candidate was scored on a 5-point scale:

1 = Rejection; 2 = Rejection with the possibility of reconsideration at a later date; 3 = Qualified acceptance in which a program or coursework adjustment was stipulated; 4 = Acceptance; and 5 = Acceptance with encouragement by a personal letter or an offer of unrequested financial aid.

Results

Figure 1 contains the results of the analysis of variance. The sex effect was in the predicted direction. Males were preferred over females, but contrary to the authors' expectation this difference was not significant ($F = 3.54, p < .06$). A significant but unexpected result was found in the joint test of interactions. At the low-ability level males were preferred over females. At the high-ability level this difference disappeared (Interaction $S = 2.39, p < .05$).

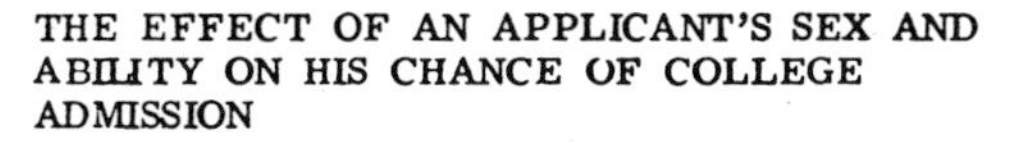
THE EFFECT OF AN APPLICANT'S SEX AND ABILITY ON HIS CHANCE OF COLLEGE ADMISSION

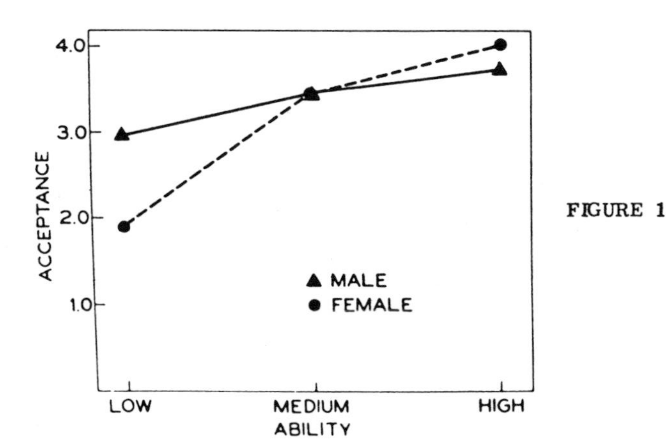

FIGURE 1

These findings have important implications. According to national norms, all three of our bogus candidates were of fairly high caliber. In the actual high-school population, students are generally less qualified than were our candidates. Since discrimination was most prevalent at the lower levels, it is clear that, overall, women are undoubtedly discriminated against in college admission. The significant sex-by-ability interaction adds support to the feminist observation (and complaint) that only a truly exceptional woman can ever hope to transcend sexual stereotypes and to be judged on an objective basis.

EXPERIMENT 2—THE EFFECT OF SEX ON HOW HIGHLY WORK IS EVALUATED

An experiment by Pheterson, Kiesler, and Goldberg tested the hypothesis that when women attempt to accomplish something, their performance will be judged more harshly than an identical performance by males.[4] Once the women become acknowledged successes, however, the authors predict that discrimination will disappear. They predict, then, that it is the woman who is *trying* to make it, rather than the woman who has *already* made it who will be discriminated against.

Experimental Design

Small groups of women college students were asked to evaluate eight paintings. Half of the time students were led to believe that the painting was created by a male artist; half of the time they believed it was created by a female artist. Whether the painting was an acknowledged success or not was also varied. (Half of the time students were told that the painting was a prizewinning painting. Half of the time they thought it was just an entry in a show.) Each subject participated in each experimental condition, evaluating eight paintings sequentially. The identity of each painting was counterbalanced among subjects so that all conditions were represented for each painting.

Procedure

The subjects were 120 freshmen and sophomore women students at Connecticut College. Women were seated in a room equipped with a slide projector and screen. Each subject was given a booklet and was told to read the following instructions:

> Slides of eight paintings will be shown in conjunction with brief biographical sketches of the artists. After viewing the slide, turn the page and answer five evaluative questions about the painting. No personal information about your identity, talents, or tastes is required. This is a study of the artistic judgment of college students.

Students first read a fictitious biographical sketch of the first artist. Half of the sketches described a female artist, and half, a male. Their age, residence, and occupations were briefly described (identical for male or female). For example, "Bob (Barbara) Soulman, born in 1941 in Cleveland, Ohio, teaches English in a progressive program of adult education. Painting is his (her) hobby and most creative past-time."

Cross-cutting the sex manipulation, half of the profiles described the painting as a contest entry (e.g., "She has entered this painting in a museum-sponsored young artists' contest."), and half described it as a recognized winner (e.g., "This painting is the winner of the Annual Cleveland Color Competition.").

After reading the biography, the students inspected the projected painting, and then they answered some questions about their reaction to the painting. Students were asked 1) how technically competent they would judge the artist to be, 2) how creative he/she seemed to be, 3) to assess the quality and content of his/her painting, 4) to estimate the emotional impact the artist instilled in his painting, and 5) to predict the artistic future of the artist.

Results

The results of the Pheterson and others[5] experiment show surprising consistency with those of Walster and others:[6] The question regarding technical competency revealed that the sex of the artist and whether or not he had been certified a success, interacted ($F= 3.99$; $df = 1, 119$; $p<.05$). When the merit of the paintings had not yet been evaluated by professionals, a given painting was evaluated more highly when a male was said to be the artist than when the identical painting was attributed to a female artist ($t = 1.99$; $p<.05$). Once experts had put their stamp of approval on a painting and it had won a prize, it was accorded the same respect regardless of whether the artist was said to be a male or a female.

Table 1

Mean Competence Ratings and Ratings of the Artistic Future of Male and Female Artists with Winning or Entry Paintings

	Sex of Artist	
Competence Ratings	Male	Female
Winner	3.48	3.48
Entry	3.56	3.35
Ratings of Artistic Future		
Winner	2.97	3.99
Entry	3.06	2.81

The question concerning the artistic future of the artist produced results paralleling the competence data. There was a significant interaction between sex and painting status ($F = 4.52$; $df = 1,119$; $p<.05$). A painting that had been entered in a contest was evaluated more favorably when attributed to a male than when attributed to a female ($t = 1.92$; $p< .06$). Evaluations did not differ significantly for the winning paintings, although evaluations tended to favor the female winners.

The authors frankly admit that significance was obtained on only two of the five questions (i.e., technical competency and artistic future). However, they speculate that, "creativity is ambiguous, and may have feminine connotations." They further suggest that judging "quality" and "emotional impact" are perhaps similarly ambiguous and, thus, unreliable measures of sex bias. The authors' interpretation of the discrepancy is summarized in the sentence, "Bias apparently was directed toward the performer, rather than toward his or her work."[7]

This pattern of discrimination is totally consistent with that detected in the first study. The authors argue: "The implications of this finding are far-reaching. The work of women in competition is devalued by other women." They point out, "even work that is equivalent to the work of a man will be judged inferior until it receives special distinction; and, that distinction is difficult to achieve when judgment is biased against female work in competition. According to the present data, and that of Goldberg,[8] women cannot expect unbiased evaluations until they prove themselves by award, trophy, or other obvious success."[9]

EXPERIMENT 3—THE EFFECT OF SEX ON THE LIKELIHOOD OF EMPLOYMENT

Recently an announcement was made regarding an opening for an assistant or associate professorship at a major university. At the conclusion of the elegantly worded description of the position, the following footnote appeared: "[This university] is guided by the principle that there shall be no differences in the treatment of persons because of race, creed, color, or national origin and that equal opportunity and access to facilities shall be available to all." One wonders whether the omission of sex was due to oversight or to foresight.

In these times of an ever-increasing surfeit of unemployed and anxious Ph.D.'s, the effect of sex on academic hiring practices becomes a question of general curiosity, if not sincere concern. The following experiment conducted by Clifford and Looft[10] was designed as a companion study to the investigation by Walster, Cleary, and Clifford in which the effect of sex on college admissions was examined.[11] As in the previously conducted study, it was predicted that male candidates would receive more interview invitations from academia than would females, and that males would be more favored at the lower level than at the higher level of ability.

Procedure

The study was conducted at a week-long meeting of the American Education Research Association. Bogus application forms were submitted to the AERA employment placement service, which operates during the convention. Applications were prepared for a high-ability and an average-level candidate. For each level forms were prepared in the name of both a male and a female candidate. The intended procedure was to record and score all requested contacts initiated by prospective interviewers.

A change in procedure, however, was adopted during the second afternoon of the convention because not a single interviewer had requested an appointment with any of the eight applicants. It was therefore decided that requests for interviews would be submitted in the name of each applicant. The prospective interviewers registered with the placement service were randomly assigned to one of the four conditions; the job availabilities allowed for twenty observations for each sex at each level of ability, or a total of eighty independent observations. Interview contacts were then attempted via message-forms commonly used by prospective applicants for this purpose.

Independent Variables

The application forms indicated that all potential employees had attended the same Big Ten university and received the same degrees; all were seeking employment in either academic or research institutions; all had special interests in learning and human development.

The sex variable was manipulated by the choice of names for each applicant. Last names were carefully chosen so no two bogus applications were found in close priximity in the alphabetized handbooks made available to employers. In the high-ability condition the subject was presented as having two published articles, one paper presentation, one article in preparation, an NDEA fellowship, and one year of teaching experience at the college level. In the average condition the applicant claimed only one paper presentation and two years' work as a teaching assistant.

Dependent Variable

The main dependent variable was the interview opportunity an applicant was offered or the response he (she) received to the requested interviews. Each of the twenty observations per cell (i.e., interview inquiries by the candidates) received one of the following scores: 0 = no reply, or a reply indicating that no interview was desired with the applicant; 1 = a request to send a vita to the interviewer; 2 = a scheduled interview indicating time and place; 4 = a scheduled interview plus a follow-up message requesting a future contact. (Obviously, the original appointment was not kept.)

It was felt that the last response category indicated such strong interest in the applicant that a double weighting was appropriate.

Results and Discussion

An analysis of variance was used to examine the main effects and interactions.

Figure 2 presents the mean interview opportunity for each of the four cells. The data seem to indicate that ability effect is relatively greater for the female than for the male candidate.

Contrary to expectation, the predicted Sex by Ability Interaction was not secured ($F = .99$, $df = 1/72$; $p < .32$). Thus, it can only be said that the patterning does resemble that found in the first two studies. Ability was the only factor that resulted in significance beyond the .05 level ($F = 6.48$; $df = 1/72$; $p < .01$).

Although there is *no* statistical confirmation of the authors' hypothesis in this last study, the modest interaction trend becomes important in view of the fact the authors were unable to secure the necessary N (i.e., 268 subjects would have been required to test the hypothesis with a power of .90 and a significance level of .05 [15]). The interaction trend, combined with the fact that their results are consistent with the findings of Walster and others[12] and Pheterson and others[13] led the authors to conclude: "In short, this experiment *suggests* that . . . females of less than outstanding ability appear to be in need of vocational rehabilitation."[14]

CONCLUSION

All three of these studies provide evidence that women generally have a disadvantage in higher education and professional activities. In spite of the head start displayed during the years of compulsory education, the average female can anticipate being rated second-best after that. The only possibility of escape seems to lie in superb performance or public recognition. One explanation for the professional underachievement of women has been a prejudicial evaluation of their work by men.[15] There seems to be evidence, however, that women are also culpable for the crimes of sex discrimination of which they are victims.

REFERENCES

Ames, L. B., and Ilg, F. L. 1964. Sex differences in test performances of matched girl-boy pairs in the five-to-nine-year-old range. *Journal of genetic psychology* 104: 25–34.

Clifford, M. M., and Looft, W. R. 1971. Academic employment interviews; effect of sex and race. *Educational researcher* 22: 6–8.

Eisenman, R., and Platt, J. J. 1968. Birth order and sex differences in academic achievement and internal-external control. *Journal of genetic psychology* 78: 279–85.

Goldberg, P. A. 1968. Are women prejudiced against women? *Transaction* 5 (April 1968) : 28–30.

Havinghurst, R. J., and Breese, F. F. 1947. Relation between ability and social status in a midwestern community, III primary mental abilities. *Journal of educational psychology* 38: 241–47.

Klein, V. 1950. The stereotype of femininity. *Journal of social issues* 6: 3–12.

Lee, L. C. 1965. Concept utilization in preschool children. *Child development* 36: 221–27.

Lovejoy, C. E. 1968. *Lovejoy's college guide*. New York: Simon and Schuster.

Maccoby, E. E. 1966. *The development of sex differences*. Stanford, Calif.: Stanford University Press.

Northby, A. S. 1958. Sex differences in high-school scholarship. *School and society* 66: 63–64.

Pheterson, G. I.; Kiesler, S. B.; and Goldberg, P. A. Evaluation of the performance of women as a function of their sex, achievement, and personal history. *Journal of personality and social psychology*.

Schienfeld, A. 1944. *Women and men*. New York: Harcourt, Brace.

Stroud, J. B., and Lindquist, E. F. 1942. Sex differences in achievement in the elementary and secondary schools. *Journal of educational psychology* 33: 657–67.

Walster, E.; Cleary, T. A.; and Clifford, M. M. 1971. The effects of race and sex on college admissions. *Sociology of education* 44: 237–44.

Walster, G. W., and Cleary, T. A. 1970. The use of statistical significance as a decision rule. *Sociological methodology*.

NOTES

1. This research was supported in part by the National Science Foundation Grant GS 2932 and National Institute of Mental Health Grant MH 16661. We would like to thank Drs. T. Anne Cleary, P. Goldberg, Sara Kiesler, William Looft, and Gail Pheterson.
2. E. Walster, T. A. Cleary, and M. M. Clifford, "The Effects of Race and Sex in College Admissions," *Sociology of Education* 44 (1971) : 237–44.
3. C. E. Lovejoy, *Lovejoy's College Guide* (New York: Simon and Schuster, 1968) .
4. G. I. Pheterson, S. B. Kiesler, and P. A. Goldberg, "Evaluation of the Performance of Women as a Function of Their Sex, Achievement, and Personal History," *Journal of Personality and Social Psychology.*
5. Ibid.
6. Walster, Cleary, and Clifford, "Effects."
7. Pheterson, Kiesler, and Goldberg, "Evaluation."
8. P. A. Goldberg. "Are Women Prejudiced Against Women?", *Transaction* 5 (April 1968) : 28–30.
9. Pheterson, Kiesler, and Goldberg, "Evaluation."
10. M. M. Clifford and W. R. Looft, "Academic Employment Interviews: Effect of Sex and Race," *Educational Researcher* 22 (1971) : 6–8.
11. Walster, Cleary, and Clifford. "Effects."
12. Ibid.
13. Pheterson, Kiesler, and Goldberg, "Evaluation."
14. Clifford and Looft, "Academic Employment."
15. V. Klein, "The Stereotype of Femininity," *Journal of Social Issues* 6 (1950) : 3–12; and A. Schienfeld, *Women and Men* (New York: Harcourt, Brace, 1944) .

Sex Bias in Selective College Admissions*

GARY R. HANSON, NANCY S. COLE and RICHARD R. LAMB

In 1837 Oberlin College admitted the first female college students in the United States.[1] In 1972, just 135 years later, over three million women were enrolled in college. That relatively brief history of college education for women has been filled with contradictions and conflict. Even today, although the equal rights of women to higher education are widely acknowledged, women do not participate in institutions of higher education to the same extent as men. In 1970, for example, women earned about forty percent of the bachelor degrees, about a third of the master's degrees, and about a tenth of the doctorates.[2]

There are many factors that probably contribute to the lower level of involvement of women in higher education. However, because selection of students does occur at many colleges and universities, it is important to examine the effects of possible selection strategies on the proportions of women and men in entering college classes. Selection strategies commonly include (among many types of variables) the use of test scores and high-school grades. These variables are often the primary-quantified variables in college admissions and are used in various ways in conjunction with other considerations. The purpose of this study is to examine the effect of various selection strategies using these two common variables (test scores and high-school grades) on the proportion of women and men admitted to undergraduate higher education.

* Reprinted with the permission of Gary R. Hanson, Nancy S. Cole, and Richard R. Lamb. This article is a revised version of a paper presented at the 1973 Annual Meeting of the American Educational Research Association, New Orleans.

SELECTION STRATEGIES AND THE ISSUE OF FAIRNESS IN SELECTION

In this section is examined several possible selection strategies that might be followed in selective college admissions. However, it is important to note that probably few, if any, selective colleges today follow any of the strategies described. There are often restrictions of various types on the number of women that override test scores, high-school grades, or other qualifications. For example, in some colleges the number of women is restricted by available dormitory space; in others, a desired ratio of men to women is implemented. Thus, as the implications of the different selection strategies on the proportion of women and men are described, it is possible to compare the hypothetical resulting representation of men and women with the representation commonly existing in American colleges. Such comparisons may show best which strategies are clearly *not* in common use.

Separate Regression Strategy

The traditionally espoused fair-selection strategy has been the procedure of selecting the so-called best qualified students as determined by the regression of college grades on test scores and high-school grades. Individuals with high-predicted college grades are preferred for selection over those with low-predicted grades. When separate within-group (within sex) regression equations are used, this procedure is fair in the sense that there is no average error or bias in the grade predictions of either group. This strategy has been supported by Cleary and others in the recent debates of test bias or test fairness in selection.[3]

Combined Regression Strategy

It is possible that an institution might apply the basic regression strategy but not analyze the data separately for women and for men. If there were no differences in the regressions for the sexes, the combined regression strategy would be identical with the separate regression strategy. However, there are usually sex differences in test scores and grades; consequently, the implications of ignoring such differences must also be examined. We know of no psychometrician who argues that the combined-regression strategy is statistically sound or fair when group differences exist. However, such a strategy might be implemented through convenience or lack of sufficient data on one sex.

Thorndike's Constant-ratio Strategy

Several authors have examined the separate-regression idea of fairness described above and concluded that it is but one of several possible appropriate ideas of fairness depending upon one's values and goals.[4] One of the alternative models of fairness of Thorndike's required that applicants from each group should be selected in proportion to the rate at which selectees from that group succeed, once selected.[5] While the separate-regression strategy places primary emphasis on selecting successful students, the constant-ratio model emphasizes the fair opportunity for selection within a group.

Cole's Conditional Probability Strategy

Cole suggested that the group most deserving of concern in many selection situations is the group of applicants who, if selected, could succeed.[6] Thus, the proposed conditional probability strategy requires that the conditional probability of selection given success be the same in each group. Here the emphasis is put on the fair opportunity for selection within each group for those who can succeed if selected.

Other Strategies

Several other models of fairness have been proposed that should be noted here, although the empirical analyses of this study are limited to the four already described. Einhorn and Bass defined fairness in terms of equal-estimated chances of success of individuals based on regression equations.[7] Because the Einhorn-Bass model is conceptually similar and yields almost identical empirical results to the separate-regression strategy, it is not treated separately in this sudy.

Darlington proposed a strategy that combines subjective value judgments related to each group with regression methodology by predicting not the criterion (college grades) alone but the criterion adjusted by some social-value weighting.[8] Because the adjustment may take on any value, depending upon one's subjective values, no single form of the strategy is meaningful as a general representation. Consequently, no computations were made based on the Darlington model. However, when the special adjustment is zero, the model reduces to the separate-regression strategy. Thus, as one or the other sex group was favored, the proportion of the favored sex would be increased from the separate-regression proportion and the nonfavored sex decreased.

Quota models of fairness are sometimes explicitly proposed and probably more often implemented. Some of the possible bases of sex quotas were mentioned above. Quotas represent a concern with the proportional representation of different groups and involve the assignment of the desired representation, a priori. Thus, a proponent of a particular quota judges a procedure as fair if the desired quota is met. The relation of any desired quota to the other models described can be examined in the empirical data by considering the proportional representation of women and men under each model. If the desired sex representation is 60% men

—40% women, 50% men—50% women, or any other distribution, the degree to which any of the four strategies approximates such quotas can be examined from the data.

Comparison of the Strategies

The different selection strategies are expressions of different value judgments in the selection situation. The separate-regression strategy is an expression of the traditional idea of selection of the best qualified. Its use places high value on the selection of highly successful students for college, but the strategy is limited by the predictor variables used since other equally "qualified" students may have been identified by the use of other variables. By contrast, the Thorndike and Cole strategies express primary concern with fair group opportunity for selection. While these strategies provide types of fair opportunity, they may result in lower success in one group than another (or lower overall success rates), thus conflicting with a primary goal of the separate-regression strategy. In the case of men and women, we must also consider the use of the combined-regression strategy, the implications of which depend upon the sex differences in the data, and the possibilities of quotas on the representation of women in entering college classes that derive from values on desired sex representation.

Method

The method employed was to analyze data on first-year men and women students at a number of colleges, and on the basis of those analyses to apply, *post hoc,* the different strategies described. The basic output data was then the proportion of men and women who would have been selected under each selection strategy.

Data

Data on freshmen students at nineteen colleges participating in the 1969 ACT Research Services were analyzed. The colleges were chosen from four levels of colleges (two-year colleges to universities) throughout the nation that enroll both men and women students. A brief description of each college is given in Table 1. Data were available on the four ACT tests (English, mathematics, social studies, and natural science), four student-report high-school grades (from the ACT record) in the same four subject areas, and overall first semester grade-point average.

Procedure

For each college, eight-variable (four ACT test scores and four high-school grades) regression equations (and the related multiple correlations) were calculated first separately for men and women and then for the total group combined. Next, using the appropriate regression equations, the necessary cutting points were calculated according to the operational definitions of each strategy (see Cole for the statistical methodology).[9]

These calculations required several assumptions. First, multivariate normality of the predictors and criterion was assumed. This assumption is a common and apparently reasonable one in this type of data. However, the assumption is not crucial to the strategies but a convenience for computation. Thorndike's and Cole's strategies require a college-grade pass-point and within each college the pass-point was set at one-half standard deviation below the combined (or total) group mean. Since approximately 70% exceed this point, this seemed an appropriate and realistic choice. Finally, for all the strategies, it was necessary to specify the proportion of applicants from each sex group and the proportion of total applicants to be selected. Because this information was not available for the colleges being analyzed, the arbitrary assumption of 50% men applicants and 50% women applicants at each college was made. It was further assumed that 50% of the total group of applicants could be selected. (Thus, for example, if there were 1000 applicants, 500 were assumed to be men and 500 women, and only 500 places were assumed to be available in the entering class.) These figures were chosen to represent common college-admission situations, but other values examined yielded highly similar results.[10]

Finally, the prescribed cutting points for each strategy were applied to a hypothetical applicant group with predictor-criterion data as observed in each college and with proportions of applicants of each sex as assumed. The result was a selected class composed of certain percentages of men and of women. These percentages or proportions of the selected group belonging to each sex according to each strategy was the primary outcome data. For further comparison of the strategies, the expected success rates within each selected sex group were computed, as were the conditional probabilities of selection given success. Finally, the actual sex composition of the freshman class at each of the nineteen colleges was obtained.

Results

Any selection process using test scores and high-school grades is based on the assumption that these variables are valid predictors of college grades. Thus, the first consideration in examining the results from the nineteen colleges was the appropriateness of this assumption.

Level of Prediction

The median-multiple correlation, based on the eight-variable equation and predicted grade, with achieved college grade-point average using separate regression equations was .55 (range: .27 to .71) for men and .61 (range: .51 to .73) for women. The median-standard errors of estimate were .67 and .64 for men and women respectively. These results indicate the commonly found tendency of better prediction of women's college grades than of men's.

Proportion of Men and Women Selected

The proportion of selected applicants of each sex under each of the four selection strategies are presented in Table 2. Under each of the four strategies, more women would have been selected than men. This result is a function both of the higher mean-predictor scores for women and the higher level of correlation between predictor and criterion variables. Use of the most widely espoused selection strategy, the separate-regression strategy, would have resulted in the most disparate sex distribution, only 30% men and 70% women—a distribution matched by few colleges in the nation.

The sex representation required by each of the four strategies can be compared with the actual sex representation in the freshman class at each of the colleges also given in Table 1. The discrepancies indicate that none of the four strategies was implemented—at least not without additional restrictions limiting the acceptance of women students.

Conditional Probability of Selection

The conditional probability of selection given success is the basis of one definition of fairness (Cole's conditional probability strategy). Table 3 presents the conditional probability of selection for men and women under each of the four strategies. While these conditional probabilities are the same for men and women as required under the Cole strategy, there are great differences in the other strategies. For example, the men have far less opportunity for selection given success under the separate-regression strategy (.42 to .81) than the women.

Conditional Probability of Success

The conditional probability of success given selection is also reported in Table 3. Expected success rates are usually of great importance to colleges because they relate to how many students will remain in college or drop out for academic reasons. The separate-regression strategy incorporates the desire to maximize overall success rates and results in .86 and .88 expected success rates for men and women respectively (or .87 overall). By contrast, the Thorndike and Cole strategies that are concerned with group opportunity not success rates per se, result in discrepant success rates by sex but comparable overall success rates.

Discussion

There are several key results of this study. First, there would be wide differences in the resulting representation of men and women in entering college classes under different selection strategies based on different ideas and values about fairness in selection. These differences range from median values of 30% men, 70% women under the separate-regression strategy to 48% men, 52% women under Cole's conditional probability strategy.[11]

Second, in order to select more men (under the combined regression-constant ratio or conditional probability strategies) than the 30% selected under the separate-regression strategy, the expected success rates of men will be considerably lower than the expected success rates of women. Only 81% of the men would be expected to succeed, while 93% of the women would be expected to succeed under the conditional probability strategy, for example. Thus, the concerns of the institution for high-success rates (sometimes called institutional standards) would have to be

Table 1

Identification of Colleges Analyzed
Sex Group Analyses

Code	Description of College	Men N	Women N
A	A southwestern state-supported 2-year college	458	241
B	A western public-community college	346	288
C	A mountain-state college	316	110
D	A state-supported western college	400	216
E	An eastern-state college	365	273
F	A southern state-supported college	303	290
G	A southern state-supported university	838	613
H	A midwestern state-supported university	645	845
I	A midwestern-state college	322	255
J	A midwestern state-supported university	845	529
K	A midwestern state-supported university	514	180
L	A southwestern-state university	1026	677
M	A large southwestern-state university	741	540
N	A midwestern state-supported university	699	336
O	A large southern-state university	807	542
P	A midwestern state-supported university	931	647
Q	A large midwestern-state university	2581	1568
R	A midwestern state-supported university	711	346
S	A western-state university	788	432

Table 2

Proportion of Selected Applicants by Sex
for Different Models of Fair Selection

College	Combined Equation		Regression Model		Equal-risk Model		Constant-ratio Model		Conditional Probability Model	
	M	*W*	*M*	*W*	*M*	*W*	*M*	*W*	*M*	*W*
A	.37	.63	.15	.85	.14	.86	.42	.58	.48	.52
B	.44	.57	.33	.67	.33	.68	.46	.54	.48	.51
C	.40	.60	.21	.80	.19	.82	.45	.55	.50	.49
D	.38	.63	.28	.73	.26	.75	.44	.56	.47	.52
E	.34	.66	.24	.77	.20	.81	.42	.58	.47	.53
F	.39	.61	.29	.70	.29	.70	.43	.57	.45	.54
G	.42	.79	.29	.72	.27	.74	.44	.56	.47	.52
H	.45	.54	.41	.58	.38	.62	.48	.52	.50	.49
I	.37	.64	.29	.72	.26	.75	.43	.57	.47	.52
J	.38	.63	.18	.83	.18	.83	.42	.58	.47	.52
K	.47	.54	.43	.58	.42	.59	.48	.52	.49	.50
L	.47	.53	.36	.65	.34	.67	.46	.54	.49	.50
M	.49	.51	.40	.60	.40	.61	.47	.53	.48	.52
N	.41	.60	.29	.71	.26	.74	.43	.57	.46	.52
O	.48	.53	.40	.61	.37	.63	.47	.53	.49	.50
P	.34	.67	.25	.76	.22	.78	.43	.57	.46	.53
Q	.47	.54	.42	.58	.40	.60	.48	.52	.49	.50
R	.41	.60	.30	.70	.23	.72	.44	.56	.46	.52
S	.52	.48	.44	.56	.43	.58	.48	.52	.49	.50
Median Value	.41	.60	.29	.70	.27	.72	.44	.56	.48	.52

downgraded if more men than the typical 30% are to be accepted. Further, for the typical institution with 60% men and 40% women, the expected success rates will be even more discrepant than the 81%-93% noted above.

Third, if the values of the separate-regression strategy are espoused (as they frequently are in discussions of fairness where the variable of concern is racial-ethnic membership), then entering freshman classes would typically be composed of 30% men and 70% women. Since we know that few classes have this sex composition, it is clear that the arguments of maintaining high standards and selecting the most qualified often used in other settings are not applied in practice when the variable of concern is sex not race.

Finally, the results indicate the likelihood of the existance of quotas for women in undergraduate admissions. The data indicate that women are not being excluded because of objective, quantified qualifications such as test scores and high-school grades. Even if fewer women than men applied, our analyses suggest that women would make up the greater portion of entering classes under all four strategies. Consequently, other variables or restrictions must be operating. Some of these restrictions are public quotas on women; others probably represent more subtle restrictive factors. Since we prefer at least openly stated admission policies, we deplore the latter private restrictive factors based on sex. While quotas based on sex may sometimes be consistent with institutional policy and facilities, we believe the conditional probability strategy to be consistent with the goals and values of many colleges and universities. The implementation of such a stragegy with regard to racial-ethnic group membership and sex results, we believe, in logical consistency for both variables, a reasonable idea of fairness, and desirable outcomes in the selection of students for college.

Table 3

Median Conditional Probabilities of Selection Given Success and Success Given Selection for Different Models of Fair Selection*

	Combined Equation		Regression Model		Equal-risk Model		Constant-ratio Model		Conditional Probability Model	
	M	*W*	*M*	*W*	*M*	*W*	*M*	*W*	*M*	*W*
Conditional Probability of Selection, Given Success Pr (Selection/ Success)	.55	.68	.42	.81	.41	.81	.58	.64	.61	.61
Conditional Probability of Success, Given Selection Pr (Success/ Selection)	.83	.91	.86	.88	.87	.88	.82	.92	.81	.93

* Median values based on 19 colleges described in Table 1

REFERENCES

Cleary, T. A. 1968. Test bias: prediction of grades of negro and white students in integrated colleges. *Journal of educational measurements* 5: 115–24.

Cole, N. S. 1973. Bias in selection. *Journal of educational measurement* 1:237–55.

Cole, N. S.; Hanson, G. R.; and Munday, L. A. 1974. Social issues of selection in education and employment. Unpublished manuscript, N. S. Cole, American College Testing Program, Iowa City, Iowa.

Darlington, R. B. 1971. Another look at "culture fairness." *Journal of educational measurement* 8: 71–82.

Einhorn, H. J., and Bass, A. R. 1971. Methodological considerations relevant to discrimination in employment testing. *Psychological bulletin* 75:261–69.

Linn, R. L., and Werts, C. E. 1971. Considerations for studies of test bias. *Journal of educational measurement* 8: 1–4.

National Center for Educational Statistics. 1970. *Earned degrees conferred: 1969–70 Institutional data.* Washington, D. C.: U. S. Government Printing Office.

Newcomer, M. 1959. *A century of higher education for American women.* New York: Harper and Brothers.

Thorndike, R. L. 1971. Concepts of culture-fairness. *Journal of educational measurement* 8: 63–70.

NOTES

1. M. Newcomer, *A Century of Higher Education for American Women* (New York: Harper and Brothers, 1959).
2. National Center for Educational Statistics, *Earned Degrees Conferred: 1969–70 Institutional Data* (Washington, D. C.: U.S. Government Printing Office, 1970).
3. T. A. Cleary, "Test Bias: Prediction of Grades of Negro and White Students in Integrated Colleges," *Journal of Educational Measurement* 5 (1968): 115–24.
4. R. L. Thorndike, "Concepts of Culture-fairness," *Journal of Educational Measurement* 8 (1971): 63–70; R. B. Darlington, "Another Look at 'Culture-fairness,'" *Journal of Educational Measurement* 8 (1971): 71–82; R. L. Linn and C. E. Werts, "Considerations for Studies of Test Bias," *Journal of Educational Measurement* 8 (1971): 1–4; and N. S. Cole, "Bias in Selection," *Journal of Educational Measurement* 10 (1973): 237–55.
5. Thorndike, "Concepts."
6. Cole, "Bias."
7. H. J. Einhorn and A. R. Bass, "Methodological Considerations Relevant to Discrimination in Employment Testing," *Psychological Bulletin* 75 (1971): 261–69.
8. Darlington, "Another Look."
9. Cole, "Bias."
10. A more detailed explanation is provided in *Assessing Students on the Way to College: Technical Report for the ACT Assessment* (Iowa City, Iowa: American College Testing Program, 1973).
11. Additional analyses were also done within liberal arts and science curriculum to insure that these results were not due to curriculum differences. Comparable proportions (30% men, 70% women) were obtained within each curriculum ground under the separate regression strategy.

Continuing Education for Women: Factors Influencing a Return to School and the School Experience*

HAZEL MARKUS

During the past five years, there has been an impressive increase in the number of special programs designed to aid adult women returning to school. A 1971 survey by the U.S. Department of Labor listed 435 different continuing education programs for women. This represents an 80% increase over the number of programs reported three years earlier.

A woman's decision to continue her education by returning to school may be the result of a number of situational or social pressures, chief among them present or anticipated economic need. This decision, however, may be viewed as a self-initiated attempt by the woman to actively change and improve her life. Studies of adult socialization rarely focus on these types of self-initiated changes. Most investigations, whether of children or adults, view the socialization process as one in which social groups or persons transmit values or train the individual for some existing role. It is difficult, of course, to separate the determinants of an individual's decision, and external demands are important in almost every decision. Nevertheless, more attention should be given to any decision that involves some elements

* Hazel Markus, "Continuing Education for Women: Factors Influencing a Return to School and the School Experience," reprinted with the permission of Hazel Markus and the Center for Continuing Education of Women, University of Michigan, Ann Arbor, Michigan.

of goal-setting and self-induced change, and to those activities that are more a result of one's own efforts than a result of the demands of others.[1] The motivation for these changes and their outcomes need to be systematically investigated.

Brim claims that self-initiated socialization, such as a return to school, stems from greater affluence of the average adult and, thus, an increase in what one can expect from life in terms of personal gratification and self-fulfillment.[2] Several specific social and economic changes are related to the growth in educational programs for women: technological advances lightening household tasks and giving women more free time; longer life expectancy and earlier marriage and childbearing; and, probably most importantly, a clarification and expansion of the various life-styles and roles open to all women.

Contacting a center for continuing education can be viewed as a decision point where anticipated self-initiated life changes and the motivations for these changes can be studied. This report is based on a sample of women who have contacted the Center for Continuing Education of Women at The University of Michigan. It will focus on 1) making a decision to continue education: why women come to the Center, characteristics of women contacting the Center, the decisions made, and differences between those women returning to school and those not returning; and 2) the school experience itself: changes in home and family life, institutional problems encountered, and factors important to success.

The Center for the Continuing Education of Women at Michigan was established in 1964 and has counselled over 4,000 women. It provides individual and vocational guidance to women whose schooling has been interrupted. The Center is available to all women of the community, but it is primarily designed to help women with family and/or employment responsibilities resume their higher education.

From statistics compiled by existing continuing education programs and a few studies of mature women graduate students, we know something about the population of women that return to school.[3] The first continuing education programs seemed to attract women who were relatively affluent, educated through high school or beyond, and without clear-cut goals other than expanding their realm of interests beyond the home. Usually these women wanted to prepare for employment and needed help in thinking through the problems involved in returning to school. In a related area we know that women who have completed their education in order to pursue a career often identify with parents who adhered to nontraditional sex roles, or with adults outside the family. In addition, such women tend to have developed career and intellectual interests in college, to be more autonomous and individualistic, and to have developed a feeling of independence and internalized criteria for esteem.[4]

There has been almost no research, however, on the reasons behind a woman's decision to continue her education. Research on a related question, reasons underlying a vocational decision, is vague and equivocal, suggesting only that a choice of vocation is in some way related to a desire to implement the self-concept.[5] For college women in the typical undergraduate age range (18-22), going to college is beset by role-conflict problems, i.e., achievement orientation versus the prescribed feminine role.[6] For many college women, achieving independently and occupationally only becomes important when affiliative needs are met and feminine identity is achieved.[7] For older women, married and with children, this feminine identity is assured, and returning to school seems to mark a period of determination and goal setting, a phase of achievement unhindered by worries over affiliative needs. Some women, of course, may gratify achievement needs through the task of creative childrearing.[8] However, as the children grow older and childrearing is not such a demanding task, a return to school may be viewed as an alternative means of engaging achievement expectancies.

A study by Baruch indicates that there is a temporal cycle in the achievement motive associated with the age and family situation of college-educated women.[9] A period of high-achievement needs before beginning a family is followed by a period of decline in achievement needs corresponding to a phase of high family involvement. When the family is grown, there is a return to the previous high level of need for achievement. These findings suggest that a return to school, at least for the older woman, may be an attempt to reclaim the ground many women lose in personal development and self-esteem during the middle years of adulthood.[10] Several studies of returning women graduate students find that becoming a better person and developing one's potentials are, in fact, the chief motivating factors in returning to school.[11] For other, especially younger, women, the vocational uses of continuing education are most important.[12]

Exploration of the school experience itself, its impact on home and family, and general factors important to successful completion of goals has been sparse. A considerable amount of study has been given to the working woman, however. Generally, working mothers (working from choice), compared to homemakers, report greater life satisfaction and self-esteem.[13] It is reasonable to expect that similar reports could be elicited from women returning to school.

The several studies available on women returning to school suggest that although women do experience the anticipated problems with combining school responsibilities and family responsibilities, most find ways to manage.[14] A critical factor in continuing a program, as well as the decision to begin school, appears to be the husband's favorable attitude.[15]

Investigations of programs for women have found considerable discrimination against older or part-time students. The returning woman student often is confronted with a questioning of her motives and capabilities. Most faculty members are not prepared to deal with the problems of returning women students.[16] Usually, however, the returning woman student has strong motivation, seriousness of purpose, persistence, and adaptability.[17] She performs well in school, often better than other groups of women.[18]

More systematic information is needed on women returning to school, how they succeed in meeting the goals they set for themselves, and the problems they face. Research indicates that a return to school is basically motivated by a need for independent achievement in other than interpersonal areas. This need for achievement is evidenced by setting new goals and attempting to meet them. In this study it was hypothesized that women who are successful in returning to school are likely to have support from the immediate social environment, adequate child-care facilities, an equitable distribution of household chores within the family, and hold the view that family responsibilities can be successfully combined with other responsibilities. The eventual impact of a return to school also should be affected by the institutional problems encountered. The number of these problems should increase with age and the amount of time away from an academic environment. To the extent that women are successful in returning to school they should experience renewed feelings of competence and self-esteem.

The achievement need and self-esteem are used as global concepts rather than as more specified sets of related concepts. The achievement need is interpreted as a motive for success in performing tasks, and self-esteem as the evaluation an individual places upon himself. For many women, especially those that have at least some college education before beginning a family, the traditional feminine role often does not allow them to fulfill their perceived potential or to achieve independently and may result in lowered self-esteem. It was hypothesized that women not returning to school should be relatively less satisfied with themselves than women returning to school, unless they have experienced gratification of independent achievement needs through career employment.

METHOD

The subjects for this study were a sample of women who had contacted the Center for Continuing Education of Women from 1964-1972. A contact usually involved filling out an information sheet and an appointment with a counselor. Approximately 4,000 women have contacted the Center since it was established. A random sample of 150 subjects was drawn by selecting every 24th name from the alphabetical file. A mail questionnaire was specifically developed by the author for this study, incorporating questions used by Judith Birnbaum for her study on life patterns, personality style, and self-esteem in gifted, family-oriented, and career-committed women,[19] and questions developed by Elizabeth Douvan.[20] Subjects were asked to complete the questionnaire to help understand something about how helpful the Center is in meeting the various educational needs of women, the problems and experiences of women returning to school, as well as some more general attitudes and feelings of women.

The questionnaire itself was divided into three parts. The first section dealt with the visit to the Center, goals at that time, reasons for contacting the Center, and the outcome of this contact. The second section explored the school experience itself, reasons for returning, problems encountered, factors important in success, and how school was combined with family responsibilities. The third section focused on the background of the subjects, activities, attitudes, and values. There were questions on family occupational and education status, attitudes toward marriage and children, involvement in community organizations, achievements and satisfactions, and attitudes toward combining marriage and career. This section also included self-rating on characteristics like attractiveness, competitiveness, and dependence, a twenty-one-item, self-esteem measure, and a five-item test of social desirability.

The questionnaire was sent under the auspices of the Center for Continuing Education of Women. Subjects were asked to complete the questionnaire whether or not they returned to school. A stamped, self-addressed envelope was provided. Anonymity and confidentiality were assured. Of the 150 questionnaires that were mailed out, approximately 30 were not received. In most of these cases, the potential respondents had moved and had not provided the Center with a new address. Of the 120 received, 83 were returned, after a postcard and two telephone call follow-ups. This amounted to a response rate of 69%. There was, of course, the problem that the nonrespondents may have differed significantly from the respondents, in which case estimates based on the latter would be biased. Checking the sample against total population figures kept by the Center on such items as age, marital status, and educational background, indicated that the sample was representative of the Center's population, with one possible exception. Those under 25 comprised only 9% of the sample. Statistics kept by the Center indicate that the percentage of younger people contacting the Center is somewhat larger than this number, especially in recent years. These younger people are the most mobile and transient members of a university community, the people most likely to have moved since their initial Center contact, and may account for a large portion of the unreturned questionnaires.

The open-ended questions were content analyzed and then coded with the remainder of the questionnaire. Scores on the self-esteem measure ranged from 34 to 117 with a mean of 86.9. There was a .01 correlation between the self-esteem scores and the social-desirability scores. This low correlation between scores on these two scales may indicate that the self-esteem scale is tapping an underlying personality trait and not just a subject's desire to present herself as socially desirable.

It should be emphasized that this study was largely exploratory, although guided by some basic questions based on related work. An attempt was made to uncover salient overall patterns and to accumulate some systematic information on the returning woman student.

FINDINGS

Who are the women that contact the Center?

In this sample, 53% of the women are between 30 and 40 years of age, 76% between 30 and 50 years of age. Those under 25 comprised 9% of this sample. The majority of the women are married (80%) and 84% of them have children, 70% two or more children, 45% with three or more children.

The majority of women returning to school (71%) already have some college credit. These percentages compare favorably with those collected by the Center during its seven years of operation and indicate that this sample is fairly representative of the Center's population.

The parents and husbands of these women also are well educated. Seventy-three percent of the husbands of these women have at least a B.A. degree, and 39% have a professional degree (MD or JD) or a doctorate. Less than 17% have husbands without a college education. The initial suggestion might be that a highly educated group of men supports the continuing education of their wives. Seventy-five percent of the husbands are earning over $10,000 a year, with 57% earning more than $15,000 annually. Looking at the family educational background of these women, 67% of their fathers, and 42% of their mothers have at least some college education. These women are representative of the highly select group that uses the Center. As suggested earlier, a return to school appeared to be a by-product of relative affluence. The economically and educationally disadvantaged are not included.

The majority of these women appear to be leading full and active lives at the time of contacting the Center. Seventy-three percent belong to at least one volunteer organization and 49% to two or more.

Contacting the Center and making a decision

Women contacting the Center were seeking a variety of assistance including clarification of goals, thinking through their problems in returning to school, and securing admission and registration. The goals they set for themselves ranged from mentions of specific aims—finishing a degree (32%), training for a future job (30%)—to the more general aims of planning future education (31%) and self and family enrichment (37%). Some came to the Center with precise goals in mind, while others expected their further education to crystallize their goals for them. The vast majority, however, appear to have at least a general goal in mind and some ideas about how to realize it.

A clear majority (70%) of these women indicated that the Center was at least somewhat helpful to them. Sixty-five percent were in the process of making a decision to return when they contacted the Center. Others were seeking help in transferring or scheduling, information on child care and financial assistance, or help in finding a job. Eighty-eight percent of the women contacted the Center only once or twice, and 45% of them reached an immediate decision that involved the pursuit of continuing education. Thirty-six percent decided at the time of their initial contact not to return to school. Many of these women (46%), however, returned to school at some later point. Of those deciding not to return, 51% decided either to get a job or to continue in their present occupation. Twenty-one percent decided to postpone the decision regarding further education for a specific period. The reasons most frequently given for not returning included family and financial burdens, and other opportunities, notably employment.

Reasons for returning to school

When given a choice between two primary reasons for continuing their education, 58% of the women stated that they were interested in goals like finding stimulation, enlarging their own interests and pleasures, and increasing skills as a wife and mother, while 29% stated that finding an interesting and satisfying job was the most important goal. Thirteen percent felt that both goals were equally important.

The specific reason most often given for returning to school usually has two aspects. There is the desire for expansion and personal enrichment coupled with the hope that the stimulation and expanded horizons provided by a return to school may one day be given some practical, useful application. Although, for the majority of women, general goals and values of education may appear as the most important factor in continuing education, rarely was self-enrichment given as a goal without tying it to some more concrete aim. The frequently mentioned specific reasons for returning to school included obtaining a degree (26%), training for a new job, career, or gaining some specific skill (47%), advancing in present job (10%), and insuring financial security (3%).

These women are attuned to the potential for general self-development and growth provided by further education, but they also are able to define fairly specific goals to be achieved through continuing their education. To grow or develop in some vague and unspecified way is clearly not enough for these women. In most cases, their commitment is fairly long term and much more inclusive than just getting out of the house or finding a new part-time activity. These findings, along with those from the majority of studies of returning women, clash sharply with any suggestion that continuing education involves rusty ladies finding something to do with free Tuesday and Thursday afternoons. Controversies over whether facilities for education should be used for "the production of cultured and enlightened mothers" are largely moot: few women want an education for this purpose alone. No systematic relationships were discovered, however, between the type of goal that was set or the reason for returning and how well these women did in school, or the impact of the school experience in home and family life.

The school experience

As noted in several earlier studies, the advice and opinions of others, especially the husband, often are critical in making a decision to return to school, and once returning, staying in school. During the time these women were in school as adult returnees, 82% reported that they received some help and encouragement from their husbands, with 58% reporting a great deal of help and encouragement. The majority of women also felt that they received at least some help and encouragement from their children and friends.

In an attempt to relate various measures of success in school to the amount of encouragement received, a clear pattern emerged between drop-out and perceived encouragement. Although the reasons for dropping out are varied, dropping out can be viewed as a lack of success in returning to school. The various reasons given for leaving school will be discussed later. As Table 1 indicates, the more help and encouragement the returning student felt that she received from her husband, the greater the likelihood she would stay in school. Although cell frequencies are small, the pattern is unambiguous.

Table 1

Perceived Husband's Encouragement and Drop-out

	Encouragement			
	None at all	Very little	Some	A great deal
Drop-out	100.0% (3)	50.0% (3)	41.7% (5)	39.3% (11)
No Drop-out	0.0% (0)	50.0% (3)	58.3% (7)	60.7% (17)

These results suggest that, even though a return to school is a self-initiated attempt at change prompted by internal needs and motives, there is still a great need for a supporting social, interpersonal environment. Brim, for instance, has noted that when an adult seeks change, the immediate social environment is crucial to the outcome of the change.[21] Less immediate support—but nevertheless important to drop-out decisions—is the help and encouragement of instructors and advisers, and employers (see Tables 2 and 3).

Similar patterns emerged with the perceived encouragement from children, friends, parents, and neighbors. To combine this information into an index of encouragement, scores from each of the seven items (husband, children, parents, neighbors, friends, advisers, and employers) were standardized, summed, and divided by seven. (Missing data was assigned a score of zero, i.e., the mean of the standardized score. Individuals with missing data on more than three items did not receive an index score.). The resultant index scores were collapsed into two groups, those less than the mean value of zero, and those greater than or equal to the mean value of zero. The result is summarized in Table 4.

It is possible, of course, that in reviewing the school experience some women may see their dropping out as a result of lack of support from the

Table 2

Perceived Employer Encouragement and Drop-out

	Encouragement			
	None at all	Very little	Some	A great deal
Drop-out	88.9% (8)	50.0% (1)	50.0% (3)	16.7% (1)
No Drop-out	11.1% (1)	50.0% (1)	50.0% (3)	83.3% (5)

Table 3

Perceived Instructor Encouragement and Drop-out

	Encouragement			
	None at all	Very little	Some	A great deal
Drop-out	71.4% (5)	57.1% (4)	35.3% (6)	50.0% (9)
No Drop-out	28.6% (2)	42.9% (3)	64.7% (11)	50.0% (9)

Table 4

Index of Perceived Encouragement and Drop-out

	Encouragement		
	Low	High	Total
Drop-out	68.2% (15)	37.5% (9)	52.2% (24)
No Drop-out	31.8% (7)	62.5% (15)	47.8% (22)

$X^2 = 4.33$, $p < .05$

social environment, when it is actually a result of personal lack of interest, motivation, or ability. However, it seems that one of the factors important to success in a return to school is a sense of continual support and encouragement from important others.

Returning to school does pose some problems for most women. As would be expected, these usually center around the management of time and how family responsibilities can be juggled to accomodate the pressures and demands of classes. Sixty-four percent of the women reported that spending less time with children created some problem. Fifty-six percent felt that spending less time with their husbands also was some problem. Spending less time with friends (44%), neglecting housework (53%), and putting extra responsibilities on husband and children (42%), also posed some problem for returning women. Only a few women, however, reported major problems in any of these areas.

Apparently, for these women, returning to school does not cause radical changes in their patterns of responsibilities and is viewed as another activity that must be integrated into the existing family life-style. Forty-seven percent indicated that going back to school did not affect the distribution of household chores in the family. Another 45% reported that the family shared the chores. However, when the distribution of housework among the woman, her husband, and children before a return to school is compared with the distribution after a return to school, very little difference is observable, suggesting that if the family shared the chores it was because they had always done so and this was not a redistribution based on the woman's return to school. Before entering school, 86% reported doing all or most of the housework. While in school, 67% of the women did all or most of the housework. Only 10% of the husbands did as much as half of the housework before their wives returned to school, and only 17% were reported as doing half the housework when these women returned to school.

Although a return to school may not have brought about a more equitable distribution of family responsibilities, 58% of these women reported that there were some changes in their home and family life, and 18% said there was a great deal of change. These changes reflect a concern with managing extra responsibilities and perhaps some guilt feelings over not doing all that is expected of them. Not surprisingly, 74% of the women reported that there was not enough time for housework, entertaining, or other home-related or social activities. Thirty-three percent mentioned that there was not enough time for family. Changes were most evident for large families.

A relationship between age and the change reported in home and family life was observed. There was more change in home life for older women returning to school. See Table 5.

As could be expected, more change also was reported in the home and family life of those women with children. See Table 6.

Typically there were mentions of "messier houses," "simpler meals," and a "more stressful life." These comments, however, were embedded in

Table 5

Age and Change in Home and Family Life

	Change	
	Some	None
Age: 20–29	55.5% (10)	44.4% (8)
30–39	85.7% (12)	14.3% (2)
40+	84.6% (22)	15.4% (4)

Table 6

Number of Children and Change in Home Life

	Change	
	Some	None
No children	42.9% (3)	57.1% (4)
One child	87.5% (7)	12.5% (1)
Two or more children	86.5% (32)	13.5% (5)

the context of more general positive comments like "my life had new dimensions which my husband didn't share. He and I enjoyed this—because I had new things to bring to him which enlarged his life as well as my own, new interests, ideas, friends, and perspectives," or "I had to work doubly hard to keep the house clean, cooking, and still find time for homework, but my family had a happier wife and mother."

The comments of these women returning to school hint at one of the major findings of this survey. A return to school, in almost all cases, is an enjoyable, valuable experience. The positive impact of this particular self-initiated change on the individual appears almost unquestionable. Eighty-five percent of the women reported that they enjoyed school (or are enjoying school) very much. Seventy-five percent felt that it changed their lives in significant ways. Sixty-six percent mentioned increased knowledge, understanding, and qualification for a specific job as the significant contributions of continuing their education. Sixty-one percent mentioned that a return to school gave them a sense of accomplishment and achievement, or gave them new confidence and self-respect. The feeling of accomplishment gained from a return to school seems to offset many of the external, concrete problems encountered and probably contributes significantly to the overall positive evaluation of the school experience. This finding is not unexpected and supports the hypothesis that there is a loss of self-esteem and a decrease in feelings of competence and efficacy associated with a routine, unchallenging job, or centering life completely around home and children that can be regained with a return to school. A return to school presents an integrative challenge. Mentions of small failures in fulfilling the housewife role may reflect the respondent's feeling that now she is concerned with higher, more important values and has moved beyond a preoccupation with household tasks. The fact that they are mentioned at all suggests that they are not major problems and are the expected result of meeting the responsibilities of both family and school. Attempting to fulfill both sets of responsibilities seems to engender a feeling of competence best explained as a feeling of managing, of control, of being able to organize and utilize all of one's resources to accomplish various tasks.

This renewed feeling of accomplishment should be especially evident for women who attended a college or university before stopping their education. These women are probably most aware that their need for achievement and involvement is not being met and that something is missing in their lives. Seventy-one percent of the women that returned to school completed at least some college before stopping their education for the first time.

A return to school not only satisfied a desire for achievement for many women, but it also was perceived as enhancing existing interpersonal relationships. A particularly forthright and thoughtful response given by a woman who returned to school after twelve years to work on an MSW degree illustrates this finding: "It provided new perspectives, direction, and structure to my life. I discovered, or rather rediscovered, enjoyable talents in myself and gained a greater poise and self-confidence as a result of my feeling of competence and knowledgeability. It enabled me to establish a more sharing relationship with my children that crossed parent-child boundaries and it enabled me to share common interests and work with my husband (a psychologist) and to enrich the excitement we feel for each other."

Another woman wrote: "I gained a sense of self-respect, felt more able to converse with people. I began to appreciate myself as having more ability than I realized. I had a sense of accomplishment and achievement for myself and my efforts, and this knowledge gave me more insight into family problems." More directly, another woman stated: "I have less time to devote to unimportant areas. I am more interesting to myself and others. I have goals other than child rearing. I don't harp on the children but rather get to my own work."

Other significant changes that were reported included gaining greater respect from family (17%) and gaining new friends (10%). Enjoyment of school also was related to high scores on the encouragement index discussed earlier. More enjoyment of school was reported by women who perceived substantial support from their social environment (see Table 7).

Table 7

Encouragement Index and Enjoyment of School

	Encouragement	
	Low	High
Did not enjoy school	29.4% (5)	4.5% (1)
Enjoy school very much	70.6% (12)	95.5% (21)

Reports of significant positive changes in one's life were most prevalent for the older women in the sample (see Table 8).

Table 8

Age and Significant Positive Changes in Life

Age:	Some change	No change
20–29	64.7% (11)	35.3% (6)
30–39	76.9% (10)	23.1% (3)
40+	80.8% (21)	19.2% (5)

One can suggest that this result stems from the fact that an older woman's life contains more elements that could be changed by schooling when compared wih the life of a younger woman. Just as returning to college effected the greatest change in the day-to-day life of the older woman, so it is that this group was most likely to be more profoundly affected by the college experience as well. In line with several other findings, relatively fewer young women have experienced periods of doubt related to self-esteem and achievement motivation, and accordingly a return to school does not produce noticeable changes for them. These women also have been out of school for a relatively shorter time and reintegration is a much simpler process.

The enjoyment of the school experience noted by the respondents was reflected in their academic performance. Ninety-one percent of the women did at least as well in their schoolwork as they had the last time they were in school. Fifty percent reported grades better than the grades they received earlier. Forty-two percent received some type of a degree. Twenty percent received a B.A. degree, 52% an M.A. degree, 16% received both a B.A. and an M.A., and 4% earned a Ph.D. Thirty-seven percent of these women are still attending school either part- or full-time.

On the whole, these women did not report many problems directly related to the school experience itself. Sixty-three percent reported liking their fellow students very much upon their return and 76% felt accepted and comfortable with the other students. The majority of the students did not report any problems in "fitting in" to the school environment. The problems that were mentioned included acceptance by professors, counselors, and advisers (16%), not feeling a part of the university (28%), and resentment by other students (7%). Some of the women reported that their motives in taking classes were questioned and that they were discouraged from trying to undertake a program of study if they could only attend classes on a part-time basis. Most reports of not feeling a part of the university centered around not having enough time to spend on campus to take part in extra activities. Some women who were only taking one or two classes and could devote a great deal of time to them noted that some other students resented their hard work and felt that the returning women had an unfair advantage. It was the women aged 30 and older who were most likely to report these types of problems (see Table 9).

Table 9

Age and Problems Encountered*

Age:	Acceptance by Professors	Not feeling a part of the University	Resentment by other students	None	Other
20–29	11.8% (2)	29.4% (5)	0.0% (0)	64.7% (11)	5.9% (1)
30–39	23.1% (3)	38.5% (5)	15.4% (2)	38.5% (5)	7.7% (1)
40+	24.0% (6)	32.0% (8)	8.0% (2)	52.0% (13)	0.0% (0)

* Due to multiple responses, percentages do not sum to 100.

Many students reported more concrete problems in returning to school. Hours of classes was the problem most frequently mentioned, followed by problems with parking and libraries, notably reserve books.

Over half of the returning women reported some initial disappointments with the school experience. That these disappointments were not later labeled as problems suggests that most women were able to deal with some gap between previous expectations and the actual experience and were able to overcome it. The main disappointments were with the structure of the university, the majors available, and red-tape problems. These disappointments are not, of course, peculiar to returning women students. Consistent with a general trend, older women were somewhat more likely to report these disappointments than were younger women (see Table 10).

Table 10

Age and Disappointment with School

	Yes	No
Age:		
20–29	47.1% (8)	52.9% (9)
30–39	64.3% (9)	35.7% (5)
40+	56.0% (14)	44.0% (11)

Fifty-seven percent of the women reported at least some second thoughts after returning to school. These doubts fell into two basic categories: those related to family and home (41%), e.g., "am I neglecting my home and family?", and doubts related to ability to succeed (52%), e.g., "can I do it?" or "am I too old?" Although there is a trend for more second thoughts of this type to be expressed by older women, the pattern is not pronounced.

Table 11

Age and Second Thoughts Related to School

	Yes	No
Age:		
20–29	50.0% (8)	50.0% (8)
30–39	50.0% (7)	50.0% (7)
40+	65.0% (17)	34.6% (9)

Second thoughts were also related to scores on the self-esteem measure. The scores on this measure were dichotomized at the mean. Those with higher self-esteem scores were less likely to report second thoughts when returning to school.

Table 12

Self-esteem and Second Thoughts Related to School

	Second Thoughts?	
	Yes	No
Low self-esteem	78.8% (18)	22.0% (5)
High self-esteem	38.0% (12)	62.0% (20)

$X^2 = 7.39$, $p < .05$

Overall, 64% of the women stated that a return to school made positive changes in them and their lives, and 41% rate the change as very positive and as improving their lives in many ways. Twenty-two percent saw a return to school as having both positive and negative aspects. Only one person indicated that returning to school had a totally negative impact upon her life. Although older women experienced more problems, more disappointments, and second thoughts, it was the older women who reported the most positive overall evaluation of the school experience. The younger women were most likely to report mixed or negative changes associated with a return to school (Table 13). As noted earlier, perhaps the problems and difficulties experienced by older women are viewed as a test or as a challenge. Meeting this challenge results in a feeling of competence gained from organizing one's resources to initiate a change or a goal and achieving it.

Table 13

Age and Evaluation of School Experience

Age	*Mixed or Negative Reaction*
20–29	55.6%
30–39	25.0%
40+	26.9%

Another behavioral measure of the overall impact of a return to school and the success of this self-initiated life change is the attrition or drop-out rate discussed earlier. Forty-eight percent of all women returning to school dropped out of school at least once since their return. The reasons given for dropping out are fairly diverse and do not seem to revolve around any one particular issue. In order of frequency, the reasons mentioned included personal problems, e.g., illness, marriage, or pregnancy (31%), financial problems (21%), lack of interest, motivation, or changed goals (21%), school did not leave enough time for family responsibilities (17%), moved away, suitable program not available elsewhere (14%), and difficulty with school (3%).

School drop-out was related to a general fate-control question, suggesting that success in school may be influenced by some general attitudes and beliefs as well as by more immediate factors like encouragement and support.

Table 14

Fate Control and Drop-out

	A man can make long-range plans for his life, but a woman has to take things as they come	
	True	*False*
Drop-out	66.7% (12)	39.5% (15)
No Drop-out	33.3% (6)	61.5% (23)

An alternative interpretation deserves mention. Rather than reflecting a fairly stable attitude about life control, it may be that a woman's response to this item may itself have been influenced by her being forced to disrupt her school plans to accommodate her family or others.

There also was some indication that those women with higher self-esteem scores were less likely to drop out of school. A t-test on the mean self-esteem scores of these two groups did not, however, reach significance. The drop-out rate also was slightly higher in the middle-age group (30–39) than in either of the other two age groups. Those in this age group also reported more problems with acceptance as adult returnees (see Table 9) and more disappointment upon returning (see Table 10). These findings could be interpreted as suggesting that it is this stage of the life cycle (30–40) when women are most likely to be defining themselves in terms of others and are most likely to experience a loss in self-esteem. This loss in self-esteem might be manifested in greater difficulties with a return to school. Women in the younger group have only been away from school for a relatively few years, have a realistic view of the school experience, and have little difficulty "fitting in." Older women usually have defined themselves as older women returning to school and expect not to fit in to the general student population. Women in the middle group, however, are probably least sure about fitting in and about their own goals and expected achievements. The mean self-esteem score of the 30–39 group was lower than the mean self-esteem score of the 20–29 group or the 40+ group. However, an analysis of variance performed on the self-esteem scores of the three age groups did not reach significance.

General attitudes and values of women contacting the Center

Looking at the total sample of women who contacted the Center, it was observed that only 10% see themselves as doing all the things they would really like to be doing. Those with the highest self-esteem scores are most likely to place themselves in this category. The others report that various aspects of their life are unfilled. Basically two things are missing: (1) a sense of accomplishment, purpose, "a job I could do well in," "a project of my own," "challenge and creative involvement," and, closely related, (2) time, usually for creative endeavors. There were relatively few mentions of friendship, interpersonal closeness, time for family, money, or travel. The majority of these women are married and presumably secure in some type of family relationships. Perhaps, as Bardwick suggests,[22] these women have satisfied the affiliative goals and can now look in other directions, notably to personal development and achievement. Accordingly, when asked "what would make you happiest?" or "what do you imagine as the most satisfying thing that could happen in your life in the next five years?", 61% mentioned having a happy husband and/or children, or helping some family member realize their potential, but 88% also mentioned some intellectual achievement, e.g., finishing education. This is in marked contrast to the results of a study of college-age women completed by Bardwick in which she observed that not one respondent referred to her own academic or professional role as a source of happiness.[23]

The responses of these women best describe the concern for interpersonal matters that is now infused with a motive to achieve independently: "To feel needed and effective, that my children would turn out well with a life and career of their own, and that I would have a satisfying job of my own and recognition in my own right." "It would satisfy me to achieve more recognition because of my work. I'm assuming, of course, that everything goes as well as it has at home so far, the children are developing, my marriage is satisfying, and I see no radical changes."

When asked "what kinds of things have you done in your life which you think of as accomplishments and achievements?", 86% of these women mention some type of academic or vocational achievement besides the usual mention of success in interpersonal relationships and internal development found to characterize the responses of young college women.[24]

Generally, the women who have contacted the Center, whether or not they returned to school, describe themselves as independent, intellectual, competitive occupationally, and attractive. In this and several other respects, these women resemble the composite given by Birnbaum to describe the married professional more closely than the composite describing the homemaker.[25] Birnbaum studied three groups of University of Michigan alumnae graduating between 1945 and 1955: 1) homemakers, married women with intact families and children at home, with no degree beyond the bachelor's level, and not currently in school, 2) married professionals, women with the highest degree in their particular field; and 3) single professionals. Birnbaum compared the life patterns, personality style, and self-esteem of these three groups of women.

As a group, the women who contacted the Center believe in the general aims of the women's liberation movement, egalitarian marriages, and that the worker and mother role can be successfully and creatively combined. Again, in these areas they resemble the married professionals more closely than the homemakers described by Birnbaum (see Tables 15 and 16).

Table 15

	CEW women	Married Professionals	Homemakers
A working mother can establish just as warm and secure a relationship with children as a mother who does not work:			
True	88%	100%	65%
False	12%	0%	35%
	(73)	(25)	(29)

Table 16

	CEW women	Married Professionals	Homemakers
It is more important for a wife to help her husband's career than to have one for herself:			
True	23%	25%	71%
False	77%	75%	21%
	(73)	(25)	(29)

Generally the women who contact the Center have successfully integrated the important goals in their lives and have resolved the question of their independence and individuality. They do not appear as independent, assertive, and self-assured as the married professionals, but they are certainly not like the homemakers with motherhood as a focal life-role and little faith in their competence and self-worth. Just a decision to contact the Center for Continuing Education for Women, regardless of outcome, is indicative of reaching a point where the need for independent achievement has become a goal in its own right. If this goal conflicted with goals of interpersonal closeness and approval in the past, it seems that the conflict has been resolved prior to a decision to contact the Center. The clients of the Center generally are not in need of psychological counsel, or help in resolving feminine role conflicts or in formulating life goals. This finding is supported by the observation that there are few attitudinal differences between the women who continue their education after contacting the Center and those that do not.

There are no striking differences in attitudes toward marriage, children, combining marriage and career, or achievement and satisfaction between those who decide to continue their education and those that do not. The two groups also are distributed similarly with regard to background and descriptive factors. This suggests that the decision not to continue education after contacting the Center is largely the result of external family and financial problems.

It was hypothesized that women who do not return to school might be more satisfied with their job or perceive themselves as more successful in their occupation than those women returning to school. No difference was observed in this area, however.

One difference that does emerge centers on the life-changing role of marriage. The women who did not return to school are more likely to hold polarized views of how marriage changes a woman's life. They focus on either the fulfilling, enriching aspects of marriage or on the restricting, self-sacrificing aspects of marriage. In contrast, women who returned to school are more likely to hold a balanced view of marriage, mentioning the enlarging aspects as well as the narrowing, loss of freedom aspects of marriage.

One interpretation of this finding is that women who do not have marriage as the focal point of their lives and are involved in projects and activities outside the home are more likely to hold a realistic view of its advantages and disadvantages.

One interesting difference was observed in the self-esteem scores of these two groups. Women who returned to school had higher self-esteem scores. A t-test on the mean self-esteem scores of these two groups revealed a significant difference ($t = 2.13$, $p < .05$). As noted earlier, there is no ground for inferring a causal relationship between self-esteem and a return to school. Several explanations for this relationship could be offered. Perhaps a return to school and consequent increases in feelings of competency and achievement results in a somewhat higher self-esteem score.

Table 17

Return to School and View of Marriage

	More positive than negative responses	Both negative and positive responses	More negative than positive responses
Women who did not return to school	45% (9)	15% (3)	40% (8)
Women who returned to school	24% (13)	47% (26)	27% (16)

$X^2 = 6.77$

Or, just as plausibly, perhaps there is a selection factor operating. Those with higher self-esteem are more sure of themselves, perceive themselves as more able to cope with the problems of continuing their education, and are the ones that make the decision to return to school. Nevertheless, the positive relationship between returning to school and higher self-esteem needs further systematic study.

Conclusions

A return to school can be viewed as a self-initiated life change. The women in this study are relatively affluent, come from relatively well-educated families, already have at least some college education themselves, and are returning to school solely because they want to. These women usually have fairly clear-cut goals. The goals they set for themselves range from the specific, getting a degree, to the more general, self and family enrichment. Yet in probing for reasons for return, we find that almost all women have a relatively specific, long-term goal in mind (obtaining a degree, training for a new job or career, gaining some specific skill) and some ideas about how to achieve it. A return to school is seen as a generally enriching experience, but also as a vehicle for a specific change.

Although a return to school is a self-initiated activity, one of the most important factors related both to enjoyment of the school experience and to remaining in school is the perceived support from the important others in the immediate social environment. This usually means the help and encouragement received from husbands, children, friends, and instructors and advisers. The more support a woman receives, the more likely she is to return to school, to stay in school once returning, and to enjoy school.

The major problems encountered in a return to school center on managing time so that both family demands and school responsibilities can be accommodated. A return to school is regarded as just another activity that must fit into the existing pattern of responsibilities. Some shifting of responsibilities to other family members is noted, especially for older women and women with two or more children, but no radical changes are found. A return to school is a woman's own idea, she expects to be able to manage it successfully without major disruptions in her roles as wife, mother, or worker, and she usually does. Most women note some worries over not having enough time for their families, but these worries are generally embedded in a context of positive comments about the school experience.

The most significant life changes reported as a result of a return to school include not only achieving stated goals, getting a degree, and gaining some specific skill, but also gaining a sense of achievement and accomplishment. These feelings of renewed self-confidence and competency, which are consistently reported, seem to more than offset the family problems encountered or problems with school itself, and contribute significantly to the finding that returning to school is a positive, enjoyable experience.

These women perform well in school, feel accepted and comfortable with other students, and usually report few problems or institutional barriers. The problems that are mentioned include acceptance by professors, resentment by other students, and fitting into the university environment. It is generally the older women who report these types of problems and who experience more disappointments and second thoughts upon returning to school. Yet despite these problems, the older students are more likely to describe the return to school in more glowing, positive terms, presumably because of the overall feelings of independent achievement that are experienced. Younger women, less likely to feel that accomplishment and achievement are missing from their lives, do not generally view a return to school in these terms and report more mixed reactions to the school experience. There also was some indication that women in the 30–39 age group have the most uncertain self-conceptions and the most difficulty fitting into the school environment.

Overall, regardless of age, a return to school appears to have a positive impact on these women, at least in terms of their feelings about themselves. They also report that their families benefit as well. Data is now needed on whether these renewed feelings of self-confidence and achievement have behavioral correlates, that is, whether they are translated into success in careers or jobs, or into observable changes in relations with their families.

This study also found that, unlike typical college-age women, women who have interrupted their education and are contemplating a return to school, view academic and professional accomplishments as a source of satisfaction and happiness, and as notable achievements in life. These women see themselves as being independent, competitive, and intellectual. They feel that the worker, mother, and wife roles can be successfully combined. Very few differences were found between those women that returned to school and those who did not. Higher self-esteem scores were obtained from those women that returned to school, however. More investigation of the relationship between self-esteem and a return to school is needed to determine the direction of this relationship.

The results of this study suggest that women contacting the Center for the Continuing Education of Women are usually seeking to do just that—continue their education. Conflicts over fulfilling the traditional feminine role and developing their own ability are either not relevant or have been resolved. Consistent with viewing a return to school as a self-initiated life change, these women are not in need of psychological counsel, but rather in need of support, encouragement, and specific goal-related advice.

Further studies in this area should concentrate on women who return to school on a full-time basis and should investigate more systematically the pattern of drop-out and return. More investigation is also needed on the differential experience of women in the 30–39 age group. Further study on the achievement motivation of women who have returned to school and have satisfied affiliative goals associated with the feminine image also would be valuable.

REFERENCES

Addis, M. E. 1967. Problems of administrative change in selected programs for the reeducation of women. Unpublished Ph.D. dissertation, Harvard University.

Bardwick, J. M. 1971. *Psychology of women: A study of bio-cultural conflicts.* New York: Harper and Row.

Baruch, R. 1967. The achievement motive in women: implications for career development. *Journal of personality and social psychology* 5: 260–67.

Birnbaum, J. 1971. Life patterns, personality style, and self-esteem in gifted family-oriented and career-committed women. Unpublished Ph.D. dissertation, The University of Michigan.

Brim, O. G., Jr. 1968. Adult socialization. In *Socialization and society,* ed. J. A. Clausen. Boston: Little, Brown and Company pp. 182–226.

Burton, L. K. A follow-up study of the mature women clients at the University of Colorado Women's Center, 1964–1966. Unpublished MPS thesis, University of Colorado.

Campbell, J. 1974. Women drop back in: educational innovation in the Sixties. In *Academic women on the move,* ed. Alice Rossi. Russell Sage Foundation.

Davis, N. Z. 1966. A study of 42 women who have children and who are in graduate programs at the University of Toronto. Preliminary Report, University of Toronto. Mimeographed.

Doty, B. A. 1966. Why do mature women return to college? *Journal of the national association of women deans and counselors* 29, no. 4: 171–74.

Douvan, E., and Gold, M. 1966. Model patterns in American adolescence. In *Review of child development research,* vol. 2, ed. M. L. Hoffman and L. W. Hoffman. New York: Russell Sage Foundation, pp. 469–528.

Fagerburg, J. E. 1967. A comparative study of undergraduate women in relation to selected personal characteristics and certain effects of educational interruption. Unpublished Ph.D. dissertation, Purdue University.

Ginzberg, E., and Yohalem, A. M. 1966. *Educated American women: self-portraits.* New York: Columbia University Press.

Gurin, G.; Veroff, J.; and Feld, S. 1960. *Americans view their mental health.* New York: Basic Books.

Horner, M. S. 1968. A psychological barrier to achievement in women—the motive to avoid success. Symposium presentation at the Midwestern Psychological Association, May 1968, Chicago.

Likert, J., ed. *Conversations with returning women students.* Ann Arbor, Michigan: University of Michigan Center for Continuing Education of Women.

Lipinski, B. Sex-role conflict and achievement motivation in college women. *Dissertation abstracts* 26: 4077.

Maccoby, E. 1963. Women's intellect. In *The potential of women*, ed. S. M. Farber. New York: McGraw-Hill.

Marlowe, D., and Crowne, D. P. 1961. Social desirability and response to perceived situation demands. *Journal of consulting psychology* 25: 109–115.

Murphy, L. B., and Raushenbush, E., eds. 1960. *Achievement in college years: a record of intellectual and personal growth.* New York: Harper and Brothers. 1967.

Newcomb, T. M. 1967. *Persistence and change: Bennington College and its students after twenty-five years.* New York: Wiley.

Nye, I., and Hoffman, L. W. 1963. *The employed mother in America.* Chicago: Rand McNally.

Rossi, A. S. 1968. Transition to parenthood. *Journal of marriage and the family* 30: 26–39.

Schletzer, V. M.; Cless, E. L.; McCune, C. W.; Mantini, B. K.; and Loeffler, D. L. 1967. *A five-year report, 1960–65, of Minnesota plan for the continuing education of women.* Minneapolis: University of Minnesota.

Super, D. E. 1963. *Career development: self-concept theory.* Princeton, N. J.: College Entrance Examination Board Research Monograph no. 4.

Tiedman, D. V., and O'Hara, R. P. 1963. *Career development: choice and adjustment.* New York: College Entrance Examination Board Monograph no 3.

Westervelt, E. M. 1971. *Education, vocation, and avocation in women's lives. What is happening to American women.* Atlanta: Southern Newspaper Publishers Association Foundation, pp. 57–93.

Withycombe-Brocato, C. J. 1969. The mature woman student: who is she? Unpublished Ph.D. dissertation, United States International University.

Women's Bureau. 1971. Continuing education programs and services for women. Pamphlet 10, Rev. Washington, D. C.: U.S. Government Printing Office.

NOTES

1. O. G. Brim, "Adult Socialization," in *Socialization and Society,* ed. J. A. Clausen (Boston: Little, Brown, and Company, 1968) : 182–226.
2. Ibid.
3. V. M. Schletzer, et al., *A Five-year Report, 1960–1965, of the Minnesota Plan for the Continuing Education of Women* (Minneapolis: University of Minne-

sota, 1967) ; N. Z. Davis, *A Study of 42 Women Who Have Children and Who Are in Graduate Programs at the University of Toronto, Preliminary Report* (mimeographed, University of Toronto, 1966) ; L. K. Burton, "A Follow-up Study of the Mature Women Clients at the University of Colorado Women's Center, 1964–1966" (M.P.S. thesis, University of Colorado) ; C. J. Withycombe-Brocato, "The Mature Woman Student: Who Is She?" (Ph.D. diss., United States International University, 1969) ; J. Likert, ed., *Conversations with Returning Women Students* (Ann Arbor, Mich.: University of Michigan Center for Continuing Education of Women) ; and E. M. Westervelt, *Education, Vocation, and Avocation in Women's Lives: What Is Happening to American Women* (Atlanta: Southern Newspaper Publishers Association Foundation, 1971) : 57–93.

4. T. M. Newcomb, *Persistence and Change: Bennington College and Its Students After Twenty-five Years* (New York: Wiley, 1967) ; E. Ginzberg and A. M. Yohalem, *Educated American Women: Self-portraits* (New York: Columbia University Press, 1966) ; L. B. Murphy and E. Raushenbush, eds., *Achievement in College Years: A Record of Intellectual and Personal Growth* (New York: Harper and Brothers, 1960) ; Schletzer, "Five-year Report"; and J. M. Bardwick, *Psychology of Women: A Study of Bio-cultural Conflicts* (New York: Harper and Row, 1971) .
5. D. E. Super, *Career Development: Self-concept Theory* (Princeton, N. J.: College Entrance Examination Board, 1963) ; and D. V. Tiedman and R. P. O'Hara, *Career Development: Choice and Adjustment* (Princeton, N. J.: College Entrance Examination Board, 1963) .
6. E. Douvan and M. Gold, "Model Patterns in American Adolescence," in *Review of Child Development Research,* vol. 2, eds. M. L. Hoffman and L. W. Hoffman (New York: Russell Sage Foundation, 1966) , pp. 469–528; E. Maccoby, "Women's Intellect," in *The Potential of Women,* ed. S. M. Farber (New York: McGraw-Hill, 1963) ; and M. S. Horner, "A Psychological Barrier to Achievement in Women—The Motive to Avoid Success" (Paper delivered at the Midwestern Psychological Association, Chicago, May 1968) .
7. Bardwick, *Psychology.*
8. G. Gurin, J. Veroff, and S. Feld, *Americans View Their Mental Health* (New York: Basic Books, 1960) .
9. R. Baruch, "The Achievement Motive in Women: Implications for Career Development," *Journal of Personality and Social Psychology* 5 (1967) : 260–7.
10. A. S. Rossi, "Transition to Parenthood." *Journal of Marriage and the Family* 30 (1968) : 26–39; and Gurin, Veroff, and Feld, *Americans.*
11. Withycombe-Brocato, "Mature"; and B. A. Doty, "Why Do Mature Women Return to College?", *Journal of the National Association of Women Deans and Counselors* 29 (1966) : 171–74,
12. Westervelt, *Education.*
13. I. Nye and L. W. Hoffman, *The Employed Mother in America* (Chicago: Rand McNally, 1963) ; Gurin, Veroff, and Feld, *Americans;* and J. Birnbaum, "Life Patterns, Personality Style, and Self-esteem in Gifted Family-oriented and Career-committed Women" (Ph.D. diss., University of Michigan, 1971) .
14. Davis, "A Study."
15. Ibid.; and Westervelt, *Education.*
16. M. E. Addis, "Problems of Administrative Change in Selected Programs for the Reeducation of Women" (Ph.D. diss., Harvard University, 1967) .
17. J. Campbell, "Women Drop Back In: Educational Innovation in the Sixties,"

in *Academic Women on the Move,* ed. Alice Rossi (New York: Russell Sage Foundation, 1974), pp. 93–124.

18. J. E. Fagerburg. "A Comparative Study of Undergraduate Women in Relation to Selected Personal Characteristics and Certain Effects of Educational Interruption" (Ph.D. diss., Purdue University, 1967).
19. Birnbaum, "Life Patterns."
20. Douvan, "Model Patterns."
21. Brim, *Adult.*
22. Bardwick, *Psychology.*
23. Ibid.
24. B. Lipinski, "Sex-role Conflict and Achievement Motivation in College Women," *Dissertation Abstracts* 26 (1966), p. 4,077A.
25. Birnbaum, "Life Patterns."

Overt and Covert Forms of Discrimination Against Academic Women

JANICE POTTKER

INTRODUCTION

Prejudice against women in higher education is a vastly complex and multifaceted problem. It is often difficult to understand the insidious paths discrimination takes. The various methods of overt and covert discrimination are covered here in the hope of drawing attention to the complexity of this issue, because only when the various forms of discrimination are identified can successful strategies be devised to eliminate them.

This study deals, in many of its aspects, with the concept of institutional discrimination. Institutional discrimination is the bias that stems from the normal structure and functioning of the institution itself, as opposed to the bias that is caused by the beliefs, attitudes, and behaviors of the actors within that institution. It is the *practices* of the organization that are analyzed when looking at institutional discrimination, whether or not these practices are manifest (intended) or latent (unintended).

Some of the overt and covert aspects of discrimination against academic women are closely tied to forms of institutional discrimination. For example, university nepotism rules that forbid the employment of faculty wives is used as a device to forbid employment to certain women. This nepotism rule is part of university policy and functions from the normal operations of the university. In fact, its bureaucratic function is to remove possible roles from individual actors: they need not act of their own accord when they deny women employment, because they have an institutional policy as their rationale. It is true that ". . . the individual only has to conform to the operating norms of the organization and the institution will do the discriminating for him."[1]

It is not the intent of this study to trace institutional discrimination in higher education, however, this concept should be kept in mind during any analysis of institutional procedures. This study deals primarily with the overt forms of bias against women, those that are most easily recognized, such as promotions, as well as the covert or less obvious forms of discrimination against women, such as maternity-leave regulations.

OVERT MEANS OF DISCRIMINATION

Not Hiring

The easiest way to discriminate against a faculty woman (or a potential faculty woman) is to not hire her. This is the most basic form of discriminatory action. Nationally, women represent about 20% of the faculty of four-year universities, 10% of the faculty of large, elite universities, and only 1% or 2% of its tenured faculty.[2] Although there are a disproportionately low number of women hired by American universities, certain types of universities have worse male-female ratios than do others.

When the male-female ratio of different universities is compared, it is obvious that the elite schools hire fewer women than the average university. Rossi states: "An inverse relation is indicated between prestige standing of the university and the proportion of women on the full-time faculty at each of the top three ranks in the academic hierarchy."[3]

The exceedingly small number of faculty women at some schools does not even approach the level of tokenism. Columbia University is a good example of this:

Table 1

Sex and Rank at Columbia University, 1970[4]

School	Professor	Associate Professor	Assistant Professor	Instructor
Columbia College	1/133 (0.7)	0/68 (0.0)	7/101 (6.5)	8/76 (9.5)
School of International Affairs	3/87 (3)	0/27 (0.0)	1/17 (6)	0/1 (0.0)
Grad Faculties	7/367 (2.0)		10/74 (12)	7/52 (12)
Barnard	11/38 (22)	12/12 (50)	21/12 (64)	15/16 (48)

(The figures given are the ratio of women to men in that category. The figure in parentheses below this ratio is the percentage of the total number of teachers represented by women.)

Harvard presents an even more discriminatory picture:

Table 2

Sex and Rank at Harvard University
Faculty of Arts and Sciences, 1970[5]

Title	Total	Women	Percent Women
Full professors	444	0	0
Associate professors	39	0	0
Assistant professors	194	9	4.6
Instructors	18	3	16.7
Teaching fellows	1104	226	20.5

Students in Arts and Sciences: Men, 2480; Women, 600.

However, to be fair to Harvard, it recently appointed three women to be professors, which, out of the entire university faculty "more than doubled the number of women professors on its faculty."[6] And Yale "named two women—one of them black—as the first female members of the Yale Corporation since the university's founding 270 years ago."[7]

Table 3 lists the number of faculty members at the University of Chicago by rank and sex. What is not shown in this table is that although Chicago has eleven female full professors, six of these women are in the Social Service school.

Table 3

Sex and Rank at the University of Chicago, 1970[8]

	Prof.	Assoc. Prof.	Assist. Prof.	Instructor
Female	11	16	45	15
Male	475	217	308	102

At Stanford under five percent of the entire faculty is female, with only two percent of the full professors being women.[9] Out of 540 faculty members, Princeton has seventeen women faculty members of the professorial rank.[10]

Brandeis University, possibly the most prestigious of all of the young universities, fares no better.

Table 4

Proportion of Faculty Positions Held by Women at Brandeis University Faculty of Arts and Sciences, 1970[11]

Rank	Percent
Professor	6.0
Associate Professor	6.0
Assistant Professor	13.2
Instructor	21.6
Lecturer	27.7
Total	11.0

It is more difficult to obtain a faculty position at certain high-ranking schools than at lower-ranking schools, and therefore there is more discrimination against women at these high-ranking schools. This is evidenced by the low ratio of black to white faculty members as well as by the low ratio of women to men faculty members.

These schools, because of the high talent they can pull in from the male rank, possibly have the least to lose from excluding women from the faculty. For the fifteen men Harvard appoints on any one day, there are fifty equally as good men and women who were not appointed. Because Harvard, and other Ivy League schools, have the largest field of selection (since almost any candidate would choose to teach in any Ivy League school), and since they employ relatively few people, Harvard can afford, in one sense, not to hire women. This is, of course, unfair to the women who aspire to Harvard positions, but this policy hurts Harvard less than it would Boston University.

One way the Ivy League universities associate well-known women scholars with them is to have the women's colleges that are part of the university (for example, Radcliffe at Harvard) hire women. Internationally known scholar Mirra Komarovsky is a professor at Barnard College, not Columbia College. However, hiring well-known women faculty at least provides role models for these college's female students.

Although men are given preferential treatment in hiring at men's Ivy League schools, women are not preferred at the Seven Sisters schools.

> Only Wellesley, in fact, of the Seven Sisters colleges has more female than male in tenured ranks and in chairmanships. In the rest, male faculty dominate the upper levels and in some cases the lower levels as

well. At Vassar women have dropped from 55.6% of the faculty in 1958–9 to 40.5% in 1969–70. The number of women with full professorships has dropped from 35 to 16. At Vassar it was thought that a coeducational facility provided a healthier atmosphere for women students. The reverse does not apparently apply to Harvard, Princeton, Yale, or Brown. Barnard has two more female than male full-time faculty but the men have 78% of the full professorships and chairmanships.[12]

Although men can seek and find jobs at men's schools, women's schools, and coeducational schools, women can only seek jobs at women's schools and coeducational schools, which limits their job market. Their market is further limited when it is realized that when they do compete for jobs at women's and coeducational schools, men are given preferential treatment.

There exists bias against women's employment at public state schools as well as private schools. Simpson's study found that, "When all variables were equal except sex, the male candidate (for the faculty position) was typically chosen for employment."[13]

The University of Maryland was the first school to be charged with sex discrimination under Executive Order 11246 as amended. Bernice Sandler, the main force behind this action (and who was not rehired after her report was issued but who now heads the Association of American Colleges' Project on the Status and Education of Women), stated that eight percent of the full professors at the University of Maryland were women, and only twelve percent of assistant professors, associate professors, and full professors were women.[14]

Other state schools also show that discrimination is not limited to private colleges. For example, Table 5 shows the number of male and female faculty at California State College at Fullerton.

Table 5

Sex, Rank, Tenure, and Ph.D.s at Fullerton[15]
1959–1969

	Male	Female
Full professor	94	10
Associate prof.	86	29
Assistant prof.	141	27
Instructor	11	8
Lecturer	40	12
Total	372	86
Tenured	120	21
Ph.D.s issued	373	256

And at the University of Illinois, ten women are full professors as compared to 244 men, nine are associate professors as compared to 100 men, twenty-four are assistant professors as compared to 136 men, and forty-eight women have teaching positions below the rank of assistant professor as compared to ninety-one men. The total number of faculty women hired is ninety-one; the total number of faculty men hired is 541.[16]

Nationally, there does not seem to be any increase in the hiring of women faculty members within the last ten years (1963–1973): "except for instructors, women as a percentage of instructional faculty have remained about the same."[17]

Not promoted

The first conclusion reached after looking at the male-female faculty rankings is that few women are hired. The next realization is that women tend to be clustered in the lower ranks of faculty: very few women are tenured professors, and very many women are instructors. As the level of faculty position increases, the percentage of women employed decreases. In 1972–73, roughly forty percent of academic women were instructors, twenty-four percent were assistant professors, sixteen percent were associate professors, and only ten percent were full professors.[18]

In an analysis of fourteen studies of women's promotion within academe, Robinson concluded that, "Every institutional analysis of promotion that examined length of time in rank showed that women progressed through the ranks at a significantly slower rate than men."[19] For example, it took women faculty at the University of Indiana at Bloomington one and a quarter years longer in a specific rank than men to be *recommended* for promotion, and again over one and a half years longer than men before they *achieved* this promotion.[20]

Academic women are cognizant of their low rank: one-third of faculty women report promotion discrimination.[21] The effects of promotion discrimination become stronger at the higher ranks: the American Association of University Women found that the "percentage of women decreases as rank increases," and that "women infrequently hold departmental chairmanships."[22]

Parrish found that "*there are almost no women of full professorial rank in twenty-eight major disciplines in twenty leading U.S. universities.*" (Emphasis his.) He concludes that "the failure of women to advance up the academic ladder appears rather striking in view of their substantial contributions at lower rank levels. For example, in mathematics seventeen percent of all instructors but less than one percent of professors are women. Similarly, in bacteriology twenty-one percent of instructors but only two percent of professors are women."[23]

Alice Rossi reports that "a full forty-two percent of the men with a doctoral degree are full professors, compared with only sixteen percent of the women with a doctoral degree."[24] Rossi describes the effect this must have on the women graduate students. "To be one of sixty-four women doctoral students in a department that has only three women on nontenure, junior appointments can scarcely be an encouragement to the younger women students. It is more likely to communicate the view that graduate sociology departments are places women can 'buy' from (as students) but not 'work' in (as faculty.)"[25]

There are always reasons given for the low number of faculty women in high positions. George Frakel, Dean of Graduate Faculties at Columbia University, stated that women at Columbia do not hold tenured university appointments because this "requires a tremendous amount of dedication and time that interferes with our normal idea of a women's role in the family."[26] And at Columbia, "well over fifty percent of the men who earned their Ph.D.s in 1963 and 1964 have been given tenure," although "none of the women in that group has been promoted to that rank."[27]

There is also evidence that women who do achieve a certain rank must be more qualified than the average man in that rank. An assistant at Columbia University's School of Architecture stated that a woman's folder could not be submitted to the dean unless it was "absolutely excellent."[28] "Most women faculty members are not promoted unless they are 'obviously superior' to competing males."[29]

It is recognized that as the reputation of the school increases, the percent of women hired decreases. Two-year institutions employ approximately thirty-three percent women, while other four-year schools have over twenty-three percent women on their faculty, with universities hiring only sixteen percent women.[30] Women and men are also hired at different ranks: for example, of all faculty hired at Stanford University, under ten percent of the women were hired at the professor or associate professor level, while over fifty percent of faculty men were hired at this rank.[31]

But it is sometimes impossible for any woman, no matter how high her qualifications, to be hired at certain schools. A Harvard department head stated that he has "men on the staff who will vote against a woman for a job just because she is a woman. They just don't want women around."[32]

The University of Chicago committee was given four explanations, or "concealed assumptions," explaining why women are in lower faculty positions. Some of the report's answers to these assumptions were conservative, and a group of young radical sociology graduate students dissented from the answers.[33]

The first assumption was that "women are more often lecturers or research associates because they do not have the qualifications to fill regular faculty positions," a statement that the committee countered with a lack of evidence.[34] The second assumption was that "many women research associates and lecturers are married and hence represent a 'captive labor force' of persons who can not bargain effectively for other positions."[35] However, the percentage of married faculty women is the same in all ranks, therefore disproving this statement. (Although not pointed out by the committee, there is evidence that faculty men discriminate more against married women than single women.)

The third assumption is that "women are research associates and lecturers because these positions are the best that a male-dominated society will allow them."[36] The committee women stated that they would be "hard put to make a case for overt discriminatory attitudes among male faculty," even after one *chairman* stated that "women's physiological nature was a restraint on their potential," and while another *chairman* stated that women can not succeed in top positions "because they become too emotionally involved and are thus unable to make difficult decisions."[37]

"Women otherwise qualified for regular faculty positions are lecturers and research associates because they find these positions more convenient than positions on the academic ladder," was the fourth assumption.[38] The committee did find women who were happy staying in the lower ranks, but instead of addressing this statement more directly (how many women wanted to climb the ladder as compared to how many women who did not want to), the committee women divided into an interesting and insightful discussion. It is suggested that this discussion was typical of the different factions among faculty women.

The caucus of graduate sociology women looked at the women who were happy in terminal positions, and stated that these women had the "false consciousness of an oppressed class of women who have accepted the ideology of dominant males and who give socially acceptable responses."[39] The older faculty women (most of whom were not sociologists) stated that these terminal-position women may be stating the "*true consciousness* of a woman who has opted to retain responsibiliy for her house and children."[40] (Emphasis mine.)

Alhough not meaning to denigrate those women who apparently opt out of competition, it is obvious that the faculty women quoted do not understand the term *consciousness,* nor do they pay much tribute to the processes of socialization. They also support the status quo of a woman assuming that home duties are paramount in a life.

When discussing the failure to promote women, it also must be realized that the process of not promoting women keeps them from policymaking positions, whether as a tenured faculty member, a department head, or as an administrator. These policymakers are the people who, if only through inaction, keep women from assuming higher positions within the university structure. Promoting women to be policymakers would have a double effect in alleviating discrimination: there would be women in high positions, and these women would hopefully be willing to allow equal competition between men and women for faculty ranks.

Salary Differences

"Women on campus make $150 to $200 million less per year than men in comparable positions."[41] There are several ways of discriminating against women in terms of salary. The most apparent means of discrimination is paying women faculty members less money than male faculty members of the same rank. Kreps states that the NEA 1965–1966 survey showed that "the median academic yearly salary for women in all institutions was about 17% lower than that for men. Larger differences appeared in the larger universities, within which women on the average earned less than 80% of the men's salaries."[42] Forty percent of faculty women thought that they were paid a lower salary than a similarly qualified man.[43]

Women faculty average almost $2,500 a year, or seventeen percent, less than their male counterparts, as shown in Table 5A. This table also confirms Robinson's analysis that ". . . the largest dollar differences occur at the full professor rank."[44]

Table 5A

Rank and Sex by Average Salary, 1973[45]

Rank and Sex	Average Salary	Women's Salary As Percent of Men's Salary
Total		
Men	$14,352	
Women	$11,865	82.7%
Professor		
Men	19,128	
Women	16,950	88.6
Associate Professor		
Men	14,481	
Women	13,704	94.6
Assistant Professor		
Men	12,233	
Women	11,437	93.4
Instructor		
Men	10,964	
Women	10,089	92.0

The pay disparity between men and women's salary at private universities is even greater; women's average salary at private universities is only 76.7 percent of men's salary.[46] The American Council on Education states that in 1969, while only twenty-eight percent of faculty men earned under $10,000 a year, sixty-three percent of faculty women earned less than that amount.[47]

Different universities have different levels of pay for men and women. For example, the University of Kansas pays female instructors, on the average, $7,005, and male instructors $7,840; female assistant professors $8,341, male assistant professors $9,423; female associate professors $10,029, male associate professors $10,664; and female professors $11,282 and male professors $13,053.[48]

Graduate assistants also receive different salaries according to sex. A University of Michigan graduate student and research assistant began a lawsuit against the University of Michigan when she learned that she was being paid $9,100 while a male research associate (whom she claims is less qualified) is being paid $12,500 and that "the amount for her own salary in the projects budget is $13,200, or $4100 more than she receives."[49]

The evidence shows that women faculty members receive lower salaries than male faculty members. This is even more devastating when it is realized that women receive fewer promotions than do men, and that they are therefore receiving less money than they should for being in a lower position than they should occupy. It is believed by many that pay differences between men and women decrease each year, yet Dowding suggests that these salary differences are *increasing* each year.[50] (This increasing difference in faculty salaries is similar to the American labor market as a whole: not only do American women earn less than American men, but they earn less and less each year.)

There are also other reasons why women earn less money that are not as clear as the reasons already mentioned. One is that women tend to work in smaller universities, and these universities pay less money than do larger universities.[51]

Another less discernible reason for academic women's lower salary is their (forced) participation in the women's branch of a university. For example, Barnard pays less than Columbia: Kate Millett was paid only $4,000 a year for teaching at Barnard.

The *Report from the Committee on Discrimination Against Women Faculty, Columbia University,* states under the division "Barnard College and what it indicates":

> The role of Barnard as an equalizer in the otherwise male-dominated Columbia community is worth examining for other clues about the position of women. Although 78% of Barnard's full professors are men, by and large the number of men and women employed in full-time teaching is almost equal.
>
> All these women's colleges lack the endowment of their male equivalents; all of them have fewer facilities; all pay lower salaries to their faculty. The difference between Barnard and Columbia College salaries are well known, varying from an average difference of over $5,500 at the Full Professor level to $1,765 at Assistant Professor level. Not only the absolute but also the percentage differential in compensation between Columbia and Barnard increases with rank. These salary differences do not measure relative excellence, but rather punish those engaged in the education of women. They are a direct reflection of the value society places on women's education and on women's role in society.[52]

Equal pay for equal work is stated as a basic American tenet of fair play: very few would agree that those who make equal contributions should receive unequal rewards. Yet American colleges and universities do not operate under this belief: in fact, pay differences for male and female academicians is so disparate that it would seem that universities are openly defying this tenet. It can only be hoped that since this argument is a dollars and cents issue that hits women, it will be the first of those issues that will be taken up by academic women in demanding equal rights from higher education institutions.

Teaching Responsibilities, Marginal Appointments, and Tenure

Table 6 shows that, nationally, one-fifth more women faculty members than men taught only undergraduate students. Almost twice as many male faculty taught only graduate students as did women faculty. In universities the difference between the proportion of men and women who teach only undergraduates increases, so that almost twice as many women teach undergraduates as do men.

Table 6

Teaching Responsibilities by Sex and Institution, 1969[53]

Teaching Responsibilities	All Institutions		Universities		4-Year Colleges		2-Year Colleges	
	Men	Women	Men	Women	Men	Women	Men	Women
Entirely Undergraduate	48.2%	68.6%	24.3%	48.1%	67.5%	75.5%	96.0%	96.2%
Some Undergraduate, Some Graduate	35.1	19.6	49.6	31.8	25.1	16.6	1.0	.8
Entirely Graduate	12.3	6.8	20.2	13.2	4.8	4.0	.0	.0

This difference in teaching responsibilities highlights an overt form of discrimination against women. Those with any knowledge of academia realize that teaching undergraduates is considered less prestigious than teaching graduate students. Teaching undergraduates is also associated with those faculty who have a low rank and who do little research. It is identified as a "dead-end" job.

Within the national academic community, academics who teach only undergraduates are outside the prestige network. They have no bright student to sponsor through a doctoral program and on to a high-ranking job, which limits their ability to make essential contacts with colleagues in other schools. They are considered less competent by their colleagues because, it is thought, fewer skills and less sophistication are needed to teach undergraduates. They also have a talent supply of very few students whom they know to draw upon when they need assistants for their own professional work.

This can be used as a rationale to keep women from receiving higher ranking and tenure: they are assigned, differentially from men, to low-status teaching jobs. They therefore have a difficult time entering into academic competition that is saturated with male values. It is then inevitable that academic women remain settled at the bottom of the status ladder.

One way to combat this is to give women faculty more graduate classes to teach. A reemphasis in colleges and universities on teaching skills as a major criteria for tenure, rather than on research and publication competence, would also raise the academic woman's status and value within the community.

Another status difference between men and women in academe is shown by marginal appointments. These appointments are often to nonfaculty ranks that permit women to teach or do research, but are not on the promotions ladder since they are not considered part of the regular faculty appointments. There is a ". . . tendency to appoint women to positions variously referred to as *marginal, soft-line, irregular, nonladder, part-time, exceptional,* or *fringe*.[54] Morlock points out that "women are much more likely than men, and married women more likely than single women, to hold such nonladder positions as research associate."[55]

The holders of these positions do not receive the same privileges as do holders of the universities' regular positions: salaries are not comparable, tenure is not granted, fringe benefits are not given, and so on. In fact, since many of these positions are funded through "soft-money" or "slush funds," in time of economic pressure these positions are the first to be cut.

Yet they exist precisely because they cost the university less than would supporting a greater number of people in regular ranks. Rather than hiring several full-time faculty at high expense to teach introductory courses, the universities can turn to a pool of qualified but cheap labor and hire part-timers from this group. It is no coincidence that "the Columbia University report points out that although women are almost invisible in the regular faculty ranks, they constitute the majority of part-time employees."[56]

The differing tenure rates for men and women are shown in Table 7. The proportion of faculty men who receive tenure and the proportion of faculty men who do not receive tenure are roughly equivalent, but twenty percent more women do not have tenure than women who do have tenure. The difference within universities is even more striking: about eighteen percent more faculty men have tenure than do women, while about eighteen percent more women than men do not have tenure. Also, more university faculty men (9.4%) are tenured than are not, while twenty-seven percent more faculty women are not tenured than who are tenured.

Since tenure is essential for survival within academia, any bias against women that comes out in the different types of requirements for the granting of tenure can be fatal to their careers. Emphasis is placed on research and publication when determining tenure, while it has been shown that

Table 7

Type of Appointment by Sex and Institution, 1969[57]

Type of Appointment	All Institutions Men	All Institutions Women	Universities Men	Universities Women	4-Year Colleges Men	4-Year Colleges Women	2-Year Colleges Men	2-Year Colleges Women
Regular with Tenure	51.1%	39.4%	54.7%	36.4%	46.6%	40.9%	48.8%	42.4%
Regular without Tenure	48.9	60.6	45.3	63.4	53.4	59.1	51.2	57.6

academic women are more often assigned undergraduate classes, which results in less leverage when tenure is considered. The burden of teaching undergraduate courses also allows women less time for research, which is an important criterion for tenure.

The "beauty" of this system is that it provides an institutionalized method of discrimination against women. Women are assigned lower-status undergraduate classes, and therefore have academic interests and duties that do not automatically lead them into research and publishing. Then tenure is denied them by the university that judges through supposedly objective criteria. The university committees can then say that it is not their fault that women do not meet the mark, ignoring the present pervasive system of institutional sexism.

COVERT MEANS OF DISCRIMINATION

Covert means of discrimination against academic women are more subtle and less visible methods of bias. Most likely there are many administrators in academe who do not realize that certain institutional policies are major impediments to women's careers. Yet as these policy impediments are pointed out, these administrators must respond either by being flexible and changing covertly discriminatory policies, or by responding in a way that as much as condones sex discrimination.

Nepotism

Nepotism is one of the most visible and structured ways a university can discriminate against women. Nepotism is understood, however, usually only by faculty members, and then only if it affects them. The general public, and certainly most college students, have seldom realized the existence of nepotism regulations.

Nepotism rules "prohibit the employment at the same university of two or more persons who are related by blood or marriage."[58] This restricts the hiring of one spouse in a marital pair. There has been little discussion, even in feminist circles, of why husbands do not give up their position in favor of their wives. It is generally assumed that if two faculty members marry, the *wife* loses her job. Since the woman is discriminated against in so many other ways in academia when the man is not, it would seem more fair if the husband would give up part of his advantaged position. But it will suffice to say that women, at this time, are affected by nepotism rules more greatly than are men.

Pierre Van Den Berghe, in *Academic Gamesmanship,* describes nepotism:

> The best thing that the unmarried female student can do is to become the mistress or wife of a professor, but then to drop any pretense of real academic competition with him. In most cases "nepotism" (in effect, antifeminist) rules will prevent her from doing so anyway. Many universities do not hire both husband and wife, at least in the same department. In practice, it means the wife gets no job, or one that is clearly inferior in status to that of her husband. And when he changes jobs, she has to follow him, almost never the other way around.[59]

More seriously, Simon et al. found that nepotism was not so much a barrier to the *entry* to the academic world as it was a barrier to achievement, in terms of advancement, tenure, and salary.[60] Nepotism had the following effect on the academic community; first, since full faculty status or tenure was withheld, this had the effect of making a wife's job "temporary" in nature. Second, married women who were hired were considered as stop-gap faculty members rather than career personnel. Third, when wives were hired, only one member of their family (either themselves or their husbands) was allowed to vote in policy matters. Finally, these wives had retirement and medical insurance plans, sabbatical leaves, and fringe benefits denied them.[61]

In showing salary and rank differences between faculty husbands and wives in universities with nepotism rules, Simon found that eighty percent of these husbands earned more money and had a higher rank than their wives, and sixty percent were hired before their wives were, when they had both received their Ph.D.s in the *same* year.[62]

Nepotism rules affect careers of women in four different ways. The first is shown by:

> women claim they can work at the same university, in some instances, in the same department as their husbands, but under "special" circumstances. These special circumstances involve such things as: temporary employment with no possibility of being considered for tenure; part-time employment; semester by semester hiring on an emergency basis; lower salary than colleagues with comparable rank and experience; no voting privileges; must secure salary from research grants; no professorial rank; change of field or specialty.[63]

Illustrations of this are shown by the two following quotations:

I am the only person to my knowledge with the Ph.D. who wasn't hired as an assistant professor. I also hold one of the lowest salaries in the department. This is my tenth year of teaching and I am publishing. An instructor with a doctorate earns more.

The nepotism rules at the University of . . . was directly responsible for my shifting my focus of interest from experimental child psychology in order to acquire service skills to make me employable at institutions near the University where my husband will work. This set back my career, requiring an additional postdoctoral year as a clinical trainee, beyond the one already completed in experimental child psychology. Then, I had to work one addition year in a low-level staff position usually open to a new clinical Ph.D.[64]

Because women are forbidden under nepotism regulations from teaching at the same college as their husbands, they are forced to obtain teaching jobs at another college in the area. If this is not possible, they must find a job outside of teaching or drop out of the labor market completely. Examples of this are illustrated by the statements:

Our move to . . . was largely determined by the erroneous judgment of my husband's chairman that I could be employed. When this was ruled out by the President, I found myself another job at a college within commuting distance.

My husband has recently been appointed to a professorship in the Department of Zoology at . . . University. Unfortunately, I cannot be appointed to any position in this department because of the nepotism rules. This makes it rather difficult for me to pursue my teaching career since this is the main university in. . . ."[65]

Another effect nepotism has on married women is in limiting the mobility of themselves and their husbands. Certain universities that have nepotism rules are not considered a place for possible appointments for either of them. For example:

We are affected in this sense—nepotism rules elsewhere limit our chances to make a move. My husband has had invitations to apply for positions elsewhere, but when we are told that nepotism rules were enforced, or feelings were strong against hiring wives, we did not pursue these invitations. I received an invitation to apply at. . . ; but there is a nepotism rule that would prevent my husband's consideration.[66]

There are some women who are not affected by nepotism rules because they were lucky enough to have had tenure before their marriage, or they were research associates and received their salaries from grants. For example:

I had tenure at the time of my marriage. I retained my tenure. However, if I had not had tenure at that time, I would have not been eligible for it.[67]

Table 8 gives the rank of full-time academic women in universities by marital status. It is hypothesized that married women's lower academic rank is due, in part, to academic nepotism regulations. This table shows that married women "are more likely to be represented in the lower ranks of instructor and lecturer and less likely to be represented in the associate and full professor ranks than are unmarried women and men; that married women are more likely to be hired as research associates; and that unmarried women are just as likely as men to hold associate and full professorships."[68]

Table 9 shows that married women are also less likely to have tenure than are unmarried women or men: note that there is no difference in the last two categories.

Table 8

Professional Ranks Among Respondents Who Are Employed Full-time At Colleges and Universities[69]

Rank	Women Presently Affected by Anti-nepotism Rules	Women with Husbands in Academia	Women with Husbands *Not* in Academia	Single Women	All Men
Instructor	9.6	12.4	9.3	2.9	3.1
Lecturer	6.4	2.4	2.4	1.3	1.1
Ass't Professor	37.7	48.4	43.9	36.5	35.1
Assoc. Professor	20.4	11.6	21.1	30.9	40.9
Professor	4.2	8.6	8.6	20.0	15.7
Research Associate	18.1	14.7	12.6	7.2	4.0
No answer	3.2	1.9	1.7	1.3	.9

The American Association of University Women (AAUW) reports that "almost 355 of the schools reporting indicate that they have specific policies against nepotism in hiring of faculty. Nepotism policies are most evident on campuses of large schools, least evident at private and women's colleges and small campuses."[70] Table 10 shows that "there appears to have been some liberalizing of nepotism regulations in the public institutions in the past ten years, but little change in the private sector."[71]

Table 9

Percent of Respondents With Tenure Among Those Employed Full-time At Colleges and Universities[72]

Tenure	Women Presently Affected by Anti-nepotism Rules	Women with Husbands in Academia	Women with Husbands Academia *Not* in Academia	Single Women	All Men
Yes	25.0	24.8	34.4	48.4	48.4
No	75.0	75.2	65.5	51.6	51.6

Table 10

Policies on Nepotism Rules[73]

	Have Policy Against (Percentage) Yes	No
Private schools*	27%	73%
Public schools	45	55
Schools under 1,000*	15	85
Schools over 10,000	56	44
Women's Colleges	78	22
Coed schools	36	64
Total (No. R.s 414)	35	65

*Exclusive of women's colleges.

Morlock states that

"departments that are bound by university antinepotism policies (written or unwritten) tend to have lower percentages of women at all ranks in comparison to departments that are not subject to such rules. Departments bound by regulations prohibiting the *supervision* of one relative by another (e.g., a husband who is a chairman recommending for promotion a wife who is a departmental staff member) tend to fall between those departments with and those without antinepotism regulations in respect to proportions of women at each rank. Furthermore, among those departments that are not restricted by university rules, those with antinepotism policies of their own have lower proportions of women full-time faculty at each rank than departments without such regulations."[74]

Horror stories are told about faculty women under the effects of nepotism rules:

> At a state university in the Midwest, the psychology clinic is headed by a man who holds both a Ph.D. and an M.D. degree. His wife, who also holds a Ph.D. degree in psychology, has established a national reputation in her own right. Although she would be happy to teach a course in the medical school in the same university—a course in which the book she wrote is used as a text—university regulations preclude her appointment, much to her regret and to the detriment of students who could benefit from her vast knowledge.[75]

And:

> Consider the case of Margaret Harlow, who was an assistant professor of psychology at the University of Wisconsin when she married another professor in the department in 1948. Faced with a university rule against nepotism, she resigned her post. She spent most of the next 17 years assisting her husband and his colleagues in their research without formal recognition or pay.
>
> In 1965, the university bent its regulations enough to allow Prof. Harlow to be a *lecturer* in another department. But it wasn't until 1970 —22 years after she was forced to resign—that the university finally agreed to make her a full professor. "I could cry when I think of all the years I lost because of that silly rule," she says.[76]

Fascinating aspects of nepotism emerge when looked for. At the University of Maryland, where spouses can be faculty members as long as they are not both at least at the rank of associate professor, if two spouses are both being considered for the rank of associate professor, one administrator stated that the husband "automatically" receives the promotion.[77]

Another aspect of nepotism emerges when it is realized that while nepotism may not be an official university policy, it is touted as such when convenient:

> One recent case at Columbia illustrates both sexual discrimination and covert nepotism rules (many institutions claim not to have them and do not print them in official literature). A brilliant European couple were invited to teach in one department, for they specialize in different areas. He did not have a Ph.D.; she did. He had not published a book; she had. He was hired as a visiting Associate Professor; she, after considerable hassle, as a visiting Assistant Professor. Throughout the negotiations, they were told that the nepotism rule would prevent Columbia's offering her a full-time position in the same department as her husband, although in reply to a questionnaire circulated by the AAUW

a few years ago, Columbia declared that it did not have any nepotism rules. Clearly Columbia thinks that it should not have any nepotism rules.[78]

One response to nepotism rules is for women not to marry, as might be the trend today. However, as a result of recent complaints about nepotism regulations by women, certain universities, for example, the universities of Stanford,[79] Arizona, Michigan, and Wisconsin,[80] have abolished these rules.

The University of Chicago currently does not proscribe nepotism, "but warns against it"; however, few people in the university system knew of this change. Despite the fact that the committee women of the University of Chicago report on women were "gratified" by this warning, there are many other women who would resent this warning, which sounds suspiciously like changing the rule but keeping the practice.[81]

The University of Chicago, the University of Maryland, and the Columbia University examples previously mentioned have shown how devious and tricky cases regarding nepotism can be. It seems apparent that this is an area where the universities should be watched with vigilance.

We have seen how often, and in what forms, married women are affected by nepotism rules. The effect that this could have on families might be enormous. Some consequences might be in choosing one area or one university in preference to another, so that both husband and wife might find suitable employment. More serious consequences for the family might be in bitterness and acrimony between husband and wife: one might feel that the other had negatively affected that person's career. Certainly one example of this might be the case of the late Margaret Harlow.

What is especially interesting about these rules is how they punish either academic women who marry, or else wives who are academics. Obviously the roles of college teacher and wife are incompatible in the universities' eyes, although of course the roles of college teacher and husband are not. The university also punishes the egalitarian husband who considers his wife's job possibilities as well as his own. But most of all, it would seem that the university would have the most to lose: the university limits its own talent pool by nepotism rules. Perhaps the only way the universities will change their rules is by realizing, since there are more egalitarian marriages today than ever before, that they are losing talented men as well as women because of their nepotism regulations.

Visibility

It is recognized that universities are prejudiced against hiring people of certain races, religions, ethnic-group background, and sex. There is an additional disadvantage women have in this system, which is that certain people who want to hide their background can change their name or even pass for another race, but women's visibility factor is very high. A person can change his or her name to disguise his or her ethnic-group status, as many academics have done, but a woman cannot easily similarly disguise her sex. Many women do use initials instead of their first name when submitting papers for publication, which shows the need women feel to become less visible as a member of their particular sex.

Unwritten quotas

There are unwritten and undisclosed quotas on the number of women faculty in certain departments. "The existence of such quotas is difficult to prove, but it is easy to infer from employment figures."[82] However, *prima facie* evidence is now being accepted in courts and by the federal government in discrimination cases.

Husband factor

Another unwritten policy that discriminates against women is another problem that only *married* women face. According to the University of Chicago report, there are frequent instances of a woman being not considered as a possibility for an appointment if she lives in a different geographic region, since it is automatically assumed that her husband will not want to move.[83]

Matina Horner, President of Radcliffe College, speaks: "On another occasion, at another, similar (faculty) meeting, the names of one or two women were tossed out for faculty-appointment consideration. Of one of these women, a professor I know well, said, 'Forget it. Her husband won't come here.' I exploded. 'For Heaven's sake,' I said, 'You've got to stop doing that. You've got to stop making those assumptions.' "[84]

Opposition to Inbred-Hiring

Many universities dislike hiring graduates of their own university. This situation is extremely disadvantageous to graduate women who marry faculty members,[85] and to those women who attend the school in which their husbands work. Opposition to inbred-hiring also harms women who matriculate in an area where their husbands work, since it would be difficult for them to move to a different area to find employment in another college.

Academic Women Perceived As Wives and Mothers

It is clear that part of the problem women face with male university administrators and faculty is these men's insistence and inability to view women as anything but wives and mothers. Women's key status is perceived as being that of a wife or mother, sometimes even when women do not hold either status. Women's roles as wife and mother are tantamount in some men's minds to any other role women might play.

The husband factor, as mentioned earlier, describes how women are not considered for faculty positions due to the assumption of the knowledge that their husbands will not want to move. This is a view of women that shows how many academic men (and some academic women) view an academic woman's status of wife as being comprised of certain restrictive roles that conflict with the roles of any other status she might hold.

Shaffer and Shaffer report on restrictive rules regarding married women's employment in colleges. "Other support for restrictive rules can undoubtably be traced to traditional views and attitudes regarding differences between the sexes. In any case, tradition has it, woman is biologically destined and emotionally constituted primarily to bear and raise children."[86]

Bernice Sandler has stated: "Essentially our universities punish women for being women. They punish women not only for having children, but even for having the potential to bear children."[87]

It is obvious that university men see university women as wives and mothers, even when they are not already married. It is interesting to note that women who are mothers are told that they should devote themselves fully to the role of mother, and that married women without children are often told that they are not hired because they will become pregnant (obviously here pregnancy and motherhood are reason for not employing women), and single women are told that if hired, they will soon get married and move anyway.

Interestingly, an American Council on Education study has found that only twenty percent of faculty women have interrupted careers for more than a year for nonacademic reasons, while twenty-five percent of men have done this.[88]

The view of women as wives and mothers is so strong that any woman is seen as a potential wife and mother. This would not be as restrictive as it is if women were not punished for being wives and mothers. Mead states that "the academic world is fundamentally hostile, by tradition . . . to those aspects of femininity which involve child bearing."[89]

Perhaps the best example of punishing women for bearing children is the maternity-leave regulations enacted by universities, and the child-care facilities provided.

Maternity Leave and Child Care

"When Ruth Weintraub, now the dean of social sciences of Hunter College, found that she was pregnant, she recalled she was delighted and 'would have liked to cherish it' for awhile. Instead, she had to notify the college president of her pregnancy 'forthwith.' "[90]

Such rules are typical of the regulations affecting faculty members who become pregnant. Since, in almost all instances, maternity leave with pay for even short periods of time is not granted to women in academia, women have to plan (hopefully) to have their babies between semesters or over the summer. If this does not occur, leaves of absence must be taken. These leaves are often harmful to progress on the career ladder, especially since years worked towards tenure often must be repeated if there is a break in employment.

"The single most critical problem for women" as stated in the *Report of the Subcommittee on the Status of Academic Women on the Berkeley Campus*[91] was the lack of child-care facilities for the members of the university community.[92] Graham notes that "for women to have a place where they can leave their children, confident that they will be well cared for, would be a tremendous help."[93]

It seems that colleges and universities are trying very hard to ignore the pressing needs of those faculty members who happen to be mothers. If all academic women are viewed primarily in terms of two statuses, wife and mother, and if they are then punished for enacting these two roles, something seems askew in American male-female relations.

Male-Female Sex Role Strain

Part of the reason for discrimination against women in American universities, and possibly the underlying cause of discrimination against women, is that many men tend to be confused and anxious in their relations with women, which actualizes itself in hostility toward women. This hostility results, in part, in employment discrimination against women.

Simpson found that men who rejected women for employment "typically expressed negative attitudes toward women" on the Open Subordination of Women Attitude Scale.[94]

It would be interesting to see the results of this attitude scale given to a sample of faculty men. A survey of male faculty in medical schools brought forth the following comments:

> In this school we have not been overly impressed with the women that have been admitted to medicine even though academically they are entirely satisfactory. I think they ordinarily have so many emotional problems that we have not been particularly happy with their performance. In this medical school we screen all women applicants as carefully as possible, in order to be as certain as we can concerning their motivation for studying medicine.[95]

And:

> I have enough trouble understanding my wife and daughters without attempting to explain the questions in this paragraph.[96]

Van Den Berghe sums up the general pyschological disposition of faculty men toward women:

> Most professors being males, female students have an obvious advantage, and they should make the most of it because this is the last occasion where being a woman in academia is an advantage. Generally,

> the academic world is strongly antifeminist, not to say misogynous. Male professors love female graduate students who pay them homage, but dislike female colleagues, especially if they are brighter than themselves. Even the female graduate student must be careful to appear bright enough to appreciate the subtleties and witticisms of her professors, but never to show any signs of outshining them. (This applies to all students, but even more to women.)[97]

And he continues:

> If you are a woman, these considerations hold even more, for then you will not only have to demonstrate your humility as a junior but also stay in your place as a member of the inferior sex. It is bad enough that you should aspire to be an academic instead of getting domesticated and pregnant like most of your kind, so you cannot afford to be aggressive, nor even to seem too bright. If you must appear bright, then let it be in support of an even brighter male colleague. Otherwise, just play the role of the sweet female; smile and be vivacious, but never ironical.[98]

Professional socialization

Academic women are excluded from the full effect of certain processes. One of these is professional socialization. White defines this as consisting of "learning the roles, the informal values and attitudes, and the expectations which are an important part of real professional life."[99]

These processes occur during graduate school and the beginning of professional life, and they set women's self-identity and perceptions of themselves as scholars and professionals. Women in the university system are women in a male world. Therefore, these women sometimes feel out of place and self-conscious about being women. Epstein suggests that women worry about how they will be received in this situation, and concludes that the woman's male role-partner is also uncomfortable with her, which results in compensatory behavior on his part (for example, solicitousness and courtliness).[100] This behavior does not help the woman feel more at ease, nor does it denote, on the man's part, an egalitarian attitude toward women coworkers.

Attitudes toward women faculty can be inferred from reported attitudes toward women graduate students. A study using data from the 1969 American Council on Education-Carnegie Commission higher-education survey showed that the faculty attitudes toward women doctoral candidates "contributed significantly to their emotional stress and self-doubts. Interaction with faculty, while related to general satisfaction with graduate school for both men and women doctoral students, revealed a bias in favor of men." One out of three women graduate students reported that they felt stress due to faculty's negative attitudes toward women.[101] Obviously, this is partially the result of there being few women faculty members.

Sponsorship and aid

Sponsorship is vital in terms of self-image, professional recognition, and future jobs. Women can be in a situation where they are not sponsored as strongly as are men. This is due to the male sponsor's image of her as a woman before that of a professional. He also might be threatened by her as a woman, believe that she is less dedicated than a man (and therefore be afraid her lack of dedication reflects on him), and he might even perceive her (or have his wife perceive her) as a sexual threat or temptation.[102]

In data based upon a sample survey by the Carnegie Commission and the American Council on Education, over ten percent more male faculty members than female faculty members reported that during graduate school they had a faculty sponsor for jobs, as shown in Table 11.

The difference by sex increased as did the quality of the institution in which they were enrolled as graduate students. There was less than a one percent difference in sponsorship rates between male and female students in two-year colleges, with more than a five percent difference between male and female sponsorship rates in a four-year college, while there was a *fourteen* percent difference between male and female sponsorship rates in universities.

There were also significantly important differences between the percentages of males and females who were teaching assistants, research assistants, or who were awarded fellowships of over $1,000 during graduate school. The greatest male-female difference, overall, among these characteristics was in being a research assistant.

Table 11

Sponsorship and Aid by Sex and Institution, 1969[103]
(Percent)

During Graduate School	All Institutions		Universities		4-Year College		2-Year College	
	Men	Women	Men	Women	Men	Women	Men	Women
Had faculty sponsor for job	38.1	27.7	46.2	32.2	32.0	26.6	19.1	20.0
Was teaching assistant	55.8	41.3	63.3	49.1	53.3	39.7	29.1	27.3
Was research assistant	38.2	18.9	48.5	24.6	31.0	18.8	12.9	6.3
Was awarded fellowship over $1,000	38.1	27.7	46.2	32.2	32.0	26.6	19.1	20.0

The Club

Women are less apt to feel like a participating member in their own particular reference group, or the group within which they work, whether it is a discipline, department, research center, or university. White states that, indeed, women are not a member of the club,[104] and Epstein points out that only one of fifty-seven presidents of the American Sociological Association have been women.[105] Not being in the club keeps women from participating in the informal communications network that is of vital importance to scholars.

Employment Grapevine

Purposely or not, women do not hear about job openings. This may be because they are denied access to the club, where such things are discussed, or because their sponsor has not told them of it, or because they were purposely not told of it because the position was not open to them as women. Another reason women are excluded from the employment grapevine is because there is often a pervasive male undertone to it.

> The cliché opening, "Do you know a good man for the job," results in continuous but largely unconscious discrimination against women. Most of the men who use this phrase would deny vigorously that they are discriminating and would not also consider a "good woman," but the "good man" is an effective subconcious roadblock because the image we all tend to carry in our minds of a scholar is a masculine one.[106]

Women are also not privy to the employment grapevine because they are out of the prestige system. Caplow and McGee note that "women tend to be discriminated against in the academic profession, not because they have low prestige but because they are outside the prestige system entirely and for this reason are of no use to a department in future recruitment."[107]

Informal Communications

Merton points out that the communications system is one of the major mediums for the exchange of knowledge.[108] Menzel's list of the functions of scientific communication includes the areas of adding to knowledge, understanding new trends and areas in the field, verifying reliability of known information, and obtaining critical response to one's own work.[109]

Menzel states that although informal communication appears to be an unplanned mechanism, taken in the aggregate it constitutes a regular mechanism,[110] and is of great importance. When women are excluded from informal communications, as they are in their restrained relationships with male colleagues, they (and their colleagues) suffer from the genuine absence of exchange of knowledge.

Career Concepts

Some academic women have different concepts of career lines than do academic men. An example of this would be willingness to work part-time. But women in universities are being forced to fit into male lines: they can best combat discrimination against them due to their sex by acting like men. The less said in the university setting by academic women about their problems in maintaining a university career and, for example, raising children, the better. Academic women go to great lengths, out of necessity, to deny certain aspects of their femininity. They must deny that raising small children (in a community that provides them with few or no facilities for child care) presents problems when one is pursuing full-time professional work.

The most prevalent question being asked today is "how can women fit into the male structure of the university?" This is partially due to the fact that many of the women who are currently publishing on women's problems in academia seem to be older women who are more eager to follow a male model.

Certainly the first and possibly the easiest way for women to obtain university psoitions is to adapt to the male model. But perhaps with a greater number of women employed in higher education, women can shape the university so that it is more adaptable to their needs. There is certainly a place for futuristic speculation on what the university, with women well-represented within it, might be. This thinking will probably have to come from the younger members of society, since their needs are currently the greatest.

INDICATIONS FOR THE FUTURE

The "Carnegie Commission on Higher Education expects it will take until the year 2,000 'under reasonable assumptions' (which is to say where there is *no* discrimination) before women will be proportionately represented in academic life."[111] This means, of course, that women will not be proportionately represented until past the year 2,000, since it is an unreasonable assumption that the present discrimination against women will immediately disappear.

At this point, women constitute a disproportionately small number, under one-third, of graduate students. The Carnegie Commission's *Opportunities for Women in Higher Education* notes that more women must be recruited as graduate students.[112] Another problem in increasing the number of women faculty members is that there will be a relatively lower proportion of academics hired in the 1980s. The declining college enrollment and the increases in the number of persons receiving doctorates will increase the difficulty of women obtaining academic positions. However, these problems over which institutions have little control should not be allowed to overshadow current policies (such as hiring and promotion) that higher education can control.

Although there are realistic future problems to be dealt with regarding why there are so few women academics, these problems have received attention out of proportion to the more pressing critical areas of discrimination against women today. It is easy for speculative theories to be spun about issues regarding women in the year 2,000, especially when this happens at the expense of hardhitting solutions to the ongoing bias against professional women in 1975. When it is realized that one of the country's most eminent schools of education (Teachers College, Columbia University) will not be able "even to replace those women now on the faculty"[113] due to previous discriminatory hiring practices, the supposed need for attention spent on solving anything other than immediate problems rings false.

There are also too few toughminded analyses and answers as to how the male-oriented and inflexible structure of today's universities can be amended. If futuristic thinking may include solutions to such far-out questions as how women's needs can change the university structure, then attention should be spent on these problems that need immediate attention. Academic women must also stop feeling grateful to institutions of higher education when they allow women to adapt to their structure. Academic women have the right to demand that the universities adapt to their needs.

CONCLUSIONS

Women service the universities. They enter its ranks as paying undergraduate and graduate students, receive an education, and then are either denied jobs with alma mater or if they are hired, are paid less and promoted less often. The problem lies in that universities view women primarily as wives and mothers. But if all women did as the universities seem to want them to do, that is, not become part of the professional labor force, and therefore also drastically cut the college enrollment figures, the universities would flounder.

What is also interesting about this scheme is that the universities are supposedly so concerned about the husbands and children of academic women, yet they do everything possible to hinder their well-being. Universities resist setting up day-care facilities, they resist restructuring work loads so that both mothers and fathers can raise children, and they resist allowing wives and husbands to plan careers together, uninterrupted by factors such as nepotism regulations.

It is obvious that women who are married or have children are being penalized by the university. In doing so, the university harms itself, by limiting its talent supply. But certainly this discrimination against married women performs a function, latent though it might be, and it is in understanding this function that we can understand the true basis of discrimination against women, and its consequences.

Women are not really being penalized by the university for being, or having the potential to be, wives and mothers. The fact that women have children comes after the fact of their discrimination by universities. We know that women are in fact *hired* by the university; they are just not promoted and paid equal salaries. What the university is doing is using the somewhat socially acceptable explanation that the roles of wife and mother supersede any other role women might play. The university uses this explanation in order to obtain what the universities want: cheap, yet talented, labor.

Women have always been in the position of being paid less than their talents deserve. This exploitive situation exists in the university, and is supported through the men (and sometimes women) of it who are either adherents of the status quo, or who want to protect their own status position and can do this through a limited contest for status positions.

It is therefore in the best interest of those who benefit in the present system (usually men) to resist voluntary changes in the current discriminatory treatment of women academics. Too much is personally at stake for most people in the universities to end discrimination against women. It will not end voluntarily; it must be required.

NOTES

1. Harold Baron, "The Web of Urban Racism," in *Institutional Racism in America,* eds. Louis L. Knowles and Kenneth Prewitt (Englewood Cliffs, N. J.: Prentice-Hall, Inc., 1969).
2. Nancy E. Dowding, letter to George P. Shultz, in *Discrimination Against Women,* Hearings Before the Special Subcommittee on Education and Labor, House of Representatives, 91st Congress, 2nd Session, June–July 1970, p. 313.
3. Alice S. Rossi, "Status of Women in Graduate Departments of Sociology, 1968–1969," *The American Sociologist* 5 (February 1970): 6.
4. Rachel DuPlessis, et al., *Report from the Committee on Discrimination Against Women Faculty, Columbia University* (New York: Columbia Women's Liberation, 1970).
5. The Women's Faculty Group, *Preliminary Report on the Status of Women at Harvard* (Cambridge, Mass.: Harvard University Women's Faculty Group, 1970).
6. "Women's Lib Victories," *Phi Delta Kappan* 52 (September 1971): 71.
7. Ibid.
8. Committee on University Women, *Women in the University of Chicago* (Chicago: University of Chicago Committee on University Women, 1970).
9. Alberta E. Siegel, "Education of Women at Stanford University," in *The Study of Education at Stanford,* vol. 12 (March 1969).
10. Nancy Hicks, "Women on College Faculties Are Pressing for Equal Pay and Better Positions in Academic Hierarchy," *New York Times,* 21 November 1971, p. 41.
11. Pauli Murray, statement, in *Discrimination Against Women,* Hearings, p. 338.
12. Ann Sutherland Harris, statement, in *Discrimination Against Women,* Hearings, R. 252.

13. Lawrence Simpson, "A Myth Is Better than a Miss: Men Get the Edge in Academic Employment," *College and University Business* 48 (February 1970) : 72–73.
14. Bernice Sandler, "Sex Discrimination at the University of Maryland," in *Discrimination Against Women,* Hearings, pp. 1,024–29.
15. National Organization for Women North Orange County Chapter, "Report on Women at the California State College at Fullerton," in *Discrimination Against Women,* Hearings, pp. 203–209.
16. Women's Research Group, "Women at Wisconsin," in *Discrimination Against Women,* Hearings, pp. 190–200.
17. National Center for Educational Statistics, Office of Education, U. S. Department of Health, Education, and Welfare, *Bulletin,* March 1973, no. 14, p. 1.
18. Ibid., p. 2.
19. Lora H. Robinson, "Institutional Variation in the Status of Academic Women," in *Academic Women On The Move,* eds. Alice S. Rossi and Ann Calderwood (New York: Russell Sage Foundation, 1973), p. 208.
20. Ibid., p. 215.
21. Alan E. Bayer and Helen S. Astin, "Sex Differences in Academic Rank and Salary Among Science Doctorates in Teaching," in *Discrimination Against Women,* Hearings, p. 1,031.
22. Ruth Oltman, *Campus 1970: Where Do Women Stand?* (Washington, D. C.: American Association of University Women, 1970), p. 17. See Appendix for the complete results of this study.
23. John B. Parrish, "Women in Top-level Teaching and Research," *Journal of the American Association of University Women* 55 (January 1963) : 99–103, 106–107.
24. Rossi, "Status of Women," p. 7.
25. Ibid., p. 5.
26. Minda Bikman, "Where Do All The Women Ph.Ds Go?" *The Village Voice,* 21 May 1970, p. 42.
27. Harris, statement, in *Discrimination,* p. 253.
28. Bikman, "Where Do All The Women," p. 42.
29. Hicks, "Women on College Faculties," p. 41.
30. National Center for Educational Statistics, *Bulletin,* p. 2.
31. Robinson, "Institutional Variation," p. 208.
32. Susan B. Miller, "Female Academicians Claim Careers Curbed By Male Chauvinists, *Wall Street Journal,* 30 June 1971, p. 1.
33. Committee on University Women, *Women in the University of Chicago,* p. 26.
34. Ibid., p. 25.
35. Ibid.
36. Ibid., p. 26.
37. Ibid.
38. Ibid.
39. Ibid.
40. Ibid.
41. "Making Haste Slowly: The Outlook for Women in Higher Education," *Carnegie Quarterly* 21 (Fall 1973) : 50.
42. Juanita Kreps, *Sex in the Marketplace: American Women at Work* (Baltimore: Johns Hopkins University Press, 1971), p. 52.
43. Bayer and Astin, "Sex Differences," p. 1,031.
44. Robinson, "Institutional Variations," p. 221.

45. National Center for Educational Statistics, Office of Education, U.S. Department of Health, Education, and Welfare, *Preliminary Data* (February 1973), p. 4.
46. Ibid., p. 7.
47. Miller, "Female Academicians," p. 1.
48. Committee on the Status of Women, "Salary Study at Kansas State Teachers College," in *Discrimination Against Women,* Hearings, pp. 1,226–41.
49. "Sex Discrimination on Campus: Michigan Wrestles With Equal Pay," *Science* 173 (16 July 1971): 214.
50. Dowding, letter, in *Discrimination,* Hearings, p. 313.
51. Kreps, *Sex in the Marketplace,* p. 53.
52. DuPlessis, *Report.*
53. National Center for Educational Statistics, *Digest of Educational Statistics, 1972* (Washington, D.C.: U.S. Government Printing Office, 1973), p. 91.
54. Robinson, "Institutional Variation," p. 212.
55. Laura Morlock, "Discipline Variation in the Status of Academic Women," in *Academic Women on the Move,* eds. Alice S. Rossi and Ann Calderwood (New York: Russell Sage Foundation, 1973), p. 272.
56. Robinson, "Institutional Variation," p. 212.
57. National Center for Educational Statistics, *Digest, 1972,* p. 90.
58. Leo Kanowitz, "The Professor and His Wife," *McCall's* (August 1971), p. 42. *See also,* Leo Kanowitz, *Women and the Law* (Albuquerque, New Mexico: University of New Mexico, 1969).
59. Pierre Van Den Berghe, *Academic Gamesmanship* (New York: Abelard Press, 1970), p. 31.
60. Rita Simon, Shirley Clark, and Larry Tifft, "Of Nepotism, Marriage, and the Pursuit of An Academic Career," *Sociology of Education* 39 (Fall 1966): 344.
61. Ibid., p. 345.
62. Ibid., p. 347.
63. Ibid.
64. Ibid., pp. 347–48.
65. Ibid., p. 348.
66. Ibid., p. 349.
67. Ibid.
68. Ibid., p. 353.
69. Ibid., p. 352.
70. Oltman, *Campus 1970,* p. 21.
71. Ibid.
72. Simon, Clark, and Tifft, "Of Nepotism . . . ," p. 353.
73. Oltman, *Campus 1970,* p. 21.
74. Morlock, "Discipline Variation," p. 265.
75. Harry G. Shaffer and Juliet P. Shaffer, "Job Discrimination Against Faculty Wives," *Journal of Higher Education* 26 (January 1966): 10.
76. Miller, "Female Academicians," p. 25.
77. Sandra Fleishman, "University May Drop Antinepotism Policy," *Diamondback* 65 (18 February 1971): 3.
78. Harris, statement, *Discrimination,* Hearings, pp. 254–55.
79. Hicks, "Women on College," p. 42.
80. Miller, "Female Academicians," p. 25.
81. Committee on University Women, *Women in the University of Chicago,* p. 7.

82. National Organization for Women, "Women at California State College at Fullerton," pp. 203–209.
83. Committee on University Women, *Women in the University of Chicago,* pp. 17–18.
84. Vivian Gornick, "Why Radcliffe Women Are Afraid of Success," *New York Times,* 14 January 1973, p. 61.
85. National Organization for Women, "Women at California State College at Fullerton," pp. 203–209.
86. Shaffer and Shaffer, "Job Discrimination," p. 13.
87. Bernice Sandler, statement, *Discrimination,* Hearings, p. 325.
88. American Council on Education, *American Universities and Colleges* (Washington, D.C.: American Council on Education, 1973).
89. Kreps, *Sex in the Marketplace,* p. 51.
90. "City University Accused of Bias Against Women at Hearing," *New York Times,* 1 March 1972, p. 45.
91. Subcommittee on the Status of Academic Women on the Berkeley Campus, "Report," in *Discrimination Against Women,* Hearings.
92. Esther Manning Westervelt, *Barriers to Women's Participation in Postsecondary Education* (Washington, D.C.: U.S. Office of Education, 1973), p. 66.
93. Patricia Graham, "Women in Academe," *Science* 169 (25 September 1970): 1,289.
94. Simpson, "A Myth," pp. 72–73.
95. Harold I. Kaplan, "Studying Attitudes of the Medical Profession Toward Women Physicians," in *Discrimination Against Women,* Hearings, p. 559.
96. Ibid., p. 560.
97. Van Den Berghe, *Academic Gamesmanship,* pp. 30–31.
98. Ibid., pp. 68–69.
99. Martha S. White, "Psychological and Social Barriers to Women in Science," *Science* 170 (23 October 1970): 413.
100. Cynthia Fuchs Epstein, "Encountering the Male Establishment," *American Journal of Sociology* 75 (May 1970): 980.
101. Engin Ihel Holmstrom and Robert W. Holmstrom, "The Plight of the Woman Doctoral Student," *American Educational Research Journal* 11 (Winter 1974): 1.
102. See Epstein, "Encountering," pp. 969–71; White, "Psychological," p. 414.
103. National Center for Educational Statistics, *Digest, 1972,* p. 90.
104. White, "Psychological," pp. 414–15.
105. Epstein, "Encountering," p. 976.
106. Harris, statement, in *Discrimination Against Women,* Hearings, p. 6.
107. Theodore Caplow and Reece J. McGee, *The Academic Marketplace* (New York: Basic Books, 1958).
108. N. Kaplan and N. Storer, "Scientific Communication," *International Encyclopedia of the Social Sciences,* 1968, p. 14.
109. Ibid.
110. Herbert Menzel, "Planned and Unplanned Scientific Communication," in *The Sociology of Science,* eds. Bernard Barber and Walter Hirsch (New York: Harcourt, Brace, and World, 1962), p. 439.
111. "Making Haste," *Carnegie Quarterly,* p. 4.
112. Carnegie Commission on Higher Education, *Opportunities for Women in Higher Education* (New York: McGraw-Hill, 1973).
113. "Women Professors at Teachers College," Office of Institutional Studies, Teachers College, Columbia University, p. 1.

Characteristics and Attitudes of Women Trustees*

RODNEY T. HARNETT

A summary of some of the more important biographical characteristics of female trustees is presented in Table 1, where the characteristics of trustees of women's colleges are reported separately and data for male trustees are also provided. From these data two general points can be made. First, there were important differences between women who served on boards of women's colleges and those who were trustees of other institutions. Second, both of these groups—or, in other words, women trustees generally—differed in numerous significant ways from their male counterparts.

In terms of the male-female comparison, women trustees less often had advanced degrees, more often held positions in "helping" occupations (for example, community volunteer work, education) than in business, and were more likely than the men to be Democrats and liberal. The education and occupation differences were not surprising, of course, and probably are reflections of certain kinds of biases operating in these other areas.[1] But the ideological difference is one that has not been apparent and is worth exploring in more detail. In what ways, for example, might this ideological difference between male and female trustees be reflected in their attitudes and behaviors as trustees? The data in Table 2 offer a clue.

When compared to men, the women trustees—whom we've already described as being more liberal—were more in favor of free faculty expression of opinion and more opposed to administrative control of the student newspaper and loyalty oaths for faculty members. They were more likely to agree that the institution ought to be actively engaged in solving

* Rodney T. Harnett, "Characteristics and Attitudes of Women Trustees." © Copyright 1970, Educational Testing Service, from Rodney T. Harnett, *The New College Trustee: Some Predictions for the 1970s* (Princeton, N. J.: Educational Testing Service, 1970). Reprinted with the permission of Educational Testing Service and Rodney T. Harnett.

social problems and less enamored with organized fraternities and sororities as a positive influence for undergraduates. Curiously, they differed very little from men in their attitudes about who should be served by higher education, but in this case both groups so strongly favored broad access to higher education that differences between the two groups are minimal.

Table 1

Distribution of Male and Female Trustees of Four-year Colleges and Universities by Selected Biographical Characteristics (in percentages)

	Female Trustees		Male Trustees
	Women's Institutions	Other Institutions	
	(N=230)	(N=289)	(N=3943)
Age			
Under 40	3.9	2.4	4.8
40–49	22.2	16.3	21.0
50–59	37.8	33.6	37.0
60–over	35.7	47.4	36.7
Level of Education			
No Bach. degree	7.4	17.6	9.7
Bach. and/or Master's	67.0	66.1	47.4
Prof. or Ph.D.	22.6	14.6	39.4
Occupation			
Business related	1.2	6.7	42.5
Education (all levels)	36.5	18.0	11.3
Community volunteer	26.1	30.0	0.2
Foundation executive	8.7	5.5	3.3
Other	14.3	20.8	5.0
Alumnus(a) of Institution			
No	28.3	51.6	50.8
Yes, B.A., B.S.	65.2	34.9	38.7
Yes, other degree	3.9	11.8	9.3
Political Party			
Republican	31.3	52.6	61.3
Democrat	56.5	37.4	31.1
Other	5.2	5.5	4.5
Political Ideology			
Conservative	6.5	12.1	21.7
Moderate	67.0	57.8	61.3
Liberal	22.2	25.3	14.8

Table 2

Educational Attitudes of Male and Female Trustees at Colleges and Universities
(in percentages) *

Educational Attitudes (Statements in table abridged and modified.)	Female Trustees				Male Trustees	
	Women's Institutions		Other Institutions			
	(N=230)		N=289)		(N=3943)	
	Agree**	Disagree	Agree	Disagree	Agree	Disagree
Academic freedom:						
Faculty members have right to free expression of opinions	83	10	78	16	66	29
Administration should control contents of student newspaper	16	77	21	69	42	50
Reasonable to require loyalty oath from faculty members	35	59	43	47	54	37
Who should be served by higher education:						
Attendance is a privilege, not a right	93	5	91	4	93	4
Academic aptitude should be the most important admissions criteria	76	19	69	24	74	21
Should be opportunities for higher education for anyone who wants it	91	6	89	6	84	12
Colleges should admit disadvantaged not meeting requirements	62	26	68	18	66	23
Others:						
Institution should attempt to solve social problems	65	23	70	17	61	25
Students punished by local authorities for off-campus matters should also be disciplined by the college	33	52	43	45	50	38
A coeducational institution provides a better educational setting	31	54	69	19	67	20
Fraternities/sororities provide positive influence	27	66	36	43	47	34

*Excluding junior colleges.

**Percentage "Agree" is a combination of those responding "Strongly Agree" and "Agree." Percentage "Disagree" is a combination of those responding "Strongly Disagree" and "Disagree." Percentages do not add to 100 because of those responding "unable to say."

Differences between the two groups of women trustees suggest that those on boards of women's colleges tended to be somewhat more disposed toward academic freedom, not surprisingly more optimistic about the advantages of single-sex colleges, and less enthused about the value of fraternities and sororities.[2]

In any event, it is clear that the educational attitudes of female trustees differed substantially from the men's attitudes in many important areas. Whether such differences are best explained in terms of their occupations (they were far more often involved in "helping" occupations), a "feminine outlook," or whatever, is relatively unimportant. What is important is that their appointment to trusteeships will probably contribute a more liberal viewpoint to most governing boards.

NOTES

1. For a view of the status of women in higher education generally, see a special report, "Women in Higher Education: Challenging the Status Quo," in *The Chronicle of Higher Education,* 9 February 1970.
2. The differences between the female groups must be interpreted with great care, since characteristics other than sex makup of the student body might be the major source of the difference. Women's colleges, for example, are nearly always private. Thus, the differences between these groups in terms of academic freedom, for example, may simply be a reflection of their type of control.

State and Local Studies of Sex Bias in Public Education

As the movement for equal rights for women has grown in recent years, the operation of state and local education systems has fallen under close scrutiny by individuals concerned about the existence of sex discrimination in the schools. As a result of this examination, studies aimed at identifying sex bias in local school-district policies and practices have been undertaken in a large number of communities, usually by ad hoc groups of parents or by a community-based women's organization.

The Dayton Public Schools studies, "The Time is Now" and "Choices" are exceptions to most previous studies in that they were undertaken at the request of the superintendent of schools and were conducted by the school district staff. As a result, the Dayton studies have a larger scope and more accurate data than studies made of other school districts. The Dayton studies did not suffer from problems of inaccessibility of school district information or lack of cooperation from staff, due to the official sanction of the study. Inaccessibility to data and lack of cooperation were frequently the problems that plagued others who were conducting studies without the approval of their school system.

The Dayton studies are also impressive because they are far more objective in their style of presentation than is often the case with studies of sexism in local school systems. In addition, the Dayton studies use the findings as a means of supporting the changes that are being recommended. As such, the emphasis of the studies is on bringing about positive changes. While the studies of the Dayton Public Schools should not be viewed as the definitive case study in either its methodology or scope, it does offer an example of how examinations of local school systems can be conducted.

In contrast to the local level, where studies of sex discrimination in education are quite numerous, the study of the Massachusetts education system is probably the only such state-wide treatment undertaken to date. As was the case in Dayton, the Massachusetts report was officially undertaken, this time at the request of the Governor. Because it had formal sanction, the study carried the legitimacy that otherwise would have been lacking. The Massachusetts report, like the Dayton reports, is objective and uses the information derived from the data collected to support the changes being recommended. Again, the Massachusetts study is not presented as a definitive model, but rather as an excellent illustration of how a study of an entire state's education system can be conducted.

The Time Is Now*
Report A
The Women's Rights Committee

DAYTON PUBLIC SCHOOLS

INTRODUCTION

The Committee on Women's Rights was established at the request of Superintendent Wayne Carle in September 1972. As its goal the committee was to make a study and write a subsequent report addressing the following objectives:

(1) Review and appraisal of current statistics on the employment and assignment of women
(2) A subjective assessment of the status of women in Dayton Public Schools
(3) Recommendation of an Affirmative Action Program for the employment, assignment, and promotion of women
(4) Assessment of the curricular and extracurricular activities of the schools in the light of women's rights.

The superintendent first appointed three women who were knowledgeable and sensitive to the issue. That nucleus then made recommendations to him on additional members. The ten who made up the group were represen-

---

* Reprinted with the permission of Joyce S. Kaser, Dayton Public Schools, Dayton, Ohio.

tative of the district's professional and nonprofessional staffs, teachers, administrators, and black/white, male/female employees. (Committee members are listed at the end of the report.)

At its initial meeting the group decided to deal with charges one through three during the first half of the school year and with sexism in curricular and extracurricular activities in the second term.

During the study, two related issues came to light: discriminatory items in printed forms used by the schools and in the Board of Education's *Master Agreement* with the Dayton Classroom Teachers Association. Since both are primarily administrative matters, they were examined along with the employment and assignment of women, a subjective assessment of the status of women in the district, and recommendations on an Affirmative Action Program.

What follows is a report on the group's study. Included is an outline of the approach that was used for studying sexism in the curriculum.

REVIEW AND APPRAISAL OF THE CURRENT STATISTICS ON THE EMPLOYMENT AND ASSIGNMENT OF WOMEN[1]

Although women make up 63.1 percent of the total staff in Dayton schools, they are distributed unevenly through various employment categories. For example, 80.5 percent of the elementary teachers are women but only 42.3 percent are at the secondary level. Women make up 97.9 percent of the clerical staff but only 26.1 percent of the administrative staff. All of the nurses are women but only 3.7 percent of the custodial staff are female. (*See* Tables 1, 2, and 3.)

Table 1

Total Staff (Male and Female)

		Male		Female	
		No.	%	No.	%
Administrative Staff		189.5	73.9	67.0	26.1
Regular Teachers		668.0	33.2	1345.0	66.8
Traveling Teachers		46.6	44.3	58.5	55.7
EMR Teachers		20.0	15.5	109.0	84.5
Visiting Teachers		9.0	64.3	5.0	35.7
Librarians		6.0	9.7	56.0	90.3
Counselors		34.0	33.3	68.0	66.7
Food Service		10.0	2.9	333.0	97.1
Custodial		387.0	96.3	15.0	3.7
Security Guards		13.0	86.7	2.0	13.3
Nurses		0.0	0.0	38.0	100.0
Clerical		6.0	2.1	282.0	97.9
TOTAL STAFF	(3767.6)	1389.1	36.9	2378.5	63.1

Table 2

Elementary/Secondary Teachers, Principals/Assistant Principals (Male and Female)

	Male		Female	
	No.	%	No.	%
Elementary and Middle School Teachers	253.0	19.5	1041.0	80.5
Secondary Teachers	415.0	57.7	304.0	42.3
Elementary Principals	40.0	76.9	12.0	23.1
Middle School Principals	5.0	100.0	0.0	0.0
Secondary School Principals	11.0	100.0	0.0	0.0
Elementary-Assistant Principals	12.0	75.0	4.0	25.0
Middle School Assistant Principals	7.0	70.0	3.0	30.0
Secondary School Assistant Principals	18.0	78.3	5.0	21.7

The similarity is striking in comparing local data with national figures (*see* Table 4). Dayton has slightly higher percentages of women as principals, assistant principals, and central office administrators, but no difference exceeds 10 percent.

In analyzing the extraduty assignments, a similar unbalanced situation exists. For example, 86.3 percent of the elementary house or unit leaders are female, while only 43.6 percent of the high-school department heads are women. Only four women hold positions as secondary vocal music, orchestra, or band directors; but all but two cheerleader/drill-team sponsors are female. In varsity sports women constitute only 19.6 percent of the coaching staffs and then may coach only girls' teams with the exception of fencing and gymnastics (*see* Table 5).

There are several causes to which these discrepancies may be attributed, all of them exhibiting some degree of sex bias:

(1) *The presence or lack of women in a particular area.* One could explain the greater number of women elementary house or unit leaders as compared to high-school department heads on the basis that there are more women in elementary schools. That does not go far enough, however. One then must ask why there are fewer females in our secondary schools?

(2) *Sex stereotyping within schools: this job is for males; this one, for females.* Men make up 70.8 percent of the elementary safety patrol advisors; 91.2 percent of the elementary cheerleading advisors are female. This may reflect a subtle stereotyping that safety patrolling is more a man's job, while cheerleading is a woman's.

(3) *Sex stereotyping both within and outside the schools.* Society's sex bias is certainly reflected in 100 percent female nursing staff, while 96.3 percent of the custodial staff is male. Male nurses are looked

upon with suspicion, usually thought to be effeminate. Maids who supposedly perform light work may be women, but custodians who do the heavy work must be male.

(4) *Lack of specific recruiting.* An outgrowth of sex stereotyping is the lack of specific recruiting. We tend to select from what is most readily available instead of actively seeking members of the sex that is in the minority; *e.g.,* librarians or food service workers.

(5) *Overt discrimination.* The athletic department, along with building principals, is working toward a more equal athletic program for girls (even though we know the fallacy of separate but equal). Yet to date they have maintained segregated programs. Thus, a woman wanting a position as athletic director or track coach would probably not be greeted with élan.

Table 3

Administrative Staff (Male and Female)

	Male		Female	
	No.	%	No.	%
Superintendent	1.0	100.0	0.0	0.0
Clerk-Treasurer	1.0	100.0	0.0	0.0
Administrative Assistant	0.0	0.0	0.0	0.0
Assistant Superintendent	3.0	100.0	0.0	0.0
Executive Director	2.0	100.0	0.0	0.0
Director	7.0	100.0	0.0	0.0
Associate Director	5.0	83.3	1.0	16.7
Supervisor and Assistant Supervisor (Certificated)	19.0	63.3	11.0	36.7
Supervisor and Assistant Supervisor (Noncertificated)	18.0	78.3	5.0	21.7
Coordinator	9.0	75.0	3.0	25.0
Program Director and Coordinator (Spec. Asst.)	9.0	56.3	7.0	43.7
Resource Teacher	2.0	66.7	1.0	33.3
Psychologist	10.0	58.8	7.0	41.2
Child Accountant	0.0	0.0	1.0	100.0
Other	6.0	66.7	3.0	33.3
Supervising Principals or Facilitators	2.5	33.3	5.0	66.7
Total Central Office and Service Building	94.5	68.2	44	31.8
Principals	56.0	82.4	12.0	17.6
Assistant Principals	37.0	75.5	12.0	24.5
Total Principals and Assistant Principals	93.0	79.5	24.0	20.5
TOTAL ADMINISTRATIVE STAFF	187.5	73.9	68.0	26.1

Table 4

Comparison of National and Local Statistics (Male and Female)

	National		Local	
	Male %	Female %	Male %	Female %
Total Teaching Staff	32.8	67.2	33.2	66.8
Principals	84.7	15.3	82.4	17.6
Assistant Principals	85.0	15.0	75.5	24.5
Central Office Administrators	74.1	25.9	68.2	31.8
TOTAL PROFESSIONAL STAFF	36.1	63.9	37.2	62.8

Table 5

Extra Duty Assignments (Male and Female)

	Men		Women		
	No.	%	No.	%	Total
School Assignments–Elementary and/or Middle School					
Treasurer	10	20.0	40	80.0	50
Safety Patrol Advisor	34	70.8	14	29.2	48
Audio Visual Chairman	5	31.2	11	68.8	16
Student Council	14	32.6	29	67.4	43
Cheerleader Advisor	3	8.8	31	91.2	34
House/Unit Leader–Elementary	11	13.7	69	86.3	80
House/Unit Leader–Middle School	11	47.8	12	52.2	23
	88	30.0	206	70.0	294
School Assignments–Secondary School					
Band Director	8	88.9	1	11.1	9
Orchestra Director	7	71.4	2	28.6	9
Vocal Music Director	7	71.4	2	28.6	9
Play Director	5	55.5	4	44.5	9
Newspaper Advisor	3	37.5	5	62.5	8
Yearbook Advisor	3	42.9	4	57.1	7
Class Advisor–Seniors	8	72.7	3	27.3	11
Juniors	4	36.4	7	63.6	11
Sophomores	3	33.3	6	66.7	9
Freshmen	6	66.7	3	33.3	9
Cheerleader/Drill-team Sponsor	2	12.5	14	87.5	16
Student Government Advisor	8	88.9	1	11.1	9
Bookroom Supervisor	2	22.2	7	77.8	9
Department Heads	62	56.4	48	43.6	110
	128	54.5	107	45.5	235

Varsity Sports					
1971–72 Football	55	100.0	0	0.0	55
1971–72 Basketball	33	100.0	0	0.0	33
1972–73 Basketball (Girls)	0	0.0	11	100.0	11
1971–72 Cross Country	11	100.0	0	0.0	11
1971–72 Wrestling	22	100.0	0	0.0	22
1971–72 Baseball	11	100.0	0	0.0	11
1971–72 Gymnastics	2	28.6	5	71.4	7
1971–72 Track	22	100.0	0	0.0	22
1971–72 Tennis	10	100.0	0	0.0	10
1971–72 Golf	10	100.0	0	0.0	10
1971–72 Tennis (Girls)	0	0.0	9	100.0	9
1971–72 Fencing	0	0.0	7	100.0	7
1971–72 Volleyball (Girls)	0	0.0	11	100.0	11
	176	80.4	43	19.6	219
Intramurals 1971–72 (By Season)					
December 1971					
Elementary	26	72.2	10	27.8	
Secondary	8	66.7	4	33.3	
March 1972					
Elementary	27	67.5	13	32.5	
Secondary	9	60.0	6	40.0	
June 1972					
Elementary	35	72.9	13	27.1	
Secondary	10	58.8	7	41.2	
	115	68.5	53	31.5	

The low number of women in administration is a complex situation with several factors at work. A close look at the administrative statistics shows that there are very few of the 26 percent in major decision-making positions in central office or in the schools. The majority come in the supportive ranks where they are responsible for carrying out decisions made by their superiors or are themselves responsible for lower-level decision making. This appears to be outright discrimination, and in part is, but factors of self-image and capabilities enter in.

Dr. Thomas Graham, assistant superintendent for staff development, indicated in an interview with the committee chairer that he keeps an active list of both males and females interested in administrative positions. Many women, when requesting that their names be placed on the list, qualify the kind of job they want. Most indicate assistant principal, curriculum facilitator, or a similar position. Interestingly, women are placing limitations on themselves in the administrative strata. Why?

(1) *A woman may have the bulk of family responsibilities thrust upon her.* Since society traditionally gives homemaking and childrearing to the distaff, she may already be working two full-time jobs. Assuming additional duties is virtually impossible.

(2) *She may lack the skills necessary for the higher decision-making positions.* For example, many males on the sheer basis of height and weight, use threats, force, and intimidation in discipline. Women, however, usually must develop more sophisticated techniques to gain the cooperation and rapport of young people. (It is hoped that all would use techniques that are more humane than intimidation, verbal, and physical abuse.) If a woman has not developed these techniques, she then may not want a job with those responsibilities.

In another example, women may not see themselves as having skills for fast, on-the-spot decision making. Having been taught to be emotionally and intellectually dependent much of their lives, women many times have not had opportunities for making major decisions rapidly without consulting others.

(3) *Professional women also lack models that might provide incentive.* Since few women are in decision-making positions, especially in the upper echelons, others do not see themselves in these positions and thus fail to aspire.

A different situation exists for the supportive staff. A school clerical worker who has attained the rank of Secretary 1 with more than five years' experience finds no place to advance unless she moves to Central Office. A Secretary 3 and an executive secretary in the administrative offices are in a similar position. Most frequently these staff members are in a liaison position between the schools and Central Office, carrying responsibilities beyond that of a secretary. In reality, they are functioning more as an administrative aide or supervisor's assistant.

A SUBJECTIVE ASSESSMENT OF THE STATUS OF WOMEN IN THE DISTRICT

As employees of the Dayton Board of Education, women have found and do find themselves subject to less discrimination than women in many areas of business and industry.

Historically, the Board of Education has been somewhat responsive to the needs of women. In 1937 the Board refused to adopt a salary schedule that would have paid men teachers more than women, and in 1941 all restrictions against married women teaching were removed. Also, in recent times, the district has had two female high-school principals, and four of its schools are named for women.

Throughout the years the maternity leave has become more liberal until last year when the Board made the matter essentially the decision of a woman and her physician. (At one time women were required to take a minimum of two years' leave.) Most recently, women on maternity leave were granted paid group life and hospitalization/medical coverage for a period of time up to ninety days prior to the expected date of delivery and extending up to ninety days past the date of delivery.

Although women serve in a variety of professional roles, receive equal pay for equal assignment, and receive most of the same benefits as men, discrimination is still readily evident.

Over the past years the number of women principals has dropped drastically. In 1955, 41.4% were women; 1964, 25.4%; today, 17.6%. As indicated previously in this report, in terms of advancement, women are hemmed in: noncertificated women because there is no place to go; certificated women because they may lack the skills and motivation needed to make that push forward or because certain areas are closed to them.

Further, neither certificated nor noncertificated women (or men) receive assistance and encouragement in terms of ongoing training programs or internships. Those with major family responsibilities find limited aid in flexibility in hours and no day-care centers for children.

Moreover, women who work in male-dominated organizations generally find that they must have a more extensive background, exhibit a higher level of skills, and outperform their male coworkers if they want to be considered at promotion time. Women who "make it" must be "superwomen"—similar to "superblacks" who "make it" in white society.

June Gabler, the only woman school superintendent in Ohio, was once told by a dean of education that she would work twice as hard as any man and that it would be questionable whether or not she would ever get into central-office administration—were that her interest.[2]

That admonition certainly applies to a Dayton staff member who currently is serving as acting head of the curriculum development department, the first woman to serve in an executive capacity on the Superintendent's cabinet. Although the Superintendent has recommended this eminently well-qualified woman to the position of executive director of the department, the Board of Education has refused to make the appointment. Currently, she is in an untenable position by directing department operations while still handling many of the duties of her former position at a salary of $5,000 less than her male predecessor.

Another area of discrimination is professional organizations and social/recreational activities sponsored directly or indirectly by the schools. Men and women have separate coaching associations, separate lounges in some schools, and two different bowling leagues, the Schoolmasters and the Schoolmarms.

In summary, the committee feels that the sexism that exists in the district is subtle, frequently submerged, many times the result of omissions rather than commissions. However, they do find encouraging the current administration's awareness of and concern about the issue.

Perhaps because discrimination is not overt and rampant that women in Dayton schools, and in education in Ohio, have not yet responded to the national movement. At this time the women's rights movement seems to have barely touched Dayton schools. The following are cited as possible benchmarks of the level of awareness in the district:

1. When potential membership for the committee was surveyed, the attempt was made to select those who were knowledgeable and committed to women's rights. During the following weeks, three of the ten resigned. Each cited other responsibilities that may in part indicate that women's rights just does not have that high a priority.

2. When a high-school teacher showed a blatantly sexist film that he and his students had made, few saw the discrimination and even fewer were concerned. When one of the committee members made the charge, the teacher defended the film by saying that "not one female teacher or female student (in his school) felt that the examamples of sexism . . . were significant."[3] However, an article in that school's paper recently reported that girls, previously excluded from a school club, had pushed for and won the right to be members next year.[4]

3. The committee chairer has received few serious inquiries from fellow staff members concerning the group's work. In fact, she has had more written and verbal requests from people outside the district than from those within. When she called to ask questions about procedures, on two occasions she was asked, "Don't you have something better to do?" Others have commented, "We have enough problems around here now; we don't need you coming up with another one."

   Other members reported such questions as: "What's the need?" "Is there really a women's rights committee?" "Is it subversive?" "Who started this committee?"

   On the other hand, those who provided much of the data for this report, specifically, staff development department, management services department, and the athletic office, were at all times extremely cooperative.

4. The Superintendent asked a panel of women to make a presentation on women's rights to his Teacher Advisory Group and to the schools' administrative and supervisory personnel on January 15 and 17 [1973], respectively. The teachers seemed receptive to the panel; they were attentive with good discussion following. However, some administrators and supervisory personnel appeared less interested, even to the point of being rude. Although members of the panel received personal thanks of several teachers and administrators, as of this time no one has requested the panel to come to a school to make a similar presentation to either faculty or students. In fact, one high-school principal refused to have panel speak to a group of social studies students after tentative arrangements had been made. He would not give a reason, saying only that if he wanted the panel, he would call them.

5. Although not surveying the schools, the group knows of no other committee, building, or central office department where staff have

added women's studies (the contributions and current status of women) to the curriculum, have screened text and/or trade books for sex bias or stereotyping, or have banded together to push for equal rights for themselves or for their students.

6. The committee has also become aware of an interesting mental phenomenon in this district: many individuals sensitive to racism and ethnic and religious prejudice who appear totally insensitive to sexism. Somehow they have managed to compartmentalize prejudice, excluding discrimination against women. The district's level of awareness of sexism is probably at a similar point where racism was five years ago before the current administration.

DISCRIMINATORY ITEMS IN FORMS USED IN DAYTON PUBLIC SCHOOLS

The printed forms used in Dayton Public Schools are relatively free of discriminatory questions and language. Items that might be classified as discriminatory fall into three categories: (1) titles, (2) questions on marital status, and (3) the use of the masculine gender.

The committee makes the following recommendations:

(1) *Writing one's name according to personal preference should be the option of every person.* For many, identity is attached to a name so that an incorrect address may become a personal affront. Thus, Ms. should be added to such forms as "Application for Employment" and "MDECA Elementary and Secondary New Student Information" and all others that have titles preceding a name line.

A possible alternative would be to drop all titles and use just first, middle (or initial), and last names, the style of many computer printed items. Since titles do change, this may be a more practical approach.

(2) *Questions on marital status on such forms as "Application for Employment" should be dropped.* With the variety of relationships existing today, including all categories would be cumbersome and also possibly an invasion of privacy. Also, why should one's marital status be important to an employer?

Also, questions dealing with spouse's name, spouse's place of employment, and similar information should be deleted. However, "In case of emergency, contact" is a legitimate item that in no way discriminates.

"My dear Mr. & Mrs.", which appears on many report cards, should be dropped. Perhaps, "Dear Parent or Guardian," would be more appropriate.

The "Kindergarten Registration Blank" includes several items (questions on nationality, parents' place of birth, and marital status) that may discriminate. This form should be evaluated and such items eliminated.

(3) *Delete unessential use of the masculine noun, pronoun, or pronominal adjective when the sex could be either male or female or is unknown.* For example, on the telephone message blank the *his* of, "His Telephone," and the *he* of, "He will call back," are totally unnecessary. On the "Application for Employment" *his* could easily be dropped from the italicized statement at the bottom of the first page. The message to parents on the front of many report cards is rampant with *he, his,* and *him,* occurring eleven times in four short paragraphs, many of which could be eliminated.

The constant use of the masculine gender in such situations smacks of sexism, especially when such use is not necessary. However, the alternative of *he/she* is awkward, probably worse than the constant use of *he.* Until our language coins a new word that refers to either sex, the use of the masculine should be minimized.

(4) *Since the Manual does not include every form used in the district, the committee suggests that all departments scrutinize their forms for discriminatory items.* Perhaps some changes could be made by hand where convenient and others incorporated at the next printing.

DISCRIMINATORY ITEMS IN THE MASTER AGREEMENT BETWEEN THE BOARD OF EDUCATION AND THE DAYTON CLASSROOM TEACHERS ASSOCIATION

The committee notes the following concerns:

(1) Although the term *professional staff member* was developed to eliminate discrimination, the *Master Agreement* still contains excessive use of the categorical *he, him,* and *his.* Dealing with this problem, usually in a legal document, is most difficult, pointing out again the need for a word that would refer to both sexes.

(2) *Articles 16.01 A 4e vs 16.01 A 5e and 16.01 A 6.* These articles grant less planning time to primary teachers, most of whom are women. (No primary teachers were represented at the time of negotiations for the contract. Were they not women, they might have been more visible and might have received equal planning time.)

(3) *Article 26.14.* According to this item, teachers may take two visitation days a year with the approval of the principal and if no substitute is required. This discriminates against primary teachers, again mostly women. At all other levels there are teachers with

planning periods who can reciprocate class coverage. This, however, might be partially, but not entirely, offset by the fact that some primary schools have teaching teams that could cover for an absent member or upper-elementary teachers who could help out.

(4) *Article 26.31.* Provisions for leave for adopting a child indicate that professional staff members must have completed three years of service and if the child is less than six months old, can not return "earlier than the beginning of the semester following the date on which the child is six months old." These terms are more stringent than those for maternity leave: three years as compared to one and minimum leave as compared to no time restrictions except that "maternity leave of more than two weeks for any remaining part of the semester in which it occurs shall continue for one semester."

(5) *Appendix A 14.03.* Head coaches of football and basketball plus athletic directors, all exclusively male positions, are paid $1,300 per year. Women coaches are paid on a lower level: *e.g.,* women coaching girls' basketball received $760 a year. No one would quarrel with the fact that the head coach of a boys' basketball team is more demanding than coaching a girls' team at this point and that a salary differentiation is justified. The point is, however, that separate athletic programs are not, and probably never can be, equal.

(6) The Board of Education's contract with Blue Cross/Blue Shield states that the father is head of the family and that his insurance company must take the primary responsibility for payments. Women have no reason to be automatically classed as nonhead of the family because they happen to remain in the same household with their husbands. This may especially discriminate in some black homes, where although husband and wife both have degrees, the female as a teacher may be earning more than her husband, who might be employed elsewhere.

(7) State Teachers' Retirement System pays fewer benefits to widowers of female teachers than to widows of male teachers. A key issue here appears to be a classification of "dependent" and "nondependent" widower, which goes back to the "head of household" issue. (Currently a class action suit on this matter has been filed in U.S. District Court in Dayton.)

As many of these items as possible should be taken care of through the DCTA/Administration Mutual Concerns Committee. Those that cannot be resolved through this group should be handled in the next negotiations session or brought to the attention of the appropriate agency as is the case of #6 and 7.

The Committee reviewed the *Agreement* between the Board of Education and the Ohio Association of Public School Employees and found nothing discriminatory. All bargaining units should check their agreements with the Board in light of items that would discriminate against either men or women.

RECOMMENDATIONS ON AN AFFIRMATIVE ACTION PROGRAM FOR WOMEN

The Board of Education should adopt a comprehensive affirmative action plan including guidelines for its implementation, which ensures that there will be no discrimination on the basis of race, creed, color, sex, age, or national origin. (This should be one document with appropriate subdivisions rather than one policy dealing with minorities, another with sex, etc.)

It should ensure no discrimination (1) in recruiting, hiring, training, and promoting, and (2) in other personnel actions such as pay, benefits, transfers, layoffs, in-service training, social, and recreational programs.

Specifically in regard to women, the affirmative action plan should contain the following:

(1) A statement of compliance with Title VII of the Civil Rights Act of 1964 along with the "Guidelines on Discrimination Because of Sex" published by the U.S. Equal Employment Opportunity Commission, 31 March 1972.

(2) An analysis of areas in which women are either under- or over-utilized.

(3) A line of progression within the ranks of both certificated and noncertificated employes that is based on qualifications, experience, and years of service.

(4) Objectives for achieving better utilization of women along with a timetable. (The number of women in all job classifications, including administration, should be proportionate to the total number employed by the district. Preferential hiring of both sexes should be used in areas of imbalance.)

(5) Details of an internship program that would (a) search out potential female leadership talent and (b) provide training to help the women develop skills needed for educational supervision and administration.

(6) Procedures for disseminating the affirmative action plan.

(7) An evaluation that would measure effectiveness of the total program.

One additional recommendation would be to request that the City of Dayton's Human Relations Council add a question or questions on sex to Item 12 of the "Affirmative Action Assurance," which companies doing business with the Board must submit.

Since national employment statistics on females parallel in many instances those on minorities, the provisions in the affirmative action program for both groups should be similar.

GENERAL RECOMMENDATIONS TO ASSURE FEMALE/MALE EQUALITY

The goal of these recommendations is to provide equality for men and women in this district. Thus, they apply to both sexes equally unless otherwise noted. In cases where a service, benefit, or consideration is currently not provided to either sex, the result of the omission is discrimination primarily against women.

(1) *Open all employment categories to both sexes.* In areas where one sex is underutilized, use preferential hiring. Women should be actively recruited for positions generally closed to them: athletic directors, track, basketball, golf, tennis, and other coaching positions, regardless of whether the team is male or female.

(2) *Establish a line of progression for both certificated and noncertificated employes.* Example: differentiated staffing for teachers and higher level positions within the clerical ranks.

(3) *Establish an internship program* that would recruit potential female leadership talent and provide training to develop skills necessary for supervision and administration. Such a program would be open to males, but preference would be given to females until they were represented in administration in proportion to their total numbers in the district.

(4) *As a caring institution, provide flexibility in assignment.*

(a) Extend a reasonable measure of flexible hours to those with major family responsibilities if they so request. If certain jobs do not necessarily require the people who fill them to be on duty the regular hours, then allow for some variation if that would aid an individual.

(b) Considering both the district's need and those of the employe, permit half-time assignments to teachers in all subject areas. One may very well get more work from two half-time people than one full-time and working half-time may very well aid those with family responsibilities.

(5) *Provide in-service training for both certificated and noncertificated staff to raise level of awareness of the contributions and status of women.* This should be an on-going training program rather than a single experience.

(6) (a) *Affirm compliance with Section 1604.10* of the "Guidelines on Discrimination Because of Sex," which indicates that pregnancy should be treated the same as any other disability. A pregnant woman could use the number of sick-leave days she had accumulated but would not be permitted to draw upon those yet unearned. (Ironically, now a woman can use sick leave for a miscarriage or any other pregnancy-related condition except the birth of a healthy child.)

(b) *Provide parental leave for males.* Such leave would give a father the opportunity to assist his wife one or two weeks right after the birth of a child or to assume family responsibilities for six months or a year while his wife works. Parental leave would be without pay.

(7) *Investigate establishing day-care centers* in selected schools for children of Dayton Schools' employes. A day-care center in a school can serve the needs of staff and perhaps community, while providing a living-learning laboratory for young people. Classes in home economics, health, child care, or psychology could work in the lab, receiving credit for time spent. Once established, the centers should be self-supporting.

(8) *All professional organizations and social/recreational activities should be open to both males and females.* This includes the coaches associations, the school bowling leagues, intramural teams (regardless of the sport), faculty luncheons, and all other social events.

(9) *Separate lounges for males and females should be eliminated.* The usual justification for their existence:

(a) That members of the opposite sex can hear others using the restroom facilities,

(b) That men should not see sanitary napkins or internal sanitary protection, or

(c) That men need a place to "talk male talk"; or females, "woman talk," reflect an immature level of social development. Faculty should be setting a more mature example for students.

(10) *A means of channeling complaints on sex bias should be available to every staff member* and that means well publicized. Perhaps consideration should be given to resurrecting the Human Relations Coordinating Committee for this purpose and for promoting within the district a greater awareness of the contributions and status of women. This group could also serve as the liaison with outside agencies such as colleges and universities, which tend to perpetuate institutional sexism much as public education does.

Also, freedom from sex bias should be incorporated into the district's evaluation forms for all employes as these forms are being developed.

PROPOSED PLAN FOR STUDYING SEXISM IN CURRICULAR AND EXTRACURRICULAR PROGRAMS

Although the Superintendent's first three charges dealt with in this report are certainly important, the fourth charge—assessing the curricular and extracurricular activities of the schools in light of women's rights—is by far more important. Eliminating sex bias and stereotyping for 50,000 young people will reap returns beyond those coming from the elimination of discrimination for 3,800 staff members.

During the remaining months the committee will be concerned in determining if

(1) Students experience instruction by both sexes equally at the elementary, middle, and high school levels

(2) All course offerings and extracurricular activities are open to both sexes and that both are encouraged to make a choice based on interest and talent

(3) Athletics and physical education programs are free from arbitrary distinctions in sports based on sex and not ability (includes staffing, participants, and facilities)

(4) Vocational guidance presents all career possibilities without sex bias to both girls and boys

(5) Text and trade books are screened with the goal of providing schools with materials that present the contributions of women in an unbiased manner and are free from sex stereotypes

(6) Women's studies are incorporated into the curriculum and that both boys and girls are presented with opportunities to expand their levels of awareness.

CONCLUSION

The committee may be charged that it has created another problem to be dealt with, the last thing needed in urban education today. We respond with an analogy: We know that the all-white suburban community that says it has no race problem is blind to its own situation; those who say there is no discrimination against women in Dayton schools are just as myopic.

Sexism is not just another problem to solve. Whether it be racism, anti-

Semitism, sexism, religious, or ethnic prejudice, all are forms of discrimination. Perhaps each has a few characteristics of its own, but similarities far exceed differences. One who is part of the army battling for human rights must carry all the banners; he cannot choose to leave one behind. As Shirley Chisholm says:

> Every American who believes in liberty and justice for all must join the struggle for equal rights for blacks and Indians, Puerto Ricans and Chicanos, and women. Progressive Americans should join in the struggle to end *all* forms of discrimination in America and to end the narrow-minded approach of assigning stereotypic roles to particular groups. Human beings cannot be assigned so easily, since we are unique in our individual abilities and characters. Liberation in American must therefore transcend ending discrimination against a particular race. It must entail ending discrimination because of sex, origin, and religion as well.[5]

Committee Members

Mary Arnold
Jean Booker
Nancy Brown
Theresa Brytus
Virginia Carter
Ronald Jones
Billie Mason
Elaine Stephens
Dale Van Tine

Joyce Kaser, Chairer

NOTES

1. "Professional Women in Public Schools, 1970–71," *NEA Research Bulletin* (Oct. 1971), pp. 67–8.
2. "Sex Discrimination in Schools is a Two-sided Issue," *Ohio Schools* (22 December 1972), pp. 11–12.
3. Charles Scott, personal letter, 4 October 1972.
4. "Libbers Hit Students," *The Wright Plot* (Dayton) (21 December 1972), p. 2.
5. Shirley Chisholm, 'Sexism and Racism: One Battle to Fight," *Personnel and Guidance Journal* (October 1972): 123–25.

Choices*
Report B
The Women's Rights Committee

INTRODUCTION

The Committee on Women's Rights was established at the request of Superintendent Wayne Carle in September 1972. It was charged with studying and reporting on the following objectives:

(1) Review and appraisal of current statistics on the employment and assignment of women.

(2) A subjective assessment of the status of women in Dayton Public Schools.

(3) Recommendation of an Affirmative Action Program for the employment, assignment, and promotion of women.

(4) Assessment of the curricular and extracurricular activities of the schools in light of women's rights.

Initially the committee dealt with the first three objectives and filed a report entitled *The Time Is Now* (8 February 1973). This report reviews data and makes a series of recommendations for providing more equal opportunities for men and women in the district. Copies are available from

---

* Reprinted with the permission of Joyce S. Kaser, Dayton Public Schools, Dayton, Ohio.

the school-community services division, administration department, Dayton Board of Education.

This second report examines sex bias and stereotyping in curricular and extracurricular activities in Dayton schools. The committee felt that although the first three charges were important, the fourth, assessing sex bias and stereotyping in the schools, was of the most consequence. Eliminating bias and discrimination should ultimately reap returns for 50,000 students far beyond those accruing for 3,800 adult staff members.

In this study, the committee wanted to determine if:

(1) Students experience instruction and support services by both sexes equally at the elementary, middle, and high-school levels.

(2) All course offerings and extracurricular activities are open to both sexes and that both are encouraged to make a choice based on interest and talent.

(3) Athletics and physical education programs are free from arbitrary distinctions in sports based on sex.

(4) Vocational guidance presents all career possibilities without sex bias to both young women and men.

(5) Text and trade books are screened with the goal of providing schools with materials that present the contributions of women in an unbiased manner and are free from sex stereotypes.

(6) Women's studies are incorporated into the curriculum and that both young men and women are presented with opportunities to expand their levels of awareness.

The following report presents data and makes recommendations for eliminating any sex bias and discrimination found.

OBJECTIVE 1: STUDENTS EXPERIENCE INSTRUCTION AND SUPPORT SERVICES BY BOTH SEXES EQUALLY AT THE ELEMENTARY, MIDDLE, AND HIGH-SCHOOL LEVELS

As the first report detailed, the male/female distribution of administrators, teachers, and support personnel is uneven throughout the district. For example, women make up 63.1 percent of the total staff, but that percent jumps to 80.5 for teachers in the elementary and middle schools and drops to 42.3 percent for secondary teachers. The number of male principals in the elementary schools totals 76.9 percent and 100 percent for middle and high schools.

In regard to support services, 80.3 percent of all librarians are female along with 100 percent of the nurses. However, 88.9 percent of the high-school band directors are male along with 80.4 percent of the coaches.

Clerical staff is almost entirely women (97.9%), while the custodial staff is almost all male (96.3%).

RECOMMENDATIONS

(1) A detailed analysis should be made of the areas in which women and men are either under- or overutilized.

(2) All employment categories must be open to both sexes and active recruiting conducted until all areas are balanced roughly in the percentage of the total number of men and women on the staff. That number should approximate 50 percent male, 50 percent female.

OBJECTIVE 2: ALL COURSE OFFERINGS AND EXTRACURRICULAR ACTIVITIES ARE OPEN TO BOTH SEXES AND THAT BOTH ARE ENCOURAGED TO MAKE A CHOICE BASED ON INTEREST AND TALENT

Elementary: Curricular and Extracurricular

To determine types of sex bias in the elementary grades, the committee sent a questionnaire (at end of article) to fifty schools. Data from the eighteen responding points out some specific instances of sex bias and role stereotyping:

(1) Sex stereotyping exists in assigning duties. Young men carry furniture and have flag duties; young women serve as hostesses and teacher helpers.

(2) In instruction, students are frequently separated for physical education, home economics, and industrial arts, which, because of scheduling problems, may lead to segregated classes in art, music, academic areas, and even homerooms.

(3) Students are divided into separate lines for lunch, dismissal and restroom breaks.

(4) Discipline may be determined, in part, by the sex of the offender.

Several respondents indicated that they felt their colleagues were unaware of their bias as they separated sexes or set different expectations for young women and men.

This data supports the personal observations of the committee members that sex bias does exist in the elementary schools. Also, there appears to be a low level of awareness of stereotyping on the part of the teaching and supportive staffs.

RECOMMENDATIONS

(1) All instructional programs should be integrated including physical education, music, art, home economics, industrial arts, and academic classes.

(2) Students should not be segregated for lining up, seating, or for forming opposing teams. Neither should they be listed by sex in grade books or on other records.

(3) Beginning in the earliest grades, all students should have opportunities to work with construction tools and to learn basic housekeeping and body maintenance skills.

(4) All school service groups (safety patrol, hall monitors, audio-visual aides, etc.) must include members of both sexes in approximately the same numbers.

(5) Discipline policy should be formulated and implemented without regard to the sex of the offender.

(6) Schools should not participate in contests in which females compete with one another in categories of charm, grace, dress, or figure.

High School

Curricular

The vocational program was the committee's main area of concern at the secondary level. To determine if students were enrolling in vocational courses according to traditional sex-role patterns, data was gathered from three schools: Belmont, Patterson Cooperative, and Roth high schools. Patterson is the district's cooperative high school; the other two are comprehensive high schools with extensive vocational programs.

Table 1 shows that young women select cosmetology, medical arts, and office education; young men, auto mechanics, drafting, and graphic arts. Only in commercial art, distributive education, occupational work adjustment, and occupational work experience do students and program start to become sexually unidentifiable.

The committee also reviewed three publications of course descriptions to check for sex labeling. Patterson Cooperative High School's "Courses of Study," the district's handbook for incoming freshmen, "Mission Possible," and the district-wide "Courses Offered in Comprehensive High Schools," were relatively free of sex distinctions. However, the latter did list a total of six courses in music, home economics, and career exploration open to only one sex.

Although on paper only six courses are limited to one sex, segregated classes are the rule in vocational education, health and physical education, industrial arts, and trades and industries. This may, however, be the result of sex-role patterning rather than overt discrimination. *See* Objective 2: Elementary and High School: Special Programs, and Objective 3.)

Table 1

Number of Students Enrolled in Vocational Courses in Three Selected High Schools

	BELMONT		PATTERSON		ROTH	
	Male	Female	Male	Female	Male	Female
Business and Office Education	0	77	12	106	0	50
Distributive Education	20	35	59	96	26	31
Occupational Work Adjustment	22	8			36	39
Occupational Work Experience	39	11			25	0
Auto Mechanics	20	0	30	0		
Body and Fender			33	0		
Occupational Drafting			33	2	28	0
Machine Shop			42	0	18	0
Sheet Metal			16	0		
Electrical			15	0		
Industrial Electronics			41	0		
Cosmetology			0	31	0	34
Dental Assisting			0	50		
Nursing Assistance			19	7		
Commercial Art			14	19		
Graphic Arts			58	2		

RECOMMENDATIONS

(1) Course descriptions should be screened for sex labeling. No student should be excluded from a course solely on the basis of sex.

(2) Both sexes should have equal exposure to all vocational areas with each presented to them as a viable option. Vocational staff should have a long-range goal of roughly equal enrollment of sexes in each instructional area. Thus, eventually programs and students could not be identified by sex.

(3) Vocational staff may need to alert employers to the federal laws against sex bias and discrimination and assist them in the hiring and assignment of the minority sex.

Extracurricular Activities

High schools were asked to list their extracurricular organizations, specifying whether each was open to one or both sexes. If open to both, the approximate male/female membership was to be indicated.

Although ten of the eleven high schools reported, there were some discrepancies in data since what one school classified as extracurricular, another did not. However, the following patterns emerged:

(1) Almost every school has four organizations that are exclusively female, although they may or may not be open to both sexes. These are cheerleading squads, drill teams, majorettes, and pep clubs. Simply saying that both young men and women can join a group doesn't mean that they will do so.

(2) Most schools have vocational and/or special-interest clubs, many of which are sexually segregated because the instructional program traditionally is identified with one sex. These include cosmetology, electronics, auto mechanics, clerical, dental arts, and similar clubs that draw their membership from students enrolled in such programs. As long as the program is segregated, the club will be also.

(3) Almost every school has at least one club, in most cases a service organization, that limits membership to one sex. Young men have the Key Club, Hi-Y, Civitan, Jrs., and the Fellowship of Christian Athletes; young women, T-Teens, Arcessimus, and similar organizations.

(4) All schools have organizations that are freely open to both sexes: Spanish, Latin, and French clubs; student councils; art and drama groups; honor societies; and the Junior Council on World Affairs.

To get some indication of how many young men and women participate in segregated groups, the committee tabulated data from one high school with a wide gamut of extracurricular activities. Of the young men participating, 42% were in groups exclusively male, while 84% of the females were in segregated groups. Had athletic organizations been included, the percentage of boys in segregated groups would have increased substantially.

RECOMMENDATIONS

(1) Cheerleading squads, pep clubs, drill teams, and majorettes should be open to both sexes and both *actively* recruited for membership.

(2) All vocational and/or special-interest clubs should be open to both sexes and both recruited for membership. This situation will partially remedy itself as the instructional programs that generate these clubs become integrated.

(3) Schools should evaluate the continuation of segregated service clubs in light of sex discrimination, duplication of effort, and the eventual passage of the Equal Rights Amendment.

ELEMENTARY AND HIGH SCHOOL: SPECIAL PROGRAMS

Because of their traditional sex-role emphasis, home economics, industrial arts, and music require special mention.

Home Economics and Industrial Arts

Dayton schools have a practical arts program for students in grades seven and eight in all but two elementary buildings and a limited program in three of the five middle schools. Practical arts students take industrial arts and home economics alternately with the majority in sexually segregated classes. However, the option of mixed or separate classes belongs to the principal. Curriculum supervisors indicate the instructional program is identical for both sexes.

At the high-school level, a variety of courses are available in both home economics and industrial arts. However, males taking home economics will usually have special courses designed for them (such as foods and nutrition for young men), as will females enrolling in industrial arts (home repairs for young women, for example).

A total of 172 young men are enrolled in home economics courses and 46 in job training (food service) as compared to 2,623 young women in home economics and 140 in job training (child care, fabrics, and community service). Of these 218 young men, 144 are in segregated classes.

The vocational staff (division of career education) was unable to provide comparable data for enrollment in industrial arts. However, if data on enrollment in vocational units is a gauge of females taking industrial arts courses, then the number is very small. Figures show only three young women in graphics and two in drafting.

RECOMMENDATIONS

Practical Arts (Grades 6–7–8)

(1) All students should take both home economics and industrial arts and classes should be mixed.

Industrial Arts and Home Economics (High School)

(2) Courses designed for one sex should be eliminated. All classes should be free from sex-role goals.

Total Program (6-12)

(3) Goals in home economics and industrial arts should place emphasis on all persons being able to handle basic body maintenance, homemaking, and home care both individually and cooperatively rather than through traditional role assignment.

(4) Classes at all levels should provide a wide variety of experiences that would appeal to both sexes. Sewing should include costume design and upholstery in addition to basic clothing. Cooking should range from hamburgers to haute cuisine. Woodworking should offer refinishing and antiquing. Electronics should include repair of small appliances.

Music

The committee looked at two aspects of the music program: vocal groups and the kinds of instruments students play.

A survey of the vocal music organizations in all schools shows that the majority of participating students are in mixed groups (Table 2). Only two schools have groups for one sex without having a mixed group. However, eighteen schools reported no vocal music organizations at all.

Table 3 shows the instruments selected by young women and men in Dayton schools. Choices follow the stereotyped patterning: females choose strings and woodwinds; males, brasses and percussion.

One other problem is the existence of some segregated music classes in the elementary schools as mentioned previously.

Table 2

Vocal Music Groups

Number exclusively for young women		24
Number of young women enrolled	451	
Number exclusively for young men		11
Number of young men enrolled	86	
Number of mixed groups		105
Number of young women enrolled	2,367	
Number of young men enrolled	1,835	

Table 3

Instruments Played By Dayton Students

	Young Men	Young Women
String	222	325
Woodwinds	244	808
Brasses	359	94
Percussion	361	82
Other (Piano and Guitar)	109	119

RECOMMENDATIONS

(1) All music classes should be sexually integrated.

(2) If a school has only one vocal (or instrumental) group, it should be open to both sexes.

(3) Music teachers should use a variety of methods in attempting to match students and instruments in an instrumental program. Every student should have some exposure to each type of instrument: woodwinds, percussion, brass, and strings—before making any selection. At no time should students be steered toward one instrument because of their sex.

(4) Additional opportunities should be made available to both young men and women in such areas as composing and conducting to encourage them to select music as a career. This is especially true for young women, who are represented to a lesser extent in music than in any other fine arts area.

SOURCES OF SEX BIAS AND STEREOTYPING

Much of the sex bias and stereotyping in schools is subtle, conveyed covertly by teachers' attitudes and actions in the classroom. The following lists serve as references for many of the common kinds of stereotyping all educators need to guard against. The lists could also serve as the basis for group discussions of school staff members who are attempting to heighten their awareness in order to provide a full range of opportunities for both sexes.

List 1[1]

Differing expectations by teachers of the students in regard to

(1) Temperament—do teachers expect and tolerate more independence, aggressiveness, loudness, restlessness from boys? more dependence, whining, giggling from girls?

(2) Intellectual abilities—do teachers believe that girls are more verbal, boys more mathematical? that aggressive curiosity is more to be expected from boys?

(3) Socialization—do teachers expect girls to be more "mannered" in the conventional sense and encourage them to be "feminine" (passive, dependent)? do they encourage boys to be "gallant" (move the girls' chairs, etc.)? do they expect the girls to be more religious and moral, boys to be more loyal and ethical?

(4) Language use—do teachers expect and tolerate more slang, rough language from the boys?

(5) Dress—do teachers expect girls to be neater, follow fashion styles, and seasonal changes more closely? do they pity girls who are unable or unwilling to play the fashion game? do they reinforce those who do? . . . do they stress modesty for girls?

(6) Health—do teachers expect boys to be more robust, less complaining, and reinforce girls for being "sick" monthly? do they encourage a healthy respect and confidence in their bodies in boys and a morbid anxiety and fear on the part of girls?

(7) Athletics—why are boys and girls segregated if they are in their athletic activities? do teachers expect competence from boys and failure from girls? are the terms "sissy" or "tomboy" ever applied?

(8) Interests—do teachers expect girls to be more interested in child care, home, and family? do they expect boys to be interested in cars, sports, building, and creating with permanent materials (rather than food and cloth)?

(9) Career goals—do teachers expect boys to be doctors, girls nurses? do they encourage the continual sorting out of career options by boys and overlook the need in girls?

(10) Sexual attitudes—do they think boys have stronger sexual urges and interest and therefore expect and tolerate more from them in the way of questions, jokes, masturbation?

(11) Monitorial duties—do teachers expect girls to do light housework and secretarial chores in the classroom, boys to do the heavy work and executive duties?

List 2

(1) Seating arrangement—is it sex segregated or arranged, e.g., girls in even rows, boys in odd; girls on the right side, boys on the left, etc.?

(2) Classroom chores schedule—is it sex specific? does the schedule work chart, or work wheel reserve certain jobs for boys, e.g., window monitor, passing out books, chalkboard monitor, cleaning erasers; and certain jobs for girls, e.g., watering plants, dusting, doing errands?

(3) Work displays—are bulletin boards with "good work" or special projects sex segregated, e.g., "girls' good work," "boys' good work," "royal work: kings and queens," etc.?

(4) Classroom library—are books arranged according to sex, e.g., books for boys, books for girls?

(5) Free play or special privileges schedules—are they sex segregated, e.g., painting: Monday—girls, Tuesday—boys; girls free play from 9-9:30, boys from 9:30-10, etc.?

(6) Pictures around the room—do they depict males and females in typically sex-typed situations, e.g., girls playing with dolls, boys with blocks, women with babies, men in manual labor or executive jobs?

(7) Sex-segregated or special teams at recess—e.g., girls baseball team and boys baseball team, or girls jump-rope squad, boys football squad, etc.?

OBJECTIVE 3: PHYSICAL EDUCATION AND ATHLETICS ARE FREE FROM ARBITRARY DISTINCTIONS BASED ON SEX

The committee examined the three components of the total program: physical education, intramurals, and interscholastic athletic competition.

Physical Education

Elementary

Currently schools provide physical education for students in grades four through eight two days per week. The program offers basic skill development and the beginning of team sports in segregated classes with males teaching young men and females teaching young women.

There are exceptions to this standard program. One school (McGuffey) had twelve of sixteen physical education classes integrated this year, including those for grades seven and eight. The principal mixed classes because he saw no reason to segregate and because it facilitated scheduling of other classes. He did this with limited facilities, including no shower rooms. He indicates receiving no complaints from students or parents and only a few from teachers.

High School

All ninth- and tenth-grade students take physical education two days a week. The program is basically segregated with teachers instructing those of their sex. At this level students are putting their skills to use through team sports and some coeducational activities in rhythmics and life-time sports. The program for eleventh and twelfth graders depends on each school's facilities. The curriculum is life-time sports with emphasis on coeducational activities in square and folk dancing, archery, tennis, golf, badminton, shuffleboard, table tennis, and bowling. All schools provide some life-time sports, but there is great variation from school to school.

Roosevelt High School offers a coeducational program for all students except seniors. Young people are scheduled by lot and given their choice of five different activities. Teachers team for instruction, each working with a maximum of thirty-five students. Staff, administration, and students indicate that approach is working well.

Intramurals

Schools can provide intramurals for students in grades five through twelve by writing a program and submitting to the physical education and athletic office (division of human welfare and development). Generally, teams are segregated with coaches directing activities of their like sex. However, the program does include coed volleyball, life-time sports, and recreational games.

During 1972–73 schools could request funds for fall, winter and/or spring programs. Nineteen schools did not submit any requests during the year while three sponsored a program only once. All other schools held programs for at least two of the three sessions. Only $18,000 of the $28,000 allotted for intramurals was spent.

Interscholastic

Seventh and Eighth Grades

The interscholastic program at this level is for young men only. Twelve football centers are set up for the entire city with the student participating at his nearest center. For basketball, every school may have a coach and team and participate in city leagues.

High School

The following activities are available for students:

Young Men	*Young Women*	*Both*
Football	Basketball	Fencing
Basketball	Volleyball	Gymnastics
Baseball	Tennis	
Cross Country	Track (73–74)	
Track		
Tennis		
Wrestling		

The athletic office has exhibited an increasing awareness of providing more opportunities for young women as evidenced by adding basketball this year and track next. Also, athletic staff has pushed for equal salaries for women coaches and for a policy (through the Athletic Board of Control) to insure females greater use of facilities.

The following are some of the committee's concerns of a segregated program in physical education, intramurals, and interscholastic competition:

(1) Separate classes reinforce the false assumption that females must participate only in less-demanding physical activities, while males are equipped physically and psychologically for more strenuous sports. As a result, young women may not develop physical skills to the maximum extent.

(2) The female's inadequate opportunities to develop physical skills supports the stereotype that women are defenseless and must be protected by men.

(3) Lack of opportunities for advanced skill development means that few young women get athletic scholarships and that few scholarships are available for them.

(4) Lack of adequate number of female coaches means that sometimes young women may be without an intramural program because the physical education teacher or coach already has so many extra-duty assignments (cheerleaders, drill team, Girls Athletic Association) that she cannot take on more responsibilities.

(5) Both the physical education and intramural programs are financed by the Board of Education (General Fund). Since expenditures are not divided according to the sex of students, determining the amount spent for young men and for young women is difficult. The interscholastic program (with exception of coaches' salaries) is supported from proceeds of young men's football and basketball. Thus, opportunities for young women are determined, in part, by the financial success of the young men's varsity teams.

(6) Scheduling facilities for physical education, intramurals, and interscholastics is difficult. Although the Athletic Board of Control has established a procedure on facility use, young women still are not getting prime time. Young men's basketball and football continue to take precedence.

(7) There is no official female representative on the Athletic Board of Control with the exception of a Board of Education delegate. Although the president of the women coaches association sits as a voting representative, the Board of Education has never officially approved her membership or that of the president of the men coaches association.

(8) Dayton has no women athletic directors ($1,300 per year). Head coaches of young women's teams are paid on the level of assistant coaches for basketball and football. As a result, women basketball coaches are receiving $540 less than their male counterparts.

(9) In varsity sports during 1971–72, women held 19.6% of the coaching positions; men, 80.4%.

(10) Out of the top 25 people earning extra-duty pay[2] in Dayton schools, two are women and 23 are men. Top man makes $3,595; top woman, $2,055. Out of a total of $56,000, women receive only $3,885.

EFFORTS TO INTEGRATE

On May 4 the Ohio High School Athletic Association (OHSAA) sent a memo saying that the U.S. Sixth District Court of Appeals had issued a ruling that young women could not be denied participation on young men's teams in noncontact sports. This decision nullified OHSAA's regulation that prevented mixing sexes on interscholastic teams.

On 7 May 1973 Superintendent Wayne M. Carle wrote the following letter to the director of physical education and athletics:

In light of the Sixth Circuit Court of Appeals ruling in the Michigan sex discrimination case and the rules change of OHSAA to integrate all noncontact sports, please implement the desegregation by sex of physical education and athletics in the Dayton schools to be effective with the opening of the 1973–74 school year.

1. Please develop rules and procedures to assure that:

   a. Qualified males and females are admitted without regard to sex to enrollment in all physical education programs and participation on all intramural and interscholastic teams. If exceptions are proposed, as for the contact sports of football, basketball, and wrestling, such exceptions must be based on objective and legal criteria.

   b. Qualified males and females are recruited, employed, and assigned without regard to sex as teachers, coaches, and game officials in all physical education programs and intramural and interscholastic athletics.

   c. Meets, leagues, and tournaments are conducted bisexually.

2. As minimum preparation for needed changes, please provide for:

   a. Written explanations suitable for distribution to students, staff, and parents.

   b. Orientation meetings for principals, coaches, teachers, game officials, and student bodies to acquaint them with the revised programs and advise them of their rights and opportunities.

   c. A written plan for implementation, noting objectives, time schedules, and critical points for checking progress.
   d. Involvement of representatives of groups affected, in developing

plans and procedures. Such involvement is to include equal numbers of males and females at all times.

e. An affirmative action program of dated goals for increasing participation of female students, teachers, coaches, and officials in integrated physical education and athletics.

3. The following guidelines should be observed:

a. Where students have been enrolled for physical education by sex for next year, consider reassignment by lot.

b. Women are to be assigned to head coaching positions as frequently as men.

c. Separate male and female coaching staffs are to be discontinued.

d. Where males and females are competing for the first time, some form of handicapping should be used to assure that females are not excluded on the basis of inequitable qualifications or requirements.

e. Recognizing the results of past emphasis on male sports to the exclusion of women, special programs to qualify more women for team membership, coaching, and officiating should be planned and conducted.

Since that time, physical education and athletic personnel have expressed opposition to the Superintendent's request, citing the following problems:

(1) Lack of facilities, funds, and coaches.

(2) Basic physiological differences between males and females with possibility of injury.

(3) Fear of discipline problems in class and in locker rooms.

(4) Belief that opportunities for both sexes are equal in physical education and growing more equal in intramurals and athletics.

(5) Fear that one sex cannot teach or coach members of the opposite sex.

When this report was finalized, the issue remained unsolved. Considering both positions, the Women's Rights Committee suggests the following:

RECOMMENDATIONS

Physical Education

(1) The primary and elementary program should be integrated with

opportunities for separate activities, especially at the sixth-, seventh-, and eighth-grade levels. This program should continue to emphasize individual skill development.

(2) The secondary program should also be integrated with opportunities for separate activities. This program should provide some team participation, but the emphasis should be upon life-time sports. Students need many opportunities to select activities of their choice.

Intramurals

(3) All schools serving students in grades five through twelve should either provide an intramural program or enable students to participate in another school's program.

(4) The program should be integrated with opportunities for separate activities. Emphasis should be on enjoyment and recreation rather than competition.

Interscholastic

(5) In light of the Sixth Circuit Court's ruling, young women should be permitted to play on young men's teams in noncontact sports if there are no female teams.

(6) Young women should have as many opportunities for interscholastic competition as young men. For example, football could be balanced by soccer or sports emphasizing balance, skill, and coordination rather than strength.

(7) Sports in which strength is not a key factor (flag football, bowling, fencing, archery, table tennis) should be integrated.

(8) If there are separate teams for sports in which strength is a key factor, each team should have equal status. For example, both basketball teams should constitute the varsity team. Each should play on the same night and their scores combined to determine winner of the game.

(9) Some sports might be added on the cluster or district basis rather than each individual school sponsoring its own team.

GENERAL RECOMMENDATIONS

(10) Teachers, coaches, and athletic directors should be hired and assigned on basis of skill, interest, and certification rather than on sex. (Doing otherwise would put the schools in violation of Title VII of the Civil Rights Act of 1964 and Title IX of the Educational Amendments of 1972.)

(11) To make up for past inequities, special encouragement should be given to young women and young men outside the interscholastic program to develop skills to maximum extent.

(12) The physical education and athletic office should hold in-service training for all physical education teachers and coaches to help them expand their awareness of the physical abilities of young women and to help them break down some of the traditional sex stereotypes which pervade instruction which has been sexually segregated.

(13) A specific recruiting program should be undertaken to increase the number of female coaches. The physical education and athletic office might consider training nonphysical education majors to coach areas in which they have special skill and talent.

(14) Coaches salaries for each sport should be equal. Thus, those coaching young women's basketball should receive the same amount as coaches of the young men's teams.

(15) Women should be officially represented on the Athletic Board of Control and the professional staff of the physical education and athletic office should be integrated sexually.

OBJECTIVE 4: VOCATIONAL GUIDANCE PRESENTS ALL CAREER POSSIBILITIES WITHOUT SEX BIAS TO BOTH BOYS AND GIRLS

To evaluate vocational counseling in light of sex bias, the committee focused on three areas: the Consortium of Community Consultants, counseling procedures, and vocational interest testing.

The Consortium of Community Consultants (3C's) is a cooperative project between the schools and the Chamber of Commerce by which speakers from area business and industry visit classes to talk with students about careers. The 3C's handbook lists job titles from which a teacher makes a choice. The school counselor then contacts the counseling and guidance office, which secures a speaker for the class from the community.

An analysis of requests filled during September-December 1972 revealed the following:

(1) In K–8 schools men talked to mixed groups about policework, banking, medicine, dentistry, the FBI, law, auto mechanics, and telephone service. Women usually talked about cosmetology, secretarial work, nursing, and modeling. In most cases women spoke primarily to females rather than to mixed groups.

(2) In high schools (9–12) men talked to mixed groups about careers in banking, insurance, engineering, law, meat cutting, and tool-and-die work. Women spoke to mixed groups about secretarial work, medical technology, nursing, and cosmetology.

(3) Presentations on how to apply for a job, career opportunities in Dayton, or the importance of attitudes in job performance were made twice as often by men as by women.

In summary, men talk to students about careers more frequently than women; speakers usually talk about careers traditional to their sex; and that although men talk to mixed groups, women may talk only to female students.

The counseling and guidance office explains that speakers on nontraditional roles are not readily available and that business and industry has the option as to whom they will send. Schools must accept the speakers assigned to them.

Thus, the 3C's program perpetuates sex-role stereotyping in jobs by furthering the status quo rather than exposing students to men and women representing a wide range of careers.

To determine possible sex bias in vocational counseling procedures, the committee sent a questionnaire (at end of article) to all counselors in the district. Out of 104 forms, 21 were returned (seven from high schools, fourteen from K–8 schools).

Although the 20% return was lower than the committee had hoped for, it followed through on tabulating responses and evaluating data where appropriate. Major findings include the following:

(1) Young men see the counselor for discipline, personal problems, and vocational guidance; young women, for personal problems, discipline, and vocational guidance—all in the order listed. Both discipline and personal problems take precedence over vocational counseling.

(2) Counselors say they provide options not necessarily restricted to traditional sex roles when presenting career information to students. However, when students request information on careers, their choices are usually traditional to their sex.

(3) Young women in grades K–8 seem attracted to careers atypical of their sex (medicine, law, business, art, law enforcement); but by the time they reach high school, their interests are more traditional. According to the survey, there were no career choices for young men at either the middle or high-school levels atypical of their sex.

(4) Counselors indicate that they provide the same kind of information to both sexes. However, many mentioned that they also alert students to obstacles or limitations they might encounter in working in a specific area.

In summary, although counselors may be willing to provide the same information to both sexes, students already have definite areas of interest that parallel their sex. Also, counselors may be expressing unconscious sex bias in mentioning obstacles and limitations of certain fields.

The major instrument used by the schools to help students determine career choices is the Ohio Vocational Interest Survey (OVIS). A close look at this test reveals a built-in sex bias.

Although the questionnaire is identical for both young men and women, there is a different interpretation of scoring for each sex. Out of twenty-four different job areas, five differentiate according to sex. These include care of people and animals, inspecting-testing, crafts and precise operations, training jobs, and sales representative. For example, only a man can be a bricklayer, heating engineer, or flying instructor; only a female can be a chief airline stewardess, charm-course instructor, or a buyer.

Thus, students scoring high in one particular area—crafts and precise operations, for example—are restricted to certain jobs.

RECOMMENDATIONS

(1) The counseling and guidance office should make a specific effort to recruit women as speakers. Although schools may be obligated to take speakers provided by business and industry, nothing precludes the counseling and guidance staff from expressing a preference for women. Also, the staff should compile a list of women speakers to complement the 3C's program. (The Women's Rights Committee has already started a drive to obtain names.)

(2) The counseling and guidance office should also make a specific effort to send speakers who work in areas atypical of their sex: females who are in law enforcement, business administration, science; men who are in cosmetology, social work, food service.

(3) All speakers should address mixed groups. Segregating sexes is flagrant bias.

(4) The counseling and guidance office should provide in-service training for counselors in techniques to eliminate sex bias in vocational counseling to promote a wider choice of careers for young people.

(5) Supervisors of career motivation (K–6), career exploration (7–8), and career orientation (9–10), have attempted to provide equal opportunities for all students to investigate many areas of work. Their efforts could be strengthened by in-service training for teachers who carry out the programs and by a review of materials in light of sex bias.

(6) All testing material related to vocational guidance, including the Ohio Vocational Interest Survey, should be reevaluated. If evidence of sex bias is found, the counseling and guidance staff should contact the publisher of the test and request elimination of the bias.

OBJECTIVE 5: TEXT AND TRADE BOOKS ARE SCREENED WITH THE GOAL OF PROVIDING SCHOOLS WITH MATERIALS THAT PRESENT THE CONTRIBUTIONS OF WOMEN IN AN UNBIASED MANNER AND ARE FREE FROM SEX STEREOTYPES

Several studies on the representation of females in text and trade books have been conducted across the country. One study of 2,760 stories in 134 books revealed the following:

(1) For every six biographies of males, there was one of a female.

(2) Ration of boy-centered to girl-centered stories was five to two.

(3) Adult-male character stories outnumbered those of adult-female three to one.

(4) The image portrayed by females was seldom accurate. Initiative, strength, bravery, and cleverness were traits shown primarily by males.

(5) Careers for young women were limited to teaching, nursing, clerical, and motherhood, while those for young men were more varied.[3]

Another study of twelve American history textbooks (including *The Adventure of the American People* used in Dayton schools), revealed that many women of importance were omitted while the cultural, legal, and social disabilities they faced were minimized.

This author concludes that "the treatment of women simply reflects the attitudes and perjudices of society,"[4] so women are slighted because male activities are considered more important, just as minority groups are slighted.

To see if the conclusions of these studies apply to books used in Dayton schools, the committee examined a number of texts:

SCIENCE

An examination of the illustrations in eight elementary science books revealed the following disproportionate figures:

Basic Science 1
(Harper & Row, 1963)

Male	181
Female	68
Male occupations	12
Female occupations	2
Minority groups	0

Basic Science 5 (continued)

Female occupations	8
Minority groups	3

(Three Polynesians are the only nonwhites in this book.)

Basic Science 6
(Harper & Row, 1963)

Basic Science 2
(Harper & Row, 1963)

Male	185
Female	108
Male occupations	12
Female occupations	4
Minority groups	0

Basic Science 3
(Harper & Row, 1963)

Male	190
Female	59
Male occupations	13
Female occupations	4
Minority gsoups	0

Basic Science 4
(Harper & Row, 1963)

Male	183
Female	62
Male occupations	22
Female occupations	3
Minority groups	0

Basic Science 5
(Harper & Row, 1963)

Male	217
Female	81
Male occupations	24

Male	167
Female	37
Male occupations	15
Female occupations	1
Minority groups	4

(One Oriental, two Indians, and one dark-skinned fisherman are the only nonwhites in the book.)

Science You Can Use 7
(Prentice-Hall, Inc., 1961)

Male	116
Female	75
Male occupations	8
Female occupations	2
Minority groups	8

(Two youths listed as brown-and yellow-skinned, two Arabs on a flying carpet, and four Indians weighing an elephant are the only nonwhites in the book.)

Science in Action 8
(Prentice-Hall, Inc., 1964)

Male	51
Female	7
Male occupations	4
Female occupations	1
Minority groups	0

In these eight books, females are seen in thirteen occupations as compared to 110 for males. This supports the statement that "the school shares a responsibility for the diminished aspirations of its female student."[5]

READING

The following reading books were found to contain a disproportionate number of male-centered, majority group stories and poems featuring illustrations of males.

Roads to Everywhere—4
(Ginn & Co., 1961)

Male-centered stories	24
Female-centered stories	3
Male-illustrated poems	9
Female-illustrated poems	0

(One woman is included with thirteen men in "A Nation's Strength.")

Minority group main character	6

(Oriental, Indian, Costa Rican, North African Arab)

Trails to Treasure—5
(Ginn & Co., 1961)

Male-centered stories	30
Female-centered stories	6
Male-illustrated poems	10
Female-illustrated poems	0
Minority group main character	2

(Indian, Mexican-American)

Wings to Adventure—6
(Ginn & Co., 1961)

Male-centered stories	28
Female-centered stories	6
Male-illustrated poems	2
Female-illustrated poems	1
Minority group main character	2

(Indian, Mexican-American)

Adventure Bound—7
(Houghton Mifflin, 1961)

Male-centered stories	45
Female-centered stories	10
Male-illustrated poems	12
Female-illustrated poems	3
Minority group main character	9

(Berber, Mexican, Indian, Lebanese, African, Chinese, Arabian, Polynesian)

Journeys into America—8
(Houghton Mifflin, 1961)

Male-centered stories	42
Female-centered stories	8
Male-illustrated poems	20
Female-illustrated poems	0
Minority group main character	4

(Egyptian, Indian, Arabian, Japanese)

LITERATURE

The following figures reveal the disparity between the number of male and female authors included in representative literature books.

Adventures in Appreciation—9
(Harcourt, Brace, & World, Inc., 1967)

Male authors	55
Female authors	4

Perspectives—10
(Scott, Foresman, & Co., 1963)

Male authors	41
Female authors	12

Accent: U.S.A.—11
(Scott, Foresman, & Co., 1965)

Male authors	41
Female authors	7

The Idea of Man—12
(Harcourt, Brace, & World, Inc., 1967)

Male authors	28
Female authors	1

SOCIAL STUDIES

The following comparison of the number of men and women cited in representative social-studies textbooks supports the study cited earlier.

You and Regions Near and Far—4
(Benefic Press, 1969)

Men	7
Women	0

Geography—United States and Canada—5
(D. C. Heath, & Co., 1966)

Men	80
Women	2

You and the Americans—6
(Benefic Press, 1967)

Men	90
Women	4

You and the World—7
(Benefic Press, 1966)

Men	142
Women	7

The Free and the Brave—8
(Rand McNally, 1967)

Men	340
Women	6

A Global History of Man—10
(Allyn & Bacon, 1966)

Men	207
Women	6

The Adventure of the American People—11

Men	640
Women	41

The Challenge of Democracy—12
(Webster Division, McGraw-Hill Book Co., 1966)

Men	145
Women	5

RECOMMENDATIONS

Stereotyping such as that found in the textbooks surveyed must be eliminated. Materials must, as urged in Scott, Foresman's *Guidelines for Improving the Image of Women in Textbooks,* "more accurately represent reality, encourage tolerance for individual differences, and allow more freedom for children to discover and express their needs, interests, and abilities."[6]

To promote the use of nonstereotypic materials, the following recommendations are offered:

(1) The committee examined only a few of the textbooks used in Dayton schools. All others should be screened for sex bias and stereotyping and those blatantly sexist should be removed from the approved list of texts.

(2) Amend *Process for Curriculum Development Committees* by adding the following statement to Item 14, which refers to "suitable material," but does not define the word "suitable."

> The material conforms to the following guidelines, adapted from the Ohio Department of Education's *Multi-cultural Materials: A Guide to the Selection of Curriculum Material for Schools in a Pluralistic Society* (January 1969), and from Scott, Foresman's *Guidelines for Improving the Image of Women in Textbooks* (1972).

(a) The subject matter is approached in a scholarly and realistic manner, and materials about women and minorities, chosen for their relevance, are woven into the fabric of the book or other instructional media.

(b) The achievements of women and of various minority groups in fields such as politics, the sciences, and the arts are recognized.

(c) Both illustrations and content clearly indicate that the United States is a pluralistic nation.

(d) Women, as well as the various cultures, races, and ethnic groups, are portrayed in a manner that will help develop understanding, respect, empathy, and acceptance.

(e) Conflict situations are honestly and objectively presented with the emphasis on possible solutions to intergroup tensions.

(f) The material avoids stereotypic distortions—ethnic, racial, religious, and sexual—in content and illustrations. Abilities, traits, interests, and activities are not assigned on the basis of such stereotypes.

(g) The material reflects the basic philosophy of a democratic society as it relates to civil rights and intergroup relations.

(h) The material reflects respect for personal and cultural differences and the worth and importance of the individual.

(i) The material is designed to help students understand, appreciate, and develop democratic values.

(Copies of this revision should be sent to all publishers with which the schools do business.)

(3) To aid in the selection and utilization of nonstereotypic materials, in-service training for librarians, media-center teachers, and media-center aides must be provided. In addition, materials such as the following bibliography should be purchased for each library and learning-center teacher or director.

Feminists on Children's Media, comp. *Little Miss Muffet Fights Back: Recommended Non-sexist Books About Girls for Young Readers.* New York: Feminists on Children's Media, 1971.

(4) To aid educators in developing understanding of the women's rights movement, materials should be purchased for the professional section of each library and learning center.

(5) Omission of women occurs in audio-visual material as well as in text-

books. Of 88 biographical films in the *Instructional Materials Catalog for Secondary Schools,* 81 subjects are men and only 7 are women. It is recommended that more audio-visual materials reflecting the roles of women be purchased.

OBJECTIVE 6: WOMEN'S STUDIES ARE INCORPORATED INTO THE CURRICULUM AND THAT BOTH YOUNG MEN AND WOMEN ARE PRESENTED WITH OPPORTUNITIES TO EXPAND THEIR LEVELS OF AWARENESS

All students in Dayton schools need to gain a clear perspective of women in history, the role of women today, new concepts of masculinity and femininity, the potential of women, the relationship between men and women, and related topics. This objective can be achieved by the following:

RECOMMENDATIONS

(1) Teachers at all grade levels and in all subjects should incorporate the achievement and contributions of women into their studies. Their efforts should be aided by in-service training.

(2) All high schools should offer a separate mini-course that would examine the role and contributions of women historically and in present-day society. (Currently a group of high-school teachers and one student are developing a nine-week course entitled "Women in American History," which will be piloted second semester of the 1973–74 school year.)

FUTURE OF THE WOMEN'S RIGHTS COMMITTEE

Although much has been accomplished during this past year, the committee has a strong commitment to follow through on its responsibilities. The group sees itself:

(1) Helping to implement the recommendations of Report A and Report B.

(2) Functioning as a monitoring agency alert to sex bias and discrimination within the schools.

(3) Assisting in planning and conducting in-service training for staff.

(4) Serving as liaison with community agencies in matters of sex discrimination and stereotyping.

COMMITTEE MEMBERS

Mary Arnold
Jean Booker
Theresa Brytus
Nancy Brown
Ronald Jones
Margaret Peters
Dale Van Tine

Joyce Kaser, Chairperson

NOTES

1. National Organization for Women, *Report on Sex Bias in the Public Schools* (N. Y.: National Organization for Women, 1971).
2. Extraduty includes all extra assignments, most of which are in athletics.
3. Ann McFeatters, "Beautiful Princess Gone From Children's Books," *Rocky Mountain News,* 12 April 1973.
4. Janice Law Trecker, "Women in U.S. History High-school Textbooks," *Social Education* 35 (March 1971) : 260.
5. Ibid., p. 250.
6. Sexism in Textbooks Committee of Women at Scott, Foresman, and Company, *Guidelines For Improving The Image of Women In Textbooks* (Glenview, Ill.: Scott, Foresman, and Company, 1972), p. 40.

QUESTIONNAIRE ON SEX BIAS AND STEREOTYPING IN ELEMENTARY SCHOOLS

Are all the activities in your school geared to eliminate sexist overtones? Please answer the following questions and return by April 13.

1. Are there extracurricular activities for only boys, only girls, or both?

Traffic patrol ________	Flag patrol ________
Hall duty ________	Door duty ________
Chair setup ________	Teacher helper ________
Student store ________	Volleyball team ________
Baseball ________	Basketball ________
Track ________	Gymnastics ________
Audio-visual ________	Learning-center aides ________
Pages ________	Office helpers ________
Hosts ________	Yard duty ________
Cheerleaders ________	Hockey ________
Fire patrol ________	Chess club ________

Tutors ______________ Chorus ______________
Choir ______________ Pep club ______________
Clean-up committee ______________ Other ______________ (Name)
Speech ______________

2. Are there any activities in the classroom that are restricted to males or females except restroom usage? If so, please list.

____

____

3. Are students separated by sex for any of the following:
In line ______________ Seating ______________
Practical Arts ______________ Home Economics ______________
Gym ______________ Entering and/or
Moving furniture ______________ leaving a room ______________
Washing boards ______________ Carrying things ______________
Grading papers ______________

4. Do you have any areas in your texts that seem blatantly sexist. If so, please list text title, author, publisher, and pages.

____

____

____

5. Are there any particular practices in your school that seem to be sex oriented? Please list.

____

____

____

6. Do you use materials that show women in other than the typical role of housewife, cook, laundress, head-patter?

____

____

7. Do you use materials that depict men in roles of human warmth: cooking, nursing, showing emotion, holding a baby?

____

____

8. In what nonstereotyped roles are women depicted in your materials?

____

____

9. Do you or your fellow teachers tell pupils that some activities are only or especially for boys or for girls?

____

____

10. THANKS for answering this.

FROM: ______________
(Your school)

____

VOCATIONAL COUNSELING SURVEY

Name (optional) ________________________ School K–5 K–8 6–8 9–12

1. The average number of girls counseled at your school during a week's time. __________
2. The average number of boys counseled at your school during a week's time. __________
3. The average number of self-referrals for personal problems during a week's time. boys ________ girls ________
4. The average number of individual students who request information on vocations or careers during a week's time. boys ______ girls ______
5. The average number of individual students who are referred by someone other than themselves. boys ________ girls ________
6. List by order of frequency the reason for referral. 1. discipline, 2. vocational guidance, 3. personal problems

boys	girls
__________	__________
__________	__________
__________	__________

7. List the three vocational areas that girls in college preparatory programs seem to be most interested in when interviewing.

   __________ __________ __________

   (list others if you feel it is necessary)
8. List the three vocational areas that boys in college preparatory programs seem to be most interested in when interviewing.

   __________ __________ __________

   (list others if you feel it is necessary)
9. List the three vocational areas that girls not in college preparatory programs seem to be most interested in when interviewing.

   __________ __________ __________

   (list others if you feel it is necessary)
10. List the three vocational areas that boys not in college preparatory programs seem to be most interested in when interviewing.

    __________ __________ __________

    (list others if you feel it is necessary)
11. When interviewing students about careers, what options do you provide?
    a. Vocational areas that are generally related to careers of their sex.
    b. Vocational areas that are not related to careers of their sex but fit their interest.
12. Please comment:
    A girl comes to you requesting information in the medical field. She

has a very high academic ability. What information would you provide for her?

What would you say to a boy?

13. Please comment:

    A boy requests information on careers in clothing design. He is an excellent artist. What information would you provide for him?

    What would you say to a girl?

Governor's Commission on the Status of Women* Task Force on Education Report Commonwealth of Massachusetts

BLANCHE FITZPATRICK

When Governor Sargent established the Commission on the Status of Women, he expressed his commitment to the full development of the potential of each Massachusetts citizen, both as a basic right, and as essential to the economic development of the Commonwealth. The Task Force on Education, in carrying out the Governor's charge, conceived its role to be twofold:.

> First, to encourage in a girl or woman a sense of unlimited aspiration—the confidence to follow educational paths to any career to which she is attracted.

* Blanche Fitzpatrick, "Report of the Task Force on Education, Governor's Commission on the Status of Women, Commonwealth of Massachusetts." Reprinted with the permission of the Governor's Commission on the Status of Women, Commonwealth of Massachusetts, and Blanche Fitzpatrick.

Second, to open up opportunities in the field of education for women—to remove any discriminatory practices that set a limit to achievement as student, faculty, or member of the administration.

The basic Task Force study was directed to both academic and vocational areas, including a sample of public-school systems, colleges, universities, and professional schools, as well as business, trade, and technical schools. (*See* sample and methodology right after notes.) Although studies have been made in recent years of the status of women in individual schools and school systems, we believe that there has been no overall assessment of opportunities for vocational and academic education for an entire state. This study thus makes a modest beginning in the direction of setting forth the total options open to a woman within a limited political sphere. This in turn makes possible appropriate political action to remedy discrimination or other practices that hinder the full development of all citizens and the economic development of the state.

The major findings of the study are given in the section immediately following: supporting data and expanded discussion of these points will be found in the body of the report.

SUMMARY OF FINDINGS

The Task Force on Education has found that girls and women are not given equal educational opportunities with boys and men in Massachusetts's schools, colleges, and universities, both public and private, as students, faculty, and administrators.

Finding Number 1: Public Schools

In public education below the college level, although student bodies are almost universally coeducational, with roughly equal numbers of boys and girls, higher level administrators and faculty are overwhelmingly male. Thus girls are provided with few female-role models to encourage aspiration to a variety of occupations. Curriculum distinctions, and texts in use have served to weaken girls' confidence in their abilities, in sports, manual skills, and mathematics and physical sciences.

Expenditures for boys' sports outrun similar expenditures for girls' sports by ratios as high as 100:1, with dollar differentials as high as $150,000 per year. Women faculty receive lower salary increments than their male counterparts for identical sports with differentials up to $1,000 per year among male and female basketball coaches.

Despite the passage in 1971 of chapter 622 forbidding discrimination by sex in Massachusetts schools, at least 25% of responding schools in the sample replied that both sexes were not admitted to all courses; even where no administrative prohibition was reported, shop classes were largely male, and home-economics classes largely female.

Finding Number 2: Colleges and Universities—Undergraduates

Although numbers of boys and girls in high-school graduating classes are roughly equal, only 1/3 of the enrollment in Massachusetts universities are women. It is understood that universities because of size, endowment, or budgetary allotments, can offer a wider range of courses, better libraries, more fully equipped laboratories, greater opportunity and incentive to students for continuing on to graduate or professional studies. Yet Massachusetts girls are channeled to state colleges, where they constitute 2/3 of the enrollment. Despite highly competent and dedicated faculty at these institutions, lack of facilities effectively narrows vocational choices for young women undergraduates to public schoolteaching, and opportunities for advanced study are extremely slight.

Finding Number 3: Universities—Graduate and Professional Study

In admission to advanced study, young women again fare worse, since so few have a background of university undergraduate education, an important factor in admission to graduate study. Few women aspire, and even fewer are accepted to graduate study; only about 26% of all graduate students in Massachusetts, on a full-time basis, were women. Similarly, of first professional degrees conferred by Massachusetts institutions, 1969–70, women received only 5% in law; 8% in medicine; 8% in architecture; and in other fields, women recipients were a similarly low percentage.

Yet women presented slightly higher undergraduate records than did men applicants to graduate study in 1971, according to a few fields reported by responding institutions to Task Force questionnaires; on Graduate Record Examinations, men scored slightly higher. Greater correlation has been found between undergraduate grade averages and performance in graduate school than for any other indicator.

Finding Number 4: Trade and Technical School

In the area of high-school or post-high-school vocational education, there are few places for women. In the newly built, highly modern regional vocational schools, there are more than four times as many places for men as for women. In the terminal-occupational courses in Massachusetts Community Colleges, there are about 40% more places for men; there are four times as many places for boys in vocational schools linked with high schools. Only in the business courses did women predominate, by a 4 to 1 ratio. Thus girls are being trained for the relatively low-paid jobs in which women have always predominated.

Finding Number 5: Faculty and Administrative Positions—Colleges and Universities

Most high-level administrative positions, and top-ranking faculty positions are held by men. This serves to waste the potential of those women who have persevered through graduate school, and further inhibits the aspiration of the next generation of women students.

Possible Explanations for Second-Class Status of Women in the Field of Education

Massachusetts has a long and proud history in the field of education, with a claim to the first public school, the first college, and many other notable achievements. If it appears, then, that Massachusetts is not offering equal educational opportunities to its girls and women, it is necessary to investigate possible reasons for these inequities. Several hypotheses can be offered to explain differential treatment of the sexes:

A.

The first, and most appealingly simplistic explanation, is that when girls are compared to boys, or women to men, the former are inferior with respect to intelligence, manual dexterity, physical strength, or other qualities needed in studies or employment.

B.

A second possibility is that the females are equal in ability to males, but do not try to achieve success because of social constraints, poor image, or lack of female-role models.

C.

Another possibility is that the females are equal in ability, do in fact try to achieve success, but are barred by discriminatory practices.

D.

A final possibility to be considered (more could probably be advanced) is that society, through the state, explicitly accepts discriminatory practices in the educational system because girls and women do not "need" academic or vocational education as much as do boys and men. This explanation assumes that women will be provided for throughout their lives by father or husband or son, and will not need to provide for themselves or anyone else.

Any or all of the above possible explanations of differential education offered to the sexes may be accepted by many men and women of the Commonwealth who elect the members of the school committee and the legislators who control school budgets, or legislate tax exemption and grant policies. But especially in an area so fundamental as education, we must not accept ideas from the past without testing their validity. Is there evidence to support these explanations? A remark by President Kennedy at the 1962 Yale commencement is appropriate here:

> "The great enemy of the truth is very often not the lie—deliberate, contrived, and dishonest—but the MYTH, persistent, persuasive, and unrealistic. Too often we hold fast to the clichés of our forebears. We subject all facts to a prefabricated set of interpretations. We enjoy the comfort of opinion without the discomfort of thought."

In the light of that quotation, we must search for evidence or discard the explanations listed above—some of them may indeed be myths whose day is past. The average Massachusetts citizen and taxpayer has little time to spare from his working day to investigate the philosophy and operations of the state's educational system. The Task Force on Education has applied itself to investigate these statements, to discover any available evidence, and to present these findings in the report that follows:

Where is the evidence that girls are inferior to boys with respect to intelligence?

> "There is no difference in intellectual development; there is complete equality between boys and girls." Jean Piaget[1]

With respect to the belief that boys are naturally brighter than girls, or "catch up" and surpass after a slower start in the elementary grades, we could find no objective proof. What evidence there is of objective performance as measured by grades, in fact, seems to imply the contrary. Psychological testing as summed up by Maccoby has found there is no conclusive proof that either sex is superior.[2] Piaget, one of the most eminent of current students of child development, finds no difference in intellectual development, as quoted above.

It was not possible to obtain comparative achievement test scores of boys and girls in Massachusetts schools since sex classifaction has been eliminated to avoid the appearance of discrimination, according to Mr. Clement Perkins of the Massachusetts Department of Education Research Division. It is also alleged that Horace Mann, first among Massachusetts notable educators, did not require that schools keep records on girls' attendance or grades, since they were deemed uneducable. More boys than girls "drop out" before high-school graduation, but this may well reflect boys' greater independence, culturally accepted, and dissatisfaction with institutionalized learning. Nevertheless, the major argument used by opponents of equal admission to Boston Latin on the basis of test scores was that Boston Latin would then have a majority of girls.[3]

In applications for entrance to Massachusetts State Colleges, the median secondary-school grades of women who were admitted was about 50 points higher than for men,[4] although this may only reflect discriminatory admissions to Massachusetts universities.

In applications for entrance to graduate school, only a few fields were reported on by the institutions responding to the Task Force questionnaire (Form 2). In those fields reported, however, women applicants slightly surpassed men in thirty-one fields in undergraduate grade-point average, did equally well in five fields, and less well in three fields. (Table 17) On the Graduate Record Exam, in a similarly small group of scores reported, men surpassed women by a slight margin in twenty-four instances, and were lower in twelve instances. (Table 18)

Universities were apparently unwilling to report on scores at the professional level (law, medicine, etc.). However, the Dean of the Harvard Law School reported that women on the average presented slightly better undergraduate grades, while men did slightly better on the preprofessional examinations.[5]

Thus, at all age levels, available data suggests that relative academic performances of girls and boys, men and women, do not differ significantly. Moreover, the differences within each sex, between the brightest boy or girl, and the dullest of the same sex, is much greater than the differences between the sexes.

Intelligence and achievement measured by school grades and examination scores is not the only relevant characteristic to be looked at when considering the investment of state funds in the educational area. In vocational education, an aptitude for mechanical problems and manual dexterity, as well as physical strength may be required. Is it worth while, or even possible to train girls and women in technical and trade occupations?

To quote Piaget once more, girls on the average made a poorer showing on his tests in mechanical problems. Piaget commented, "I never saw any reason for this retardation except for lack of interest. I can't imagine any other explanations."[6] To account for this lack of interest by girls would involve recapitulation of the entire socialization process whereby the female child is given dolls and dishes while the male is given trucks and chemistry sets. Suffice it to say that those girls with requisite interests may be presumed equally competent in mechanical operations. The Bureau of Apprentice Training of the U.S. Department of Labor in 1970 reported women apprentices placed in over 100 skilled occupations ranging from auto mechanic to universal equipment operator. Over 1,800 women were in registered apprentice programs in 1970, working as plumbers, operating engineers, shipfitters, aircraft mechanics, and machinists.[7]

A.

The question of physical strength is also important in assessing the ability of women to enter into technical and trade occupations, even in a push-button age of automated technology. Although some girls are much weaker physically than the average boy of the same age, some are stronger, as indicated by the recent women's Olympic Teams. Again, the range of physical strength between the strongest and weakest boys is greater than the variation in physical strength between boys and girls of average abilities. It is possible for some women to choose occupations that require physical abilities not possessed by all women.

Thus, it does not appear from available evidence that women are inferior in physical or mental abilities required to pursue either academic or vocational studies. Yet the study by the Task Force on Education found women to be only a small minority of the skilled trades, in graduate study, of the professions. Can the explanation be lack of aspiration?

B.

What is the evidence that women, although equal in ability to men, do not try to achieve success because of social constraints, poor self-image, or lack of female-role models?

"It's easy. Even I can do it. And you know how stupid I am!"[8]

A recent unpublished study of toys at one of the larger children's-goods stores in the Boston area emphasized the difference in toys designed to be purchased for boys or girls, that is showing pictures of boys or girls on the cover or instructions or toy itself. The girls' toys were adult life-models, dolls and dishes, carpet sweepers and carriages; boys' toys were trains, trucks, chemistry sets, often electrically- or battery-powered, which can be worked with, or taken apart, to foster curiousity about mechanical and physical problems.[9]

If as Montessori believed, the child is working in his play, "making himself," the girls have less to work with, and are constrained to make themselves into wives and mothers. Boys' toys foster creative and skill development. A recent study showed that both boys and girls, given a choice, select male activities and toys up to about the fifth grade.[10]

Trade books and texts alike further the concept of girls as weaker, more timid, less physically and mentally capable than the male counterparts in children's stories.[11] The Caldecott Medal winners in the past five years show a ratio of 7:2 of male to female characters. Boys are shown in exciting and adventurous activities, in a variety of tasks. "Not one of the women in the recent Caldecott sample has a job or profession. At a very early age, then, children are being taught that boys grow up to act and do, while women grow up to serve, have children, and be feminine."[12]

The Task Force is in the process of analyzing children's trade books and readers used in Massachusetts schools. Publishers' response to questionnaires indicate recognition of this problem.[13] At the college level, a study of freshmen English essay anthologies has been made by the Task Force, reflecting both inadequate treatment of women as subject, and a predominance of male editors (related to higher faculty status).[14]

A 1971 study of violence on children's television programs noted also that few women were present.[15] A Task Force member who had participated in that study undertook an analysis of the content of TV commercials, news, and entertainment programs with respect to presentation of women. The image of women in monitored programs reflected the stereotype of the female. The women appearing in TV programs were frequently only shown, while an authoritative male voice-over explained the virtues of the product; such women appear to have no thoughts or problems not associated with cleaner laundry or personal charm. In entertainment programs women are usually shown in a number of subordinate roles as secretary, wife, or maid, while men on the programs are doctors, teachers, U.S. marshals. The only women appearing on the newscasts monitored were: a murdered nurse; a captive bride; a young tennis star.[16]

Thus, stereotypes of not-too-bright females are presented throughout the formative years, through a variety of media. The stereotypes presented in school texts and illustrations weaken the confidence and interest of girls in scientific studies and mechanical problems, as well as participation in sports. By showing only boys as protagonists in adventures, by frequent textual disparagement of girls' mental and physical abilities, the girl is led to narrow her options to fields in which she may excel because few boys will compete —i.e., home economics, English, good behavior.

Moreover, the Task Force study of the distribution of faculty and administration of the public-school systems of the state serve to reinforce the concept of male leaders and female followers. The sample of school systems surveyed revealed no woman superintendents of schools (the one woman among 351 Massachusetts cities and towns did not appear in the sample); only 6% of the high-school principals were women; 9% of the assistant and associate superintendents were women. (See Table 13.) Similar distribution of upper ranks of faculty and administration are found at the college and university level. (*See* Table 15.) Among the 9 private universities, there is no woman president. Among the 35 private four-year colleges, 6 (all women's colleges) were headed by women, 4 of whom are members of a religious order. Of the 19 two-year colleges, including 8 women's colleges, none are headed by a woman. There is no woman president at any of the state-run colleges or universities, and the administration generally follows suit.

Preliminary findings of a study of Massachusetts guidance counselors, who are themselves frequently graduates of Massachusetts schools and colleges, indicated that both male and female counselors admit to some feelings of ambivalence with regard to counseling girls to aspire to nontraditional fields and professions.[17] Another Task Force study, directed to school committee chairmen, reveals a dearth of female selections for higher administrative posts.[18]

Even with respect to use of athletic equipment and facilities, girls are conditioned to accept the fact that gymnasium and playing fields will only be made available to girls when the boys do not need them. In the Task Force sampling of school systems, half the women faculty coaches receive less than 2/3 the increments of male coaches in the same sport, basketball. (Table 11.) Only one school system reported spending as much as $10,000 on girls' sports in 1971 yet 80% of the sample reported spending over $10,000 on boys' sports. (Table 10.)

After a student lifetime in the educational system now in force in Massachusetts, it would be surprising if many young women emerged with confidence in their ability to complete with young men in physical or intellectual competition. A recent study indicated that "from elementary school through college, females have comparably lower expectancies about their intellectual and academic accomplishments than males do, despite the fact that their performances are typically as good or better than those of their male counterparts."[19]

Despite the passage of chapter 622 forbidding discrimination in admission to all classes in Massachusetts public schools, response to the Task Force questionnaire indicates little affirmative action to encourage both sexes to enroll in shop classes and home-arts classes. (Table 9.) Thus, while the girls are "protected" by school and society from difficult or dangerous situations, their skills and self-confidence in ability to handle mechanical problems are correspondingly diminished. Yet when the Task Force queried school departments and colleges in other states, it was learned that several have introduced "Education for Living" courses that prepare both sexes for practical aspects of operating and maintaining a variety of mechanical and electrical appliances and equipment.[20] Under the present Massachusetts system in practice, young girls have no opportunity to discover their own interests and skill in areas leading to future jobs in the skilled trades.

C.

What evidence can be found of explicit discrimination against women in education?

"Bok Calls for 2.5 to 1 Ratio in Undergraduate Admissions."[21] The limitations discussed in sections A and B above do not always imply discrimination against women per se. If in most school systems eighth-grade girls are automatically enrolled in a cooking class, it does not seem to reflect a conscious design to prepare all women for lives as cooks, but the persistance of the wisdom of an age that has disappeared. It was true as recently as 50 years ago that there was little opportunity for women to work outside the home; most women would marry and have several children, with neither funds nor public facilities to assist in caring for these children. In these circumstances, the ability to cook was probably the most essential skill a woman could possess, and in many cases a source of satisfaction as one of the few creative acts possible in a daily round of cleaning, washing, and making do. But it is in major vocational and academic areas going far beyond the outmoded division of boys and girls into shop and cooking classes that discrimination has been found by the Task Force on Education within the Massachusetts system. Girls and women do not receive an equal education in terms of dollars spent, courses provided, or higher educational opportunities offered; women faculty and administration are concentrated at lowest ranks, at salaries below male counterparts.

One of the curious and unexpected findings of the toy study referred to above was that the great majority of expensive ($15 or more) toys and games were illustrated by pictures of boys on the cover and instructions. This could be explained by the different material costs or technological equipment required for a model railroad as compared to a doll or cooking set. But, given the inclination of toymakers, like other businessmen, to maximize profits, it is more likely that this indicates that adults, even equally loving parents, are less willing to purchase expensive toys for girls. There is a subconscious acceptance that items that may be "good enough" for a girl, will not suffice for a boy.

Is the same principle operative in evidence that the new handsomely equipped regional vocational-technical schools have been designed primarily for the education of young men? There are four times as many places for men as women in these schools. (Table 2.) Vocational training for women continues mainly in aging high schools. There are almost 50% more places for men in the occupational courses in the Massachusetts community college system. There are four times as many places for boys as for girls in vocational schools tied-in with high schools. Only in business courses do girls predominate, in a 4 to 1 ratio. *Total* places for men in vocational training in Massachusetts public schools are almost three times in number the places for women.

Within the vocational program, men are enrolled in technical and trade programs—automotive repair, sheet metal, carpentry, welding; these programs will lead to well-paid jobs in skilled trades. Women are enrolled in secretarial programs, while men are enrolled in "administrative and management" programs. Women are enrolled in health-technician programs, men in data-processing. (Table 3.) As the Bureau of Labor Statistics pointed out in its projection of "manpower demands" in the 1970s, half of all women workers were employed in only 21 occupations in 1969; for men, half of all workers were employed in 65 occupations.[22] This concentration reinforces and exacerbates the low wages traditionally associated with women's work, since there are too many trained for the same field. It is at this level of vocational training that social distinction between girls' and boys' roles becomes the foundation for life-long income distinctions between men and women. "Women who work at full-time jobs the year round earn, on the average, only $3 for every $5 earned by similarly employed men."[23] Vocational training channels women into clerical and low-paid service work while men predominate as craftsmen, managers, and blue-collar workers.

In undergraduate education also, women are channeled into state colleges where they represent 2/3 of the enrollment, and discriminated against in admission to universities where they represent only 1/3 of the enrollment. The 1972 "Guide to Financial Admissions Information of the Massachusetts State College System" suggests to prospective applicants for each of the nine state colleges that they compare their high-school grade-point average with similar averages for those admitted to that college. An example is given for "Carol" who with a high-school G.P.A. of 2.8 would have a 50% chance for admission; but Tom, Dick, or Harry with the same 2.8 average would have an 81% chance of admission.[24] It is not the obvious discrimination that is most offensive; the reason that the girls' average so greatly outdistances that for boys is that the brighter boys, corresponding to the brighter girls, have applied and won admission to the universities, public or private. And the usual corollary also applies—tuition at the state colleges averages about $200, at the state university about $600, and at the private universities about $2,000.

Just as with the distribution of courses at the vocational schools, the state colleges' concentration on education courses leads to large numbers of graduates narrowly oriented to public schoolteaching. This is at present worsened by the declining demand for teachers, so that the system will turn out many more graduates with this specialty than the system can absorb, thus depressing salaries, or slowing increases, for those already in the field. When we compare the annual output of trained teachers, or nurses, to the tightly controlled output of doctors, we already have a partial explanation of salary differentials between these professional groups.

Even if the numbers are accepted, and discrimination admitted by the private colleges and universities (as Harvard explicitly states its ratio as 5:2) some may question the right of outsiders to insist on nondiscriminatory policies. These are *private* institutions; can the state interfere in undergraduate selection policies without destroying the quality of these institutions?

The excellence of Massachusetts private universities is not in question. But this very excellence, coupled with vigorous lobbying against competition by public institutions, has left Massachusetts with a very much smaller and weaker collection of state colleges and universities than is true of any other state in the union. Therefore, like the shoemaker's children who go without shoes, Massachusetts young women (and to some extent young men, since our excellent institutions attract a large out-of-state enrollment) go without high-level education, graduate study, and professional opportunity. Is this unfortunate situation then the responsibility of private enterprise?

The answer is that "private enterprise" in education, as in aircraft manufacture or railroad transportation, is somewhat of a myth, and growing more so daily, as the very hard-pressed private schools seek federal and state aid for financial survival. Education is a matter of fundamental concern to the state and nation; as such we cannot begrudge public assistance to the institutions that provide the education. This assistance takes many forms; property tax exemption; research grants; scholarship funds. Thus, the state or federal government already "interferes" with private enterprise in education to a considerable degree. Is it not reasonable that the taxpayer who provides the wherewithal have the right to insist on nondiscriminatory admissions policies? If private institutions forego tax-derived funds, they may admit whomever they please. But if they wish to administer the distribution of our tax monies, they must do so fairly. Sex-blind undergraduate admissions were defeated in the pending Higher Education Bill at the federal level as the result of strenuous lobbying by private universities and colleges. Our only remedy in Massachusetts where the private institutions constitute such an important sector of our total educational system, is to enact legislation at the state level ensuring equal-admissions policies. As Representative Green indicated, without equal admissions at the undergraduate level, nondiscriminatory policies at the graduate levels are meaningless.[25]

Admission applications to Harvard Law School, for example, are rated on a point scale depending on the excellence of the undergraduate school, and the record of previously admitted students from the same school. Because of a lack of major library facilities at the state colleges, it is unlikely that many of the young women graduates will think of applying to law school; but it is even more unlikely that they would be admitted.

Even setting aside the question of undergraduate preparations, there is evidently discrimination in admissions to the Harvard Law School. (The repeated use of Harvard is not intended to imply that Harvard is any more discriminatory in its graduate and professional admissions than many other private institutions in Massachusetts; its activities, however, are better publicized.) Total applications to Harvard Law were 6,170 in 1971, of whom women were 844 (13½%). Women admitted were 107, also 13½%.
"Our present policy with respect to women applicants is to try to treat them exactly on a par with male applicants. . . . We have . . . satisfied ourselves that in fact we admit virtually the same proportion of women applicants as of men applicants at every level of objective qualification. . . . Women applicants have a slight edge in undergraduate grades while men present slightly better LSAT scores—but on the whole these are minor."[26]

It is well that Harvard male administrators, faculty, and admissions committee have "satisfied themselves" that their admissions policies are fair. Certainly they probably strove to select the best of the women applicants. But of that self-selected group of young women applicants who rose above the limitations of societal discouragement and overt discrimination to apply to Harvard Law School, are not a very large proportion likely to do well? What is Harvard's responsibility for the situation when the President of the United States cannot nominate a woman for the Supreme Court because of the "small pool" of women lawyers from which to make a selection—and this most prestigious of the nation's law schools can only admit women at the level of 13% of its admissions? Especially since, according to Dr. Chase Peterson, Director of Admissions, the reason for increased applications to Harvard undergraduate status by women this year was that formerly women saw little chance of admission to the smaller Radcliffe?

To look at the other side of education, the lack of women at higher ranks of faculty and administration is true in Massachusetts as it is nationwide. A young woman student in Chemistry will not be inspired or emboldened to enter Ph.D. studies leading to college teaching if she observes no women faculty in her field, or finds them given only low rank and slow promotion. The lack of tenured women professors is an overt example of discrimination. Likewise the women faculty without representation as deans or college presidents find the route to advancement more difficult. (Tables 15, 20, 21, 22, 23, 24, 25).

Salaries for women at all faculty ranks are lower than for their male counterparts at both four-year colleges and universities. Since federal agencies, HEW and OFCC are moving only slowly to require equalization of salary schedules, and because the forthcoming Higher Education bill covers public institutions only, Massachusetts must take action to prevent discrimination in rank and salary against women faculty and administrators.

In other less widely recognized areas also, discrimination against certain groups of women, or ignorance of their needs, has hampered their educational progress. In some Massachusetts schools, because of grade-structure patterns in predominantly black schools, black girls are channeled into predominantly black high schools, where there is less emphasis on college preparatory courses and vocational training is limited to low-paid, semi-skilled trades.

The "Project Hope" report "Children in the Streets" using data compiled by Sister Francis Georgia estimates that almost half of Boston's Spanish-speaking school-age children are "out of school." Parents are handicapped by ignorance of opportunity for bilingual education; the inadequacy of bilingual programs in grades 7–12 also effectively limits opportunities for vocational training for skilled jobs, and destroys aspiration for college education.

For women in prison, also, educational opportunities are more restricted than for the average woman. Instruction at the Framingham Institution is provided by just one teacher from elementary through high-school levels; the woman offender must request permission from her social worker to attend classes, and must first complete work assignments for the day. (Of an average 280 inmates in 1971, school enrollment was 89). Study leading to the GED high-school equivalency diploma is hampered by the Department of Education rulings that no one under age 19 may receive a GED certificate. Since education would remove handicaps to employability, it might prevent return to old ways and habits. Thus, it is doubly unfortunate that resources allotted to education at women's institutions are so limited.[27]

D.
Women do not "need" education as much as male "breadwinners"

> "Women with some college education, both white and Negro, earn less than Negro men with 8 years of education. Women head 1,723,000 impoverished families. . . ."[28]

Even though evidence has been presented in the preceding sections that women are equally capable as men for training and education in a variety of fields; that women are hindered in aspiring to highly skilled and professional work by a poor self-image fostered by societal pressures, structured by school texts, curriculum pattern, and male leadership of the Massachusetts educational system; and that women are discriminated against in admission both to vocational schools and colleges and universities at undergraduate and graduate levels, yet another tired cliché may raise its head: Does a woman "need" the education as much as a man of similar ability? Is not the man the breadwinner? If we set aside for a moment the very important question of development of human potential, and look merely at the economic aspect, still we find only another hard-dying myth.

Nowhere is the general reluctance to accept the changing society more apparent than in the persistent myth that women work only for "pin money." It is still widely believed, flying in the face of recorded labor-force data, that a woman will work for only a few years after high school, will then marry, and will never again need to support herself or anyone else. But if we look at the evidence: according to the Department of Labor, married women in the past decade have been the fastest-growing component of the labor force. Of the 37 million women who worked at some time in 1968, 17% were widowed, divorced, or separated; many of these women were raising children in a fatherless home. Another 23% of women workers were single. An additional 30% had husbands present whose incomes were below $7,000, at a time when a low standard of living for a family of four was estimated at $6,567.[29] Thus about two-thirds of working women were supporting themselves and often children or other dependents as well.

Some families are well provided for by the earnings of husband and father; many are not. Since no woman can foresee her future status with respect to widowhood, divorce, or separation, in economic terms alone it is shortsighted for Massachusetts to restrict the educational opportunity and thus the earning power of women. The costly AFDC welfare program reflects in part the lack of training and opportunity for women.

The average working woman will spend twenty-five years in the labor force; over such a time span, women must have equal opportunity for advancement and adequate pay. Without academic or vocational education, women are effectively barred from achieving advancement.

RECOMMENDATIONS OF THE TASK FORCE ON EDUCATION

The studies of the Task Force on Education have demonstrated that women have the ability to pursue any field of training or education in which they are interested; that aspirations are discouraged by the differentiated curriculum and administrative and faculty structure of the Massachusetts public and private school system; that there exists discrimination against women in admission to private colleges and universities; that women faculty and administrators receive lower pay and rank than male colleagues; that women are not admitted in equal numbers to graduate and professional study, partly because they are not admitted to undergraduate status in universities; and finally that a Massachusetts woman will need all the education she can obtain in order to provide economic security for herself and other dependents throughout life. Therefore the Task Force on Education has made recommendations below for executive and legislative action to remedy the situation.

We believe the Massachusetts Governor and Legislature have been unaware of the unequal educational opportunity given to Massachusetts girls and women. Yet state fiscal practices, tax exemptions, grants and scholarship funds have permitted the creation of great inequality of places for women in vocational and academic education. It is asking too much of the seventeen-year-old high-school girl to expect her to cope with the institutionalized injustice of discriminatory admissions policies. Thus, the young woman is closed out of a variety of occupational fields before her working life has begun. Such young women may blame themselves for lack of diligence, or parents may blame themselves for excessive permissiveness, but the true fault lies with the Commonwealth itself. We cannot afford to make Ph.D.'s or tool-and-die makers of all our young people, nor would most high-school graduates wish to take those roads. What we can and must do, however, is to alter our entire educational structure, public and private, so that our scarce state funds may be allocated to the best advantage. We must insist that all our schools which benefit so greatly from tax exemptions, state scholarship funds, and other grants, perform the function for which the Commonwealth awards these funds and exemptions. That is, these institutions must educate the best qualified of our youth without discrimination as to sex.

1.

Discrimination in admission on account of sex should be forbidden to all institutions, public and private. Private institutions are granted tax exemptions by local government, and awarded grants, scholarship funds, and other financial aid in return for the service performed in educating young Massachusetts citizens. That service is not well performed when half the youthful population is denied equal access to educational opportunity.

2.

The Secretary of Educational Affairs should require affirmative action by Massachusetts educational institutions to ensure that numbers and percentages of women in administrative and faculty positions are increased. He should be empowered to require an annual report from all schools, colleges, and universities with respect to admissions by sex, and distribution by sex of faculty and administration; he should be granted authority to deny funds and tax exemptions to institutions that discriminate in admissions or hiring or promotion because of sex.

3.

The Massachusetts Commission Against Discrimination should be funded to permit enforcement of existing antidiscrimination legislation with respect to educational institutions in the area of sex bias in hiring, promotion, and salary policies.

4.

The Department of Education should develop a curriculum of Career Education, so that from the lowest grades young boys and girls will be aware of all occupational possibilities, and develop motivation toward career goals.

5.

The Massachusetts Department of Education should set up a separate school district, adequately funded, for those in custodial institutions, and should carry out a high-level, year-round program of academic and vocational education for inmates, to improve employability on release; should provide special instruction for women with learning disabilities.

6.

The Department of Education should assist local school districts in setting up a program of instruction from K–12 for both boys and girls, dealing with "Education for Living"—the maintenance of houses, household appliances, automobiles; as well as instruction in legal, medical, and other problems associated with the new age eighteen majority.

7.

The Department of Education should expand its activities in the area of Equal Educational Opportunity, to include an interest in women and girls; should seek out and encourage minority women to aspire to skilled and professional careers, and to persevere in education toward these goals; should increase its employment of black, Spanish-speaking, and minority women.

8.

The Massachusetts Department of Employment Security should continue and increase its programs for encouragement of women, particularly minority women, to enroll in vocational training.

9.

There are many other areas of concern to women that, for reason of lack of time and no funds, the Task Force was not able to investigate. We would, therefore, further recommend that the Massachusetts Department of Education set up a permanent committee on the changing role of women, which would be charged to: follow up efforts for legislative reform; look into creation of flexible curricula for women with family responsibilities; study and suggest texts and curriculum pattern to portray women in favorable light in public schools; take affirmative action to improve the percentage of women at top levels in the Department of Education; request M.A.C.E. to study the status of women in Massachusetts schools and institutions of higher education.

10.

The Governor's Commission on the Status of Women should be adequately funded to permit continuing studies of needs of women and to assure communication between interested groups and state administration and legislature.

11.

The Board of Education should be directed to assure the implementation of chapter 622 banning discrimination in Massachusetts schools on account of sex.

12.

The Department of Education should establish an information center to follow developments in education for women and disseminate information on financial resources available to independent study groups; should require schools and school districts to maintain records of students, faculty, and administration by sex, in order to identify inequities; establish a committee to make annual reports on action by state agencies with respect to hiring and promotion of women; provide for the dissemination to school systems and other interested persons the findings of the six task forces of the 1971–1972 Commission on the Status of Women.

Task Force on Education

Members
Blanche Fitzpatrick, Chairwoman
Kay Bourne
Argelia Hermenet
Carol Nadelson, M.D.
Barbara Solomon

Consultants
Ruth Bean
Barbara Beelar
Mildred Berman
Ruth Broder-Ennis
Janet Bryant
Helen Chin

Joanne Coakley
Velia DiCesare
Anna Hart
Ellen Jackson
Gail Kleven
Judith Leff
Mary Ness
Marion Rhodes
Carol Reines
Carol Springer
Rosemary Tobin
Carolyn Tribe
Rosemary Trowbridge

Sample and Methodology

Type of School	Number in State	Sampling Ratio	Number in Sample	Returns	Returns as %
[1] University	14	1:1	14	12	86%
Public	3*			3*	
Private	9			7	
Four-Year Colleges	44	1:3	14	14	100%
Public	9		3		
Private	35				
Women	13		4		
Coed	18		6		
Men	4		1		
Two-Year Colleges	34	1:3	11	9	82%
Public	15		5	5	
Private	19				
Women	11		3	3	
Coed	8		3	1	
Special Degree** Issuing	12	1:1	12	7	62%
Public	2			2	
Private	10			5	
Theology	9	1:1	9	1	11%
[2] Private Business Schools	31	1:1	10	6	60%
[3] Technical and Trade Schools					
[5] Public	11	1:1	11	6	55%
Private	58	1:3	20	11	55%

[4] Hospital School of Nursing	47	1:4	12	7	62%
[5] Public Schools	351				
Enr: 10,000 & +	20	1:1	20	16	80%
5,000–9,999	43	1:3	15	11	76
500–5,000	182	1:8	22	17	81
Nonops & Under 500	106				
Regionals	47	1:8	6	3	50+

* 5 locations ** Art, Maritime, Optometry, etc.

THE COMMONWEALTH OF MASSACHUSETTS
Governor's Commission On the Status Of Women

December 27, 1971

FRANCIS W. SARGENT
GOVERNOR

CHAIRMAN
ANN BLACKHAM

VICE CHAIRMAN
DOROTHY PENDERGAST

Gentlemen:

In order to employ all state resources to maximum advantage, as well as to ensure equal opportunity for development of all citizens, Governor Sargent last spring appointed a Commission to study the Status of Women in the Commonwealth. A Task Force on Education was set up within the Commission to look into this important area.

As part of the Task Force study, questionnaires are now being distributed to a sample of schools, colleges, and universities throughout the Commonwealth, in order to provide the Governor with factual data. Would it be possible for someone on your staff to respond on the attached forms as to the comparative numbers and status of men and women in your organization and student body? These data will be held in strict confidence and released only in aggregate form for the state as a whole. Completed questionnaires should be returned to Room 268, State House, Boston, as soon as possible (no later than January 20, 1972). Additional comments would be most welcome.

Thank you.

Sincerely,

Blanche Fitzpatrick
Chairwoman
Task Force on Education

Study: Status of Women in Education

INSTRUCTIONS: JUNIOR COLLEGES
COLLEGES
UNIVERSITIES

I. UNIVERSITIES, COLLEGES, JUNIOR COLLEGES:

Forms 1a and 1b	*Undergraduates.* Please provide requested data as of September 1971 for undergraduate schools and colleges in this institution.
1a Q 3A &B	The distinction between administrative and clerical positions should be made on the basis of your best judgment as to responsibilities and type of duties performed. A person who fills both administrative and faculty positions should be reported only *once,* in the area in which work time is primarily spent.
Form 2	*Graduate students.* Please provide requested data, by department for graduate enrollment in September 1971.
Form 3	*Professional Schools.* (LAW, MEDICINE, etc.) Please complete a separate Form 3 for each professional school within the institution.
	NOTE*:* With respect to faculty salary for the 1971–72 academic year, the median should be derived on the basis of the annual salaries contracted for, regardless of any Phase I or II adjustments. If this cannot easily be provided, please specify basis of figures.

II. COLLEGES, JUNIOR COLLEGES

Form 5 Q.3	Please supply requested data as to vocational courses offered. Since only a few representative occupations could be included on the form, it would be appreciated if you would note on the reverse of the form the three occupations of greatest enrollment in your institution, distributed by sex, for faculty and students.

Study: Status of Women in Education
INSTRUCTIONS: PUBLIC CITY/TOWN SCHOOL SYSTEMS
PUBLIC REGIONAL VOCATIONAL SCHOOLS

I PUBLIC SCHOOL SYSTEMS—Town/City:

Form 4 — Please supply requested data on Form 4.

Q 1-c — Please report data for faculty and administration of *academic* high school only.

Q.2 — If sports budgets can only be provided on calendar rather than academic year basis, please specify time perior used.

Form 5 — For those schools receiving Form 5, please provide requested data on vocational or industrial arts *high school only*.

II REGIONAL VOCATIONAL SCHOOLS

Form 5 Q.2 — Please supply requested data as to distribution of faculty, administration, and staff, by sex.

ALL SCHOOLS—Form 5

Form 5 Q.3 — Since only a few representative occupations could be included, it would be appreciated if you would note on the reverse of the form, the three occupations of greatest enrollment in your institution, distributed by sex, for faculty and students.

Study: Status of Women in Education

INSTRUCTIONS: Business Schools
Technical and Trade Schools

Form 5 Q.2 — Please supply requested data as to distribution of faculty, administration, and staff, by sex.

Q.3 — Since only a few representative occupations could be included, it would be appreciated if you would note on the reverse of the form, the three occupations of greatest enrollment in your institution, distributed by sex, for faculty and students.

Table 1

Academic Places For Women

Full-time Undergraduate Places For Women In Massachusetts
Four-year Colleges and Universities: 1970[1]

Type of Institution	*Numbers enrolled* *Men*	*Women*	*Women as % of Total*[2]
Universities			
Public	16,362	9,699	37.2%
Private	35,442	19,093	35.0%
Total	51,804	28,792	35.7%
Four-Year Colleges			
Public	9,315	16,226	63.5%
Private			
Men's (Rel. Affil)	2,408[3]		0
(Non-Relig)	3,424		0
Coed (Rel. Affil)	2,955	1,976	40.0%
(Non-Relig)	11,313	3,994	26.1%
Women (Rel. Affil)		4,513	100%[3]
(Non-Relig)		9,632	100%
Total	29,415	36,341	55.2%
TOTAL PLACES Universities and Four-Year colleges	81,219	65,133	44.6%

1. SOURCE: U.S. Office of Education: *Fall Enrollment 1970,* Institutional Data Table 1, pp. 30–32. Excludes specialized schools—theology, optometry, maritime, etc.
2. *See also,* Table 8.
3. Classified as Men's or Women's in *New England Board of Higher Education 1971–72 "Facts" Listing.* (Actually very small number of opposite sex in some of these institutions.)

Table 2

Vocational Places For Women

Total Enrollment In Public Vocational Schools and Terminal/Occupational Courses Public Two-Year Colleges: 1971

Type of School	*Total Enrollment*	
	Men	*Women*
Regional Vocational School[1]	6,926	1,583
Community College (Terminal/[2] Occupational Course)	5,241	3,673
Public High School[1]		
Vocational	15,671	3,496
Business[2]	442	1,736
	28,280	10,488

SOURCE:

1. Mass Dept. of Education, *Directory of Public Schools, Fall 1971,* computer runoff, untotaled.
2. Mass. Dept. of Education: Mr. Frank Merola, Research Division; these represent unedited rough totals from questionnaire returns by school officials.

Table 3

Types of Vocational Courses, By Sex

1971—Distribution of Course Offerings, By Sex—Community College[1] Terminal/Occupational

Type of Course (Selected courses)	*Enrollment*	
	Men	*Women*
01 Agriculture	32	
04 Distribution	253	142
07 Health Care and Dental Technician	135	1135
09 Home Economics	51	343
14 Office Occupations	2512	1906
Admin & Mngmnt.	1,200	177
Secretarial		1,300
Data Processing	462	
Accounting & Computer	729	
16 Technical & Trade	1,358	27
Law Enforcement	900	128
Other		
Total	7,632	5,158

Table 4

1971—Distribution Of Course Offerings, By Sex—Public Vocational Schools[1]

Type of Course (Selected courses)	*Enrollment* *Men*	*Women*
04 Distribution	36	25
07 Health Care	19	631
09 Home Economics	169	57
14 Office Occupations	245	351
16 Technical	183	28
Trade & Industry	8,222	664
Automotive		
Sheet Metal		
Carpentry		
Welding		
Other	600	
Total	9,474	1,756

1. SOURCE: Mass Dept. of Education; Mr. Frank Merola, Research Division; these represent unedited rough totals from questionnaire returns by school officials.

Table 5

Enrollment In Graduate Studies Full-time Students

Graduate Enrollments in Massachusetts Institutions of Higher Education: Full-time, 1970[1]

	Total Full-time Graduate Enrollment	In Massachusetts Universities	In Massachusetts State Colleges
Men	15,496	14,307	76
Women	5,558	4,752	75
Total	21,054	19,059	151
Women as % of Full-time Graduate Enrollment			
	26%	25%	50%

SOURCE:

1. U.S. Office of Education: *Fall Enrollment 1970,* Institutional Data, Table 1, pp. 30–32.

Table 6

First Professional Degrees Conferred, By Sex

Massachusetts: First Professional Degrees Conferred, 1969–70: By Profession, and Sex[1, 2]

Profession	*Total Degrees*	*Men*	*Women (%)*		*Granting Institutions*
Dentistry	119	119	0	(0)	Harvard, Tufts
Medicine	327	302	25	(8%)	Boston University, Harvard, Tufts
Law	1,135	1,075	60	(5%)	Boston College; Boston University; Harvard; Suffolk; N.E. School Law
Optometry	34	33	1	(3%)	Mass. College of Optometry
Architecture	36	33	3	(8%)	Harvard
Theology	208	200	8	(4%)	Andover Newton; B.C.; B.U.; Episcopal Theological; Harvard; Hellenic; St. John's; Tufts
Total	1,859	1,762	97	(5%)	

[1] U.S. Office of Education, Earned Degrees Conferred; First Professional. 1969–70 Table 3 (Institutional Data).

[2] NOTE: Other fields in which women constitute a larger percent of advanced degree recipients (Social Work, Education, Library Science, Nursing) are not listed in Professional Degrees conferred).

Table 7

Residence and Migration Of College Students In Massachusetts: 1968

Ratio of Massachusetts Residents to Total Student Enrollment in Private Institutions of Higher Education (1968)[1]

All Students—Privately controlled institutions of Higher Education

Type of Institution		*Massachusetts residents*	*All Students*	*Mass. residents as % of total*
All Private	Men	64,373	110,037	58.5%
	Women	32,134	62,495	51.3%
Private 4-year	Men	58,757	102,263	57.6%
	Women	28,890	54,475	53.0%
2-year	Men	5,616	7,774	72.0%
	Women	3,244	8,020	40.0%

1. SOURCE: U.S. Office of Education: *Basic State to State Matrix Tables, Fall 1968,* Tables 5, 6, and 7.

Table 8

Percentage Distribution Of Full-time Undergraduate Students
In Privately Controlled Institutions

Places Open For Massachusetts Women Full-time As Undergraduates
In Privately Controlled Institutions Of Higher Education: 1968[1]

Type of Institution		*Massachusetts Residents*	*All Students*	*Mass. Residents as % of Total*
Privately controlled				
	M	29,981	58,930	50.7%
	W	19,241	44,264	43.3%

SOURCE: 1. U.S. Office of Education, *Basic State to State Matrix Tables, Fall 1968*, Table 15, p. 32–33.

Table 9

Enrollment In Shop and Domestic Arts Courses: By Sex

A)

Percent	Enrollment In 1971–72 Shop Course[1] Girls as % of Boys taking	Enrollment In 1971–72 Domestic Arts[1] Boys as % of Girls taking
0	21	23
Under 2%	6	4
2–10%	9	3
Over 10%	1	6
Total schools reporting	37	36

B) Response to question: Are both sexes permitted to register for all courses offered by school?

Yes 31

No 10

1. SOURCE: Response to Questionnaire by Governor's Commission on the Status of Women, Task Force on Education. Forty-one replies to sample of sixty-three school systems queried; *see* methodology.

Table 10

Expenditures On Sports, School System, By Sex (1971)

Total Expenditures On Sports, By Massachusetts School Systems, By Sex (1971)[1]

Distribution Of School System Expenditures On Sports 1971	Boys	Girls
Under $1,000	0	5
$ 1,000– 1,999	2	12
$ 2,000– 4,999	2	12
$ 5,000– 9,999	2	7
$10,000–24,999	12	1
$25,000–49,999	9	0
$50,000–74,999	8	0
$75,000–99,999	1	0
$100,000 and over	1	0
	37	37

1. SOURCE: Response to Questionnaire by Governor's Commission on the Status of Women, Task Force on Education. Forty-one replies (37 this item) from sample of sixty-three school systems queried.

Table 11

Faculty Coaching Increment: Basketball Coach, By Sex

Increment Of Woman Faculty Basketball Coach Relative To Man Faculty Coach (1971)[1, 2]

Total responses:	Increment of Woman Faculty Basketball Coach	Relative to Man Faculty Basketball coach at same school: Not more than % of salary increment shown: 10	20	30	40	50	60	70	80	90	100%	Greater
2	Under $100										1	1
3	$ 100–299					1					2	
10	$ 300–499		1	3	1		1	1	1	1		1
9	$ 500–799		1			4	1	1	1		1	
	$ 800–999											
1	$1,000 and over										1	
25			2	3	1	5	2	2	2	1	5	2

Median: ↑

1. SOURCE: Response to Questionnaire by Governor's Commission on the Status of Women, Task Force on Education. Forty-one replies to sample of sixty-three school systems queried.
2. Numbers of male coaches generally exceed numbers of female coaches by substantial margin; not tabulated.

Table 12
Places For Women Administrators and Faculty
Massachusetts School System 1971

A) Distribution Of Professional Administrators, By Sex, By Highest Degree:[1] (1971–72)

Professional Administrators	*Men*		*Women*	
by degree held:	*Number*	%	*Number*	%
Doctorate	81	7%	32	7%
Master's	1,080	89	366	83
Bachelor's	50	4	37	8
Total[2]	1,211	Distrib. of those with reported degree	435	Distrib. of those with reported degree

B)

Teaching Staff by degree held:	*Men* Number	%	*Women* Number	%
Doctorate	61	1%	25	.002%
Master's	3,524	54	4,008	32
Bachelor's	2,777	43	8,240	66
Total[2]	6,362	Distrib. of those with reported degree	12,273	Distrib. of those with reported degree

1. SOURCE: Response to Questionnaire by Governor's Commission on the Status of Women, Task Force on Education. Forty-one replies to sample of sixty-three school systems queried.
2. Some personnel reported as less than bachelor's degree; items do not add to total.

Table 13

Selected Positions, School Systems: Distribution By Sex (1971)

Percentage Distribution of Selected Positions in Massachusetts School Systems: By Sex, 1971[1]

Central Administration	*% Women*
Superintendent	0
Assoc., Asst. Supt.	9
Supervisor	34
Curriculum Development	30
Social Worker	29
High School	
Principal	6
Deputy, Asst. Principal	15
Head, Guidance Dept.	34
Asst. Guidance	47
Head Librarian	87
Asst. Librarian	74
Coach	12
Dept. Head	26
Classroom Teacher (H.S.)	42
All system— Classroom teacher	65

1. SOURCE: Response to Questionnaire by Governor's Commission on the Status of Women, Task Force on Education. Forty-one replies to sample of sixty-three school systems queried.

Table 14

Places For Women In Private Technical and Trade Schools (Fall 1971)

Estimated % Of Places For Women In Private Technical and Trade Schools In Massachusetts (Fall 1971):

	Men	*Women*	*Women as %*
Private Technical and Trade[1, 2]	1,638	396	19%
Private Business[1, 3] Secretarial and Data Processing	796	1,441	64%

SOURCE:
1. Mass. Dept. of Education, Division of Occupational Information: *List of Licensed Private Trade Schools; American Trade Schools Directory* (Queens Village, N.Y.: Croner Publications, Inc.); *Patterson's School Directory,* 1970. Systematic sample drawn from composite list from above sources; see Appendix A for methodology.
2. Based on returns from 11 of 18 private Technical and Trade Schools; no total enrollment in state available.
3. Based on return from 6 of 10 Mass. Business schools queried; no total enrollment in state available.

Table 15

Massachusetts Universities—Distribution Of Faculty By Rank and Sex

Massachusetts Universities: Faculty Distribution and Median Salary, By Rank and Sex (1971)[1]

Full-Time

A) Numbers of faculty in rank:[1, 3]

Rank	Men	Women	*Tenure noted*[2] Men	Women
Professor	1,151	47	772	23
Assoc. Prof.	1,098	117	387	36
Assist. Prof.	1,198	257	85	23
Instructor	335	140	9	5

B) Median salaries of Full-time faculty (Median institution):

Professor	$22,300	$18,500
Assoc. Prof.	16,600	16,000
Assist. Prof.	12,900	11.900
Instructor	10,700	9,800

1. SOURCE: Listing in *New England Board of Higher Education "Factbook" 1970.* All 14 universities (including U. Mass., 3 campuses) were queried. All responded with some data except Tufts and Harvard; officials at these institutions have promised data.
2. Not all institutions noted tenure status; those that included data for both men and women within rank have been included.
3. Numbers reported by 10 universities; salaries by 9.

Table 16

Graduate Admissions To Massachusetts Universities 1971

Distribution Of Applications and Acceptances To Graduate Study In Massachusetts Universities, By Sex: Fall 1971

Graduate Status	*Men*	*Women*
Number of applications[1]	13,626	5,155
Number accepted and enrolled[1]	2,729	972
Acceptances as % of applications	20%	19%
Women enrolled in[2] full-time graduate programs as % of total full-time graduates	15,496	5,558 26%

SOURCE:

1. Response to Questionnaire. Data from 9 universitiy responses.
2. Table 1, Office of Education; *Fall Enrollment 1970, Institutional Data,* pp. 30–32.

Table 17

Undergraduate Grades Of Persons Admitted To Graduate Study In Massachusetts Universities, By Sex: 1971

Distribution Of Undergraduate Grades Of Persons Admitted To Graduate Study, Mass. Universities: Relative Grades By Sex: (1971)

Average Undergraduate GPI of Men admitted relative to Women admitted:[1]

Relative standing	*Number*
Higher	3
Same	5
Lower	31
Total	39

SOURCE:

1. Response to Questionnaire by Covernor's Commission on the Status of Women, Task Force on Education. Only five of the institutions reported usable data, and only for some fields of graduate study; a more comprehensive response will provide greater reliability.

NOTE: Only three of the Massachusetts universities with one or more professional schools returned Form 3; therefore no comparative scores of men and women applicants could be shown.

Table 18

Graduate Record Exam Scores Of Persons Admitted To Graduate Study, Massachusetts Universities By Sex, 1971

Distribution Of Graduate Record Exam Scores Of Persons Admitted To Graduate Study, Mass. Universities
Relative scores by sex: (1971)

Average GRE scores of men accepted[1] relative to scores of women accepted:

	Math	*Verbal*	*Other*	*Total*
Higher	6	1	17	24
Same	—			
Lower	2	3	7	12

SOURCE: 1. As noted on Table 17 only 5 of reporting institutions supplied usable data for a few fields.

Table 19

Heads Of Academic Departments, Massachusetts Universities: 1971

Distribution Of Department Heads, By Sex: 1971[1]

	Men	*With Tenure*	*Women*	*With Tenure*
Dept. Head	140	88	5	3
Range of Median salaries	$18,400–30,000		$16,300–20,200	

1. SOURCE: Response to Questionnaire by Governor's Commission on the Status of Women, Task Force on Education. Based on responses from six universities.

Table 20

Administrative Positions Held In Massachusetts Universities

Distribution By Administrative Title, Selected Positions By Sex, 1971[1]

	Men	Women	Total
Private Universities			
University President	6*	0	
Vice-President	16	0	
Assistant to President; Vice-President	3	4	
Dean	17	3	
Associate Dean	7	1	
Assistant Dean	14	6	
Student Advisor—Head	8	2	
Director of Admissions	4	0	
	76	16	
Public Universities			
University President**	3	0	
Vice-President/Chancellor	5	1	
Assistant to President; Vice-President; Vice-Chancellor	6	0	
Dean	21	3	
Associate Dean	13	0	
Assistant Dean	7	2	
Student Advisor—Head	4	2	
Admissions Director	4	0	
	63	8	
Universities, Public and Private Total	138	24	162
Women as % of listed administrative positions***			14.8%

SOURCE: 1. Response to Questionnaire by Governor's Commission on the Status of Women. Response from 10 of 14 universities.

* All 9 presidents of Masssachusetts private universities are men.

** University of Massachusetts President heads campuses at Amherst, Boston, Worcester; SMU; LTI.

*** Where responding institutions suggested additional administrative positions held by women, these were included.

Table 21

Massachusetts Universities, Administrative Distribution

Distribution of Selected Administrative Positions, Salary, By Sex, Massachusetts Universities, 1971:[1]
(Public and Private combined)

	Number		Over $20,000		$15,000–20,000		$10,000–14,999		Under $10,000	
Title	*Men*	*Women*	*M*	*W*	*M*	*W*	*M*	*W*	*M*	*W*
President	6	0	6							
Vice-Pres./ Chancellor	10	1	10	1						
Asst. to Pres. or Vice-Pres. Vice-Chancellor	8	3	5		2		1	2		1
Dean	28	4	26	3	1		1	1		
Assoc. Dean	16	0	14		1		1			
Asst. Dean	9	6	7	2			2	4		
Head, Student Advising	6	2	3		2	1	1	1		
Director Admissions	7	0	3		3		1			
Total Men	90		74		9		7		0	
Total Women		16		6		1		8		1
Salaries not reported	48	8								
Total	138	24								

SOURCE:

1. Response to Questionnaire by Governor's Commission on the Status of Women; responses from 10 of 14 universities salary data.

Table 22

Administrative and Clerical
Massachusetts Universities

Distribution Of Administrative and Clerical Personnel, By Sex: (1971)[1]

	Number		*Median Salary*	
Full-time Employees	*Men*	*Women*[1]	*Men*	*Women*[2]
Professional Administrators	1,182	322	$16,230	$10,650
Clerical	321	3,083	6,700	6,600

SOURCE: 1. Response to Questionnaire by Governor's Commission on the Status of Women. Response from 10 of 14 universities.
2. Response from 10 of 14 universities.

Table 23

Massachusetts Four-year Colleges
Administration, Faculty, Clerical

Distribution Of Faculty, Administration, Clerical
By Sex, Median Salary (1971)[1]

Type	Numbers		Median Salary		(Median at Institution)
	Men	Women	Men	Women	
Full-time faculty	783	422	$12,600	$11,600	
Administration	240	189	15,900	10,400	
Clerical	38	672	6,500	5,600	

SOURCE:

1. Response to Questionnaire from 14 of 14 sample members; some missing items. Includes 4 women's colleges; 1 men's college.

Table 24

Four-year Colleges In Massachusetts
Faculty Distribution By Sex

Rank Distribution Of Full-time Faculty
Four-year Colleges In Massachusetts By Sex (1971)[1]

	Number, Full-time Faculty: All Reporting Colleges[2]		Number Full-time Faculty All Reporting Colleges Excluding Women's Colleges[2]	
	Men	Women	Men	Women
Full Professor	158	86	102	15
Assoc. Professor	214	76	161	32
Assist. Professor	344	146	228	68
Instructor	99	108	81	58
TOTAL	815	416	572	173

SOURCE:

1. Response to Questionnaire by Governor's Commission on the Status of Women.
2. Data from 12 of 14 institutions, including 4 women's colleges, 1 men's college, as classified by *New England Board of Higher Education "Fact-book," 1970.*

Table 25

Four-year Colleges In Massachusetts
Administrative Distribution

Distribution of Administrative Positions, 1971[1]
By Sex, Title, Salary

Title	MEN All Colleges	MEN Excluding Women's Colleges	WOMEN All Colleges	WOMEN Excluding Women's Colleges
President	12	9	1	0
Vice-President	10	7		
Asst. to Pres. or to V.P.	6	5	4	1
Dean	17	14	4	1
Associate Dean	4	3	1	1
Asst. Dean	6	4	11	2
Head, Student Advising	6	5	3	1
Asst. Student Adv.			4	2
Director Admissions	9	9	4	1
Other Admissions	1	1	1	0
Other			3	2
	71	57	36	11

Salary Distribution of Administrative Positions

	MEN All Colleges	MEN Excluding Women's Colleges	WOMEN All Colleges	WOMEN Excluding Women's Colleges
Over $20,000	37	29	6	3
$15,000–20,000	18	15	7	2
$10,000–14,999	10	8	12	2
Under $10,000	—	—	11	4
Salary not reported	6	5	—	—
	71	57	36	11

SOURCE:

1. Response to questionnaire of Governor's Commission on the Status of Women, Task Force on Education; 13 of 14 institutions responding.

NOTES

1. Sidney Weinheimer, "How to Teach Your Child to Think—An Interview with Jean Piaget," *Redbook,* March 1972, p. 118.
2. Eleanor E. Maccoby, ed., *The Development of Sex Differences* (Stanford, Calif.: Stanford University Press, 1966).
3. "Hearing on Amendments to Chapter 622 Before the Massachusetts House/Senate Committee on Education and Labor," *Boston Globe,* 7 February 1972, p. 48.
4. *Guide to Financial and Admissions Information, The Massachusetts State College System,* 1972 (Princeton, N. J.: College Entrance Examination Board, 1972), p. 7.
5. *Harvard Gazette* 67 (March 31, 1972): 4.
6. Weinheimer.
7. Bureau of Apprenticeship and Training, U.S. Department of Labor, "Women in Apprenticeship, August 1970," pp. 1–6.
8. Women on Words and Images, *Dick and Jane as Victims* (Princeton, N. J.: P.O. Box 2163), p. 65.
9. Susan Kannenberg and Sarah Lockeretz, unpublished study of toys and games, 1972. Available from Task Force on Education, Governor's Commission on the Status of Women.
10. Bonnie Spring, unpublished paper given at Massachusetts Guidance Counselors Association Conference, Hyannis, Massachusetts, 6 May 1972, p. 6.
11. Women on Words and Images, pp. 64–66.
12. Spring.
13. Judith Leff, Study of Children's Books. Conducted for Task Force on Education. Available from Governor's Commission on the Status of Women.
14. Ruth Broder-Ennis, Study of College Freshman Literature. Conducted for Task Force on Education. Available from Governor's Commission on the Status of Women.
15. Earle F. Barcus, *Saturday's Children.*
16. Carol Springe, Study of Presentation of Women on TV. Conducted for Task Force on Education. Available from Governor's Commission on the Status of Women.
17. Joanne Cookley, Study of Massachusetts Guidance Counselors Attitudes. Conducted for Task Force on Education. Available from Governor's Commission on the Status of Women.
18. Anna Hart, Study of School Committee Selection Process. Conducted for Task Force on Education. Available from Governor's Commission on the Status of Women.
19. Spring.
20. Carol Rines, Study of Education for Living. Conducted for Task Force on Education. Available from Governor's Commission on the Status of Women.
21. Derek Bok, quoted in Harvard *Crimson,* 6 October 1971, p. 1.
22. J. N. Hedges, "Women Workers and Manpower Demands in the 1970s," *Monthly Labor Review* (June 1970): pp. 19–20.
23. Women's Bureau, U.S. Department of Labor, *Fact Sheet on Earnings Gap* (Washington, D.C. Women's Bureau, 1972).
24. Guide to Financial and Admissions Information, p. 7.

25. U.S. Congress, House of Representatives, *Congressional Record,* 4 November 1971, p. 10365.
26. Harvard *Gazette* 67 (31 March 1972) : 4.
27. Kay Bourne, Study of Education for Women in Prison. Conducted for Task Force on Education. Available from Governor's Commission on the Status of Women.
28. Presidential Task Force on Women's Rights and Responsibilities, *A Matter of Simple Justice* (Washington, D.C.: Task Force on Women's Rights and Responsibilities, 1970) .
29. Women's Bureau, U.S. Department of Labor, *Underutilization of Women Workers* (Washington, D.C.: Women's Bureau, 1971) .

Appendixes
The Sexist Control of Education: A Statistical Portrait

Women in Educational Governance: A Statistical Portrait*

ANDREW FISHEL and JANICE POTTKER

Information on the sex of educational leaders is not collected in any uniform or systematic fashion. However, through the use of published and unpublished sources it is possible to compile statistics that reflect the sex of individuals holding positions of authority in education at the national, state, and local levels.

NATIONAL LEVEL

Decision-making positions in both the U.S. Office of Education (OE) and the National Institute of Education (NIE) tend to be held by men.

Reprinted with the permission of American Educational Research Association and the authors, from *Educational Researcher* 3, no. 7 (July/August 1974) :4–7.

* Tables 1 and 2, reprinted with the permission of the U.S. Department of Health, Education, and Welfare, Washington, D. C.

Table 3, tabulations of the state boards of education reprinted with the permission of the National School Boards Association; and state departments of education tabulations based on *Education Directory-State Governments, 1971–73* (Washington, D. C.: U.S. Office of Education, 1971).

Table 4, reprinted with the permission of the National Education Association, Research Division, *26th Biennial Salary and Staff Survey of Public-school Professional Personnel, 1972–73* (Washington, D. C.: N.E.A., 1973), © copyright 1973 by the National Education Association.

Table 5, reprinted with the permission of the National School Boards Association, *Women on School Boards* (Evanston, Ill.: NSBA, 1974).

Table 1

Sex of U. S. Office of Education Staff By Grade, 1974

Grade	Total	No. of Women	Percent Women
01	8	5	63%
02	63	47	75
03	148	125	84
04	184	153	83
05	219	190	87
06	227	214	94
07	263	202	77
08	66	57	86
09	150	116	77
10	5	3	60
11	164	107	65
12	181	91	50
13	373	92	25
14	420	72	17
15	248	23	9
16	27	2	7
17	10	2	20
18	4	0	0
Total	2,760	1,501	54%

In OE in 1974, 54% of the employees are women, but only 18% of those in senior-grade positions (GS–13 to GS–15) and 10% of those in super-grade positions (GS–16 to GS–18) are women. The average civil-service grade for women in OE as of January 1974 was GS–7, while the average grade for men was GS–12. Table 1 shows male-female frequencies in the OE by grade level. The same pattern holds for the NIE. While 59% of the employees of NIE are women, only 23% of the employees at the GS–13 level or above are women. The average civil-service grade for women in NIE as of January 1974 was GS–8, while the average grade for men was GS–12. Table 2 shows the male-female ratios of the NIE by grade level.

In both OE and NIE women constitute a majority of the employees at all grade levels until GS–13, but are a distinct minority of the employees from GS–13 to GS–18.

Table 2

Sex of National Institute of Education Staff By Grade, 1974

Grade	Total	No. of Women	Percent Women
01	0	0	—
02	2	2	100
03	6	4	67
04	10	10	100
05	29	25	86
06	33	33	100
07	48	39	81
08	7	7	100
09	32	22	69
10	0	0	—
11	25	16	64
12	29	17	59
13	49	18	37
14	52	10	19
15	27	2	7
16	0	0	—
17	0	0	—
18	0	0	—
Total	349	205	59%

STATE LEVEL

Table 3 shows male-female frequencies of state boards of education and state department of education leaders.

Five states have no women at all on their state board of education and 15 other states have only one woman on the board. Out of 485 state board of education members in the country, 95 or 20% are women. Only one state had a woman chief state school officer and in only four states was a woman a deputy superintendent, associate superintendent, or assistant superintendent. Out of the 236 deputy, associate, and assistant state superintendents in the U.S., 2% are women.

Table 3

Sex of State Education Leaders By State, 1972

State	State Brd. of Ed.		% St. Bd. of Ed Members Women, 1972	State Dept. of Education				
				Chief State School Officer		Deputy Supt. Assoc. Supt. Assist. Supt.		% All St. Dept. of Ed. Leaders Women, 1972
	No. of Men	No. of Women		No. of Men	No. of Women	No. of Men	No. of Women	
Ala.	5	3	38	1	0	0	0	0
Alaska	3	4	57	1	0	1	0	0
Ariz.	8	1	11	1	0	8	0	0
Ark.	9	0	0	1	0	3	0	10
Calif.	7	2	22	1	0	7	0	6
Colo.	4	1	20	1	0	4	0	8
Conn.	5	4	44	1	0	3	0	0
Del.	5	1	17	1	0	4	0	8
Fla.	7	0	0	1	0	3	0	0
Ga.	8	2	20	1	0	4	0	3
Hawaii	9	2	18	1	0	4	1	19
Idaho	7	1	13	1	0	5	0	0
Ill.	—	—	—	1	0	15	0	4
Ind.	15	3	17	1	0	3	0	8
Iowa	5	4	44	1	0	6	0	5
Kans.	7	3	30	1	0	5	0	11
Ky.	7	0	0	1	0	7	0	11
La.	10	1	9	1	0	5	0	11
Maine	8	1	11	1	0	3	0	14
Md.	5	2	29	1	0	8	1	26
Mass.	8	2	20	1	0	7	0	7
Mich.	6	2	25	1	0	6	0	0
Minn.	7	2	22	1	0	4	0	3
Miss.	3	0	0	1	0	0	0	0
Mo.	7	1	13	1	0	5	0	2

Mont.	8	3	27	0	1	2	0	0
Nebr.	6	2	25	1	0	4	0	11
Nev.	6	3	33	1	0	6	0	0
N. H.	6	1	14	1	0	5	0	15
N. J.	7	5	42	1	0	3	0	6
N. Mex.	8	2	20	1	0	3	0	22
N. Y.	14	1	7	1	0	9	0	5
N. C.	12	2	14	1	0	6	0	15
N. Dak.	7	0	0	1	0	2	0	18
Ohio	20	4	17	1	0	6	0	4
Okla.	7	1	13	1	0	4	0	0
Ore.	6	1	14	1	0	4	1	5
Pa.	14	3	18	1	0	6	0	2
R. I.	8	1	11	1	0	2	1	25
S. C.	15	1	6	1	0	3	0	0
S. Dak.	4	3	43	1	0	6	0	0
Tenn.	14	1	7	1	0	6	0	8
Tex.	21	3	13	1	0	8	0	6
Utah	6	3	33	1	0	3	0	0
Vt.	4	3	43	1	0	1	0	22
Va.	7	2	22	1	0	3	0	4
Wash.	10	4	29	1	0	4	0	7
W. Va.	9	1	10	1	0	5	0	16
Wis.	—	—	—	1	0	7	0	4
Wyo.	6	3	33	1	0	4	0	7
Total	390	95		49	1	232	4	

NOTE: The number and percentage of men and women in State Department of Education positions was calculated from the names of the individuals holding the positions as listed in *Education Directory-State Governments, 1971–73* (Washington, D.C.: U. S. Office of Education, 1971). Individuals for whom initials were given instead of a first name were not counted, nor were persons with names that were likely to be held by both men and women. The titles of the positions in State Departments of Education were not always comparable. Therefore, for some states it was necessary to determine the organizational hierarchy of the State Department of Education and categorize the individuals in these states by the titles applied to their level position in the majority of the states.

Women are not significantly better represented at the next level of leadership in state departments of education. At the director level, women constitute 99 out of 1,090 or 9% of the individuals holding this position. Of those women who are directors, 30% are directors of library services, home-economics education, or school-lunch programs. Of all state department of education leaders, including chief state-school officers, deputy superintendents, associate superintendents, assistant superintendents, and directors in the country, 92% are men and 8% women.

LOCAL LEVEL

The national distribution of men and women in various positions in local school districts has been estimated and is shown in Table 4. While 66% of the 2,110,368 public schoolteachers in the country are women, only 13.5% of the principals and 12.5% of the assistant principals are women. Almost all of the women who are principals hold this position at the elementary-school level. Out of all the women who are principals, 95% are elementary-school principals.

Although women comprise 84% of elementary schoolteachers, only 20% of elementary-school principals are women. Of all the men employed in elementary education, one in five is a principal or assistant principal. In contrast, of all the women in elementary education, only one in one hundred is a principal or assistant principal.

Women comprise 46% of the secondary schoolteachers in the country, but constitute only 3% of the principals of junior-high schools and 1% of the principals of senior-high schools. Thus, one out of thirteen men in secondary education is a principal or assistant principal, while only one out of two hundred fifty women in secondary education is a principal or assistant principal. While 19% of all men in elementary education and 8% of all men in secondary education are principals, only 1% of all women in elementary education and .4% of all women in secondary education are principals.

Since women are rarely appointed to principalships, it is not surprising that few women become local superintendents of schools. Still the fact that 99.9% of all local superintendents, 94% of all deputy and associate superintendents, 95% of assistant superintendents are male suggests that the few women who do manage to be appointed principals advance no farther in the organizational hierarchy. Out of 13,037 local superintendents in the U.S., 65 are women. Out of 19,227 superintendents, deputy superintendents, associate superintendents, and assistant superintendents in the country, 401 or 2% are women.

The only category where women are visable in local educational governance is in general central-office administrative positions. Of the administrators responsible for general administration, finance and school plant, pupil personnel services, instruction administration, and special-subject areas, 35% are women. As a result of the presence of women in these general

Table 4

Estimated Number and Percent Distribution of Full-time Public-school Professional Employees, 1972–73, by Sex

Position	Number of persons			Percentage distribution		
	Total	Men	Women	Total	Men	Women
1	2	3	4	5	6	7
Instructional Staff						
Teachers	2,110,368	709,084	1,401,284	100.0	33.6	66.4
Principals						
Elementary (including teaching principals)	48,196	38,750	9,446	100.0	80.4	19.6
Junior high	9,374	9,102	272	100.0	97.1	2.9
Senior high	15,827	15,605	222	100.0	98.6	1.4
Total principals	73,397	65,457	9,940	100.0	86.5	13.5
Assistant principals						
Elementary	6,483	4,486	1,997	100.0	69.2	30.8
Junior high	7,817	7,223	594	100.0	92.4	7.6
Senior high	13,289	12,439	850	100.0	93.6	6.4
Total assistant principals	27,589	24,148	3,441	100.0	87.5	12.5
Other instructional staff						
School librarians	40,540	3,324	37,216	100.0	8.2	91.8
Counselors	49,770	26,378	23,392	100.0	53.0	47.0
School nurses	17,074	239	16,835	100.0	1.4	98.6
Other*	33,691	16,812	16.879	100.0	49.9	50.1
Total other instructional staff	141,075	46,753	94,322	100.0	33.1	66.9
Total instructional staff	2,352,429	843,442	1,508,987	100.0	35.9	64.1
Central-office Administrators						
Superintendents	13,037	12,972	65	100.0	99.9	0.1
Deputy and associate superintendents	853	800	53	100.0	93.8	6.2
Assistant superintendents	5,337	5,054	283	100.0	94.7	5.3
Other central-office administrators**	48,488	31,614	16,874	100.0	65.0	35.0
Total central-office administrators	67,715	50,440	17,275	100.0	74.4	25.6
Total Full-time Professional Employees	2,420,144	893,882	1,526,262	100.0	37.2	62.8

* Includes heads of departments, social workers, visiting teachers, psychologists, and psychometrists.

** Includes central-office administrator for General Administration, Finance and School Plant, Pupil Personnel Services, Instruction—Administration, and Special Subject areas.

administrative positions, the sex ratio for all central-office administrative personnel is not as one-sided as the male occupancy of superintendency positions would indicate. Out of all central-office administrators, 26% are women.

Women are also not well represented on local boards of education. Of 98,642 local school-board members, 11,763 or 12% are women. Table 5 shows the sex of local board members by state.

Table 5

Sex of Local School-board Members by State, 1972

State	No. of Men	No. of Women	% Local Bd. of Ed. Members Women, 1972
Ala.	611	39	6
Alaska	98	64	40
Ariz.	769	151	16
Ark.	2,034	37	2
Calif.	4,640	1,160	20
Colo.	962	76	7
Conn.	959	360	27
Del	151	20	12
Fla.	306	41	12
Ga.	1,068	46	4
Hawaii	9	2	18
Idaho	501	46	8
Ill.	7,195	755	10
Ind.	1,498	112	7
Iowa	2,216	189	8
Kans.	2,100	77	4
Ky.	912	48	5
La.	670	27	4
Maine	1,200	480	29
Md.	119	39	25
Mass.	1,580	408	21
Mich.	3,827	473	11
Minn.*	2,575	208	8
Miss.	780	25	3
Mo.*	3,148	311	9

Mont.*	2,099	110	5
Nebr.*	4,480	729	14
Nev.	92	15	14
N. H.	553	217	28
N. J.	4,023	683	15
N. Mex.	435	20	4
N. Y.	4,300	700	14
N. C.	901	113	11
N. Dak.	1,618	119	7
Ohio*	3,243	572	15
Okla.	2,100	150	7
Ore.	1,998	300	13
Pa.	4,268	388	8
R. I.	159	51	24
S. C.	1,117	33	3
S. Dak.	1,381	120	8
Tenn.	894	54	6
Tex.*	6,925	1,223	15
Utah	198	9	4
Vt.	820	366	31
Va.	675	85	11
Wash.*	1,360	151	10
W. Va.	250	25	9
Wis.	2,741	289	10
Wy.	321	47	13
Total	86,879	11,763	

NOTE: States marked with * are estimated figures.

In the nation's fifty largest city-school districts women are better represented than they are in the nation as a whole, but they are still a definite minority.[1] Five of the largest city-school districts in the country have no women school-board members and twenty-two have only one woman on the board. In no large city is there a majority of women on a school board.

The sex of educational leaders is important and highly relevant information, and as such, should be easily available in a form that guarantees accuracy. While the information in this article provides the basis for analyzing the current status of women in educational governance, there is still a need for a more systematic collection of data in this area.

NOTES

1. National School Boards Association, *Survey of Public Education in the Nation's Big City School Districts* (Evanston, Ill., 1972).

Women in Academic Governance*

RUTH OLTMAN

POSITIONS OF LEADERSHIP ON CAMPUS

Analysis of campus offices (*see* Table 1) most likely to be held by women on campus show that women students are most frequently found in positions that are primarily nonelective or appointive, such as editor of the yearbook or literary magazine, or chairman of the activities committee or freshman orientation—all positions requiring special skills, such as writing, and detail work. Greater opportunities for leadership are open to women on small campuses (under 1,000) or at private institutions (and women's colleges not included in this tabulation) than at very large, public or coeducational institutions.

Men are most likely to hold the elective, political offices such as president of the student body, class president, chairman of the Campus Judicial Board or Union Board of Governors—all positions with much power and influence. Again, these trends are accentuated on the large campuses and at public or coeducational schools. There is a tendency toward cochairmanships (men and women) for positions such as chairman of freshman orientation or activities committee, some editorships, or judicial boards.

---

* Reprinted with the permission of the American Association of University Women and Ruth M. Oltman, © copyright 1970 by the American Association of University Women from *Campus 1970: Where Do Women Stand?* (Washington, D. C.: American Association of University Women, 1970).

DEPARTMENT HEADS

It should be noted that 90 percent of the schools surveyed answered "yes" to the question, "Our promotional policies are the same for men and women faculty." Data show, however, that women infrequently hold department chairmanships. Thirty-four of the schools in this study indicate no women as heads of academic departments, and the average number of women in such positions in all schools was 2.6 per school. When they are department chairmen, they are found primarily in the fields of home economics, physical education, English, languages, nursing, and education. The opportunities in the women's colleges, however, are greater than in other schools, particularly in areas of the sciences, math, history and government, and art. Table 2 gives all department categories mentioned two percent or more of the total listings.

WOMEN ADMINISTRATORS

In answering the question, "It is our policy to include women in a). top-level administrative positions" and b). "policymaking decisions," 87 to 92 percent of the total sample indicated affirmative responses. The most positive responses came from the sample of women's colleges, the large universities with enrollments over 10,000 stating more reservations.

In spite of such affirmative policy, however, this actual participation of women in administrative policymaking in higher education is conspicuously lacking, as Table 3 demonstrates. The position of women in administration is similar to that of women students—they are working at jobs requiring skills and attention to detail but without much relationship to policymaking or influence. Generally they are in positions at middle management level or that involve sex stereotypes, such as Dean of Nursing.

The study points up the comparatively greater opportunities for women in the administration of women's colleges and in schools with under 1,000 enrollment, especially in certain categories. In addition to the position of Dean of Women, women are most likely to hold positions such as head librarian, director of placement, director of financial aid, or college counselor. They are least likely to be found in the positions of president, vice-president, director of development, business manager, academic dean, dean of students, director of counseling, and college physician.

It should be noted that women are less likely to be head librarians in schools with enrollment over 10,000 and in public institutions than in private schools or schools with enrollment under 1,000. The same holds true for the positions of placement director, director of counseling, dean of students, assistant academic dean, and director of financial aid. Categories such as president, director of development, college physician, and business manager show little differential among institutions, despite size or type, except at the women's colleges, where women do hold many positions of responsibility.

Further evidence of the lack of utilization of women power in college administration is seen in the answers to an open-sided question that asked for a list of all positions in the administrative staff for which qualified women are generally sought. Only 19 percent of the schools indicated that they specifically seek "qualified persons, regardless of sex, except for Dean of Men and Dean of Women" and another nine percent answered generally "any position." The 454 schools in the survey listed only 427 such positions, an average of less than one position per school. Table 4 shows the distribution of responses in ten categories including all positions listed at least two percent or more. Again, there appear to be broader opportunities in women's colleges, fewer in the large universities.

WOMEN TRUSTEES

More and more is being heard about the appointment of women trustees in our colleges and universities but they still are not represented as fully as they should be in view of enrollment of women and number of alumnae, particularly at the large public universities. Twenty-one percent of the schools surveyed had no women trustees and the percentage in this category is much higher for institutions with over 10,000 enrollment (32 percent), public schools (26 percent), and coeducational schools (24 percent). (*See* Table 5.)

Twenty-five percent of the total sample have a token woman on the board, with the percentage of those having only one woman again shown as much higher at large public schools. Sixty-six percent of the women's colleges and sixteen percent of the schools with under 1,000 students have six or more women trustees, but only two percent of schools with 10,000 or more students and three percent of the public institutions. The overall governance of an institution is obviously reflected in its policies. Does the lack of women in the top governing board have a relationship to some of the differentials among institutions that have been previously noted? This is an area meriting further research.

Table 1

Students In Campus Leadership Positions (1967–70) **

Position	Coed Schools (376)			Public Schools (189)			Private Schools* (207)			Schools over 10,000 (63)			Schools under 1,000* (53)		
	% Men 3 yrs.	% Women 2–3 yrs.	Total Re-sponses	% Men 3 yrs.	% Women 2–3 yrs.	Total Re-sponses	% Men 3 yrs.	% Women 2–3 yrs.	Total Re-sponses	% Men 3 yrs.	% Women 2–3 yrs.	Total Re-sponses	% Men 3 yrs.	% Women 2–3 yrs.	Total Re-sponses
President Student Body	84	5	370	86	4	188	77	12	204	92	2	63	67	18	51
Class President	76	6	294	75	8	138	69	13	179	80	5	41	60	22	45
Chrmn, Union Board of Governors	65	12	209	64	13	125	63	15	92	62	11	47	69	16	19
Captain, Debate	65	8	170	60	13	96	68	10	85	79	3	38	77	8	13
Chrmn, Campus Judicial Board	68	12	252	77	13	124	55	17	147	74	6	46	55	18	33
Editor, Yearbook	17	49	362	19	46	183	15	54	201	25	48	61	12	52	50
Chrmn, Activities Committee	47	27	259	47	30	128	43	31	150	42	22	36	33	38	42
Chrmn, Freshman Orientation	40	24	259	44	26	124	35	29	156	44	28	43	40	32	35
Editor, Literary Magazine	39	30	263	43	23	127	33	41	153	49	16	49	17	63	30
Editor, Campus Paper	39	25	373	40	24	186	36	31	209	53	18	62	23	46	52

* Exclusive of women's colleges.

** To provide a clear picture of women's participation, instances are tabulated in which women held these offices at least 2/3 of the time during 1969–70. Instances of incumbency for one year only are not shown.

Table 2

Departmental Chairmanships Held By Faculty Women**

Department	Total Group (454)		Coed Schools (376)		Women's Colleges (59)		Schools over 10,000 (63)		Schools under 1,000* (53)		Public Schools (189)		Private Schools* (207)	
	%	No. R's	%	No. R's	%	No. R's	%	No. R's	%	No. R's	%	No. R's	%	No. R's
None	3	1217	4	913	—	248	1	199	5	131	3	438	4	509
Home Economics	13		15		6		21		8		21		10	
Physical Education	9		10		7		14		6		15		7	
English, Journalism, Speech, or Theater Arts	8		8		9		4		11		8		8	
Languages	8		8		10		4		12		6		11	
Nursing	8		9		4		11		5		10		7	
Education	6		6		6		3		7		2		7	
Business Administration and/or Economics	6		6		3		4		5		7		6	
Mathematics	4		4		6		0		8		3		5	
Fine Arts, History of Art	5		4		6		1		6		4		5	
Biology and/or Earth Science	4		3		9		8		3		3		3	

History, Government, and/or Political Science	4	4	6	4	2	3	4
Physical Science	4	2	7	1	4	1	4
Sociology and/or Anthropology	4	3	4	2	3	2	3
Psychology	3	3	4	9	5	3	3
Music	2	3	2	1	2	2	2

* Exclusive of women's colleges.
** Percentages represent proportion of total number of chairmanships listed.

Table 3

Women In College Administration**
(1967–70)

	Total Group (454)			Coed Schools (376)			Women's Colleges Only (59)			Schools over 10,000 (63)		
	% Men 3 yrs.	% Women 2–3 yrs.	Total Re-sponses	% Men 3 yrs.	% Women 2–3 yrs.	Total Re-sponses	% Men 3 yrs.	% Women 2–3 yrs.	Total Re-sponses	% Men 3 yrs.	% Women 2–3 yrs.	Total Re-sponses
President	88	11	441	95	5	366	50	47	56	100	—	58
Vice-president	93	4	290	97	2	246	69	17	29	100	—	55
Director of Development	95	4	381	97	2	314	86	6	50	98	—	52
Business Manager	90	9	437	93	5	362	66	32	56	98	2	58
College Physician	82	8	397	82	7	325	82	13	55	68	10	60
Director Financial Aid	70	23	440	79	15	364	21	67	57	85	12	61
Director Placement	64	28	429	72	21	355	22	73	55	80	10	59
Director Counseling	76	19	319	82	13	273	30	67	30	92	5	61
Dean of Students	71	23	419	82	12	343	12	83	57	86	5	57
Head Librarian	57	35	445	63	29	368	23	61	57	85	8	61
Academic Dean	69	18	432	76	10	359	31	62	55	50	17	60
Asso. or Asst. Academic Dean	68	17	261	74	12	223	32	44	25	63	12	60
College Counselor	36	25	318	38	17	265	27	51	41	18	16	49

** To provide a clear picture of women's participation, instances are tabulated in which women held these offices at least 2/3 of the time during 1969–70. Instances of incumbency for one year only are not shown.

Table 3 (Continued)

	Schools under 1,000* (53)			Public Schools (189)			Private Schools* (207)		
	% Men 3 yrs.	% Women 2–3 yrs.	Total Re-sponses	% Men 3 yrs.	% Women 2–3 yrs.	Total Re-sponses	% Men 3 yrs.	% Women 2–3 yrs.	Total Re-sponses
President	87	13	53	97	3	184	92	8	200
Vice-president	85	8	26	98	—	123	94	4	138
Director of Development	98	3	47	96	1	140	97	3	189
Business Manager	92	4	53	97	1	180	90	9	200
College Physician	95	5	42	80	9	162	83	7	179
Director Financial Aid	61	32	51	84	9	183	71	23	201
Director Placement	59	33	49	80	14	179	62	30	196
Director Counseling	61	32	28	88	9	150	73	20	138
Dean of Students	70	26	50	85	9	174	76	18	189
Head Librarian	36	62	53	69	22	184	56	37	204
Academic Dean	77	15	52	74	8	178	76	14	198
Asso. or Asst. Academic Dean	67	20	15	73	11	121	72	16	116
College Counselor	58	26	31	35	19	140	39	22	139

* Exclusive of women's colleges.

Table 4

Administrative Positions For Which Qualified Women Are Sought**

Question	Total Group (454)		Coed Schools (376)		Women's Colleges (59)		Schools over 10,000 (63)		Schools under 1,000* (53)		Public Schools (189)		Private Schools* (207)	
	%	No. R's	%	No. R's	%	No. R's	%	No. R's	%	No. R's	%	No. R's	%	No. R's
Qualified persons regardless of sex, except Deans of Men and Women	19	427	19	347	17	53	17	64	13	38	22	184	16	186
Women's Counselor	10		10		6		8		8		10		11	
Asso. Dean of Students	10		11		6		5		21		11		11	
Any position at all	9		8		17		2		13		7		9	
Dean of Nursing	8		9		2		16		—		12		5	
Dean of Students	5		2		23		5		8		2		3	
Dean of Home Economics	5		6		—		14		3		9		2	
Registrar	4		5		—		—		8		1		8	
Director of Admissions	3		2		8		3		—		3		2	
Librarian	3		3		4		—		5		3		3	
Director of Placement	2		3		2		2		—		3		2	
Asst. to Dean	2		2		2		5		3		2		2	

* Exclusive of women's colleges.
** Percentages represent proportion of total positions listed.

Table 5

Women Trustees

	Number	Total Group (454)		Coed Schools (376)		Women's Colleges (59)	Schools over 10,000 (63)		Schools under 1,000* (53)		Public Schools (189)		Private Schools* (207)	
	%	No. R's	%	No. R's	%	No. R's	%	No. R's	%	No. R's	%	No. R's	%	No. R's
		438		365		53		60		53		184		201
None	21		24		4		32		21		26		22	
1	25		29		2		42		11		41		17	
2	18		19		8		16		15		19		19	
3	10	Mode	11	Mode	7	Mode	6	Mode	13	Mode	7	Mode	13	Mode
4–5	10	= 2	9	= 2	13	= 7	2	= 1	24	= 3	4	= 1	15	= 2
6–9	10		6		38		0		10		2		10	
10 or more	6		2		28		2		6		1		4	

* Exclusive of women's colleges.

Appendixes
Opinion Polls

Equal Rights for Women*

NATIONAL EDUCATION ASSOCIATION

The vast majority of the nation's public schoolteachers favor a Constitutional amendment that would guarantee equal rights for women. Over half *strongly* favor such an amendment, and an additional 3 in 10 *tend* to favor it. Fewer than 10 percent are opposed.

These are findings of a Teacher Opinion Poll, which in spring 1971 asked a nationwide sample of classroom teachers the following question:

"Do you favor or oppose an amendment to the federal Constitution providing that equality of rights under law shall not be denied or abridged by the United States or by any state on account of sex?"

Responses show a higher percentage of women than of men (85 compared with 80 percent) in favor and also a noticeably larger proportion of women than of men (56 percent compared with 46 percent) who *strongly* favor a Constitutional amendment to this effect.

	Total	Men	Women
Strongly favor	52.5%	46.0%	56.4%
Tend to favor	30.5	33.8	28.5
Tend to oppose	6.2	7.6	5.4
Strongly oppose	3.3	5.5	2.0
No opinion	7.5	7.1	7.7

Regional analysis of responses reveals that more teachers in the Northeast (87 percent) and the Middle section of the country (85 percent) than in the Southeast or West (80 percent each) favor an equal rights amendment. The Northeast stands out from other regions of the country

* Reprinted with the permission of the National Education Association, Research Division, © copyright 1971 by the National Education Association from *Today's Education* 60 (October 1971): 9.

in having a particularly large percentage (61 percent) who *strongly* favor such an amendment.

	Northeast	Southeast	Middle	West
Strongly favor	61.4%	46.3%	52.9%	49.1%
Tend to favor	25.1	33.7	31.8	30.9
Tend to oppose	5.7	5.6	5.9	7.7
Strongly oppose	3.0	4.1	2.8	3.7
No opinion	4.9	10.3	6.7	8.6

Proportions of urban, suburban, and rural teachers in favor of an equal rights amendment are generally similar. However, larger percentages of urban and suburban teachers *strongly* favor such an amendment, while more rural schoolteachers say they *tend* to favor it.

Schoolbook Sex Bias: Seek and Ye Shall Find?*

from NATION'S SCHOOLS

Sexism in textbooks may be a hot topic with ladies who like Ms. in front of their names but not with school administrators. They don't think that sort of sex bias even exists—in spite of the fact that they haven't really looked for it lately.

Results from this month's poll, however, seem to show a correlation between the lookers and the finders. Nearly the same number of administrators who believe textbooks to be sexually biased (16 percent) indicated they had recently reviewed texts for such bias (17 percent). Apparently, then, only 1 percent who actually searched for "sexism" failed to find some instances of it.

Why are so few searching? "This is a new issue and I haven't had the chance to evaluate it," a Vermonter explains. Other schoolmen apparently don't think it's worth the effort.

"Sex bias? Hogwash!", claims a Californian. A Virginia administrator calls it "just a figment of some feminist's frustrated imagination."

Many indicated they were unaware of any evidence of sexism in curricular materials—a response that suggests that women's groups publicizing their evidence haven't gotten it out to school administrators.

Judging from poll results, few administrators will turn a deaf ear if presented with convincing arguments and some textbook examples actually showing sex bias. A full 70 percent of poll respondents say that if reviews of their texts pinpointed negative portrayals of girls and women, they *would* stop using those books, finances permitting.

Also, nearly 40 percent agree that sex bias will be a more important consideration than ever when they next select textbooks. The figure seems likely to increase considerably once schoolmen learn more about sexism.

What's important for feminists to remember, points out a Michigan schoolman, is that whatever bias exists is largely "an innocent variety" and not a "grand scale conspiracy to keep women down." Texts should change with the times, he declares, but "can hardly be faulted for not anticipating women's liberation."

HOW ADMINISTRATORS VOTED

1. Recent studies report that many elementary-school textbooks present a "biased" and negative view of girls and women, i.e., girls generally portrayed as "passive and emotional," while boys are depicted as "aggressive and logical." Do you think this type of sex bias exists in curriculum materials? *16%* Yes, *84%* No.

2. Have you recently made an effort to review long-used textbooks regarding their portrayal of women? *17%* Yes, *83%* No.

3. If finances permitted and if reviews of your own textbooks showed sex bias, would you stop using these books? *70%* Yes, *30%* No.

4. Will sex bias be of greater importance to you than ever before when you next select textbooks? *38%* Yes, *62%* No.

5. Do you plan any study units or courses in women's studies? 6% Yes, *86%* No, *8%* Already have them.

This opinion poll survey, based on a five percent proportional sampling of 14,000 school administrators in 50 states, brought a 37 percent response.

Participation in Sports by Girls*

GEORGE H. GALLUP

Should girls be permitted to participate in noncontact sports—track, tennis, golf, baseball, and the like—*on the same teams with boys?*

	National Totals	No Children In Schools	Public School Parents	Parochial School Parents	High School Juniors & Seniors
	%	%	%	%	%
Yes	59	58	59	66	76
No	35	34	37	30	22
Don't know/ no answer	6	8	4	4	2
	100	100	100	100	100

Should girls have equal financial support for their athletic activities as boys?

	National Totals	No Children In Schools	Public School Parents	Parochial School Parents	High School Juniors & Seniors
	%	%	%	%	%
Yes	88	87	88	96	89
No	7	7	8	4	9
Don't know/ no answer	5	6	4		2
	100	100	100	100	100

 Appeared in George H. Gallup, "Sixth Annual Gallup Poll of Public Attitudes Toward Education," *Phi Delta Kappan* 56, no. 1 (September 1974) : 29.

What, If Anything, Impedes Women from Serving on School Boards?*

NATIONAL SCHOOL BOARDS ASSOCIATION

THE SURVEY SAMPLE

In January 1974 NSBA Research mailed a four-page questionnaire to a nationwide group of approximately 750 male and 750 female school board members. This initial population was selected to reflect the percentage of men and women serving on school boards in each state.†

Two hundred-twelve men from 39 states, and 320 women from 47 states, currently serving on school boards, responded to the questionnaire. Geographically, this sample of 532 school-board members closely resembles

* Reprinted with the permission of James A. Mecklenburger, © National School Boards Association, 800 State National Bank Plaza, P.O. Box 1496, Evanston, Illinois 60204. From National School Boards Association, *Women on School Boards* (Evanston, Ill.: NSBA, 1974).

† The first appropriate name (male or female) on each page of the October 1973 *The American School Board Journal* subscription list was chosen. For only two states—Texas and Vermont—was the number of female subscribers to the *Journal* lower than the desired sample. While we should have selected 78 women from Texas, we could select only 36; while we should have selected 23 women from Vermont, we sould select only 18. Thus, questionnaires were mailed to 705, rather than 750, women.

the actual distribution of school-board members in the nation. The smallest district serves 15 students; the largest district serves 1,000,000 students.

The 212 male respondents are, approximately, 1 of every 410 male school-board members in the nation. The 320 female respondents are 1 of every 37 female school-board members in the nation.

Table 1

Sample Compared To All School-board Members, By Region

	percentage of all board members		*percentage of sample*	
region	*male*	*female*	*male*	*female*
Northeast	20.9	31.6	20.3	27.8
Southern	18.7	14.9	18.9	10.3
Central	31.5	25.1	30.2	27.8
Western	17.8	12.3	20.3	15.0
Pacific	11.1	16.1	10.4	19.1
total	100.0	100.0	100.1	100.0

HANDICAPS IN SEEKING SCHOOL-BOARD OFFICE

Roughly one-third of all board members in this study—39.2% ot men and 32.2% of women—indicated they experienced *no* handicaps in seeking school-board office. Seventeen women elaborated with comments such as:

"Believe it or not, no problems."
"Not at all. It was a very easy process."
"Aside from carving time from a busy way of life, I feel that being elected was natural and easy."
"I felt no particular handicaps—had been (was) very visible to townspeople via newspaper over four years—had a good profile . . ."
"Frankly, it was a cinch, as the only candidate, but I was pleased with the number of votes I received, as often, with just one candidate, a lot of people don't bother to check the boy."

Approximately two-thirds of the school-board members in this study felt they were handicapped by one problem or another as they sought school-board office. Women were most troubled by time required by the office (18.8%) and not enough speechmaking experience (16.9%); discouragement by school-board members (13.4%); and cost of election campaigning

(10.9%). Not surprisingly, the problem of enough time led the list for men as well, but for proportionately more men than women—37.3%. Men also mentioned lack of relevant experience (16.5%) more frequently than women.

Table 2

At the time, did you have to overcome any particular *handicaps* in order to seek or to accept school-board office (*212 male and 320 female respondents*)

	responses		*percentage*	
*particular handicaps**	*men*	*women*	*men*	*women*
Discouragement by school-board members	14	43	6.6	13.4
Discouragement by school administrators	11	30	5.2	9.4
Discouragement by friend/neighbor	16	10	7.6	3.1
Discouragement by spouse/family	20	19	9.4	5.9
Discouragement by political party	5	13	2.4	4.1
Discouragement by the press	9	9	4.3	2.8
Discouragement by school-related group	4	5	1.9	1.6
Discouragement by nonschool-related group	2	9	0.9	2.8
Costs of election campaigning	16	35	7.6	10.9
Time required by the office	79	60	37.3	18.8
Not enough speechmaking experience	21	54	9.9	16.9
Not enough relevant experience	35	30	16.5	9.4
No handicaps	83	108	39.2	33.8

* This checklist was provided on the questionnaire.

One hundred-two women (31.9%) and 19 men (9.0%) either elaborated on their responses, or indicated other problems, in response to the open-ended portion of this survey question that called for "other."

Among the 19 men

The most frequent concern is time.

"If I could only find the time."
"Sacrifice of time from my family."
"I had vague notions of the amount of time that was required for a part-time school-board membership. However, until involved and participating, no one can possibly understand the number of hours required."

Also frequent were the fears of a newcomer to the board.

"I felt overwhelmed by the ability of the other board members and administrative staff."
"Political naiveté and lack of community-wide exposure."
"Giving opinions and making decisions when representatives of the press were present."

In addition, one was troubled by the nominating petition process, another by the wealth of his opponent, another by the negative attitude of his employer toward school-board service. Two expressed difficulty at being a newcomer in a Southern community.

Among the 102 women (61 full-time homemakers and 41 women employed full-time outside of the home)

The most frequent concern is their sex. Many said they were the first woman on their school board, or to ever hold a public office in their community, for many years:

"Having the community see the need to have a woman on the board. There hadn't been one for 30+ years."
"There had not been a woman serving on the board before."
"No woman had ever served on the school board in our community."
"They had not had a woman on the board in 40 years since they went to the county system."
"Being the first woman on our board of education, I had to earn the respect for my convictions . . ."
"At this time our town was a small town, that had never had a woman serving in a public office."

Others said they were confronted with stereotypical attitudes, based upon their sex:

"Being a woman." (Five responses)
"Had one man try to defeat me because I was a woman."
"Only the fact that I was a woman."
"I was pregnant. Many people, especially women, seemed to feel that this would hinder my effectiveness on the Board."
"My three smallest children are 'triplets.' Many people felt that I had no business seeking a public office. My opposing candidates particularly hammered at my lack of time."
"Question raised as to a 'woman' being able to fulfill Board duties adequately (!!) . . ."
"Convincing voters that a woman could know as much about a topic as could a man. Maybe more."
"The traditional and almost universal feeling that women should run against each other for *the one* woman's seat on the Board."

Also frequent were the fears of a newcomer to the board, or to the community itself:

"I felt I had a great deal to learn about taxation, state legislation, negotiations, and school organizations."
"Had to seek further education on setting up budgets, state school laws, how to negotiate for salary for teachers."
"I was considered a 'newcomer' to the community."

Some were concerned about their temperament:

"By nature I am thin-skinned and shy."
"Only my reticence to becoming more of a public figure . . ."
"I just had to stir my self-confidence a bit!"
"I tend to see both sides of a situation, and wondered if I could make up my mind and take a stand on anything."
"A feeling of inadequacy in publicly expressing my views, especially off-the-cuff."

Some were concerned about the effects of their candidacy on their husband's job or position in the community, and some were concerned about the effects upon caring for their children:

"With my husband teaching in the school system, they did not like the idea that I run."
"Also discouraged by my husband's friends who felt my involvement might hurt his political future."
"Children very young (three and six then), and it was difficult to find happy babysitting arrangements."

In addition, some women were concerned about personal characteristics: lack of a college degree, physical handicap, health, being an American Indian, being black, religion, politics and age—too young at eighteen, and too old at sixty-five. A few others were concerned that their outlook on race relations—such as one woman's involvement in open housing, one white couple's adoption of a black child—would hinder their candidacy.

And several others were troubled that the school board either received little community support, or that it was a "thankless and discouraging position."

EFFECTS OF SEX UPON CHANCES FOR ELECTION OR APPOINTMENT TO SCHOOL BOARD

A clear majority of men (64.9%) believe that being a woman makes no difference in a candidate's chances for election or appointment to a school board. Women, on the other hand, appear to be rather evenly divided over whether being a woman makes no difference (42.6%) or hurts one's chances (40.1%).

An even larger majority of men (72.5%) believe that being a man makes no difference in a candidate's chances for election or appointment to the board. Women again are somewhat divided over whether being a man makes no difference (50.7%) or helps one's chances (44.7%).

But while most school-board members in this study appear to believe that the sex of a school-board candidate makes no difference in his or her chances for election or appointment, inconsistency emerges: substantial numbers of men and women indicated that being a woman can hurt her chances for getting on the school board (20.9% men, 40.1% women), but hardly any men or women indicated that being a man can hurt his chances (1.4% men, 2.2% women).

These questions proved to be the litmus test for uncovering some deeply held attitudes about women serving on school boards. Frequently both men and women in this study volunteered the observation that a qualified woman candidate might *not* be elected or appointed to the school board if there were already a woman—or women—serving on that board. This the Commission termed an "informal quota system." (Question #13 showed that out of 532 boards in this study, only fourteen had more women board members than men, and only one consisted of all women.)

Table 3

In your experience or judgment, is the fact that a candidate for school-board service is a *woman* likely to affect her chances for appointment or election? If so, in what ways?

effect of	*responses*		*percentage*	
being a woman	*men*	*women*	*men*	*women*
It helps	16	40	7.6	12.5
It hurts	44	128	20.8	40.0
It makes no difference	137	136	64.6	42.5
Blank/Unusable	15	16	7.1	5.0
total	212	320	100.1	100.0

MEN AND WOMEN SCHOOL-BOARD MEMBERS ON THE EFFECTS OF BEING A WOMEN

Many expressed the idea that women school-board candidates have to prove themselves more than men:

"She had better be stable and know the art of discretion." (Woman)

"She must demonstrate much more specifically her knowledge, seriousness of purpose, and general stability. Men are assumed the reverse until proven otherwise." (Woman)

"The majority of men who become board members seem to feel women are definitely inferior to men. Some preconceived idea of women as flighty, nervous, empty-headed, housewives exists. Even when a woman proves herself, that preconceived idea still hangs in there." (Woman)

"I don't think people accept the judgment of a female as well as a male." (Man)

"If she's nice, she can't stand the heat. If she isn't, no one wants her." (Man)

"A woman's place is in the home and she must be very unusual to be suitable to serve on a school board." (Man)

"She must be twice as knowledgeable as a male candidate with the ability to hide this genius from a part of the electorate, most of the teachers, and all of the administration." (Woman)

As mentioned in the opening text, many indicated that even a qualified woman candidate is likely to run into difficulty if there is already one or several women serving on the school board:

"An asset, if no other women are on the Board." (Woman)

"We're now 3–2 (men/women). The voters probably would balk at a 1–4 or 0–5 female board. Even this white-collar professional community isn't that 'enlightened' yet." (Woman)

"It has been my experience to often hear 'two women on a board is enough' expressed. The one time a third woman ran, her opponent used this remark (subtly, of course), and she lost." (Seven-person board)

"Being a woman is an asset in a bedroom community where the men are honest enough to know that they don't have the time. . . . However, the sex issue is more of a sleeping giant than I am indicating. If a man wanted to run against any one of the three women on our board and put up a fight—we'd probably lose. The town feels we've got our 'token' woman—*plus!* They could sacrifice any one of us. . . ." (Five-person board)

"It is felt that our board is 'safe' with two women. More than that and the board loses status. I've tried to get women appointed when we had two women on and enough of the men openly said that they would reject *all* women candidates despite their qualifications; that year none was appointed." (Seven-person elected board)

"Although most people express a desire to have women *represented* on the board, I feel that they have reservations about women's capabilities in some business dealings and would be reluctant to elect a majority of women." (Woman)

Some indicated that being a woman can be an advantage:

"At first it was detrimental. Now with a good campaign and public relations, it is no problem." (Man)

"Since women are the mothers of children, the prime concern of school boards, they are perhaps more likely to be thought appropriate as members of a school board than in some other types of public bodies." (Woman)

"It helped in '72 because there was a stronger 'put women in there' mood . . ." (Woman)

"She has an advantage if she is not employed outside of the home, because the electorate will assume she will have more time to spend on school affairs, is more readily reached, and is easier to talk to about personal problems." (Woman)

"Right now, I think a woman has a better chance of being elected than a man." (Woman)

"I feel that our community—and perhaps many over the country—is anxious to involve women, therefore, a less qualified person might receive the benefit of being a woman." (Man)

"Feeling seems to be that women should be 'represented.' Much the same with a black member." (Man)

Table 4

In your experience or judgment, is the fact that a candidate for school-board service is a *man* likely to affect his chances for appointment or election? If so, in what ways?

effects of being a man	*responses*		*percentage*	
	men	*women*	*men*	*women*
It helps	45	143	21.2	44.7
It hurts	3	7	1.4	2.2
It makes no difference	153	162	72.2	50.6
Blank/Unusable	11	8	5.2	2.5
total	212	320	100.0	100.0

MEN AND WOMEN SCHOOL-BOARD MEMBERS ON THE EFFECTS OF BEING A MAN

Most of the written comments suggested that men do have an advantage over women in seeking a seat on the school board:

"A man is naturally looked upon as the head of the family, the leader in the community . . . he was chosen first even by God . . . it is simply the natural thing to expect the man to be the best candidate." (Woman)

"Many voters do not have confidence in a woman's sense of finances, and, of course, many expect a woman to be unpredictable, unstable, and unwilling to compromise in any situation. Men are pictured as having both feet squarely on the ground." (Woman)

"The assumption is made a man won't get the wool pulled over his eyes by administration." (Woman)

"Men are more likely to be trusted as business managers regardless of their real talents in this regard." (Man)

"I feel that the general public would not question his credibility to the degree they would a woman's." (Woman)

"A man is more likely to be judged by his ability, a woman by her personality." (Woman)

"I would like to say that service on a school board is not discriminatory as far as sex is concerned, but I cannot." (Woman)

On the other hand, many insisted that a man's sex makes little difference:

"In eleven years I've seen good and bad board members of both sexes —neither has a monopoly on certain traits." (Woman)
"No—I won over a man!" (Woman)

And in one instance, where the majority of board members on a three-person board were women, a woman replied:

"It is generally felt at least one man should serve on the Board."

And many indicated that the sex of a candidate did not make a significant difference:

"People today want qualified 'people.' Believe me, if I was only elected, reelected and reelected because I am a woman, I wouldn't take the job—I am on the Board because I am a good school-board member and I know what I am doing." (Woman)
"I am presently sponsoring two women for two seats." (Man, on a five-person elected board)
"Depends on the woman. Leadership experience in civic organizations and in business are essential." (Man)
"We have a woman board member, and have had for 50 years." (Man)
"Only problem I see is that many haven't any business experience, and today school boardmanship is much more business management than before." (Man)
"Only in that, on our board, both men and women tend to think of men first when a vacancy occurs." (Man)

DIFFERENCES BETWEEN MALE AND FEMALE SCHOOL-BOARD MEMBERS

Eighty-eight men and 75 women insisted either that there are no differences between male and female school-board members—in terms of their interests, attitudes, capabilities, or behaviors—or that any differences depend entirely upon the individual.

However, 85 men and 234 women indicated that they perceive some differences that *do* exist between male and female board members.

Some men said that men were more capable than women as board members in business and financial matters. Men also indicated that men generally are "tougher" board members: women are not as critical nor as pragmatic as men. Women, men said, are better than men at community relations; they are people oriented and have the time to devote. Women are also more curriculum oriented than men, men said.

Many women indicated that women are more interested in children and people than men, and that they have more time, are more accessible to the community, and are better informed than men. They criticized men for not being as education oriented as women, and for having less time to devote.

Men criticized women for being too concerned with the day-to-day operational details of the school system. Women "nitpick," and often "meddle with administrative concerns," some men said.

Table 5

In your experience, what ways, if any, do *male and female school-board members differ* from each other in their interests, attitudes, capabilities or behavior?
(194 male and 309 female respondents)

differences between male and female members	*responses*		*percentage*	
	men	*women*	*men*	*women*
No differences, or any differences related to sex are unimportant	88	75	45.4	24.3
"Don't know," or no experience with a female school-board member	21	n/a	10.8	n/a

Table 6

Characteristics Expressed About Female School-board Members
(85 male and 234 female respondents)

Men said *women* tend to:

be better at community relations, more people oriented (26)
have more time to devote (16)
be more concerned with the day-to-day operational details of the school system (14)
be more curriculum oriented (12)
be more emotional (9)
have less business experience (8)
be better informed (5)
be less critical (4)
be less aggressive (4)
be less pragmatic (3)
drink more at conferences (1)

Women said *women* tend to:

be more interested in children, people (139)
have more time to devote (49)
be more accessible to community (21)
be better informed (13)
ask more questions (5)
be more emotional (5)
have less business experience (4)
be less aggressive (4)
be more concerned with detail (3)
be more flexible (3)

Table 7

Characteristics Expressed About Male School-board Members
(85 male and 234 female respondents)

Men said *men* tend to:

- be better in business and financial matters (24)
- be better in physical plant matters (8)
- be better, generally speaking, because more realistic, more capable, tougher (8)
- be better at being a board member, because of a greater understanding of policymaking (5)
- be better at dealing with the administration (4)
- be better in athletic and vocational education matters (3)
- have less time to devote (1)

Women said *men* tend to:

- not be education oriented (111)
- have less time to devote (26)
- have more rigid attitudes (9)
- not want to rock the boat (9)
- be politically motivated (6)
- be more defensive, more protective of their egos, and hold more grudges (6)
- be more business and finance oriented (6)
- be more practical (4)
- not ask enough questions of the administration (4)
- be more decisive and more outspoken (3)

"MEN AND WOMEN SCHOOL-BOARD MEMBERS *DO* DIFFER . . . "

Some representative comments offered by both men and women:

"[Men and women] vary greatly. The two [women] I have observed are more interested in nuts and bolts of building and classroom mechanics. They tend to play educator rather than evaluate and formulate policy. Little interest and no expertise in budgets, negotiations, personnel evaluation, etc. They do have more interest and time for communicating Board actions to community groups, PTA, etc." (Man)

"Female pluses: 1. Time—We are better able to devote time to school affairs during the school hours. We prefer this because it is easier on our families. Men are busy with their businesses.

2. Child oriented, human emphasis—As a parent we deal with the child much more and are more aware of "what's going on," "where it's at."

3. Woman's point of view—Not always business oriented. Need to ask questions many a man wouldn't get away with, but extremely important.

4. Community input—From other women. Availability on the telephone. People don't feel they are 'interrupting' your very important business. (They sometimes are!) " (Woman)

"The women nitpick details to death—become too immersed in trivia. They seem less inclined to seek middle-ground solutions. Time seems relatively unimportant to them. Males may have some of the same attributes, but they are less apparent." (Man)

"Interest:	Men	Women
Attitude:	Financial	Academic
	Passive	Active
	Rely on administrative recommendation	Desire in-depth information

Capability: Little difference except that the male board members are more apt to represent 'special interest' groups within their area of expertise

Behavior:	Statistics and rationale are important	People are important." (Woman)

"The female members are interested in the input of teachers and the achievement of the student. The male members have the same interests, but to a lesser degree. Their interests are directed more to upkeep and condition of equipment, buildings—and sports. And don't you think that is a nice balance of interests?" (Woman)

"MEN AND WOMEN SCHOOL-BOARD MEMBERS *DON'T* DIFFER . . . "

Some representative comments offered by both men and women:

"Male or female has nothing to do with ability. Things like being a businessman, professional, etc., can be advantages over someone without this background and it just happens that quantitatively more men than women have this experience. However, I know many women are much more qualified than many men. Each candidate must be judged on their own merits and not according to a male-female, black-white, Jewish-Catholic, or any other coincidental label." (Man)

"Differences are due primarily to background, education, work experience, character and temperament rather than to sex." (Woman)

"Each member brings their own personality to a meeting. I know more about school law than the president of a construction company, but he knows more about reading the blue prints for a new school than I do. I know more about milleage than our truck driver, but he knows when we're being overcharged on bus repair. This is a give-and-take business and if you get one person or one group that knows it all—male or female—then you have lost the freedom of education." (Woman)

"I have not noticed any real differences. We all complain. We all seem to be dedicated to our children." (Man)

Appendixes
Sex Differences in Educational Attainment

Sex Differentials in School Enrollment and Educational Attainment*

CHARLES E. JOHNSON, JR., and
JERRY T. JENNINGS

Although at the compulsory attendance ages almost all of the boys and the girls are enrolled in school, there are still significant differences between boys and girls in the number and percent enrolled above and below the compulsory attendance ages, in modal grade of enrollment, in the proportion who go on to college and graduate or professional school, and in the level of education attained when their schooling is finished.[1]

In the fall of 1969, 99% of the children in the United States aged 6 through 15 were enrolled in school.[2] This enrollment rate was the same for both the girls and the boys. However, among those of the very youngest enrollment age, 3 years old (the age when children can begin nursery school), girls were slightly more likely to be enrolled than were boys. At age 3, 9 percent of the girls and 8 percent of the boys were enrolled in school, or 166,000 girls and 149,000 boys. Three-year-old children comprise nearly one-third of the total of 860,000 pupils enrolled in nursery school.

At age 4, the girls still had a slight edge over the boys in enrollment rate—24 percent and 22 percent, respectively—with 444,000 girls and

* Charles E. Johnson, Jr. and Jerry T. Jennings, "Sex Differential in School Enrollment and Educational Attainment," © copyright 1971 by Russell N. Cassel and Robert E. Hoye, from *Education* 92 (September-October 1971) : 84–87; reprinted with the permission of Russell N. Cassel and Robert E. Hoye, and Charles E. Johnson, Jr. and Jerry T. Jennings.

436,000 boys enrolled in school. The majority of both the four-year-old boys and girls who were enrolled in school were enrolled at the nursery-school level, but the girls were somewhat more likely than the boys to be enrolled in kindergarten—47 percent and 43 percent, respectively—probably because a slightly larger percent of the girls had had nursery-school training when they were three years old.

At age five, when most children can enroll in public kindergartens, the girls still had a higher enrollment rate than the boys—80 percent of the five-year-old girls were enrolled in school compared with 77 percent of the boys. Their numbers enrolled were nearly equal with around 1.6 million five-year-old boys and a like number of five-year-old girls in school. The modal enrollment grade for the five-year-old children was kindergarten and around 85 percent of both sexes were enrolled at this level, around two percent were still enrolled in nursery school, and around twelve percent in the first grade.

Since there are slightly more boys than girls in the population at the compulsory attendance ages, 6 to 15 years old, there were slightly more boys than girls of this age enrolled in school in the fall of 1969, 20.6 million boys versus 20.0 million girls.[3] At each level of school from the first grade through high school there were more boys enrolled than girls with the relative distribution being around 51 percent boys and 49 percent girls. At the primary level (grades 1 to 6), there were 13.2 million boys and 12.5 million girls; at the junior high-school level (grades 7 and 8), there were 4.1 million boys and 4.0 million girls; and at the high-school level (grades 9 to 12), there were 7.4 million boys and 7.2 million girls.

Boys may be in the majority but girls are likely to be further advanced in school. Among the students enrolled at the elementary-school ages (6 to 13 years old), girls were more likely to be enrolled above the modal grade for their age, 11 percent, than were boys, 9 percent. Conversely, boys were more likely to be enrolled below the modal grade for their age, 21 percent, than were girls, 14 percent.

Just beyond the compulsory attendance ages, among those 16 and 17 years old, 92 percent of the boys were still enrolled in school, but the percent of the girls enrolled had declined to 88 percent. These 16-and-17-year-old boys and girls who were not enrolled usually left school without graduating from high school. Girls of this age who were not enrolled were about twice as likely as boys to have finished high school. Of the 16-and-17-year-old girls not enrolled in school in the fall of 1969, 26 percent were high-school graduates compared with only 14 percent of the not-enrolled boys of this age. Also among those of college age (18 to 21 years old) who were not enrolled in school, women were more likely to be high-school graduates, 75 percent, than were the men, 66 percent. The difference between the education of the men and women 18 to 21 years old is not, however, as striking as these figures might indicate. Men are more likely than women to go on to college and many of the male high-school graduates of this age are likely to be in the Armed Forces and excluded from the school enrollment and educational attainment universe included in the October Current Population Survey of the Bureau of the Census, which is restricted to the civilian noninstitutional population. Among those aged 25 to 29 years, 74 percent of both the men and women who were not enrolled in school in the fall of 1969 were at least high-school graduates.

Approximately 1.6 million men and 2.0 million women, between the ages of 14 to 24, left school between the fall of 1968 and the fall of 1969. Of the men who left school, around one in four left without completing high school as compared with only one in five of the women. A little less than half, 45 percent, of these men left after completing the 12th grade and a little over half, 52 percent, of the women left at this level. In the adult population in 1970 (persons 25 years old and over) men and women were about equally likely to have dropped out of school without completing high school.[4] There are, of course, relatively fewer high-school dropouts now than in the past. Among the men and women 20 to 24 years old in 1970, only around 20 percent had failed to complete high school as compared with 45 percent of the men and women 25 and over.

At the primary ages of college attendance, 18 to 21 years, over half of the men but only one-third of the women were still enrolled in school in the fall of 1969. However, the women of college age who were enrolled in school were somewhat more likely to be enrolled in college, 87 percent, than were the enrolled men of college age, 82 percent. Although the percent still enrolled in school drops sharply among persons over 21, the men of this age were more than twice as likely as the women to still be enrolled in school. For instance, among the 22 to 24 year olds, 23 percent of the men were still enrolled in school, but only 9 percent of the women; among the 25 to 29 year olds, 11 percent of the men were still enrolled in school, but only 5 percent of the women; and among those 30 to 34 years old, 6 percent of the men were still in school as compared with 4 percent of the women.

Women are more likely than men to have completed high school without having gone on to college. Among persons 25 years old and over in 1970, 38 percent of the women and 30 percent of the men had completed high school without having gone on to college. The men were more likely to have gone on to college. Among adult men, 25 percent had completed some college, including 14 percent who had completed 4 years of college or more, whereas among the adult women, 18 percent had completed some college, including 8 percent who had completed 4 years or more. The younger women, 20 to 24 years old, were more likely than the younger men to complete high school without going on to college, just as the older women were more likely than the older men to have completed exactly 4 years of high school. Forty-seven percent of the younger women had completed high school only as compared with 38 percent of the younger men. Both the younger men and women were more likely to have completed some college than were the older men and women. About 42 percent of the younger men and 34 percent of the younger women had completed some college as compared with 25 percent of the older men and 18 percent of the older women.

Although more men and women are continuing their education into college now than in the past, it appears that most of the gain comes from increased numbers of high-school graduates rather than from increases in the percent of high school graduates going on to college. Among women high-school graduates 20 and 21 years old in 1970, 44 percent had completed some college, not far different from the 40 percent of the women high-school graduates 75 years old and over who had completed some college. Among young, male high-school graduates, 59 percent have completed some college, also not far different from the 54 percent of the older, male high-school graduates who had completed some college.

Of all the students enrolled in college in the fall of 1969, the 4.4 million men comprised 60 percent of the total and the 3.0 million women comprised 40 percent. There was a more nearly equal distribution of the sexes among those enrolled in the first two years of college, with the men comprising 56 percent of the total enrollment and the women 44 percent. However, among those enrolled in the last two years of college, the division of the sexes was 61 percent men and 39 percent women, and at the graduate level, the fifth year of college or higher, the 792,000 men enrolled comprised 70 percent of the total and the 345,000 women comprised only 30 percent.

Among both men and women enrolled in college at the undergraduate level, a little over 80 percent were enrolled on a full-time basis. At the graduate level, however, a considerably smaller percentage were attending full-time. Over half of the men enrolled in the fifth or higher year of college were attending full-time and only a little over one-third of the women. It is likely that many of the women attending graduate school on a part-time basis were schoolteachers working towards an advanced degree in education.

The men enrolled in college are more likely than the women to be married. Of the 4.4 million men enrolled in college in the fall of 1969, 1.2 million, 26 percent, were married and living with their wives. Of the 3.0 million women enrolled in college, a little over 500,000, 18 percent, were married and living with their husband. The percent of college students who are married has not varied appreciably in the past decade. The students attending college on a part-time basis were far more likely to be married than were the full-time students. Of the men attending college on a part-time basis, 67 percent were married and living with their wife compared with only 16 percent of the men attending on a full-time basis. And 50 percent of the women attending on a part-time basis were married as compared with only 8 percent of the women attending college on a full-time basis.

The men 18 to 24 years old who were attending college full-time and living with their wife had a considerably smaller family income than did the married men of this age who were not enrolled in school. Nearly half of these married men in college had a family income of less than $5,000 as compared with less than one-third of the married men of this age who were not enrolled in school. Of course, the men who complete college can expect to have a considerably larger life-time earnings than the men who do not complete college.[5] Of the married women of this age who were attending college full-time, nearly half had a family income of less than $5,000, just as did the married men attending college, but only around one-fourth of the married women who were not enrolled in school had family incomes at this level. The lower percentage of the not-enrolled women with a relatively low family income when compared with the not-enrolled men is likely the result of the women marrying older, better-educated men.

At all levels of school, except nursery school, both the boys and girls are more likely to be enrolled in public schools than in private schools. At the nursery-school level in the fall of 1969, only 28 percent were enrolled in public schools, but 82 percent of the kindergarten pupils, 88 percent of the elementary-school pupils, 92 percent of the high-school students, and 73 percent of the college students were enrolled in public schools. There were, however, some differences in the percent of boys and girls in public and private schools. At the nursery-school level, both the public and private schools had an equal distribution of the sexes. At the kindergarten level, the distribution was even in the public schools, but the private kindergartens had more boys than girls. Of the 594,000 pupils enrolled in private kindergartens, 56 percent were boys and 44 percent girls. At the elementary-school level there was an even distribution of the sexes in both the public and private schools. In the public high schools the sexes were evenly distributed, but in the private high schools there were more girls, 53 percent, than boys, 47 percent. The higher proportion of girls in private high schools may be due to a preference of the parents that their daughters attend an all-girl school during their adolescence. At the undergraduate level of college in both public and private colleges the sex distribution was 58 percent men and 42 percent women. However, among students enrolled in the fifth or higher year of college, the private colleges were more highly male, 76 percent, than were the public colleges, 66 percent. The greater predilection for women enrolled at the graduate level to be enrolled in public colleges rather than in private colleges is likely due in part to the relatively high proportion of women who are education majors and attend state-supported colleges.

The only age level at which Negro boys and girls were more likely to be enrolled in school than were white boys and girls was among the three and four year olds. Around 21 percent of both the Negro boys and girls were enrolled in school in the fall of 1969 as compared with 15 percent of the white boys and girls. The Head Start program that provides nursery-school and kindergarten training for the disadvantaged has helped increase the enrollment of the three-and-four-year-old Negro children.[6] The only difference between the races or the sexes at the compulsory-attendance ages was that the Negro boys and girls were just slightly less likely to be enrolled than the white boys and girls, but nearly 99 percent of both races were enrolled. Just after the compulsory-attendance ages, however, there are differences in attendance rates between the races and the sexes. Among those 16 and 17 years old, the percent enrolled declines to 92 percent for the white boys, 88 percent for both the Negro boys and white girls, and to 84 percent for the Negro girls. At the next older age group, the 18 and 19 year olds, there is a greater dispersion in enrollment rates between the white and Negro men than between the white and Negro women. Still enrolled in school in 1969 at ages 18 and 19, were 61 percent of the white men and 50 percent of the Negro men; but only 42 percent of the white women and 40 percent of the Negro women were still enrolled. White men have the highest enrollment rate among the 20 and 21 year olds, 49 percent, Negro men and white women have about the same enrollment rates, 28 percent and 26 percent, respectively, and Negro women have the lowest enrollment rate, 20 percent.

The role of the sexes diverge in many instances after the completion of schooling. Men generally enter the labor force and women, marrying at a younger age than men, raise the children and maintain the home. Yet in many ways the roles of the sexes are converging with more and more women entering the labor force and with more men sharing the responsibility for child and home management. This diversity of future roles requires the American educator, who has provided the nation's population with an extensive education for all ages from the three year olds in nursery school to the over thirties in graduate school, to provide the type of training of greatest relevance to each sex when they have completed their formal education.

NOTES

1. For a description of trends in school enrollment see Charles E. Johnson, Jr., and Aurora A. Zappolo, "Recent Trends in U.S. School Enrollment," *School and Society* 98 (February 1970) : 2323, and Dawn D. Nelson and Charles E. Johnson, Jr. "School Enrollment: October 1968 and 1967," U.S. Bureau of the Census, *Current Population Reports,* Series P-20, no. 190, 1 October 1968. For a description of trends in educational attainment see Aurora A. Zappolo and Charles E. Johnson, Jr., "Educational Attainment: March 1969," U.S. Bureau of the Census, *Current Population Reports,* Series P-20, no. 194, 19 February 1970.
2. The 1969 school-enrollment data in this article are based on the report "School Enrollment in the United States: 1969," *Current Population Reports,* Series P-20, no. 199, 22 April 1970, and unpublished data collected by the Bureau of the Census in the Current Population Survey of October 1969. Detailed tables are to be published in a forthcoming census report.
3. The sex ratio for live births has changed very little in the past 30 years, ranging from 104.7 to 105.8 males per 100.0 females. Due to higher mortality among males, by age 6 the sex ratio is 104 and by age 16 it is 100. See "Monthly Vital Statistics Report: Advance Report, Final Natality Statistics, 1968," U.S. Department of Health, Education, and Welfare, Public Health Service (30 January 1970) : 11.
4. The 1970 educational attainment data in this article are based on unpublished data collected by the Bureau of the Census in the Current Population Survey of March 1970. Detailed tables are to be published in a forthcoming Census Bureau report.

5. Murray S. Weitzman and Mitsuo Ono, "Annual Mean Income, Lifetime Income, and Educational Attainment of Men in the United States, for Selected Years, 1956 to 1966," U.S. Bureau of the Census, *Current Population Reports,* Series P-60, no. 56. 14 August 1968.
6. For a description of the Head Start program and its participants see Sar A. Levitan, *The Great Society's Poor Law: A New Approach to Poverty* (Baltimore: The Johns Hopkins Press, 1969) ; and Barbara D. Bates, *Project Head Start 1965–1967: A Descriptive Report of Programs and Participants,* U.S. Department of Health, Education, and Welfare, Office of Child Development.

Proportion of Doctorates Earned by Women, by Area and Field, 1960-1969*

COUNCIL FOR UNIVERSITY WOMEN'S PROGRESS AT THE UNIVERSITY OF MINNESOTA

* Prepared by the Council for University Women's Progress at the University of Minnesota, June 1971, for Women's Equity Action League (WEAL). Distributed by the Project on the Status and Education of Women, Association of American Colleges, 1818 R Street, N. W., Washington, D. C. 20009. Reprinted with permission of the Association of American Colleges.

PROPORTION OF DOCTORATES EARNED BY WOMEN, BY AREA AND FIELD, 1960–1969*

	Total Number of Doctorates Earned 1960–1969	Total Number of Doctorates Earned by Women 1960–1969	Percentage of Doctorates Earned by Women 1960–1969
Agriculture, Total	4,462	79	1.77
Agriculture, General	115	1	.87
Agronomy, Field Crops	966	5	.52
Animal Science	872	21	2.41
Dairy Science	262	4	1.53
Farm Management	13	0	.00
Fish, Game or Wildlife Management (1961–1969) [1]	209	2	.96
Food Science	385	16	4.16
Horticulture	539	11	2.40
Ornamental Horticulture	14	0	.00
Poultry Science	211	7	3.32
Soil Science	568	2	.35
Agriculture, all other fields	308	10	3.25
Architecture	50	4	8.00
Biological Sciences, Total	17,708	2,448	13.82
Premedical, Predental, and Preveterinary Sciences	25	2	8.00
Biology, General	1,949	395	20.27
Botany, General	1,653	186	11.25
Zoology, General	2,262	318	14.06
Anatomy and Histology	633	116	18.33
Bacteriology, etc.[2]	2,096	355	16.94
Biochemistry	2,695	417	17.48
Biophysics	429	32	7.46
Cytology	30	9	30.00

* SOURCE: U.S. Department of Health, Education, and Welfare. *Earned Degrees Conferred: Bachelor's and Higher Degrees.* A publication of the Bureau of Educational Research and Development and the National Center for Educational Statistics, Washington, D. C.: U.S. Government Printing Office. (All public and private colleges and universities in the United States known to confer doctoral degrees are included in the survey. Professional doctoral degrees, such as M.D., however, are not listed.) The consecutive bulletins from which these original data were obtained are located in the Wilson Library, Documents Division.

	Total Number of Doctorates Earned 1960–1969	Total Number of Doctorates Earned by Women 1960–1969	Percentage of Doctorates Earned by Women 1960–1969
Ecology (1961–1969 only)	37	2	5.41
Embryology	45	11	24.44
Entomology	1,097	46	4.19
Genetics	672	61	9.08
Molecular Biology (1968–1969 only) [3]	32	6	18.75
Nutrition (1961–1969 only)	156	45	28.85
Pathology	271	15	5.54
Pharmacology	783	87	11.11
Physiology	1,145	168	14.67
Plant Pathology	692	19	2.75
Plant Physiology	203	12	5.91
Biological Sciences, all other fields	803	92	11.46
Business and Commerce, Total	3,046	86	2.82
Business and Commerce, General	1,372	33	2.41
Accounting	268	18	6.72
Finance, Banking (1967–1969 only) [4]	53	1	1.89
Marketing (1967–1969 only) [5]	66	1	1.52
Real Estate, Insurance (1967–1969 only) [6]	2	0	.00
Transportation (1967–1969 only)	7	0	.00
Business and Commerce, all other fields	1,278	33	2.58
City Planning (1966–1969 only) [7]	44	2	4.55
Computer Science and Systems Analysis, Total (1964–1969 only) [8]	158	4	2.53
Computer Science	99	3	3.03
Systems Analysis	22	1	4.55
Computer Science and Systems Analysis, all other fields	37	0	.00
Education, Total	26,369	5,230	19.83
Physical Education	1,143	313	27.38
Health Education	88	26	29.55
Recreation	30	4	13.33
Education of the Mentally Retarded	118	36	30.51
Education of the Deaf (1964–1969 only) [9]	6	4	66.67
Speech and Hearing Impaired	339	67	19.76
Education of the Visually Handicapped (1964–1969 only) [10]	3	1	33.33
Education of the Emotionally Disturbed (1965–1969 only) [11]	24	6	25.00

	Total Number of Doctorates Earned 1960–1969	Total Number of Doctorates Earned by Women 1960–1969	Percentage of Doctorates Earned by Women 1960–1969
Administration of Special Education (1968–1969 only) [12]	14	4	28.57
Education of Other Exceptional Children[13]	391	126	32.23
Agricultural Education	228	2	.88
Art Education	194	52	26.80
Business or Commercial Education	300	89	29.67
Distributive Education, Retail Selling	28	6	21.43
Home-economics Education	124	123	99.19
Industrial-arts Education, Nonvocational	224	1	.45
Music Education	548	75	13.69
Trade or Industrial Education, Vocational	181	8	4.52
Specialized Teaching Fields, all other	756	261	34.52
Nursery or Kindergarten Education	14	12	85.71
Early Childhood Education	22	20	90.91
Elementary Education	1,199	459	38.28
Secondary Education	966	154	15.94
Combined Elementary and Secondary Education	21	4	19.05
Adult Education	303	46	15.18
General Teaching Fields, all other	445	97	21.80
Education Administration, Supervision, Finance[14]	7,242	931	12.86
Counseling and Guidance	2,357	488	20.70
Rehabilitation and Counselor Training (1964–1969 only)	80	14	17.50
History of Education, etc. (1964–1969 only) [15]	488	99	20.29
Education, General	6,286	1,183	18.82
Educational Psychology (1964–1969 only)	875	224	25.60
Physical Education, Nonteaching (1964–1969 only)	36	9	25.00
Education, all other fields[16]	1,296	286	22.07
Engineering, Total[17]	18,572	82	.44
English and Journalism, Total	6,471	1,541	23.81
English and Literature	6,322	1,523	24.09
Journalism	149	18	12.08
Fine Arts and Applied Arts, Total	4,035	678	16.80
Art General	99	18	18.18

	Total Number of Doctorates Earned 1960–1969	Total Number of Doctorates Earned by Women 1960–1969	Percentage of Doctorates Earned by Women 1960–1969
Music, Sacred Music	1,473	199	13.51
Speech and Dramatic Arts	1,978	314	15.87
Fine and Applied Arts, all other fields	485	147	30.31
Folklore (1965–1969 only)	29	8	27.59
Foreign Languages and Literature, Total	4,158	1,186	28.52
Linguistics	551	133	24.14
Latin, Classical Greek	506	128	25.30
French	768	311	40.49
Italian	47	17	36.17
Portuguese	14	3	21.43
Spanish	668	217	32.49
Philology and Literature of Romance Languages	380	93	24.47
German	678	171	25.22
Other German Languages	27	5	18.52
Philology and Literature of Germanic Languages	52	9	17.31
Arabic	5	1	20.00
Chinese	14	2	14.29
Hebrew	23	1	4.35
Hindi, Urdu (1961–1969 only)	2	0	0.00
Japanese	12	2	16.67
Russian	116	28	24.14
Other Slavic Languages	68	20	29.41
Foreign Language and Literature, all other fields	227	45	19.82
Forestry	558	1	18
Geography	663	37	5.58
Health Professions, Total	1,831	168	9.18
Hospital Administration	20	1	.50
Medical Technology	2	0	.00
Nursing, Public Health Nursing	18	17	94.44
Optometry	16	1	6.25
Pharmacy	563	24	4.26
Physical Therapy, Physiotherapy	1	0	.00
Public Health	418	62	14.83
Radiologic Technology	3	0	.00
Clinical Dental Services	24	4	16.77
Clinical Medical Services	302	31	10.26

	Total Number of Doctorates Earned 1960–1969	Total Number of Doctorates Earned by Women 1960–1969	Percentage of Doctorates Earned by Women 1960–1969
Clinical Veterinary Services	250	4	1.60
Health Professions, all other fields	214	24	11.21
Home Economics, Total	514	392	76.26
Home Economics, General	104	101	97.12
Child Development, Family Relations	174	87	50.00
Clothing and Textiles	53	52	98.11
Foods and Nutrition	134	108	80.60
Institution Management or Administration	6	6	100.00
Home Economics, all other fields	43	38	88.37
Law	268	12	4.48
Library Science	140	38	27.14
Mathematical Sciences, Total	6,166	401	6.50
Mathematics	5,538	348	6.46
Statistics	781	53	6.79
Philosophy, Total	1,701	188	11.05
Philosophy	1,520	155	10.20
Scholastic Philosophy	181	33	18.23
Physical Sciences, Total	25,736	1,179	4.58
Physical Sciences, General	93	3	3.23
Astronomy	421	29	6.69
Chemistry	12,963	884	6.82
Metallurgy	213	0	.00
Meteorology	245	2	.82
Pharmaceutical Chemistry (1961–1969 only)	289	13	.50
Physics	8,415	163	2.00
Geology	2,143	53	2.47
Geophysics	203	3	1.48
Oceanography	222	4	1.80
Earth Sciences, all other fields[18]	170	2	1.18
Physical Science, all other fields	359	18	5.01
Psychology, Total	9,135	1,845	20.20
General Psychology	7,071	1,365	19.30
Clinical Psychology (1961–1969 only)	651	163	25.04
Counseling and Guidance	138	33	23.91
Social Psychology (1961–1969 only)	309	68	22.01
Rehabilitation Counselor Training (1964–1969 only)	36	8	22.22
Educational Psychology	137	37	27.01

	Total Number of Doctorates Earned 1960–1969	Total Number of Doctorates Earned by Women 1960–1969	Percentage of Doctorates Earned by Women 1960–1969
(1964–1969 only)			
Psychology, all other fields (1964–1969 only)	793	171	21.56
Religion, Total	2,825	141	4.99
Religious Education, Bible	368	49	13.32
Theology	1,417	49	3.46
Religion, Liberal Arts Curriculum	860	39	4.54
Religion, all other fields	180	4	2.22
Social Sciences, Total	18,662	2,072	11.10
Social Sciences, General	261	27	10.34
American Studies, Civilization, Culture	257	41	15.95
Anthropology	942	202	21.44
Area or Regional Studies	384	46	11.98
Economics	3,898	219	5.62
History	4,943	579	11.71
International Relations	425	33	7.76
Political Science or Government	2,876	253	8.80
Sociology	2,361	403	17.07
Agricultural Economics	1,165	12	1.03
Foreign Service Programs	11	1	9.09
Industrial Relations	96	4	4.17
Public Administration	283	23	8.13
Social Work, Social Administration	480	174	36.25
Social Science, all other fields	280	55	19.64
Trade or Industrial Training	84	0	.00
Broad General Curriculums and Miscellaneous Total	726	107	14.74
Arts, General Programs	39	9	23.08
Sciences, General Programs	84	9	10.71
Arts and Sciences, General Programs	40	5	12.50
Teaching of English as a Foreign Language	27	10	37.04
All Other Fields of Study[19]	536	74	13.81
Total *All* Fields (areas) reported:	154,111	17,929	11.63

NOTES

1. When information was available from 1961–1969 (this field was not given as a separate category in 1960–1961), proportions were computed based on information available. If the field was not listed as a separate category for more years than 1960–61, the information was included in the residual category. Exceptions are noted.
2. Includes Bacteriology, Virology, Mycology, Parasitology, and Microbiology.
3. The status of this field prior to 1968, when it was considered separately, is not clear.

4, 5 & 6. As in 3, the same observation applies.

7 & 8. These entire areas are new.

9, 10, 11, & 12. Subsumed under other categories in earlier years.

13. Includes Special Learning Disability, Education of the Crippled, Education of the Multiple Handicapped.
14. Includes Curriculum Instruction as well. These fields were separated for all but year 1963–1964, so it was necessary to combine them.
15. Includes History, Philosophy, and Theory of Education.
16. Includes the recently listed field of Education Specialist.
17. A breakdown on Engineering was omitted from *Earned Degrees Conferred: Bachelor's and Higher Degrees* for the four academic years 1960 through 1964. Other sources investigated provided breakdown by field but not by sex.
18. Includes recent field, "Earth Sciences, General."
19. Includes recent field, "Interarea Fields of Study."

Notes on Contributors

William C. Bingham is currently Professor of Education, Graduate School of Education, at Rutgers University. He received his Ed.D. from Teachers College, Columbia University, in Counseling Psychology, and served as President of the National Vocational Guidance Association from 1971–1972.

Margaret M. Clifford holds the rank of Associate Professor in Educational Psychology at the University of Iowa. She received her Ph.D. in Educational Psychology from the University of Wisconsin.

Nancy S. Cole is the Assistant Vice-president for Research and Development at the American College Testing Program. She received her Ph.D. in Psychometrics from the University of North Carolina.

James S. Coleman is Professor of Sociology at the University of Chicago. He received his Ph.D. in Sociology from Columbia University. Coleman received the American Educational Research Association's Distinguished Research Award in 1974.

Doris R. Entwisle is Professor of Social Relations and Engineering Science at Johns Hopkins University, from which she received her Ph.D.

Jane Faggen-Steckler is a lecturer at the City University of New York Graduate School. She received her M.S. from Cornell University and will be receiving her Ph.D. in Educational Psychology from C.U.N.Y.

Blanche Fitzpatrick is Associate Professor in the Department of Economics, Boston University. Fitzpatrick received her Ph.D. in Economics from Harvard University. She is a member of the Governor's Commission on the Status of Women, and chaired the Task Force on Education. Her forthcoming book, *Give Her A Chance* (Ronald Press), deals with women's unemployment and work power.

Donald W. Felker is Professor and Department Head of the Department of Child Development and Family Life at Purdue University. He received his Ph.D. in Education from Indiana University.

A. J. H. Gaite is Professor and Head of the Department of Educational Psychology at the University of Oregon. He received his Ph.D. in Educational Psychology from the University of Toronto.

Mary J. Gander is Assistant Professor of Psychology at the University of Wisconsin-La Crosse. She received her Ph.D. in Educational Psychology from the University of Wisconsin-Madison.

Jane Goodman holds the titles of Counselor and Research Associate at the Continuum Center for Adult Counseling and Leadership Training at Oakland University in Michigan. She received her M.Ed. in Guidance and Counseling from Wayne State University.

Selma Greenberg received her Ed.D. degree from Teachers College, Columbia University, and holds the rank of Associate Professor at Hofstra University. She is a contributing editor to the *Journal of Educational Research.*

Ellen Greenberger is Principal Research Scientist in the Center for Social Organization of Schools and the Department of Human Relations at The Johns Hopkins University. She received her Ph.D. degree from Radcliffe College in Clinical Psychology. Her present research program involves an investigation of family, school, and peer influences on psychosocial development.

Ruth E. Hartley is a Professor in and the Chairperson of the Department of Growth and Development at the University of Wisconsin-Greenbay. She received her Ph.D. in Clinical Psychology from Columbia University.

Rodney T. Hartnett holds the title of Research Psychologist at Educational Testing Service, where his research area is higher education. His Ph.D. degree in Psychology is from Michigan State University.

Gary R. Hanson is the Assistant Director of Research at the American College Testing Program. He received his Ph.D. in Counseling Psychology from the University of Minnesota.

Elaine W. House is Chairperson of the University Department of Undergraduate Teacher Education at Rutgers University. She received her Ed.D. degree in Vocational-technical Education from Rutgers. House is both Trustee of the National Vocational Guidance Association and National Chairperson of its Commission on the Occupational Status of Women.

Lynne B. Iglitzin is Assistant Director of Undergraduate Studies at the University of Washington, where she currently teaches a course entitled, "Women and Patriarchal Politics." Her Ph.D. degree in Political Science was received from Bryn Mawr College.

Winifred Jay is Curriculum Specialist in Elementary Education in the Hawaii Department of Education. She received her Ph.D. degree from the University of Oregon in Curriculum and Instruction.

Jerry T. Jennings holds the title of Statistician at the Population Division of the Bureau of the Census. His B.A. degree in Sociology is from Guilford College, and he has done graduate work at Duke University.

Carole Joffe is Assistant Professor at the Graduate School of Social Work, Bryn Mawr College. She received her Ph.D. degree in Sociology from the University of California at Berkeley.

Charles E. Johnson, Jr., is Assistant Chief of the Population Division of the Bureau of the Census. He received his M.A. degree in Sociology from The American University. Johnson has authored numerous articles on school enrollment and population trends.

Richard S. Kay is Assistant Professor of Educational Psychology at Brigham Young University. He received his Ph.D. degree in Educational Psychology and Child Development from Purdue University. Kay's present research is in the area of self-concept, and he is currently writing a book on self-concept development and change.

Richard L. Krebs, who holds a Ph.D. degree in Clinical Psychology from the University of Chicago, is in private practice and also is on the staff of Ascension Lutheran Church and Sinai Hospital in Baltimore.

Richard R. Lamb holds the title of Counselor at the Iowa Lake Community College. He received his Ph.D. degree in Student Personnel from the University of Iowa. He previously had been on the staffs of the American College Testing Program and the University of Iowa.

Karen McCarthy is Director of Research, Testing, and Evaluation at the White Plains Public Schools, New York. She will receive her Ph.D. degree in Educational Psychology from the City University of New York.

Hazel Markus holds the title of Research Assistant at the Research Center for Group Dynamics, Institute for Social Research, University of Michigan. She will receive her Ph.D. degree in Social Psychology from the University of Michigan.

Ruth M. Oltman is Dean of the Graduate Program at Hood College. She received her Ph.D. degree in Counseling Psychology from Western-Reserve University. Oltman had previously been Assistant Director of the Higher Education Program at the American Association of University Women.

John J. Pietrofesa is Associate Professor of Counseling and Guidance at Wayne State University. He received his Ed.D. degree in Counseling from the University of Miami, Florida. Pietrofesa has authored numerous articles on sex roles, sexuality, and counselor education.

Cheryl L. Reed is Statistical Associate of the Higher Education and Career Programs at Educational Testing Service. She received her Ph.D. degree in Educational Research from Purdue University. Her research interests include sex bias in testing, and measurement theory for criterion-referenced tests.

Nancy K. Schlossberg is Professor in the Department of Counseling and Personnel Services at the University of Maryland. She received her Ed.D. degree in Guidance and Student Personnel from Teachers College, Columbia University. She is also consultant to the Maryland State Department of Education.

Claire Lynn Fleet Siegel is Assistant Professor in the Counseling Center and Department of Psychiatry, Michigan State University. She received her Ed.D. degree in Counselor Education from Boston University.

Douglas J. Stanwyck is Assistant Professor of Educational Psychology at the University of Maryland, Baltimore. He received his Ph.D. degree in Educational Psychology and Research from Purdue University. Stanwyck's areas of interest are self-concept, mental health, and classroom climate.

Anne Steinmann is President of the Maferr Foundation, Inc., and is also a psychotherapist in private practice. She received her Ph.D. degree in Psychology from New York University. Steinmann has published many articles on male and female sex roles.

Suzanne Saunders Taylor is Director of Research at the Connecticut Education Association. She received her Ph.D. degree in Educational Administration from the University of Connecticut. Taylor is currently the Commissioner of the Connecticut Commission on the Status of Women.

Carol Kehr Tittle is Associate Professor in the School of Education at Queens College, C.U.N.Y. She received her Ph.D. degree in Measurement and Evaluation from the University of Chicago. Tittle is chairperson of the American Educational Research Association's Committee on the Role and Status of Women.

Elaine Walster is Professor of Sociology and Psychology at the University of Wisconsin. She received her Ph.D. degree in Social Psychology from Stanford University.

Index